# THE SAGE IN ISRAEL
### AND
# THE ANCIENT NEAR EAST

# THE SAGE IN ISRAEL
## AND
# THE ANCIENT NEAR EAST

edited by

*John G. Gammie*
and
*Leo G. Perdue*

Eisenbrauns
Winona Lake
1990

Library of Congress Cataloging-in-Publication Data

The Sage in Israel and the ancient Near East / edited by John G.
   Gammie and Leo G. Perdue.
      p.   cm.
   Includes bibliographical references.
   ISBN 0-931464-46-3
   1. Wisdom literature—Criticism, interpretation, etc. 2. Wis-
dom—History. 3. Middle Eastern literature—History and criti-
cism. 4. Bible. O.T.—Extra-canonical parallels. I. Gammie,
John G. II. Perdue, Leo G.
BS1455.S32     1990
296.6′1′09394—dc20
                                                      90-30764

# CONTENTS

# PREFACE

This volume seeks to make a modest contribution to the intellectual and social history of Israel and the ancient Near East. As the title of the volume suggests, the focus is upon those wise men and women in ancient Israel who composed Israel's wisdom literature, counseled her kings, and consoled—and sought to guide—her people on the basis of Israel's sapiential tradition. The debate over the identity of the sages in Israel has largely centered on the question of whether they were primarily intelligent individuals who functioned in a variety of social roles and locations, or whether they were a professional class active mainly in the court, temple, and school and who shaped their own distinctive literary and philosophical tradition.

As is well known, the Israelite and Jewish composers in the sapiential tradition drew deeply upon literary and social models from the ancient Near East. To begin to formulate, therefore, conceptions of the Israelite sage and of the sage in emerging Judaism, it is requisite to take note of how the female and male sage elsewhere in the ancient Near East functioned and viewed the world. Accordingly, the first section of this volume is devoted to an examination of the sage as he or she appears in ancient Near Eastern literature, while the second section carries forward that examination to the social location to inquire how the sage functioned in royal court, family, tribe, and school. Sections three and four are devoted to an exploration of how the sage is portrayed in Israel's wisdom literature and in other biblical texts. The fifth section of the volume presses the inquiry concerning the portrait of the sage into Hellenistic—and to a limited extent, Roman—philosophy and literature, as well as into two deuterocanonical wisdom texts, select apocalyptic and pseudepigraphic texts, Qumran, the New Testament, and finally a noted rabbinical text. The volume concludes with three essays that seek to record and reflect on changes in the images and symbols employed by Israelite and Jewish sages in the course of the first millennium B.C.E. and slightly beyond. Each of the final essays has a slightly different focus. The opening essay of this section seeks to clarify the nature of the shift in the self-understanding of the sage that transpired in the course of the postexilic era and the beginning of the Roman era as one moves from biblical authors to the rabbis; the second explores the symbolic universe of the biblical sages and, in the light of

ix

that examination, suggests conclusions that would follow as to the social location of the biblical sages; and the third, in the light of a brief summary of the types and forms of wisdom, seeks to describe several important transformations in the sages' social construction of reality as one moves from canonical to deuterocanonical texts.

Each of the essays appears here for the first time and all except one were composed explicitly for this volume. Contributors have employed a variety of methodologies in the endeavor to throw light on the meaning and function of the sage in Israel and the ancient Near East. Accordingly one will find below thematic surveys of the sage in literature, philological studies, sociological analyses, and historical-literary analyses. One essay also contains a bibliographic survey, because the ground being covered is so new; on the other hand another author has chosen primarily to review current scholarship in his assigned area. In quite a few of these essays authors have drawn upon the fruits of a lifetime of study of particular books and areas, and a number contain fresh soundings on the nature and function of the sage. Some of the issues that have engaged scholars for the past several decades are discussed herein—notably, whether "sage" constituted a separate class, whether there were schools in Israel comparable to the schools in ancient Egypt and Mesopotamia, and whether the evidence permits the drawing of conclusions on the social location of the sage-authors of Israel's several types of wisdom literature. Hardly unique to this volume in substance, but unique in emphasis is the stress placed upon distinguishing the distinctive ways in which female sages functioned within and outside Israel.

Just as the methodologies employed by the contributors to this volume are diverse, so are their findings with respect to the nature and function of the sage. Some would reserve the designation for an exceedingly wise person, whereas others, including both editors, have taken the starting point for a definition of sage as one who has composed a book or piece belonging to the wisdom literature of the ancient Near East. In not a few instances below it will be seen that the sage was often a scribe or minister in the employ of a royal court. Even in instances where the philological evidence does not seem to warrant the conclusion that the sages constituted a professional class, the repeated praise of royalty as "wise" would seem to suggest that the ancient authors using such terminology knew whence their bread was buttered. Modern readers of the literature are thus not amiss in concluding that the authors of such eulogies stood in some state of dependency to royalty. A case in point is provided by the Aramaic *Words of Ahiqar* wherein the sage Ahiqar is addressed several times as a "wise scribe," "counselor of all Assyria," and "master of good counsel."[1] Scribe in this text from the late preexilic period is tantamount to minister and connotes considerably more than clerk, amanuensis, or transcriber. To this minister Ahiqar are attributed the slightly more than one hundred proverbs, riddles, aphorisms, animal fables, etc., that comprise the second part of the "words." This attribution is not certain, but a number of the phrases in *The Words of Ahiqar* and a cluster of proverbs pertaining to the king and deportment before him lend credence to the conclusion that at least a portion of the sage-authors of the wisdom literature in the ancient Near East came from among the ranks of scribes who served in some capacity in the royal bureaucracies of antiquity. As the Egyptian texts "In Praise of the Learned Scribes" (ca. 1300 b.c.e.) and "The Satire on the Trades" (which probably dates back to the Middle Kingdom, ca. 2150–1750 b.c.e.) make plain, the term scribe in the ancient Near East has a venerable history.[2]

To multiply or list further the various findings of authors below would exceed the proper task of a preface. The contributors to this volume will feel well rewarded if it serves to sharpen our understanding of the subtle and diverse meanings attached to the sage in antiquity, and not least if it also serves to enhance our understanding of the variety of ways in which the sage-authors of the biblical and extrabiblical sapiential texts functioned—whether in or outside the precincts of royal courts.

It remains a task for others to explore further the role and understanding of the sage in several biblical texts (especially Esther and the Song of Songs), deuterocanonical texts (especially Tobit, Judith, and Baruch), and extrabiblical texts (especially *The Words of Ahiqar*) not examined in this collection. Likewise, only a beginning has been made in the exploration of the sage in the New Testament.

With the keen interest on the part of several authors and the editors of this volume to draw upon the sociology of knowledge in explicating the sages of antiquity, their world construction and world maintenance, their legitimations of social institutions and their social locations, it perhaps will not be amiss to mention that in the eyes of the editors such an inquiry neither replaces nor precludes the necessity and importance of theological analysis.

1. For an accessible and persuasive analysis of this text, see J. M. Lindenberger, "The Words of Ahiqar," *The Old Testament Pseudepigrapha* (ed. J. H. Charlesworth; 2 vols.; Garden City, NY: Doubleday, 1983–85), 2:479–507. The phrases alluded to above are found in lines 12, 18, 35–36, and 42. For the Aramaic text, see A. Cowley, *Aramaic Papyri of the Fifth Century b.c.* (Oxford: Clarendon, 1923) 212–26.

2. For a translation of these two texts, see *ANET* 431–34.

The Select Bibliography focuses on wisdom, the sage, and the scribe in the ancient Near East and Israel. For the most part essays and articles which concentrate on specific exegetical problems within the biblical sapiential books have been omitted. Similarly, short shrift has been given to the subjects of creation in wisdom theology and to the bearing of the latter on the contemporary concern for ecology. For the latter, readers are referred to the excellent bibliographies of Henning Graf Reventlow and Bernard W. Anderson.[3] Responsibility for the final selection is the editors', but we would like to thank the following for scrutinizing our initial list and making suggestions: Claudia V. Camp, James L. Crenshaw, Michael Fishbane, Steven D. Fraade, Roland E. Murphy, and Samuel Terrien.

A special word of thanks is also due to Betty Creech of the University of Tulsa for her kindly and manifold assistance, to Steve Holloway of the University of Chicago for bibliographic tracking, to David Aiken, copyeditor at Eisenbrauns, for his meticulous reading and preparation of typescripts, and to Jim Eisenbraun for many manifestations of his deep commitment to the maintenance of high standards in the publication of scholarly works pertaining to the ancient Near East.

3. H. G. Reventlow, *Problems of Old Testament Theology in the Twentieth Century* (Philadelphia: Fortress, 1985) 134–86; B. W. Anderson, *Creation versus Chaos* (Philadelphia: Fortress, 1971) 196–206; and idem, *Creation in the Old Testament* (Philadelphia: Fortress, 1984) 172–78.

✿　　✿
✿

It is with a profound sense of loss that we report the death of coeditor John G. Gammie on December 26, 1989, while the book was in the final stages of preparation for the press. During most of the editorial and typesetting stages of production, John was battling cancer. He underwent several operations, and while we could sense his body weakening and energy flagging, he expressed a positive spirit and remained involved in the publication of this book (and several others) to the end. We, and scholarship, will miss him.

THE PUBLISHER
AND COEDITOR

# ABBREVIATIONS

| | |
|---|---|
| AB | Anchor Bible |
| *AEL* | M. Lichtheim, *Ancient Egyptian Literature* (3 vols.; Berkeley: University of California, 1973-80) |
| *AfO* | *Archiv für Orientforschung* |
| *AHw* | W. von Soden, *Akkadisches Handwörterbuch* (3 vols.; Wiesbaden: Harrassowitz, 1965-81) |
| *ANET* | J. B. Pritchard (ed.), *Ancient Near Eastern Texts Relating to the Old Testament* (3d ed. with supplement; Princeton, NJ: Princeton University, 1969) |
| AS | Assyriological Studies |
| *BA* | *Biblical Archaeologist* |
| *BASOR* | *Bulletin of the American Schools of Oriental Research* |
| BETL | Bibliotheca Ephemeridum Theologicarum Lovaniensium |
| BKAT | Biblischer Kommentar: Altes Testament |
| *BWL* | W. G. Lambert, *Babylonian Wisdom Literature* (Oxford: Clarendon, 1960) |
| BZAW | Beiheft zur Zeitschrift für die alttestamentliche Wissenschaft |
| *CAD* | *The Assyrian Dictionary of the Oriental Institute of the University of Chicago* (Chicago: Oriental Institute, 1956–) |
| *CBQ* | *Catholic Biblical Quarterly* |
| CBQMS | Catholic Biblical Quarterly Monograph Series |
| *HUCA* | *Hebrew Union College Annual* |
| *IW* | John G. Gammie et al. (eds.), *Israelite Wisdom: Theological and Literary Essays in Honor of Samuel Terrien* (Missoula, MT: Scholars Press for Union Theological Seminary, 1978) |
| *JAOS* | *Journal of the American Oriental Society* |
| *JBL* | *Journal of Biblical Literature* |
| *JCS* | *Journal of Cuneiform Studies* |
| *JNES* | *Journal of Near Eastern Studies* |
| JPSV | Jewish Publication Society Version (1985) |
| *JQR* | *Jewish Quarterly Review* |
| JSOTSup | Journal for the Study of the Old Testament Supplement Series |

| | |
|---|---|
| LCL | Loeb Classical Library |
| NAB | New American Bible |
| NEB | New English Bible |
| OBO | Orbis Biblicus et Orientalis |
| *Or* | *Orientalia* |
| OTL | Old Testament Library |
| *RB* | *Revue Biblique* |
| RSV | Revised Standard Version |
| *SAIW* | J. L. Crenshaw (ed.), *Studies in Ancient Israelite Wisdom* (New York: Ktav, 1976) |
| SBLDS | Society of Biblical Literature Dissertation Series |
| SBT | Studies in Biblical Theology |
| *UF* | *Ugarit-Forschungen* |
| *VT* | *Vetus Testamentum* |
| VTSup | Supplements to Vetus Testamentum |
| *WIANE* | M. Noth and D. Winton Thomas (eds.), *Wisdom in Israel and in the Ancient Near East: Presented to Professor Harold Henry Rowley* (VTSup 3; Leiden: Brill, 1955) |
| WMANT | Wissenschaftliche Monographien zum Alten und Neuen Testament |
| *ZAW* | *Zeitschrift für die alttestamentliche Wissenschaft* |

# PART I

---

*The Sage*
*in Ancient Near Eastern Literature*

# THE FEMALE "SAGE" IN MESOPOTAMIAN LITERATURE (WITH AN APPENDIX ON EGYPT)

## Rivkah Harris

### INTRODUCTION: NATURE OF THE SOURCES AND METHODOLOGY

Mesopotamia was a traditional patriarchal culture whose traditions are chiefly known through male authors and male-oriented visual materials. The evidence suggests that in Mesopotamia home, family, and domestic life were central and crucial to women.[1] The arenas for male status and public prestige—palace, military, and priestly offices—were largely, if not entirely, closed to women. Inasmuch as education was a significant avenue to power and status, lack of educational opportunities was then, as it always has been, a way of curtailing female influence and authority.

Although neither ancient Mesopotamian nor Egyptian women lived the sexually dimorphic or circumscribed lives such as those lived by women in classical Athens, "real women, like other muted groups, are not to be found so much in the explicit text of the historical record as in its gaps and silences."[2] This absence of direct accessibility produced, as M. B. Skinner has put it, "a circumstance that requires the application of research methods based largely upon controlled inference."[3] Additionally exacerbating the problem of the researcher is one noted by Leo Oppenheim, namely, the "remoteness from the realities of everyday life" that characterizes the cuneiform material.[4] Given the limitations of

Rivkah Harris is Associate Professor of Liberal Arts at the School of the Art Institute of Chicago.

1. These traditional roles are best summed up in a verse of "The Gula Hymn of Bulluṭsa-rabi," published by W. G. Lambert in *Or* 36 (1967) 121:65: "I am daughter, I am daughter-in-law, I am spouse, I am housekeeper [*mārāku kallāku hīrāku u abrakkāku*]."

2. M. B. Skinner, "Introduction" to *Rescuing Creusa: New Methodological Approaches to Women in Antiquity*, ed. M. Skinner, a special issue of *Helios* 13/2 (1987) 3. This comment by Skinner, a classicist, is as applicable to ancient Near Eastern women as to Greek and Roman women.

3. Ibid.

4. *Ancient Mesopotamia: Portrait of a Dead Civilization* (Chicago: University of Chicago, 1964) 301.

3

male dominance and remoteness of the sources, I herewith draw together a few preliminary observations based on my own research and
that of others. I say "preliminary," for Near Eastern women's roles in
history is only now beginning to receive the scholarly attention it
merits.[5]

The term "sage" when preceded by the adjective female must be
put in quotations marks, for it is highly questionable whether women in
the ancient Near East were ever considered to be culture creators, or
whether any mirrored "in themselves the ideals of wisdom" or were
"folk heroes of the wisdom tradition."[6] The usual term in Akkadian for
sage is *apkallu*, but apart from its application to goddesses such as Gula
and Damkina, *apkallatu* is limited in its usage to males, whether divine,
mythological, or mortal.[7] Does the ancient view that a goddess might
be an *apkallatu* imply, even if there is no such example to date attested,
that a mortal woman might also have been regarded as an *apkallatu*?
One must be very cautious and not infer, as have others, that the world
of goddesses is a direct reflection of everyday life.[8] Indeed, "female"
and "sage" were contradictions in terms in the ancient Near Eastern
world.

A more fruitful and probably the only viable approach to the topic
for now is by way of the rich vocabulary for wisdom and its derivatives,[9] as it was actually used *or might be inferred* in reference to
women and their activities.[10] One of the key terms, *nēmequ*, is defined

5. For example, *Frauen in altsumerischer Zeit* (Bibliotheca Mesopotamica 18;
Malibu, CA: Undena, 1985) by J. M. Asher-Greve is an exhaustive study of women,
focusing on the approximately nine hundred years of Uruk IV through Early Dynastic III
periods. There is no comprehensive study at present on Egyptian women, but see B. S.
Lesko's *The Remarkable Women of Ancient Egypt* (Providence: B. C. Scribe, 1987) and
the essays in *Histoire mondiale de la femme: préhistoire et antiquité* (ed. P. Grimal; Paris:
Libraire de France, 1957). A woman's role and function in the ancient Near East were
always tied to the status of her family, both natal and marital. But the kinds of sources
available on women for any given period skew the information. In my judgment women's
position in Mesopotamia, as in Egypt, probably changed far less than is frequently
assumed.

6. These "definitions" are given by G. Buccellati, "Wisdom and Not: The Case of
Mesopotamia," *JAOS* 101 (1981) 42.

7. For references see *CAD* A/2 171. For more on the Akkadian term for sage, see
the work of Ronald Sweet in this volume.

8. See my review of J. Ochshorn, *The Female and the Nature of the Divine* in *BA*
47 (1984) 124–25 for a discussion of this issue.

9. For an excellent entrée into Mesopotamian wisdom literature, its terminology,
and problems, as well as an extensive bibliography, see the Ph.D. dissertation of S. D.
Bolle, "Wisdom in Akkadian Literature: Expression, Instruction, Dialogue" (University of
California, Los Angeles, 1982).

10. Given the social structure and ideals of Mesopotamian and Egyptian societies I
find it unlikely that women, with the exception of those who like Enheduanna lived
outside of the traditional norms, would be permitted or even wish to devote themselves

in the *Chicago Assyrian Dictionary* as "knowledge, experience, wisdom (referring to the body of experiences, knowledge, skills, and traditions which are the basis of a craft or occupation, or form the basis of civilization as a whole), skill, cunning."[11] The adjective *emqu* is translated "experienced, skilled, educated, wise, wily."[12] Other derivatives of *emqu* also have meanings that fall within the range of skill and experience. It is significant that terms for housekeeper, such as *ēmiqtu* and *emuqtu*, imply that the woman who manages a household is a prudent woman.

The Greek *mētis* is close in its range of meanings to *nēmequ* for it "implies a complex but very coherent body of mental attitudes and intellectual behavior which combine flair, wisdom, forethought, subtlety of mind, deception, resourcefulness, vigilance, opportunism, various skills and experience acquired over the years."[13] So too does the Hebrew *ḥokmâ* incorporate a similar diversity of meanings.[14]

It is therefore within the parameters of the multifold connotations of the wise/wisdom vocabulary that the activities of the female "sage" are accessible to us in varying degrees. Included here are women as scribes and composers of written and oral literature, as healers, as musicians (vocal and instrumental), as mantics, and lastly as advisors in informal settings.

## FEMALE SCRIBE AS BUREAUCRAT

Leo Oppenheim in his seminal article, "The Position of the Intellectual in Mesopotamian Society,"[15] noted the many problems inherent in the study of scholarship, learning, and the art (and science) of writing. He provides a useful framework for examining the female as scribe: the

---

full time to scholarship and learning. At the same time one must not be too dogmatic if one bears in mind the results of recent studies on ancient Greek women. For example, K. Wider, "Women Philosophers in the Ancient Greek World: Donning the Mantle," *Hypatia: A Journal of Feminist Philosophy* (Spring 1985) 21ff., demonstrates that women were consistently involved with philosophy throughout antiquity, ancient and modern views notwithstanding.

11. *CAD* N/2 160.

12. *CAD* E 151.

13. M. Detienne and J. P. Vernant, *Cunning Intelligence in Greek Culture and Society* (Atlantic Highlands, NJ: Humanities, 1978) 3. These authors note (4–5) that although philosophical thinking marked a break with the earlier understanding of *mētis* it nevertheless continued "to operate in large areas such as politics, the military art, medicine, and the skills of the artisan." Even Adapa, the Mesopotamian sage *par excellence*, was wise in practical matters as well as outstanding in scholarly achievement, as shown by B. R. Foster, "Wisdom and the Gods in Ancient Mesopotamia," *Or* 43 (1974) 344ff.

14. See J. L. Crenshaw, "Prolegomenon," *SAIW* 4.

15. *Daedalus* 104/2 (Spring 1975) 34–46.

scribe as bureaucrat, the scribe as poet, and the scribe as scholar. The bureaucrat is usually connected with the two "great organizations"—the palace and the temple. The complex and lengthy training required to master reading and writing of necessity precluded (most men and) almost all women, who very early on, first as children and then as adults, took on the responsibilities of household tasks. It is therefore intriguing that it was a goddess Nisaba (Nidaba was her Sumerian name) who was for so many centuries the patron goddess of scribes and the scribal art.[16] And yet only exceptionally could women read or write. Nisaba is "the lady with cunning intelligence" who provides the scribe "with wisdom and intelligence."[17] Goddesses are attested as scribes, especially of the netherworld.[18]

Only sporadically and meagerly, though for centuries, is the female bureaucrat scribe attested. There is the one reference to a female scribe receiving rations in an Ur III text,[19] which suggests that she was perhaps a slavegirl belonging to the temple force. Much better evidenced are the nadītu women of the cloister (gagû) of Sippar who served as scribes.[20] Several of these have Sumerian names and were the daughters of scribes.[21] These female scribes acted as recorders of and witnesses to the transactions of nadītu women only. They are attested only for the earlier part of the Old Babylonian period and then disappeared from the scene at some time in the reign of King Samsuiluna. This was the time too when nadītus served in other official capacities in the cloister

16. So too is a goddess, Seshat, the patroness of writing in ancient Egypt. Note that the patron saint of the faculty of the medieval faculty of arts was Saint Katherine, and yet medieval women were not permitted to enroll in institutions of higher learning. For this see M. H. Shank, "A Female University Student in Late Medieval Krakow," *Signs: Journal of Women in Culture and Society* 12 (Winter 1987) 373.

17. Å. W. Sjöberg, "The Old Babylonian Eduba," *Sumerological Studies in Honor of Thorkild Jacobsen on his Seventieth Birthday* (ed. S. Liebermann; AS 20; Chicago: University of Chicago, 1975) 175, 173.

18. For references see *AHw* 1395.

19. A. L. Oppenheim, *Catalogue of the Cuneiform Tablets of the Wilberforce Eames Babylonian Collection* (American Oriental Series 32; New Haven: Yale University, 1948) 21–22.

20. For the names and functions of these scribes, see my "The Organization and Administration of the Cloister in Ancient Babylonia," *Journal of the Economic and Social History of the Orient* 6 (1963) 138–39, and *Ancient Sippar: A Demographic Study of an Old Babylonian City (1894–1595 B.C.)* (Istanbul: Historisch-archeologisch Instituut, 1975) 196–97, 288.

21. This is important for it suggests the possibility that scribes in the Old Babylonian period and later too may have taught their craft to their daughters, as well as to their sons. The question is whether women, apart from the special instances discussed, ever put their knowledge to professional use. Male scribes may have deliberately chosen Sumerian names to demonstrate their learning but whether this was so for the nadītu scribe is difficult to say.

administration. They and the female scribes apparently disappeared with the growing concentration of property and power in the hands of a few male administrators.[22] The cloister administration, which handled the affairs of its residents, the *nadītu* women,[23] celibate devotees in Sippar of the god Shamash and his consort Aya, was itself under the jurisdiction of the administrators of the Shamash temple, Ebabbar, the "great organization" of Sippar. With the *nadītu* scribe we have therefore a situation where women serve other women. There is no evidence that they functioned outside of the confines of the *gagû*.

The extensive "correspondence féminine" of Mari is well known. Published in Archives royales de Mari 10, it has served as the basis for the excellent study by B. F. Batto, *Studies on Women at Mari*.[24] These letters are nowhere said to have been written by their senders. They were for the most part probably dictated, as was generally the case in Mesopotamia. However, there is now evidence that at least ten women did serve as scribes in the Mari texts. One list mentions nine who received rations alongside others who worked in the harem; they were therefore slaves or at least of low status.[25] Nothing is known about the training they received. At times a Mari princess leaving her natal home to marry a ruler of another town might be given a slavegirl trained as a scribe as part of her dowry.[26] It would seem therefore that slavegirls might be specially trained to serve the correspondence needs of the harem women and princesses leaving Mari. They would thereby perform the important function of curtailing harem women's contacts with non-kin males, namely male scribes.

22. See my "Organization and Administration of the Cloister," 131–38, 141.

23. For more on this remarkable institution see, in addition to the publications cited above in n. 20, my article on "The *nadītu* Woman," *Studies Presented to A. Leo Oppenheim* (ed. R. Biggs and J. A. Brinkman; Chicago: University of Chicago, 1964) 106–35.

24. Baltimore: Johns Hopkins University, 1974. Batto states (5) that the woman at Mari "might receive an extensive education and serve as a scribe." S. Dalley, *Mari and Karana: Two Old Babylonian Cities* (London/New York: Longman, 1984) 110, comments that the number of female scribes "is enough to show that men did not hold a monopoly of literate skills." I contend that "extensive education" was rare for anyone, but especially so for women. In Mari it was for slavegirls who were trained for the specific concern of their owners: to limit access to harem women by non-kin males.

25. These nine scribes are named in M. Birot, "Textes Economiques de Mari," *Revue d'assyriologie* 50 (1956) 5ff. S. Dalley in *Mari and Karana*, 110, refers to them as female secretaries. But their slave status is significant and should not be forgotten.

26. See J.-M. Durand, "Trois études sur Mari, *Mari—Annales de Recherches Interdisciplinaires* 3 (1984) 167 n. 41. See his article "Les dames du palais de Mari à l'epoque du royaume de haute-Mesopotamie," *Mari—Annales de Recherches Interdisciplinaires* 4 (1985) 419, where a female scribe is considered as part of the household of the princess of Qatna.

We learn no more about female bureaucrat scribes. In a study of
Neo-Babylonian scribes by the Russian Assyriologist M. A. Dandameyev,
not a single female scribe occurs among the more than 3,000 known
scribes![27]

## FEMALE SCRIBE AS POETESS

The female scribe as poetess is also rarely attested to in the texts. But it
is in this category that Enheduanna, high priestess of the moongod
Nanna and the remarkable daughter of the Akkadian ruler Sargon,
belongs. The Sumerologists A. Falkenstein, W. W. Hallo, and Å. W.
Sjöberg all believe that she wrote and compiled a collection of Sumerian
hymns to temples. Hallo has described her "as a kind of systematic
theologian, well-versed in the subtleties of a—perhaps already traditional—set of Sumerian beliefs, and capable of adapting them to a new
point of view."[28] In a line of her magnificent nin-me-šár-ra hymn to the
goddess Inanna, Enheduanna refers all too briefly to the process of her
creativity as "I have given birth."[29] Her creative agony is compared to
labor pains, a fitting metaphor for a poetess.[30]

More than four centuries later another princess, priestess, and
poetess, also the daughter of a founder of a dynasty, appears on the
scene—Ninshatapada, daughter of Sin-kashid, founder of the Old
Babylonian dynasty of Uruk. The letter-prayer that she composed and
wrote to Rim-Sin of Larsa, conqueror of the city in which she had
served and from which she was exiled, became part of the scribal
curriculum. Hallo notes that this document adds new historical information: "She thus stands in a long tradition of princely women of Sumer
who enriched Sumerian literature with their creative talents."[31]

27. See the English summary in *Vavilouskie Pisci* (Moscow: Nauka, 1983) 237.
It must be stressed that this datum should not be taken as evidence of the deterioration of women's legal and economic status. Women continued throughout all of
Mesopotamia history to participate in the economic life of their community. They
also continued, I maintain, to be excluded from educational opportunities. Nor
should we assume that they regarded this negatively either.

28. *The Exaltation of Inanna* (New Haven: Yale University, 1968) 4.

29. Ibid., 33:138.

30. The extent to which Enheduanna's work reveals a specifically *female* style
and rhetoric remains to be explored. Appearances to the contrary, was she locked
into traditional male canons and forms?

31. For details of this text see Hallo's "Sumerian Historiography," *History,
Historiography, and Interpretation: Studies in Biblical and Cuneiform Literatures*
(ed. H. Tadmor and M. Weinfeld; Jerusalem: Magnes, 1983) 17. Note that Hallo
comments that "its very language was that of the royal scribes who formulated the
hymns, inscriptions, and date-formulas of the dynasty." The possibility therefore
remains that, although Ninshatapada was the author of the letter, she may have
dictated it.

In an informative article on "The Women of Sumer," W. W. Hallo calls attention to a moving lament to Ur-Nammu who died in battle; the lament, Hallo suggests, may have been composed by his widow.[32] S. N. Kramer considers the wife of King Shulgi of Ur the possible authoress of a lullaby to her son the future king. He attributes a love song to the *lukur* Kubatum, the concubine of Shu-Sin, son of Shulgi.[33] Indeed, a very good case could be made for the female authorship of lullabies and love songs. Along with work songs, stories, and proverbs,[34] they fit into the types of oral literature that have traditionally and cross-culturally belonged in the domain of women. The question remains however whether women themselves would have been able to write down any of their compositions.

## FEMALE SCRIBE AS SCHOLAR

There is to my knowledge one single tantalizing piece of evidence concerning a Mesopotamian female scribe. A fragment of the vocabulary text Proto á=A is known from its colophon to have been written by a female scribe named Belti-remenni. It has been assumed that she was a *nadītu* of the Sippar cloister mainly because "the existence of female scribes during the OB period is attested only in Sippar." The same scribe probably wrote an extant literary tablet.[35] Whether the woman who "wrote" the partly preserved requests for an oracle from the god Lahar on behalf of King Ashurbanipal was a scribe is unknown. She says, "Disregard that it is a (mere) woman who has written and submitted (this) to you." [36]

It is certainly within the realm of possibility that the *nadītu* scribes not only served the needs of their sister *nadītu*s but that they and other

32. *The Legacy of Sumer* (ed. D. Schmandt-Besserat; Bibliotheca Mesopotamica 4; Malibu, CA: Undena, 1976) 32.

33. See *ANET* 651–52 and 644–45. In the latter instance Kramer notes that "this poem seems to be a song chanted by a chorus of *lukur*-priestesses . . . , probably on the occasion of *hieros-gamos* celebration." I am not sure if Kramer still considers Kubatum to have been the authoress as he did earlier in *ANET* 496. Also see below in the appendix the strong possibility that women composed some Egyptian love songs.

34. Note, e.g., the Sumerian proverb, "My mouth makes me comparable with men," which, as W. G. Lambert rightly observes, "suggests that a woman may be speaking" (*BWL* 236, 238).

35. See *Materials for the Sumerian Lexicon* (ed. B. Landsberger et al.; Rome: Pontifical Institute, 1967), 9:148–49. She does not appear in any other Sippar text.

36. L. Waterman, *Royal Correspondence of the Assyrian Empire* (4 vols.; Ann Arbor: University of Michigan, 1930), 2:453:1367, 1368. This self-deprecation by a woman also is found below in the letter by princess Kiru to her father. The question remains whether she actually *wrote* these texts. In tone they are reminiscent of Shiptu's concern for her husband in a similar context.

celibates such as the *entu* priestesses Enheduanna and Ninshatapada living outside of the embroilment of wifely and motherly demands had the leisure (motivation and capacity) to devote themselves to learning and scholarship as did many a medieval nun.[37]

## FEMALE PERFORMING ARTISTS

Another area that should be noted if only in passing is women's participation in the performing arts—in dance and music (vocal and instrumental). King Shulgi of the Ur III period regarded the playing of complex musical instruments and the composing of songs as much a part of learning as was the learning of the scribal art.[38] One must be careful to separate the performers from the musicologists. It is doubtful whether singers and songstresses could read or write. It was rather the male *galmāḫu*, chief singer of temple dirges, who was trained in the scribal school.[39]

Very little is known about the training of men and women as singers. There may have been a kind of music academy for upper-class girls (and boys) to judge from a few references.[40] But what if any were the differences in training for free individuals and slaves, for men and women? It seems likely that royal and upper-class women (and men) received instruction in singing and playing of musical instruments as part of their education (which in Mesopotamia did not usually include reading and writing).

37. The case of the palace attendant (ˢᴬᴸSUHUR.LAL) who was the author or co-author of several Luwian purification rituals in the Hittite material is also of interest. See H. G. Güterbock, "A Hurro-Hittite Hymn to Ishtar," *JAOS* 103 (1983) 159. Her low status is significant.

38. G. R. Castellino, *Two Šulgi Hymns* (Rome: Pontifical Institute, 1972) 47:155ff. See also Sjöberg, "The Old Babylonian Eduba," 168–70, for music as part of school instruction. But again it must be noted that women would not receive their learning in this masculine institution. S. Pomeroy, *Goddesses, Whores, Wives, and Slaves: Women in Classical Antiquity* (New York: Schocken, 1975) 17–18, points out that being well read in Greek literature is associated with playing the lyre and dancing.

39. See Sjöberg, "The Old Babylonian Eduba," 170 n. 39, for references.

40. See Archives royales de Mari 1 64 discussed by Batto (*Studies on Women at Mari,* 51) where Shamshi-Adad advises his son to send his grown daughters to Shubat-Enlil to learn the art of singing (*nārūtu*). CAD Z 40 notes that the *zammeru* connotes "either an untrained singer or a singer of popular songs," in contrast to the *nāru* "who performed in palace and temple, singing to the accompaniment of various musical instruments." There is a group of Kassite letters that reports on the illnesses of young women in a music academy attended by princes and princesses. This is discussed by E. K. Ritter, "Magical Expert (*āšipu*) and physician (*asū*)," *Studies in Honor of Benno Landsberger on His Seventy-fifth Birthday* (AS 16; Chicago: University of Chicago, 1965) 317–18. For a discussion of songstresses in Zimri-Lim's harem see Durand, "Les dames du palais de Mari," 390ff.

## WOMEN AS HEALERS

Turning now to women as healers, an area frequently "assumed to be a mere extension of wifely functions and so female practitioners are often taken for granted." Female healers are "more likely to define themselves as informal practitioners, to operate within the home and not fit the model of medical knowledge, practice, and advancement."[41]

For Leo Oppenheim, "Mesopotamian medicine is shown to be a typical folk medicine . . . the *materia medica* consists mainly of native herbs of many kinds. . . ."[42] He points out that the two medical traditions and schools of Mesopotamia can be divided into the "scientific" and the "practical."[43] Women may safely be assigned only to the latter; the former presupposes a modicum of literacy. But once again we are at the mercy of the anonymity and the elusiveness of the women we seek.

There is the rare reference to a female physician (*asātu*): one appears in the palace at Larsa in the Old Babylonian period.[44] In a Mari letter (Archives royales de Mari 10 72:14-15) a secondary wife is in charge of an unnamed female physician who is remiss in her job of caring for the women of the harem.[45] Perhaps she too, like the female scribes of Mari, functioned to curtail access of male non-kin to women of the harem and did not serve male members of the court.

Leo Oppenheim has insisted that the goddess Gula who was associated with healing is "a deity of death and healing . . . and has no function as a patron deity."[46] He perhaps overstates the case. Goddesses and women cross-culturally have been regarded ambivalently (by men), linked with both healing illness and causing illness.[47]

The status and training of the female practitioner who was undoubtedly important throughout Mesopotamian history—the midwife (*šabsūtu*)—are little known.[48] Her techniques were not part of its *written*

41. S. A. Sharp, "Women as Keepers and Carriers of Knowledge," *Women's Studies International Forum* 9/3 (1986) 247-48.

42. *Ancient Mesopotamia*, 292.

43. Ibid., 290-92, for a discussion of their different methods of healing.

44. *Musée du Louvre—Département des antiquités orientales: textes cunéiformes* (Paris: Geuthner, 1926), 10 107:27.

45. Dalley, *Mari and Karana*, 122, who implies that a "medical practitioner might be of either sex." I doubt there were ever many female physicians.

46. *Ancient Mesopotamia*, 304-5.

47. See, e.g., *Women in Ritual and Symbolic Roles* (ed. J. Hock-Smith and A. Spring; New York: Plenum, 1978) 21, for this cross-cultural ambivalence.

48. See T. Jacobsen, "Notes on Nintur," *Approaches to the Study of the Ancient Near East*, ed. G. Buccellati, a special issue of *Or* 42 (1973) 290-93, for information on the tasks of the midwife. Cf. also W. von Soden, "Die Hebamme in Babylonien und Assyrien," *AfO* 18 (1957) 119-21.

medical traditions. It is likely that as was the case with the Hittites so
with the Mesopotamians the midwife was "the wise woman."[49] In a late
Babylonian poem to the greatness of Marduk and his city, Babylon
mention is made of "the *nadītu* women who with skill [*nēmequ*] save
the foetus."[50] It is unknown whether the *nadītus* ever functioned as
midwives during their heyday. It is more likely that it was their con-
temporaries, the *qadištu* women, who did.[51] Although so little can be
said about Mesopotamian midwives I would suggest that theirs was a
profession that may well have covered the services of a modern gyne-
cologist, obstetrician, and pediatrician. Perhaps they also served to
advise and help with family problems. Their knowledge was presumably taught by mothers to daughters and other relatives.

## WOMEN AS MANTICS

The penultimate area to be considered under the rubric of female
"sage" is the mantic. For men, divination and the profession of the
diviner (*bārû*) are central. The diviner's lore, the wisdom (*nēmequ*) of
the gods Shamash and Adad,[52] was closed to women. The goddess Gula
might be addressed as "a wise woman, a diviner, an exorcist."[53] But
there is to date only one Old Assyrian reference to a group of female
diviners (*bārīatu*) who are consulted, significantly by a woman, along
with female dream interpreters and spirits of the dead, to learn whether
the god Ashur continues to care for her.[54] On the basis of this one

49. J. Pringle, "Hittite Birth Rituals," *Images of Women in Antiquity* (ed. A. Cameron
and A. Kuhrt; Detroit: Wayne State University, 1983) 133. M. Lefkowitz and M. B. Fante,
*Women's Life in Greece and Rome* (London: Duckworth, 1982) 162-63, include Roman
texts that demonstrate the "elaborate professional skill involved in an exclusively female
profession." Of interest too is the case of the biblical midwives in Exod 1:15 who
outwitted the Egyptian authorities. Detienne and Vernant, *Cunning Intelligence*, 309,
mention that Aristotle was impressed with the "quickwittedness" needed by the midwife
"when she cuts through the umbilical cord . . . the skill of the midwife is no different from
the subtlety of the politician."

50. For more on this passage see my article, "The *nadītu* Woman," 135.

51. The *qadištu* woman is customarily associated with wetnursing (see *CAD* Q 48-
49), but may have been a midwife too.

52. Bolle, *Wisdom in Akkadian Literature*, 75, discusses at length the "intermeshing
of cult with the more speculative problems of existence that renders any definition of
'wisdom' in Mesopotamia fairly tenuous." It is the consequence and biases of Greek
philosophical thinking that makes this problematic for us. Detienne and Vernant in
*Cunning Intelligence* are very helpful in clarifying the issues.

53. *CAD* B 112 under *bārītu*. This too points to the distance of the world of
goddesses from the world of human women.

54. *Musée du Louvre—Département des antiquités orientales: textes cunéiformes*
(Paris: Geuthner, 1911), 2 5:5. See A. L. Oppenheim, *The Interpretation of Dreams in the*

reference nothing can really be said about female diviners except that the Old Assyrian letter may represent an atypical situation.

It is rather in the realm of dream interpretation that we find women. The *šā²iltu*, the oneiromancer, apparently functioned mainly outside and below the domain of the official, temple-centered religious life.[55] Leo Oppenheim has surveyed the role of female dream interpreters such as Ninsun, divine mother of Gilgamesh, in the epical literature. Dream interpretation in this genre is an aspect of maternal concern for men, as well as illustrative of women's advisory functions.[56] Oppenheim stresses that the methods of the dream interpreter "were interpretive rather than technical."[57] So again years of scribal training were not required. It is noteworthy that *entu* priestesses, such as Enheduanna, were dream interpreters.[58] It is not surprising that it is a goddess, Nanshe, who was the patroness of dream interpretation.[59]

I bypass the Mari phenomenon of prophetesses, which has been extensively studied by B. F. Batto.[60] It, along with the occurrences of "the Assyrian prophetesses of the goddess Ištar (of Arbela and even of Assur) . . . are deeply alien to the eastern, Mesopotamian, attitude toward the god-man relationship."[61]

Attention however should be called to the belief, especially evidenced for the late Assyrian period, that women might have a far greater propensity for sorcery than do men. A rich vocabulary exists for witches and sorceresses who are thought to possess great powers and esoteric knowledge. The compendia utilized by the exorcist priest, the *āšipu*, Shurpu and Maqlu, abound in terms for women who are regarded as powerful, disruptive elements in the social order, enemies of the order and well-being of the community.[62] And yet as S. D. Walters notes in "The Sorceress and Her Apprentice," "not only are prosecutions for sorcery lacking, prosecutions of accusations of sorcery are lacking as well."[63] He suggests that many cases of suspected sorcery may have

---

*Ancient Near East* (Transactions of the American Philosophical Association 46/3; Philadelphia: American Philosophical Society, 1956) 221–22, for a discussion of this text.

55. Oppenheim, ibid.

56. I enlarge on these in a forthcoming study on "The Images of Women in the Gilgamesh Epic."

57. *Interpretation of Dreams*, 225.

58. Hallo, *Exaltation of Inanna*, 59–60.

59. *Wörterbuch der Mythologie* (ed. H. W. Haussig; Stuttgart: Ernst Klett, 1965) 109.

60. Batto, *Studies on Women at Mari*, 119ff.

61. Oppenheim, *Ancient Mesopotamia*, 221–22.

62. See S. Rollins, "Women and Witchcraft in Ancient Assyria (c. 900–600 B.C.)," *Images of Women in Antiquity* (ed. A. Cameron and A. Kuhrt; Detroit: Wayne State University, 1983) 34–45, for a discussion of some of the issues.

63. *JCS* 23 (1970) 28.

been handled at lower levels of authority or even *sub rosa*. It must be emphasized that no witch is ever designated by name.[64] Women remained outside the ranks of the exorcists (*āšipu*) who required lengthy training in difficult texts.

## WOMEN AS COUNSELORS

Lastly, and most importantly for our topic, is the role of women of intelligence and cunning in advising and assisting men in their activities and enterprises. Further study is needed here. Despite the oft-expressed ambivalence toward women, the literary and epistolary materials particularly can reveal much.[65] I don't know if one will find, as C. V. Camp did for Israel,[66] the topos of wise woman. But capable, even remarkable women, are found at all times especially and not surprisingly from the royal and upper class—but not confined to it, as is evidenced perhaps most clearly in Siduri, the tavernkeeper who advises Gilgamesh on how to cope with the realities of death.[67] The women of Mari have already received well-deserved attention. The case of Kiru the princess giving advice to her father on political matters might be noted. In a letter to her father she reminds him that he had previously disregarded her advice. This time he ought to pay attention to her "even if she is only a woman."[68] Is this self-deprecation her own view of herself, the male view generally of women, or a way of appealing subtly to male prejudice in order to achieve what she wants to achieve?

## APPENDIX: SOME NOTES ON THE
## FEMALE "SAGE" IN EGYPT

R. J. Williams noted in his article "Scribal Training in Ancient Egypt" that "girls received training in specialized arts like singing, dancing, and the playing of musical instruments, yet we do occasionally come across references to female scribes. This suggests that sometimes provision

---

64. Even the special classes of women of the Old Babylonian period such as the *nadītu ištarītu kulmašitu* are lumped together in *Maqlû* (3:44) as evildoers. There is, it would seem, a general malaise and suspicion about these earlier groups of women who lived lives different from most women.

65. For some examples of ambivalence see my article, "Woman in the Ancient Near East," *Interpreter's Dictionary of the Bible: Supplement* (ed. K. Crim; Nashville: Abingdon, 1976) 963b.

66. "The Wise Women of 2 Samuel: A Role Model for Women in Early Israel," *CBQ* 43 (1981) 14–29. The Hittite sources are worthy of study from this perspective.

67. See *The Epic of Gilgamesh*, 3:1ff., in *ANET* 90.

68. See Batto, *Studies on Women at Mari*, 44, for a discussion of Archives royales de Mari 10 31.

was made for girls to receive the same type of education as boys."[69] To my knowledge, there is no evidence that girls ever attended schools alongside boys. They would probably have received private tutoring. Nowhere in his later article on "The Sages of Ancient Egypt in the Light of Recent Scholarship," does Williams mention a woman.[70]

Of recent interest to some Egyptologists has been the question of literacy among the ancient Egyptians. J. Baines in "Literacy and Ancient Egyptian Society," suggests "that in most periods not more than one percent of the population was literate."[71] But he does not include women in his figure, for he thinks women were probably not literate.[72] In another essay written with C. J. Eyre, he states that "there is no normal iconographic or textual context in which women would be presented as writing . . . but this simply shows that female writing was not part of the official, public life represented by monuments and documents. It leaves open the question of female literacy in other spheres."[73] They add a very significant comment: "Women's administrative titles in general belong to the service of women for women."[74] (This was very much the same situation for female scribes and perhaps for female physicians in Mesopotamia.)

Most recently Betsy M. Bryan has discussed the data for female literacy in the New Kingdom period.[75] This is the era, especially in the 18th Dynasty, when a remarkable group of women, such as Hatshepsut, Tiy, and Nefertiti, play *atypical* public roles. Bryan describes the "continuing, if somewhat rare, motif for literate women found in five tombs spanning a period of some three hundred years: scribal kits appear beneath women's chairs in the artistic representations of deceased women as they do for men." These tombs "provide the visual proof of non-royal female literacy."[76] Baines and Eyre, and certainly Bryan, are prepared to allow for literate women's contribution to "high culture" and accept the possibility that women wrote letters and composed poetry. Bryan is even open to the "professional use of literacy" by women. New data may yield firmer, more explicit information perhaps demonstrating that the relatively high legal and economic status of

69. *JAOS* 92 (1972) 220.

70. *JAOS* 101 (1981) 1-19.

71. *Man* n.s. (London: Royal Anthropological Institute of Great Britain and Ireland, 1983) 572-99, replete with bibliography.

72. Ibid., 584.

73. "Four Notes on Literacy," *Göttinger Miszellen* 61 (1983) 81.

74. Ibid., 82.

75. "Evidence for Female Literacy from Theban Tombs of the New Kingdom," *Bulletin of the Egyptological Seminar* 6 (1985) 17ff.

76. Ibid., 25.

Egyptian women was accompanied by accessible avenues for intellectual achievement. It is noteworthy that it is a goddess—Seshat—who
is the patroness of scribes and writing.[77]

As was suggested above, there was undoubtedly an ancient Near
Eastern oral literature to which women contributed. M. V. Fox, who
has studied Egyptian love songs, pinpoints some of these women as the
"songstresses of Hathor, goddess of love. It is quite likely that these
women composed songs as well as sang them . . . there is no reason to
assume that poetic composition was the exclusive province of men in
the ancient Near East. The scribes of the manuscripts were probably
men—all professional scribes were—but the authors may well have
been women."[78]

Meager evidence exists, but only for the Old Kingdom period, that
there were female physicians. The name of one overseer of female
physicians is known—Peseshet.[79] Apart from occurrences in myths and
stories nothing is known about the midwife.[80]

There are fragmentary texts that mention "a wise woman," literally
"a knowing one" ($rh.t$), who "may have been a kind of intermediary for
problematical affairs in the village community."[81]

The great deity of magic (and healing) was the goddess Isis who
healed her own injured son Horus. In a folk tale version of the myth she
refers to herself as "a knowing one [$rh.t$] in her town" who was taught
the knowledge by her father of how "to dispel a poisonous snake with
her oral powers." J. F. Borghouts suggests that "the $rh.t$ would appear

---

77. Baines and Eyre ("Four Notes on Literacy," 86) and H. Brunner (*Altägyptische
Erziehung* [Wiesbaden: Harrassowitz, 1957] 46) touch on the paradox of a goddess being
associated with writing, but they don't really come to grips with this intriguing but elusive
issue. Note the comment by H. G. Fischer, *Egyptian Studies I: Varia* (New York:
Metropolitan Museum of Art, 1976) 78, that Seshat is the only female shown holding or
using scribal equipment in the Old Kingdom and Middle Kingdom periods. He refers to
an 18th Dynasty graffito at the Step Pyramid "which condemns the graffiti left by earlier
visitors by comparing them to 'the work of a woman who has no mind' [lit. 'whose
counsel does not exist']." See also n. 16 above.

78. *The Song of Songs and the Ancient Egyptian Love Songs* (Madison: University
of Wisconsin, 1985) 56.

79. P. Ghalioungui, "Les Plus Anciennes Femme-Médecins de l'Histoire," *Bulletin de
l'Institut Français d'Archéologie Orientale* 75 (1975) 163.

80. For example, in W. K. Simpson, "King Cheops and the Magicians," *The Literature of Ancient Egypt* (New Haven: Yale University, 1973) 16–30. Relevant too are the
references in W. A. Ward, *Essays on Feminine Titles of the Middle Kingdom and Related
Subjects* (Beirut: American University of Beirut, 1986) 22ff., 76ff.

81. J. F. Borghouts, "Divine Intervention in Ancient Egypt and its Manifestation
($b3w$)," *Gleanings from Deir el Medīna* (Leiden: Brill, 1982) 84–85. I am grateful to
Barbara Lesko of Brown University for this reference.

to have had the function of a diviner and healer in Egyptian society."[82] He does not believe she was an ecstatic. She seems to me to be very much like the ubiquitous female practitioner who knew the curing powers of herbs and words.

In Egypt there were myths and stories that told of cunning as well as wicked wives.[83] In one, "The Tale of the Doomed Prince,"[84] the daughter of the Prince of Nahrin compels her father to accede to her wishes to marry the prince by various threats. She uses a ruse to prevent a snake from killing her husband by making it drunk—a theme similar to how the god Re prevented the goddess Hathor from entirely destroying mankind.[85]

82. Ibid., 26.
83. The women in "The Tale of the Two Brothers" (in Simpson, *Literature of Ancient Egypt*, 93-107) deserve far more study.
84. Ibid., 85ff.
85. See J. A. Wilson, "Deliverance of Mankind from Destruction," *ANET* 10-11.

# THE SAGE IN
# EGYPTIAN LITERATURE

## Ronald J. Williams

Early Greek travelers, overwhelmed by the magnificence of the pyramids, temples, and colossal statues that they encountered in Egypt, returned home with glowing accounts of the achievements of the inhabitants. Both Hecataeus of Abdera and Plato expressed their admiration of the sagacity of the Egyptians. For some centuries after 1500 B.C.E. Palestine was under Egyptian domination, and biblical writers in later ages also referred to the renown of Egyptian wisdom (1 Kgs 4:30 [5:10]; Acts 7:22). Moreover, the enigmatic hieroglyphic inscriptions that fascinated all visitors to Egypt added to their wonder and evoked feelings of awe and mystery.

The invention of this writing system shortly before 3000 B.C.E. was a tremendous achievement that made possible the development of a literary élite into whose hands the government of the land was entrusted. During the Old Kingdom period (ca. 2686–2160 B.C.E.) a large educated body of scribes was required to staff the civil service. High officials who were mostly of royal blood trained their successors in their own homes, and in the course of time organized classes were held at the royal court.

## WRITINGS OF THE SAGES

For purposes of instruction some teachers prepared didactic treatises designed to provide pupils with materials for practice in reading and writing and at the same time to inculcate rules for acceptable conduct and habits of speech. The earliest named author of such a work (which unfortunately has not survived) was Imhotep, the architect and chancellor of King Djoser of Dynasty 3 (ca. 2650 B.C.E.). Only the conclusion remains of the "Teaching for Kagemni," which purports to have been composed ca. 2600 B.C.E. by a vizier (whose name is lost) for his pupil

Ronald J. Williams is Emeritus Professor of Egyptology at the University of Toronto.

who was destined to become a vizier.[1] A similar work, the "Teaching of Hardjedef," was attributed to a son of King Khufu (Cheops) of Dynasty 4, ca. 2570 B.C.E. Only the beginning of this treatise has so far been pieced together from excerpts written by schoolboys some fourteen and a half centuries later (*AEL* 1:58–59). The one complete example recovered from the Old Kingdom, the "Teaching of Ptahhotpe," is ascribed to the vizier of King Isesi of Dynasty 5 (ca. 2400 B.C.E.; *AEL* 1:61–80).

For a variety of reasons scholars regard some or all of these works as pseudonymous. The association of texts with famous figures of an earlier age in order to endow them with a greater authority was a common feature of antiquity. The Egyptians had an enormous respect for the past, combined with a high esteem for the written word. In his teaching the aged Ptahhotpe says to the ruler, as he requests royal permission to train a successor: "Let me tell him the words of those who took heed, the counsels of the ancients, those who once listened to the gods." The king replies: "Do teach him about the words of former times. . . . No one is born wise" (*AEL* 1:63). Similarly, Merykarē's father urges him: "Emulate your forefathers, your ancestors. . . . You see, their words remain in [their] writings; open, that you may read and copy their wisdom" (*AEL* 1:99).

This last citation comes from the "Teaching for Merykarē" (*AEL* 1:97–109), a composition produced ca. 2050 B.C.E., after the collapse of the Old Kingdom. It was probably commissioned by Merykarē and ascribed to his father after the latter's demise. It is entitled a *sbōyet* 'teaching', like the other works, but differs from its predecessors in two ways: it displays a strong political motivation in its advice to the new ruler in stressful times, and it concludes with a hymn of praise to the creator-god.

Perhaps as early as the period between 2180 and 2130 B.C.E. a new type of composition appeared that may be characterized as pessimistic and cynical, boldly confronting established ways of thinking. This lengthy but poorly preserved work, the "Admonitions of Ipuwer" (*AEL* 1:149–63), describes a time of troubles in the land, a theme that was soon to become a literary topos for later writers. Toward the close of the text a dialogue ensues between the sage and the creator-god in which the deity is blamed for the state of the nation. The work received later editorial additions in Dynasty 13.

Two more texts of this kind from the same period may be mentioned. The "Tale of the Eloquent Peasant" (*AEL* 1:169–84) portrays a

---

1. English translation in M. Lichtheim, *Ancient Egyptian Literature* (3 vols.; Berkeley: University of California, 1973–80), 1:59–61 (hereafter *AEL*).

humble oasis-dweller confronting the Chief Steward of the land and, in a series of nine speeches, demanding his rights when robbed by a tenant farmer. This eloquent plea for social justice is said to have been made during Dynasty 9. The other is a poem that the Egyptians called a "Harper's Song" (*AEL* 1:194–97), copied from the tomb of a ruler named Inyotef, very likely early in Dynasty 11. It deprecates the costly and elaborate preparations made for the afterlife.

The reunification of the land late in Dynasty 11 ushered in the Middle Kingdom (ca. 2040–1786 B.C.E.). Prosperity brought with it the need for an enlarged bureaucracy and hence more scribes. Some schools still continued at the court. For the purpose of instruction new materials were prepared, such as a manual of epistolary greeting formulas, useful phrases, and advice to the young known as *Kemyt* 'Compendium'. Shortly after, a renowned scribe by the name of Khety produced a work called "Satire on the Trades" (*AEL* 1:184–92). Still introduced as a "teaching," its novel feature was the glorification of the career of scribe in comparison with all other occupations, which gave rise to many later imitators. Both of these compositions were studied and copied for at least a thousand years.

Dynasty 12 was founded by a usurper who assumed the throne as Amenemhet I ca. 1990 B.C.E. In order to bolster his claim to sovereignty he had a tractate written, referred to as the "Prophecies of Neferty" (*AEL* 1:139–45). This sage of Dynasty 4 predicted during the reign of King Snofru that a future time of troubles would be followed by a return of national stability on the accession of Ameny (the hypocoristic of Amenemhet). This did not take the form of a teaching but, like some texts already mentioned, belongs to the pessimistic and reflective writings of the sages.

Yet another politically inspired document appeared as a posthumous royal testament after the assassination of Amenemhet I. The "Teaching of Amenemhet" (*AEL* 1:135–39) was addressed to his son and successor Senwosret I, confirming the latter's legitimacy. However, a papyrus from Dynasty 19 records about the aforementioned "scribe Khety . . . , the one of excellent and choice phrases. I commend his name to eternity. He it was who composed a scroll, namely the Teaching of the King of Upper and Lower Egypt Sehtepibrē [i.e., Amenemhet I], when he had gone to rest, that he might join heaven and enter among the lords of the necropolis."[2] Clearly this too was a pseudepigraph.

Two more instructions were created during the Middle Kingdom, both political in nature, urging allegiance to the crown. The "Loyalist

---

2. Papyrus Chester Beatty 4:6:12–14. Translated in A. Gardiner, *Hieratic Papyri in the British Museum* (3d series; 2 vols.; London: British Museum, 1935), 1:43.

Teaching" eulogizes the ruler and calls on the readers to be loyal subjects.[3] The second has proved to be very lengthy, but is still being assembled from fragments that leave many gaps. It is entitled the "Teaching of a Man for His Son" and is uniquely anonymous among other teachings.[4]

With the pessimistic writings of this age or slightly earlier should be included what it is customary to call the "Dispute of a Man with His *Bai*" (*AEL* 1:163-69). The latter term, often mistranslated as 'soul', means 'power' and refers to the vital forces that leave the body at death to be united once more in the afterlife existence. This imaginative debate between the two is a skeptical attack on the efficacy of funerary preparations. Four fine poems were incorporated into the dialogue. Because of the lost beginning of the work the author is unknown. Somewhat later a Heliopolitan priest in the "Lament of Khakheper-rēsonbe" (*AEL* 1:145-49) returned to the well-worn but by then probably irrelevant theme of national woes. In accordance with the Egyptian love of eloquence he longs for new and different means of expression. It may well be that what we possess is merely part of a much larger work now lost.

During the New Kingdom (ca. 1567-1085 B.C.E.) the armies of Egypt drove north and south to create an empire that extended from Napata in Nubia to the Euphrates. This called for an expanded civil service, and scribal schools proliferated. In addition to the palace they were now located in temples. Teachers compiled anthologies of model letters, warnings to pupils against laziness and dissipation, eulogies of teachers by students, adulations of the sovereign, and countless variations of the "Satire on the Trades" theme. Seventeen of these testify to their great popularity (for example, Papyrus Lansing; see *AEL* 2:168-75). Extensive lexicographical lists of professions, titles, plants, and animals, as well as geographical and meteorological terms, known as *Onomastica*, were also drawn up.

Didactic treatises continued to be written, but were no longer attributed to members of the aristocracy. Political propaganda did not serve as a motive and such works were permeated by a new emphasis on personal piety. Probably composed in Dynasty 18, the "Teaching of Any" (*AEL* 2:135-46) was the creation of a temple scribe. The conclusion of the work presents a debate between Any and his pupil concerning

3. Translated by G. Posener, *L'Enseignement loyaliste: sagesse égyptienne du Moyen Empire* (Centre de recherches d'histoire et de philologie 2: Hautes études orientales 5; Geneva: Droz, 1976).

4. The beginning is translated in K. Kitchen, "Studies In Egyptian Wisdom Literature: The Instruction by a Man for His Son," *Oriens Antiquus* 8 (1969) 189-208.

the differing degrees of students' comprehension of the nature of instruction. The "Teaching of Amennakhte" was perhaps contemporary with it. Unfortunately, the beginning alone is preserved.[5]

The only fully intact treatise, the "Teaching of Amen(em)ope" (*AEL* 2:146–63), is ascribed to a minor official. Because of the likelihood that it was the source of Prov 22:17–23:14 it has become familiar to most biblical scholars. Later copies reveal that the text must now be dated to the twelfth century B.C.E. or even slightly earlier. It is noteworthy for the lofty ethical tone that characterizes it.

The didactic treatise survived as a living form down into the Greco-Roman period. By the middle of the seventh century B.C.E. demotic had come into vogue. This term is used both for the current vernacular form of the Egyptian language and for the more cursive form of script in which it was written. Evidence for the existence of as many as a dozen works of instruction has come to light. Of these, three have been sufficiently recovered and published to receive mention here.

Two important differences from their predecessors must be noted. First, the two-line units or "verses" of the earlier period have been replaced by short one-line sentences called "aphoristic monostichs."[6] Second, there are clear indications of cultural influences from outside Egypt, predominantly Aramaic and Greek.

The "Teaching of Ankhsheshonqy" (*AEL* 3:159–84) was composed no later than the second century B.C.E. The framework of the story has its fictional setting in Dynasty 22. It narrates how Ankhsheshonqy, a priest of Rē, was unjustly accused of involvement in a plot against the pharaoh's life and thrown into prison. While there he wrote out instructions and counsels for his son. The theme is akin to that of Ahiqar, and many of the maxims are similar.

A short composition, the "Teaching of Pordjel" is probably slightly later since it cites several lines from the "Teaching of Ankhsheshonqy," unless both works were indebted to a common source. This text seems to be a random collection of miscellaneous aphorisms.[7]

"Papyrus Insinger" (*AEL* 3:184–217), a manuscript of the first century C.E. is the longest known text of its kind, and several more columns have been lost from the beginning. We are thus ignorant of the author's name, although the reference to a certain Phibhor at the close of the text may pertain to him. Five other fragmentary papyri, all of

---

5. For a translation, see W. K. Simpson, *The Literature of Ancient Egypt* (2d ed.; New Haven: Yale University, 1973) 341–42.

6. M. Lichtheim, *Late Egyptian Wisdom Literature in the International Context: A Study of Demotic Instructions* (OBO 52; Fribourg: Fribourg University, 1983) 1–12.

7. English translation in Lichtheim, *Late Egyptian Wisdom*, 94–98.

Roman date, preserve portions of the text and exhibit many variant readings and dislocations of lines and sections. These features testify to its popularity and resulting editorial activity. In the work great emphasis is placed on the wise or godly man, on the one hand, and the fool or impious man, on the other. Moderation and self-control are central to the attainment of wisdom.

These didactic works were studied, copied, and memorized for many centuries. For instance, a scrap of papyrus dating from between Dynasty 26 and Dynasty 30 bears a portion of the text of the "Teaching of Amenemhet." This means that the little tractate was still being read and copied some fourteen to seventeen centuries later! Almost all of the early works are represented by copies from the Ramesside period on ostraca or papyri. Moreover, some have been the objects of editorial activity. In addition to the revision of the "Admonitions of Ipuwer" in Dynasty 13 mentioned above, the "Teaching of Ptahhotpe" underwent two later recensions, the "Teaching of Any" is known in two versions, and the teaching in "Papyrus Insinger" shows evidence of redaction in the later manuscripts.

Anonymity was the rule in the literature of ancient Egypt. The only exception to this appears to have been the writings of the sages to which real or fictitious names were usually attached. These ascriptions to well-known figures of antiquity were intended to lend authority to the document. The real or putative authors were revered long after their demise. The "Harper's Song" declares, probably as early as Dynasty 11: "I have heard the words of Imhotep and Hardjedef, much recounted as their own sayings" (*AEL* 1:196).

Nearly a millennium later, a papyrus of Ramesside date has preserved a long encomium of some of the illustrious writers:

> Those learned scribes since the time of those who existed after the gods, those who predicted what was to come, have become persons whose names endure forever. They have departed, having ended their lives, and all their kinsmen have been forgotten.
>
> They did not make themselves pyramids of copper having stelas of iron. They could not leave heirs as children [ . . . ] pronouncing their names. They made themselves heirs out of writings, of teachings which they had composed. They provided themselves with [the papyrus-roll as a lector]-priest and the writing-board as a loving-son. Teachings are their pyramids, the reed-pen their child, the stone surface a wife. . . .
>
> Is there one here like Hardjedef? Is there another like Imhotep? No one has appeared among our kinsmen like Neferty or Khety, the foremost of them. I mention to you the names of Ptahemdjehuty and Khakheper-rēsonbe. Is there another like Ptahhotpe or Kaires also?
>
> These sages who predicted what was to come—what issued from their mouths happened. It has been found as an utterance, written in their

scrolls. The offspring of other people have been given to them for heirs as their own children. They hid from everyone their magic (to be) read in their teaching.[8]

All the ancient scribes named in this passage have been discussed above, with two exceptions. Ptahemdjehuty is so far unattested elsewhere, and it has been suggested that he might have been responsible for the "Loyalist Teaching"; Kaires, associated in the list with Ptahhotpe, is thought to be a likely candidate as author of the "Teaching for Kagemni."

A welcome supplement to this text is a wall relief from a tomb at Saqqarah, apparently dated to Dynasty 19. Now destroyed, two blocks were photographed and copied by G. Daressy.[9] Three rows of persons are depicted: the top register consists of seated kings, their names now lost; the second and third registers are devoted to standing mummiform figures accompanied by their names and titles, including viziers, high priests of Ptah, lector-priests, and chief embalmers. Among the viziers Imhotep and Kaires are included, while a horizontal line of hieroglyphs between the second and third rows refers to the chief singer Ipuwer. The bottom register identifies the lector-priest Khakheperrēsonbe and Khety.


ROLES AND FUNCTIONS OF EGYPTIAN SAGES

These sages were all learned scribes, steeped in the texts usually designated as wisdom literature, and in many cases authors or compilers of such works. To later generations they embodied all the virtues of their teachings. Some, such as Prince Hardjedef of Dynasty 4, were even accorded divine honors. In addition to their influence on the moral climate of Egypt, they were in the forefront of the scholarship of the day. Many of them held positions at the court where they served as royal advisers.

During Dynasty 18 there were several instances of such persons. Queen Hatshepsut's chief steward and most valuable courtier, Senenmut, recorded in one of his inscriptions at Karnak: "Moreover, I had immersed myself in all the writings of the prophets. There was nothing I did not know about what had transpired since the dawn of creation so

8. Papyrus Chester Beatty 4:2:5–3:11 (see n. 2).
9. See J. Yoyotte, "A propos d'un monument copié par G. Daressy," *Bulletin de la Société Française d'Égyptologie* 11 (1952) 67–72. Photograph of one block is in Simpson, *Literature of Ancient Egypt*, pl. 6, and of the second block in H. G. Fischer, *Egyptian Studies I: Varia* (New York: Metropolitan Museum of Art, 1976) pl. 6 and 64 n. 26.

as to perpetuate antiquity."[10] Rekhmirē, the vizier of Thutmose III, stated: "Every sage is one who will heed what the earlier ancestors have said."[11]

Another such was Amenhotpe, the son of Hapu, who held the offices of royal scribe and overseer of royal works under Amenhotpe III. So influential was he at court that he outshone the vizier. The sovereign, out of gratitude for his services, endowed him with a handsome mortuary temple in the royal compound. An inscription speaks of him as "one who was advanced because of the excellence of his plans, whom the king exalted above his peers, the virtues of whose character the Two Lands [i.e., Egypt] knew, truly beloved intimate of the king, whose wisdom advanced his family."[12] In the Greco-Roman period he was to be deified and linked with Imhotep, the sage of Dynasty 3, as a god of healing. Citing Manetho, Josephus described him as one "who seemed to share the divine nature on account of his wisdom and foreknowledge of things to come" (*Against Apion* 1:232).

After elementary instruction in the schools, most promising pupils underwent a period of apprenticeship for more advanced training, especially in trades and crafts. Further specialized education was necessary for those scribes who aspired to administrative positions in the government, temple, or army, or who sought a career in such areas as medicine, astronomy, sorcery, or dream interpretation. Such tuition could be obtained in the palace or temple, or from competent practitioners elsewhere.

A variant reading on one ostracon of the "Teaching of Amennakhte" gives the author's title as "scribe of the House of Life."[13] Later in the text Amennakhte says to his apprentice: "May you be a scribe and frequent the House of Life!" Clearly this was a place to which one ought to aspire. Late in Dynasty 20, the compiler of one of the *Onomastica* describes himself in his introduction as "a scribe of the god's book(s) in the House of Life."[14] Even the pharaoh was not averse to

10. K. Sethe, *Urkunden der 18. Dynastie* (4 vols.; Urkunden des ägyptischen Altertums 4; Leipzig: Hinrichs, 1906), 2:415.14–16. The title *ḥm-nṯr*, literally 'god's servant', was applied to a grade of temple priest. It was rendered in Greek translations by the term *prophētēs*, i.e., one who interpreted the divine will.

11. Ibid., 4:1084.8.

12. H. W. Helck, *Urkunden der 18. Dynastie* (Urkunden des ägyptische Altertums 4, fascs. 17–22; Berlin/Gratz: Akademie Verlag, 1955–61), 21:1817.1–5.

13. This ostracon in the Cairo Museum contains only the opening title of the work. See G. Posener, "Les richesses inconnues de la littérature égyptienne," *Revue d'Égyptologie* 6 (1951) 42 (55), and idem, "L'exorde de l'Instruction éducative d'Amennakhte," *Revue d'Égyptologie* 10 (1955) 64 (C).

14. A. Gardiner, *Ancient Egyptian Onomastica* (2 vols; Oxford: Oxford University, 1947), 1:2*.

availing himself of its archives, as seen in an inscription in the Wady Hammamat, which says of Ramesses IV: "Of excellent understanding like Thoth, he was immersed in the annals . . . , having scrutinized the writings of the House of Life."[15] In a demotic document of the Persian period, Peteēse, priest of Amūn of El Hibeh, on being urged to accompany the pharaoh on an expedition to Syria, is told: "You are a scribe of the House of Life. There is nothing they will ask you which has no answer."[16]

The institution known as the House of Life had not one but many locations, usually—but not exclusively—in the proximity of temples. It was more than a mere scriptorium or library, although it was a center for the composition, preservation, study, and copying of texts. These were mainly of a religious nature, intended for cult use. However, the range of works extended to magical and medical texts, dream-books, and hemerologies. Academy may be an inaccurate as well as an anachronistic term for it, but it was the resort of the intellectuals of the day. That some instruction took place there is evident from a Middle Kingdom scarab in Cairo that identifies its owner as a "teacher of the House of Life."[17]

From the variety of works available in the House of Life, it is apparent that scholarship was not narrow in its scope. The Egyptian term $rḫ-(i)ḫt$, which means literally 'one who knows things', is the most frequently employed epithet for the sages. Originally it meant a knowledgeable person, as in the description of the ruler in the "Teaching for Merykarē": "The ⟨Lord⟩ of the Two Banks is knowledgeable" (*AEL* 1:105). But the same term is applied to Neferty, "that sage of the east," who is "a great lector-priest of Bastet . . . , a citizen with a capable arm, a scribe with excellent fingers, a wealthy man with greater possessions than any of his peers" (*AEL* 1:140). By demotic times the term had been replaced by $rmt-rḫ$ 'wise man', although in one trilingual temple decree the hieroglyphic $rḫw-(i)ḫt$ was rendered in the demotic version as 'scribes of the House of Life'.[18] The corresponding Greek version translated the word by *hierogrammateis*.

15. K. A. Kitchen, *Ramesside Inscriptions: Historical and Biographical* (7 vols.; Oxford: Blackwell, 1969-), 6:10, 15–16.

16. Papyrus Rylands 9:14, 21. Translated in F. Griffith, *Catalogue of the Demotic Papyri in the John Rylands Library* (3 vols.; Manchester: Manchester University, 1909), 3:64–105.

17. P. Newberry, *Scarab-shaped Seals* (Catalogue général des antiquités égyptiennes du Musée du Caire; London: Constable, 1907) pl. xiii.34. Discussed by J. Černý, "An Alternative Etymology of the Bohairic Word for Interpreter of Dreams," *Journal of Egyptian Archaeology* 50 (1964) 184.

18. In the Canopus decree from Tanis, line 3. See W. Spiegelberg, *Der demotische Text der Priesterdekrete von Kanopus und Memphis (Rosettana), mit dem hieroglyphischen und griechischen Fassungen* (Heidelberg: Carl Winter, 1922) 4.

As seen above, many of these sages were authors of works in which moral instruction was prominent. In urging their readers to live in conformity with ma$^c$at, the 'order' established by the gods in primeval times, they were transmitting the teachings of past generations. The "Teaching for Merykarē" declares: "An intelligent man is a [store]house for nobles. Those who know that he knows do not attack him. No [harm] occurs where he is, but ma$^c$at comes to him well-strained in accordance with what the ancestors have said" (AEL 1:99).

However, the sages were believed not only to be cognizant of the past and the present, but also to be able to peer into the future. In the encomium of the sages quoted earlier, the "learned scribes" are described as "those who predicted what was to come."[19] Neferty had been depicted as just such a figure. In Dynasty 12 Nedjemusonbe, chief physician during the reign of Amenemhet III, spoke of himself as "a pupil of Horus [i.e., the king], lord of the palace, student of Horus, lord of the Two Lands, one who predicts before it comes, who sees before it happens."[20]

In Dynasty 18 Thuty, the royal butler and herald of Queen Hatshepsut, recorded on his stele: "I investigated a time and predicted what was to come, (being) one who was skilled in looking at the future, aware of yesterday and thoughtful concerning tomorrow, ingenious regarding what would happen."[21] The Egyptian soothsayer was no prophet in the biblical sense. In his case there was no divine inspiration, but rather the prediction of events by a sage who was fully conversant with the essential nature of ma$^c$at, the divinely ordained order of the cosmos.

The wise man was also expected to be a practitioner in the arts of magic, a field that assumed great importance in the ancient world. The hymn in praise of the creator-god appended to the "Teaching for Merykarē" includes the statement: "He made magic for them [i.e., mankind] to be a weapon to ward off contingencies which are watched over by night and by day" (AEL 1:106). A series of tales concerning sorcerers is contained in the "Westcar Papyrus." At the court of Khufu (Cheops) two of the ruler's sons recount feats of magic by two chief lector-priests. Finally his third son, Hardjedef, produces a living sorcerer named Djedi, learned in the magical writings, who demonstrates his

19. See n. 8.
20. Stele Leyden V:7. See P. Boeser, Beschreibung der ägyptischen Sammlung des niederländischen Reichsmuseums der Altertümer in Leiden (12 vols.; The Hague: Nijhoff, 1905–25), 2:7, lines 3–4 of the vertical inscription on the right.
21. Lines 11–12 of the North Stele of Thuty; see N. Davies, "Tehute: Owner of Tomb 110 at Thebes," Studies Presented to F. Ll. Griffith (ed. S. R. K. Glanville; London: Egypt Exploration Society, 1932) 279–90 (text on pl. 39, translation on p. 287).

prowess. At the same time he proves to be equally adept at prediction, when he foretells the birth of triplets who are destined to inaugurate Dynasty 5. This same Hardjedef, renowned as an author, was reputed to have discovered magical spells in the temple of Hermopolis according to rubrics in the *Book of the Dead*.

In the Greco-Roman period a cycle of demotic stories revolves about Prince Khaemwēse, a famous son of Ramesses II and high priest of Ptah at Memphis. He and other participants are referred to as "learned scribes" and "sorcerers." The demotic term for 'sorcerer' is *ḥry-tp*, an abbreviation of the earlier title *ḥrw-ḥbt ḥry-tp* 'chief lector-priest'. This demotic term is now regarded as the source of the Hebrew word *ḥarṭummîm* 'magicians', closely associated with the term "wise men" in the Bible (Gen 41:8; Exod 7:11).[22]

## CONCLUSION

Despite the fact that so small a part of the written material from ancient Egypt has survived, sufficient evidence has been recovered to suggest the importance of learned scholars in the development of Egyptian civilization. On their testimony, the Old Kingdom witnessed the beginnings of a system of education for the children of the aristocracy, which in time became open to all with the requisite ability. It was sponsored by some of the most important individuals, whose names were to be remembered for long ages. They were the polymaths of their generations.

Any consideration of their contribution to the intellectual and spiritual life of ancient Egypt must take account of one significant fact. Tomb inscriptions of nobles in the Old Kingdom consisted of a brief listing of the titles and achievements of the deceased, with some emphasis on his funerary gifts. However, in Dynasty 6 one is suddenly confronted with longer "autobiographies," which include self-laudatory statements designed to ensure immortality to the occupant. One example must suffice, taken from the tomb of Neferseshemrē, a priest of the pyramid of King Teti, ca. 2340 B.C.E.:

I executed *maʿat* for its lord [i.e., the deity], satisfied him with what he desired, spoke truly, did *maʿat*, spoke what was good, repeated what was

22. Some scholars have supposed *ḥry-tp* to be an abbreviation of the earlier Egyptian title *ḥrw-ḥbt ḥry-tp*, customarily rendered as 'chief lector-priest'. More recently this view has been examined by J. Quaegebeur, "On the Egyptian Equivalent of Biblical *Ḥarṭummîm*," *Pharaonic Egypt: The Bible and Christianity* (ed. S. Israelit-Groll; Jerusalem: Magnes, 1985), 162–72, who believes *ḥry-tp/b* to be an independent title in this case rather than an attributive element.

good, seized the opportune time, wishing that thereby it might go well with people. I judged between two persons in order to reconcile them. I rescued the oppressed from one more powerful than he as far as I was able. I gave bread to the starving and clothing ⟨to the naked⟩, a means of landing to him without a boat. I buried him who had no son. I made a ferry-boat for him who had none. I was respectful to my father, kind to my mother, and I brought up their children.[23]

Many of the same phrases are to be found in other tombs and will become clichés. They reflect the ethical norms of Egyptian society. One may doubt the veracity of every statement attributed to the tomb occupant, but the important fact is the expression of what he regarded as ideal conduct.

What was the stimulus that gave rise to such a development? It was prior to this period that the first didactic treatises were produced. The sages believed that morals could be taught. Their writings had a profound and lasting effect on the intellectual and ethical life of ancient Egypt, which was to reach far beyond the small number of those who were literate. The sages left their mark on the tomb biographies, the *Coffin Texts*, and the *Book of the Dead*, in addition to a number of quotations and allusions in later ages.

The learned scribes of the Old Kingdom and First Intermediate Period who first attempted to put their thoughts and convictions into writing made remarkable progress in creating literary forms suitable to their purpose. They also initiated some of the themes that were to remain central to wisdom literature for more than two millennia. For instance, the concept of the *gr* 'silent one', a term that implies discipline and self-control, appears in the "Teaching for Kagemni" and the "Teaching of Ptahhotpe," and assumed an ever larger role in subsequent ages. The first clear formulation of a final judgment is found in the "Teaching for Merykarē," but it has been shown that even this passage is based on the earlier words of Ptahhotpe.[24]

23. K. Sethe, *Urkunden des Alten Reiches* (Urkunden des ägyptische Altertums 1.3; 2d ed. Leipzig: Hinrichs, 1933) 198. 14–199. 7. For a translation see *AEL* 1:17.

24. G. Fecht, *Der Habgierige und die Maat in der Lehre des Ptahhotpe, 5. und 19. Maxime* (Abhandlungen des Deutschen Archäologischen Instituts Kairo 1; Glückstadt: Augustin, 1958).

# THE SAGE
# IN SUMERIAN LITERATURE:
# A COMPOSITE PORTRAIT

## Samuel Noah Kramer

"Before the Flood" there were, according to a Sumero-Akkadian tradition of a much later day, sages known as *abgals*, such as Adapa, who brought culture and civilization to Sumer and humankind. But virtually nothing is known of these *abgals*, and what little is known is vague, legendary, and obscure.[1] The first true sages, one may surmise, were the temple priests and administrators in the city of Erech who, toward the end of the fourth millennium B.C.E., originated the semipictographic system of writing, together with an embryonic system of teaching related to these newly invented signs. Very real sages too were no doubt the later high temple functionaries in the various cities of Sumer who transformed these semipictographic signs of their predecessors into a phonetic system of syllabic and ideographic script, and developed the educational system that this transformation required. But nothing is known of these early sages except what can be surmised or inferred from the hundreds of administrative tablets that have been recovered from these early days.[2]

Beginning about 2500 B.C.E., however, as is evident from numerous lexical and literary documents excavated at Fara (ancient Šuruppak) and Tell Abu-Salabikh, there must have been an educational institution, a place of learning, known from later days as the *edubba* 'tablet-house', in a number of Sumerian cities.[3] In the course of the centuries that followed, the *edubba* developed and matured as the center of culture and learning. In the *edubba*s of Nippur and Ur, for example, there

Samuel Noah Kramer is Emeritus Curator of Tablet Collection at the University Museum, University of Pennsylvania.

1. Cf. *CAD* sub *apkallu* for details and bibliographical references.
2. Cf. A. Falkenstein, *Archaische Texte aus Uruk* (Leipzig: Harrassowitz, 1936); and E. Burrows, *Archaic Texts* (Ur Excavation Texts 2; London: British Museum, 1935).
3. Cf. R. D. Biggs, *Inscriptions from Tell Abū Ṣalabikh* (Chicago: University of Chicago, 1974).

flourished the scholar and man of letters, the academic and humanist, who studied, enlarged, and expanded whatever linguistic, literary, and theological lore was current in his day.[4]

At the head of the *edubba* was the wise, word-knowing, all-knowing *ummia*, the savant *par excellence*, and over the centuries it was he and his associates in the *edubba* who originated, planned, and devised a wide-ranging curriculum for the purpose of training the students in such basics as reading, writing, arithmetic, and music both vocal and instrumental; preparing them for recording the complex and diversified administrative documents of temple and palace; teaching them how to become accomplished archivists and chroniclers (and thus helping preserve important historic events for future generations); and guiding them in the copying, studying, and redacting of a wide variety of literary works that had come down from earlier days, as well as in the art of composing new ones when the appropriate occasion arose.

Once the students had completed their training and graduated from the *edubba*, and in one way or another had succeeded in becoming dominant and influential officials in the temple or palace, they helped guide and direct Sumerian intellectual and spiritual life. These are the ones who are envisaged as sages throughout this essay, beginning with the sages as educators and humanists, continuing with their role in the temple, and concluding with their role in the palace.

## THE SAGE AS EDUCATOR AND HUMANIST

An important secular part of the *edubba* curriculum consisted of the copying and studying of hundreds of proverbs, precepts, and maxims that were selected, redacted, and arranged according to various criteria by the *ummias* and their associates.[5] Many of these no doubt went back to early oral and written sources, but not a few were probably originated and put in literary form by various *ummias* of later days. As even a cursory survey of this "wisdom" material indicates, the *ummias* were in some respects secular humanists whose aim was not only to imbue the students with proper ethical and practical values (and thus mold them into decent, sensible, likable, and healthy human beings), but also to help them apprehend and comprehend the ambiguous, ambivalent nature of the human condition, and the rather bitter irony of fate, thus

4. For the *edubba* cf. Å. W. Sjöberg, "The Old Babylonian Edubba," *Sumerological Studies in Honor of Thorkild Jacobsen* (ed. S. Lieberman; AS 20; Chicago: University of Chicago, 1975) 159–79, where all essential bibliographical details will be found.

5. For a detailed treatment of the Sumerian proverb collection, cf. R. S. Falkowitz, "The Sumerian Rhetoric Collection" (Ph.D. diss., University of Pennsylvania, 1980), which includes all essential bibliographical material.

saving them perhaps from disillusionment and frustration. By and large these proverbs and precepts may be divided into two categories: those that relate to human values both ethical and practical, and those that concern the paradoxical and contradictory aspects of human destiny. Thus, there are numerous maxims and sayings that stress the beneficial effects of teamwork, patience, clarity of vision, firmness of resolve, realization of one's limitations, faithful execution of one's craft and handiwork, cleanliness, and tactful, friendly, truthful speech. Many others highlight the harmful effects of greed, gluttony, lying, extravagance, arrogance, contention, and controversy. These were the practical and ethical values necessary for the sages to cultivate in order not only to perform their official, professional functions successfully and well, but also to achieve well-being in everyday existence.

There are other aphorisms, however, that tend to demonstrate that despite people's best efforts to live properly and do what is right, they are often doomed to failure, disappointment, and frustration because of the paradoxical character of human nature and the inevitability of fate. Take, for example, the dilemma of choosing between wealth and poverty. Though the rich have many possessions, these are fleeting and evanescent, and, moreover, make their nights sleepless. But the poor are certainly no better off: their food is never adequate and satisfying, their clothes are ragged and torn, and their debts lay them low with worry and pain.

Marriage and its deterioration provide another example of the ambiguities and contradictions that often characterize human conduct. Marriage in Sumer usually began with a tender, affectionate, harmonious relationship between husband and wife. But as time went on it had its ups and downs, its loving kisses and its hateful beatings. Often, some proverbs indicate, the husband became disillusioned with the marriage, especially if the wife was quarrelsome and discontented. Mutual accusations of infidelity and deception were not infrequent, so that the husband thought of divorce, and the wife looked back longingly to the days when her husband was still a wooing bridegroom.[6]

The sages also reflected on family life, which also has its contradictory, antithetical aspects. There was the harmonious family whose members were mutually respectful and affectionate. But there was also the family that had been infected by the blight of the "generation gap," with constant bickering and squabbling between older sister and brother,

6. Cf. my "The Woman in Ancient Sumer: Gleanings from Sumerian Literature," *La Femme dans le Proche-Orient antique* (ed. J.-M. Durand; Compte Rendu, Rencontre Assyriologique Internationale 33; Paris: Editions Recherche sur les Civilisations, 1987) 107–12.

between son and mother, and between father and son.[7] A vivid example
of the ambivalent, fluctuating father-son relationship is provided by a
composition that may be entitled, "A Scribe and His Delinquent Son."
It consists almost entirely of a father's bitter, abusive denunciation of his
ungrateful son who, he claims, hates school, learning, and the scribal
art; who is perverse and looks not to his humanity; and who constantly
pursues materialistic success and distracting, worldly, depraved pleasures. But instead of ending his diatribe with a curse against the ingrate,
as might have been expected, he proceeds to bless him with divine
favor, exalted humanity, and leadership among the city's savants. Evidently the scribe's fatherly feeling proved to be stronger than his anti-
pathy and disappointment.[8]

Another secular, humanistically oriented component of the *edubba*
curriculum consisted of a rather unusual group of "disputations" in
which the *ummias* presented their perceptive reflections on various
aspects of the human scene and its environmental horizon.[9] These
included the comparative value and usefulness of human-made artifacts,
the two seasons of the year, and the varied components of the animal
and vegetable world that surround humans and circumscribe their
activities. In the "Disputation between the Hoe and the Plow," for
example, the author, some anonymous *ummia*, argues that it is the
unattractive, ungainly, mud-wallowing hoe that builds dams and dykes,
mends walls and roofs, straightens roads, digs ditches, cleans canals,
drains marshland, rips out weeds, builds temples and palaces, and digs
wells that make gardens fruitful. To be sure, the plow, too, is necessary
and useful, and kings and nobles recognize its value by celebrating the
planting season with feasts and banquets. The grain sheaves it produces
present a picturesque scene in the field, and the stacks and mounds of
ripened grain are full of allure. Moreover, the fallen scattered seeds are
gleaned by the orphan, the widow, and the destitute to sate their
hunger. But it takes four men and six oxen to work the plow; it labors
only four months out of the year; it breaks down again and again and
has to be fixed by carpenter and mended by leather-workers. Hence
the author adjudged the lowly hoe the victor.

7. For additional details and bibliographical references, cf. my "Modern Social
Problems in Ancient Sumer," *Gesellschaftsklassen im Alten Zweistromland und in den
angrenzenden Gebieten* (ed. D. O. Edzard; Compte Rendu, Rencontre Assyriologique
Internationale 18; Munich: Bayerischen Akademie der Wissenschaften, 1972) 113–21.

8. For the edition of this document, cf. Å. W. Sjöberg, "Der Vater und sein
missratener Sohn," *JCS* 25 (1973) 105–69.

9. The sketch of the contents of the disputations that follows is based on the (as of
yet) unpublished editions of the documents prepared by Miguel Civil for the *Sumerian
Dictionary*. For the "fish-lover" composition, see M. Civil, "The Home of the Fish," *Iraq*
23 (1961) 154–75.

Just as the muddy, slimy, ungainly hoe was deemed more valuable than the rather finicky, aristocratic plow, so the rather crude, rude "mighty Copper" was deemed more useful than attractive, seductive "Silver." At least this was so according to the *ummia* who composed the "Disputations between Silver and Mighty Copper." He pronounced copper the victor because it is the copper mattock that breaks up the ground for irrigation; it is the copper adze that helps fashion the seed-planting plow; it is the copper axe that cuts the firewood that brings warmth to the cold wintry days; and it is the copper sickle that cuts the standing grain at harvest time. As for silver, its only use is as ornaments for the palace and gifts for the grave.

One moral that may be drawn from the two disputations treated above is that one should not judge by surface appearances. This is also true in the "Disputation between Summer and Winter," whose author concluded that it was the harsh, rigorous, violent Winter that was superior to the mild, tranquil, indulgent Summer. It was frosty Winter that made possible the annual overflow of the Tigris and Euphrates, which made the fields productive and the farms prolific, which generated the marshes where birds and fish thrive, and the canebrake with its invaluable reeds of diverse types; it was during Winter that all animals, domestic and wild, give birth to their teeming young.

The nature, role, and function of the animal world that pervaded the human scene generated much thought and reflection among the *edubba* personnel, as is evident from the numerous extant animal fables. These concern some sixty species of animals, including the greedy dog, the predatory wolf, the boastful, cowardly fox, the hibernating bear, the thieving mongoose, the preying lion, and the foolish donkey. But it was the struggle between the bird and fish that seemed to fascinate them most. And not surprisingly it was the beautifully ornamented bird who walked about in the palace like a jewel, chirping sweetly, that was adjudged superior to the fish with its ugly face, crawling body, and foul smell. Nevertheless, there was also the dedicated and devoted lover of fish whom some savants envisaged and romanticized as having constructed a special home for the fish, spacious and secure, and provided it with fine food and drink, with beer and sweet cookies, a place where all fish could live in peace safe from preying birds and sharklike predators.

In the vegetable kingdom it is the differences between the tree and the reed that attracted one *ummia*'s attention and preoccupation. After due reflection, this sage concluded that the tree with its rich fruit and sturdy timber from which were constructed palaces and thrones, boats and chariots, footbridges and plank-walks, was superior to the infirm, shaky reed used for making drab mats, although admittedly it did provide fuel in winter, styluses for the scribe, and flutes for the musician.

The most valuable products from the vegetable worlds are, of course, the cereal grains such as barley, emmer, and wheat. But pressing hard to equal recognition are cattle, large and small, as is evident from the "Disputation between Cattle and Grain," which, however, concludes with a resounding victory for grain. For as the author sees it all, even those who have great wealth and much cattle must stand and wait patiently at the gate of him who possesses grain. After all, it is grain from which bread and beer are produced, the two essentials of a joyous life.

As is evident from the "Disputation between Cattle and Grain," it was the farmer who was deemed the most important contributor to Sumer's prosperity and well-being, the backbone and mainstay of its agriculturally based economy. The *ummias* therefore introduced in the *edubba* curriculum a kind of farmer's handbook in the form of a father's instructions to his son that would guide him throughout his yearly farming activities, beginning with the inundation of the field in May-June and ending with the gleaning and winnowing of the freshly harvested crops the following April-May.[10]

This annual gathering of the harvest in the late spring was a time of feasting and rejoicing accompanied by merry drinking songs. At least one of these was part of the *edubba* curriculum, a hymn to the beer-goddess Ninkasi, consisting of two parts. The first describes the various steps in the brewing process, beginning with the preparation of a cooked mixture of dough and aromatic herbs and ending with the pouring of the fermented liquid in special beer vats and jars. The second begins with a merry, joyous toast to these beer-filled vessels, and ends on what seems to be an erotic note involving Inanna, the goddess of love.[11]

So much for the mundane, worldly wisdom imbibed and absorbed by the students of the *edubba* from the secular and humanistic ingredients of the *edubba* curriculum. But there were two other professionally more useful and practical components of the curriculum designed for those graduates of the *edubba* who intended to enter the service of the palace or temple. One of these consisted of collecting, compiling, and arranging a large diversified group of archival, historical, and legal documents, such as royal inscriptions, lists of year-names used for dating purposes, lists of kings and dynasties, royal correspondence that

10. Cf. for the present chap. 11 of my *History Begins at Sumer* (3d ed.; Philadelphia: University of Pennsylvania, 1981).

11. For the edition of this composition, cf. M. Civil, "A Hymn to the Beer Goddess and a Drinking Song," *Studies Presented to A. Leo Oppenheim* (ed. R. Biggs and J. Brinkman; Chicago: Oriental Institute, 1964) 67–89.

had accumulated over the years, model legal contracts of varied content, and law-codes promulgated by one ruler or another. The other, and spiritually and culturally the most significant, ingredients of the *edubba* curriculum related to the hundreds of literary documents that had been composed, revised, and redacted over the centuries beginning with the middle of the third millennium: myths and epic tales, hymns, divine and royal, prayers and chants, and laments of diverse character and categories. It was the cumulative, comprehensive, collective, encyclopedic content of these literary works that shaped the students' theological and cosmological opinions and views, inspired religious beliefs and tenets, and molded moral and ethical ideals. All of these the students were to inculcate, in one way or another, in the minds and hearts of kings and courtiers, of priests and temple administrators, once they had graduated from the *edubba* and risen to high office in temple or palace.

That at least some of the *edubba* graduates would become leading functionaries and respected sages can be assumed from their social origins as well as their aggressive personalities. Most of the students belonged to the upper strata of Sumerian society. They were the children—chiefly sons—of kings, governors, "city elders," ambassadors, temple administrators, high military officers, sea captains, scribes, archivists, and accountants. The personalities of these *edubba* graduates had been deeply affected by, and imbued with, the competitive, aggressive drive for preeminence and prestige, for victory and success, that characterized much of Sumerian behavior, and was fostered and nurtured by the teachers of the *edubba* who composed quite a number of school essays and dialogues in which the poor, failing student was mercilessly ridiculed and reviled, while the good, promising student was encouraged to become "the leader among his brothers, the chief among his friends, the highest among his fellows."[12]

## THE SAGE AND THE TEMPLE

As is well known and documented, the temple played a predominant role in Sumerian religious life.[13] In charge of the temple and its cult was a numerous and diverse clergy consisting of priests high and low, diviners, and exorcists. Among the leading temple functionaries were

12. Editions of these school essays and dialogues are to be published by Miguel Civil in the near future.

13. For more details cf. chap. 4 of my *The Sumerians* (Chicago: University of Chicago, 1963), and section 3 of *Le temple et le culte* (Compte Rendu, Rencontre Assyriologique Internationale 20; Leiden: Nederlands Historisch-Archeologisch Institut te Istambul, 1975) 31–172.

the high priest or high priestess known as *en*, and the chief temple administrator known as *sanga*. It is not unlikely that they, and other high functionaries of the temple, had attended the *edubba* in their youth, or had received comparable private instruction from some renowned *ummia*. It was therefore the teaching and indoctrination of these *ummias* that dominated the thought and practice of these high temple officials. Over the centuries, it is not unreasonable to surmise, it was the eminent, far-famed *ummias* and the top temple functionaries trained and educated by them who originated and developed the intellectual constructs and spiritual concepts that provided the groundwork and framework of the religious thought and practice of the Sumerians. These included their cosmological assumptions and theological credos, their belief in the existence of an invisible anthropomorphic pantheon, their ideas about its organization and method of operation, their notions about the creation of humanity and their role as the servant of the gods and the builder of temples. It is the sage's dark vision of humanity's place in the universe that will be sketched briefly in the pages that follow.

The Sumerian sages, in line with their world view, had no exaggerated confidence in humanity and human destiny. They were convinced that humans were fashioned of watery clay and created for one purpose only: to serve the gods by supplying them with food, drink, and shelter, and thus freeing them for their divine activities. Human life was beset with uncertainty and haunted by insecurity, since people could not know the destiny decreed for them by the inscrutable and unpredictable gods. When they died their emasculated spirits descended to the dark, dreary netherworld, where life was but a dismal wretched reflection of its earthly counterpart.

As if this pessimistic view were not enough to humble and distress human beings, the sages introduced and taught the doctrine that human suffering and misfortune were the consequence of sins and misdeeds and furthermore that no one was without sin. There were no cases of unjust, undeserved human suffering. To help brighten and alleviate somewhat this dark, dismal view of humanity and human fate, the sages granted one ray of hope—they taught and propagated the credo of the existence of a personal god, a kind of good angel and divine parent for every family head. It was to this personal god that sufferers must bare their hearts in prayer, and it was through this god that they would find salvation.

But woe to those who did not acknowledge and value their personal god. They were in grave danger of being made to walk the road to a house of lament, a kind of hell on earth where hostility, hatred, discord, and madness predominate, a house filled with tears and groans that rips the wicked apart and grants life only to the righteous. This, according to the composition "Nungal in the Ekur," actually happened to one foolish fellow who was caught by the goddess Nungal, the Queen of the Ekur, at the gate of her temple.[14] Fortunately the merciful and compassionate side of the goddess came to his rescue, and she brought him out of the hellish prison and returned him to her "house of life" where he soothed the heart of his god with tears of prayer. Only then did Nungal forgive him. She made him as pure as refined silver and returned him to the protection of his god, who, according to the author, would show his gratitude by praising and exalting Nungal's name unto distant days.

The Ekur was the most revered and hallowed temple of all Sumer, since it was the house of Enlil, the leading deity of the Sumerian pantheon throughout most of Sumer's recorded history. It was situated in Nippur, Sumer's holy city, which was the fearful, awesome, terrifying guardian of humanity's moral and spiritual values. The preordained divine laws of the Ekur were shrouded in mystery; its rites and rituals conducted by an expert priesthood were enduring and eternal; it was filled with prayers, incantations, and favorable omens; its festivals overflowed with milk and cream, and its banquets and feasts were celebrated from sunrise to sunset. It was the king himself who provided all the necessities for the food offerings and animal sacrifices, and saw to it that the conquered foreign land brought heavy booty to the Ekur's storehouses. In brief, as the sages saw it, it was the breath of life, the protective shade of all peoples, foreigners as well as Sumerians, so that all lands bowed their heads to it, and all lords and princes brought there their sacrifices, prayers, and gifts.

The Ekur was not the only temple in Sumer that was hallowed and revered—every major city had a holy shrine dedicated to its tutelary deity.[15] All were glorified and exalted in poetic, metaphorical, imaginative hymns composed by the poets and bards who, if not themselves sages, were guided and governed by the theological views and beliefs propagated by the sages.

But about 2000 B.C.E., during the reign of Ibbi-Sin, the last king of the Third Dynasty of Ur, Sumer suffered a catastrophic calamity: the Elamites and their allies overwhelmed and destroyed the capital Ur, led off the king into captivity, and ravaged and devastated many of the

---

14. For the edition of this composition, see. Å. W. Sjöberg, "Nungal in the Ekur," *AfO* 24 (1976) 19-46; and for its interpretation and implication, see T. Frymer, "The Nungal Hymn and the Ekur Prison," *Journal of the Economic and Social History of the Orient* 20 (1977) 78-89.

15. Cf. Å. W. Sjöberg and E. Bergmann, *The Collection of the Sumerian Temple Hymns* (Texts from Cuneiform Sources 3; New York: Augustin, 1969).

temples of Sumer despite their hallowed sanctity. This tragic event left
a bitter, distressing, harrowing mark on the Sumerian psyche that led to
the creation of the image of the pitiful, grieving, suffering goddess, a
mythic invention by the sages and poets of Sumer that mirrored the
distress of the Sumerians at the sight of their ruined temples that had
been so lovingly planned and built by the king with such high hopes
and joyous promise of divine blessings for the prosperity of the land
and its people, but now were no more.[16]

## THE SAGE AND THE PALACE

Just as the sages shaped and developed the ideological and religious
concepts that governed the temple, so they shaped and developed the
symbolic constructs and inspirational sentiments that governed the palace, and especially its dominating figure, the king. Kingship, the sages
believed and propagated, came down from Heaven, once before the
Flood, and once again after it. Along with it came its *me*, that is, the
divine laws and controls that related to the king's authority as the vicar
of the gods, as well as to his insignia and regalia. It thus seems that the
Sumerian sages assumed that kingship came "full blown, full grown" to
Sumer, and they had no idea that it originated early in Sumerian history
and evolved only gradually over the centuries until by the end of the
third millennium B.C.E. it had become the very hallmark of civilized
society. And this they believed in spite of the fact that there was at their
disposal a vast group of contemporary historical documents that had
accumulated over the centuries: hundreds of royal building and votive
inscriptions on clay, stone, and metal; many date-formulas recording
important religious and political events; quite a number of letters between the king and high palace officials that reveal the temptations,
rivalries, and intrigues that pervaded the palace and at times embittered
the spirit. From all these, it is quite clear that the Sumerian kings
differed widely in their accomplishments and achievements, in their
character, temperament and personality, and in their physical appearance, carriage, and courage.

But different as they may have been, there was one psychological
trait they all had in common, a characteristic that was fostered and
nurtured over the centuries by the sages: all the Sumerian kings had a
compulsive need for glorification and celebration, for fame and name,
for acclaim and renown. This is quite evident from the vast and varied
assortment of extant royal hymns created by the court poets who had

16. For the texts relating to the grieving goddess, see my "The Weeping Goddess:
Sumerian Prototypes of the *Mater Dolorosa*," BA 46 (1983) 69–80.

been educated in the *edubba*, an institution that was no doubt supported in part by the king.[17] These hymns, which glorify and celebrate the ruler in hyperbolic diction and extravagant imagery, were no doubt instrumental to a large extent in shaping the king's thoughts, molding his ideas, inspiring his psyche, and imbuing him with the conviction that all his acts and deeds—conducting wars, building and rebuilding temples, maintaining the cult, digging and clearing canals, constructing and repairing highways, promulgating law codes—all had one supreme goal: to make his people happy, prosperous, and secure. As the poets put it, the king is the farmer who fills the granaries, the shepherd who enriches the stalls and sheepfolds. He is the high protecting wall of the land; the people look up to him as their father and live securely in his sweet shade. And as a consequence of these noble achievements, they reiterate again and again, his name will be honored and exalted in all the lands unto distant days and especially by the scribes of the *edubba*.

The portrait of the ideal king that emerges from the royal hymns, and that the king presumably cherished, cultivated, and emulated, may be briefly sketched as follows. The king was of divine parentage and thus himself divine; he came in to the world blessed from the womb, and received numerous additional blessings from the gods, especially from Enlil, on the day of his coronation, or when about to conduct a campaign against Sumer's enemies. These divine benedictions related to everything essential for an ideal reign: a throne that is governed by divine laws, an enduring crown, a scepter that exercizes firm control over the people, overflow of the rivers, fertility of the soil and fecundity of the womb, and tribute from the lands near and far. Having attended the *edubba* faithfully and zealously, he was literate and learned, an expert in poetry and music. He was the complete and perfect man: physically powerful and distinguished looking; brave and courageous in battle and in the chase; he was wise, understanding, astute, and psychologically penetrating; he was devoted to the cult, knew how to serve the gods, and saw to it that the temple rites and rituals were properly consummated, especially during the various monthly holidays and the day of the New Year when the sacred marriage between the goddess Inanna and him was celebrated. One of his prime concerns related to equity and social justice, to law and litigation: he was a judge who did not tolerate iniquity; he did not permit the powerful to oppress the weak, or the noble to mistreat the commoner. He saw to it that the poor

17. For more details and bibliographical references, see my "Kingship in Sumer and Akkad: The Ideal King," *Le palais et la royauté: archéologie et civilisation* (ed. Paul Garelli; Compte Rendu, Rencontre Assyriologique Internationale 19; Paris: Geuthner, 1974) 163-76.

were not afraid to talk back to the rich, that there was no bribed verdict or twisted word, that the cry of the wronged, the orphan, and the widow was not in vain, and that family life was affectionate, respectful, and harmonious.

Were there any Sumerian rulers who measured up to this portrait of the ideal king? Actually there may have been several, but as of today the most eligible candidate is undoubtedly Šulgi, the second ruler of the Third Dynasty of Ur.[18] According to numerous reliable contemporary historical documents, he fought and won a series of bloody military campaigns, made a number of sweeping constructive administrative reforms, built numerous temples throughout Sumer, was probably the promulgator of the first extant Sumerian law code (hitherto commonly known as the Ur-Nammu Law Code), and played a major role in the formation of the politico-religious institution of divine kingship. It is not surprising therefore that the poets glorified his name and spread his fame in a large number of hymns, diverse in content and form—more than twenty of these have been studied and analyzed to date—and one of the longest and most informative of these is especially relevant for the Sumerian concept of the ideal king. It consists of what purports to be a self-laudatory "autobiography" in which Šulgi portrays himself as an exemplary, messianic type of ruler, a rare combination of sage, soldier, sportsman, diviner, diplomat, patron of learning and literature, and happy provider of all good things for his land and people.[19]

Šulgi begins with his education, claiming that as a young prince he had studied zealously the scribal art and that none of his fellow students among the nobility could write a tablet as well as he. He next depicts his soldierly qualities and skills: he possessed extraordinary physical strength and courage, was an expert in handling all sorts of weapons, marched ahead of his troops in battle, and terrorized all the foreign lands with the fame of his military triumphs. He was also immensely brave in hunting wild game in the steppe in order to make it safe for

18. For Šulgi as the ideal king, see now J. Klein, *The Royal Hymns of Šulgi, King of Ur: Man's Quest for Immortal Fame* (Transaction of the American Philosophical Society 71/7; Philadelphia: American Philosophical Society, 1981). For Šulgi rather than Ur-Nammu as the first lawgiver, see my "The Ur-Nammu Law Code: Who was its Author?" *Or* 52 (1983) 433–56.

19. It is quite unlikely that the author of the autobiography was Šulgi. In all probability the author was the poet who introduced it with the assertion that Šulgi the king of Ur, the son of the goddess Ninsun, had been especially granted the "wisdom of the future" in order that he might make known unto future generations his preeminent power and wisdom—a statement that was no doubt intended to convince skeptics that the king could actually compose the autobiography that followed. But no matter who composed it, there is no reason to doubt that at least some of its contents are authentic and trustworthy.

the shepherd and his flock. When he killed a lion he did so "face to face," not hiding in ambush behind a safety fence, or wielding his weapons from afar. On returning from the hunt, he brought the game to his divine mother Ninsun as a good son should.

Šulgi next boasts of his role as a master diviner, as an expert in extispicy and the art of recognizing and identifying the will of the gods in order to make appropriate decisions in critical cultic and political situations. In fact he could read the divine instructions concerning the entire universe in the entrails of a single sheep. He was also very proud of his musical talent, claiming that he was an accomplished singer familiar with all types of songs and melodies. He could tune and play every known musical instrument, even those that had fallen into disuse over time. He thus brought great joy to all, and especially to his mother Ninsun who shared his happiness in the palace.

Šulgi next elaborates on his political wisdom and tact—in the assembly everyone sought his wise counsel. As a judge he was greatly admired because he knew several languages and needed no interpreter to respond to any foreign litigants. His inspiring eloquence promoted peace and harmony in the land.

Most of the rest of the autobiography concerns Šulgi's efforts to insure that his fame and glory never fade in hymn and song. Following a rather remarkable assertion that he never suppressed any traditional human knowledge, and that he encouraged the continuous performance of the hymns and songs glorifying earlier kings, whether they were Sumerians, Akkadians, or even oppressive Gutians, he exhorts future kings to see to that songs glorifying his wisdom and bravery are recited continuously and repeatedly in their palaces. But most of all it is the *edubba* that concerns him. It is there that his hymns, psalms, and prayers will be perpetuated unto the end of days. He therefore built the two most important *edubba*s of Sumer, one in his capital Ur and the other in the land's religious center, Nippur.

This essay will conclude with the role of the king in the cultic ceremony commonly known as the "Sacred Marriage Rite," which in the course of time came to be celebrated in various Sumerians cities.[20] It was probably originated by the sages of Erech who first conceived of the attractive idea that, in order to make the land fruitful and fecund, it was the duty of the king to wed the Venus-goddess Inanna, the tutelary deity of their city, who was also the goddess of love and procreation.

20. For full details, see my *The Sacred Marriage Rite* (Bloomington, IN: Indiana University, 1969); and now the revised French version translated and adapted by J. Bottéro, *Le mariage sacré à Sumer et à Babylone* (Paris: Berg International Editeurs, 1983).

The first king to perform this joyous function was, to judge from the chants of a much later day, Dumuzi, one of the kings of Sumer's heroic age, who lived in the first half of the third millennium B.C.E. Just how the cult grew and developed in the following centuries is unknown. But by the time of Šulgi there is clear evidence that the kings of Sumer celebrated their marriage to Inanna as Dumuzi incarnate, a sexual union that was believed to insure not only the land's fertility and fecundity, but also the king's immortality. To be sure, according to the long-known myth "Inanna's Descent to the Nether World," his immortality could last for only half the year, since he had to spend the other half as a surrogate for Inanna who was held captive there because of the violation of its *me*. Sumerian mythographers, however, are not noted to the absolute consistency of their plots and motifs. According to a British Museum tablet published very recently, Dumuzi does not die at all, but goes up to heaven instead.[21] Perhaps therefore there were some sages who believed that the king, like Dumuzi, became a heavenly star, and thus achieved an immortality of sorts.

21. See my "BM 88318: The Ascension of Dumuzi to Heaven," *Recueil de travaux et communications des etudes du Proche-Orient ancien* 2 (1984) 5–9.

# THE SAGE
# IN AKKADIAN LITERATURE:
# A PHILOLOGICAL STUDY

## Ronald F. G. Sweet

This essay has two purposes: first, to identify the Akkadian words that can be translated "wise man" (sage), "wise," and "wisdom" (what will be called the vocabulary of wisdom); and, second, to establish the classes of person to whom these terms were applied in Mesopotamian society as reflected in Akkadian literature. The question to be answered is: Who was called wise and who was said to possess wisdom?

Since the ultimate point of reference for the essays in this volume is the sage in ancient Israel, the Akkadian terms selected will be those that mean "wise" in the general sense of Hebrew *ḥākām*. For this word BDB recognizes the following meanings: (1) skillful in technical work, (2) wise in the administration of affairs, (3) shrewd, crafty, cunning, (4) pl. class of learned and shrewd men, including astrologers, magicians, and the like, (5) prudent, (6) wise, ethically and religiously.[1] The dominant concerns of the present volume tempt one to restrict attention to the possible Akkadian correspondences of items (4) and (6) in this list of meanings, and in particular to the latter's sub-meaning b(2): "as a wise teacher, a sage." But this would allow a preconceived notion of what is meant by "wise man," and allow a notion taken from another culture, to determine the selection of the Akkadian evidence and would risk distorting the testimony of the Mesopotamian sources. Mesopotamian ideas as to who might be called wise may have differed from those of ancient Israel.

To distinguish a variety of nuances for a term, as BDB has done for *ḥākām*, inevitably involves a measure of interpretation and subjectivity. Not everyone may agree with the distinctions of meaning proposed in BDB or with the suggested distribution of the *Belegstellen* among these

Ronald F. G. Sweet is Professor of Assyriology in the Department of Near Eastern Studies at the University of Toronto.

1. F. Brown, S. R. Driver, and C. A. Briggs, *A Hebrew and English Lexicon of the Old Testament* (Oxford: Clarendon, 1907) 314–15; hereafter cited as BDB. Abbreviations used in this essay that are not listed above on pp. xiii–xiv may be found in *The Chicago Assyrian Dictionary* (*CAD*).

meanings. The situation is no different with Akkadian terms. For the purposes of this essay, it has therefore been thought prudent not to restrict too narrowly the Akkadian data presented, nor to press distinctions of meaning that cannot be clearly demonstrated.

Some restrictions on the data, however, are permitted, indeed required, by the topic. Since the concern of this volume is with the wise human being in the societies of the ancient Near East, references to deities as wise will generally be ignored. So also will references to legendary wise men of the past, such as the Seven Sages, Adapa, or Atra-ḫasīs ('Surpassing-in-Wisdom'), the survivor of the Flood.[2] Statements about gods or legendary figures may reveal something about ideas as to the nature of wisdom, but they do not speak directly to the question of the identity and social role of the wise person. In general they signify no more than that wisdom was highly regarded in the society that produced the myths and legends. Other textual data that are of interest for Mesopotamian ideas about the nature of wisdom, but which yield no information about the wise person, will also be ignored.

The evidence presented is from Akkadian literature. But it must be remembered that the higher culture of Mesopotamia was always bilingual, and the distinction between texts composed in Sumerian and texts composed in Akkadian is often artificial and difficult to maintain. The problem is particularly acute with bilingual compositions. When such texts are quoted in this essay, the Sumerian version is ignored because the evidence of the Sumerian texts is considered in a separate essay.

The quotations and references given below are intended as a representative sampling of the relevant evidence. For justification of the translations of the terms of the wisdom vocabulary and for information on the use of these terms in other contexts, reference should be made to the two modern standard dictionaries of Akkadian, W. von Soden's *Akkadisches Handwörterbuch* (*AHw*, 1958–81) and *The Chicago Assyrian Dictionary* (*CAD*, 1956–), which are invaluable not only as dictionaries but, taken together, as the closest approach to a concordance of Akkadian literature available today. The present essay is heavily indebted to them. It has not been possible to maintain a uniform translation for each of the wisdom terms, in part because of the requirements of English idiom but especially because of the frequent proximity

2. For the Seven Sages, see E. Reiner, "The Etiological Myth of the 'Seven Sages,'" *Or* 30 (1961) 1–11, and J. Van Dijk, UVB 18 (1962) 44–52. For a fairly recent study of Adapa, see B. Kienast, "Die Weisheit des Adapa von Eridu," *Symbolae Biblicae et Mesopotamicae F. M. Böhl dedicatae* (ed. M. A. Beek et al.; Leiden: Brill, 1973) 234–39. For Atra-ḫasīs, see W. G. Lambert and A. R. Millard, *Atra-ḫasīs: The Babylonian Story of the Flood* (Oxford: Clarendon, 1970).

of synonyms in the Akkadian texts. Both *eršu* and *mūdû*, for example, can properly be translated 'wise' when standing alone; but when they stand side by side, another translation has to be found for one of them.

## THE VOCABULARY OF WISDOM

The terms listed below in this section are those used in the texts quoted in the next two sections of this essay. Because they are limited to terms used with reference to human beings, they do not represent all the vocabulary of wisdom found in Akkadian literature. For example, no reference is made under *ḫasīsu* to *atra ḫasīs* or *atar ḫasīsa* 'surpassing in wisdom', because the epithet is applied only to the hero of the Flood legend, Adapa, and the eaglet that warned its parent against acts of folly in the *Etana Epic*. Other terms that are omitted are learned terms of high diction known only in the native lexical tradition or rare terms with more theoretical than practical relevance to the task in hand. Such are the adjectives *adapu*, *angallu*, *āšišu*, *eppešu*, *itpušu*, *muštēpišu*, *ṭāmu*, and *ummuqu* ('wise'), and the substantives *eršūtu*, *ḫassūtu*, *mūdûtu*, and *naklūtu* ('wisdom'). However, the list includes a number of terms that have reference to wisdom only by extension or as one meaning among many. Such are the terms for parts of the body regarded as the seat of thought, understanding, and so wisdom: *ḫasīsu*, *karšu*, *libbu*, *ṣurru*, and *uznu*. Wise has been taken to include the meanings "skillful in technical work" (the first of the definitions of *ḫākām* in BDB), intelligent, and informed, and words with these primary meanings have been admitted. The translation given in the heading of the relevant entry in *CAD* and *AHw* is noted (sometimes in abbreviated form) for each of the Akkadian terms in the list. When no translation from *CAD* is given, it is because the pertinent volume has not yet appeared. Cross references are given in the list to the notes in which the sources are cited to enable the reader to locate the texts in the essay. The list concludes with a verb, but the adverbs derived from adjectives have been omitted.

Because of the loose definition of wisdom accepted here, the English terms wise, wise man, and wisdom are to be understood *lato sensu*.

1.0  *Substantives meaning wise man*

1.1  *apkallu* "1. wise man, expert, 2. (a mythological) sage, 3. (a priest or exorcist)" (*CAD*); "Weiser" (*AHw*). The term is rare with reference to human beings, but see nn. 69 and 79. Most commonly it refers to gods or legendary sages, and examples incidentally occur in texts quoted below. For examples referring to gods, see nn. 17,

34, 37. For examples referring to legendary sages, see nn. 19 and 37. The term also refers to a human being in the compound *apkal šamni* 'oil diviner' (see nn. 37, 72, 73).

1.2 *emqu* See 2.1 (adjective as substantive).

1.3 *eršu* See 2.2 (adjective as substantive).

1.4 *igigallu* "1. wise person, 2. wisdom" (*CAD*); "Weiser, Weisheit" (*AHw*). See n. 21.

1.5 *mār ummâni* "member of the *ummânu* class, craftsman, expert." See *ummânu* sub 1.7. See nn. 56, 57, 58, 59, 68, 76, 81.

1.6 *mūdû* See 2.7 (adjective as substantive).

1.7 *ummânu* "Feldmesser; Handwerker, Fachmann, Künstler, Gelehrter; Geldgeber, Gläubiger" (*AHw*, *ummiānu(m)*); note especially meanings 8–11 for texts of the first millennium B.C.E.: "Fachmann, Gelehrter (genaue Funktion oft unklar)"). Translated below as 'expert' (nn. 36, 38, 66, 67, 74, 86, 93), 'skilled craftsman' (n. 55), and 'scholar' (nn. 37, 96). See *mār ummâni* sub 1.5.

2.0 *Adjectives meaning wise*

2.1 *emqu*, var. *enqu* "experienced, skilled, educated, wise, wily" (*CAD*); "weise, klug" (*AHw*). See nn. 33, 40, 44, 45, 50, 51, 53, 59, 61, 63 (stative), 65, 71, 84, 89, 90, 93, 97. Used as substantive meaning 'wise man' (nn. 6, 88, 94, 98).

2.2 *eršu* "wise" (*CAD*, *eršu* A); "weise" (*AHw*, *eršu(m)* I). See nn. 11, 12, 16, 26, 43, 54, 64. Used as substantive meaning 'wise man' (n. 95).

2.3 *ḫāsisu* "intelligent" (*CAD*); "klug, verständig" (*AHw* sub *ḫassu*, as variant). Used absolutely in status rectus (n. 16), and in status constructus before an objective genitive (nn. 33, 40, 50).

2.4 *ḫassu* "intelligent" (*CAD*); "klug, verständig" (*AHw*). See nn. 32, 58, 73. Used as substantive meaning 'wise man' (n. 93) and in *lā ḫassu* 'fool' (n. 98).

2.5 *itpēšu* "wise, expert" (*CAD*); "erfahren, tüchtig" (*AHw*). See nn. 18, 23, 25, 26, 32, 33, 49, 50, 73.

2.6 *lēʾû* "able, capable, skilled" (*CAD*); "tüchtig, fähig" (*AHw*). See nn. 19, 32, 37, 38 (stative), 57, 83 (stative).

2.7 *mūdû* "1. knowing (something or somebody), expert in a specific craft, wise, competent, learned, knowledgeable, expert, 2. acquain-

tance" (*CAD*); "wissend, klug" (*AHw*). Serves as participle of the
G stem of the verb *idû* 'to know'. For examples of *mūdû* used
absolutely in the status rectus with the meaning 'expert, wise', see
nn. 3 (stative), 16, 32, 40, 45, 46, 51 (stative), 52, 54, 66, 67, 70
(stative), 73, 74, 76, 82, 86. For examples of *mūdû* in the status
constructus with an objective genitive meaning 'knowing (something or somebody)', see nn. 7, 11, 23, 27, 35, 48, 53, 57, 64. Used as
substantive meaning 'learned man' (nn. 85, 87, 88, 92).

2.8  *naklu*  "ingenious, clever, artistic, artful, sophisticated, complicated"
(*CAD*); "kunstreich, -voll" (*AHw*). See n. 23.

2.9  *palkû*  "weit," 4. "kenntnisreich" (*AHw*). Apparently an abbreviation of *palkû ḫasīsi/uzni*, literally 'wide of ear', thus 'of wide
understanding, wise'. See nn. 35, 80. For *palkû* as an attributive
adjective qualifying terms for wisdom, see nn. 17, 24, 28, 34, 37 for
*ḫasīsu* (3.2); n. 20 for *mērešu* (3.10); and n. 20 for the dual of *uznu*
(3.20).

2.10  *telēʾû*  "überaus tüchtig, fähig" (*AHw, teleʾû*). See n. 46.

## 3.0  *Substantives meaning wisdom*

3.1  *emqūtu*(?)   Not recognized in *CAD* or *AHw*. See n. 94.

3.2  *ḫasīsu*  "1. aperture of the ear, ear, 2. (faculty of) hearing, 3. understanding" (*CAD*); "Ohr, Weisheit" (*AHw*). See nn. 15, 17, 20, 24,
28, 34, 37. For *pet(i)ḫasīsi* in nn. 15 and 19, see *uznu* (3.20).

3.3  *ḫissatu*  "1. intelligence, understanding, 2. mention" (*CAD*); "Verstand, Erwähnung" (*AHw*). See nn. 13, 14, 15, 20, 62.

3.4  *igigallu*  See 1.4 and nn. 4, 5, 7, 9.

3.5  *igigallūtu*  "wisdom" (*CAD*); "Weisheit" (*AHw*). See nn. 30, 34, 41.

3.6  *inû*  "knowledge, technical lore of a craft" (*CAD, inu* B); "etwa
'Berufsarbeit'" (*AHw*). See nn. 19, 38.

3.7  *kabattu*, var. *kabittu*  "1. inside (of the body), liver(?), 2. emotions,
thoughts, mind, spirit" (*CAD*); "Leber, Gemüt" (*AHw*). See n. 29.

3.8  *karšu*  "1. stomach, belly, womb, body, 2. mind, heart, plan, desire" (*CAD*); "Bauch, Magen; Inneres, 3.b. Verstand" (*AHw*). See
nn. 22, 23, 28, 35, 39.

3.9  *libbu*  "1. heart, abdomen, entrails, womb, 3. mind, thought, intention, courage, wish, desire, choice, preference" (*CAD*); "Leib, Inneres; Herz" (*AHw*). See nn. 13, 14, and esp. 41.

3.10 *mērešu* "knowledge, wisdom" (*CAD*, *mērešu* B); "Weisheit" (*AHw*, *mērešu* II). See nn. 20, 29, 41.

3.11 *nēmequ* "knowledge, experience, wisdom (referring to the body of experiences, knowledge, skills, and traditions which are the basis of a craft or occupation, or form the basis of civilization as a whole), skill, cunning" (*CAD*); "Weisheit" (*AHw*). See nn. 8, 10, 16, 19, 20, 31, 36, 37, 39, 42, 47, 51, 60, 62, 77, 78, 91, 93, 96.

3.12 *nikiltu*, pl. *niklātu* "1. ingenuity, skillful work, ingenious or clever idea, 2. trick, cunning, deception" (*CAD*); "kunstvolle, listige Gestaltung" (*AHw*). See nn. 17, 20 (pl.), 29.

3.13 *pakku* "etwa 'Überlegung'" (*AHw*). See n. 41.

3.14 *pīt ḫasīsi* "Weisheit" (*AHw* sub *pītu* 'Öffnung' #6). See n. 22.

3.15 *ṣurru* "insides (of the human body), heart, center (of an object)" (*CAD*, *ṣurru* B); "Inneres, Herz" (*AHw*, *ṣurru(m)* II). See n. 23.

3.16 *tašīmtu*, pl. *tašīmātu* "Einsicht, Verständnis" (*AHw*). See nn. 11, 18, 20, 35, 48.

3.17 *ṭēmu* "etwa Planungsfähigkeit, Entschluß (kraft); Verstand; Anweisung, Bescheid" (*AHw*). See nn. 21, 29, 41, 64, 97.

3.18 *ummânūtu* "Handwerkskunst, Gelehrsamkeit" (*AHw*). See n. 31.

3.19 *uršu* "Verlangen" (*AHw*, *uršu(m)* II, connecting the word with the verb *erēšu* 'to request, desire'). But see *naqbu* #2.a in *AHw* for the translation 'Weisheit', connecting *uršu* with the adjective *eršu* (2.2) and the substantive *mērešu* (3.10). See also *nagbu* B.d in *CAD* for the translation 'knowledge'. See n. 6.

3.20 *uznu* "Ohr; Weisheit, Verstand" (*AHw*). See nn. 4, 17, 20 (dual), 24, 29, 34, 37, 39, 59. In the phrase *pet(i) uz(u)ni*, literally 'opened of ear', thus 'with informed understanding', nn. 15, 16 (*pet(i)* understood as status constructus of an adjective *petû* 'opened', a word not recognized in *AHw*; cf. *pet(i)ḫasīsi* [3.2]; for *ḫasīsu* and *uznu* as the object of the verb *petû* [G and D stems respectively], see nn. 34 and 88). In the phrase *rapša rapaš uzni* it means 'broad of understanding, with wide understanding' (nn. 23, 35). In the phrase *lā bišīt uzni* it means 'ignorance' (n. 56).

4.0 *Verbs meaning to be wise*

4.1 *ḫasāsu* "1. to think of a deity = to heed a deity, be pious, 6. to be intelligent, understanding" (*CAD*); "gedenken, sich erinnern," G.II.3 "verstehen" (*AHw*). See n. 56 (*lā ḫasās amāti* 'lack of understanding').

In the next two sections texts are presented in which the epithets wise man or wise are applied to human beings, or in which men are said to possess, or be connected with, wisdom. The person most often called wise is the king, and it has been found convenient to divide the material into statements about the king and statements about members of other classes, who will collectively be called commoners. Unless indicated otherwise, the texts may be presumed to date ca. 700 B.C.E.

## THE KING AS WISE MAN

Evidence for the belief that the king possessed a special degree of knowledge may be found already in the early Sargonic period (ca. 2340 B.C.E.) in the personal name Šarru-mūda 'the-king-is-wise'.[3] The king's wisdom was regarded as god-given, to judge from the words of Kudurma-bug of Yamutbal, father of Hammurapi's rival, Rim-Sin of Larsa, some five hundred years later. It was, he tells us, "with the wise understanding [uzun igigallim] that the god had given him" that "he skillfully [emqiš] made a search" and, on a chosen spot, "built a temple of baked bricks."[4]

Hammurapi (1792–1750 B.C.E.) similarly acknowledged that his wisdom (igigallum) had been decreed for him by a god.[5] He claims to be "a wise man [emqum] who gets things done, one who has attained all wisdom [uršum]."[6] The claim is made in the prologue to the Laws, where Hammurapi lists his pious benefactions to the cities under his rule; the passage shows the typical Mesopotamian understanding of wisdom as the intelligence and skill that enable one to perform practical deeds, particularly deeds for the benefit of the gods. Hammurapi is "one who understands wisdom [mūde igigallim]"[7] and it is by his wisdom (nēmequm) that he protected his subjects.[8] His son, Samsuiluna, similarly boasts of his wisdom; it was by means of his own strength and "great wisdom [igigallum rabûm]" that he rebuilt ruined cities for their patron deities.[9]

3. Sar-ru-mu-da (Nikolski 2 35 ii 6). For the date, see B. R. Foster, Umma in the Sargonic Period (Memoirs of the Connecticut Academy of Arts and Sciences 20; Hamden, CT: Archon, 1982) 2–7. The text belongs to Foster's Group A. The name also occurs with the writing Sar-ru-GAL.zu; see MAD 3 18.

4. ina uzun igigallim ša ilum iddinūšum emqiš ištīma . . . bīt agurrim . . . īpuš (RA 11 92 i 8–14).

5. ina igigallim ša Ea išīmam . . . nakrī eliš u šapliš assuḫ 'I ousted the enemy north and south with the skill that Ea had decreed for me' (CH xl 26–31).

6. emqum muttabilum šu ikšudu nagab uršim (CH iv 7–10).

7. CH iii 17.

8. nišī māt Šumerim u Akkadîm . . . ina nēmeqīja uštapziršināti 'I protected the people of Sumer and Akkad by my wisdom' (CH xl 50–58).

9. LIH 97 ii 39–40. A claim to have built a city with the wisdom (igi-gál) given by a god is also made in Ammiṣaduqa's eleventh year-name (Sumerian); see RLA 2 190 no. 259.

The high value placed on wisdom is shown by the wish of the author of the Agum-kakrime text on behalf of the early Kassite ruler of that name (sixteenth century B.C.E.): "May Ea, the god of the depths, grant him perfect wisdom [*nēmequm*]."[10] In the late thirteenth century B.C.E. the *Tukulti-Ninurta Epic*, which is at pains to present the Assyrian king in a favorable light in contrast with his Kassite rival, Kaštiliaš, refers to Tukulti-Ninurta on one occasion as "the wise [*eršu*] shepherd who understands [*mūdû*] good judgment [*tašīmtu*, pl.]."[11] The adjective *eršu* occurs again a century later in a long list of imposing epithets claimed by Aššur-reš-iši I of Assyria.[12]

The king's wisdom or cleverness could be applied to the arts of war. "Using my clever mind [*ḫissat libbi*], I set up forts round about it," reports Adad-nirari II (911–891 B.C.E.), referring to an enemy city.[13] Aššurnaṣirpal II (883–859 B.C.E.) also speaks of his *ḫissat libbi*, but in his case it was used to fashion an image of the god Ninurta[14] and, on another occasion, to rebuild a temple of the goddess Ishtar.[15] This is a king who made a most emphatic claim to wisdom: "Wise [*eršu*], learned [*mūdû*], clever [*ḫāsisu*], perceptive with the understanding (and) wisdom [*pet uzni nēmeqi*] that Ea the king of the Deep has decreed for me," runs one string of his epithets.[16] Another Assyrian king who boasts of using his wisdom for a peaceful pursuit is Tiglath-pileser III (744–727 B.C.E.): "With the clever wisdom [*uzun nikilti*] and wide understanding [*ḫasīsu palkû*] which the wisest [*apkallu*] of the gods, the noble Nudimmud, has given me, I built a palace of cedar wood in Calah."[17]

The claims to royal wisdom are particularly insistent in the highly literary royal inscriptions from the period of the Sargonid dynasty. Speaking of his plans to make his kingdom prosper by populating

10. *Ea bēl nagbim nēmeqam lišaklilšu* (5R 33 viii 15–18).

11. *[r]ē⁾û eršu mūdû tašīmāti* (P. B. Machinist, "The Epic of Tukulti-Ninurta I: A Study in Middle Assyrian Literature" [Yale thesis, 1978] 86:7 [= *KAR* 303 obv. 7]).

12. A. K. Grayson, *Assyrian Rulers of the Third and Second Millennia B.C.* (Royal Inscriptions of Mesopotamia: Assyrian Periods [= RIMA] 1; Toronto: University of Toronto, 1987) 310:4.

13. *ina ḫissat libbīja . . . ālāni battubattēšu addi* (*KAH* 2 84:54–55).

14. *[e]nūma ṣalam Ninurta šuātu . . . ina ḫissat libbīja [la]massi ilūtīšu rabīti . . . lū abni* 'at that time, using my clever mind, I fashioned this statue of Ninurta as a representation of his great divinity' (*AKA* 210 18–20). Shalmaneser III (858–824 B.C.E.) also states that he made (*epēšu*) the image of a deity *ina ḫissat libbi* (*KAH* 2 103:4–6).

15. *ina ḫissat libbīja ša Ea šar apsê peti uzuni ḫasīsi išrukanni ana šâši bīt Kidmuri šuātu ana eššūte abni* 'with my clever mind that Ea, king of the Deep, perceptive in understanding and wisdom, had given me, I rebuilt this temple of Kidmuri for her' (*KAH* 2 164:22–25).

16. *eršu mūdû ḫāsisu pet uzni nēmeqi ša Ea šar apsî išīmanni ana jâši* (*KAH* 2 197:5–7).

17. *ina uzni nikilti ḫasīsi palkê ša išruka apkal ilāni rubû Nudimmud ekal erēni . . . ina qereb Kalḫi ēpuš* (Rost Tigl. III p. 72:17–18).

virgin territory, planting orchards, putting undeveloped land under cultivation, and installing irrigation works, Sargon II (721–705 B.C.E.) calls himself "a wise [*itpēšu*] king who devises beneficent plans."[18] He claims to be "a wise [*pet ḫasīsi*] king, skilled in all learning [*lēʾi inî kalâma*], the equal of the Sage (*apkallu*), who grew up in wise counsel [*milik nēmeqi*] and attained full stature in good judgment [*tašīmtu*]."[19] Referring to his efforts to build his capital, Dūr-Šarrukīn, he states:

> I planned and labored night and day using my broad wisdom [*mērešu palkû*] which, at the command of the divine King of the Deep, the lord of wisdom [*bēl nēmeqi*, i.e., Ea], has been adorned with good judgment [*tašīmtu*] and is full of cleverness [*niklātu*]—also my wide-ranging intelligence [*ḫissat uznī palkâti*], my understanding [*ḫasīsu*] which Ninmenanna, the creatress of the gods, has made to surpass that of my royal ancestors.[20]

As "the wisest [*igigallu*] of the rulers of the whole world who had been created by (the operation of) counsel [*milku*] and understanding [*ṭēmu*],"[21] Sargon acted "with the wisdom [*pūt ḫasīsi*] and breadth of understanding [*šadāl karši*]" that Ea and Bēlet-ilī had assigned him.[22] This was on the occasion when, advancing into the mountains of Urartu, he equipped troops in the vanguard with hammers that they might smash the rocks to make a path for his army.

Merodach-baladan II (721–710, 703 B.C.E.), who claimed the throne of Babylon in defiance of both Sargon and Sennacherib, claims to have been

> a wise [*itpēšu*] ruler of broad understanding [*rapša uzni*], a clever [*naklu*] leader, one who knows [*mūdû*] everything, (possessed of) a far-reaching mind [*ṣurru šadlu*] (and) a thoughtful disposition [*karaš šitūlti*], one given to careful consideration.[23]

The connection between wisdom and piety is very clear:

> With the lofty understanding [*uznu*] that the divine Craftsman, Ea, creator of all, granted him (and with) the profound wisdom [*ḫasīsu palkû*] which

18. *šarru itpēšu muštābil amat damiqti* (Lyon Sar. 6:34).

19. *šarru pet hasīsi lēʾi inî kalâma šinnat apkalli ša ina milki nēmeqi irbûma ina tašīmti išeḫ[u]* (Lyon Sar. 6:38). The Sage is the legendary Adapa.

20. *ina mērešīja ⌜palkî ša⌝ ina qibît ᵈšar apsî bēl nēmeqi tašīmta zunnunūma malû niklāti u ḫissa[t uznīja palkâ]te ša eli šarrāni abbīja Ninmenanna bānīt ilī ušāteru ḫasīsī ... urru u mūšu akpud aṣrim* (Lyon Sar. 7:48–8:49). For the restoration *ḫissat uznīja palkâte*, see Winckler Sar. pl. 40:13.

21. *igigalli malkī ša kiššati ša ina milki u ṭēmi ibbanû* (*TCL* 3 115).

22. *ina pūt ḫasīsi u šadāl karše ša Ea u Bēlet-ilī išīmūni* (*TCL* 3 23).

23. *malku itpēšu rapša uzni massû naklu mūdû kal šipri ṣurru šadlu karaš šitūlti māliku ramānīšu* (VAS 1 37 ii 47–51).

Ninšīku bestowed on him, his mind [*uznu*] was set on carrying out ceremonies (in places) where rituals (are performed) and on renovating the sanctuaries and dwellings of the great gods of the land of Akkad.[24]

Sennacherib (704–681 B.C.E.) presents himself as a "wise shepherd [*rēʾû itpēšu*],"[25] a "wise and clever king [*šarru eršu itpēšu*],"[26] one "who understands every craft,"[27] one to whom "Ninšīku gave wide understanding [*karšu*] and equality with the Sage, Adapa, and granted profound wisdom [*palkû ḫasīsu*]."[28] The knowledge and skill shown by Sennacherib in making copper castings in the course of his building projects were seen as evidence of god-given wisdom.

With the clever understanding [*uzun nikilti*] that the noble Ninšīku has granted me and (with much) deliberation [*šitūlti ramāni*], I gave careful consideration to executing that task and, with my judicious counsel [*milik ṭēmi*] and wisdom [*mēreš kabitti*], I had copper casting(s) made and performed the clever procedure [*nikiltu*].[29]

Elsewhere, and again with reference to his building projects, he speaks of acting with the wisdom (*igigallūtu*) that the god Aššur had given him.[30] Two generations later it was believed that Aššur had once told Sennacherib in a dream: "You have surpassed the wisdom [*nēmequ*] of the Deep and all the skill of the experts [*ummânūtu*]."[31]

Like Sennacherib, Esarhaddon (680–669 B.C.E.) also lays claim to wisdom when reporting activities that gave practical evidence of his piety—building temples and making cultic objects. He was a king who was "skillful [*lēʾû*], clever [*itpēšu*], intelligent [*ḫassu*], wise [*mūdû*], whom the great gods had elevated to kingship in order to renovate (the images of) the great gods and to complete the shrines of all the cult centres."[32] He was "a wise [*emqu*] and clever [*itpēšu*] prince, one who

24. *ina uzna ṣīrtu ša Ea mummu bān kala iqī[šū]šu ḫasīsa palkâ ušatlimuš Ninšīku ana šullum parṣī ašru kidudê uddu[š] māḫā[zī] u ešrēt gipar ilī rabûti ša māt Akkad uzunšu ibši*; see C. J. Gadd, "Inscribed Barrel Cylinder of Marduk-Apla-Iddina II," *Iraq* 15 (1953) 123:19–22.

25. OIP 2 23:3.

26. OIP 2 66:1.

27. *mūde šipri kalâma* (OIP 2 109 vi 90–91).

28. *Ninšīku iddina karšu ritpāšu šinnat apkalli Adapa išruka palkâ ḫasīsu* (OIP 2 117:4).

29. *ina uzni nikilti ša ušatlima rubû Ninšīku ina šitūlti ramānīja ana epēš šipri šuātu rabîš amtallikma ina milik ṭēmīja u mēreš kabittīja pitiq erî ubaššimma unakkila niklassu* (OIP 2 109 vii 1–8). Similarly OIP 2 133:77–79.

30. OIP 2 145:11.

31. *tušātir nēmeqi apsî u gimir ummânū[ti]* (ABL 923:9).

32. *lēʾû itpēšu ḫassu mūdû ša ana udduš ilī rabûti u šuklul ešrēti ša kullat māḫāzī ilī rabûti iššûšu ana šarrūti* (Borger Esar. 45:18–21).

understood [ḫāsisu] every art, who put in place those things needed in the great cult centres and ordered the liturgy aright."³³ He tells how, before beginning to renovate the images of the gods and restore their temples, he offered prayers

> with the broad understanding [uznu rapaštu] (and) profound wisdom [ḫasīsu palkû] that the wisest [apkallu] of the gods, prince Nudimmud, gave me, (and) with the wisdom [igigallūtu] which (I gained when) Aššur and Marduk opened my understanding [ḫasīsu].³⁴

This is probably the king who is described in the Assyrian crown prince's "Vision of the Underworld" as "one who knows [mūdû] (many) things, of broad comprehension [rapaš uzni], with wide and discerning understanding [palkû karaš tašīmti], one who studies the design of what holds the earth together."³⁵

Ashurbanipal (668–627 B.C.E.) has left a lengthy account of how he acquired wisdom and learning while still residing in the crown prince's residence (bīt redûti). "There I learned the wisdom [nēmequ] of Nabû, I studied all the scribal craft (and) the teachings of absolutely all the experts [ummânu]," he states.³⁶ Later he remarks:

> Marduk, the wisest [apkallu] of the gods, gave me wide understanding [uznu] and extensive intelligence [ḫasīsu] (and) Nabû, the scribe (who knows) everything, granted me his wise teachings [iḫzī nēmeqi]. . . . I learned the art of the Sage [apkallu], Adapa, (so that now) I am familiar with the secret storehouse of all scribal learning, (including) celestial and terrestrial portents. I can debate in an assembly of scholars [ummânu] and discuss with the clever [lēʾû] oil diviners [apkal šamni] (the treatise) "if the liver is a replica of the sky." I used to figure out complicated divisions and multiplications that have no solution (in the text). Time and again I have read the cleverly written composition in which the Sumerian is obscure and the Akkadian is difficult to interpret correctly. I have studied inscriptions on stone from before the Flood which are a mixture of kakku sakku.³⁷

33. rubû enqu itpēšu ḫāsis kal šipri ša ina māhāzū rabûti simāti ištakkanu uštēširu šuluḫḫa (Borger Esar. 74:24–25).

34. ina uzni rapašti ḫasīsi palkê ša išruka apkal ilī rubû Nudimmud ina igigallūti ša Aššur u Marduk ana udduš ilī rabûti iptû ḫasīsī (Borger Esar. 82:10–12).

35. mūde amâti rapaš uzni palkû karaš tašīmti ša uṣurāti ša mark[as] qaqqari ḫī[ṭu]; see W. von Soden, "Die Unterweltsvision eines assyrischen Kronprinzen," ZA 43 (1936) 18:66.

36. qerebšu āḫuz nēmeqi Nabû kullat ṭupšarrūti ša gimir ummânī mala bašû iḫzīšunu aḫīṭ (Streck Asb. 4:31–33).

37. [Mar]duk apkal ilī uznu rapaštu ḫasīsu palkû išruka ⟨ana⟩ širikte Nabû ṭupšar gimri iḫzī nēmeqīšu iqīšanni ana qīšti . . . šipir apkalli Adapa āḫuz niṣirtu katimtu kullat ṭupšarrūte ittāt šamê u erṣeti amrāku šutaddunāku ina puḫur ummânī šutābulāku šumma

He sums up his accomplishments a few lines later with the statement: "I am the most able [*lē⁾û*] of all the experts [*ummânu*]; as one (of them) I study their great learning [*inû*]."³⁸ He is described as

> the favorite of the great gods to whom Šamaš and Adad imparted broad understanding [*uznu*], who learned the art of divination, the secrets of heaven and earth, (and) the wisdom [*nēmequ*] of Šamaš and Adad, and whose mind [*karšu*] pondered (these things).³⁹

Šamaš-šum-ukīn, the brother of Ashurbanipal who reigned as king of Babylon (667–648 B.C.E.), claimed to be "wise [*emqu*] and learned [*mūdû*], one who understood [*ḫāsisu*] everything."⁴⁰

Similar claims to wisdom were made by the kings of the Neo-Babylonian dynasty that came to power with the decline of the Sargonid line. Describing how he set about restoring the ziggurat of Marduk's temple in Babylon, Nabopolassar (625–605 B.C.E.), the founder of the dynasty, states:

> I gave (the matter) careful thought with the widom [*mērešu*] (given me) by Ea, with the expertise [*igigallūtu*] (given me) by Marduk, with the understanding [*ṭēmu*] (given me) by Nabû and Nisaba, with the very broad comprehension [*libbu*] the god who created me had bestowed on me, (and) with my great mental power [*pakku*].⁴¹

Part at least of what Nabopolassar understood by wisdom is made clear when he adds: "I purified this place by means of the craft of exorcism (which is) the wisdom [*nēmequ*] of Ea and Marduk."⁴²

Nebuchadrezzar II (604–562 B.C.E.), whose inscriptions consist almost entirely of commemorations of the building of temples, includes among his many epithets the following that refer to wisdom: "wise and skillful [*eršu itpēšu*],"⁴³ "wise and prayerful [*emqu mutnennû*],"⁴⁴

---

*amūtu maṭṭ(a)lāt šamê itti apkallī šamni lē⁾ûti upaṭṭar igê arê itgurūti ša lā išû pīt pāni aštassi kammu naklu ša šumeru ṣullulu akkadû ana šutēšuri ašṭu ḫīṭāku miḫišti abnī ša lām abūbi ša kakku sakku ballû* (Streck Asb. 254:10–256:18, with Bauer Asb. 2 84 n. 3). For *kakku sakku*, see S. Parpola, "Assyrian Library Records," *JNES* 42 (1983) 22.

38. *lē⁾āku ša gimir ummânī kalîšunu inûšunu rabû ištēniš alammad* (Streck Asb. 256:25–26).

39. *narām ilī rabûti ša Šamaš u Adad uzna rapaštu ušāḫizūšūma bārûta piršti šamê u erṣeti nēmeqi Šamaš u Adad īḫuzūma uštābilu karassu* (Hunger Kolophone no. 325:2–3).

40. *enqu mūdû ḫāsis kal šipri* (ArOr 7 [1939] 314:9).

41. *ina mērešu ša Ea ina igigallūtu ša Marduk ina ṭēm ša Nabium u Nisaba ina libbim šundulu ša ilu bānīja ušaršânni ina pakkīja rabiu ušataddin* (VAB 4 62:14–23).

42. *ina šipir kakugallūtu nēmeqa Ea u Marduk ašrum šâtim ullil* (VAB 4 62:41).

43. VAB 4 104 no. 13 i 5, 140 no. 16 i 2, 150 no. 19 A i 16, 176 no. 20 i 5.

44. VAB 4 86 no. 7 i 11, 150 no. 19 A i 19, 196 no. 29 i 3, 198 no. 32:3.

"learned and wise [*mūdû emqu*],"⁴⁵ "learned and capable [*mūdû telēʾû*],"⁴⁶ "considerate, one who has learned wisdom [*muštālu āḫiz nēmeqi*],"⁴⁷ "one who knows good judgment [*mūde tašīmti*],"⁴⁸ and "wise ruler [*šakkanakku itpēšu*]."⁴⁹

Nabonidus (555–539 B.C.E.) calls himself "a wise [*emqu*] prince who understands [*ḫāsisu*] everything, an exalted governor who renovates all the cult-centers, a clever [*itpēšu*] prince who makes the sanctuaries perfect."⁵⁰ The Nabonidus Verse Account represents him as claiming:

> I am wise [*emqu*], I am learned [*mūdû*], I have seen what is hi[dden]; I do not understand the impressions made by a stylus, (but) I have seen se[cret things]; the god Ilteʾri has shown me everything, I have found out [secret lore]; in respect of all wisdom [*nēmequ*] I surpass (the treatise) "The Lunar Crescent of Anu and Enlil" which Adapa composed.⁵¹

The conclusion to be drawn from this evidence is clear. In Mesopotamian society the king was regarded as possessing an unusually large measure of god-given wisdom, and was thought to manifest that wisdom by performing deeds pleasing to the gods, in particular the building of temples. The Israelite tradition of King Solomon, the wise king whose greatest achievement was the building of a temple, reflects a similar point of view.

## THE COMMONER AS WISE MAN

The nonroyal persons to whom the various terms for wise and wise man are applied, or to whom wisdom is attributed, belong to a wide range of professions.

*Craftsmen.* One group of persons associated with wisdom can be classed as craftsmen. A carpenter can be described as *mūdû*,⁵² and a

45. VAB 4 98 no. 11 i 4.
46. VAB 4 150 no. 19 A i 11–13.
47. VAB 4 62:88 no. 9 i 4, 122 no. 15 i 7. Neriglissar (559–556 B.C.E.) also used this epithet (TLB 2 22:6).
48. VAB 4 176 no. 20 i 7.
49. VAB 4 120 no. 14 iii 45. This epithet was also used by the late Assyrian king, Sin-šar-iškun (?–612 B.C.E.) (Böhl Leiden Coll. 3 34:10).
50. *rubû emqa ḫāsis mimma šumšu iššakku ṣīri muddiš kal māḫāzū malku itpēšu mušaklil ešrēti* (VAB 4 252 no. 6 i 3–4).
51. *enqēk mūdâka ātamar ka[timtu] miḫiṣ qan ṭuppu ul īdi ātamar ni[ṣirtu] ušabrâ ilum Ilteʾri kullat ūta [piristu] uskār Anim Enlila ša ikṣuru Adapa elīšu šūtuqāk kal nēmequ* (BHT pl. 8 v 9–13).
52. *naggāru mūdû* 'skilled carpenter' (BWL 178:33).

metal worker is found with the epithet *emqu*.[53] The word for 'potter' (*paḫḫāru*) is listed after two terms meaning wise (*eršu*, *mūdû*) in the lexical series *Igituḫ*, which suggests that the adjectives in question connote skillful in the sense that a craftsman is skillful.[54] The noun *ummânu* 'expert', which sometimes denotes someone expert in knowledge and understanding and, as such, is to be translated 'wise man', at other times denotes someone who seems to be more an expert in manual skills. In these contexts the word must be translated 'craftsman', 'skilled tradesman', or 'specialist'. Esarhaddon and Ashurbanipal mention *ummânu*s among the conscripts with special skills who were included in the army, listing them alongside blacksmiths.[55] Sennacherib speaks of *mārī ummâni* 'members of the *ummânu*-class' making copper statues by what was evidently the *cire perdue* method; these were metal workers.[56] Esarhaddon seems to use the same term inclusively of the "carpenter(s), stone-cutter(s), copper-smith(s), (and) seal-cutter(s)" that he employed in temple building.[57]

*Architects and builders.*    Members of the building trades are often found described as wise and their professional skill is called wisdom. Thus Tiglath-pileser III (744–727 B.C.E.) applied the adjective *ḫassu*

53. *gurgurru enqu mūde šipri rabî* 'the wise metal worker who understands the great art' (*CT* 16 38 iii 10, referring to the making of objects required in a religious ritual).

54. šu.GAL.AN.ZU = *er-šu, mu-du, pa-ḫa-ru* (*Igituḫ* 108–10, quoted in *CAD* E 313b).

55. *ina muḫḫi . . . ša mugirre qurubte pitḫal qurubte šaknūte maᵓāsse šūt rēše [kit]kittû ummânī kallābu arīte dajjālu ikkaru rēᵓû nukaribbu eli em[ūqī]* ᵈ*Aššur gapšāte . . . [uradd]i* 'I added (new troops) to the . . . , the chariot-drawn guards, the mounted guards, the stable masters, the quartermasters, the blacksmith(s), the skilled craftsmen, the light infantry, the shield bearer(s), the scout(s), the farmer(s), the shepherd(s), and the orchardmen, (in short,) to the powerful forces of Aššur' (Borger Esarh. 106 iii 16–20); *ṣāb qašti arīti ummânī kitkittû . . . eli kiṣir šarrūtīja uraddi* 'I added bowmen, shield bearer(s), skilled tradesmen, (and) blacksmith(s) to my Royal Regiment' (Streck Asb. 60 vii 2–5, cf. 56 vi 86–89). *kiškattû* 'blacksmith', of which the *kitkattû* of these two passages is a variant, also occurs together with *ummânu* in the *Gilgamesh Epic* (vi 168), referring to people who were taken on board the great boat to preserve civilization.

56. *ša ultu ulla šarrāni abbīja ṣalam erî tamšīl gattīšunu ana šūzuzi qereb ekurrāti ibnûma ina epištīšunu ušānīḫū gimir mārī ummâni ina lā bišīt uzni lā ḫasās amāti ana šipri ḫišiḫtīšunu šamna iškuru nalbaš ṣēni uqqirū qereb mātātīšun* 'Whereas from earliest times my royal ancestors made copper statues in their likeness, to be set up in the temples, and (thus) by their action tired out all the craftsmen—through their ignorance and lack of understanding these made oil, wax, and fleeces scarce throughout their lands because of what they needed' (OIP 2 108:80–88, also 122:14–19).

57. *naggāru zadimmu gurgurru [purkullu mārī] ummâni lēᵓūti mūde piristi ina bīti . . . lū ušērib* 'I brought carpenter(s), stone-cutter(s), copper-smith(s), (and) seal-cutter(s), skilled craftsmen who understand the secrets (of their trades), into the building' (Borger Esar. 83 r. 29–30). All the terms are plural in the duplicate on which the restoration is based. Line 28 indicates that "the building" in question was the Bīt Mummu, for which see n. 89.

'wise' to *mārī ummâni* employed to build a palace,[58] and Esarhaddon chose the adjective *emqu* to describe the *mārī ummâni* who were to build him a sanctuary (*atmānu*), praying that the gods might grant them "a high (degree of) wisdom [*uznu*]."[59] Shamshi-Adad I (ca. 1800 B.C.E.) refers to the work that had gone into the construction of a temple as an example of "the wisdom [*nēmequ*] of the architect's craft,"[60] and Sennacherib states that he had two palaces built in Nineveh "by the handiwork of wise [*emqu*] architects."[61] A court scribe (*ṭupšar šarri*) of the time of Aššur-uballiṭ I (fourteenth century B.C.E.) has recorded that he put up a structure of baked bricks "with the cleverness (born) of wisdom [*ina ḫissat nēmeqi*]."[62]

*Soldiers.* Another profession requiring practical skills to which the vocabulary of wisdom was applied is that of the soldier. "Be wise [*emqu*] and lead (your followers) well," the king tells his military officers in the Hittite legend, known to us in Akkadian, about the siege of Urshu.[63] Šamši-Adad V (823–811 B.C.E.) calls his senior general "a wise [*eršu*] commander-in-chief who understands [*mūdû*] warfare, a man of good judgment [*ṭēmu*]."[64] It was probably a reputation for skill in strategy that led to the application of *emqu* 'wise' to Išum, the herald of the gods (*ālik maḫri ilī*) who leads the forces of Erra, god of pestilence, in the *Erra Epic*.[65]

*Cult officials.* Wisdom terms are often applied to cult officials. The official who inspects the ox that is to supply the hide for the recovering of a temple drum in a late ritual is called a 'learned expert' (*ummânu m[ū]dû*).[66] The same phrase is used of the officiants in a ritual for the repair of the statue of a god.[67] More common is the term *mār ummâni* 'member of the *ummânu*-class', which is used, for example, of clergy who officiated at the New Year ceremonies in Babylon,

58. *gimir mārī ummâni ḫassūti* 'all the skilful craftsmen' (Rost Tigl. III p. 74 r. 20).

59. *mārī ummâni enqūti . . . uzni ṣīrtu šurkāšunūti* 'grant the wise craftsmen a lofty understanding' (Borger Esar. 82:18–19).

60. *šubat Enlil bēlīja ša ina šipir nēmeq itinnūtim šuteṣbû* 'the dwelling of Enlil my lord which was carefully constructed with workmanship (that displays) the wisdom of the architect's craft' (RIMA 1 49:29–34 [see n. 12] = AOB 1 22 ii 6–11).

61. *ina šipir šitimgallī enqūti* (OIP 2 129 vi 57).

62. AOB 1 40:14.

63. *lū emqēt u damqiš u²²era* (KBo 1 11 obv. [!] 25). The king was probably Hattusili II of the seventeenth century B.C.E.

64. *rab-ša-rēši eršu mūde tuqunti amēl ṭēme* (1R 30 ii 17–18).

65. *enqu* <sup>d</sup>*Išum ša mili[kš]u damqu* 'wise Išum whose counsel is good' (Caqni Erra 1:108).

66. RAcc 10:3.

67. TuL p. 111:18.

performing such functions as serving Nabû with a table spread with food and drink offerings.[68] The term *apkallu* 'sage', which was used of the legendary Seven Sages of remote antiquity, was also used of an officiant in the ritual for the Opening of the Mouth performed on the statue of a god.[69]

*Diviners.* The vocation of the diviner (*bārû*), which required a knowledge of the voluminous omen literature, was a learned profession, and it is not surprising that wisdom was ascribed to its practitioners. "I am a diviner, I am a man of learning [*mūdû*]," runs a line in a broken text, which, its editor suggests, may be a fable.[70] The phrase "wise [*emqu*] member of the guild of diviners' occurs in the damaged introduction to a ritual of the diviner.[71] The noun *apkallu* 'sage' is used of the diviner in the title *apkal šamni* 'oil diviner', a profession whose ancestry was thought to go back to antediluvian times.[72] The reputation for wisdom enjoyed by this class of diviner is clearly expressed in words that describe a new member of the profession: "the clever [*itpēšu*], wise [*ḫassu*], and learned [*mūdû*] member of the diviners' guild, the oil diviner."[73] The master who had trained the apprentice diviner is called "the learned expert [*ummânu mūdû*] who guards the secret lore of the great gods."[74] Reference has already been made to Ashurbanipal's boast of his ability to discuss scholarly omen texts with "the expert [*lē'û*] oil diviners."[75]

*Exorcists.* The exorcist was also deemed worthy of the epithet wise. When the officiant of the *bit mēseri* ritual had recited an incantation (*šiptu*) before Lugal-irra (a deity described as "the exorcist of all the gods"), "Lugal-irra heard the words of the wise expert [*mūdû mār ummâni*]."[76] The body of knowledge that this wise expert was expected

68. *mārī ummânu* (*RAcc* 143:404-7. Cf. also 142:372, 384, and 144:414.
69. *išippu pašīšu apkallu abriqqu ša Eridu ina* [. . .] *erēni šur'īni sebet adi šina pīka ip[tû]* 'a purification priest, an anointed priest, a sage, (and) an *abriqqu*-priest of Eridu have twice times seven opened your mouth with a [. . .] of cedar and cypress' (K.2946 i 14-15, quoted in *CAD* A/1 626). For the participation of the *apkallu* in the Washing of the Mouth and the Opening of the Mouth rituals, see the references given in *CAD* under *apkallu* 3.a.
70. *bārâku mūdâku* (*BWL* 211:16).
71. *enqu mār bārû* (Craig *ABRT* 1 60:2).
72. *apkal šamni zēru dārû pere' Enmeduranki šar Sippar* 'the oil diviner, (scion of) an eternal lineage, offspring of Enmeduranki, king of Sippar' (*BBR* no. 24:23). This king appears in the antediluvian section of the Sumerian King List.
73. [*mār*] *bārî apkal ⌈šamnī⌉ itpēšu ḫassi mūdû* (*MCT* 140 V 7).
74. *ummânu mūdû nāṣir pirišti ilī rabûti* (*BBR* 24:19).
75. See above n. 37.
76. *išmēma Lugal-irra amat mūdê mār ummâni* (*AfO* 14 [1941-44] 146:107). The god himself is also called *mūdû mār ummâni* (144:70). The description of the god quoted above (*mašmaš ilī kalîšunu*) occurs in 142:32.

to master is summed up in a catalog of the exorcist's curriculum as "all the depths of wisdom [*nēmequ*] (and) the secret lore of exorcism."[77] Sennacherib speaks of "the wise lore [*nēmequ*] of exorcism" when alluding to the apotropaic rituals carried out when the foundations of his palace were laid.[78] The association of wisdom with exorcism is further suggested by the grouping of the terms *āšipu* 'incantation priest' and *išibgallu* 'chief purification priest' with *apkallu* 'sage' in the native lexical tradition.[79]

*Musicians.* Musicians are also described as wise or skilled. A hymn to the goddess Nanāya states that "skilled [*palkû*] singers kneel before her."[80] "Singers of laments and musicians" are mentioned together with "members of the *ummânu*-class" ("experts") and exorcist-priests as cultic personnel of a temple.[81]

*Physicians.* It was also thought appropriate to call a physician wise (*mūdû*), as shown by another line in the Nanāya hymn just mentioned.[82] In the "Tale of the Poor Man of Nippur" the mayor, who was so easily taken in when the poor man posed as a physician, unquestioningly told his officials, "The doctor is clever [*lēʾû*]."[83]

*Scribes.* As might be expected, the terminology of wisdom is often associated with the scribe. "Let expert [*emqu*] scribes read your stele," says the king in the epilogue to the "Cuthean Legend of Naram-Sin," addressing a future ruler.[84] The words recall those of Nebuchad-rezzar II: "Let the learned man [*mūdû*] read over and over all my deeds that I have written in (my) foundation document."[85] In this context the learned man must have been literate and almost by definition was a scribe. When the buried ruins of the Ebabbara temple in Larsa were discovered in the reign of Nabonidus, "a learned expert [*ummânu mūdû*] examined the foundation document where they came upon it

77. *kullat nagbi nēmeqi niṣirti kakugallūti* (KAR 44 r. 7).

78. *ina šipir išippūti nēmeq kakugallūti . . . uššīšu addi* 'I laid its foundations while rites of divination (and) the wise lore of exorcism (were performed)' (OIP 2 137:31). Similar statements are made by Nabopolassar (VAB 4 62 ii 40) and Nabonidus (VAB 4 220:52).

79. *Erimḫuš* 5:7–9, quoted in CAD A/2 171a and 431a, also I 242b.

80. *nārī palkê* [*palkûti* expected] *maḫarša kamsū* (Craig ABRT 1 54; K.3600 i 7).

81. *mašmaššī kalî nārī u mārī ummânu* (RAcc 79:45).

82. *asû mūdû* (Craig ABRT 1 54 no. 4 iv 7).

83. *asû lēʾīma* (O. R. Gurney, "The Sultantepe Tablets V: The Tale of the Poor Man of Nippur," AnSt 6 [1956] 156:126).

84. LÚ.DUB.SAR *enqūte liskurū narâka* (O. R. Gurney, "The Sultantepe Tablets IV: The Cuthaean Legend of Naram-Sin," AnSt 5 [1955] 108:173 (SB).

85. *kala epšētija ša ina narê ašṭuru mūdâ lītammar* (VAB 4 76 ii 51, cf. also 110 iii 5).

and studied the figures represented."[86] The man of learning might be privy to knowledge denied those outside the ranks of the professional scribes. Such may be inferred from the formula found in the colophons of esoteric works: "An expert [*mūdû*] should show (this only) to an(other) expert [*mūdû*]; a non-expert must not see (it)."[87] Indeed, scribes who had been trained in the more esoteric branches of knowledge fully deserve the title of scholar. The wise (*emqu*) and the learned (*mūdû*) who are called on to discuss together the fifty names of Marduk in the epilogue to *Enuma Elish* must have been scholars trained in the higher branches of learning, for only they could have appreciated the learned Sumerian etymologies of the names.[88]

In the inscriptions of Nabonidus the epithet wise (*emqu*) is on one occasion bestowed on scribes specializing in mensuration—what may be called mathematicians or surveyors. When excavations were being carried out to locate the long buried Ebabbara temple in Sippar, the king sent "wise [*emqu*] mathematicians resident in the Bīt Mummi who guard the secrets of the great gods and uphold the royal rule" to provide advice.[89] Surveyors or, to give the word its more general meaning, accountants, are found deserving of the same epithet by the author of the Assyrian crown prince's "Vision of the Netherworld."[90]

---

86. *ummânu mūdû ašar ušta*[*m*]*ḫir temenna iḫīṭūma uṣappû simātim* (VAB 4 240 ii 56–57). Because of the lack of concord in number between subject and verb in the main clause, one should perhaps read *ummânū mūdûti*. The meaning of *uštamḫir* is not clear, and a subjunctive form is expected.

87. *mūdû mūdâ likallim lā mūdû lā immar* (Hunger Kolophone no. 40:1–2). For the various forms of this formula, found from the Middle Babylonian to the Seleucid periods, see p. 163 sub *idû*.

88. *liṣṣabtūma maḫrû likallim / enqu mūdû mitḫāriš limtalkū / lišannīma abu mārī lišāḫiz / ša rēˀî u nāqidi lipattâ uznašun* 'let them [i.e., the wise and learned] engage together (in discussion) and let the senior (scholar) give an explanation; let the wise and the learned discuss (the names) together; let the master [lit., father] repeat (them) and teach the pupils [lit., sons]; let him open up the understanding of shepherd and herdsman' (*Enuma Elish* vii 145–48). If "shepherd" and "herdsman" are metaphors for kings, the teacher whom the author had in mind must have been a high-ranking scholar entrusted with the education of royal princes.

89. *ṭupšar minâti enqūtu āšib bīt mummu nāṣir piršti ilī rabûti mukīn pān šarrūtu* (VAB 4 256 i 32–33). *ṭupšar minâti* is literally 'scribe(s) of measurements'. Their function is stated in line 34: *ana mitlukti ašpuršunūti* 'I sent them to (give) advice'. *bīt mummi*, translated "workshop (used to make and repair ritual objects)" in *CAD*, cannot be understood apart from *CAD*'s *mummu* A 2, i.e., a "school for scribes, workshop." The scribes referred to in this passage were clearly scholars from the academy in Babylon.

90. *šassukkī enqūti nāṣir* [*piriš*]*ti bēlīšu*[*n*] 'wise accountants who guard the secrets of their lord'; see W. von Soden, "Die Unterweltvision eines assyrischen Kronprinzen," *ZA* 43 (1936) 13:3. *šassukku* renders Sumerian dub-sar a-šà-ga 'scribe of the field' in MSL 12 99:143, and is explained as *ṭupšarru* 'scribe' in the synonym list *LTBA* 2 no. 11 i 11.

*Counselors.* One might expect the large corpus of Akkadian literature to yield evidence that persons with a reputation for wisdom were
consulted for advice and teaching. Diviners were certainly consulted for
their technical knowledge. But the evidence is slim that sages were
consulted for advice on more general matters. "You have all wisdom
[*nēmequ*] in your power," said the sufferer to his friend in the "Babylonian Theodicy," "and you give advice to people."[91] But this may have
been spoken in irony, and the proffered counsel may have been unsoli-
cited.[92] A proverb alludes to a lord (*bēlu*), probably to be identified as
the king, having need of a clever expert (*ummânu emqu*). Was the
wisdom (*nēmequ*) of the expert of value to his master as advice, and is
there here a reference to a royal counselor? Perhaps—but the wisdom
could equally well have been technical knowledge. The proverb reflects
on the injustice of life but concludes by affirming confidently that virtue
will eventually be recognized and rewarded.

> A rogue is a tenant (of a house), but a wise man [*ḫassu*] does not (even)
> reach old age. Yet the wise expert [*ummânu emqu*] whose wisdom
> [*nēmequ*] his lord has not remembered, and any eminent person whom his
> lord has forgotten, will be needed and will be reinstated.[93]

Skill as a counselor to the pharaoh clearly accounts for Rib-Addi's
description of Ḫaya the Egyptian vizier (*pazitu*) as wise (*emqu*) in an
Amarna letter: "See, you are a wise man [*emqu*] at the king's side and it
is because of your wisdom(?) [*emqūtu*] that the king has sent you as a
commissioner."[94] But in this case, although the language is Akkadian,
the social setting is Syrian, not Mesopotamian.

An opinion as to the social standing of a wise man, and the esteem
in which he should be held, can be found in the proverb that states:
"The wise man [*eršu*] is clothed in fine raiment, but the fool is dressed
in a blood-stained rag."[95] This, of course, is the opinion of a scribe.

91. *kaššāta kullat nēmeqi nišī tamallik* (*BWL* 82:200).

92. Irony is perhaps found already in the first stanza of the composition where the
sufferer says to his friend: "Where did a learned man [*mūdû*] (ever) compete with you?
[*ajjiš mūdû iššanin ištīka*]" (*BWL* 70:6).

93. *aššāb raggu / ul ulabbar ḫassu / ummâna emqa / ša nēmeqšu bēlšu / lā ḫassu / u
mamma aqra / ša bēlšu / imšûšu / ibbašši ḫišiḫtašūma / innašši rēssu* (*BWL* 241:54-63).
The composition is bilingual.

94. *amur atta emqu* [written LÚ *em-qú*] *idi šarri u ina em-⟨qú⟩-ti-ka ištaparka šarru
ina rābiṣi* (*EA* 71:7-10). Since *emqu* is used substantivally elsewhere (see nn. 6, 88, 98), the
LÚ has been understood as a determinative. The suggestion that a word *emqūtu* 'wisdom'
be found in this passage goes back to W. F. Albright ("Cuneiform Material for Egyptian
Prosopography 1500–1200 B.C.," *JNES* 5 [1946] 12), but the word is not known elsewhere.

95. *nanduq eršu ṣubāt balti / nu'û ulāp dāmi labiš* (*BWL* 228 iii 13-14). The proverb
is bilingual.

*Teachers.* It was said above that there is little evidence that wise men were sought out for their teaching. But in one passage, unfortunately broken but thought by its editor to be the beginning of the "Counsels of Wisdom," a scholar (*ummânu*) calls on a pupil (*māru* 'son') to heed his teaching. "A scholar . . . in wisdom [*nēmequ*] . . . , 'Come, my son . . . [give heed] to the teaching which . . . , accept my advice. . . .'"[96]

Whether or not these lines in fact form the beginning of the "Counsels of Wisdom," that document may be taken as a sample of what the scholar's teaching and advice would have been. The teaching would have been intended to develop a "wise [*emqu*] and modest understanding [*ţēmu*]," as the following lines imply. By stating what would corrupt such an understanding, the passage suggests the nature of the wisdom that the scholar would have attempted to impart— prudent good judgment in decisions affecting social relations and everyday conduct.

> Do not converse with a mocker; do not go for counsel to a worthless fellow who does nothing; through friendship you will take on their way of thinking [*ţēmu*]; you will be slack at your work and will abandon your path; you will corrupt your wise and modest understanding.[97]

Is the one passage quoted in which a wise man acts as a teacher sufficient evidence for believing that a distinct professional group of wisdom teachers existed in Mesopotamia? Hardly. Nor are the texts that refer to wise counselors sufficient to support the idea of a distinct class of professional counselors. Both sets of evidence are better subsumed under the more general heading of scribe.

*Nonspecific.* Many references to wise men in Akkadian literature do not indicate the occupation or social standing of the persons so designated. Such references are, of course, worthless for the task of establishing the social groups, functions, and status of the wise men of ancient Mesopotamia, which has been a concern of the sections on the king and commoner above. But one example of that class of references will be quoted, partly because it illustrates the inconclusiveness of the evidence, and partly because it defines a wise man by contrasting him with his opposite and in so doing shows *ḫassu* to be a synonym of *emqu*. The passage, also of interest for hinting at one aspect of Mesopotamian wisdom, is in the epilogue to the Laws of Hammurapi where

96. *ummânu i*-[. . . / *ina nēmeqi* [. . . / *alka mār*[*ī* . . . / *ana urti š*[*a* . . . / *milkī lim*[*ad* . . . (*BWL* 106–7).

97. [*itti ēpi*]*š namûti ē tuštāmi* / [*ana r*]*īqi lā bābil šipri ana šitūlti ē tallik* / *ina ţubbâtīma ţēnšunu taššakkin* / *tuštamaţţi šipirkāma uruḫka tezzib* / *enqu baṣṣâ tusarrar ţēnka* (*BWL* 99:21–25).

the king says that his words and deeds "are devoid (of meaning) only for the stupid [*lā ḫassum*—the non-*ḫassu*]; for the wise man [*emqum*] they are spoken of (only) in praise."[98] Who is this wise man? Presumably any Babylonian subject, but he cannot be defined more precisely. The grounds for calling him wise, however, are clear. He recognizes the significance of the king's achievement in issuing fair legal decisions and promoting the welfare of the people. The wise man was a man of insight.

## CONCLUSION

Who, on the evidence of Akkadian literature, was the wise man in ancient Mesopotamia? If the answer is to be decided by a frequency count of claims to wisdom, or by the passion and eloquence of the claims, the answer cannot be in doubt: the king was the wise man *par excellence*. Yet only three kings claim to have been literate in two thousand years of Mesopotamian history.[99] The wisdom of kings was therefore not a bookish or intellectual affair. It was largely a matter of recognizing the supremacy of the gods and performing deeds pleasing to them. Reverence for the gods was the beginning of wisdom.

The evidence has also shown that the vocabulary of wisdom was applied to certain classes of the king's subjects. What is common to the classes so identified is that they are all in some way professions that required an obvious and special skill, ranging from carpentry through the leadership of armies to vocations requiring mastery of writing. It is interesting that wisdom terms are not applied to agricultural workers, shepherds, or boatmen, for example. Such people certainly required professional skills, but they were the widely shared skills of daily life. If the wise man of Mesopotamia is to be defined as the man who is called wise in Mesopotamia, the definition must emphasize his possession of special know-how, whether in the realm of material concerns or in affairs of the unseen world of the gods.

What is not found here is evidence that the Akkadian wisdom terms were used with special frequency for a "class of learned and shrewd men, including astrologers, magicians, and the like" or for persons who were "wise, ethically and religiously," including the "wise teacher, sage" (to revert to definitions of *ḥākām* in BDB with which this essay began). Akkadian literature knows of such persons, but it does not single them out as especially deserving of the vocabulary of wisdom.

98. *ela ana lā ḫassim rīqā ana emqim ana tanadātim šūṣâ* (CH xli 103–xlii 1; the subject is *awâtū᾿a* 'my words' and *epšētū᾿a* 'my deeds' in xli 99).

99. Šulgi, Lipit-Ištar of Isin, and Ashurbanipal. See F. R. Kraus, *Vom mesopotamischen Menschen der altbabylonischen Zeit und seiner Welt* (Amsterdam: Noord-Hollandsche, 1973) 19 n. 22.

# A SURVEY AND READING GUIDE TO THE DIDACTIC LITERATURE OF UGARIT: PROLEGOMENON TO A STUDY ON THE SAGE

## Loren R. Mack-Fisher

Students of Ugaritic literature know that Ugarit was a great center of learning; they know that Ugarit has yielded a rich treasure of didactic literature. For some strange reason this common knowledge has not penetrated the writings of most biblical scholars—not even the writings of those who specialize in wisdom literature. It was excusable but inaccurate in 1955 for W. F. Albright to say that "we do not possess any didactic literature from Ugarit,"[1] but why has this statement been repeated so many times? I thought that after 1968, when the bulk of this material was published by Jean Nougayrol and Emmanuel Laroche in *Ugaritica* V,[2] the statement by Albright would no longer influence the thought and writings of modern scholars. But this was not the case. Instead the statement is often used with little modification except to introduce the confusion of the terms Canaanite and Ugaritic, as the following fairly typical citation illustrates.

Loren R. Mack-Fisher carries out his research at the Double Bar A Ranch in Covelo, California.

The following special abbreviations are used in this essay:

CTA   A. Herdner, *Corpus des tablettes en cunéiformes alphabétiques* (2 vols.; Mission de Ras Shamra 10; Paris: Geuthner, 1963)
PRU   *Le palais royal d'Ugarit* (vols. II and III; Mission de Ras Shamra 6, 7; Paris: Imprimerie Nationale, 1957, 1955)
RS    siglum for tablets discovered at Ras Shamra (Ugarit)
UT    C. H. Gordon, *Ugaritic Textbook* (Analecta Orientalia 38; Rome: Pontifical Biblical Institute, 1965)

1. W. F. Albright, "Some Canaanite-Phoenician Sources of Hebrew Wisdom," *WIANE* (1955) 7. Note below the texts found in the early fifties were published in 1955.
2. *Ugaritica* V (Mission de Ras Shamra 16; ed. C. F. A. Schaeffer; Paris: Imprimerie Nationale, 1968).

Canaanite wisdom has not survived, except indirectly through an Akkadian text in which a father offers advice about life's journey to his son
who is set to venture forth beyond the safety of home. Of course, there are
some allusions to El, the chief god of the pantheon, as wise, and Dan²el is
credited with concern for widows and orphans—traditional wisdom language—but this sort of evidence is useless.[3]

This statement requires correction and points to the need for a brief
reading guide on the didactic literature of Ugarit.

In the present guide I will include items that most scholars would
include, but at a later time it may be important to subtract from or add
to this list. Some of the texts that are listed in this guide will also be
discussed.

## AKKADIAN AND HURRIAN MATERIALS

1. RS 15.10.  As early as 1955 Jean Nougayrol began to publish Babylonian
   literary and wisdom texts from Ugarit with the appearance of *Le palais
   royal d'Ugarit* III,[4] which contained the interesting "Tablette bilingue accado-
   hourite" (RS 15.10). Nougayrol commented on the Akkadian part of the
   text and Laroche on the Hurrian section (*PRU* III: 311–24). In 1960 W. G.
   Lambert included this text in his *Babylonian Wisdom Literature* under the
   section "Precepts and Admonitions" (*BWL* 116). In addition Nougayrol
   published in *PRU* III the first of the "school texts" [pp. 211–14].)

Next, Jean Nougayrol published the following essays on this subject: *(a)* "L'influence babylonienne à Ugarit, d'après les textes en cunéiformes classiques," *(b)* "Les sagesses babyloniennes: Études récentes et
textes inédits," and *(c)* "Nouveaux textes d'Ugarit en cunéiformes babyloniens."[5] All of this discussion in the early sixties was an important

3. J. L. Crenshaw, *Story and Faith* (New York: Macmillan, 1986) 288. For an earlier
statement where the confusion is less pronounced, see his "Prolegomenon" to *SAIW* 8. Of
the many instances of a fairly uncritical following of Albright's statement that could be
given, see, for example, R. B. Y. Scott, *Proverbs; Ecclesiastes* (AB 18; Garden City, NY:
Doubleday, 1965) xvi; R. N. Whybray, *Wisdom in Proverbs* (SBT 45; London: SCM,
1965) 85; and D. F. Morgan, *Wisdom in the Old Testament Traditions* (Atlanta: John
Knox, 1981) 42. Whybray, who in fact disagreed with Albright as to the "Canaanite-
Phoenician character" of Proverbs 8 and 9, still followed Albright's statement concerning
the lack of wisdom examples.
4. Paris: Imprimerie Nationale, 1955. For a helpful list of the Akkadian texts see
Cord Kühne, "Eine Analytische Liste der Akkadischen Ugarittexte," *UF* 6 (1974) 129–56.
5. *(a)* = *Syria* (1962) 28–35; *(b)* = *Les sagesses du Proche-Orient ancien* (Bibliothèque des Centres d'Études supérieures spécialisés; Paris: Presses Universitaires de France,
1963) 41–51; *(c)* = *Des Annales Archéologiques de Syrie* 14 (1964) 39–50. Nougayrol also
published other essays, e.g., "'Vocalises' et 'Syllabes en Liberté' à Ugarit," *Studies in
Honor of Benno Landsberger on His Seventy-fifth Birthday* (AS 16; Chicago: Oriental
Institute of the University of Chicago, 1965) 29–39.

prelude to the material published in 1968 in *Ugaritica* V. There are many texts in *Ugaritica* V that should be listed in this guide, but I will list here only the obvious ones, starting with chap. 1: "Textes suméro-accadiens des archives et bibliothèques privées d'Ugarit" (by Nougayrol).

2. Text 15 (RS 17.10 and 17.80; pp. 23–28). A composition on the art of writing in the form of a letter; in both Sumerian and Akkadian.
3. Texts 16 and 17 (RS 17.81 and 17.155; pp. 29–40). These are medical/magical texts. Text 17, an appeal to "the Sage [*apkallu*] of the gods, Marduk," is a bilingual in Sumerian and Akkadian.
4. Text 18 (RS 20.24; pp. 42–64; also see text 170 [RS 26.142; p. 321]). The pantheon of Ugarit.[6]
5. Text 19 (RS 20.06; pp. 64–65). A conjuration for bad eyes.
6. Texts 109–18 (RS 21.03 E, RS 21.210 rev., RS 20.177, RS 22.220 rev. III–V, RS 20.135, RS 20.139 rev. III–V, RS 22.218, RS 20.196 C, RS 21.63 C, RS 14.128; pp. 199–210). This group of texts or language manuals is the Syllabary Sa.
7. Texts 119–29 (RS 20.121, RS 20.195 A, RS 23.495, RS 17.85, RS 24.309, RS 22.344 + 23.24, RS 5.302 A, RS 20.175, RS 20.136 A, RS frag. B, RS frag. C; pp. 210–30). Another list of gods known as "List AN."
8. Texts 130–42 (RS 20.149, RS 20.426 G + 201 G, RS 20.189 B, RS 23.493 B, RS 20.426 D, RS 21.62, RS 21.63 D, RS 20.123 [+ seven more], RS 20.426 B, A, F, RS 20.185 C, RS 20.197 F; pp. 230–51). These texts are important vocabularies arranged in four columns: columns I and II are for the classical languages—Sumerian and Akkadian; columns III and IV are for the local languages—Hurrian and Ugaritic. With these texts one can go to school with the students of Ugarit. Nougayrol and Laroche have listed all of the Akkadian, Ugaritic, and Hurrian words from these vocabularies (see pp. 349–52 and 448–62).
9. Texts 143–52 (RS 20.160 N, RS 21.10, RS 20.196 A, RS 20.161 D, RS 21.05 D, RS pt. 1844, RS 20.14, RS 21.63 A, RS 21.07 H, RS 6.X; pp. 251–57; also see text 173 [RS 25.511 B; p. 324]). Tables of weights and measures.
10. Text 162 (RS 25.460; pp. 265–73). Nougayrol calls this text "(Juste) Souffrant," and compares it with *Ludlul bêl nêmeqi* or, to use Lambert's title, "The Poem of the Righteous Sufferer."[7] Nougayrol thinks that this text from Ugarit (dated ca. 1300 B.C.E.) is a copy from the early Cassite period or earlier. He also thinks that the *Ludlul* and this text have an ancient common source.
11. Text 163 (RS 22.439; pp. 273–90). I would change Nougayrol's title, "Sagesse," to "The Counsels of Shubeʾawilum." This is a very important text, and Nougayrol thinks it possible to equate Shubeʾawilum with

---

6. Entries 4–10 come from the library of Rapʾanu, who was a very important scribe at Ugarit—perhaps a sage! I will deal in some detail with him in my essay "The Scribe (and Sage) in the Royal Court at Ugarit" in section 2 of this volume.

7. *BWL* 21–62. Note that Lambert thinks that this seventh-century text from the libraries of Ashurbanipal was a copy of an earlier text from the the Cassite period (*BWL* 26).

Shuruppak and hence with the wisdom of the preflood sages.[8] Another interesting thing about this text is that there is a Hittite translation of it (see *PRU* III: 779-84 for Laroche's translation). Nougayrol says, "Pour 163, comme pour tous les textes babyloniens littéraires de Ras Shamra et de Boghazkeuï, la source commune, ultime, c'est, naturellement, la Mésopotamie" (*PRU* III: 277).

12. Texts 164-66 (RS 25.130, RS 23.34 + 23.484 + 23.363, RS 25.424; pp. 291-300). Nougayrol calls this important group of texts "Sagesses en dictons." They are both Sumerian and Akkadian, and they are usually related to Babylonian "pessimism," which seems to me more like realism. (RS 23.484 will be listed again under Ugaritic texts because there is a text in Ugaritic on the reverse.)

13. Text 167 (RS 22.421; pp. 300-304). "Récit du déluge" (Nougayrol's title) is important for many reasons, including the new information that it makes available for any discussion of the problem of the Flood tradition in the *Epic of Gilgamesh* or in the Atra-ḫasīs story.[9]

14. Text 168 (RS 22.219 + 22.398; pp. 304-10). Nougayrol calls this text "'En marge' de Gilgameš[??]"; it may be a tradition that relates to the youth of Gilgamesh—the young rebel.

15. Text 169 (RS 25.421; pp. 310-19). "Signalement lyrique" (Nougayrol's title) was probably imported from Boghazköi. It is written in four columns: column I is in normal Sumerian, II in phonetic Sumerian, III in Akkadian, and IV in Hittite (see Laroche's translation of the Hittite in *PRU* III: 773-79). It describes the poet's (?) mother.

The following texts come from chap. 2 of *Uqaritica* V, "Documents en langue hourrite provenant de Ras Shamra" (nos. 16-20), and the addendum, "Textes de Ras Shamra in langue hittite" (nos. 21, 22) (both sections by Laroche).

16. Text RS 20.123 (pp. 448-62). This is a detailed, helpful discussion of the Hurrian column of the vocabularies mentioned under no. 8 above.

---

8. That Shuruppak was a preflood sage (and not simply a place-name as the reader of the *Epic of Gilgamesh* may be inclined to conclude) is apparent from the "Instructions of Šuruppak" (see *BWL* 92-95), where Shuruppak is the father of Ubartutu, who in turn is the father of Ziusdra. Note, however, even in the *Epic of Gilgamesh* (9:23), Utnapishtim is addressed as "*man* of Shuruppak, son of Ubar-Tutu" (*ANET* 93).

9. This may be an independent Flood tradition, but I would like to see a serious discussion of the matter rather than Tigay's short statement that it "was probably part of neither *Atrahasis* nor *Gilgamesh*"; see J. H. Tigay, *The Evolution of the Gilgamesh Epic* (Philadelphia: University of Pennsylvania, 1982) 215 and n. 5. For a better treatment of this "Babylonian Flood story," see W. G. Lambert and A. R. Millard, *Atra-Ḫasīs: The Babylonian Story of the Flood*, (Oxford: Clarendon, 1969) 6, 24, 40, and esp. 131-33. For additional comments on this text and others in this list see the sections entitled "*Ugaritica* V: Rezensionsartikel" in *UF* 1 (1969) 119-95 and 2 (1970) 283-327. The most important of these comments for the present discussion is W. von Soden's "Bemerkungen zu einigen literarischen Texten in akkadischer Sprache aus Ugarit," *UF* 1 (1969) 189-95. The article is too brief, but he does say that text 168 is not related to Gilgamesh.

17. Text RS 15.30 + 49 (h.6) (pp. 463–64). This hymn to the moon-goddess Nikkal is the now famous Hurrian song and score. Anne Kilmer has studied this text in great detail.[10] (Also see *PRU* III: 334.)

18. Text RS 24.295 (pp. 508–9). Another list of gods.

19. Text RS 24.278 and RS 24.285 (pp. 510–16). Two more hymns, compared by Laroche with *CTA* 168 and 169.[11]

20. Text *CTA* 166: "The Hurrian Pantheon," (pp. 518–27). Here Laroche discusses an old text in light of new information.

21. Text RS 25.421 (pp. 773–79). This text is the Hittite column of text 169 (no. 15 above), with discussion and notes.

22. "Sagesse bilingue" (pp. 779–84). This is a translation of text 163, a Hittite text referred to above (no. 11). Such a Hittite translation is helpful in understanding the Akkadian text.

23. In *Ugaritica* VI there is a very important essay by Jean Nougayrol, "La *lamaštu* à Ugarit."[12] He not only discusses this magical text as a literary text but as a practical text (RS 25.256 A + 25.440 + 25.445 + 25.420 + 25.447). He also has a good discussion of Babylonian texts at Ugarit, and it is clear that there are more to come.[13]

## UGARITIC MATERIALS

There is not much material to list in this part of the reading guide, and my comments here will be brief. Following the list I discuss my reasons for including some of these texts here.[14]

1. School Texts: *UT* 16 (*CTA* 112) and *UT* 1019 (*PRU* II: 19) are student practice texts. The ABC texts are *UT* 401, 320, and 1186–89 (*PRU* II: 184–89). The last text of this series correlates the Ugaritic alphabet with Akkadian syllables. *Ugaritica* VII contains one more (RS 24.281; pp. 63–64).[15]

10. Kilmer recently sent me a fifty-item bibliography on ancient Near Eastern music (thirteen of which she contributed to or wrote). Perhaps the place to start is with Kilmer's "The Cult Song with Music from Ancient Ugarit: Another Interpretation," *Revue d'Assyriologie* 68 (1974) 69–82. Also see C. H. Gordon, "The Ugaritic Texts: Half a Century of Research," *Biblical Archaeology Today: Proceedings of the International Congress on Biblical Archaeology, Jerusalem, April 1984* (Jerusalem: Israel Exploration Society, 1985) 492–501. See p. 498 where Gordon discusses the possibility that the named writer of the Hurrian hymn, ʿAmmurapiʾ, may have been the last king of Ugarit (if not some scribe by the same name).

11. A. Herdner, *Corpus des tablettes en cunéiformes alphabétiques* (Paris: Geuthner, 1963) 259, 260.

12. *Ugaritica* VI (ed. J.-C. Courtois; Mission de Ras Shamra 17; Paris: Geuthner, 1969) 393–408.

13. In *Ugaritica* VII (Mission de Ras Shamra 18; Paris: Geuthner, 1978), Schaeffer says (p. 402) that additional texts will be published from the thirty-fourth campaign, i.e., from 1973.

14. For the Ugaritic texts below I use the numbering system in *UT*.

15. In *Ugaritica* VII: 405, Schaeffer says that there is a Ugaritic lexical text, but Dennis Pardee thinks that this may be a mistake (the text is RS 34.180 b + c); see D. Pardee, "Ugaritic," *AfO* 28 (1981/82) 262.

2. The Ugaritic Pantheon: *UT* 17 (*CTA* 29).
3. An Astronomical Text: *UT* 143 (*PRU* II: 162). According to some this is a report of a total eclipse of the sun.[16]
4. Magical Texts: *UT* 607 and 608 (*Ugaritica* V: 7, 8 or RS 24.244, RS 24.251). These are the serpent charms. There are also some magical texts from Ibn Hani: 78/20 and 78/14.[17]
5. Hippiatric Texts: RS 17.120 (*Ugaritica* V: pp. 625-27),*UT* 55 and 56 (*CTA* 160 and 161), and RS 23.484. This last text is the same text described above (no. 12) as text 165 in *Ugaritica* V: p. 297.[18]
6. "The Poem of Aqhat:" *UT* 1 Aqht, 2 Aqht, 3 Aqht (*CTA* 19, 17, 18). Aqhat's father, Danʾel, had a well-known place among the wise, but Ezekiel (14:12–20) creates an unfortunate misunderstanding when he describes Noah, Danʾel, and Job as "righteous"—they were three wise men. Of course Ezekiel does know something of Danʾel's wisdom, as can be seen by his satirical remark to the Prince of Tyre: "Yes, you are wiser than Danʾel" (28:3). Obviously, this was not the case. Yes, one must be wise to be a good business man, but to be really wise—to be a sage—one needs to know the difference between gods and humans, plus one needs to know that humans are mortal—this is the main thrust of the "Poem of Aqhat."

The above reading guide lists most of the texts that one should consider in any discussion of the sage in the literature from Ugarit. These texts were used in the scribal schools for didactic purposes. I do not consider in this list the texts produced by the scribes for others, e.g., letters, court cases, land grants, or treaties. (This literature will be

16. J. F. A. Sawyer and F. R. Stephenson, "Literary and Astronomical Evidence for a Total Eclipse of the Sun Observed in Ancient Ugarit on 3 May 1375 B.C.," *Bulletin of the School of Oriental and African Studies* 33 (1970) 467–89.

17. On the serpent charms see M. C. Astour, "Two Ugaritic Serpent Charms," *JNES* 27 (1968) 13–36. Astour says that the author had a "thorough acquaintance with Babylonian magic lore and technique of apotropaic and purificatory rites. . . . We should not be surprised, therefore, by finding the essential features of a Babylonian *namburbû* in Ugaritic text. What is remarkable is the skill with which the Babylonian element has been organically incorporated into an incantation that is purely West Semitic in its language, background poetic structure, terminology, and the gods acting and invoked" (p. 28). On the texts from Ibn Hani see P. Bordreuil and A. Caquot, "Les textes en cunéiformes alphabétiques découverts en 1978 à Ibn Hani," *Syria* 57 (1980) 346–50 (on 78/20, with secondary literature on p. 367), 352–53 (on 78/14; the authors see this text as a "Texte de présages").

18. There is a very good work on these four texts by Chaim Cohen and Daniel Sivan, *The Ugaritic Hippiatric Texts: A Critical Edition* (American Oriental Series, Essay 9; New Haven: American Oriental Society, 1983). I have not seen Dennis Pardee's *Les Textes Hippiatriques* (Ras Shamra-Ougarit 2, Mémorie no. 53; Paris: Editions recherche sur les civilisations, 1985). I have also dealt with these texts in a forthcoming essay (to appear in a festschrift for Stanislav Segert in a special issue of *Maarav*): "From Ugarit to Gades: Mediterranean Veterinary Medicine." Since this reading guide is intended for readers from various specialities, I also include the *KTU* numbers for these four texts from M. Dietrich, O. Loretz, and J. Sanmartin, *Die keilalphabetischen Texte aus Ugarit* (Alter Orient und Altes Testament 24; Neukirchen-Vluyn: Neukirchener, 1976): 1.85, 1.71, 1.72, and 1.97.

important when I discuss below in section 2 of this volume "The Scribe (and Sage) in the Royal Court of Ugarit.") These texts do, of course, contain some sayings or stories from the didactic tradition. For example, Nougayrol published a text in *Ugaritica* V (text 35 [RS 20.216; pp. 108–10]) from the King of Carchemish that contains a Hittite parable,[19] but I have really not made any complete search for this sort of thing.

Also, I have not listed much secondary literature in this guide, but two additional items are important to this discussion: "Wisdom Genres in RS 22.439," by Duane E. Smith, "Wisdom," by John Khanjian, both in *Ras Shamra Parallels* II.[20] Even if the suggested parallels to Hebrew wisdom were to be dismissed, these chapters contribute to an understanding of didactic literature at Ugarit. At the very least it would seem that in the time since the publication of these two essays there might have been more recognition on the part of scholars that in fact there is a great deal of didactic literature at Ugarit.

In the future, new texts will be published, and we will be able to deal with many new issues, but this present list is representative. It allows us to understand the nature of this material, and the place of the scribe and the sage.

## ASSESSING THE CORPUS: CLASSIFICATION AND THE BABYLONIAN FACTOR

Most books on wisdom start with a definition of the term. I have read these and have remained confused, thus it may be the better part of wisdom to leave all definitions for later. For the present, I will continue to be descriptive, and refer to this literature as didactic (as I have in the above material). Some may complain that this terminology is too narrow, but I doubt this. After all what is in a good teaching library? I would suggest that the above lists have everything (and more) that most people have included in their definitions and descriptions, except perhaps oral/clan wisdom (and this is perhaps included if it were incorporated into literary developments in the distant past). On this point Duane Smith says,

---

19. This parable packs quite a metaphorical punch in lines 5–11: "A parable of the Hittites says: A certain man was a prisoner in a prison house for five years. Then they said to him: 'In the morning they will give you freedom.' But alas! He had hung himself." A parable/fable in the letter of Jehoash to Amaziah (2 Kgs 14:9) is another example of this sort of thing, but it does not contain such metaphorical force in part because it is immediately allegorized. It reads: "The thistle in Lebanon sent to the cedar in Lebanon saying: 'Give your daughter to my son for marriage.' But a wild beast in Lebanon passed by and trampled the thistle." This is an interesting fable in that the thistle not only claims equality with the cedar by its request but superiority by being first in the formal address.

20. *Ras Shamra Parallels* (ed. L. R. Fisher; Analecta Orientalia 50; Rome: Pontifical Biblical Institute, 1975), 2:215–47 (Smith), 371–400 (Khanjian).

The sages of Ugarit and Israel worked within a common tradition, they used common structures and structural devices in their teaching. . . . The structure of wisdom literature was fully evolved and available in its Babylonian dress in the Levant before the advent of Israel. If paraenesis had its origin in tribal society and tribal instruction, this origin and the evolution which is of often associated with it pre-dates RS 22.439 [i.e., the "Counsels of Shube²awilum"] and therefore Israel. The genre was already fully developed.[21] One sometimes forgets that Israel was late on the scene, and this is also true for Ugarit.

Didactic literature is at the center of interest in this essay, and table 1 summarizes the contents of the list given above. Note that three texts in each column have no corresponding version in the other column. Nevertheless, it still remains a fact that most of this collection is in the Babylonian tradition. This being the case, I am even more certain that we should not use the term "wisdom," remembering what W. G. Lambert wrote: " 'Wisdom' is strictly a misnomer as applied to Babylonian literature. As used for a literary genre the term belongs to Hebraic studies and is applied to Job, Proverbs, and Ecclesiastes" (*BWL* 1). I think that the same thing could be said concerning this collection of materials. But, why is this collection so Babylonian?

Scholars have been saying for many years that wisdom was international. One of the better statements of this was made by Aage Bentzen: "The OT is well aware of the fact that Wisdom literature has roots in foreign countries and peoples. . . . The Scribes then are mediators of an *international culture* in the same manner as modern academicians. Their education they got at *schools* which we know both from *Babylonia* and *Egypt*, and *Ugarit*."[22] On the one hand we did know about such things, but I do not think that we were really prepared for the extent and the importance of the Babylonian traditions. Many may have thought that such material would have been translated into the local language. At centers like Ugarit and Boghazköi this was sometimes done, but rarely. Also, large-scale translation projects were just not important. Such things come late, not only in the history of a text, but in the history of a particular state. Neither Ugarit nor Boghazköi had a "late" period; they were

21. Ibid., 218–19.
22. A. Bentzen, *Introduction to the Old Testament* (2d ed.; Copenhagen: Gad, 1952), 1:169, 171. This English translation is poorly done but even so the word "Ugarit" looks tacked on to the original. But he does refer to Schaeffer's treatment of didactic literature from Ugarit (*The Cuneiform Texts of Ras Shamra-Ugarit* [Schweich Lectures 1936; London: Oxford University, 1939] 37–42). The first edition of this work was published in 1941, fourteen years before the statement by Albright (see n. 1 above).

Table 1. Didactic Literature of Ugarit

| Subject Matter | Classical Languages | Local Languages |
|---|---|---|
| **1. Sumero-Babylonian literature** | | |
| The Sufferer | text 162 (Akkadian) | (?) Aqhat (Ugaritic) |
| Counsels | text 163 (Akkadian) and RS 15.10$^a$ (Akkadian) | RS 15.10$^a$ (Hurrian) |
| Existential sayings | texts 164–66 (Sumerian and Akkadian) | (?) Aqhat (Ugaritic) |
| The Flood | text 167 (Akkadian) | —— |
| Gilgamesh(?) | text 168 (Akkadian) | (?) Aqhat (Ugaritic) |
| Descriptive poetry | text 169 (Sumerian, Akkadian, and Hittite) | —— |
| **2. Encyclopedic literature** [some not published] | | |
| Astronomy | —— | *UT* 143 (Ugaritic) |
| Pantheon | text 18 (Akkadian) | *UT* 17 (Ugaritic) and RS 24.295 (Hurrian) |
| **3. Language helps** (school texts) | | |
| | Sumerian and Akkadian | Hurrian and Ugaritic |
| **4. Magical/medical texts** | | |
| | texts 17, 19, and Lamashtu (Akkadian) | *UT* 607 and 608 (Ugaritic); Ibn Hani 78/20 (Ugaritic) |
| **5. Musical texts** | —— | RS 15.30 (Hurrian) (+ Hurrian hymns) |
| **6. Professional literature** | | |
| The Art of Writing | text 15 (Sumerian and Akkadian) | —— |
| Hippiatrica$^b$ | —— | RS 23.484 (Ugaritic) |

$^a$ 15.10 is written in both Akkadian and Hurrian.
$^b$ One of the hippiatric texts is written on the back of a Sumero-Babylonian text containing some "sayings."

destroyed about 1200 B.C.E.[23] The scribes at Ugarit did produce some "western" forms of Babylonian texts, but for the most part one must stand amazed before their learning and their use of the Babylonian materials. Egypt was not unimportant for eastern Mediterranean didactic literature, but at Ugarit the Babylonians were their teachers.

The strong Babylonian factor is important in several ways for an understanding of this material. It certainly explains the presence of magical texts in which gods, kings, and sages were skilled in such things as exorcism: they could curse, and they could bless (which sounds very much like Danʾel, David, and Solomon). The language helps are of course what one would expect. However, I think that most people were really not prepared for the importance of the Hurrian element. I do not refer only to the vocabularies but of rituals, music, and didactic sayings. The encyclopedic texts remind one of this emphasis in the Babylonian tradition and of the so-called "nature wisdom." All of the above is welcomed, but the real classics are also present: *Epic of Gilgamesh*, the Flood story, the "Counsels of Shubeʾawilum." There are words about suffering; there are traditional and orthodox answers; and there are the questions that challenge. In the "Akkado-Hurrian Bilingual" (RS 15.10) there are words that fit perfectly into the arguments of Job's "friends." I can hear them saying, "One who acknowledges no guilt rushes to his god" (Lambert's translation in *BWL* 116). It is the Babylonian factor that gave to the schools of Ugarit not only the humanistic challenge to the bulk of its traditional answers to human problems, but also its emphasis on the fact that human beings are mortal. This point was very important at Ugarit. In fact, the Aqhat texts pick up on this point and improve on it in the same way that the Book of Job improves on the problem of the righteous sufferer.

I think that usage has a great deal to do with classification. For example, the Kret epic is similar in some ways to the Aqhat epic, but my studies of Kret indicate that it was used by the royal house of Ugarit in order to bless the royal line. It is a patriarchal story that leads to kingship. The Aqhat epic is also a patriarchal story (with an emphasis on the heir), but it is used for quite another matter. It is a similar situation to the use, in the Hebrew Bible, of the patriarchal cycles of Abram, Jacob, Judah, and Joseph for the purposes of the Monarchy, but the patriarchal story of Job is used by the poet for quite another

23. Much later and for various reasons there are some major translation projects: *The Words of Ahiqar* was translated into Aramaic; didactic literature of Jerusalem (via Egypt) was translated into Hebrew; and much later Magon's works, which include Ugaritic and east Mediterranean materials, were translated into Latin (more on this below). As mentioned earlier, the Hittites did translate the "Counsels of Shubeʾawilum."

matter. Aqhat does not have to go through all that Gilgamesh went through. He does not start with that heroic idealism or any kind of search for immortality. From the beginning he is realistic, skilled, and he knows that he will die—all humans die. Thorkild Jacobsen says that "The Gilgamesh Epic is a story about growing up."[24] The Aqhat epic knows what that means. By the way, there is no resurrection. So, it is style, theme, and use that cause me to put Aqhat with the didactic literature at Ugarit.[25] Someone has taken this Babylonian factor and has made a creative advance.

## PROFESSIONAL LITERATURE—TRACING THE ALMANAC TRADITION

The Babylonian factor lends help in another matter. The Babylonians were interested in what I have called "professional literature." A. Leo Oppenheim has called such manuals "procedural instructions." He said, "Under unknown circumstances, the technical lore of certain artisans which catered to the need of the court was fixed in writing, presumably upon a royal order. Once admitted to and incorporated into the corpus of traditional writings, these texts continued to be copied by tradition-conscious scribes and kept in private or royal libraries."[26] I knew that didactic collections would contain things like the "art of writing," but Oppenheim made me realize that the hippiatric texts should also be in this collection. The fact that one of these texts is copied on a text with "sayings" makes all of this very clear. But none of this prepared me for the next step. I, as others, traced the Ugaritic hippiatric texts to Magon of Carthage (usually referred to as Mago), but I did not know that this westward journey would take me to Rome, to become acquainted with Marcus Terentius Varro (116–27 B.C.E.), and to Gades, to meet Lucius Columella (4 B.C.E.–65 C.E.), both of whom have taught me a great deal concerning Magon. Magon's twenty-eight volumes on agriculture were translated into Latin by order of the Roman senate about 146 B.C.E.,

24. T. Jacobsen, *The Treasures of Darkness* (New Haven: Yale University, 1976) 219.
25. I did not come to my views of the Aqhat epic through the interesting studies of Simon B. Parker ("Interpretation of Aqhat") and B. Margalit ("The Ugaritic Poem of Aqhat"; both papers were presented to the Ugaritic Studies Group of the Society of Biblical Literature), but I find that their works are very helpful; I intend to finish my own work on these epics in the near future. Also see S. B. Parker, "Death and Devotion: The Composition and Theme of *Aqht*," *Love and Death in the Ancient Near East* (ed. J. H. Marks and R. M. Good: Guildford, CT: Four Quarters, 1987) 71–83.
26. A. L. Oppenheim, "Introduction" to A. L. Oppenheim et al., *Glass and Glass-making in Ancient Mesopotamia* (Corning, NY: Corning Museum of Glass, 1970) 6. Also note that Cohen and Sivan, *Ugaritic Hippiatric Texts*, 1–2, use the term "professional instruction literature." Also see my forthcoming "From Ugarit to Gades."

with only a few quotes from that translation still extant. But Varro and
Columella do more than quote Magon—they honor him as one of the
ancients, as one of the sages. I understand Magon to be Magon I, the
founder of the Magonid family (before 500 B.C.E.) and, at the present,
my studies of Magon indicate that he collected a lot more than veterinary manuals from the eastern Mediterranean. In his works there are
proverbs, instructions, calendars, and good counsel. Borrowing from
Samuel Noah Kramer's terminology, I now call Magon's works a
"Farmer's Almanac." Kramer says in his discussion of the "Farmer's
Almanac from Nippur":

> Before the Nippur discovery, two similar farmer's "handbooks" were
> known from ancient days: Virgil's far-famed and highly poetic *Georgics*
> and Hesiod's *Works and Days*. The latter, which is by far the earlier of the
> two, was probably written in the eighth century B.C. On the other hand, the
> newly restored Sumerian clay document was actually inscribed about 1700
> B.C., and thus antedates Hesiod's work by approximately a millennium.[27]

The handbook begins, "In the days of yore a farmer gave (these)
instructions to his son." This Nippur text contains the beginnings of an
almanac tradition, and it continues by way of Ugarit, Hesiod, Magon,
Varro, Virgil, Columella, and Pliny. I am not alone in relating professional literature and didactic collections. But once again, it all begins
with the Babylonian factor. I cannot leave this subject without quoting
Columella, who indicates from whom he receives instruction:

> To the other injunctions we add one which one of the Seven Sages
> delivered to posterity for all time: that measure and proportion be applied
> to all things, and that this be understood as spoken not only to those who
> are to embark on some other enterprise, but also to those who are to
> acquire land—not to want to buy more than a regard for their reckoning
> allows. For this is the meaning of that famous maxim of our own poet:
> "Admire large farms, but yet a small one till." This precept, which a most
> learned man has expressed in verse, is, in my opinion, a heritage from
> antiquity, inasmuch as it is agreed that the Carthaginians, a very shrewd
> people, had the saying that the farm should be weaker than the farmer;
> for, as we must wrestle with it, if the land prove the stronger, the master is
> crushed.[28]

27. Samuel Noah Kramer, *From the Tablets of Sumer* (Indian Hills, CO: Falcon's
Wing Press, 1956) 61–62. Also see P. Walcot, *Hesiod and the Near East* (Cardiff: University
of Wales, 1966), and especially his chapter on "Didactic Literature in Greece and the Near
East." I am certain that he would now want to add a great deal to this discussion.

28. H. B. Ash, *Lucius Junius Moderatus Columella: On Agriculture* (LCL: Cambridge: Harvard University, 1941), 1:47–49) (*Res rustica* 1:3:8–9).

Granted, this is Columella's opinion, but it even suggests Virgil's sources. One last word on Magon. In later tradition he was seen as a collector, in some ways similar to the view of Solomon in 1 Kgs 5:9–14. Yes, they could both speak about trees, beasts, birds, creeping things, and fishes. But, Magon published.

## THE SAGE

So, after all of this, where is the sage in Ugaritic literature? This is a hard question, because there were many scribes (including teachers, practicing scribes, and students) but few sages. When I think about sages, the following words come to mind: preflood, dead, ancient, the bold few, and disclosure. When I think about scribes there is a different set of words: religious, traditional, orthodox, skilled, old men teaching the young to be old, closure, and alive. But this may be the wrong way to start. Remembering the Babylonian factor, it is no doubt better to recall their thoughts about sages (also see the essays on Sumerian and Akkadian literature in this volume).

Recently, Anne Draffkorn Kilmer has written an essay about the Akkadian *apkallu* and the Hebrew *nepilîm* (of Gen 6:1–4). She says, "In general, however, the pre-flood sages are called *apkallu* and their traditional number is seven, while the post-flood sages are called the *ummiānu*." Kilmer compares the semidivine *apkallu* to the Nephilim, pointing out well-known preflood sages like Adapa and Atra-ḫasīs, and comparing them to Adam and Noah.[29] Nougayrol sees a connection between Shuruppak, Shubeʾawilum and Atra-ḫasīs; and, in addition, there is other Atra-ḫasīs material at Ugarit. So, in the literature at Ugarit there is at least one preflood sage and perhaps his instructions or counsels. But what of the postflood sages? Here, I would list the patriarch Danʾel. In addition, note that there are some sages among the gods: Marduk, El, and Kothar-wa-Ḫasīs. But where are the historical sages—the kings and the poets? Again, I want to say that the collections of didactic literature are more important than any "author"/ sage. That does not mean that I am uninterested in making a search for such a sage. For now one can dream about some old poet behind the "Poem of Aqhat" (or even of Job), but work should be directed to the court of

29. A. D. Kilmer, "The Mesopotamian Counterparts of the Biblical *Něpīlîm*," *Perspectives on Language and Text: Essays and Poems in Honor of Francis I. Andersen's Sixtieth Birthday* (Winona Lake, IN: Eisenbrauns, 1987) 39. It is interesting to note that the Greeks historicized their Seven Sages. They could assign one of the cherished spots to someone like Solon, and of course in the stories of ancient Israel or Carthage Solomon and Magon could be seen as the great Sages. Again, I must say that these kinds of developments could have happened at Ugarit, but Ugarit was destroyed.

Ugarit. One needs to understand the "special scribes," and then study
the terms applied to them. Perhaps they will qualify as sages.[30]
    So with a promise to continue the search, I summarize as follows:

> Before scribes there were Sages,
> Oh yes, seven before the flood.
> And after? a few from out the mud.
> But now, scribes by the myriad.
> And the Sage? What? Oh, gone for ages.

30. For this study see my essay in section 2 of this volume.

# THE SAGE IN
# ANCIENT IRANIAN LITERATURE

## James R. Russell

### THE PROPHET-SAGE ZARATHUSHTRA AND HIS MESSAGE

The Persians enter the annals of Assyria in 843 B.C.E. and emerge into the full light of history only with the ascent of the Achemenian dynasty of Cyrus to power in 550 B.C.E.; but the roots of the strong, young kingdom that was to make an indelible impression on the life and thought of the Near East lay in the remote northeast, in central Asia, where in the mid-second millennium the great prophet-sage Zarathushtra (Greek Zoroaster) had preached his dramatic, dualistic vision.[1] The nomadic pastoralists of the Prophet's time seem to have adhered to a system of beliefs similar to those of the Vedic people (to whom they were kin): the universe was inhabited by a multitude of gods, many of them embodying abstract concepts. Some, like the Vedic Indra, exemplified the brute force of a young, drunken warrior exulting in his strength; others exercised the more subtle power of *maya-*, magical strength, deriving from a base meaning 'measure'. People at once propitiated and sustained the gods through priestly ritual: the recitation of *mantras* (Avestan *manthra-*), words of mental power, and the offering of sacrifices through the medium of fire. In this way the balance of cosmic order, *ṛta-* (Avestan *aṣa-*), was maintained. It seems that priests were also reputed to possess healing powers, and, like the shamans of central Asia and Siberia of recent centuries, they could journey to and from the spirit world.

James R. Russell is Associate Professor in the Department of Middle East Languages and Cultures at Columbia University.

1. The first-millennium date of Zoroaster as 258 years before Alexander, based on one of several ancient computations, is rather misleadingly called the "traditional" one. It may have resulted from a mistaken equation with Cyrus, according to A. S. Shahbāzī, "The 'Traditional Date of Zoroaster' Explained," *Bulletin of the School of Oriental and African Studies* 40 (1977) 25–35; on the life of the Prophet and the religious conceptions of the early Iranians, see M. Boyce, *A History of Zoroastrianism*, vol. 1 (Handbuch der Orientalistik 1.8.2.2a; Leiden: Brill, 1975). Perhaps Pliny's assertion that there were two Zoroasters represents an attempt to rationalize the tradition of an ancient prophet and a recent historical figure reckoned to be of the same name.

Zarathushtra in his hymns, the *Gāthās*, calls himself a priest (*zaotar-*; cf. Vedic *hotar-*) and a knower, or sage (*vidvah-*); it seems that devastating assaults on his community by cattle raiders (called *mairya-* 'young men' in the later Avesta) compelled him to withdraw into solitude and to contemplate the value of all he had learned: the old system of cosmic order could scarcely account for the undeserved suffering he beheld. At the age of thirty he came to revelation; the Holy Immortal (*Aměsha Spěnta*) of the Good Mind (Avestan *Vōhū Manah*) conducted him into the presence of Ahura Mazdā (the Lord Wisdom), and Zarathushtra set out thereafter to preach his vision of a dualistic universe in which the forces of good, light, truth, and life—all belonging to the creator Ahura Mazdā—are locked in combat with Angra Mainyu (the Destructive Spirit; Middle Iranian Ahriman), an alien being wholly inimical to Ahura Mazdā, this world, and humans, and whose invasion has brought evil, darkness, lying, and death.[2]

The peculiar power of the Prophet's message is reliant upon the dramatic cosmology described in the *Gāthās* (*Yasna* 30); were the present struggle between good and evil a permanent state, the Zoroastrian message should inspire at best a bleak Stoicism, at worst a resignation to a fatalistic gloom. Zarathushtra regarded the world, however, as essentially good, a joyous fulfillment of the impulse of the creator to fill his spiritual realm with material being. The Pahlavi (Middle Persian) *Bundahishn*, or "Book of Creation," elaborates this theme: Ohrmazd (Ahura Mazdā), as Wisdom par excellence, intended the world for people, but warned the still unembodied souls that Ahriman would invade it. Humans affirmed a preeternal covenant to struggle (Iranian *Bundahishn*, MS. TD2 fol. 21b, chap. III.24), knowing that the end should be the reward of a perfect life, with Ahriman banished forever from the possibility of manifestation; and with death no more, the dead should rise anew.

It is evident that Ahriman, holding no real hope or attraction for humans, can subvert them to his purposes only through deceit: the Pahlavi *Dēnkard*, or "Acts of the Faith," an encyclopedic compilation of the ninth century C.E., explains that Ahriman's chief desire of people is "that you do not know me . . . for if they know me, no one will follow me [*ku-m mā šnāsēd . . . ku-m agar šnāsēnd kas-iz az pas ī man ne bawēd*]."[3] Wisdom is in the Zoroastrian system a power in the mental and physical war against evil: this perpetuates an ancient Indo-European

2. On the cattle raiders, see B. Lincoln, *Priests, Warriors, and Cattle* (Berkeley, CA: University of California, 1981), and most recently M. Boyce, "Avestan People," *Encyclopedia Iranica* 3 (1987) 63–64.

3. See S. Shaked, *The Wisdom of the Sasanian Sages (Denkard VI)* (Boulder, CO: Westview, 1979) 14–15.

concept—for Avestan *khratu-* 'wisdom, counsel' is cognate to Greek *kratos* 'power'—but with particular and novel force. In the Avesta—the Zoroastrian sacred Scripture—two kinds of wisdom are specified: innate (*āsna-*) and acquired (*gaošō.sruta-*, lit. 'heard by the ear'). To the first belongs spiritual insight, or, perhaps, on a less exalted plane, instinctual knowledge of various kinds enabling humans to live in this world. To innate wisdom belong both the instinct that good and evil exist and the capacity of prophetic insight into their cosmic origins, while the various means of improving the world are learned (that is, acquired wisdom). Rather like the primitive shamanist peoples of Asia and America, the early Iranians believed that the world was a unified and animate being, everything in it possessing an iconic and symbolic value as an instrument or weapon (Pahlavi *abzār*) in the battle against the evil invader Angra Mainyu. Through learning, humans familiarize themselves with all these tools: the animals, according to the Pahlavi *Mēnōg ī Xrad*, know their *xwēškārīh* 'duty', but the innate knowledge of divine recompense is veiled from humans by Ahriman, so one must learn one's duty in the world, hence *gōšōsrūd xrad* 'wisdom heard by the ear'.

Zarathushtra was the greatest sage, endowed with every kind of wisdom; and the priest who occupied the highest rank in the clergy came to be called in Avestan *zarathuštrōtěma-* 'the one most like Zarathushtra'. There was and is no prohibition against use of the Prophet's name, and perhaps this is why confusion arose later about when Zarathushtra lived, or even how many Zoroasters there were. Although later Greco-Roman tradition attributed to the Prophet the discovery of magic, which was brought to the West by the legendary Ostanes (see below), he was held in great reverence as the first philosopher, preceding Plato by one cosmic cycle of six thousand years.[4]

4. On the two kinds of *xratu-*, see H. W. Bailey, *Zoroastrian Problems in the Ninth-Century Books* (2d ed.; Oxford: Oxford University, 1971) 98 n. 2; W. Lentz, *Yasna 28: Kommentierte Übersetzung und Kompositions-Analyse* (Abhandlungen der Akademie der Wissenschaften und der Literatur, Geistes- und Sozialwissenschaftliche Klasse 1954, no. 16; Mainz: Akademie der Wissenschaften und Literatur, 1955) 967, 1006, held that the term meant 'thinking'. Mithra himself possesses *āsna- xratu-* and is described as *aš.xrathwā-stěma* 'very much wisest' (see I. Gershevitch, *The Avestan Hymn to Mithra* [Cambridge: Cambridge University, 1967] 256); on the term *zarathuštrōtěma-* see C. Bartholomae, *Altiranisches Wörterbuch* (Strassburg: Trübner 1904) 1677. Pliny (*Natural History* 30:1) attributes to Eudoxus of Cnidos the statement that Zoroaster lived six thousand years before Plato, while Diogenes Laertius counts six thousand years between Zoroaster and the campaign of Xerxes. The number is significant in Iranian eschatology: in the six-thousandth year after creation, Ahriman invades the material world; and six thousand years more are to pass thereafter before the expulsion of evil from the cosmos and the end of mortal, reckonable time—as eternal life unfolds in undisturbed splendor. See my "Vec' hazareak mateaně Hayoc' mej" (The Book of the Six Thousand amongst the Armenians), *Erevan University Herald* (Erevan, Armenian Soviet Socialist Republic) 64

The Prophet possessed not only revelatory wisdom, but detailed
knowledge also of the world as it is. Similarities have been noted
between passages in the *Gāthās* where the Prophet asks Ahura Mazdā
about the structure of the cosmos, and verses in Deutero-Isaiah that
express the same concerns in a similar fashion.[5] Question-and-answer
compilations of this kind are commonplace in ancient literature, and it
would be rash to propose Iranian influence, were the texts not very
similar indeed; moreover, contemporary Jewish references to Cyrus as
a shepherd (Hebrew *rôʿeh*; cf. Avestan *vāstar-*), messiah (cf. Avestan
*saošyant-*), and upholder of righteousness (Hebrew *ṣedeq*; cf. Avestan
*aša-*)[6] bear the stamp of Persian religious propaganda, for all these
designations are Gāthic and find a parallel besides in Persian approaches
to the priests of Marduk at Babylon. Zarathushtra in Iranian tradition
also has visions of the future: downcast at the prospect of his approaching death, he complains to Ohrmazd, who explains to him that, were
bodily immortality to exist now, then the wicked should also never pass
away, and the final renovation (Pahlavi *frašegird*) of the world never be
attained. To prove his point, the Wise Lord gives the Prophet a drink
containing omniscience (*khrad ī harvīsp-āgāhīh*); Zarathushtra beholds
a vision of the future, including the reversals and defeats that will beset
Iran at the hands of infidels before the final victory.[7]

The pagan clergy of his people feared and hated Zarathushtra; so it
was many years before he gained a convert in Jāmāspa, the vizier of
Kavi Vīshtāspa, who eventually converted to Zoroastrianism, together
with his nobles and subjects. Like most of the monarchs depicted in the
New Persian epic *Shāh-nāmeh* by Firdousī, Vīshtāspa seems to have
been vain, foolish, and vacillating in his adherence to the new dispensa-
tion; and in the Pahlavi-Parthian *Ayādgār ī Zarērān*, an epic narrative
about the first war in defense of the faith, Jāmāspa is shown as a
prophet and counselor, showing Vīshtāspa the future and pleading with
him not to abandon the cause of righteousness. The vizier is said in the

---

(1988) 85–95; and M. Boyce, *Textual Sources for the Study of Zoroastrianism* (Manchester:
Manchester University, 1984) 20–21), for a discussion of the diffusion of the Zoroastrian
concept of the world-year in East Christendom.

5. See M. Smith, "II Isaiah and the Persians," *JAOS* 83 (1963) 415–21, on the parallels
between *Yasna* 44:3–5 and Isa 45:8, 40:12, 44:24, 40:13, and 45:7.

6. On Hebrew *ṣaddîq* and Avestan *ašavan-* ('righteous man'), see my "An Irano-
Judaic Correspondence," *Journal of the K. R. Cama Oriental Institute* (Bombay) 54 (1987)
81–84, and idem, "*Aša* in Armenia," *Handēs Amsōrya* (Vienna) 101 (1987) 85–93, with
discussion also of the parallels between the Avestan mantric prayer *Ašēm Vōhū* and
passages in the *Nicomachean Ethics* of Aristotle.

7. B. T. Anklesaria (ed./trans.), *Zand-ī Vohūman Yasn* (Bombay: privately printed,
1957) 103. Most of the vision is a resentful *vaticinatio ex eventu* of the catastrophe of
Muslim conquest, in the style of earlier such prophecies, see S. K. Eddy, *The King is Dead*
(Lincoln: University of Nebraska, 1961) 3–36.

Persian *Zardusht-nāmeh* to have received knowledge of all sciences, as well as the power to foretell the future, through the scent of a consecrated flower given him by the Prophet (*Jāmāsp dād-eš az ān yašte būy hame 'ilmhā gašt rōšan bad-ūy / be-dānest čīzī ke bāyad šodan ō tā rastakhīz ānče khwāhad būdan*).[8] Vīshtāspa's brother is fated to die in battle; but Jāmāspa tells the king that there is a bronze fortress where the heroes might take immortal refuge—at the price of failing to act against evil. The vizier's argument that one must fight for a just cause, whatever the cost, recalls strangely the counsel of Krishna to Arjuna in the *Bhagavad Gītā*: the topos of hard advice to a reluctant warrior may belong to common Indo-European tradition.[9]

Zarathushtra was famed among the Greeks as the first astrologer (a belief encouraged by the coincidence of *astrēs* 'star' in the Greek rendering of his name); and Jāmāspa in Persian tradition seems to have learned this art also from the Prophet, for a Pazand text calls him a *zīč* 'astrologer'.[10] Later Parthian (ca. 250 B.C.E.–224 C.E.) and Sasanian (ca. 224–651 C.E.) kings maintained an *axtarmārānsālār* 'chief of the stargazers' at court, and each monarch had a regnal horoscope. Political crises were regarded as inevitable at important conjunctions of the constellations; and such a coincidence at the time of the Arab invasion in the seventh century may have helped to weaken the Iranians' will to resist.[11]

Several classical authors call Zoroaster the discoverer of magic, a word that derives from the Magi—the Median priestly tribe whose name was later generally applied to the Zoroastrian priesthood—and many miraculous abilities are ascribed to the Persian priests. This oriental magic was supposed to have been introduced first to the West in the time of the invasion of Xerxes by a Persian, Ostanes, and many Hellenistic magical texts contain attributions to Zoroaster and to him. Iranian sages, the ancients believed, possessed the ability to visit the next world and return safely.[12] The locus classicus for such shamanlike journeys in

8. Cited by J. J. Modi (ed./trans.) *Jāmāspi* (Bombay: Bombay Education Society, 1903).

9. See my "Government Fellowship Lectures, II: Kavi Vishtaspa and Arjuna: Political Necessity and Sacred Duty," *Journal of the K. R. Cama Oriental Institute* 53 (1986) 90–108.

10. Modi, *Jāmāspi*, xxx. On classical traditions about Zoroaster and astrology and magic, see W. S. Fox and R. E. K. Pemberton, *Passages in Greek and Latin Literature Relating to Zoroaster and Zoroastrianism* (Bombay: D. B. Taraporevala, 1929).

11. On the astrologers at court, see A. Christensen, *L'Iran sous les Sassanides* (2d ed.; Copenhagen: Munksgaard, 1944) 396; on horoscopes, see E. Kennedy and D. Pingree, *The Astrological History of Mashā'allāh* (Cambridge, MA: MIT, 1971) vi.

12. There is a large literature on Ostanes, and it would seem that the diffusion of wisdom by a sage attached to an invading army is at once a literary topos and a historical phenomenon; cf. the journey of Plotinus to the East and the Magi in the Persian force that

Iranian literature is the *Ardā Wīrāz Nāmag*, the "Book of the Righteous Wīrāz," a Pahlavi text whose hero is mentioned briefly in the Avesta. The purpose of the journey of Wīrāz is to obtain an account of the rewards of the righteous and the punishments of the wicked in the next world in order to affirm Iranians in their faith. Wīrāz was not a priest; but the Sasanian high priest Kartīr records in inscriptions that he made the same spirit-journey for the sake of the soul of the king (who had shown too great an interest in the heretical doctrines of Mānī).[13]

## ACTIVITIES OF THE IRANIAN SAGE

### Interpreters of Dreams

Iranian sages were expected, as it seems, to be able to interpret the meaning of dreams; in the Pahlavi *Kārnāmag ī Ardašīr ī Pāpakān*, "The Book of the Deeds of Ardašīr, Son of Pāpak," an epic-legendary account of the beginning of the Sasanian dynasty, Pāpak dreams for three nights. He summons his sages (*dānāgān*) and dream-interpreters (*xwamn-wīzārān*), who explain that a son of Sāsān, that is, Ardašīr, will be king. In pre-Christian Armenia also a certain Magus was renowned as an interpreter of dreams (*mogi . . . erazahani*).[14] A king who was unable to sleep might summon the Magi and wise men to read to him from the

---

invaded Greece (mentioned by Herodotus 7:43). On Ostanes, see L. Thorndike, *A History of Magic and Experimental Science* (8 vols.; New York: Macmillan, 1923), 1:58. "King" Ostanes is said to have expressed an interest in divination by skull cups; see D. Betz (ed.), *The Greek Magical Papyri in Translation, Including the Demotic Spells* (Chicago: University of Chicago, 1986) 73; see pp. 157-58, for the figure prescribed by Ostanes to be drawn to send someone dreams, which somewhat resembles the four-winged apotropaic being in bas-relief at Pasargadae. In the pseudo-Democritean *Physica et Mystica*, the Persian sage Ostanes is said to have "died . . . having used poison to release the soul from the body"; G. Fowden, *The Egyptian Hermes* (Cambridge: Cambridge University, 1986) 90 n. 66, suggests that the alchemical context implies Ostanes was doing this for some spiritual purpose, but he does not mention the Iranian tradition of spirit-journeys, to which this legend may belong. Ostanes' name is good Achemenian Persian: ʾWSTN (= °*Ostan*) is found as the name of a Jew in Egypt; see A. Cowley, *Aramaic Papyri of the Fifth Century* B.C. (Oxford: Clarendon, 1923) 112 line 18. Lucian in his *Nekyomanteia* ascribes to the Magi the ability to travel to and from Hades at will; see J. Bidez and F. Cumont, *Les mages hellénisés* (Paris: Belles Lettres, 1938; repr. 1973), 1:113, and my "Ēr, Ara, and Ardāy Wīrāz," *Revue des Études Arméniennes*, n.s. 18 (1984) 477-85.

13. See P. Skjaervo, " 'Kirdīr's Vision': Translation and Analysis," *Archaeologische Mitteilungen aus Iran* 16 (1983) 269-306; P. Gignoux, "Les voyages chamaniques dans le monde iranien," *Monumentum Georg Morgenstierne* (Acta Iranica 21; Leiden: Brill, 1981) 244-65.

14. O. M. Chunakova (ed./trans.), "Kniga deyanii Ardashir syna Papaka" [Kārnāmag ī Ardašīr ī Pāpakān], *Pamyatniki pis'mennosti Vostoka* (Moscow) 78 (1987) chap. I; on Armenia, see my *Zoroastrianism in Armenia* (Cambridge: Harvard University, 1987) 296-97.

royal annals (cf. the Pahlavi *Xwādāynāmag*, used as a source of the *Shāh-nāmeh*), as does Ahasuerus in the Book of Esther.[15] Or the sages could offer advice; the Sasanian court had a *mogandarzbed* 'Magus chief counselor' (Armenian *movanhanderjapet*, with a Parthian element indicating the office may have existed also under the Arsacids) or *darandarzbed* 'court chief counselor'. The Pahlavi translation and commentary (*Zand*) on *Yasna* 48:8 attributes ancient origins to the office: Zarathushtra is said to have asked Ahura Mazdā to grant the office of *darandarzbedīh* to Frashaoshtra, the brother of Jāmāspa.[16]

## Makers and Compilers of Maxims

The sages presumably knew many maxims of pious and practical wisdom, called in Pahlavi *andarz*, and collections of these are attributed to several individuals: the pre-Zoroastrian sage Aoshnara, the mythical king Yima (Jamshed), Zarathushtra, the teacher Saēna (whose school flourished several generations after the Prophet's death), the Sasanian high priest Ādurbād ī Amahraspandān (who codified the Avesta and compiled the Zoroastrian prayerbook), and the late Sasanian king Khusrō I Anōsharvān (late sixth century; known in later Muslim literature as Nūshirvān the Just). A large collection of maxims is attributed to the Spirit of Wisdom (*Mēnōg ī Xrad*) itself.[17] Many precepts counsel avoidance of overindulgence in eating or hunting (*bazm* and *naxčīr*, the two most beloved activities of the nobility), and, without acknowledging an evident debt to Aristotle, prescribe the mean between extremes.[18] Other

15. On Iranica in Esther, see my "Zoroastrian Elements in the Book of Esther," *Irano-Judaica* 2 (ed. S. Shaked; Jerusalem: Hebrew University, in press).

16. See. B. N. Dhabhar (ed./trans.), *Andarj-i Aōshnar-i Dānāk* [The Counsels of Oshnar the Sage] (Bombay: Parsec Panchayet Fund, 1930) ix.

17. See M. Boyce, "Middle Persian Literature, 5: Wisdom-literature," *Handbuch der Orientalistik* 1.4.2.1 (Leiden: Brill, 1968) 51–55, with bibliography; also J. Tavadia, *Die mittelpersische Sprache und Literatur der Zarathustrier* (Leipzig: Harrassowitz, 1956) 103–10; Shaked, *Irano-Judaica* 2; and idem, "Andarz", *Encyclopaedia Iranica*, 2:11–16.

18. The Zoroastrian religion itself is identified as the Mean in the *Dēnkard* (see R. Zaehner, *The Teaching of the Magi* [Oxford: Oxford University, 1976] 83–84, 91–93); discussed recently in detail by Shaked, in "Payman: An Iranian Idea in Contrast with Greek Thought and Islam," *Transition Periods in Iranian History, Actes du Symposium de Fribourg-en-Bresgau (22–24 Mai 1985)* (Studia Iranica 5; Leiden: Brill, 1987) 217–40. Despite the obvious debt to Aristotelian learning in the Iranian doctrine of the Mean, there may be a native component in the concept of Mithra as the mediator. According to Plutarch, *De Iside et Osiride* 46 (369 b) (ed. J. Griffiths; Cardiff: University of Wales, 1970) 45, Mithras stands between Horomazes (Ahura Mazdā) and Areimanios (Angra Mainyu): *dio kai Mithrēn Persai ton mesitēn onomazousin* 'on account of which Persians call Mithras also the Mediator'. In Zoroastrian tradition, Ahura Mazdā and his adversary have made a pact for the world to exist for a stated period as a battleground between good and evil (Greater or Iranian *Bundahishn*; ed. B. T. Anklesaria, *Zand-Ākāsīh* [Bombay: Rahnumae Mazdayasnan Sabha, 1956] chap. I.27= MS. TD2 fol. 5a–b). The Avestan

maxims extol wisdom and prudence, and enjoin fortitude, even fatalistic resignation, in the face of the vicissitudes of life. Some teachings have an ascetic flavor alien to the life-affirming attitude of the Zoroastrian tradition; most, however, praise temporal enjoyment of the blessings of Ohrmazd as a means of struggle against the gloom and dearth of Ahriman's miscreations. Maxims urge the performance of certain virtuous acts peculiar to Zoroastrianism: the killing of noxious creatures, such as frogs, wolves, and snakes; next-of-kin marriage (Pahlavi *xwēdōdād*); and reverence for fire, water, and the other sacred creations. Armenian Christian polemicists, seizing upon such statements, ridiculed the Persians as "woman-crazy"; the Magi angrily responded by accusing Christian celibates of helping Ahriman to depopulate the world.[19]

## Education

To the Iranian sages was entrusted the education of the young: children of the priestly class began at a very early age to memorize the text of the *Yasna* and its accompanying ritual (*nīrang*) at the seminary (*erbadistān*), as today in the Parsi Madressas of India. Priests who had learned the entire Avesta with its *Zand* by heart were called *hamāgdēn*, a term later adopted also by the Manicheans. A Pahlavi catechism, the "Select Counsels of the Ancient Sages," advises every Mazdā-worshiper to spend a third of his or her days attending the *erbadistān* in order to enquire of the righteousness concerning wisdom (*xrad*).[20] Scribes were taught in the *dabīristān*; the *frahangistān*, or academy, seems to have been reserved for children of the nobility. Since Saēna, one of the Ancient Sages ( *pōryōtkēšān*), is reputed to have been a teacher, it is likely that Iranian education was quite sophisticated at an early date;

---

Yašt 10:2, the Hymn to Mithra, affirms that the contract (*mithra-*), whether it is made with a follower of the Lie (*drĕgvant-*) or with a righteous person (*aṣavan-*), must be kept. Mithra is renowned in tradition as the Judge, and as such exercises *miyānčīgīh* 'mediation'. In the present cosmic state of Mixture (Pahlavi: *gumēzišn*) of good and evil, Mithra as embodiment of the Mean or of moderation could have inspired further speculation on the application of the principle of the Mean in Zoroastrian ethics. Although R. Turcan, *Mithras Platonicus* (Leiden: Brill, 1975), takes into account the position of Mithra as the Iranian sun-god in the center of the sky, he does not consider the other internal Iranian evidence for the epithet *mesitēs*.

19. The Sasanian responses to Christian calumny are preserved by the Armenian historian Ełišē; see my *Zoroastrianism in Armenia*, chaps. 4 and 15.

20. On the term *hamāgdēn* see my "A Wandering Herder of Camels," *Annual of Armenian Linguistics* 8 (1987) 12 n. 8; on the elaborate rules of the *erbadistān* see S. J. Bulsara, *Aerpatastān and Nīrangastān* (Bombay: British India Press, 1915; repr. New York: AMS, 1977) 3–60; for counsel to the laity to attend the seminary see M. Kanga (ed./trans.), *Čītak Handarz ī Pōryōtkēšān* (Bombay: N.P., 1960) 21.

but Herodotus, in keeping with his view of noble savages as the pro-
genitors of empire, described the Persians of the time of Cyrus as plain-
living, plain-speaking folk, only later to be spoiled by Babylonian
luxury, who taught their young men three things only: to ride a horse, to
shoot a bow and arrow, and to speak the truth.[21] But Greeks generally
held Persian education in high regard, as in Plato's *Alcibiades*, which
praises the training of the Spartan and Persian kings:

> When the young prince is fourteen years old he is given into the charge of
> certain persons who are called the "Royal paedagogues." These are four
> Persians in the flower of their age who are selected as being reputed
> foremost in certain virtues: one is the wisest, one the most just, one the
> most prudent, one the bravest. Of these the one who is wisest teaches the
> magic of Zoroaster the son of Horomazos: this is the service of the gods.
> The same man gives instruction in kingly duties.[22]

By kingly duties is most likely meant statecraft; pre-Islamic Iran
produced the first mirrors for princes, such as the "Testament of
Ardašīr," preserved only in an Arabic version. The Persian *Siyāsat-
nāmeh* ("Book of Government") of Niẓām al-Mulk, though composed
in the eleventh century, reflects the ancient doctrine that monarchs are
granted divine favor to restore righteousness in evil times. There are a
number of anecdotes on Sasanian kings, especially Nūshirvān and his
sagacious vizier Buzurjmihr (Wuzurgmihr; Būrzōē). The text recom-
mends the old custom of the Persian kings to hold public audiences on
the Zoroastrian feast-days of Nō Rōz (the vernal New Year) and
Mihragān (the autumnal feast of Mithra), and to have the *mōbadān
mōbad* ('the chief priest', explained by Niẓām al-Mulk as 'judge of
judges') decide on the spot on cases between king and commoner. The
text urges princes to consult often with learned men—a practice frequently enjoined in Pahlavi texts also.[23]

21. Herodotus (*Histories* 1:131-71, 9:122; cf. Isa 13:17), who praises the Persians for
scorning silver and gold, is cited by M. Dandamayev and V. Lukonin, *Kuľtura i ekono-
mika drevnego Irana* (Moscow: Izd-vo "Nanka," 1980) 289-90. The authors fail adequately
to recognize that these accounts, rather like the later *Germania* of Tacitus, are highly
tendentious and cannot be taken at face value.

22. *Alcibiades* 122b, cited by J. E. Harrison, *Themis: A Study of the Social Origins
of Greek Religion* (2d ed.; Cambridge: Cambridge University, 1927) 75.

23. Khwāja Niẓām al-Mulk, *Siyar al-mulūk (Siyāsat-nāmeh)* (Tehrān, 1962), chap. 6,
p. 57; H. Darke (ed./trans.), *The Book of Government; or, Rules for Kings* (London:
Routledge and Kegan Paul, 1960) xviii, 42-43, 91. On the transmission to Islam of ancient
Iranian political wisdom, and on *hampursagīh* 'consultation of the learned', see S. Shaked,
"From Iran to Islam," *Jerusalem Studies in Arabic and Islam* 4 (1984) 33. It seems
significant that the king heard petitions on Mihragān, given the connection of the Zoroastrian sun-god with justice. The Sasanian king wore a radiate solar crown on the holiday,

## Judges and Laws

It is evident from the foregoing that the Zoroastrian priests and sages served as judges of a highly ethical code of laws; and the titulature of Sasanian seals bears this out. A common epithet given priests is *driyōšān jādagōw* 'advocate of the poor' (*driyōš*; New Persian *darvīš* 'poor man' is a term applied to the faithful generally, as those who stand in need of Ahura Mazdā; it is later adopted by the Muslim Ṣūfīs); the Armenian Christian clergy adopted this title.[24] Xenophon in *Cyropaideia* 1:2:2–3 praises the laws of the Persians in terms that indicate they had a strong religious foundation:

> These laws seem to begin with a provident care for the common good; not where they begin in most other governments: for most governments leaving each individual to educate his children as he pleases, and the advanced in age to live as they please, enjoin their people not to steal, not to plunder, not to enter a house by violence, not to strike anyone whom it is wrong to strike, not to be adulterous, not to disobey the magistrates, and other such things in like manner, and if people transgress any of these precepts they impose punishment upon them. But the Persian laws, by anticipation, are careful to provide from the beginning, that their citizens shall not be such as to be inclined to any action that is bad and mean.

Zoroastrian *andarz* texts (precepts) counsel people to guard the gates of body and soul against entry by the demons, so that the gods may find a dwelling; and they uphold the ethical triad of good thoughts, words, and deeds. One might almost see in Xenophon's list an invidious reference to the majority of negative commandments in the Decalogue, contrasted with the wisdom of the Persians.

## THE IMPACT OF PERSIAN SAGES
## IN CHRISTIAN TRADITION AND JUDAISM

The most famous Persian wise men are the three Magi who are supposed to have followed a star from the Mons Victorialis in the East to visit the infant Jesus at Bethlehem. It has been suggested that the journey of the Armenian king Tiridates I to the court of Nero served as the prototype for the legend;[25] but the historical record of a journey much more like the Christian tradition than the embassy of the Armenian monarch is found in the Jerusalem Talmud:

---

somewhat like the nimbus of the American Statue of Liberty with her torch of justice. An Aramaic version of the *Words of Aḥīqar* from Achemenian Elephantine extols the power of the king, who is "like Šemeš"—the sun (see Cowley, *Aramaic Papyri*, 223).

24. See N. G. Garsoïan, "Sur le titre de Protecteur des pauvres," *Revue des Études Arméniennes*, n.s. 15 (1981) 21–32.

25. See my *Zoroastrianism in Armenia*, 268, 279 n. 46.

Important men came up from the Persian [scil. Parthian] Empire to Yannai the King [i.e., Alexander Janneus, who reigned at Jerusalem in the first century B.C.E.]. When they were sitting and eating, they said to him, "We remember that there is here a certain old man, who used to say before us wise sayings. Let him teach us something. Send and summon him." [26]

The Jews of the land of Israel looked to Iran as a liberator from Greek and later Roman oppression; the legend of the Magi might have been calculated to impress Jews who felt Jesus offered no political salvation to his people. Zoroastrian theological books present a uniformly hostile view of Judaism, however; since ethical differences between the two faiths are not profound, and Babylonian rabbis maintained cordial relations with the Sasanian King of Kings, it would seem that the Magi with their hostile propaganda were seeking to stem the tide of conversion to Judaism among Iranians. In the *Dēnkard*, the ten good commandments of Jamshēd are contrasted to the evil Decalogue of the Jews, whose authorship is attributed to the demonic monster of misrule, Ažī Dahāka.[27]

Many Zoroastrian influences have been perceived in Judaism; most apposite is the doctrine that God created the world by *da'at*, *bînâ*, and *heśkel*—'knowledge', 'understanding', and 'perception'—which appears parallel to the Zoroastrian idea that Ahura Mazdā created and maintains the world through *dānāgīh* ('knowledge'), *frazānagīh* ('sagacity'), and *mardābagīh* ('manliness').[28] In terms of religious learning, it is intriguing to observe the similarities between the format of the Talmud (Mishnah plus Gemara commentary) the Avesta with *Zand* commentary: the latter consists of Avestan passages interlarded with literal translations and the various commentaries of prominent sages in the later Pahlavi tongue. Young Mazdean acolytes of the Sasanian period, like their Jewish counterparts, studied and memorized sacred texts by rocking back and forth and chanting loudly, to the distaste of contemporary Christian observers.

26. *Y. Ber.* 7:2, cited by J. Neusner, *History of the Jews in Babylonia* (Leiden: Brill, 1965), 1:171.

27. See my "Our Father Abraham and the Magi," *Journal of the K. R. Cama Oriental Institute* 54 (1987) 62-63; J. de Menasce, "Jews and Judaism in the Third Book of the *Dēnkart*, " *K. R. Cama Oriental Institute Golden Jubilee Volume* (Bombay: K. R. Cama Oriental Institute, 1969) 45-49; and L. H. Gray, "The Jews in Pahlavi Literature," *Actes du XIVᵉ Congrès International des Orientalistes, Alger, 1905* (Paris: Leroux, 1906), 1:177-92.

28. See Shaked, *Wisdom of the Sasanian Sages*, xxiv, on the Pahlavi system; the same author offers a perhaps overly cautious appraisal of Iranian influences in "Iranian Influence on Judaism: First Century B.C.E. to Second Century C.E.," *The Cambridge History of Judaism* (ed. W. D. Davies and L. Finkelstein; Cambridge: Cambridge University, 1984), 1:308-25.

## PERSIAN WISDOM AND GRECO-ROMAN RELIGIONS

Zoroastrian wisdom appears to have influenced profoundly certain non-Greco-Roman pagan religious systems of the ancient world. The expansion of the cult of the Semitic Baᶜal Šamîn, the Lord of Heaven, may have been influenced by the Achemenian worship of Ahura Mazdā;[29] and an Aramaic inscription from Arebsun in Cappadocia commemorates the marriage of the *mazdā* ('wise') religion of Mazdā-worship to the god Bel,[30] recalling the role of Sophia in other philosophical systems. The cosmogonic vision at the beginning of the *Poimandres*, with its confrontation of light and darkness, evidently owes much more to Zoroastrianism than to the Book of Genesis; and spirit-journeys and visions, followed by questionings of the divinity in the pseudepigraphical *Zostrianos* (a Gnostic text from Nag Hammadi), appear to be inspired by themes from the more accessible hymns of the *Gāthās*. Persian words and invocations of Mithras are scattered also through the Greco-Egyptian magical papyri, indicating that Iranian ideas were current on many levels of religious thought and practice in the Near East.

Following the Muslim conquest and the destruction of Iranian government, Zoroastrian priests found themselves the leaders of the beleaguered and diminishing communities of the faithful. A Pahlavi text, *Gizistag Abāliš*, "The Accursed Abālish," records the debate of the leader and high priest of the Zoroastrians of Fars, Ādurfarnbag ī Farrōkhzādān, with Abālish (an apostate to Islam) at the court of the Caliph Mamūn (reigned 813–33).[31] Though the defeat of the traitor is recorded in terms reminiscent of the sonorous abjuration of Ahriman himself, the progress of Islam in Iran was relentless, and within a century sages of Khorāsān guided communities of Zoroastrians out of their ancestral lands to a new home and religious freedom in India.

## SUMMARY: ON WISDOM
## AND THE ROLE OF THE PROPHET

The faith of ancient Iran was founded on the assertion that the goodness of God, and the ability of human beings to commune with the deity, rests in Wisdom; through Wisdom also, the world will be restored to its primal purity and evil expelled hence forever. The role of the prophet was necessarily that of the sage as well, and the bearer of Wisdom occupied a central position in Iranian society for the ages to come.

29. See J. Teixidor, *The Pagan God* (Princeton, NJ: Princeton University, 1977) 12.
30. See Boyce, *History of Zoroastrianism*, 2:274–75.
31. H. F. Chacha (ed./trans.), *Gajastak Abālish* (Bombay: Parsi Punchayet Fund, 1936).

# PART II

*The Social Locations*
*and Functions of the Sage*

# THE FUNCTIONS OF THE SAGE
# IN THE EGYPTIAN ROYAL COURT

## Ronald J. Williams

### Magician and Sorcerer

The natural tendency to regard sages as a normal component of an oriental court owes much to the Old Testament. For instance, the Joseph saga tells how Pharaoh, seeking an interpretation of his dream, "sent and summoned all the magicians [ḥarṭummîm][1] of Egypt and all her sages [ḥăkāmîm]" (Gen 41:8). Again, when Aaron transformed his staff into a serpent in the presence of the king and his courtiers, "Pharaoh, on his part, summoned the sages and the sorcerers [mĕkaššĕpîm], and they too, the magicians [ḥarṭummîm] of Egypt, did the same with their incantations" (Exod 7:11).

### Interpreter of Dreams

In these passages the Hebrew writers correctly portray the Egyptian wise men as both sages and sorcerers, for the learned scribes, who were frequently also lector-priests, were well-versed in the magical texts. In addition, they were proficient in the interpretation of dreams. The author of the demotic "Papyrus Insinger," in the course of a long list of benefactions by the creator-god, says that "he created remedies for curing illness, wine for curing distress of mind; he created dreams to show the way to the dreamer when he is blind [i.e., to the future]."[2]

### Adviser

Another biblical text refers to a third role of the court sage in Egypt, that of adviser to the sovereign. In derisive words directed

Ronald J. Williams is Emeritus Professor of Egyptology at the University of Toronto.

1. The Hebrew word ḥarṭōm was probably derived from demotic ḥry-tp/b 'chief, headman', a title that later came to mean 'sorcerer, magician'. See now J. Quaegebeur, "On the Egyptian Equivalent of Biblical Ḥarṭummîm," *Pharaonic Egypt: The Bible and Christianity* (ed. S. Israelit-Groll; Jerusalem: Magnes, 1985) 162–72.

2. Translated in M. Lichtheim, *Ancient Egyptian Literature* (3 vols.; Berkeley: University of California, 1973–80), 3:210–11 (hereafter *AEL*).

against the Egyptian ruling house the writer declares: "The princes of Tanis are just fools; the wisest of Pharaoh's counselors are a stupid council. How can you say to Pharaoh, 'I am a child of sages, a child of ancient kings'?" (Isa 19:11).

## Diplomat

The few clear descriptions of similar scenes at the court in Egyptian sources all occur in fictional accounts. One such is recorded on a papyrus of Dynasty 19. The story is set in the Second Intermediate Period, when the land was dominated by the Hyksos who had established themselves in the north. Apophis, the Hyksos king, seeking to provoke an encounter with his vassal ruler Seqenenrē who held sway at Thebes, called for his palace officials. On their advice he had 'his scribes and sages' (n3y.f sšw rḫyw-3ḫt)[3] compose a provocative message to be transmitted to the latter.

## Problem Solver

A second instance is to be found in another papyrus of Dynasty 19 that preserves the "Tale of Two Brothers" (AEL 2:203–11). In one episode the Egyptian king is annoyed at his washermen over a strange perfume that still pervades the royal laundry. The odor is traced to a braid of hair found floating on the water. Puzzled by this fact, the sovereign called upon 'the scribes and sages of Pharaoh' (n3 sšw rḫyw-ḫt n pr-ꜥꜣ) to identify the owner of the braid, a task that they successfully accomplished.

## Physician

The "Bentresh Stele" contains a later work of fiction that cannot have been composed earlier than the Persian period (AEL 3:90–94). It relates how the ruler of Bakhtan (Bactria?) sent an urgent request to Ramesses II of Dynasty 19 on behalf of his daughter Bentresh, the sister of Ramesses' queen. Since she was suffering from a mysterious malady he asked that a sage (rḫ-ḫt), in this case a physician (who would also be proficient in sorcery), be sent to examine her. Ramesses summoned the staff of the House of Life and the Council of the Court (qnbt nt ḫnw). The latter body was composed of the senior palace officials. From their number the royal scribe Thutemheb was selected and despatched to Bakhtan.

## Eloquent Entertainer

Yet another fictitious narrative appears in the "Prophecies of Neferty," the scene of which is laid in Dynasty 4 (AEL 1:139–45). King

---

3. 'Scribes and sages' may also be rendered 'learned scribes'.

Snofru also convoked the Council of the Court in order to have them recommend a sage who might entertain him with his eloquence. They were able quickly to produce a notable lector-priest, Neferty, who was both sage and soothsayer.

## Chancellor, Architect, Government Official

During the Old Kingdom the court officials were almost exclusively members of the royal family. Among their number were to be found men who later became renowned as sages. Such were Imhotep, the chancellor and architect of Djoser in Dynasty 3, Prince Hardjedef of Dynasty 4, and the viziers Kaires and Ptahhotpe of Dynasty 5 or 6. After this period commoners in increasing numbers were appointed to high governmental posts. Indeed, as early as ca. 2050 B.C.E. the author of the "Teaching for Merykarē" offered the following prudent advice to the new ruler: "Make no distinction between a well-born son and a commoner; rather select a man in accordance with his performance" (*AEL* 1:101).

By the New Kingdom many competent senior officials attained a reputation as learned men. Senenmut, a man of humble origin, became chief steward of Queen Hatshepsut in Dynasty 18. Amenhotpe, son of Hapu, also of nonroyal birth, became royal scribe and overseer of royal works under Amenhotpe III. He, together with Imhotep, was remembered and deified in the Greco-Roman period.

## Counselor

These wise men were undoubtedly highly regarded as counselors, although hardly a word is mentioned about this valuable function. The reason may have been reticence in view of the dogma of the ruler's divinity. A statue of Amenhotpe, son of Hapu, records the following:

> I am a great man, greatest of the great, skilled in hieroglyphs and reasoned(?) counsel, adhering to the king's plans, whose position the sovereign advanced. . . . I was appointed to be royal scribe at the palace, and moreover was introduced to the god's book(s), saw the powers of Thoth and was equipped with their secrets. I opened up all their mysteries and my advice was sought concerning all their matters.[4]

During the reign of Osorkon II of Dynasty 22 Nebneteru served as royal secretary (*sš šᶜt [n] nsw*) and attained the venerable age of ninety-six. An inscription on his statue describes him as "an official of the outer

---

4. H. W. Helck, *Urkunden der 18. Dynastie* (Urkunden des ägyptischen Altertums 4, fascs. 17–22; Berlin/Gratz: Akademie-Verlag, 1955–61), 21:1820.6–15. The expression "god's book" refers to religious or magical works regarded as sacred books.

chamber [*sr ḫnty*] who guides the land by his counsel" (*AEL* 3:21), and again as "a mouth effective at privy speech, . . . whose coming is awaited at the palace and whose sagacity has promoted his person [lit., his *ku*]" (*AEL* 3:20). It is perhaps significant that this inscription contains some maxims in the style of the wisdom texts.

# THE SAGE IN MESOPOTAMIAN PALACES AND ROYAL COURTS

## Ronald F. G. Sweet

### THE KING AS SAGE

In my earlier essay in this volume it was shown that the king must be regarded as the sage—the "wise man"—*par excellence* in Mesopotamian society, at least if the evidence of Akkadian literature is taken at face value.[1] The normal center of the king's activities was the palace, which comprised both administrative and residential quarters. Thus the proposition that the sage in Mesopotamia was normally associated with the royal court, which is the thesis of the present essay, is, with regard to the chief exemplar of wisdom in Mesopotamian tradition, simply a corollary of what was said about the king in the earlier essay.

The case for regarding the king as the wisest man in the realm depends, of course, on the tendentious claims of royal inscriptions. An unbiased observer might not always have conceded the legitimacy of the claims. James I of England was once called "the wisest fool in Christendom." In the same spirit an honest subject might, at certain junctures of Mesopotamian history, have called his king (*sotto voce*) the most foolish sage in the four quarters.[2] However, the stereotyped claims

Ronald F. G. Sweet is Professor of Assyriology in the Department of Near Eastern Studies at the University of Toronto.

1. See "The Sage in Akkadian Literature: A Philological Study" (pp. 45-65 above). J. L. Crenshaw has remarked that "it needs to be pointed out that to call one wise is not to identify him as a sage" ("Method in Determining Wisdom Influence upon 'Historical' Literature," *JBL* 88 [1969] 133 [repr. in *SAIW*]). Wisdom, however, is so problematical a genre in Mesopotamian literature that it has been decided for the purposes of this essay to regard any man who is called "wise" as a "wise man." The oft quoted words of W. G. Lambert bear repeating: "'Wisdom' is strictly a misnomer as applied to Babylonian literature" (*BWL* 1). (Abbreviations used in this essay that are not listed above on pp. xiii-xiv may be found in *The Chicago Assyrian Dictionary*.)

2. This in effect is what the author of the Nabonidus Verse Account has done (but *ad alta voce*, and only after the fall of Nabonidus). The picture of the king presented in this text is very different from that found in Nabonidus's own official inscriptions (see VAB 4 218-97). Whether the condemnation was justified, and to what extent it was

of the royal inscriptions were not without some foundation. The substance of the claims lay in the fact that the king was at the head of a governmental organization that commanded the services of the best available science, technology, and craftsmanship of the day. The king displayed wisdom, in the sense of good judgment, by ordering the use of that science, technology, and craftsmanship for the execution of deeds pleasing to the gods, in particular the construction and upkeep of their temples and the good government of the people whom the gods had entrusted to his care. He possessed wisdom, in the sense of a body of knowledge and skill, by having at his disposal the best informed experts and the most skillful craftsmen to carry out his wishes.

Even if the king was illiterate and therefore had no personal competence in those skills that, with a modern and western bias, one may be inclined to regard as the highest manifestations of Mesopotamian wisdom—divination or astronomy, for example—one should not hesitate to recognize the typical Mesopotamian ruler as a shrewd judge of people, a decisive man of action, and a skillful organizer of large-scale human and material resources who fully deserved the epithet wise.[3] Although the majority of Mesopotamian kings are little more than names, in a few cases enough is known of the intrigues and power struggles in which they were embroiled for one to be confident that a man who gained and retained a throne must normally have been someone of quite uncommon ability.[4] The apodoses of omen texts referring to the king contemplate the full range of political hazards to which a priori one might expect a king to have been exposed in the social conditions of ancient Mesopotamia—disloyalty of close associates, betrayal of state secrets, harem conspiracies, witchcraft, disaffection of the populace, assassination attempts, and revolts.[5] Only a shrewd, wily, and forceful man of action could survive the hazards. Even if one looks no further in the royal court than at the occupant of the throne, evidence is found there for the presence of the sage in a sense readily accepted by the Mesopotamians.

---

motivated by opportunism and self-serving under a new regime, is another question. A translation by A. L. Oppenheim is given in *ANET* 312–15.

3. For the extent of royal literacy, see the first paragraph of the conclusion to my first essay above (p. 65, and n. 99).

4. The reigns of Zimri-Lim (deposed and exiled), Tukulti-Ninurta I (assassinated), Sennacherib (assassinated), and Ashurbanipal (fratricidal strife with Šamaš-šum-ukīn) illustrate the kind of power struggle that could test the mettle of a Mesopotamian king—and sometimes prove his undoing.

5. See J. Bottéro, "Le pouvoir royal et ses limitations d'après les textes divinatoires," *La Voix de l'Opposition en Mésopotamie* (ed. A. Finet; Brussels: Institut des Hautes Etudes de Belgique, 1973) 119–65, esp. 140–65.

The building of temples and the furnishing of their necessary equipment (images of the gods, for example), which the kings mention most often in connection with their claims to be wise, may seem an unlikely proof of a special endowment of wisdom. But, apart from the consideration that such activities gave evidence of wisdom by showing a right order of priorities, it should be remembered that the building of a temple, at least in the case of the larger of the temples known from excavations, must have been one of the most ambitious projects of a peaceable nature that a Mesopotamian ruler could embark upon. The king was the inheritor of an impressive tradition of large-scale temple building going back to the Ubaid period.[6] The building and furnishing of a temple called for the skills of the surveyor, architect, mason, carpenter, and metal worker, not to mention the skill of organizing what must have been the scores, if not hundreds, of workers required and of ensuring the delivery of materials.[7] As the initiator of such a project and the one who directed the resources of the state to its fulfilment, the Mesopotamian ruler felt fully entitled to be considered wise.

## EXPERTS IN THE PALACE AND ROYAL COURT

The king necessarily had to depend upon subordinates for the execution of his wishes and thus became the great patron of science, technology, and the crafts. The palace must always have been the principal provider for the arts and sciences in the land, outstripping the other obvious candidates for this honor, the temples, because these themselves depended on the generosity of the king.[8] The palace was thus a natural center for experts—the wise—of every kind.

6. For a comprehensive and detailed presentation of the evidence, see E. Heinrich, *Die Tempel und Heiligtümer im alten Mesopotamien* (Deutsches Archäologisches Institut: Denkmäler antiker Architektur 14; Berlin: de Gruyter, 1982). For the building of palaces, which Assyrian kings also mention as requiring and displaying their wisdom, see E. Heinrich, *Die Paläste im alten Mesopotamien* (Deutsches Archäologisches Institut: Denkmäler antiker Architektur 15; Berlin: de Gruyter, 1984). The textual evidence for the building activities of Assyrian kings down to Tiglath-pileser III is presented in S. Lackenbacher, *Le roi bâtisseur: les récits de construction assyriens des origines à Teglathphalasar III* (Paris: Editions Recherche sur les Civilisations, 1982).

7. Note, as an indication of the careful planning that preceded the building of a temple, the architect's plans shown on Gudea's lap on the statue Louvre AO 2. See F. Johansen, *Statues of Gudea Ancient and Modern* (Mesopotamia 6; Copenhagen: Akademisk, 1978) pls. 19, 22.

8. "Royal largess, rather than the returns of its agricultural investments and the pious generosity of its worshipers, often, and especially in the later periods, provided the means the temple could utilize for the purpose of displaying the wealth of the deity" (A. L. Oppenheim, *Ancient Mesopotamia* [rev. ed.; Chicago: University of Chicago, 1977] 97).

A distinction should properly be made between "palace" and "court" when speaking of the location of experts who stood at the service of a king. By court is meant in this context the persons habitually in the entourage of the king, as against persons of lower social rank employed as servants in the palace administration. Although, as J. Bottéro has observed, Akkadian had no word for court in this sense,[9] information can be gleaned from various sources about the professional designations of persons close to the king. Professions of which at least an occasional member is explicitly described as wise in Akkadian texts seem to have been uncommon in these circles. Some of the other professions known to have been held by court officials may be assumed to have required literacy, and so to qualify for recognition as skilled, or even learned, despite an absence of direct textual evidence, but several cases must remain uncertain.[10] The skilled experts who served the king should therefore, as a general rule, be thought of as active in the workshops and administrative offices of the palace rather than as having access to the court in the narrower sense. However, individual scribes, diviners, exorcists, physicians, and singers of laments could be exempted from this generalization. Their case will be considered below.

9. "Le roi avait aussi ce que nous appellerions 'sa cour' (à ma connaissance l'accadien n'a point d'équivalent pour ce mot)" (Bottéro, "Le pouvoir royal," 132).

10. For the personnel of a royal household, see the two-part article "Hofstaat" in *RLA* 4:435–52: "A. Bis ca. 1500 v. Chr.," by J. Renger; and "B. Assyrisch," by P. Garelli (the two parts are referred to as A and B in the following notes). Apart from scribes and diviners, who are dealt with later in this essay, the following skilled professions are mentioned. A smith (s i m u g) belonged to the personal staff of the children of Lugalanda and Baranamtara at Lagash (ca. 2500 B.C.E.; A §17); for the description of metal workers as wise, see nn. 53, 56, and 57 in my essay above (p. 58). Musicians were included in the court of the god Ningirsu according to Gudea Cylinder B (ca. 2140 B.C.E.; A §11); for a description of musicians as wise, see n. 80 in my essay above (p. 61). Proto-Lu, a list of professions from the Old Babylonian period but perhaps reflecting conditions in the Ur III period (ca. 2100 B.C.E.), includes among the king's servants a craftsman (u m - m i - a, Akkadian *ummiānum*; "Handwerker" [A §9 b]) and a physician (a - z u, Akkadian *asûm*; A §9 c); for the characterization of these professions as wise, see my essay above (p. 61, and nn. 82 and 83). An u m - m i - a ("Handwerksmeister" [Renger]) is also assigned to Enlil in the god list A n = *Anum*, which reflects conditions in the Old Babylonian period (A §6). Musicians and singers (*nāru, zammāru*) are also mentioned as receiving rations in the Neo-Assyrian palace at Calah (B §5). Among the officials at court who may be assumed to have been literate, but are not explicitly so described, are the god Sin's Great Keeper of the Seal (k i š i b - l á - m a ḫ) (A n = *Anum*; A §6), the "Archivist" (š a $_x$(G Á) - d u b - b a, *šandabakkum*) of Proto-Lu (A §9 b; see also A §23 [Ur III]), and the four officials in charge of Ningirsu's economic affairs in Gudea Cylinder B (A § 11). An's counselor (a d - g i₄ - g i₄, *māliku*; A §6, cf. also A §11) was presumably chosen for his wisdom, although this may not have been an institutionalized position (cf. A §34). Local and temporal variations in the offices represented in a typical court must, of course, be expected.

## PALACE SCRIBES

The skilled professional most likely to come into contact with the king was almost certainly the scribe. The palace was a center of administration, and the scribe was indispensable for administration of the scale and complexity practiced in Mesopotamia. The title 'palace scribe' (dub-sar-é-gal) was well established by the Ur III period. The highest minister in the court at this time, the Grand Vizier (sukkal-maḫ), had a number of scribes at his service, and these were presumably employed in the administrative quarters of the palace.[11] The list of professions known as Proto-Lu, probably reflecting the social organization of the Ur III period, lists eighteen varieties of scribe in a sequence of terms that begins with the 'king' (lugal) and continues with words for court officials and royal servants. One of the terms is 'King's Scribe' (dub-sar-lugal), which suggests a private secretary of the kind to whom kings must have dictated their letters.[12] The god list An = *Anum*, which mirrors the organization of a Mesopotamian court during the Old Babylonian period, includes a type of scribe among the divine officials in the following of Enlil.[13] The term 'palace scribe', familiar from the Ur III period, occurs again in the Neo-Assyrian period in Akkadian dress.[14] Quite apart from this inner textual evidence of the presence of scribes in royal palaces, the material evidence of the hundreds of tablets excavated in palaces at sites such as Mari, Assur, Kalḫu, and Nineveh make it quite clear that many scribes were employed in palace administration.

Not all scribes at the palace were engaged in preparing routine administrative records. Royal inscriptions commemorating donations to temples and extolling the virtues of the royal donors, often with a notice of the occasion of the gift, appear already before the middle of the third millennium and gradually develop into the elaborate compositions known from the first millennium B.C.E. The palace is the obvious place where these texts were composed, and their existence witnesses to the activity of wise men—in this case experts skilled in the use of the written word—at the royal court. The same place of origin may be posited for the several collections of laws for which Mesopotamia is famous, as also for lists of year-names, king lists, and eventually chronicles.

---

11. Renger, A §23.

12. Renger, A §9 b.

13. dub-sar-zag-ga, Akkadian *zazakku*, "(a high administrative official)" (*CAD*); Renger, A §6.

14. *ṭupšar ekalli*; Renger, A §4 (p. 449a).

Palace scribes may also be identified as the anonymous authors of many literary texts. The Sumerian hymns in praise of a living ruler are obvious examples. An origin in the palace has also been suggested for the Sumerian disputation texts, the epic tales about kings of the First Dynasty of Uruk, and the antiphonal recitations (bal-bal-e) that involve the king.[15] The Assyrian *Tukulti-Ninurta Epic* is a piece of political propaganda that comes most naturally from the palace. It has been suggested that the late form of the *Gilgamesh Epic* was composed at court for the consolation of a king who, like Gilgamesh, had no son.[16] The list could easily be extended. Such suggestions can never claim more than probability, but, in the absence of more plausible alternatives, it is difficult to escape the conclusion that the palace was the place where many works of literature first took shape.[17]

15. W. W. Hallo, "The Cultic Setting of Sumerian Poetry," *Actes de la XVII<sup>e</sup> Rencontre Assyriologique Internationale (Université Libre de Bruxelles, 30 juin–4 juillet 1969)* (ed. A. Finet; Ham-sur-Heure: Comité belge de recherches en Mésopotamie, 1970) 117–19. The dispute between Silver and Copper mentions king Ur-Nammu, and Šulgi is said to have settled the disputes between the Tree and the Reed, and the Bird and the Fish.

16. Oppenheim, *Ancient Mesopotamia*, 257–58.

17. Some grounds for believing that the *Gilgamesh Epic*, the *Erra Epic*, the bilingual *Exaltation of Inanna*, and the "Babylonian Theodicy" were written under royal patronage are provided by the Seleucid period tablet published by J. Van Dijk in UVB 18 (1962) 44–52. The text is a list of scholars, beginning before the Flood with the Seven Sages and ending (if one disregards the difficult line 21) in the reign of Esarhaddon with Aba-Enlil-dari "whom the Akhlamū [i.e., the Arameans] call Aḫu-ʾaqari [i.e., Ahiqar]." Sîn-liq(i)-unnīnī, Kabtu-il-Marduk (*sic*), Taqīš-Gula, and Esagil-kīn-ubba (*sic*), who are known respectively from other sources (see below) as the reputed authors of these four works, are included in the list, each with the title *ummânu* 'scholar'. The name of each is preceded by the name of a king (or in the last case the names of two kings), clearly to be identified as the ruler in whose reign the scholar was believed to have been active. For the four scholars mentioned here, the kings are (respectively) [Gilgam]eš, [Ibb]i-Sîn, [Abī-e]šuḫ and Nebuchadnezzar I and Adad-apla-iddina. Although the dates indicated for the authors may be suspect (the placing of Sîn-liqi-unnīnī in the reign of Gilgameš is obviously fanciful), the designation of these traditional authors as *ummânu*s is significant if, as may reasonably be assumed, each is remembered in the list as the leading *ummânu* of his day. The designation is significant because *ummânu* is the title given to the high-ranking scholars whose names occasionally appear alongside royal names of the eleventh to the seventh centuries B.C.E. in a number of king lists, as mentioned later in this essay. The scholars named in the king lists were evidently the leading *ummânu*s of their day who enjoyed an official status at the court because of their learning. Whether the *ummânu*s selected for mention in the list published by Van Dijk similarly enjoyed some kind of official status is not known (the first three of the four mentioned above are assigned to reigns much earlier than the eleventh century B.C.E.), but it is not improbable. If so, it is reasonable to assume that they were close to the king and that the literary works attributed to them were written under royal patronage (see further n. 27). For the identification of Sîn-liqi-unnīnī as the author of the *Gilgamesh Epic*, see W. G. Lambert, "A Catalogue of Texts and Authors," *JCS* 16 (1962) 66 K. 9717+:10; for the identification of Taqīša-Gula as the author of the bilingual *Exaltation of Inanna* (nin-maḫ ušu-ni gìr-ra), see ibid., 64

The epithet wise must be conceded to the poet-scribes who produced these works at the court under royal patronage.[18]

## THE DIVINER (BĀRÛ) IN PALACE AND COURT

Another class of wise man whose presence at the palace is quite clear from the Old Babylonian period onward is the diviner (*bārû*). The repeated claim to wisdom found in royal inscriptions shows an awareness of the importance of knowledge for the successful ruler. If the king's knowledge could extend to the future, he would obviously be better equipped to defend his own and his people's interests. It was such intelligence that the diviner claimed to offer and it is small wonder that his services were in demand at court. In this case it can be said that at least some members of a wise profession were included among the highest officials of the court. Asqūdum, the diviner known from the Mari texts, is an example. Both Ammiṣaduqa and Samsuditana are known to have sent letters to the high-ranking military commander (*rabi sikkatim*) and "the diviner" resident in Sippar-Jaḫrurum as joint addressees.[19] The linking of these two puts the diviner close to the seat of political power.

## TESTIMONY OF NEO-ASSYRIAN LETTERS ON "SCHOLARS" AT COURT

The fullest information on the important role that could be played by a *bārû* in a Mesopotamian royal court comes from letters addressed

---

Sm. 669:6–9; for the identification of Kabtu-ilāni-Marduk as the author of the *Erra Epic*, see Cagni Erra 126 v 42, with comment on p. 254; for the identification of Esagil-kīnam-ubbib as the author of the "Babylonian Theodicy," see *BWL* 63.

18. The term poet-scribe is used by A. L. Oppenheim in "The Position of the Intellectual in Mesopotamian Society," *Daedalus* 104/2 (Spring 1975) 37–46. Oppenheim distinguished three classes of scribe on the basis of function: the bureaucrat-scribe, the poet-scribe, and the scholar-scribe. He regarded the third class as "unattached professionals" who lived either without institutional (that is, palace or temple) support or by holding "a special position at court." The first two classes he located in one of the "Great Organizations"—the palace or the temple. He saw the second class as the creators of epic and hymnic pieces, including royal hymns, and of royal inscriptions. "We have to give credit to the intellectuals, that is, to the 'scribes' attached to the court, to those concerned with administrative and bookkeeping tasks, as well as to those who formulated policies by creating in their inscriptions, hymns, etc. a self-image of the ruler and an ideological context in which he could function adequately" (p. 41).

19. See the references (with discussion) given by J. Renger, "Untersuchungen zum Priestertum der altbabylonischen Zeit, 2: *šangûm*," ZA 59 (1969) 215–17, who speaks of a successful diviner being able to make a good career "im Dienste staatlicher Institutionen oder in der unmittelbaren Umgebung des Königs." It should perhaps be noted that the *rabi sikkatim* of Sippar-Jaḫrurum may have been as qualified as the diviner for the epithet wise; see nn. 62 and 64 in my essay above (p. 59).

by "scholars" to the Neo-Assyrian kings Esarhaddon and Ashurbanipal. The almost 350 letters of this kind—70% of them fragmentary—written in the Neo-Assyrian dialect have been edited by S. Parpola (those in the Neo-Babylonian dialect still await a modern edition).[20] The scholars in question are scribes (ṭupšarru), shown by their letters to be experts in celestial and terrestrial portents, diviners (bārû), exorcists (āšipu), physicians (asû), and singers of laments (kalû).[21] The letters report on a wide range of matters: lunar and solar observations (including eclipses), intercalation, meteorological and other portents, exorcistic and ritual affairs, auspicious days for the undertaking of various activities, the health of members of the court (with prescriptions for the treatment of those that are sick), etc. Parpola estimates that "medical and exorcistic matters . . . account for more than 45% of the whole corpus."[22]

The letters provide most impressive evidence for the importance of technical experts—wise men—at the heart of a Mesopotamian royal court. By Parpola's estimate, "close to 90% of the whole corpus . . . comes from persons whose relationship to the king must be regarded as close."[23] Not all scholars in the palace could claim so intimate an acquaintance with the king. An examination of the identity of the senders of the letters led Parpola to conclude that "even though the Assyrian court housed a great many of scholarly experts specializing in the same disciplines as the 'inner circle', and even though many more similar experts were scattered all around the empire, only very few select 'wise men' could be engaged in any sort of 'regular' correspondence with the king."[24] But ample evidence remains that the king was in continuous contact with the most prominent members of the profession.

Two of the sixteen letter writers whom Parpola identifies as the "inner circle" bear the title ummânu 'scholar'. One of the two also has the title rab ṭupšarrī 'Chief Scribe'.[25] These are clearly very high-ranking sages. The importance of the title ummânu is shown by a synchronistic king list in which the names of several kings, both Babylonian and Assyrian, of the eleventh to the seventh centuries B.C.E. are

20. S. Parpola, *Letters from Assyrian Scholars to the Kings Esarhaddon and Assurbanipal* (2 vols.; Alter Orient und Altes Testament 5; Kevelaer: Butzon und Bercker/Neukirchen-Vluyn: Neukirchener, 1970–83). The summary given in this paragraph is based on Parpola's introduction in vol. 2.

21. For the description of members of these professions as wise, see my essay above (pp. 59–65).

22. Parpola, *Letters from Assyrian Scholars*, 2:xii.

23. Ibid., xiii (emphasis Parpola's).

24. Ibid., xvi.

25. Ibid., xv (Nabû-zēru-lēšir *rab tupšarrī*, and Balasî).

followed by the names of their one or more *ummânus*.[26] The singling out of these officials (they might be regarded as Ministers of Science and Technology) for mention in a king list besides the name of the king speaks eloquently of the high value placed on learning at the royal court.[27] Clearer evidence of the important role played by the sage in Mesopotamian royal courts could hardly be wished for.

## SUMMATION—THE PALACE AND BEYOND

It would be misleading to suggest that wisdom and learning in Mesopotamia were always associated with the royal court. At least to the end of the Old Babylonian period the institution known in Sumerian as the é-dub-ba-a, or in Akkadian as the *bīt ṭuppi*, the 'tablet house', played a major rôle in education and learning.[28] The many discoveries of tablets containing literary texts and scholarly compilations in private houses indicate that learning was fostered not only in the great institutions of palace and temple, but also in private families.[29] But the leisure (Greek *scholē*) necessary for scholarship required patronage as much in ancient Mesopotamia as it has in later ages and in other lands, and the palace was better able to supply that patronage than were private individuals or even the temples. The record is clear that the palace provided patronage for science and technology of all kinds throughout Mesopotamian history, and the sage, both in the narrower and the broader senses, was always a familiar and welcome figure in Mesopotamian royal palaces.

---

26. KAV 216. This is part of what A. K. Grayson terms "King List 12, Synchronistic King List" in *RLA* 6:116-21, where the complete text is given in transliteration. The section for the reigns of Sennacherib, Esarhaddon, and Ashurbanipal (iv 1-20) is translated in Parpola, *Letters from Assyrian Scholars*, 2:448-49. The names of *ummânus* of the same three kings are also found in the king list fragment KAV 182 (Grayson's "King List 17, Synchronistic King List Fragment," *RLA* 6:124-25), but without explicit description as *ummânus*. The text is given in transliteration in Parpola, *Letters from Assyrian Scribes*, 2: 449. Cf. also Grayson's "King List 14," *RLA* 6:122-23.

27. The dignity of the title *ummânu* is also shown by the text mentioned above in n. 17 (UVB 18 pp. 44-52). The seven antediluvian sages and the first postdiluvian sage are here called *apkallus*, whereas the remaining postdiluvian sages are called *ummânus*. The *ummânus* are therefore in the succession of the legendary sages of antiquity (the list is in chronological order except for a reversal in the order of Nebuchadrezzar I and Adad-apla-iddina in lines 17-18). Although the list gives the names of the kings in whose reigns the scholars were active, it does not explicitly state that they were active at the court. However, this would seem a fair inference.

28. See Å. W. Sjöberg, "The Old Babylonian Eduba," *Sumerological Studies in Honor of Thorkild Jacobsen* (AS 20; Chicago: University of Chicago, 1975) 159-79.

29. Ibid., 178-79.

# THE SCRIBE (AND SAGE) IN THE ROYAL COURT AT UGARIT

## Loren R. Mack-Fisher

At the close of my first essay in this volume, "A Survey and Reading Guide to the Didactic Literature of Ugarit: Prolegomenon to a Study on the Sage" (pp. 67-80 above), I suggested that there are divine, preflood, and patriarchal sages at Ugarit as well as at Babylon. The following comparative chart may be useful:

|  | Sumer/Babylon | Ugarit | Jerusalem |
|---|---|---|---|
| *Divine Sages* { | Ea | El<br>Marduk*<br>Kothar-wa-Ḥasīs | Yahweh |
| *Preflood Sages* { | Adapa<br>Shuruppak | Shubeʾawilum | Adam<br>Lamech |
| *Flood Sages* { | Ziusdra<br>Atra-ḥasīs<br>Utnapishtim | Zurranku | Noah |
| *Postflood Sages* { | Gilgamesh | Danʾel | Job |

*Although Babylonian in origin, Marduk features prominently at Ugarit.*

Loren R. Mack-Fisher carries out his research at the Double Bar A Ranch in Covelo, California.

The following special abbreviations are used in this essay:

PRU   *Le palais royal d'Ugarit* (vols. III, IV, and VI; Mission de Ras Shamra 6, 9, 12; Paris: Imprimerie Nationale, 1955, 1956, 1970)

RS    siglum for tablets discovered at Ras Shamra (Ugarit)

UT    C. H. Gordon, *Ugaritic Textbook* (Analecta Orientalia 38; Rome: Pontifical Biblical Institute, 1965)

The above chart may be interesting (though it is too brief), but the real question is: Where are the sages of Ugarit? Where are the Davids and Solomons? Is there a great poet? These questions remind me of the "Babylonian Theodicy" and its questions, "Where is the wise man . . . ? Where is the scholar . . . ? Where is the counsellor . . . ?"[1] It is clear that there were many scribes and few sages. But, on the other hand, there just might be a lonely sage among the scribes. My suggestion is that one should take a close look at the scribes in the royal court at Ugarit: looking at what they produced and paying attention to their titles and other information may provide some answers.

There are several scholarly writings about the scribes. The initial study was conducted by Jean Nougayrol in *Le palais royal d'Ugarit* III.[2] Then Anson F. Rainey advanced this work in "The Scribe at Ugarit."[3] Third, Nougayrol brought his studies up to date in subsequent volumes.[4] Fourth, there are several recent and forthcoming studies on the king list at Ugarit.

In the present study I will not list all of the scribes at Ugarit, because this is available in Nougayrol's volumes under "Nom d'états."[5] However I will list the scribes who are important for this study and relate them to other scribes and to the kings under whom they worked. In order to do this it is necessary to list the kings of Ugarit, for which I will use some of the results of Dennis Pardee's latest work on the Ugaritic king list for the kings in the first part of the following list.[6] Since the text is broken, I entered a gap between the first part of the list and the last kings of Ugarit, which I have reconstructed on the basis of

1. See *BWL* 71 lines 5-7.

2. Jean Nougayrol, *Le palais royal d'Ugarit* III (Paris: Imprimerie National, 1955) xxxvi-xl.

3. Anson F. Rainey, "The Scribe at Ugarit: His Position and Influence," *Proceedings of the Israel Academy of Sciences and Humanities* 3 (1969) 126-46.

4. Jean Nougayrol, *Le palais royal d'Ugarit* IV (Paris: Imprimerie National, 1956); *Le palais royal d'Ugarit* VI (Paris: Imprimerie National, 1970). Also see Jean Nougayrol, "Textes suméro-accadiens des archives et bibliothèques privées d'Ugarit," *Ugaritica* V (ed. C. F. A. Schaeffer; Mission de Ras Shamra 16; Paris: Imprimerie National, 1968), chap. 1.

5. One difficulty in using these lists is that Nougayrol corrected his readings each time, and the earlier volumes have names that have been changed in the later volumes. For a very useful list see Cord Kühne, "Eine analytische Liste der akkadischen Ugarit-texte," *UF* 6 (1974) 129-56.

6. D. Pardee, "La fête des manes," *Les textes para-mythologiques de la 24e campagne (Ras Shamra-Ougarit)* (Paris: Editions Recherches sur les Civilisations, forthcoming). I will only use Pardee's list for reference; the dates and other parts are from my work. I first saw the king list (RS 24.257) in 1969 in Paris, and I read a paper on it at the American Oriental Society meeting in 1974 and at the Society of Biblical Literature meeting in 1976. Since that time several people have worked on it, and there are many new things to consider. Another work that should be consulted is K. A. Kitchen, "The King List of Ugarit," *UF* 9 (1977) 131-42.

many texts. Since I do not know how many kings are in the gap, I have used approximate dates only on the last part of the list. The Roman numerals used to distinguish kings of the same name may have to be changed when and if the gap is filled in (these numbers differ from Nougayrol's and Kitchen's; Pardee does not use numbers).

| *Kings of Ugarit* | *Major scribes of Ugarit* |
|---|---|
| Yaqaru | |
| Niqmaddu I | |
| ꜣIbiranu I | |
| Niqmepaᶜ I | |
| ꜣIbira[nu] II | |
| Niqmepaᶜ II | |
| ᶜAmmurapiꜣ I | |
| ꜣIbiranu III | |
| Niqmepaᶜ III | |
| Yaᶜduraddu | |
| ꜣIbiranu IV | |
| ᶜAmmu⟨ra⟩piꜣ II | |
| Niqmepa IV | |
| ᶜAmmittamru I | |
| | |
| *(Break)* | |
| | |
| ᶜAmmittamru II (1390 B.C.E.) | |
| Niqmaddu II (1370) | Ilumalku, the Thaᶜite (the scribe of *UT* 51 and 127)[7] |
| | Šapšumalku (*PRU* III: 49)[8] |
| | Yarimmu (*PRU* III: 262) |
| | Yatarmu (*PRU* III: 68) |
| Arḫalbu (1342) (see *PRU* III: xxxvii–xxxviii) | Šapšumalku (*PRU* III: 77, called *ṭupšarru emqu*)[9] |
| | Ḫusanu (*PRU* III: 79)[10] |
| Niqmepaᶜ V (1336) | Šapšumalku (*PRU* III: 86)[11] |
| | Karranu (*PRU* III: 288)[12] |
| | Ḫuṣanu (*PRU* III: 102, 107) |

7. For Ilumalku, also add *UT* 62(?).

8. Also see *PRU* III: 60, 61.

9. Also see *PRU* III: 74, 79, 83, 84.

10. Also see *PRU* III: 107. Note that Ḫuṣanu is the father of Yaṣiranu, for whom see under ᶜAmmittamru III.

11. Also see *PRU* III: 109, 188, 190, 193, 195; *PRU* VI: text 26.

12. Also see *PRU* III: 99, 109.

| | |
|---|---|
| ꜥAmmiṯṯamru III (1270) | Karranu (*PRU* IV: 106, now a *sukkal šàr Ugarit*)[13] |
| | Ilumalku (*Ugaritica* V: texts 9 and 10) |
| | Ilušapšu (*Ugaritica* V: text 7) |
| | Iltaḫmu (*PRU* III: 136)[14] |
| | ꜥAbdiꜥanati (*PRU* III: 33)[15] |
| | Yarimmu (*PRU* III: 165)[16] |
| | Munaḫimu (*PRU* III: 123)[17] |
| | Naꜥamrašap (*PRU* III: 117)[18] |
| | Yaꜥadidu (*PRU* III: 120)[19] |
| | Yaṣiranu (*PRU* III: 161)[20] |
| ꜣIbiranu V (1230) | Naꜥamrašap (*PRU* VI: text 43)[21] |
| Niqmaddu III (1210) | Naꜥamrašap (*PRU* IV: 201, 203) |
| | Iltaḫmu (*PRU* IV: 182, 203; called *sukkal šarri*) |
| | Eḫlitešub (*PRU* VI: text 45; called *sakkallu*) |
| ꜥAmmurapiꜣ III (1200) | Rapꜣanu (*Ugaritica* V: text 88)[22] |
| | ꜥAmmurapiꜣ (*Ugaritica* V: 463)[23] |
| | Šipṭinârum (*Ugaritica* V: text 163)[24] |

This list contains the names of twenty scribes (in the texts there are about thirty). But this study needs more than names. Here are some interesting notes on some of these scribes.

13. The important thing about Karranu is that he is now a *sukkallu* ('vizier' or 'counselor') even though it is possible that he gained this rank in the previous administration.

14. Also see *PRU* III: 115; *PRU* IV: 32, 38, 39.

15. Also see *PRU* III: 148; *PRU* VI: text 52(?).

16. Also see *PRU* III: 137, 138, 166. Also note the reign of Niqmaddu II and *PRU* III: 62.

17. Also see *PRU* III: 125, 137, 147, 156, 166; *PRU* VI: text 40; *Ugaritica* V: texts 5 and 6 (the Munaḫimu of text 5 is a different person).

18. Also see *PRU* III: 133, 137.

19. Also see *PRU* III: 122, 145; *PRU* VI: text 31.

20. Also see *PRU* III: 131, 146, 154.

21. Also see *PRU* III: texts 42, 44; *Ugaritica* V: texts 6, 88, 98, 167. In *PRU* VI: text 43, there is some evidence that Naꜥamrašap was promoted to *sukkallu*.

22. Rapꜣanu may have been active during the reigns of the preceding three kings as well—at least his library has texts from their times (this issue is discussed in item 5 below). The library is published as texts 18–158 in *Ugaritica* V (see p. 69).

23. If this is ꜥAmmurapiꜣ III—the king—then he belongs here, but if it is another person of the same name then I do not know where to place him.

24. In *Ugaritica* V: 280 Nougayrol does not attempt to do more than read ME.DI.A.UM. But on p. 290 he does make some suggestions that I have expanded (I will discuss my reasons later). Also, I have placed this name at the end of the list because I do not know where it should be placed.

1. I have placed the very famous Ilumalku, the Thaᶜite (the scribe of texts *UT* 51 [a Baᶜal text] and *UT* 127 [a Keret text]) under Niqmaddu II. I think that for now this is the thing to do, but it would not surprise me to find out later that the "traditionalists" at Ugarit thought of this "Moses" and his scribal activity in terms of the beginning—in other words, at the time of Niqmaddu I (the second king of the dynasty).

2. Rainey has some interesting comments concerning Yatarmu (under Niqmaddu II). He translates RS 16.269, lines 7–10 as, "When Yatarmu the scribe became hostile to the king his lord, then Gabᶜānu slew him and Beqaᶜ-Ištar *was given* (back) to the king."[25] Scribes who were given cities had a lot of power. The city (in this case Beqaᶜ-Ištar) was given to such a person for all time—forever. What this really means is that the person owned the city as long as he remained a "friend" of the king (more on this below). This account reflects the many aspects of royal grants known from Ugarit and the Hebrew Bible. The city of Ziklag was given to David (1 Sam 27:6); the story of Naboth's vineyard, though different, is based on this kind of system (1 Kgs 21:1–26), as is the Ziba and Mephibosheth story with David's giving, taking, and giving (2 Sam 9:9–13; 16:4; 19:29, 30). Yatarmu is Ugarit's Ahithophel. Ahithophel, the "friend" and counselor of both David and Absalom, saw that his counsel was not heeded, and he went home to *his city*, set his house in order, hanged himself, and was buried in the tomb of his father (2 Sam 17:23). It is my guess that this text does not speak concerning his native city but rather the city of a royal grant, but his burial was not necessarily in "his city."

3. Rainey has another interesting discussion of Ḥuṣanu and his son Yaṣiranu.[26] During the reign of Arḫalbu this father and son were in trouble. The king took Yaṣiranu's estate and gave it to one of his "chariot warriors" who was also a *mûdû šarri* 'a friend of the king' (*PRU* III: 78–81). (By the way, a sage/counselor is sometimes [also in the Hebrew Bible] a "friend of the king," but I have not paid too much attention to this title. The title can be applied to several vocational groups.) Later, during the reign of Niqmepaᶜ V, Ḥuṣanu is back in business, and his son is given another estate (*PRU* III: 101, 106–7). Then under the reign of ᶜAmmittamru III, Yaṣiranu becomes a scribe, and he makes it big; he receives a city (*PRU* III: 154, 161, 146). It is clear that these two were wise. There is another father and son team during the reign of ᶜAmmittamru III, namely, Yarimmu and Munaḫimu.

4. Several scribes in the list do have important titles. Under the reign of Arḫabu, Šapšumalku is called a *ṭupšarru emqu* 'an expert

25. Rainey, "The Scribe at Ugarit," 145, or *PRU* III: 68. Also see *PRU* III: 146–47 for a royal grant of a city to the scribe Yaṣiranu.
26. Rainey, "The Scribe at Ugarit," 144–45.

scribe'. This was important, but it appears that the highest title was that
of *sukkallu* 'vizier' or 'counselor' of the king. Several of these scribes
obtained this rank. First, another father and son combination, Karranu
and Iltaḥmu, gained this title—Karranu under ꜥAmmiṭṭamru III (*PRU* IV:
90, 106, 110) and Iltaḥmu under Niqmaddu III (*PRU* IV: 203). Naꜥamrašap may have had this title (*PRU* VI: text 43), and he may be the
scribe who signed the copy of a Flood tradition (see *Ugaritica* V: text
167 and Nougayrol's comment on p. 304). If he had this title, it
was probably from the reign of ꜣIbiranu V through the time of
Niqmaddu III. The last scribe-counsellor is Eḫlitešub during the reign
of Niqmaddu III. These were some of the great scribes, and some of
them endured through as many as three administrations.

   5. In this list I have included Rapꜣanu under the last king of
Ugarit, but he could have worked under the last four kings. It is
unfortunate that we do not know more about him, but we do have this
great library (see n. 22). In *Ugaritica* V Nougayrol published 141 texts
from his library and there are still more to publish. As I have discussed
in my essay above (p. 69 n. 6), this library contained all kinds of
material—not only the didactic literature and the classics, but also
international documents and letters of great importance. Rapꜣanu was a
"somebody." What I find most interesting is that his library was found
in what appears to be his private house. Since the royal palace
contained so many documents like these, it seems odd to have them in
Rapꜣanu's library. Also it would appear that Rapꜣanu was not only very
important for all kinds of official functions, but he may have been the
dean of the academy—that is, the scribal school.

   6. Lastly, I would like to mention three from the list who stand out
as the scribes of very important works (not counting Ilumalku, see
above). The first is Naꜥamrašap whose name appears in the colophon
of the Flood tradition in text 167 (*Ugaritica* V). The second is
Šipṭinârum who is the scribe of the now famous "Counsels of Shu-
beꜣawilum" (*Ugaritica* V: text 163). Nougayrol has discussed this name
(*Ugaritica* V: 290), but he did not really finish his work on it. My
reading is perhaps the best option of several, as I see it. The problem is
with the reading of *šip-ṭi-A-um*. The A could be read as *mû* or *abu*
(that is, 'water' or 'father'). However, with names such as Šipṭiya
(*PRU* VI: text 54, line 8) and *ṭpṭbꜥl* 'Judge Baꜥal' (*UT* 2063; also found
at Alalakh and in Phoenician texts), I think that the *mû* should be read
as *nâru* (plus phonetic complement *um*), and that it should be compared to names like the epithet for Yamm in Ugaritic literature, namely,
*ṭpṭnhr* 'Judge River'. The third name is ꜥAmmurapiꜣ. At the end of the
great Hurrian musical score (with words), it says, "by the hand of
ꜥAmmurapiꜣ" (*Ugaritica* V: 463). This may be a scribe, or it could be

the last king of Ugarit. Cyrus Gordon says, "The scribe or author of the Ugaritic psalm is not called 'king' but neither is David called 'king' in the psalms attributed to him." [27] On this we do not know as yet.

One should now ask the question, who are the sages in this list? If by this is meant who are the counselors, then the answer is easy: those in paragraph 4. If someone wants to expand that to include paragraphs 5 and 6, I could understand that. In any case, we are in charge of drawing the lines, but we can be more objective concerning other factors. The scribes of Ugarit were trained in the Babylonian tradition, and they were interested in every kind of literature. Given this fact, it is best to use descriptive terms for what they studied and produced (for example, didactic, economic, etc.). But what of the question, Who is a sage? The scribes of Ugarit would look to the ancients—to "truth fully brewed" as the Egyptians would say. I have my own ways of picking the sages from the scribes. A sage should have some common sense and political know-how. This means that the sage should be able to work under more than one king; a sage should outlast a king. Ahiqar is a better sage than Ahithophel or Yatramu. However, the counselors of the king may be just too close to the establishment for my tastes—at least in my more idealistic moments. Sages should know where they stand within the traditions and they should ask interesting questions. I prefer the humanists of the ancient world—those who know that human beings are mortal and those who remain fascinated by a natural world even without justice. Also, it appears that the person who suffers is always a bit wiser than the "friend" who knows why. So, from the counselors and important scribes in this list I select Naᶜamrašap as a probable sage. He worked as a scribe and counselor during the reigns of three kings and he had some interest in the Flood tradition. This is probably a silly way to determine which scribes were sages, but it makes for clarity to state some of our likes and dislikes. Let me be the first to say, that the most important part of this exercise is finding out what they were doing in the royal court at Ugarit and who was doing it. It is important to know these things, and to be ready for new texts. I will be watching for any news concerning Naᶜamrašap.

27. C. H. Gordon, "The Ugaritic Texts: Half a Century of Research," *Biblical Archaeology Today: Proceedings of the International Congress on Biblical Archaeology, Jerusalem, April 1984* (Jerusalem: Israel Exploration Society, 1985) 498.

# THE SOCIAL SIGNIFICANCE OF SOLOMON AS A PATRON OF WISDOM

## Walter A. Brueggemann

The relationship between Solomon and wisdom is much disputed in recent scholarly discussion. A part of the dispute concerns the categories in which to consider the relationship of Solomon to wisdom. It makes a great deal of difference if the question is treated in terms of literary, historical, or sociocultural categories.

### THE PROBLEMATIC OF HISTORICAL EVIDENCE

The literary evidence for Solomon as a patron of wisdom is not extensive, nor is it difficult to identify. First, the literary evidence concerns texts embedded in the "history of Solomon" as it is portrayed in the deuteronomistic account of 1 Kings 3-11. Four texts are important: *(a)* 1 Kgs 3:3-14, Solomon's inaugural dream and prayer in which he prays for wisdom to govern, *(b)* 1 Kgs 3:16-28, a narrative in which Solomon is reported to exercise wisdom in the execution of royal justice, *(c)* 1 Kgs 4:29-34 [MT 5:9-14], in which Solomon is credited with the production of encyclopedic proverbs, and *(d)* 1 Kgs 10:1-13, concerning the visit of the queen of Sheba in which Solomon's wisdom is closely related to his power and wealth.[1]

A literary analysis of these texts requires close attention to the question of genre. It is immediately clear that these narratives reflect common narrative tendencies and strategies, so that the events reported are to be regarded as stereotypical, marked by literary convention, with evidence of legendary or fictional development or both. Thus the first narrative belongs to the genre of inaugural dream,[2] the second is a

Walter A. Brueggemann is Professor of Old Testament at Columbia Theological Seminary.

1. The grouping of wisdom, power, and riches is reflected in Jer 9:23-24 (MT vv 22-23). On the significance of this text, see my essay "The Epistemological Crisis of Israel's Two Histories (Jer 9:22-23)," *IW* 85-105.
2. On this text see Helen A. Kenik, *Design for Kingship* (SBLDS 69; Chico, CA: Scholars Press, 1983).

standard and recurring example of juridical cunning, and the fourth is filled with propagandistic comparisons between competing royal figures. It may well be that none of these narratives will carry the weight expected of a factual historical report of a concrete event. In any case whatever happened historically is cast in a narrative form, which makes factuality precarious.

R. B. Y. Scott (closely followed by James Crenshaw) has concluded that these texts provide no substantive basis for linking Solomon historically to the enterprise of wisdom.[3] Moreover, each of these texts likely serves an interest other than the assertion of a sapiential function, that is, the legitimacy and success of the monarchy. In short, they are rendered imaginatively and function intentionally as propaganda. Indeed, if the propagandistic element were absent, they would fail in their function. Such intentionally overstated material provides poor evidence for factuality. Finally, because these narratives bear some marks of deuteronomistic influence, they are likely later and not to be regarded as historically reliable.

The second cluster of evidence is found in three superscriptions in the Book of Proverbs that apparently introduce distinct collections of proverbs (Prov 1:1, 10:1, 25:1). The first of these may be regarded as a late designation by the framers of the Book of Proverbs as canonical literature.[4] The second is perhaps a late designation for an earlier, precanonical collection, and the third, Scott believes, bears witness to the time and activity of Hezekiah, but not the time of Solomon. In any case, these three superscriptions provide no basis for historical judgment, important as they are for canonical understanding.

Third, I mention in passing that in the canonical presentation Ecclesiastes and the Song of Solomon are credited to Solomon.[5] However, no critical scholar takes such connotations as evidence of authorship. While these connections to Solomon may be important for canonical intention and interpretation, they provide no clue to tenth-century historical realities. Subsequent postcanonical tradition and legend add to this ongoing later tendency to assign sapiential matters to Solomon, but none of these add to the data for a historical judgment.

Thus the literary evidence is of a fanciful kind, surely marked by legendary tendencies, useful for canonical consideration, but out of

3. R. B. Y. Scott, "Solomon and the Beginnings of Wisdom in Israel," *WIANE* 262–79 (repr. in *SAIW* 84–101); James L. Crenshaw, *Old Testament Wisdom* (Atlanta: John Knox, 1981) 42–54.

4. See Brevard S. Childs, *Introduction to the Old Testament as Scripture* (Philadelphia: Fortress, 1979) 551–52.

5. See the comments of Childs, ibid., 584 on Ecclesiastes, and 573–75 on Song of Songs. Childs characteristically urges a move from historical to canonical questions. It will be clear in the end that my argument is congruent with that of Childs.

which no certain historical judgment can be made. The direct textual evidence for my topic is precarious and is judged by some scholars as nonexistent.

## SOLOMON AS A SOCIAL MUTATION IN ISRAEL

However, to pose the question in such categories is itself open to question. An approach that moves directly from literary analysis to matters of facticity proceeds on too narrow a basis, because it assumes a simple correlation between *literary evidence* and *historical judgment.* If this topic must be treated on that basis, there is little ground for discussion. It is, however, methodologically inadequate to proceed on the basis of a simple correlation between literary evidence and historical judgment. Therefore one must not so quickly accept the negative judgement of Scott and Crenshaw, but must attend to more than literary analysis of isolated texts and historical conclusions based on that literary analysis. The text never happens in a vacuum, so that, as best one can, one must attend to the social processes and transactions that were operative and likely decisive in the formation and transmission of the text. It is more helpful to view this as a sociopolitical problem rather than simply a literary-historical problem. Indeed my topic invites such a sociocultural approach because of the word "patron" in the title, which opens up a variety of questions concerning social power, social interest, ideology, and intentionality. I am not here concerned with a historical question about whether Solomon was a wisdom teacher, but with a much larger question of the rationality and intellectual commitments of the world of which Solomon is both sponsor and benefactor. I shall not arrive at historical precision and that is not the nature of this issue.[6]

I begin with the observation that the Deuteronomist (1 Kings 3–11), the formulators of the Book of Proverbs (and some of the antecedent collections in the book), and the canonical shapers of Ecclesiastes and Song of Solomon appealed to some abiding memory of the connection between Solomon and wisdom. While that memory may not be very precise, may not be recoverable now in detail, and may not be available in factual terms, it seems plausible to assume that the connection between Solomon and wisdom is remembered and not invented—remembered, to be sure, in a way quite impressionistic and without precision. Even if the various texts to which I have referred are later, the tradition refers back to something in asserting and assuming this connection.

6. I shall argue that the canonical reading in the end has it right. The argument however is not based on historical precision, but on an understanding of the social dynamics related to Solomon. The canon makes the judgment that the role of Solomon understood sociologically is in fact who he is for the Israelite tradition and for generating its sapiential dimension.

I pose the question in this way: What is it that the traditionist remembered about the Solomonic enterprise?[7] (One can never be certain about historicality and the question may alternatively be asked: What did the traditionist postulate about the Solomonic enterprise? But because I take the traditioning process with seriousness and as having integrity, I pose the question in terms of *remembering* rather than *postulating*.) It seems plausible, given the evidence at hand, to suggest that the traditionist remembered with something like astonishment and perhaps with some dismay that Solomon represents and embodies an important *novum* in the history of Israel—a *novum* anticipated by David, but visible, consolidated, and legitimated only with Solomon. That is, Solomon is not simply a historical person, but something of a sociocultural mutation in Israel.[8]

The notion of a Solomonic *novum* has been, in a general and not very precise way, characterized by Gerhard von Rad as an "enlightenment."[9] By the term enlightenment, von Rad refers to a shifted intellectual presupposition about the world, a freshly articulated structure of human plausibility. This proposal by von Rad has been critiqued and largely dismissed by Crenshaw on two grounds.[10] First, the wisdom texts are largely legendary if not fictional. Second, the move from "sacral" to "secular" understandings cannot be sustained by means of a simple contrast before and after Solomon. I have no intention of defending von Rad's hypothesis, except as an important step to the present sociological understandings of the question before us. Concerning Crenshaw's first critique, the legendary character of the texts in itself is not important, because the argument needs to be based on much broader

---

7. "Solomonic enterprise" is a carefully chosen phrase. Solomonic refers to a large cultural movement and not simply the person of the king. To call it an enterprise means that what happened around Solomon is an identifiable "project" that has some social intentionality to it and that is a deliberate departure from the pre-Solomonic world of Israel's faith.

8. See Frank M. Cross, *Canaanite Myth and Hebrew Epic* (Cambridge: Harvard University, 1973) 237–41, and more extensively G. W. Ahlström, *Royal Administration and National Religion in Ancient Palestine* (Leiden: Brill, 1982). By using the terms *novum* and mutation I am referring to an intra-Israelite development, that is, that Solomon decisively changed the character of Israel. Notice that Norman K. Gottwald, *The Tribes of Yahweh* (Maryknoll, NY: Orbis, 1979) 489–90 and passim, treats Israel as a *novum* and a mutation in the world of Canaan. I am using the terms in the opposite sense within Israel, but my point is in agreement with Gottwald.

9. Gerhard von Rad, *The Problem of the Hexateuch and Other Essays* (New York: McGraw-Hill, 1966) 69–74, 202–4; *Old Testament Theology* (New York: Harper and Row, 1962), 1:48–56.

10. Crenshaw, *Old Testament Wisdom*, 52–54; "Prolegomenon," *SAIW* 16–20; *Gerhard von Rad* (Waco, TX: Word, 1978) 42–52; and "*Wisdom in Israel* by Gerhard von Rad," *Religious Studies Review* 2.2 (April 1976) 6–12.

sociopolitical-economic grounds than simply by reference to a few texts. Second, it is not necessary to draw a clear line between secular and sacral in order to consider a decisive shift in rationality. It is surely the case that enlightenment in retrospect is an unfortunate term to use, for it inevitably invites a parallel to the modern European Enlightenment, and that obviously is not what happened in Solomon's time.

However, I would insist that what von Rad has grasped, albeit inchoately (and what Crenshaw has neglected), are the modifications in public life, political power, social organization, ideology, technology, and its management that accompanied, permitted, and required a shift in intellectual perspective. What von Rad sensed in terms of a general cultural perspective can now be pursued more confidently in light of more recent social analysis. That social analysis was not available to von Rad, but it is clearly crucial for my general topic. Thus my methodological insistence is that the question of Solomonic wisdom must be explored in terms of a broadly based social transformation, and not on narrow literary or historical-critical grounds.

## NEW FORMS OF POWER/NEW MODES OF KNOWLEDGE

A sociocultural approach to my question will not yield historical precision, but it will yield social probability. One important development in Old Testament studies since the enlightenment hypothesis of von Rad and the negative conclusion of Scott concerns the awareness that intellectual (and therefore literary) phenomena in ancient Israel are closely linked to sociopolitical-economic-technical changes in a social organization of that community. Or to put it more succinctly, economics and epistemology are closely related to each other and decisively influence each other.

Norman Gottwald has offered the most formidable comprehensive hypothesis for understanding the social world in which the Solomonic establishment emerged.[11] He has proposed that ancient Israel in the premonarchal period, that is, from Moses to Samuel, is a radical departure from the conventional state (city-state) modes of organization best known and mostly practiced in Canaan. Israel "withdrew" from that mode of social organization and organized itself in an alternative way as a covenantal-egalitarian social experiment.[12] Not only was Israel a

11. Gottwald, *The Tribes of Yahweh*; and "Early Israel and the Canaanite Socioeconomic System," *Palestine in Transition* (ed. D. N. Freedman and D. F. Graf; Sheffield: Almond, 1983) 25–37.

12. The term "withdraw" was used in the initial hypothesis of George E. Mendenhall, "The Hebrew Conquest of Palestine," *BA* 25 (1962) 66–87 (repr. in *Biblical Archaeologist Reader*, vol. 3 [ed. E. F. Campbell Jr. and D. N. Freedman; Garden City, NY: Doubleday,

theological oddity, authorized as it was by Yahweh—an odd God in the ancient world—but Israel was also a sociological oddity in a culture characteristically organized in bureaucratic, hierarchical, and therefore exploitative ways. Because conventional orderings of society tend to control and administer conventional modes of knowledge,[13] this new social reality relies on an alternative epistemology, on "revelation" in the form of Torah, that is, directly given guidance about the orderings of communal life. Early Israel thus had no recourse to conventional modes of discernment, that is, it functioned without conventional modes of bureaucratic wisdom. Israel's radical mode of knowledge (revelation at Sinai) is appropriate to the radical substance of guidance, which is an ethos of egalitarianism rooted in the exclusive authorization of Yahweh. The radical mode and the radical substance are appropriate to Israel's peculiar character and self-understanding, which made Israel an essentially alien community in its Canaanite context. Its modes of knowledge are congruent with its modes of power and its social visions.

The emergence of the monarchy, culminating in Solomon, is not to be viewed—as is conventional—simply as a defensive organizational posture to resist the Philistines. Rather, it is reflective of a changed social position that had economic and military roots and that required intellectual, religious legitimation. Frank S. Frick, informed by Frank Crüsemann, suggests that the changes are related to social organization and technology.[14] Thus the direction of social development in ancient Israel is from a segmentary society to a chiefdom. The earlier, socially primitive community is segmented into equal units of power, goods,

---

1970] 107). See also Gottwald, *The Tribes of Yahweh*, 85, 326, 408, 469; and Marvin L. Chaney, "Ancient Palestinian Peasant Movements and the Formation of Premonarchic Israel," *Palestine in Transition* (ed. D. N. Freedman and D. F. Graf; Sheffield: Almond, 1983) 49. The term and the social proposal behind it are crucial for understanding the social significance of Solomon.

13. See Glendon E. Bryce, *A Legacy of Wisdom* (Lewisburg, PA: Bucknell University, 1979). It is important and characteristic that in the plague cycle of Exodus 5–11 the power of Egypt is mediated through the wise men of Egypt, the ones who know the techniques to manage imperial power. The alternatives of Moses and Aaron *vis à vis* the imperial wise men is telling for the epistemological crisis of the Exodus. On alternative modes of power, see Aaron Wildavsky, *The Nursing Father* (Tuscaloosa, AL: University of Alabama, 1984).

14. F. S. Frick, *The Formation of the State of Ancient Israel* (Sheffield: Almond, 1985); F. Crüsemann, *Der Widerstand gegen das Königtum* (WMANT 49; Neukirchen-Vluyn: Neukirchener Verlag, 1978). See also Eckart Otto, "Gibt es Zusammenhänge zwischen Gevölkerungswachstum, Staatsbildung und Kulturentwicklung im eisenzeitlichen Israel?" *Regulation, Manipulation und Explosion der Bevölkerungsdichte* (ed. O. Kraus; Göttingen: Vandenhoeck und Ruprecht, 1986) 73–87. J. W. Rogerson, "Was Early Israel a Segmentary Society?" *Journal for the Study of the Old Testament* 36 (1986) 17–26, rejects the hypothesis that early Israel was a segmentary society.

and leadership, with no central authority and with no power positions that could dominate others. In such a society, in which there are accommodations and associations, there is no mandatory accountability. This means there may be endless splintering into more social units (fission) with lesser or greater autonomy, all equal to each other in authority.

In ancient Israel the segmentary society, especially under the impetus of David, was transformed into a chiefdom, which is the beginning of centralized authority, the assertion of dominant power supported by military success, and therefore the accumulation of an economic surplus that began to move toward monopoly. The introduction of central power and economic surplus entails the systematic introduction of social inequality in which the chief—the one who wields the newly formed power—redistributes wealth, power, and access, and therefore develops a network of supporting alliances among the powerful and the privileged.[15]

While a chief can discourage but cannot halt splintering movements of independence, that splintered independence is completely overcome when the chiefdom eventuates in a state, in which there is a strongly centralized authority that preempts all other authority and administers the economic arrangement that is now on its way to becoming a monopoly.

While these sociological modes of analysis cannot be applied to ancient Israel with precision, there is a gathering consensus among scholars that Israel emerged from a segmentary society, to a chiefdom, and finally to a state under Solomon. This sociological paradigm is congruent with the characterization of Solomon's goverance that seems clear in the texts: a social arrangement characterized by advanced technology, highly developed social organization, and bureaucratic ordering of governmental power.[16] For those who stood at the center of this arrangement, there was a high standard of living, a high degree of political security, and a situation of social leisure.

That picture of political-economic-technical change seems reasonably secure. The question then is: What happened to Israel's intellectual life in the midst of this social transformation?[17] Two developments are claimed in the text that are congruent with the social transformation,

15. See Frick, *Formation of the State of Ancient Israel*, 78–86; and Edward Neufeld, "The Emergence of a Royal-Urban Society in Ancient Israel," *HUCA* 31 (1960) 31–53. See the summary of Norman K. Gottwald, *The Hebrew Bible: A Socio-Literary Introduction* (Philadelphia: Fortress, 1985) 323–25.

16. See Ahlström, *Royal Administration and National Religion*; and T. N. D. Mettinger, *Solomonic State Officials* (Lund: Gleerup, 1971).

17. See E. W. Heaton, *Solomon's New Men* (London: Thames and Hudson, 1974).

and which therefore I take as historically probable. First, such a social enterprise that significantly departed from the old Israelite social commitments needed religious justification and legitimacy. Religiously this required the construction of a temple and the articulation of cultic practices to link the political apparatus closely to the purposes of God.[18] While one cannot be precise, it is plausible that the practice of divine enthronement begins very early in the Solomonic liturgy, for the enthronement of Yahweh surely carries with it the legitimacy of Solomon and the dynasty.[19]

The religious machinery of temple and cult needed theological, intellectual counterparts, and this is given in "a theology of presence" whereby the God of the covenantal-liberation tradition takes up (permanent) residence in Jerusalem in the temple, and becomes patron, ally, and guarantor of the dynasty.[20] This theological adjustment articulates a radically changed definition of Yahweh, from a transformative agent to a guarantor. This theological transformation is congruent with and congenial to the sociological transformation of the community from egalitarian to bureaucratic-hierarchical, in which the economic issues have changed from survival to monopoly, in which the power questions no longer concern marginality but control and domination.

Second, in the context of the theological transformation (in the interest of legitimacy) and the sociological transformation (in the interest of political control and economic affluence), the question of wisdom under royal patronage can be freshly considered. Here one is not dependent simply on a few texts that seem easily disposed of by genre analysis for one may inquire into sociological probability. What is the likely intellectual climate of the new social situation, what was permitted and required by the new circumstance? To focus on sacral/secular distinctions as von Rad (and consequently Crenshaw) has done is not as helpful as a focus on political domination and economic surplus, which require and permit fresh intellectual perspectives. The division of labor

18. See Moshe Weinfeld, "Zion and Jerusalem as Religious and Political Capital: Ideology and Utopia," *The Poet and the Historian* (ed. R. E. Friedman; Chico, CA: Scholars Press, 1983) 75–115. On pp. 87–88 Weinfeld writes, "The establishment of the Israelite monarchy thus entailed revolutionary innovations, which in turn required religious legitimation, especially in regards to the concept of dynasty."

19. Thus Sigmund Mowinckel and A. R. Johnson are surely right (against Hermann Gunkel and H.-J. Kraus) in their argument that the enthronement liturgy was used very early and served a legitimating function for the Jerusalem establishment. On the ideological function of that liturgy, see my *Israel's Praise: Doxology against Idolatry and Ideology* (Philadelphia: Fortress, 1988).

20. On temple theology of presence, see Samuel Terrien, *The Elusive Presence* (New York: Harper and Row, 1978) 186–213; and T. N. D. Mettinger, *The Dethronement of Sabaoth: Studies in the Shem and Kabod Theologies* (Lund: Gleerup, 1982).

that accompanied a bureaucratically ordered community clearly required priests for religious legitimacy and most probably required
scribes/sages/wisdom teachers who function as the intellectual brain
trust for policy formation, as ideologues for social justification, and as
pedagogues for the young who must inherit the monopoly.[21]

## KNOWLEDGE FOR EMANCIPATION AND DOMINATION

I suggest three social functions performed by such an intelligentsia in
the practice of an epistemology congruent with Solomon's new political
domination and economic surplus.

1. There is ample evidence that Solomon's ambition was to create
an intellectual climate imitative of, and no doubt in touch with and
competitive with, the sapiental activity of other state regimes, especially
Egypt. Thus it is not accidental that 1 Kgs 4:30–31 [MT 5:10–11] mentions wisdom practices outside Israel. Surely these practices were seen,
in the purview of Israel's sapiental establishment, both as models and as
competitors. It was this intellectual enterprise that emancipated Israel
from the categories of Israel's "tribal," "peasant," and "sectarian" modes
of knowledge in order to share in more universalizing and perhaps
more speculative intellectual activity. Thus accommodation to the international practice of wisdom was not only culturally ambitious in
"being like Pharaoh" (cf. 1 Sam 8:5–20), but it may also have been
emancipatory, the kind of intellectual emancipation needed for a new
regime eager to operate effectively, legitimately, and prestigiously as a
state.[22] Christa Bauer-Kayatz has argued that the wisdom collection of
Proverbs 1–9 is very early and is closely paralleled in style, substance,
and assumption with Egyptian materials.[23]

2. The intellectual operation of wisdom, one may imagine, was
both congenial to and necessary for such a state. Albrecht Alt has
suggested that the notice of 1 Kgs 4:33 [MT 5:13] is evidence of a kind

21. On the emergence of such an intelligentsia, see R. N. Whybray, *The Intellectual
Tradition in the Old Testament* (BZAW 115; Berlin: de Gruyter, 1974); and S. Yeiven,
"Social, Religious, and Cultural Trends in Jerusalem under the Davidic Dynasty," *VT* 3
(1953) 149–65, esp. 156. See also Brian W. Kovacs, "Is There a Class-Ethic in Proverbs?"
*Essays in Old Testament Ethics* (ed. J. L. Crenshaw and J. T. Willis; New York: Ktav,
1974) 173–89; and Mettinger, *Solomonic State Officials*, 140–57. On the priesthood in the
Monarchy, see Cross, *Canaanite Myth and Hebrew Epic*, 195–215; and Ahlström, *Royal
Administration and National Religion*, 44–74.

22. The legendary account of 1 Kgs 10:1–13 surely reflects a self-awareness about
competing with and being superior to other states. This much is clear even if the account
is not taken as historically reliable, which it likely is not.

23. See C. Bauer-Kayatz, *Studien zu Proverbien 1–9* (WMANT 22; Neukirchen-
Vluyn: Neukirchener Verlag, 1966).

of cataloging activity about "natural matters."[24] It is not at all necessary to suggest that such wisdom is secular (as opposed to sacral) in order to understand why the royal enterprise would want the cataloging of data. It is now readily agreed that wisdom is "creation theology," which means not only that it is a study of creation ("nature") but that wisdom in this context is a disciplined marveling at the order of the world by God.[25] That is, these teachers can be grateful to the creator, astonished at the delicate and resilient order of the world, but nonetheless deeply curious about how this order works. Amazement is not contradictory to disciplined investigation.

Such an enterprise may be congenial to the new state, because, politically and economically, the whole world becomes "available" for study and use as it has not been in Israel heretofore. It has not been available because questions of survival limit scope and energy for investigation, and because the limited technology of the marginal excludes much of the world from one's horizon. There may well have been, in this new cultural setting, a fresh kind of energy and eagerness to explore, know, and control everything available.[26] Intellectual possibility of a new kind must have been widely recognized, embraced, and pursued. In such a context, there may have been a passion to know in disciplined ways whatever could be known.

But such an enterprise may not only be congenial, but also necessary to the new state regime. Crenshaw suggests that such an enlightenment project might be incompatible with Solomon's tyranny, oppression, and greed.[27] On the contrary, such investigation that establishes predictability leads to control, and such control is not incompatible with the fresh assertion of human centrality. Such new knowledge is indeed new power. This need not mean such investigations were under-

24. A. Alt, "Solomonic Wisdom," *SAIW* 102-12 (German original: "Die Weisheit Salomos," *Theologische Literaturzeitung* 76 [1951] 139-44). While this classifying of nature seems like an objective, scientific project, it is necessary to recognize that such an enterprise had important social significance for *ordering*. A wedge must not be driven between social ordering and natural ordering. Both aspects of ordering move in a conservative social direction.

25. See Walter Zimmerli, "The Place and Limit of the Wisdom in the Framework of the Old Testament Theology," *Scottish Journal of Theology* 17 (1964) 146-58 (repr. in *SAIW* 314-26); *Old Testament Theology in Outline* (Atlanta: John Knox, 1978) 155-66; *The Old Testament and the World* (Atlanta: John Knox, 1976) 43-52; and von Rad, *Wisdom in Israel* (Nashville: Abingdon, 1972) 74-96 and passim.

26. On such energy and eagerness, modern analogies may be found in the sixteenth-century drive in western Europe for reconnaissance of the "new world," and in the drive of John F. Kennedy in the 1960s to put "a man on the moon." Both these cases represent the drive of genuine exploration, but both have an obviously political-economic motivation, one ending in colonialism, the other ending in a new dimension of military competition.

27. Crenshaw, *Old Testament Wisdom*, 53.

taken for directly ideological reasons. In our modern context, scientists and technologists who work at research and development either for government or business need not be directly committed to the use (and misuse) of their findings, but they may be those who are genuinely attuned to the wonder, coherence, predictability, symmetry, and finally inscrutability of the world that is the subject of such sapiental investigation. One will not appreciate the use (and abuse) of such wisdom by the regime unless one first notices the emancipatory power of wonder, astonishment, and knowledge that such an enterprise might unleash.

3. Having noted the dimensions of state ambitions and scientific wonder, it is reasonable to match that positive, emancipatory factor with a critical comment about the ideological function of wisdom. Wisdom proceeds on the assumption that life-experience, human life, life in the created order is a "studiable system." That studiable system has constancy and durability, experienced as regularity and predictability.[28] That is, the proverbs observe and characterize what is continually the same. The constancy and durability of the studiable system is, for those adhering to the royal enterprise, matched by the systemic durability and constancy of the political order and the economic arrangement. Indeed, the political-economic order is experienced, in such a systemic perception, as part of the assumed order, which is not questioned or criticized and outside of which questions are not raised.[29]

It is widely held that wisdom, even clan wisdom, represents the interests and perceptions of a landed, established class.[30] The modes of knowledge operating in wisdom instruction tend to be conservative and conserving, because they seek for reliable and recurring patterns of acceptable behavior. The conserving modes thus tend to buttress the status quo as an order that is to be maintained and not disrupted. Wisdom in the clan is a study about how to maintain and not disrupt the present social arrangement. Thus proverbial wisdom in any family or clan tends to assume the legitimacy and durability of present power arrangements. Knowledge tends not to push outside such interests and such awarenesses.

28. On the theological significance of that ordering of the world, see H. H. Schmid, *Gerechtigkeit als Weltordnung* (Tübingen: Mohr, 1968); and "Schopfung, Gerechtigkeit und Heil: Schöpfungstheologie als Gesamthorizont biblischer Theologie," *Zeitschrift für Theologie und Kirche* 70 (1973) 1–19.

29. Ernest W. Nicholson, *God and His People* (Oxford: Clarendon, 1986) 193–210, has well understood the dangerous potential of creation theology when it becomes state ideology. He sees clearly that covenant faith in Israel is a frontal criticism of such state ideology sometimes expressed as creation theology.

30. See Robert Gordis, "The Social Background of Wisdom Literature," *Poets, Prophets, and Sages* (Bloomington, IN: Indiana University, 1971) 160–97; and Kovacs, "Is There a Class-Ethic in Proverbs?"

How much more is this likely to be the case in a royal court setting where political interests are much more visible and intentional, and where the entire enterprise depends on the power, access, and means of the royal budget! Thus it is plausible to suppose that wisdom teachers in the court, wittingly or unwittingly, are committed to the royal arrangements as the prism for wisdom and indeed for reality. Given that prism, the wisdom teachers inevitably perform an ideological function of establishing this present political and social order as an abiding given beyond the flux of historical choice and process.[31]

Thus it is entirely possible that the sages in the service of Solomon may have exercised at times both emancipatory and ideological functions, on the one hand channeling the energies of the regime in bold exploratory directions, on the other hand justifying present arrangements. While these functions are in tension, they are not mutually exclusive. It is cogent to imagine such court functionaries as being willing to cooperate with the regime (perhaps out of conviction, perhaps not) in order to have a chance for leisure, reflection, and exploration.

If such a sociological enterprise is plausible, I now return to two observations about the Solomonic texts on wisdom. First, this analysis of sociological and epistemological development helps to understand why the sapiental texts are so carefully placed and carefully controlled by the Deuteronomist in 1 Kings 3–11. In light of the social revolution of 1 Kings 11–12 in which the Solomonic achievement abruptly collapses, it is clear that the ideological thrust of sapiential rationality was uncritical, oppressive, and therefore unacceptable to much of the populace. It may well be that the Deuteronomist understood the tension between ideologically prone sages and the uncompromising social claims of the torah. As a result, Solomonic wisdom is characterized by the Deuteronomist in ironic ways to show that it did not work. But that Solomonic wisdom did not work either historically or covenantally-theologically is no warrant for concluding that the regime was not committed to such wisdom. Indeed, it may be an argument that the regime was indeed committed to such an ideological self-deception that brought its own ruin.[32]

31. See Kovacs, "Is There a Class-Ethic in Proverbs?"; and G. E. Mendenhall, "The Shady Side of Wisdom: The Date and Purpose of Genesis 3," *A Light unto My Path: Old Testament Studies in Honor of Jacob Myers* (ed. H. N. Bream, R. D. Heim, and C. A. Moore; Philadelphia: Temple University, 1974) 319–34.

32. It is instructive that Barbara W. Tuchman, *The March of Folly* (New York: Ballantine, 1984) 8–11, cites the crisis of Israel at the death of Solomon as an early example of "the march of folly." Her chapter heading under which she discusses that crisis is entitled "Pursuit of Policy contrary to Self-Interest." For further reflection on the Deuteronomist's perception of Solomon and the sages in line with what I have observed in this paragraph, see the essay below in this volume by P. Kyle McCarter Jr., "The Sage in the Deuteronomistic History," pp. 289–93. McCarter explores more than I do the relationship of the Torah to the sage in the final redaction of the Deuteronomistic History.

Second, if this sociocultural analysis is cogent, one may better understand the claim of the canon about Solomon and wisdom. The canon is not interested in historical concreteness, but in the memory that it was Solomon, for better or for worse, who opened Israel's way for such an intellectual enterprise. That in fact is what Solomon did for Israel. Solomon made the larger world "available" for Israel. Canonically then it is sensible to juxtapose the Song of Solomon and Ecclesiastes as derivative articulations of the two poles of Solomonic wisdom. Ecclesiastes articulates a conservative ideology that reflects social control and a concern for stability. Crüsemann has carefully probed the way in which this text reflects and serves class interests that value social stability.[33] In the interest of maintaining the status quo the text avoids criticism of an oppressive social order and characteristically supports established order. The emancipatory side of Solomonic wisdom is reflected in the embrace of creation in the Song of Solomon, the ideological dimension is articulated in Ecclesiastes. Thus I suggest a connection between the sociological-epistemological probability of Solomon and the canonical memory that continued to receive fresh articulation.[34]

## WISDOM AS THEOLOGY AND AS IDEOLOGY

Finally I consider the social function of such sages in a context like that of Solomon. It is evident that the concern of the sages is the hidden, but discernible orderliness of God's creation, an orderliness that is experienced in terms of the limits of power, the contours of responsibility, and the shapes of freedom.[35] That order concerns ethical realities,[36] but it also concerns the use and misuse of power, and therefore it addresses questions of legitimate power. The juxtaposition of ethical reality and

33. See the discerning socioeconomic analysis of Ecclesiastes by Crüsemann, "The Unchangeable World: The Crisis of Wisdom in Koheleth," *God of the Lowly* (ed. W. Schottroff and W. Stegemann; Maryknoll, NY: Orbis, 1984) 57-77.

34. On the cruciality of the canonical memory, I am helped by the wonderful phrase of Alan M. Cooper in "The Life and Times of King David according to the Book of Psalms," *The Poet and the Historian* (ed. R. E. Friedman; Chico, Ca: Scholars Press, 1983) 125: "a productive interpretive strategy." Cooper is writing about another canonical shaping of the material, but it applies here as well. That is, to credit Solomon with sponsoring wisdom is not a historical judgment but an interpretive strategy already used in the texts themselves—and now to be used by us. I have argued that this canonical strategy is grounded in sociological possibility, but it goes well beyond that initial sociological function.

35. See the shrewd analysis of Proverbs 25 by Bryce, *A Legacy of Wisdom*, 139-62, in which wisdom is hidden and found out, and hidden.

36. See the references in n. 28. Schmid has seen that such ordering as the wise discerned is not only "natural" but always has social, political, and moral dimensions. Thus even the encyclopedic wisdom of Solomon's sages is related both to morality and to political power.

legitimate power causes the wisdom teacher to reflect on deeds and consequences, that is, on justice, righteousness, and equity, on the kinds of behavior (and policies) that are politically permissible and that are tolerable to the nonnegotiable perimeters of created order.[37] Because the questions of wisdom concern behavior and policy, it is appropriate that the sages have been regularly characterized as pragmatic and utilitarian. Of course they were!

This sustained ethical reflection, which had all sorts of policy implications, is, in a word, concerned with theodicy.[38] The later sapiential materials, especially Job and Ecclesiastes, are of course concerned with the "theodic crisis," with the awareness that the old expectations and assumptions of Israel were no longer adequate. A theodic crisis occurs when the dominant social values, presuppositions, and policies no longer function meaningfully and claim assent, no longer are credited by public opinion as having foundational authority.

Solomon's time was not a time when dominant assumptions were inadequate or when values seemed meaningless. In Solomon's time, everything seemed to work. The creation functioned, as did the social system. People in the royal apparatus could discern to some extent how it functioned, and could readily observe that it functioned well "for us." Thus there is no theodic crisis. But behind every theodic crisis, there is a "theodic settlement"—a long standing consensus about how life works, how society functions, how a system of benefits is allocated, what suffering must be tolerably and inescapably borne, and by whom it must be borne.[39] The theodic settlement that decides who must "rightly" suffer is characteristically a settlement authorized and imposed by those on top of the heap, who benefit from the present social arrangement, so that the system can be legitimated as good, wise, and right. For those who benefit, it is very difficult to notice that the theodic settlement may be for someone else a theodic crisis.[40]

37. See Klaus Koch, "Gibt es ein Vergeltungsdogma im Alten Testament?" *Zeitschrift für Theologie und Kirche* 52 (1955) 1–42; trans. as "Is There a Doctrine of Retribution in the Old Testament?" *Theodicy in the Old Testament* (ed. J. L. Crenshaw; Issues in Religion and Theology 4; Philadelphia: Fortress, 1983) 57–87.

38. On theodicy see the collection of essays edited by J. L. Crenshaw, *Theodicy in the Old Testament* (Issues in Religion and Theology 4; Philadelphia: Fortress, 1983).

39. Such theodic settlements that appeal to "natural law" to keep people in their "right place" are characteristically conservative. Thus in the modern world the right place of blacks and women is that they should properly bear disproportionate cost for social order. A blatant case of such a theodic settlement in the church concerns the denial of ordination to women, which is essentially a denial of access to power.

40. Peter L. Berger, *The Sacred Canopy* (Garden City, NY: Doubleday, 1967) 59, observes, "there may be two discrete theodicies established in the society—a theodicy of suffering for one group and a theodicy of happiness for the other." Obviously a society that has two such theodicies will be in endless and relentless conflict.

It is my suggestion that long before the theodic crisis in later wisdom, widely recognized today, the Solomonic enterprise of wisdom instituted a theodic settlement that was in fact a rationalization for present systemic inequity and exploitation. People who enjoy the fruits of the present arrangement characteristically have their awarenesses trimmed to and shaped by those interests and experiences. It may be that 1 Kgs 4:20-28 [MT 4:20-5:8] articulates a naïve, uncritical theodic settlement in which Judah and Israel "ate and drank and were happy" (4:20), in which every one was secure "under his own vine and fig tree" (4:25 [MT 5:5]). Conversely 1 Kings 11 with the protest of the prophet (vv 29-39) and the action of the revolutionaries (vv 14-22, 23-25, 26-28), and 1 Kings 12 with its hard political resistance (v 4) articulate a theodic crisis that envisions and requires a deep change in the rules of society. If 1 Kgs 4:20-28 [MT 4:20-5:8] and 1 Kings 11-12 stand juxtaposed as theodic settlement and theodic crisis, then the placement of sapiential references in 1 Kgs 4:29-34 [MT 5:9-14] and 1 Kgs 10:1-13 may be strategically placed, both to show how the epistemological settlement was made (1 Kgs 4:29-34), and how it was indeed linked to a disproportion of power and wealth (1 Kgs 10:1-13).[41] One needs to ask then, not if this or that text is historically accurate, but what these texts intend to tell about "remembered Solomon" in relation to Israel's persistent and recurring question of theodicy.[42]

## CONCLUSION

I therefore conclude it is *sociologically probable* that Solomon was a patron of a wisdom that was at once emancipatory *and* ideological. Only such a conclusion can explain the *canonical memory* of Solomon, both as the one who embraced creation with joy (Song of Solomon), and as the one who also knew despair about the failure of the system of creation (Ecclesiastes).[43] As I have suggested above, Solomon is remembered as a

41. It is clear that in this episode concerning Solomon and the Queen of Sheba, wisdom now has no definite function or importance, but belongs to the properties of royal prestige. By being contextualized by power and riches, wisdom has been trivialized. The same contextualization of wisdom is evident in the triad of Jer 9:23-24. Wisdom is then rather like "intelligence" in a superpower, so that knowledge simply serves economic policy and military strategy. That is, wisdom is now instrumental for power and riches.

42. In Israel wisdom and therefore theodicy are never far removed from social reality. See my "Theodicy in a Social Dimension," *Journal for the Study of the Old Testament* 33 (1985) 3-25.

43. Following Cooper ("The Life and Times of King David"), I see in the Song of Solomon and Ecclesiastes productive interpretive strategies of the canon. To reduce these strategies to questions of historical precision would be to ignore what happens in the canonical process.

patron of a self-serving theodic settlement that permitted power, wealth, and wisdom in disproportionate measure. Thus, he was a patron of a theo-political enterprise that did have emancipatory dimensions but that in the end was also ideological.[44] For Solomon was a patron for the justification of a self-serving system that benefitted the patron and those who enjoyed his patronage. Royally formed knowledge inevitably serves royally valued interests.[45] But for all the skill of that system, Solomon did not escape the "terror of autonomy" in a regime that had violated the old covenantal vision (cf. Matt 6:29). The system designed to tame and contain anxiety ended (perhaps in 922 B.C.E., perhaps in 587) in costly public alienation.

44. On the power of such an ideological function see the quotation of François Châtelet in Henri Mottu, "Jeremiah vs. Hananiah: Ideology and Truth in Old Testament Prophecy," *The Bible and Liberation* (ed. N. K. Gottwald; Maryknoll, NY: Orbis, 1983) 239: "An ideology is a cultural formation (implicit) or a culture production (explicit) that expresses the point of view of a social class or caste; such a point of view concerns man's relations with nature, imagination, the others, and himself. Ideology presents itself as having a *universal* validity; but in reality it not only expresses a *particular* point of view, but also it tends to *mask* its particularity by proposing compensations and imaginary or fleeting solutions."

45. On the relation of knowledge and interest see Jürgen Habermas, *Knowledge and Human Interests* (Boston: Beacon, 1971). In the modern world of enlightenment, what was the interest of the dominant class was perceived as objective. While one must not press the analogy of enlightenment, it is clear that the wisdom of the royal court in Solomonic time was in the service of the royal interest and the urban monopoly. When interest shaped wisdom, one may expect a "march of folly," which was the course and outcome of the Solomonic enterprise.

# THE SAGE IN THE
# ISRAELITE ROYAL COURT

## R. N. Whybray

The terms wise (*ḥākām*) and wisdom (*ḥokmâ*) in biblical Hebrew are not restricted to one class or group of persons, but refer to natural intelligence or to acquired skill. So in Proverbs and Ecclesiastes the wise person is regularly contrasted quite generally with the fool. Even in the animal world certain creatures are credited with wisdom (Prov 6:6-8, 30:24-28), while of one it is stated that its creator has mysteriously deprived it of wisdom (Job 39:13-17). In the sense of an acquired skill, wisdom may be applied to a variety of specialized occupations: seamanship (Ps 107:27), professional mourning (Jer 9:17 [MT 9:16]), snake charming (Ps 58:5 [MT 6]), house building (Prov 24:3), craftsmanship (Exod 31:3-4, 1 Kgs 7:14), magic and divination (Dan 1:20),[1] and the interpretation of dreams (Gen 41:8).

## POLITICAL WISDOM

Political and judicial sagacity also naturally come under the heading of wisdom. This kind of wisdom was an attribute particularly desirable in kings; and Solomon was regarded as a paragon in this respect (1 Kgs 3:4-14, 16-28). The spirit of wisdom and understanding was one of the principal attributes of the ideal king (Isa 11:2), though it is noteworthy that no Israelite king other than David (2 Sam 14:20) and Solomon is specifically credited with wisdom in the Old Testament.[2]

Israelite kings, however, did not usually make important decisions without consulting their ministers or courtiers, although they sometimes chose to ignore their advice. The ability to give sound advice to the

---

R. N. Whybray is Emeritus Professor of Hebrew and Old Testament Studies at the University of Hull.

1. On this subject see H.-P. Müller, "Mantische Weisheit und Apokalyptik," *Congress Volume: Uppsala 1971* (VTSup 22; Leiden: Brill, 1972) 268-93.

2. See the essay above in this volume, "The Social Significance of Solomon as a Patron of Wisdom" by W. Brueggemann (pp. 117-32).

king was clearly an important kind of wisdom, and one would expect to find royal advisers described as wise. Strangely enough, this is not so: although the advisers of foreign kings are occasionally called "wise (men)" (e.g., Isa 19:11-12), no passage in the Old Testament unequivocally uses the term wise to describe persons serving Israelite kings. The supposition, for example, that the wise men condemned by Isaiah were royal counselors is purely inferential. No class of Israelite court officials bore the title wise men or sages.[3]

In fact, advice came to the kings from various types of people: from army commanders like Joab (e.g., 2 Sam 19:1-8), from prophets like Nathan, Elijah, Elisha, Isaiah, and Jeremiah, from priests, and from other persons. Rehoboam, for example, consulted "the old men, who had stood before Solomon his father" and "the young men who had grown up with him" (1 Kgs 12:6, 8). From this incident, in which the king had to choose between two pieces of totally contrary advice, and from the somewhat similar incident in 2 Sam 16:15-17:14, we learn something about the process of decision-making at Israelite courts. In the latter case Ahithophel, "David's counselor," and Hushai, "David's friend," gave their contrary advice at Absalom's invitation. Those present agreed that "the counsel of Hushai the Archite is better than the counsel of Ahithophel," and the king accepted this decision.

Decisions, then, were made by Israelite kings on the advice both of "experts" and of others. Ahithophel and Hushai were experts. Joab, however, who gave David the best advice of all, was not an intellectual but an army general. His wisdom was that of a sharp mind, the wisdom of common sense.

It is a historical accident that most of what we know about Israelite courts comes from the reign of David. It is also interesting to note that the use of the words wise and wisdom in Samuel and Kings is entirely confined to the reigns of David and Solomon.[4]

## THE ROLE AND FUNCTIONS OF THE COURTIER

The kings chose their advisers according to their own whims; and the extent to which their advice was accepted depended on the character of the king in question. In the last days of the Monarchy, when there were conflicting parties advocating different policies, weak kings like Zedekiah were at a loss which advice to follow. On the other hand, a

3. For the demonstration of this point see especially my work, *The Intellectual Tradition in the Old Testament* (BZAW 135; Berlin: de Gruyter, 1974).

4. For a fuller treatment of these reigns see my essay, "Wisdom Literature in the Reigns of David and Solomon," *Studies in the Period of David and Solomon and Other Essays* (ed. Tomoo Ishida; Winona Lake, IN: Eisenbrauns, 1982) 13-26.

strong king might dominate or overrule his advisers: for example, Jeroboam I "took counsel and made two golden calves." Similarly the king of Syria "took counsel with [lit., to] his servants, saying, 'At such and such a place will be my camp.'" Here the consultation seems to have been purely formal: those "consulted" were expected simply to carry out the king's orders.

The Succession Narrative shows that quick-wittedness was a necessary quality for a courtier. The degree of subtlety shown by its characters is remarkable: Nathan tricked David into condemning himself by means of a fictitious story (2 Samuel 12); Joab used a similar device through the agency of a "wise woman" to force David to accept the return of Absalom to court (2 Samuel 14; the "wisdom" was that of Joab); Hushai deliberately and very persuasively gave *bad* advice (2 Sam 17:6-14). Such wisdom was simply intelligence or cleverness, without ethical content. This is shown most clearly in the incident of Amnon's rape of his half-sister Tamar (2 Samuel 13). There Jonadab, Amnon's "friend" who engineered the crime, is described—whether ironically or not—as "a very wise man [ʾîš ḥākām mĕʾōd]" (2 Sam 13:3).

The role of Israelite courtiers is also reflected in the Book of Proverbs. There it is stressed that the making of policy, specifically military policy, depends for its success on a multiplicity of counselors (yôʿă ṣîm) (Prov 11:14, 15:22, 24:6). Importance is attached to patience and persuasiveness in advocating particular policies (Prov 25:15). At the same time, the courtier's career and the precariousness of his position are clearly portrayed. His position depends on the sometimes fickle will of the ruler: an incautious word may ruin him (Prov 10:19, 13:3). Another proverb bears directly on the career prospects of the courtier: he must refrain from thrusting himself forward at court, and must wait until he is asked for his opinion (Prov 25:6-7). But in the end an intelligent servant of the king will receive the due reward of the king's favor.

The Old Testament provides no detailed account of the composition of the Israelite court or of the functions attached to particular offices.[5] The historical books contain several lists of high officers of state

5. For helpful studies on this subject, see G. W. Ahlström, *Royal Administration and National Religion in Ancient Palestine* (Studies in the History of the Ancient Near East 1; Leiden: Brill, 1982); J. Begrich, "*Sōfēr* und *mazkir*: Ein Beitrag zur inneren Geschichte des davidisch-salomonischen Grossreiches und des Königsreiches Juda," *ZAW* 58 (1940-41) 1-29; H. J. Boecker, "Erwägungen zum Amt des Mazkir," *Theologische Zeitschrift* 17 (1961) 212-16; P. A. H. de Boer, "The Counsellor," *WIANE* 42-71; A. Cody, "Le titre égyptien et le nom propre du scribe de David," *RB* 72 (1965) 381-93; H. Donner, "Der 'Freund des Königs,'" *ZAW* 73 (1961) 269-77; A. Malamat, "Organs of Statecraft in the Israelite Monarchy," *BA* 28 (1965) 34-65 (repr. in *Biblical Archaeologist Reader* 3 [ed. E. F. Campbell Jr. and D. N. Freedman; Garden City, NY: Doubleday, 1970]

in the reigns of David and Solomon, but with no explanation of their titles: 2 Sam 8:16–18, 20:23–26; 1 Kgs 4:2–6; 1 Chr 18:14–17, 27:32–34. Certain official titles also appear in the course of the narratives. (It should be borne in mind that changes almost certainly occurred in the functions of these officials in the course of time, and also that the court of the kings of northern Israel, about which very little information has been preserved, may have been constituted somewhat differently from that of Judah.)[6] Offices that may have involved specifically intellectual activity include those of *sôpēr*, *yôʿēṣ*, and *rēaʿ / rēʿeh hammelek*.

The precise function of the 'king's friend' (*rēaʿ /rēʿeh hammelek*), only attested for the reigns of David and Solomon, is not clear. The title appears in 1 Kgs 4:2–6 as a recognized office: Zabud the son of Nathan was "priest and king's friend." Attempts have been made to connect the title with those of functionaries at Egyptian and other courts; but such identifications remain problematical. According to 2 Samuel 15–17 Hushai, as David's friend, used his wisdom to secure David's safety and Absalom's downfall, while Ahithophel, David's counselor, went over to Absalom's side, but his sound advice was overruled. The distinction between the two offices is not made clear. The term *yôʿēṣ* 'counselor', however, is clear enough in itself. Ahithophel, who was evidently *the* king's counselor *par excellence*, may have stood at the head of a body of royal counselors: *yôʿēṣ* occurs in the plural, for example, in Proverbs and Isa 1:26. It is not possible to be more definite than this.

The office that presents the fewest problems of interpretation is that of *sôpēr* 'scribe, secretary'. The profession of scribe was an essential one in all the societies of the ancient Near East that had developed writing systems, but in which the ability to read and write was confined to specialists.[7] Scribes were employed not only in royal establishments but also by private persons in the conduct of their business affairs. Scribes took dictation and read documents aloud (Jer 36:4–18) and performed various other administrative and clerkly functions (e.g., 2 Kgs 12:10, Ezekiel 9).

Both in the lists of officials and in the narratives there appears an official known simply as "*the* scribe" (though in 1 Kgs 4:3 the office

163–98); A. Van Selms, "The Origin of the Title 'The King's Friend,'" *JNES* 16 (1957) 118–23; R. de Vaux, "Titres et fonctionnaries égyptiens à la cour de David et de Salomon," *RB* 48 (1939) 394–405 (repr. in his *Bible et Orient* [Paris: Cerf, 1967] 189–201).

6. A tantalizing suggestion that this is the case is to be found in 2 Kgs 10:1, 5 where reference is made to *hāʾōmĕnîm* (i.e., 'guardians' [NAB] or 'trustees' [Koehler-Baumgartner]) of Ahab's sons. That these persons were 'tutors' (as the NEB translates) is not certain; nor is it clear that they were necessarily members of the northern, royal court. See also n. 13 and the final paragraph in this essay.

7. On scribes in other ancient Near Eastern courts, see the other essays in this section. For a carefully nuanced survey of the scribe (*sôpēr*) in Israel, see A. Demsky, "Scribe," *Encyclopaedia Judaica* (Jerusalem: Keter, 1971), 14:1042–43.

appears to be duplicated) or "the king's scribe." This title is probably somewhat analogous to modern titles like Secretary of State. These men were presumably the heads of the royal scribal establishment; but they themselves were chosen for their political ability. Under them, the scribal establishment handled the administration of the government. It must have included men able to speak and write the languages of the foreign nations with whom Israel maintained diplomatic relations. It is probable that, besides the king's scribe, some of the other high officials had had scribal training: Jonathan, David's uncle, for example, "was a counselor, being a man of understanding and a scribe" (1 Chr 27:32).

## THE ROYAL COURT AS INTELLECTUAL CENTER

In Israel as elsewhere in the ancient Near East the courts were the intellectual centers of the two kingdoms. Temples, with their staff of priests and with their own scribes, were also often centers of intellectual activity, and this was doubtless the case in Israel too. In Jerusalem, however, court and temple were very closely connected, and the chief priests are listed among the high officers of state.

There can be little doubt that much of the literature composed during the period of the Monarchy was the work of either the royal or the priestly scribes. The main types of literature that may safely be attributed to this period are annals and historical narratives, poetry (especially psalms), laws and cultic material such as the description of the Temple in 1 Kings 6, and wisdom literature such as is now extant in the Book of Proverbs. Psalms, laws, and other cultic material are probably of priestly origin, although the lack of information provided by the texts themselves about their authorship makes it impossible to draw a sharp distinction.

One of the functions of the royal scribes was to record important events in the form of annals; and these appear to have been drawn upon and expanded into a chronological framework for the Books of Kings (e.g., 2 Kgs 15:1–16:4). Other written sources composed at the royal court included the now lost Books of the Chronicles of the Kings of Judah and of Israel, specifically mentioned as providing additional information (e.g., 2 Kgs 15:6), and works such as the Succession Narrative (2 Samuel 9–20, 1 Kings 1–2) and a history of the reign of Solomon (1 Kings 3–11) now incorporated in the Books of Kings. These could hardly have been written without an intimate knowledge of the royal court. The historical books of the Old Testament testify to an immense capability of the royal scribes for historical writing.[8]

8. This capability—by no means confined to the Succession Narrative—far surpasses, in my judgement, anything previously achieved by any nation. See especially my study, *The Succession Narrative; A Study of II Samuel 9–20; I Kings 1 and 2* (SBT 2/9;

Prov 25:1 attributes 'copying' or possibly 'editing'—*he^ctîqû* hardly means 'composed'—to "Hezekiah's men." It should be noted that they are not called *wise* men and that this is the only *direct* indication in Proverbs of a connection between the royal court and the wisdom literature. This section and two others are also called "proverbs of Solomon" (Prov 1:1, 10:1)—Prov 1:1, in fact, may be intended to refer to the whole book. But this ascription of literary wisdom to Solomon, also found in 1 Kgs 4:29–34 [MT 5:9–14], belongs to legend rather than history—a legend that was certainly not the peculiar property of the royal court. Other sections of Proverbs are attributed to wise men (22:17, 24:23—there is no definite article), and again there is no reason to connect these with the royal court.

Apart from the reference to Hezekiah's men, the main evidence for a connection between Proverbs and the royal court is to be found in the proverbs that refer specifically to the king and to court life. These, however, are few in number. It has been supposed that the general similarity of parts of the book to Egyptian and other foreign wisdom, and in particular the clear dependence of Prov 22:17–24:22 on the Egyptian "Instruction of Amenemopet," also points to royal (or temple) scribes as authors; but it would be wrong to assume that no educated persons existed outside Jerusalem capable of literary activity of this kind. A large proportion of Proverbs is concerned with matters of interest to the agriculturalist rather than to the courtier.

The extent to which royal scribes were responsible for the composition and editing of Proverbs is, then, difficult to assess. Much of the material is undoubtedly traditional. In the processes of its collection, editing, and subsequent growth they certainly played a part; but it cannot be said that they have left a substantial mark on the material as a whole.

## SECULAR AND RELIGIOUS WISDOM

The royal scribes were not unaffected by the religious and other changes that took place during the period of the Monarchy, nor should it be supposed that they all thought alike. Much has been made by scholars of the secularity and amorality of some practitioners of wisdom in the reigns of David and Solomon, and of a similar attitude

---

London: SCM, 1968); and G. von Rad, "Der Anfang der Geschichtsschreibung im alten Israel," *Archiv für Kulturgeschichte* 32 (1944) 1–42 (repr. in his *Gesammelte Studien zum Alten Testament* [Theologische Bücherei, Altes Testament 8; Munich: Kaiser, 1958] 148–88; trans. as "The Beginnings of Historical Writing in Ancient Israel," *The Problem of the Hexateuch and Other Essays* [Edinburgh/London: Oliver and Boyd, 1966] 166–204.

displayed in some sayings in Proverbs;[9] and it has been supposed that the clashes between Isaiah and Jeremiah and the royal establishment on matters of national policy were in fact clashes between the godless wisdom of hardheaded politicians and the message of Yahweh proclaimed by the prophets. There is no doubt much truth in this. On the other hand, the concept of wisdom as a divine gift was a very ancient one; and its implications can be seen particularly in the deuteronomistic movement, in which it is probable that royal scribes played a part.[10] Moreover, the support and protection given to Jeremiah by the powerful scribal family of Shaphan, Josiah's "Secretary of State" (Jer 25:24, 29:3, and chaps. 39–43 passim), and other officials (śārîm in 26:16, 36:19) shows that the wisdom of some of the royal scribes was of an intensely religious and moral character.

## THE COURT AND EDUCATION

Finally, reference may be made to the royal scribe as teacher. His accomplishments presuppose a thorough education; but whether there was at the Israelite court, as in Egypt and Mesopotamia, an institution that can be described as a "scribal school" is a matter of dispute. There is no direct reference to schools of any kind in the Old Testament.[11] The few references to education are imprecise,[12] and the interpretation of some other passages is dubious, for example, the view that the 'guardians' of Ahab's sons (ʾōmĕnîm in 2 Kgs 10:1, 5) were in fact 'tutors'.[13] Scribal education may have been undertaken by fathers for their own sons in an hereditary profession.[14] It is probable, on the other hand, that some parts of Proverbs, especially parts of chaps. 1–9 and 22:17–24:22, were composed as "text books" for young pupils—though not necessarily at a royal scribal school.

9. On this topic see especially W. McKane, *Prophets and Wise Men* (SBT 44; London: SCM, 1965), and idem, *Proverbs: A New Approach* (OTL; Philadelphia: Westminster, 1970).

10. On the latter subject see the essay below in this volume by P. K. McCarter Jr., "The Sage in the Deuteronomistic History" (pp. 289–93).

11. For a treatment on the schools that is more positive than mine, see the essay by A. Lemaire in this volume, "The Sage in School and Temple" (pp. 165–81 below), as well as his *Les écoles et la formation de la Bible dans l'ancien Israël* (OBO 39; Fribourg: Editions Universitaires; Göttingen: Vandenhoeck und Ruprecht, 1981), and "Sagesse et écoles," *VT* 34 (1984) 270–81.

12. For a cautious and recent survey see J. L. Crenshaw, "Education in Ancient Israel," *JBL* 104 (1985) 601–15.

13. Though fathers taught, the context of 2 Kgs 10:1–11 does not permit the conclusion that the ʾōmĕnîm were fathers since (a) reference is made to "*your* master's sons" (vv 2, 6), and (b) the ʾōmĕnîm, along with the city officials and elders, complied with Jehu's request to behead those in their charge. See also n. 6 above.

14. Note especially the scribal family of Shaphan referred to above.

# SAGES AND SCRIBES AT THE COURTS OF ANCIENT IRAN

## James R. Russell

It is fortunate for the purposes of this study on the court roles of the sages and scribes that there was an inherent conservatism in pre-Islamic Iranian thought and practice that allows one, with, due caution, to bring together evidence of the Achemenian (ca. 550–333 B.C.E.), Parthian (250 B.C.E.–224 C.E.), and Sasanian (224–651 C.E.) periods.[1] There were two major and divergent types of courts and structures of society in ancient Iran. These types will be delineated in the first two sections below before I proceed to a survey of some of the activities of ancient Iranian sages and scribes.

### COURTS OF NOBLES—COEQUAL
### KINGS—PRIESTLY SAGES

In Arsacid (Parthian) Iran, in Armenia down to the high Middle Ages, and in Sogd down to the Arab conquest early in the eighth century, powerful noble families with large domains occupied hereditary and inalienable offices at court: in Armenia, for example, the Bagratuni *naxarar*s ('dynastic clan') held the office of *t'agadir* 'coronant'. In this system, the king was *primus inter pares*. Thus the Armenian Arsacid king celebrated Nawasard, the New Year feast sacred to the chief of the gods, Aramazd (Ahura Mazdā); but the Vahuni *naxarar*s were guardians of the great shrine at Aštišat of Vahagn (Avestan Vĕrĕthraghna-, an immensely popular god likened to the Greek Heracles and Ares). The priests of the latter temple were, presumably, answerable first to their *naxarar*-patrons, rather like the *purohita*s 'household priests' of ancient India. Priests controlled considerable wealth in their own right: the

James R. Russell is Associate Professor in the Department of Middle East Languages and Cultures at Columbia University.

1. On a number of individual sages, and on Zoroastrian conceptions of wisdom, see my earlier essay in this volume, "The Sage in Ancient Iranian Literature" (pp. 81–92 above). On the matter of continuity and discontinuity, see the next note.

entire province of Ekeɫeac[c] (Greek Akilisene) in Armenia belonged, according to Strabo, to the cult of Anahit. Such temple-estates were common in Asia Minor; and to the east, in Parthia proper, ostraca testify to the existence of a *Nanaistān—an estate or district belonging to the temple of the goddess Nana(i). Sages, drawn from the priesthood, thus operated independently or with the patronage of royal and local, noble courts alike.[2]

## ROYAL COURTS—THE KING AS CENTER—HIERARCHICAL STRUCTURE

The second pattern is rigidly hierarchical and characterizes the two great Persian dynasties—Achemenians and Sasanians—though it never displaced entirely the prerogatives of the great families: the seven coconspirators of Darius were the scions of such; and in the Sasanian period the revolt of Bahrām Čōbēn can be seen as a bid for power by the Mihran family of northwestern Iran supported by other houses hostile to the concentration of power by the king. The proto-Communist rebel Mazdak in the sixth century manipulated royal mistrust of the nobility to weaken both forces. In this second structure, the king was a cosmic figure, the first among men, his court likened to the center and mainstay of an orderly cosmos: fantastic descriptions of the throne room at Ctesiphon evoke a domed and starry sky with equipment to produce artificial atmospheric effects; the king sat behind a diaphanous curtain, his globed, winged, diademmed crown so massive that it had to be suspended by a chain from the ceiling.[3] The court directly patron-

2. On the cults of Vahagn and Anahit see my *Zoroastrianism in Armenia* (Harvard Iranian Series 5; Cambridge: Harvard University, 1987) 189–260; on Parthian and Sasanian society see R. Frye, "The Political History of Iran under the Sasanians," *Cambridge History of Iran* 3.1 (ed. E. Yarshater; Cambridge: Cambridge University, 1983) 116–80; and E. Yarshater, "Were the Sasanians Heirs to the Achaemenids?" *La Persia nel Medioevo* (Accademia Nazionale dei Lincei, quad. no. 160; Rome: Accademia Nazionale dei Lincei, 1971) 517–31, who sees a strong continuity from the Parthian to the Sasanian system. The *naxarar* 'dynastic' structure of Armenian society, inherited from the Parthians, is still substantially different from the Sasanian order: see N. G. Garsoïan, *Armenia in the Period of Justinian* (Lisbon: Calouste Gulbenkian Foundation, 1970), and my *Zoroastrianism in Armenia*, 113–52.

3. On the Revolt of Bahrām Čōbēn see K. Czeglédy, "Bahrām Čōbīn and the Persian Apocalyptic Literature," *Acta Orientalia* 8 (1958) 21–43. Such events were reduced by court astrologers to inevitabilities in a fatalistic scheme, or primitively (even for that time!) seen as signs of an apocalypse. Mazdak was himself a member of the Zoroastrian clergy, according to al-Biruni, and, like Mani's, his movement had literature. The New Persian *Dabestān-e Mazāheb*, for example, mentions a lost Mazdakite text, the *Dēsnād*; see O. Klíma, *Mazdak: Geschichte einer sozialen Bewegung im sassanidischen*

ized a correspondingly hierarchical and centralized Zoroastrian priest-hood: thus, in the Sasanian "Testament of Ardašīr," of which only an Arabic translation survives, kingship and religion are said mutually and indispensably to support each other.[4]

Although the ideal of the centralized monarchy, particularly in the Sasanian period, was to control the priesthood of a similarly all-encompassing religion, Zoroastrianism could not be molded to accom-modate this ideal: it has never encouraged proselytism, and is, like Judaism, far too strongly rooted in national traditions and rigorous, culturally-prescribed prescriptions as to the everyday behavior of its adherents to spread significantly or lastingly among alien peoples. Shapur I (ca. 240–70 C.E.) briefly patronized Manicheism as a teaching with universal pretensions, and Mani attended the king at court; but ultimately the alarmed Zoroastrian clergy, with the powerful Kartir at their head, had Mani killed (ca. 276 C.E.) and his religion suppressed within the imperial frontiers. Kartir himself, though, appears to have presented to the crown the danger of excessive concentration of power in one man at the head of a sacerdotal hierarchy over whose formation the early Sasanians themselves had presided: his name does not appear in any Pahlavi text, though the Manichean books recall him with hatred—and it appears his name was expunged from the records, for many priests are mentioned whose careers were far less impressive than his.[5]

## COURT ACTIVITIES OF ANCIENT IRANIAN SCRIBES

### Clerical Tasks

Despite such frictions, Sasanian clergymen served as regional judges, called *driyōšān jādagōw* 'intercessor for the poor'; they also ran trading companies, and the Pahlavi *Erbadistān*, a text on rules govern-ing priestly seminaries, stipulates that a clergyman must be allowed time from an academy conveniently close to his home to see to personal

*Persien* (Prague: Nakladatelství Československé Akademie, 1957; repr. New York: Arno, 1979). The sources on the appearance of the late Sasanian court are reviewed, with an imaginative analysis sadly farfetched in places, by H. P. L'Orange, *Studies on the Iconography of Cosmic Kingship* (Oslo: Aschehoug/Cambridge: Harvard University, 1953).

4. The "Testament of Ardašīr" is translated by M. Grignaschi in "Quelques speci-mens de la littérature sassanide conservés dans les bibliothèques d'Istanbul," *Journal Asiatique* 254 (1966) 1–142.

5. See V. G. Lukonin, "Kartir i Mani," *Vestnik Drevnei Istorii* (Moscow) 3 (1966) 65–81.

business matters.[6] At court, they were ubiquitous advisors, employing both political precept and astrological chart to guide the ship of state.

Friction between the crown and a strong Zoroastrian clergy seems politically to be expected; and one recalls the *magophonia* 'murder of the Magi' by the supporters of Darius, an event that, Herodotus reports, was commemorated in later years.[7] The Achemenian and Sasanian courts sought to patronize the clergy of the other religions within their realm: a policy that some historians consider the prototype of the Islamic practice that survived down to the 1840s as the "*millet* system" of the Ottoman Turks. Thus, the Achemenians at Persepolis underwrote Elamite religious rituals;[8] and the Sasanian monarch was the titular head of the Nestorian church—and in the later period of the Armenian church as well. The Talmud records a close personal friendship between the Jewish *Rēš Gālūtā* ('Head of the Exile') and the Sasanian King of Kings.[9] Achemenian support and restoration of local rituals and shrines through native or ethnically related ministers is well attested for Egypt and Israel.[10]

## Interaction with Non-Iranians in Court Matters

There is evidence of interaction between Iranians and non-Iranians on the level of the court in the various periods, particularly in matters of offices, protocol, and philosophy. Since writing was a non-Iranian invention, the scribal offices reflect such interaction in the most obvious way. The literary style of the Achemenian inscriptions seems to be inspired in large measure by Urartean, perhaps through a Median

---

6. See S. J. Bulsara, *Aērpatastān and Nīrangastān* (Bombay: British India Press, 1915; repr. New York: AMS, 1977).

7. See Herodotus, *The Histories* 3:79 (trans. A. de Sélincourt; Harmondsworth: Penguin, 1975) 238. The *magophonia* festival might have been an occasion for relief of social tension through role inversion, but it remains a problem; see M. Boyce, *A History of Zoroastrianism* (Handbuch der Orientalistik 1.8.2.2a; Leiden: Brill, 1982), 2:86–88.

8. Boyce, *History of Zoroastrianism*, 2:133–34.

9. On the Christians see N. G. Garsoïan, "Armenia in the Fourth Century: An Attempt to Re-Define the Concepts 'Armenia' and 'Loyalty,'" *Revue des Études Arméniennes*, n.s. 8 (1971) 341–52 (repr. in his *Armenia between Byzantium and the Sasanians* [London: Variorum, 1985] 341–52). Jews did not have extraterritorial loyalties and therefore fared generally better than did Christians in Sasanian Iran; see J. Neusner, "Jews in Iran," *Cambridge History of Iran* 3.2 (ed. E. Yarshater; Cambridge: Cambridge University, 1983) 913.

10. For Israel I refer, of course, to the activities of Ezra and Nehemiah. On both of these men and on Achemenian sponsorship of native ministers in Egypt see the thorough discussion of J. Blenkinsopp, "The Mission of Udjahorreshet and Those of Ezra and Nehemiah," *JBL* 106 (1987) 409–21. On Ezra in particular see the essay by Blenkinsopp in this volume, "The Sage, the Scribe, and Scribalism in the Chronicler's Work" (pp. 307–15 below).

intermediary stage: the formula "by the will of Ahuramazdā" derives from the Urartean phrase "by the will of Ḫaldi." The Cyrus cylinder in Akkadian shows an adaptation of alien literary style for Persian propaganda ends; and it is possible the Magi influenced and in a way encouraged the author of Deutero-Isaiah.[11] Middle Iranian languages were written with a complex system of Aramaic allography, which presupposes the original presence of Mesopotamian scribes at the royal chancellery.

Iranian inscriptions were also written multilingually with Greek: Herodotus records that Darius left inscriptions at the Bosphorus in "Assyrian characters" (that is, cuneiform script) and in Greek.[12] The Parthian kings, who called themselves *philhellenoi* 'lovers of Greek culture', used Greek for inscriptions, documents, and on coins; and Greek is one of the languages used in the early Sasanian trilingual inscriptions. Iranian theologians acquired and exhaustively explored the Aristotelian concept of the Mean (Pahlavi *miyān*);[13] but it would seem that they learned of it through the works of Syriac speakers rather than directly from Hellenic philosophers, even though the school of Athens sojourned briefly at Gundishapur after its closure in 529 by Justinian.

## Scribal Tasks

The scribes were responsible for taxation and record-keeping. The compilation of the royal annals of the Sasanian dynasty, the *Xwādāy-nāmag* ("Book of Kings," the germ of Ferdousi's *Šāh-nāme*), was entrusted to them. In the Book of Esther, a romance set at the Achemenian court but composed in the Parthian era, the royal annals are read to the sleepless Ahasuerus:[14] the Armenian historian Movsēs Xorenacʿi, too, has the nightmare-troubled Astyages (Armenian Aždahak) summon the Magi to his bedside. Although this is a literary topos, it may allude to the reassuring vigilance of the Magi: Zoroastrian priests perform the office of the *Vīdēvdāt* ("Law against the Demons") in the small hours; and fragrant wood must be offered to a consecrated sacred fire in all five watches of the day, including the period from midnight to dawn. Most of the scribes by the Sasanian period were members of the

11. On this point see M. Smith, "II Isaiah and the Persians," *JAOS* 83 (1963) 415–21.

12. See Herodotus, *The Histories* 4:87 (Sélincourt p. 300); for a discussion see C. H. Gordon, *Forgotten Scripts* (2d ed.; New York: Basic Books, 1982) 42.

13. Zoroastrian adoption of the concept of the mean was first noted and discussed by R. C. Zaehner, *Zurvan: A Zoroastrian Dilemma* (Oxford: Clarendon, 1955; repr. Cheshire, CT: Biblo and Tannen, 1972) 251–52. S. Shaked returns to the topic in *Transition Periods in Iranian History* (Studia Iranica Cahier 5; Paris: Geuthner, 1987).

14. On the Iranian material in Esther see my "Zoroastrian Elements in the Book of Esther," *Irano-Judaica* 2 (ed. S. Shaked; Jerusalem: Hebrew University, in press).

priestly class (*asrōnān*) trained in the *dabīristān* 'scribal academy': the short Pahlavi text *Nāmag-nibēsišnīh* ("Letter-writing"), a manual,[15] demonstrates that the niceties of address so characteristic of modern Persian existed before Islam and had to be learned, together with court etiquette (the Armenian *Gahnamak* ["Book of Seating"], a list for precedence of noble guests at banquets, has a Persian title and is based on a Persian model).[16] In the Achaemenian period when Aramaic became the *lingua franca* of the empire, it is likely that a majority of the *dabīrs*—the term refers primarily to transcribers, translators, and lower-level bureaucrats—were non-Iranian.

## Sages as Physicians

The sages were expected to cure the illnesses of their liege lords: thus did Mani advertise himself as "a physician from Babylon." Greek doctors were much in demand, and Ctesias, as one of them, had access to intimate court gossip. But Zoroastrian Magi, also, cured by "sacred word, plant, and knife" (in modern terminology: psychiatry, allopathic medicine, and surgery); and Persian doctors served the Byzantine court, as well. It has been suggested that Greek conceptions of the humors and internal balance of the body were utilized in therapy together with the Iranian approach to illness due to external infection.[17] If they did not succeed, the sages again were the priests who offered regular services for the departed soul of the king.[18]

15. See R. C. Zaehner, "*Namāk nipēsišnīh*," *Bulletin of the School of Oriental and African Studies* 9 (1937–39) 93–109.

16. On the *Gahnamak* see N. Adontz, *Studies in Christian Caucasian History* (Washington, D.C.: Georgetown University, 1970) 229–30.

17. See J. Hampel, *Medizin der Zoroastrier im vorislamischen Iran* (Abhandlungen zur Geschichte der Medizin und der Naturwissenschaften 45; Husum: Matthiesen, 1982), who collects a number of useful texts, but tends to mistranslate common terms in order to endow them with special medical meanings.

18. Arrian, following Aristobulus, reports that Magi still guarded the mausoleum of Cyrus at the time of Alexander's invasion; see D. Stronach, *Pasargadae* (Oxford: Oxford University, 1978) 24.

# THE SAGE IN HELLENISTIC ROYAL COURTS

## John G. Gammie†

### AFTER THE PATTERN OF ATHENS

The accumulated institutional experiences of the great civilizations of Egypt, Mesopotamia, and Persia left their imprint in numerous ways on the structures of the kingdoms that the military successors to Alexander the Great appropriated for themselves in Egypt and Asia upon his death in 323 B.C.E., but this did not begin to compare with the dynamic effect of the accumulated Hellenic institutional experience and far-ranging intellectual inquiries among the Greeks. Under the first overlords of Judah and Samaria after Alexander's death, the Ptolemies (ca. 323–198 B.C.E.), and the second, the Seleucids (ca. 198–63 B.C.E.), the pattern of organization of cities, the educational system, laws, and the royal court were thoroughly Hellenized.[1] The despots at Antioch and Alexandria emulated the models of the tyrants of Syracuse, the Aegean isles,

John G. Gammie was Emma A. Harwell Professor of Biblical Literature at the University of Tulsa.

I wish to express my thanks to Professor A. A. Long of the Department of Classics, University of California, Berkeley, for his helpful comments and suggestions on the first draft of this essay.

1. The best, single introduction to this period is Claire Préaux, *Le monde hellénistique: La Grèce et l'Orient (323-146 av. J.-C.)* (2 vols.; Nouvelle Clio 6; Paris: Presses Universitaire de France, 1978). P. M. Fraser's *Ptolemaic Alexandria* (3 vols.; Oxford: Clarendon, 1972) is a mine of information and painstaking analysis on the cultural composition and intellectual accomplishments of the capital city of the Greco-Egyptian empire. Still useful are the works by E. R. Bevan, *The House of Seleucus* (2 vols.; London, E. Arnold, 1902; repr. New York: Barnes and Noble, 1966), and *A History of Egypt under the Ptolemaic Dynasty* (London: Methuen, 1927; repr. as *The House of Ptolemy* [Chicago: Argonaut, 1968]). Two works especially may be commended on the relation of Judaism and Hellenism: V. Tcherikover, *Hellenistic Civilization and the Jews* (Philadelphia: Jewish Publication Society, 1959; repr. New York: Atheneum, 1970), and M. Hengel, *Hellenism and Judaism* (2 vols.; Philadelphia: Fortress, 1974). For its abundance of insights on the changes in the Roman bureaucracy and outlook after the Hellenistic empires, see Arnaldo Momigliano, *Alien Wisdom: The Limits of Hellenization* (New York: Cambridge University, 1976).

Macedonia, and western Asia Minor and sought to recreate under royal
patronage a flourishing of the arts and learning that would vie even with
Athens.[2] As Plato had visited his friend Dion and the tyrant Dionysius in
Sicily, as Aristotle had visited and labored under the hospitality and
patronage of the "tyrant" Hermeias near Assus in Asia Minor, and as
Aristotle had for seven years served in the court of Philip of Macedon
as tutor to his son, Alexander, so the successors to Alexander sought to
attract to their royal court leading philosophers of the day as tutors,
counselors, and advisers in matters of statecraft. As I shall show, they
were not always successful in luring their first choices, but their wealth
was sufficient to attract and employ sculptors, painters, poets, philolo-
gists, physicians, natural scientists, historians, geographers, mathematicians, and philosophers—the latter often as tutors for their sons and
librarians.[3] The satirist Timon of Phlius (born ca. 320–310 B.C.E.) spoke
of the assemblage of scholars in Alexandria as follows: "In the populous
land of Egypt many are they who get fed, cloistered bookworms,
endlessly arguing in the bird-coop of the Muses."[4] The reference to the
"bird-coop of the Muses" is to the Mouseion with its library, the
Alexandrian counterpart of the Academy and Lyceum, so named because of its dedication to the Muses. Of the Mouseion and library Bevan
says:

> It was to be a kind of University, modelled on the Athenian schools of
> philosophers. The men of letters and *savants* who obtained the position of
> Fellows of the Museum received their board free and were exempt from
> taxation. In this way it was hoped that men of eminence would be
> attracted to Alexandria from the rest of the Greek world. Under the
> second and third Ptolemies a very brilliant company indeed of scholars,
> scientists, and poets were to be found at the Alexandrine court. . . . In
> connection with the Museum there was formed the largest library of Greek
> books which existed in the world.[5]

Included among the sages, then, at the Hellenistic royal courts were
intelligentsia of a variety of sorts, lured to the courts not only for the
remuneration but also for access to other intellectuals and a sizeable
research library. Other libraries of note in the Hellenistic world existed
outside Alexandria at Pergamum, Tarsus, and Antioch.[6]

2. See esp. Fraser, *Ptolemaic Alexandria*, 1:305–12, and E. Bikerman [= E. J.
Bickerman], *Institutions des Séleucides* (Service des Antiquités: Bibliothèque archéologique et historique 26; Paris: Geuthner, 1938) 36–39.

3. Bikerman, *Institutions des Séleucids*, 36–39, and Fraser, *Ptolemaic Alexandria*
1:305–19.

4. Fraser, *Ptolemaic Alexandria*, 1:317; Greek text in 2:471 n. 87.

5. Bevan, *The House of Ptolemy*, 124.

6. Fraser, *Ptolemaic Alexandria*, 1:320–35; Bevan, *The House of Seleucus*, 2:276.

## PHILOSOPHERS

Despite this array of persons engaged in intellectual pursuits in the Hellenistic royal courts, the designation sage or wise man (*sophos*) applied first and foremost to the philosopher ( *philosophos*, lit. 'lover of wisdom'). Thus Diogenes Laertius in his *Lives of Eminent Philosophers* (ca. 200-250 C.E.) writes that Ptolemy—which would have been Ptolemy I Soter (ca. 323-283 B.C.E.)[7]—sought to persuade Theophrastus, the successor to Aristotle at the Lyceum, to come to Alexandria (*Eminent Philosophers* 5:37). Also according to Diogenes Laertius, the third head of the Lyceum, Straton (ca. 286-268 B.C.E.), taught Ptolemy II Philadelphus (283-246 B.C.E.) and was paid for it handsomely (*Eminent Philosophers* 5:58). The Seleucid kings, whose capital was moved from Seleucia on the Tigris to Antioch on the Orontes in 300 B.C.E. by the founding king Seleucus I (323-280 B.C.E.), also sought to have noted philosophers in residence at the royal court. Thus Antiochus II Theos (262-223 B.C.E.) invited—without success—the fourth head of the Lyceum, Lycon (ca. 268-226 B.C.E.), to come to Antioch (*Eminent Philosophers* 5:67). Lycon enjoyed especial favor with the monarchs Eumenes and Attalus of Pergamum in Asia Minor, which, for a time, was an independent kingdom between the kingdoms of Macedonia and Seleucia. The so-called Attalids were also patrons of Antigonus of Carystus, a noted third-century-B.C.E. biographer of philosophers, who was a major source of Diogenes Laertius.[8]

Not only the Peripatetics were in favor as sages in the Hellenistic courts, but also the Stoics. Thus Zeno (333-261 B.C.E.), the founder of the Stoics, declined an invitation to go to the court of Antigonus II Gonatas (ca. 320-239 B.C.E.) in Macedonia, but did send two of his pupils: Persaeus of Citium and Philonides of Thebes (*Eminent Philosophers* 7:6, 9). The former wrote a treatise, among other topics, "On Kingship," and helped Antigonus plan the conquest of Eretrea where the influence in practical affairs of another philosopher Menedemus was

---

7. The dates of rule of monarchs are taken from Bevan's *The House of Seleucus* and *The House of Ptolemy*; other dates are taken from *The Oxford Classical Dictionary* (ed. M. Cary et al.; Oxford: Clarendon, 1949). For a convenient translation of Diogenes Laertius, see R. D. Hicks, *Diogenes Laertius: Lives of Eminent Philosophers* (2 vols.; LCL; Cambridge: Harvard University, 1925).

8. See F. L. Vatai, *Intellectuals in Politics in the Greek World from Early Times to the Hellenistic Age* (London: Croom Helm, 1984) 18. Another major source of Diogenes Laertius was Timon of Phlius (born ca. 320-310 B.C.E.), whose witty, anecdotal, and doxographical biographies of philosophers called *Silloi* (*Lampoons*) were indebted to the Cynic method of satire and castigation, and for whom Pyrrho, the founder of Scepticism, was champion; see A. A. Long, "Timon of Phlius: Pyrrhonist and Satirist," *Proceedings of the Cambridge Philological Society* 204 (1978) 68-91. For more on Antigonus, see Ulrich Wilamowitz-Moellendorf, *Antigonus von Karystos* (Berlin: Weidmann, 1881).

considerable (*Eminent Philosophers* 2:125-44).[9] Persaeus died in a military position in the service of his king while commandant at Corinth.[10] Another Stoic philosopher, Sphaerus (fl. ca. 220 B.C.E.), who also wrote a tractate "On Kingship," served in the court of the Ptolemies. An anecdote is told of how the king presented Sphaerus with a waxen pomegranate and thus sought—unsuccessfully, as it turned out—to refute the thesis of the contemporary Stoic philosopher Chrysippus (ca. 282-206 B.C.E.) that it was impossible for a sage to hold false opinions (*Eminent Philosophers* 7:177). The prolific Chrysippus—more than 705 writings in logic, grammar, linguistics, rhetoric, and ethics were attributed to him (*Eminent Philosophers* 7:180)—declined the invitation of the Ptolemies, as did his teacher, Cleanthes (ca. 351-232 B.C.E.), and dedicated none of his work to a king (*Eminent Philosophers* 7:185). Plutarch in his treatise, *The Self-Contradictions of the Stoics*, would later castigate Zeno, Cleanthes, and Chrysippus for their failure to become involved in political affairs and to settle for dealing with it only on a theoretical plane.[11] This charge, however, is misleading if taken to apply to all the Stoics. Before the episode in Alexandria related above, Sphaerus served Cleomenes III (ca. 260-219 B.C.E.) in Sparta where, among other things, Cleomenes "made use of Sphaerus' talents to overhaul the Spartan educational system."[12] The recent intellectual historian F. L. Vatai expresses doubt whether the works of Sphaerus served also to instigate Cleomenes' social revolution,[13] but posits rather a different role for the philosopher, namely, that of legitimator: "as the mouthpiece of Cleomenes . . . he [Sphaerus] attempted to justify the royal revolution by historical arguments."[14]

9. W. W. Tarn, *Antigonos Gonatas* (Oxford: Clarendon, 1913; repr. in 1969) 21-27.

10. Vatai, *Intellectuals in Politics of the Greek World*, 126, who goes on to describe Persaeus as a jester, as well as a philosopher and soldier. Following L. Kowalski (*Marxism and Beyond* [London: Pall Mall, 1969] 55-56), Vatai defines a jester as one "who doubts all that appears self evident. . . . Jesters are more interested in the multiplicity of things 'often unrelated and even contradictory,'" taking the last phrase from Isaiah Berlin, *The Hedgehog and the Fox* (New York: Simon and Shuster, 1953) 1-2.

11. For further discussion on the subject, see Vatai, *Intellectuals in Politics of the Greek World*, 19-21.

12. Ibid., 126.

13. Ibid. Vatai lists, however, J. Bidez, F. Ollier, and W. W. Tarn as those who think Sphaerus was a revolutionary. Vatai also discusses the ambiguous role of the Stoic Blossius of Cumae on the social reforms of Tiberius Gracchus and the rebel king Aristonicus at Pergamum. In the latter he challenges A. J. Toynbee's designation of Blossius as "Marx's 'Hellenistic' prototype." Intellectuals, he holds, were followers rather than leaders.

14. Vatai has taken this quotation from E. N. Tigerstedt, *The Legend of Sparta in Classical Antiquity* (2 vols.; Stockholm: Almqvist and Wiksell, 1956-74), 2:73. This conclusion constitutes a rephrasing of the overall thesis and conclusion of Vatai's study of the role of the intellectual in politics: "It had [also] become a tradition that a king or a grandee have an intellectual at his elbow providing ideological and historical support" (p. 127).

The third school to send philosophers to Hellenistic courts was the Epicureans. Paradoxically, even though the Epicureans discouraged their followers from entering into public affairs, in the judgment of Plutarch (expressed in his biographies of Dion, Lycurgus, and Numa), this school had "the most to offer receptive men of power."[15] Philonides of Laodicea, mathematician and philologian, enjoyed favor in the courts of Antiochus IV Epiphanes (ca. 175–163 B.C.E.), Demetrius I Soter (ca. 163–150 B.C.E.), and Alexander Balas (ca. 150–145 B.C.E.).[16] It is also recorded of this philosopher that he appealed before Demetrius for the freedom of his city.[17] The historian of the Seleucids, E. Bikerman, records that under the influence of Philonides, Antiochus IV was converted to Epicureanism—a school for which at first he held repugnance.[18] As G. B. Kerferd has shown in his essay in this volume, Epicurus taught that the highest ideal for human beings should no longer be that of the sage in theoretical wisdom, "wise one" (sophos), but rather that of the sage in practical affairs, "prudent one" (phronimos).[19] Thus, the Epicurean Cineas, who is known more as diplomat than as philosopher, served in the court of Pyrrhus of Epirus (319–272 B.C.E.) as advisor and was sent once, possibly twice, to Rome to negotiate a peace.[20]

## THE WISE IN PRACTICAL AFFAIRS— COUNSELORS AND "FRIENDS"

Despite the prominence of purely theoretical philosophers in the Hellenistic royal courts, it would be mistaken to conclude that such were the only ones who served as counselors and confidants of the Hellenistic kings. Studies of the titulature of the bureaucracy of the Hellenistic court show that in the Antigonid kingdom of Macedonia as well as in the Seleucid and Ptolemaic kingdoms, the autocrat assembled about himself a group of persons who were called "friends of the king."[21] C. Bradford Welles notes: "By the term φίλος in the early Hellenistic period is often meant a member of the crown council."[22] As a result of

15. So Vatai, *Intellectuals in Politics of the Greek World*, 21.
16. So Bikerman, *Institutions de Séleucides*, 39. See also Vatai, *Intellectuals in Politics in the Greek World*, 123.
17. Vatai, *Intellectuals in Politics in the Greek World*, 123.
18. Bikerman, *Institutions de Séleucides*, 40.
19. G. B. Kerferd, "The Sage in Hellenistic Philosophical Literature (399 B.C.E.–199 C.E.)," pp. 319–28 below.
20. Vatai, *Intellectuals in Politics in the Greek World*, 123, and *The Oxford Classical Dictionary*, 193. Examples of philosophers serving as diplomats could be multiplied.
21. Leon Mooren, *The Aulic Titulature in Ptolemaic Egypt* (Verhandelingen van de Koninklijke Academie voor Wetensehappen, Letteren in Schone Kunsten van België, Klasse der Letteren 37 no. 78; Brussels: Paleis der Academiën, 1975) 1.
22. C. Bradford Welles, *Royal Correspondence in the Hellenistic Period: A Study in Greek Epigraphy* (New Haven: Yale University, 1934; repr. Chicago: Ares, 1974) 64.

his recent and thorough study of the Ptolemaic bureaucracy, Leon Mooren views the friends of the king as "a staff of close aides, counsellors and executive agents," which must be carefully distinguished from those who held the *honorific* titles of "friend," "first friend," "relative," or the like.[23] Three specific friends of the king of quite different character in Hellenistic Egypt may be mentioned who merit the designation of sage in the senses, respectively, of wise, shrewd, and skilled.

1. Demetrius of Phalerum (born ca. 350 B.C.E.), statesman and Peripatetic philosopher, had served as absolute governor of Athens for ten years before he was forced to flee the city. He ended up in the court of Ptolemy I as a friend of the king. There, it is recorded by the Roman historian Aelian, he "initiated a code of laws [*nomothesias ērxe*]"[24] and possibly gave oversight to the library under Ptolemy I.[25] Peter Fraser adduces evidence to show that "it is more than likely that he also advised Soter about the foundation and organization of the Mouseion."[26]

2. Sosibius, a friend of the king and highly influential adviser of Ptolemy IV Philopator (ca. 223–205/4 B.C.E.), is held to be largely responsible for turning the Egyptian army around so as to be able to inflict the defeat on the army of Antiochus III at Raphia in June 217 B.C.E. (Polybius 5:35.7–13; 36.2, 6; 37.11–12; 38.1, 3, 4, 6; 15:25.1–2). Evidently he worked his way up through the bureaucratic ranks, for under Ptolemy III Euergetes (247–221 B.C.E.) he served as a *logographos*, that is, as a prosewriter (or historian). In character he was ruthless and, from what is said of him by Polybius, dissolute.[27] After Raphia, as on other occasions, Sosibius served as envoy and negotiator for the king (Polybius 5:87.5, 8).

3. Agathocles, a partner with Sosibius in the training of an army for the encounter at Raphia (Polybius 5:63.1), was author of a commentary on king Ptolemy IV's play, "Adonis."

This sketch of the wise in theory (*sophos*) and practically sagacious (*phronimos*) in the Hellenistic courts may appropriately conclude with mention of the seventy-two young Jewish savants who utter wise

23. Mooren, *The Aulic Titulature in Ptolemaic Egypt*, 1–10.

24. See Fritz Wehrli, *Demetrios von Phaleron* (2nd ed.; vol. 4 of *Die Schule des Aristotles: Texte und Kommentar*; Basel: Schwabe, 1968) frag. 65 (p. 18). In passing it may be noted that Antigonus III Doson (ca. 263–221 B.C.E.) "employed a well-known member of the Peripatetic school, Prytanis, to draw up a code of laws for Megalopolis" (Polybius 5:93.8; Vatai, *Intellectuals in Politics in the Greek World*, 121).

25. Wehrli, *Demetrios von Phaleron*, 55. According to the pseudepigraphic *Letter of Aristeas* Demetrius was librarian under Ptolemy II Philadelphus.

26. Fraser, *Ptolemaic Alexandria*, 1:315. Demetrius was in disfavor with Ptolemy II because he had advised Ptolemy I Soter to name another son than Philadelphus as king (*Eminent Philosophers* 5:78).

27. According to F. W. Walbank, *A Historical Commentary on Polybius* (3 vols.; Oxford: Clarendon, 1957–79), 2:481, Polybius reveals considerable bias in his treatment.

apothegms in response to the king's queries on kingship, education, morality, and religion (*Letter of Aristeas* 187-92).[28] Interestingly these fictive sages extol the virtues of piety, self-control, and prudence very much in accord with Hellenistic morality.[29] The aspiring Judean intellectuals—and therefore the pseudonymous author who composed their replies—manage to sound terribly accommodating to the king and to Hellenistic values. It makes one wonder if there is not some truth in an anecdote that Pyrrho the sceptic took to heart when an Indian reproached his teacher Anaxarchus, telling him "that he would never be able to teach others what is good while he himself danced attendance on kings in their courts" (*Eminent Philosophers* 9:63).[30] On the other hand, it might be argued that the pious responses of the young sages very cleverly undercut the royal cult by stressing the power of God who is mentioned (and thus extolled) in every one of the seventy-two answers.[31]

28. The literature on *The Letter of Aristeas* is extensive. For an overview, see Oswyn Murray, "The Letter of Aristeas," *Studi Ellenistici II* (ed. B. Virgilio; Pisa: Giardini, 1986) 15-27; on its relationship to the Hellenistic kingship tractates, see idem, "Aristeas and Ptolemaic Kingship," *Journal of Theological Studies* 18 (1967) 337-71; and on its date and indebtedness to the Hebrew Scriptures, see my "The Hellenization of Jewish Wisdom in the Letter of Aristeas," *Proceedings of the Ninth World Congress of Jewish Studies* (Division A: The Period of the Bible; Jerusalem: World Congress of Jewish Studies, 1986) 207-14.

29. See John Ferguson, *Moral Values in the Ancient World* (London: Methuen, 1958), which singles out for special treatment in the Greek world the cardinal virtues, friendship, eros, humanitarianism, concord, and self-rule. In his final chapter on agape, Ferguson points (p. 230) to the occurrence of the word *agape* in *Letter of Aristeas* 229, but does not comment on the extent to which this work also reflects and summarizes the ancient morality he has been discussing.

30. In this regard it is interesting to note that Vatai comes to the conclusion that intellectuals in the ancient world were more often than not accommodating legitimators of those in power (*Intellectuals in Politics in the Greek World*, 130-32). In a recent book, *The Civilization of Christianity* (Chicago: Thomas More, 1986), John L. McKenzie makes a similar point with respect to contemporary intellectuals in the west.

31. With respect to the royal cult, two points may be noted: (1) it was more actively promoted in Ptolemaic Egypt than in the Seleucid kingdom, and (2) the gymnasia especially were the loci of celebration of the royal cult and hence centers for promoting "if not hellenization at least the cohesion of hellenism" among young males and those training for the army (see Préaux, *Le monde hellénistique*, 1:255-66. See also Bikerman, *Institution des Séleucides*, 236-57, and Martin P. Nilsson, *Die hellenistische Schule* (Munich: C. H. Beck, 1955) 83-97.

# THE SAGE IN FAMILY AND TRIBE

## Carole R. Fontaine

The location of the family and tribe as possible life-settings for the origin, use, and preservation of wisdom in Israel is well attested in the work of scholars, even where textual support is less than overwhelming. Despite the absence of specific terminology associated with sages and the wisdom movement in large portions of the Pentateuch and Deuteronomistic History, Claus Westermann and Erhard Gerstenberger in particular have pointed to the tribe/clan as a logical source for pre-monarchic wisdom traditions.[1] Viewing Israel's early folk traditions as containing urban as well as nomadic elements, Gerstenberger posits the "tribal ethos" and the extended family that valued it as one of the origins of the negative "prohibitive" form ($l\bar{o}^{\circ}$ + imperfect) that finds its way into the people's legal and cultic life (e.g., Leviticus 18, etc.).[2] Survey of the use of traditional sayings in the Deuteronomistic History provides additional evidence for this position. There one sees the purposeful transmission of "traditional sayings," generally consisting of one line rather than the two lines found in the polished literary sayings in Proverbs, used by persons in tribal leadership roles and others to defuse potentially violent situations (Judg 8:2, 21; 1 Sam 16:7, 24:14; 1 Kgs 20:11), providing a life-setting for the *use* of wisdom forms long before the literary traditions can be said to have taken final form.[3] The role of the family in Israel's wisdom traditions receives more direct support from the wisdom books themselves. Claudia Camp's recent work on the centrality of family life and concerns in the formulation of the

Carole R. Fontaine is Associate Professor of Old Testament at Andover Newton Theological School, Newton Centre, Massachusetts.

I wish to thank Jonathan Dean-Lee, Gerry Brague, and Sharon Bentley for their technical assistance in the preparation of this manuscript.

1. C. Westermann, "Weisheit im Sprichwort," *Schalom: Studien zu Glaube und Geschichte Israels* (Festschrift Alfred Jepsen; ed. K.-H. Bernhardt; Stuttgart, Calwer, 1971) 73-85; E. Gerstenberger, *Wesen und Herkunft des sogennanten 'apodiktischen Rechts' im Alten Testament* (WMANT 20; Neukirchen-Vluyn: Neukirchener, 1965).
2. Gerstenberger, *Wesen und Herkunft*, 110-19.
3. See my *Traditional Sayings in the Old Testament: A Contextual Study* (Bible and Literature 5; Sheffield: Almond, 1982).

literary figure of "Woman Wisdom" has advanced the understanding of how the ongoing institution of the patriarchal family shaped wisdom thinking and traditions.[4] Before considering in more detail the relation of the sage to these two life-settings, some preliminary remarks are in order.

## THE STATUSES AND ROLES OF SAGES

Since there is no direct evidence of anyone in the tribe and family formally called by the status designation "sage" (ḥākām),[5] my investigation will proceed by comparing the role expectations of the sage (as known from wisdom literature and extra-wisdom texts where sages appear performing "sage functions") to roles enacted within the family and tribe. A review of terminology used in role theory will aid in this consideration of Israelite society: a status or position is "a location in the social structure defined by expectations for performance by an incumbent"; and a role is the "organized set of behaviors that belongs to an identifiable position."[6] Both status and role may be ascribed (by means of age, sex, and kinship) or achieved (occupation, marriage), formalized or nonformalized, public or private. Role expectations, then, are the "rights and privileges, the duties and obligations, of any occupant of a social position (status) in relation to persons occupying other positions in the social structure," with the particular "role set" of a status referring to the entire set of complementary roles associated with the position in question.[7]

From the perspective of role theory, it is clear that the status of sage in Israel is an achieved one (that is, no one is born wise), with varying role expectations and role sets depending upon the social context in which it is played out. One would expect that a sage functioning in a well-defined, formalized, public position in the royal court or postexilic academy might operate in quite a different fashion than those filling the nonformalized role of sage in family or tribe. A role set appropriate to the king's counselor may be wholly out of place in the family, and vice versa. Similarly, the role set of the sage may be constrained by gender role expectations, based on the sage's sex (that is,

4. C. Camp, *Wisdom and the Feminine in the Book of Proverbs* (Bible and Literature 11; Sheffield: Almond, 1985).

5. For a survey of wisdom terminology appearing in the Hebrew Bible, see R. N. Whybray, *The Intellectual Tradition in the Old Testament* (BZAW 135; Berlin: de Gruyter, 1974).

6. T. Sarbin and V. Allen, "Role Theory," *The Handbook of Social Psychology* (3d ed.; ed. G. Linzey and E. Aronson; New York: Random House, 1985), 1:551, 545.

7. Ibid., 497-98.

in a patriarchal society one would not expect to see a female sage acting with the same autonomy or in the same social domains as her male counterpart).

The set of roles of the sage I will be investigating with respect to tribe and family includes the following: (1) teaching (Prov 1:2-6, etc.), (2) counseling (Prov 12:15, 15:22, 19:20, 20:18, 24:6, 25:15; 2 Sam 14-17; Job 29:21; etc.), (3) planning, especially in the sense of managing economic resources (Prov 19:15; 21:5, 22; 24:30-34; 27:23-27; 31:10-31; Qoh 2:4-8; Isa 28:23-29), and (4) settling disputes, particularly through the apt use of language and discernment (Prov 11:9, 16:23, 20:5, 24:23a-26, 31:8-9; Job 29:7-17, 31:13). Since the last two functions overlap general role expectations of those holding leadership positions in ancient society, they must be considered ancillary to the main functions of the sage, teaching and counseling.[8]

## THE FAMILY AND TRIBE

The patriarchal family is the basic unit of Israelite society, and this is true in all periods: the "tribal" settlement period, later monarchic, or postexilic times. The *bêt ʾāb*, or 'father's house', was the nuclear family, consisting of a father, his spouse(s), unmarried children, married sons and their families, and widowed daughters. Potentially, it might also include older (patrilateral) widowed or disadvantaged family members, clients, and slaves. In the earliest periods, the patriarch's power over the life of the family was absolute, as biblical stories showing the father's ability to dispense death sentences or dispose of his children to his own advantage attest (Genesis 19, 21-22, 38:24; Judges 11, 19; etc.). Later law codes limit the father's power somewhat, with Israel's more humanitarian values extending even to the treatment of female slaves, the "disposable" persons of the ancient Near East (Exod 21:7-11, etc.). The nuclear family might span up to three or four generations, and tended to break up with the death of the patriarch, as each married son began his own *bêt ʾāb*.

The *bêt ʾāb*, in turn, is grouped into clanlike *mišpāḥôt*, or (extended) 'families' sharing the same lineage and usually the same general geographical location, though the process underlying the formation of a *mišpāḥâ* is considerably more complex than a simple addition of local *bêt ʾābs*. Groupings of *mišpāḥôt* create the largest unit, the tribe (*šēbeṭ*

---

8. These are not the only behaviors falling within the sage's role set, but rather those most relevant to the social contexts under consideration. One might add authorship, redaction, administration, and other behaviors to those enacted by sages during various phases of Israel's history.

or *maṭṭeh*). All the tribes together constitute the largest political unit, the 'people' or 'tribes of Israel' (ʿam, šibṭê-yiśrāʾēl, bĕnê-yiśrāʾēl).[9] While the text occasionally shows some overlap and considerable fluidity in the use of these terms, one must envision here a network of ever-widening kinship ties that span the movement from the private domain (the *bêṯ ʾāḇ*) all the way to the public domain (ʿam / šibṭê- or bĕnê-yiśrāʾel). Within this scheme, the specifics of the role of the sage are colored by the context in which it is played out. In the private domain of the family, the role of sage is a nonformalized one; in the public domain of the tribe, it tends to become more formalized, as part of the expectations of those enacting the role of "elder."

It should be noted here that it is hardly likely that Israel's kinship networks, whether exemplified by the father's house or tribe, remained unchanged over time, even though they will be treated synchronically in the remarks that follow. As broad societal changes occurred, the impact was surely felt on family and tribe alike. The development of the monarchy with its rising classes of merchants and bureaucrats, and increasing urbanization had an ongoing negative effect on Israel's old tribal organizations. This in turn would have affected certain aspects of family life as land increasingly became concentrated in the hands of a few. In economic terms, the movement from a reciprocal, redistributive mode of production in the tribe to a (monetized) militarized economy under a centralized state must also have affected the institution of the family, producing among other things an increase in debt-slaves. Likewise, the impact of the Exile and Restoration on family organization must have been great, as is hinted at in texts of this period. Future studies on the family in Israel must attempt to delineate exactly how the changes in the sociopolitical and economic fortunes of the nation affected these basic living units, rather than viewing the institution as monolithic and unchanging over time and space. Similarly, attention to the *way* in which a text relates to the society it depicts is critical, since it cannot be assumed that the social data provided in any given text are actual representations of how the society operated unless the literary complex under consideration has been assessed positively for its "cultural verisimilitude."

## THE SAGE IN THE FAMILY

The role of the sage in the family is related primarily to the authority held by the father as head of the household. One of the obligations of

9. L. Stager, "The Archaeology of the Family in Ancient Israel," *BASOR* 260 (1985) 1–36; J. Liver, "The Israelite Tribes," *The World History of the Jewish People* (ed. B. Mazar; Israel: Jewish History Publications, 1971), 3:183–211.

this position is the instruction of sons, both in the religious traditions of the group (Exod 10:2, 12:26; Deut 4:9, 6:7, 20:21; etc.), and in preparation for a useful trade. This perspective on the father as teacher/sage underlies the frequent use of forms of address such as "my son/your father" found in Proverbs and elsewhere (Prov 1:8, 10, 15; 2:1; 3:1, 11, 21; etc.; Sir 2:1; 3:1, 17; 4:1; etc.). The "instruction" form so popular in Proverbs 1-9, while certainly deriving in part from Egyptian courtly origins, recalls the familial setting for teaching as it makes use of the parent/child imagery to describe the relationship between sage and student. Further, the association of wisdom teachings with the instructions learned from one's father comes to serve as an important locus of the authority of wisdom literature,[10] as seen in the authorizing statements introducing the instruction found in Prov 4:1-9:

> Listen, O sons, to a father's instruction [mûsar];
>     pay attention, so as to know insight [bînâ];
> for good precepts I give to you;
>     my teaching [tôrātî] do not forsake!
> For I was a son to my father,
>     tender and unique in my mother's sight,
> and he used to teach me, and told me,
>     "Let your heart grasp my words,
>     keep my commandments and live." (vv 1-4)

An unbroken line of knowledge proven to enhance the fullness of life for all is envisioned here as being passed from father to son within a family context. So strong is the authority of such teachings growing out of the life of the family that it continues to operate as a motivation to the student even when the instruction has been encoded literarily and housed within "scripture." It may well be that within the scriptural wisdom traditions, the familial terminology for direct address ("my son," "your father," "my child," etc.) has become dislodged from its (possible) original setting in the family and now functions to designate social roles within the new contexts of the academy and court.

Beyond the role of sage as family teacher, one might extrapolate other more "public," extended functions of the sage as counselor, planner, and settler of disputes likewise at work at the private level of family interaction. As one holding final authority over the life of the family, such activities would have been part of the normal behavior expected of a father. Though it is difficult to assess their historicity, accounts in Genesis and Job round out the picture of the father as sage. Abraham is shown settling disputes over land usage (both within and

10. J. Williams, *Those Who Ponder Proverbs: Aphoristic Thinking and Biblical Literature* (Bible and Literature 2; Sheffield: Almond, 1981) 26-28.

outside of the family unit) and inheritance, as well as giving counsel on securing the right bride for the heir of his house (Gen 12:8-12, 16:6, 21:25, 24:1-9). Similarly, Job's references to his former life in the "Oath of Innocence" (Job 31) depict him fulfilling roles one might typically associate with the sage in the family: he hears and settles servant's complaints (vv 13-15), sees to the distribution of goods to the poor (vv 16ff.), and manages family land properly (vv 38-39). It is not unlikely that many of these routine duties of the head of the household came to influence the conception of the roles played by elders in the tribe and city and eventually those of the sages of the royal courts and later schools.

So far, I have discussed the father and his authority as the major source of "sage functions" performed within the patriarchal family. However, the exclusion of the mother and her roles from considerations is hardly possible, given the considerable textual support for the "mother as sage" in the wisdom materials themselves (Prov 1:8; 6:20; 30:17; 31:1-9, 10-31; Job 2:9-10). Not only is the patriarchal household gynocentric, relying on the unpaid labor of women for its survival, but women played a signal role in the formation of the kinship ties that sustained and shaped tribe and family alike. As one noted anthropologist has commented, the exchange of women as marriage partners is the glue that holds tribal societies together.[11] Exogamous kinship systems may play a negative role in the pan-culturally observed low status of women by perpetuating the ongoing reification of women as commodities to be traded for their reproductive services. In the same vein, tribal kinship systems also tend to enhance the view of "woman as other," since the proper bride must not be *too* closely related to the group into which she marries. However, in this setting, the "gluey-ness" and "otherness" of women in the patriarchal family actually serve to form a power base for the wisdom of the mother.

The roles played by women in the patrilineal, patrilocal, patriarchal family all tend to be mediating ones, based on her lower status as female: women are traded as marriage partners, and remain outsiders until the production of children, preferably sons. With the birth of her child, the woman becomes the mother of a tribe/family member and moves away from her previous status as outsider.[12] Her allegiance is given to the son who will further her own survival interests (for ex-

11. C. Lévi-Strauss, *The Elementary Structures of Kinship* (rev. ed., Boston: Beacon, 1969). See also E. Janeway, "Who is Sylvia? On the Loss of Sexual Paradigms," *Women: Sex and Sexuality* (ed. C. R. Stimpson and E. S. Person; Chicago: University of Chicago, 1980) 4-20.

12. E. Leach, *Culture and Communication* (Cambridge: Cambridge University, 1976) 74-75.

ample, Rebecca's attachment to Jacob in Genesis 27), and she is motivated as well by the desire to advance the position of her child and
spouse within the extended family. As someone from outside the immediate group in question, she is a functional "native" of two groups:
her original kinship group and the one into which she has married. This
gives her access to *two* stocks of family wisdom, and her initial out-
group "observer" status may well provide her with a special vision of
the needs and predilictions of her new household. The manifold com-
petences requiring mastery in order to run the household successfully
similarly enhance the perception of her wisdom (Prov 31:10–31). In
sum, the mother has the background, the knowledge, the motivation,
and the occasion to assume authority within the private domain of the
family.

Such authority often falls into the area of "unassigned power" and
may not seem as noteworthy as the "assigned power" reserved to men
in patriarchal societies, but it exists nevertheless. Ancient Israel raised
the role and authority of the mother to a new level when compared to
her ancient Near Eastern neighbors, as exemplified in law codes where
offenses against the mother are judged as seriously as those against the
father (Exod 21:15, 17; etc.). While scholars may well view this exaltation of the mother as the natural outgrowth of Israel's increasing tendency to limit women's involvement in roles found in the public
domain (that is, restriction of women's participation in the cult, property ownership, legal matters, governments, etc.), it means that those
in wisdom studies may not reduce the prominence of the mother in the
text to mere occurrences of parallelism that fill out paternal imagery.
The "torah of your mother" is just as real and as binding as the
"instruction of your father" (Prov 1:8).

The mother's role as sage, like the father's, is rooted in her authority over the child. The early education and socialization of children,
both male and female, belonged to the mother, and was enforced
through the close bond forged between mother and child in societies
where children are not weaned until the age of three or four. As boys
grew older, their education was entrusted to the men of the household,
while girls continued to be trained by their mothers. For children of
both sexes, though, the early experiences of trust and learning must
have been, like the household itself, exceedingly "woman-centered."
Considering this primal, natal tie it becomes less astonishing that wisdom itself, like torah, should come to be personified as female. Likewise, the occurrence of the father/mother word pair in numerous
proverbs (Prov 10:1; 15:20; 20:20; 23:22, 25; 28:24; 30:11, 17) should
occasion no surprise, given both parents' share in the venture of raising
and teaching a child.

It is known from Mesopotamian cultures that royal daughters destined for diplomatic marriages were often given a fair degree of education, since it would enable them to serve as liasons and information-gatherers for their fathers. Such education also ensured their successful performance of the duties of palace administration, which often fell to royal wives.[13] It is not unthinkable that older women (royal mothers? nurses? low-level palace administrators?) would have served as tutors for some of this training, suggesting a possible role for women in "formal education" in addition to their traditional function of care-giving and teaching for toddlers and older girls. Unfortunately, the data do not permit more than speculation on this point, and given Israel's rejection of the office of "queenship" as found in other lands, [14] it seems unlikely that women's involvement in higher levels of education was common. Such a reconstruction, however, does shed light on the presence of an instruction by a royal mother preserved in Prov 31:1-9.

Along with the mother's role as teacher, women in Israelite families filled the extended roles of the sage noted in connection with the father. For women, the role of counselor must be seen in connection with their lack of direct, assigned power. The crafty use of language and the pressure exerted by such activities as "gossip" are typical of those whose status does not permit direct action to achieve their goals. Where a father may command those he counsels to follow his advice, a mother must cajole (cf. the very different modes of self-presentation used by David and Bathsheba in 1 Kings 1-2). Only in the most extreme, emergency situations does the wife-counselor act independently of her husband: Abigail may well be the voice of reason in her household, but when she appears before men of superior status she knows her place well enough to behave in a conciliating fashion (1 Samuel 25). The status held by those she counsels, relative to her own status, often has a decisive effect on the success of the mother's activities when she "opens her mouth with wisdom" (Prov 31:26a): sons *may* feel obliged to listen, husbands need not (Gen 27:5-14, Job 2:9-10).

One must move to the public domain to see women settling disputes (2 Samuel 14, 20:14-22),[15] but Rebecca's astute handling of the rift between Jacob and Esau in Genesis 27 suggests that this public role of the sage may also find its roots in family life. One can easily imagine that the ever-available mother is the first court of appeal for the settling of disputes among the nursery set. The function of wife-mother as sage-

---

13. G. Lerner, *The Creation of Patriarchy* (Oxford, Oxford University, 1986) 67-68.

14. A. Brenner, *The Israelite Woman: Social Role and Literary Type in Biblical Narrative* (Sheffield: JSOT Press, 1985) 17-32.

15. See C. Camp's essay, "The Female Sage in Ancient Israel and in the Biblical Wisdom Literature" (pp. 185-204 below).

planner and manager of economic resources is amply rehearsed in the celebration of the "woman of worth" in Prov 31:10–31. Though her own public participation "in the gates" of her people is limited, at least the praises sung there by her menfolk resist the total eclipse of the sage-mother outside the home.

## THE SAGE IN THE TRIBE

The heads of individual "father's houses" serve as the 'elders' (zĕqēnîm) of the extended family (mišpāḥâ) and tribe. Although the strength and autonomy of tribal organization were severely limited by the transition to a monarchy, the elders persisted as leaders of local municipalities (Deuteronomy 19, 21, 22, 25; 1 Sam 30:26–31; 1 Kgs 21:8; 2 Kgs 10:1, 5; 23:1). As is the case with many of the terms referring to Israel's social organization, the term elder often overlaps with other leadership terminology (especailly śārîm 'princes', as in Num 22:4f., Judg 8:6ff., etc.), seeming at times to designate the entire adult male population (Joshua 24). The functions of the elders are diverse, varying with the social context in which they are found: they stand in metonymic relationship to the whole people in political and religious activity, acting as their representatives (Exod 3:16, Deut 5:23, etc.); they appear in the company of leaders as counselors and companions when these exercise authority (Exod 3:18, Josh 7:6, etc.); they act as a governing body (Josh 9:11, 1 Sam 11:3, etc.; they serve as part of the king's royal council (2 Sam 17:4, 1 Kgs 20:11ff., etc.); and they act as a judicial body (Josh 20:4, Deut 19:12, Ruth 4:2ff., etc.).[16]

The association of elders with wisdom begins symbolically in Num 11:16ff. when God empowers seventy elders to share Moses' administrative and judicial burdens by taking some of the spirit resting upon that prophet and putting it upon them as well (cf. Exodus 18). Psalm 105 states that Joseph was made lord of Pharaoh's house in order to instruct his elders in wisdom (vv 21–22). Job 12:12 makes more explicit the source of the elders' wisdom: longevity ("wisdom is with the aged, and understanding in length of days"). However, such wisdom earned in long years of observation is not proof against the freedom and wrath of Israel's God: in Job 12:20 the Lord removes discernment from the elders, and counsel perishes from the elder in Ezek 7:26. Given that the elders appear, along with the śārîm, as oppressors of the people in Isa 3:14, they cannot expect their wisdom to afford them any special protection against the Lord who comes to judge.

Textual support is evident for the elders' enactment of the role set of the sage extrapolated from wisdom literature. It is evident, however,

16. J. McKenzie, "The Elders in the Old Testament," *Biblica* 40 (1959) 523–27.

that the shift from the private domain of the family to the public sphere of the *mišpāḥâ* and tribe has altered the weight given to each role played by the elder. Where the teaching role was primary in the consideration of the mother and father as sage, it is less prominent in the activities of the elder, though I assume that when elders are present for the reading of the law or in other circumstances, they are expected to instruct the people in the proceedings at a later time (Exod 12:21-27, Deut 31:9, Josh 8:33). Elders appear as counselors to Rehoboam and "the king of Israel" (Ahab?) in 1 Kgs 12:6-11 and 1 Kgs 20:7-12 respectively. Elders take part in economic, military, and "governmental" planning in Num 22:4-7; Judg 8:5-6, 14, 16; 11:5-11; 1 Sam 8:4; and 2 Sam 3:17. The settling of disputes seems to figure most heavily in the role expectations of the elder, and this behavior is one of those most frequently emphasized in the elder's role set. Elders are seen at work rendering decisions and enacting judicial functions in Deut 19:12, 21:19, 22:13-21, 25:7-8; Josh 20:4; Ruth 4; and Jer 26:17-19.

It should be noted that some of the roles associated with the sage are enacted by tribal leaders as well as by those occupying the position of elder. Jethro, the priest of Midian, counsels Moses (v 19) on the proper delegation of his authority for the settling of disputes in Exodus 18. Gideon directs an apt traditional saying to the Ephraimites, thereby defusing a nasty confrontation over the distribution of spoil (Judg 8:2), and David similarly engages in "proverb performance" to try to reimage his dispute with Saul in 1 Sam 24:13 [MT 24:14]. Obviously, a person's ability to play the role of the sage when needed enhances the overall perception of one's capacity for leadership, and must be considered an essential prerequisite for success. The well-known association of wisdom with kingship probably owes as much to this dynamic as it does to the royal ideology of wisdom as a divine gift to the king.

## CONCLUSION

While there is no conclusive textual evidence of a formalized position of sage in operation within the family and tribe, there is ample evidence that many of the roles associated with the sage are carried out by heads of households, mothers, elders, and other tribal leaders. Within the private sphere of the family, the most important sage roles are those that emphasize teaching, and these fall equally to father and mother. In the public realm of the tribe, the settling of disputes and planning/counseling functions predominate. It is not improbable that the way these roles were enacted in family and tribal life came to influence the conception of the later, more formalized roles of the sage in court and school.

# THE SAGE IN SCHOOL
AND TEMPLE

## André Lemaire

The search for the social groups who produced the wisdom tradition in the Bible is a difficult task, because very little is known about the life and institutions of ancient Israelite society during the Old Testament period.[1] The biblical text is clearly the main source, but it is often difficult to analyze historically. There are only a few pieces of explicit evidence that derive from Palestinian archeology, mainly in the form of paleo-Hebrew and Aramaic inscriptions, as well as hints in the ancient Near Eastern texts and pictures. Subsequently, it is little wonder that the quest for the social setting of the sages has long been and continues to be a matter of considerable debate among scholars.

Did the sages live in a rural or in an urban society? Were their sayings spoken in the family, tribe, court, temple, or school? Who wrote down the biblical wisdom tradition and when? When and where were these texts quoted, read, copied, and eventually commented upon? Scholars have sometimes tried to answer these questions in a systematic, if not in a comprehensive manner, and, countering thesis with thesis, they sometimes have not taken seriously enough the fact that ancient Israelite society was somewhat diversified. If many Israelites and Judeans lived on farms or in small villages, others resided in towns or even in the capital. There were the poor and the rich, and probably many others who considered themselves neither rich nor poor. Many were farmers, but others worked in the administration, judiciary, and army. Others were artisans and merchants. Wise people were probably found at all levels of Israelite society, and the biblical wisdom tradition may have been connected with all of them in some fashion, though probably not in the same way.

André Lemaire is Directeur d'études of Ecole Pratique des Hautes Etudes, IVe section (Paris-Sorbonne).

1. See R. de Vaux, *Ancient Israel: Its Life and Institutions* (2 vols; New York: McGraw-Hill, 1965).

Sirach 38:24–39:11 suggests that among the various social groups sages played a peculiar and important role in the shaping of the wisdom tradition:

A scholar's [sôpēr] wisdom increases wisdom [ḥokmâ],
   and the one who is not involved in business may become wise.
How can one become wise who holds the goad? (Sir 38:24–25)

How different it is with the one who devotes himself to
   and studies the instruction [tôrâ] of the Most High,
who investigates [yidroš] all the wisdom of the forefathers. (Sir 39:1)[2]

Without denying the role of wisdom of other settings, including the family or the court, my concern is to understand the part played by the school and the temple in the formation of the biblical wisdom tradition. Only then may a complete and precise picture of both the function of the sage in ancient Israel and the setting of the wisdom books be developed.

## THE SAGE IN THE SCHOOL

Come to me senseless people,
   and lodge in my school [bêt midrāšî]. (Sir 51:23)

This exhortation of the sage, Jesus son of Sira, clearly reveals that he was a teacher in his own school. This first evidence of the Hebrew expression for school, bêt midrāš ('house of research/ learning') may be dated ca. 190–175 B.C.E.,[3] and clearly demonstrates that, by this time, there were schools in Jerusalem where one could learn traditional Israelite wisdom. Furthermore, the Book of Ecclesiasticus is a textbook that contains the teaching of the master, Jesus son of Sira. One may compare this book to Ecclesiastes, "the words of Qoheleth," which is also clearly a textbook containing the teaching of another Jewish master, probably living in Jerusalem during the third century B.C.E.: "Qoheleth was a sage [ḥākām], and he taught knowledge to the people" (Qoh 12:9).

These two, rather late, biblical books clearly show that Israelite wisdom was taught by sages in the context of a school by at least the third and early second centuries B.C.E. Now the question is whether this is a late phenomenon, or whether it may be traced back to the First

2. For the Hebrew text of Ben Sira, see M. Segal, Sefer Ben Sira hashalem (2d ed.; Jerusalem: Bialik, 1972).
3. See E. Schürer, The History of the Jewish People in the Age of Jesus Christ (175 B.C.-A.D. 135 (ed. G. Vermes, F. Millar, and M. Goodman; Edinburgh: T. & T. Clark, 1986), 3.1:198–212.

Temple period. Some scholars have expressed their skepticism over the effort to trace the school back to this earlier period, because the Hebrew expression *bêt midrāš* is not elsewhere attested in the Bible. Thus, for example, R. N. Whybray thinks that "the evidence for the existence of schools with professional teachers in Israel, at any rate until late times, is, then, not conclusive."[4] Similarly J. L. Crenshaw has argued that "the bulk of education may very well have taken place in the family setting," though he recognizes that "it seems unwise to insist that all education occurred in the home, despite the paucity of evidence for royal schools"; and finally concedes that "in all probability" Israelite education was far richer than his "minimal perspective."[5]

This negative, somewhat skeptical position does not seem to be held by most scholars. In the twentieth century many have dealt with the problem of schools in ancient Israel: A. Klostermann, P. Riessler, S. Herner, L. Dürr, H. J. Hermisson, A. Demsky, and B. Lang—and their conclusions were largely positive.[6] I myself have tried to show that new evidence from paleo-Hebrew inscriptions confirms the existence of schools in ancient Israel during the First Temple period.[7] However, before presenting the main arguments in favor of the existence of schools during the First Temple period, it seems wise to clarify the issues in the scholarly debate by avoiding four misconceptions.

First, one must not think that ancient Israelite schools were similar to modern schools. One must think instead of something close to either the traditional Koranic and Jewish schools or the classical Greek and Latin schools. The teaching of the master could occur in a room, in his

---

4. R. N. Whybray, *The Intellectual Tradition in the Old Testament* (BZAW 135; Berlin: de Gruyter) 43. Cf. also F. Golka, "Die israelitische Weisheitsschule oder 'des Kaiser neue Kleider,'" *VT* 33 (1983) 257–70.

5. Crenshaw, "Education in Ancient Israel," *JBL* 104 (1985) 614. Cf. also E. Lipiński, "Royal and State Scribes in Ancient Jerusalem," *Congress Volume: Jerusalem 1986* (ed. J. A. Emerton; VTSup 40; Leiden, Brill, 1988) 157–64.

6. A. Klostermann, "Schulwesen im alten Israel," *Theologische Studien* (Theodor Zahn Festschrift; by N. Bonwetsch et al.; Leipzig: Deichert, 1908) 193–232; P. Riessler, "Schulunterricht im Alten Testament," *Theologische Quartalschrift* 91 (1909) 606–7; S. Herner, "Erziehung und Unterricht in Israel," *Oriental Studies* (Paul Haupt Festschrift; ed. C. Adler and A. Embler; Baltimore: Johns Hopkins, 1926) 58–66; L. Dürr, *Das Erziehungswesen im Alten Testament und im antiken Orient* (Mitteilungen der vorderasiatisch-ägyptischen Gesellschaft 36.2; Leipzig: Hinrichs, 1932); H. J. Hermisson, *Studien zur israelitischen Spruchweisheit* (WMANT 28; Neukirchen-Vluyn: Neukirchener, 1968) 97–136; A. Demsky, "Education in the Biblical Period," *Encyclopaedia Judaica* (Jerusalem: Keter, 1971), 6:382–98; B. Lang, "Schule und Unterricht im alten Israel," *La sagesse de l'Ancien Testament* (ed. M. Gilbert; BETL 51; Gembloux: Duculot, 1979) 186–201.

7. See my *Les écoles et la formation de la Bible dans l'ancien Israël* (OBO 39; Göttingen: Vandenhoeck und Ruprecht, 1981). See also my "Sagesse et écoles," *VT* 34 (1984) 270–81.

private house,[8] in a public building, in a public place (city gate, portico, marketplace, etc.),[9] or even in the open air (under a tree or in the corner of a courtyard).

Second, one may distinguish between wisdom texts and didactic texts.[10] In a school, one may teach many other subjects in addition to wisdom: for example, reading, writing, mathematics, history, geography, etc. However, it is clear that wisdom may be one of the subjects taught in a school, as attested by Jesus son of Sira and Qoheleth. In the higher levels of education, the wisdom teacher may even be one who is a master of philosophy or ethics. Even if a wisdom text may be didactic and used as a textbook, not all didactic texts are wisdom texts.

Third, according to Crenshaw,

> It would be less confusing to speak in terms of wisdom literature, *paideia*, and *ḥokmah*. The first would refer to Prov, Qoh, Job, Sir, Wisd of Sol, and Wisdom Pss; *paideia* would suggest the wisdom movement itself, its educational curriculum and pedagogy; *ḥokmah* would indicate a particular stance, an approach to reality.[11]

Thus, there were wise people who were not associated with wisdom schools and their teachings, even as there are wise sayings that existed outside the textbooks of wisdom schools.

Fourth, the family, tutoring, and the school may have been contemporaneous methods of education that were not exclusive of the others. For instance, a priest may have taught his own children as well as those of others. Even in the modern period, when schools are almost universal, education may be supplemented by the use of private tutors, especially in the homes of the affluent.

With these various distinctions in mind, I shall argue that schools existed in ancient Israel during the First Temple period. This may be inferred from the existence of schools in neighboring cultures, from a few paleo-Hebrew inscriptions, from several suggestive hints in the Bible, and from the literary character of certain biblical texts.

Schools are attested in Mesopotamia and Egypt as early as the third millennium B.C.E.[12] The synthesis by H. Brunner treating education in Egypt underscores very clearly the importance of schools in that

8. See H. M. I. Gevaryahu, "Privathäuser als Versammlungsstätten von Meister und Jüngern," *Annual of the Swedish Theological Institute* 12 (1981) 5–12.

9. See B. Lang, *Wisdom and the Book of Proverbs* (New York: Pilgrim, 1986), esp. 22–33.

10. See my *Les écoles*, 45.

11. Crenshaw, "Method in Determining Wisdom Influence upon 'Historical' Literature," *JBL* 88 (1969) 130 n. 4 ( repr. in *SAIW* 482 n. 4).

12. For a detailed bibliography see my *Les écoles*, 94–95.

country, delineates their various levels of learning, and traces their development through the succeeding periods.[13] Even if we do not possess a similar synthesis for Mesopotamian schools, their existence is well attested, especially by the many schoolboy exercises, which were practically the same for centuries.[14] Similar schoolboy exercises were attested in Ugarit, in both cuneiform and alphabetic script.[15]

Schools in the neighboring cultures appear to have originated from the need to train scribes to work in the governmental bureaucracies.[16] In all probability there were schools in Israel for the same purpose of training future members of the royal administration, from as early as the time of David and Solomon. The suggested similarity to Egyptian schools is all the more interesting, since Egypt exerted a strong cultural

13. H. Brunner, *Altägyptische Erziehung* (Wiesbaden: Harrassowitz, 1957). Also see R. J. Williams, "Scribal Training in Ancient Egypt," *JAOS* 92 (1972) 214–21; U. Kaplony-Heckel, "Schüler und Schulwesen in der ägyptischen Spätzeit," *Studien zur altägyptischen Kultur* 1 (1974) 227–46; R. J. Williams, "Some Fragmentary Demotic Wisdom Texts," *Studies in Honor of George R. Hughes* (Chicago: Oriental Institute, 1976) 263–71; idem, "The Sages in Ancient Egypt," *JAOS* 101 (1981) 1–19; J. Debut, "Les documents scolaires," *Zeitschrift für Papyrologie und Epigraphik* 63 (1986) 251–78.

14. See Å. W. Sjöberg, "The Old Babylonian Edubba," *Sumerological Studies in Honor of T. Jacobsen* (AS 20; Chicago: University of Chicago, 1976) 159–79; A. Westenhold, "Old Akkadian School Texts," *AfO* 25 (1977) 95–110; H. Sauren, "e₂-dub-ba Literatur: Lehrbücher des Sumerischen," *Orientalia Lovaniensia Periodica* 10 (1979) 97–107; H. L. J. Vanstiphout, "How Did They Learn Sumerian?" *JCS* 31 (1979) 118–24; A. Cavigneaux, *Textes scolaires du temple de Nabû ša Harê* (Texts from Babylon 1; Baghdad: Republic of Iraq, 1981); idem, "Schultexte aus Warka," *Baghdader Mitteilungen* 13 (1982) 21–30; K. Deller, "SST 366: Deutungsversuch 1982," *Assur* 3/4 (1983) 3–17; R. S. Falkowitz, "Round Old Babylonian School Tablets from Nippur," *AfO* 29/30 (1983/84) 18–45; A. Cavigneaux et al., *The Series Erim-Ḫuš -anantu and An-ta-gál = šaqû* (Materials for the Sumerian Lexicon 17; Rome: Pontifical Biblical Institute, 1985); M. Civil, "Sur les 'livres d'écolier' a l'époque paléo-babylonienne," *Miscellanea babylonica* (ed. J. M. Durand and J. R. Kupper; M. Birot Festschrift; Paris: ADPF, 1985) 67–78; D. Charpin, *Le clergé d'Ur au siècle d'Hammurabi (XIXᵉ–XVIIIᵉ siècles av. J.-C.)* (Hautes études orientales 22; Geneva: Droz, 1986), esp. 419–86.

15. See J. P. J. Olivier, "Schools and Wisdom Literature," *Journal of Northwest Semitic Languages* 4 (1975) 49–60; M. Dietrich, O. Loretz, and J. Sanmartin, *Die keilalphabetischen Texte aus Ugarit* (Alter Orient und Altes Testament 24; Neukirchen-Vluyn: Neukirchener, 1976), nos. 402–7; A. Herdner, "Nouveaux textes alphabétiques de Ras Shamra—XXIVᵉ campagne, 1961," *Ugaritica* 7 (Paris: Geuthner/Leiden: Brill, 1978) 1–74; W. J. Horwitz, "The Ugaritic Scribe," *UF* 11 (1979) 389–94; D. Arnaud and D. Kennedy, "Les textes en cunéiformes syllabiques découverts en 1977 à Ibn Hani," *Syria* 56 (1979) 319–24.

16. See T. N. D. Mettinger, *Solomonic State Officials: A Study of the Civil Government Officials of the Israelite Monarch* (Coniectanea Biblica, Old Testament series 5; Lund: Gleerup, 1971) 140–57; J. Bright, "The Organization and Administration of the Israelite Empire," *Magnalia Dei: The Mighty Acts of God* (G. E. Wright Festschrift; ed. F. M. Cross, W. E. Lemke, and P. D. Miller; Garden City, NY: Doubleday, 1976) 193–208, esp. 203–4.

influence on Israel, demonstrated in part by the use of hieratic numerals in paleo-Hebrew writing.[17]

The existence of schools furthermore is required by the development of literacy toward the end of the Judean kingdom (ca. 600 B.C.E.). Due to the near absence of papyrus (which cannot normally be preserved because of the Israelite climate),[18] the numerous paleo-Hebrew ostraca,[19] seals, and bullas[20] show evidence of the spread of literacy in the Judean kingdom ca. 600 B.C.E. According to A. R. Millard, "Few places will have been without someone who could write, and few Israelites will have been unaware of writing."[21] Such a spread of literacy, well beyond the circle of professional scribes, would have been difficult to attain without the institution of schools. Although still few and often fragmentary, paleo-Hebrew inscriptions include several schoolboy exercises of the First Temple period: abecedaries,[22] words written twice, lists of proper names, formulas of blessings at the beginning of a letter, lists of months, lists of numerals and various units of weights and measures, and drawings.[23] As A. R. Millard has noted, "While far from the Babylonian evidence in scope and quantity, the West Semitic abecedaries and related epigraphs make the presence of schools in the first half of the first millennium B.C. somewhat less hypothetical than has been asserted."[24] Actually, since the more ad-

17. See Y. Aharoni, "The Use of Hieratic Numerals in Hebrew Ostraca and the Shekel Weights," *BASOR* 184 (1966) 13–19; I. T. Kaufman, "New Evidence for Hieratic Numerals on Hebrew Weights," *BASOR* 188 (1967) 39–41; Lemaire, *Inscriptions hébraïques*, vol. 1: *Les ostraca* (Littératures anciennes du Proche-Orient 9; Paris: Cerf, 1977), esp. 177–81; A. Lemaire and P. Vernus, "L'ostracon paléo-hébreu n° 6 de Tell Qudeirat (Qadesh-Barnéa)," *Fontes atque Pontes: Eine Festgabe für H. Brunner* (ed. M. Görg; Ägypten und Altes Testament 5; Wiesbaden: Harrassowitz, 1983) 302–26.

18. See my "Von Ostraka bis zu Schriftrollen: Überlegungen über die Entstehung der Bibel," *XXII. Deutscher Orientalistentag: vom 21. bis 25. März 1983 in Tübingen* (ed. W. Röllig; Zeitschrift der Deutschen Morgenländischen Gesellschaft, Supplementa 6; Stuttgart: Franz Steiner, 1985) 110–23.

19. See *Inscriptions hébraïques*, vol. 1.

20. See my "Recherches actuelles sur les sceaux nord-ouest sémitiques," *VT* 38 (1988) 220–30.

21. A. R. Millard, "An Assessment of the Evidence of Writing in Ancient Israel," *Biblical Archaeology Today: Proceedings of the International Congress on Biblical Archaeology, Jerusalem, April 1984* (Jerusalem: Israel Exploration Society, 1985) 308.

22. See my "Abécédaires et exercices d'écolier en épigraphie nord-ouest sémitique," *Journal Asiatique* 266 (1978) 222–35.

23. See my *Les écoles*, 7–33.

24. Millard, "ᵓBGD . . . —Magic Spell or Educational Exercise?" *Eretz-Israel* 18 (1985) 41*. For a different view, see M. Haran, "On the Diffusion of Literacy and Schools in Ancient Israel," and E. Peuch, "Les écoles dans l'Israël préexilique: données épigraphiques"; both in *Congress Volume: Jerusalem 1986* (ed. J. A. Emerton; VTSup 40; Leiden: Brill, 1988) 81–95, 189–203.

vanced exercises were probably written on perishable papyrus and leather, one could not expect much more archeological evidence for the existence of schools in ancient Israel.

In turning to the Bible, there are a few hints that point to the existence of different types of schools during the First Temple period: royal schools (1 Kgs 12:8, 10; 2 Kgs 10:1, 5, 6; 2 Chr 17:7-9), some kind of "prophetic school" (2 Kgs 6:1-2, Isa 8:16), and schools associated with the temple (Isa 28:7-13, 2 Chr 22:11; cf. 2 Kgs 12:3).[25] Admittedly, these texts are only indirect evidence, and "in light of such ambiguous evidence within the Hebrew Bible, modern critics must decide whether the virtual silence about schools is because none existed or because they were so common that no one ever thought it necessary to mention what was obvious to all."[26] In light of the comparative and epigraphic evidence, the second alternative is clearly the more probable, since a similar reticence to refer to schools also characterizes Egyptian literature. As E. W. Heaton has noted,

> It is extraordinary that men as devoted to learning as the scribes of Egypt should have made so few explicit references to their schools and educational system. This reticence ought to encourage Old Testament scholars not to interpret the silence of their own documents in the usual negative way. Both in Egypt and in Israel, the best evidence for scribal education is its literary fruits and the existence of a complex bureaucracy.[27]

Finally a close examination of certain biblical texts suggests they may have been used as school texts. This is particularly the case for the Book of Proverbs, which

> may be the closest thing to an actual school text from the biblical period. Its explicit pedagogic goal, as well as its employment of mnemonic devices, supports this connection. The centrality of secular, royal figures (Solomon, Hezekiah, King Lemuel of Massa, "The Wise") and its affinities to non-Israelite wisdom literature further argue for its role in the education of the officialdom.[28]

Recently, in a comparative study of biblical (mainly Proverbs) and Egyptian wisdom literature, N. Shupak has shown that

> the vocabulary of the Biblical sages contains semantic equivalents of terms normally found in writings associated with Egyptian schools. . . . It would

25. See my *Les écoles*, 34-41.

26. Crenshaw, "Education in Ancient Israel," 603.

27. E. W. Heaton, *Solomon's New Men* (New York: Pica, 1975) 108.

28. A. Demsky, "Education (Jewish)," *Encyclopaedia Judaica* (Jerusalem: Keter, 1971), 6:395-96; cf. Lang, *Wisdom and the Book of Proverbs*, 15.

seem reasonable to assume, therefore, that the first schools in Israel were inspired by an Egyptian archetype; and that the Book of Proverbs—and especially its second collection—served as learning material in such schools.[29]

Although the final date of the Book of Proverbs is still a matter of dispute, the influence of the "Instruction of Amenemope" on Prov 22:17–23:12, as well as the importance of other literary contacts with the Egyptian wisdom tradition, could best be explained by a setting in either the Solomonic period or during the reign of Hezekiah.[30] Further, in my judgment this book is best understood as a wisdom teaching given in the context of a school, more precisely a royal school, during the First Temple period.

However, if there were schools in ancient Israel, that does not mean that the importance of this institution remained constant during the entire First Temple period,[31] that is, for more than four hundred years, from the time of David (ca. 1010–970 B.C.E.) to the fall of Jerusalem in 587 B.C.E. Indeed, paleo-Hebrew epigraphy reveals a development in the spread of literacy, which corresponds probably with an expansion of schools.[32] At the beginning of the first millennium B.C.E., paleo-Hebrew inscriptions are very few and extremely fragmentary. Correspondingly, there were probably very few schools, perhaps located in close proximity to the great sanctuaries, in the capitals, and in the chief towns of the provinces. From the eighth century on, the number of paleo-Hebrew inscriptions (mainly ostraca, seals, and bullas) begins to rapidly increase, and this development of the use of writing is probably to be explained by the increase in schools. Actually, 2 Chr 17:7–9 may well be an indication of some kind of royal teaching reform in Judah near the middle of the ninth century B.C.E. From the beginning of the eighth century to 587 B.C.E., schoolboy exercises have been found in royal outposts (Kuntillet ʿAjrud), fortresses (Qadesh-Barnea, Arad), and major towns (Lachish).

All of these schools were probably not of the same type. Most of them may have been "elementary schools" with a few pupils gathered around a teacher to learn reading, writing, and counting. The purposes

29. N. Shupak, "The 'Sitz im Leben' of the Book of Proverbs in the Light of a Comparison of Biblical and Egyptian Wisdom Literature," RB 94 (1987) 104, 117. However, Job 38–39 has probably nothing to do with Egyptian onomastica (see M. Fox, "Egyptian Onomastica and Biblical Wisdom," VT 36 [1986] 302–10).

30. Shupak, "The 'Sitz im Leben' of the Book of Proverbs," 118.

31. Thus, "the theory of a sudden 'cultural enlightenment' in the time of Solomon" may be accepted only with some reservation (see R. N. Whybray, "Wisdom Literature in the Reigns of David and Solomon," Studies of the Period of David and Solomon and Other Essays [ed. T. Ishida; Winona Lake, IN: Eisenbrauns, 1982] 18).

32. See my Les écoles, 45–48.

were to be able to read, write a letter or message, buy and sell, and measure harvests and rations. However, in Jerusalem there were probably schools of a higher level for the king's sons and the children of the great families in order to prepare them for important positions in the royal administration. In these royal schools, the future high officials were probably taught an international language (Phoenician or Aramaic) and, at least, rudiments of Hebrew literature, history, geography, and law, as well as some moral and civic teaching designed to help in both the difficult art of governing and in achieving success in personal and professional life. In other words, these students received some wisdom instruction,[33] and the Book of Proverbs seems very well suited for this kind of teaching. Many exhortations seem to suit teenagers, for example the warning about the "loose woman with her seductive words" (Prov 7:6ff. with the words "youths," "boys") and the importance of discipline (Prov 20:11, 22:15, 23:13) or education (Prov 1:4, 22:6). Other teachings in Proverbs appear to allude to the formation of future royal courtiers (cf. Prov 8:15-18, 16:10-15, 22:9, 25:2-15).[34] One also finds counsel for future landlords (Prov 10:5, 20:4, 27:23-27, 28:19) and leading citizens (Prov 13:4-11).

Wisdom teaching in the royal schools, and more generally in the Bible, seems to have been quite open to international contacts. Prov 22:17-23:12 is demonstrably dependent on the Egyptian "Instruction of Amenemope," while the "Sayings of Agur" (Prov 30:1-14) and the "Sayings of Lemuel" (Prov 31:1-9) appear borrowed from Transjordanian, probably Aramaic, wisdom collections.[35] Later on, Qoheleth and Ben Sira were at the same time traditional and yet open to the influence of Hellenistic and Egyptian wisdom.[36]

The Bible does not preserve the name of any wisdom teacher from the First Temple period.[37] However, the Egyptian parallels suggest that

33. Some wisdom instruction may have been given to school children in "elementary schools," perhaps in the form of proverbs or fables.

34. See R. Gordis, "The Social Background of Wisdom Literature," *HUCA* 18 (1944) 77-118; B. Kovacs, "Is There a Class-Ethic in Proverbs?" *Essays in Old Testament Ethics (In Memoriam J. P. Hyatt)* (ed. J. L. Crenshaw and J. T. Willis; New York: Ktav, 1974) 171-89, W. L. Humphreys, "The Motif of the Wise Courtier in the Book of Proverbs," *IW* 177-90; and B. V. Malchow, "A Manual for Future Monarchs," *CBQ* 47 (1985) 238-45.

35. See my "Aramaic Literature and Hebrew Literature: Contacts and Influences in the First Millennium B.C.E.," *Proceedings of the Ninth World Congress of Jewish Studies, Panel Sessions: Hebrew and Aramaic Languages* (ed M. Bar-Asher; Jerusalem: World Union of Jewish Studies, 1988) 9-24.

36. See I. von Loewenclau, "Kohelet und Sokrates—Versuch eines Vergleiches," *ZAW* 98 (1986) 327-38; and T. Middendorp, *Die Stellung Jesu Ben Siras zwischen Judentum und Hellenismus* (Leiden: Brill, 1973).

37. See the remarks below about the Shaphan family and the *liškôt* of the temple.

teachers in the royal school[38] were probably experienced officials who transmitted both traditional teaching and their own experience. From the biblical tradition as well as other ancient Near Eastern sources, the teacher was generally called "father" while he called his student "my son." More generally, the teacher was called *mōreh* 'instructor' (Prov 5:13), or *mĕlammēd* 'teacher' (cf. Prov 5:13, Ps 119:99). Of course, those in charge of the wisdom teaching (*tôrâ*:[39] Prov 28:4, 7, 9; 29:18) were known as sages (cf. *tôrat ḥākām* 'instruction of the wise' [Prov 13:14]; *dibrê ḥăkāmîm* 'the sayings of the sages' [Prov 1:6, 22:17; Qoh 9:17, 12:11; cf. Prov 12:18, 14:3, 15:27]), and the wisdom school was probably considered to be the house of the sages (cf. Prov 15:31, *bĕqereb ḥăkāmîm tālîn* 'you will lodge among the sages'; and Sir 51:23, *lînû bĕbêt midrāšî* 'lodge in my school'). Consequently, it is not astonishing that the term sage is attested more than forty times in Proverbs and that, in Jer 8:8, it is associated with the instruction (*tôrâ*) of God. If R. N. Whybray is right that people other than the wisdom teacher could be wise, he goes too far when he thinks that the term *ḥăkāmîm* in the Bible cannot be used for professional teachers.[40] For instance, Ben Sira clearly presents himself as a *ḥākām* and *sōpēr* (38:24, 50:27-28, 51:15),[41] while his book is "an instruction [*paideia*] of intelligence and knowledge" (50:27). In the same way, while anyone could certainly give advice, counsel (*ʿēṣâ*) was especially considered to reside within the domain of the sages (Jer 18:18) and the word could be used, along with *mûsār* and *leqaḥ* to indicate aspects of wisdom teaching (Prov 8:14, 19:20, etc.).

As was the case with other ancient schools, students in Israel probably had to pay to enjoy the benefit of this instruction. This may be suggested in Prov 4:7 (cf. also 3:14, 8:10, 16:16). While students sometimes had to copy parts of a textbook, teaching was essentially oral and traditional,[42] consisting of some kind of oral commentary on the proverb (*māšāl*), parable (*mĕlîṣâ*), sayings of the sages, and their riddles

38. See my *Les écoles*, 54-57.

39. On the use of this word for wise 'instruction' as well as priestly instruction, see J. Jensen, *The Use of tôrâ by Isaiah: His Debate with the Wisdom Tradition* (CBQMS 3; Washington, DC: Catholic Biblical Association, 1973); and my *Les écoles*, 76-77.

40. Whybray, *The Intellectual Tradition*, 31-48. See also J. Blenkinsopp, *Wisdom and Law in the Old Testament* (New York: Oxford University, 1983) 11: "The sages in Israel were primarily teachers."

41. See J. Marböck, "Sir. 38:24-39:11: Der schriftgelehrte Weise. Ein Beitrag zur Gestalt und Werk Ben Siras," *La sagesse de l'Ancien Testament* (ed. M. Gilbert; BETL 51; Gembloux: Duculot, 1979) 296-311.

42. The traditional character of wisdom teaching is evidenced by the books of Qoheleth and Sirah. However, their authors opened up new lines of thought with their own comments (see R. N. Whybray, "Conservatisme et radicalisme dans Qohelet," *Sagesse et religion* [Strasbourg: Presses Universitaires de France, 1979] 65-81; E. Jacob,

(*ḥîdotām*) (Prov 1:6). It is clear that most of the proverbs were not created by the wisdom teachers, but were taken from everyday life and popular wisdom, collected, shaped, and then commented upon. The original setting of most orally transmitted proverbs, riddles, and short numerical sayings was probably popular wisdom in a traditional society. They were transmitted, however, in another setting, the wisdom tradition in the schools where they were collected, placed in written form, and interpreted. The original setting of proverbs is traditional society, but the setting of written collections is the wisdom school.[43]

To make their teaching more effective, sages made use of a variety of pedagogic techniques, and they probably did not hesitate to use reprimand and beatings:

> Do not withhold discipline [*mûsār*] from a boy (*naᶜar*);
>   If you hit him with the stick [*šēbeṭ*], he will not die. (Prov 23:13)

> Rod and reprimand [*tôkaḥat*] impart wisdom,
>   But a boy who runs wild brings shame to his mother. (Prov 29:15; cf. 10:13, 29:17)

Actually, the rod and physical punishment are well attested in all the ancient schools. It was a way to obtain proper behavior,[44] especially by youths who were to become courtiers and royal functionaries. However, ancient teachers also used more positive pedagogic means. They stressed the importance of their teaching for the success of life[45] and made their teaching attractive and vivid with well balanced sentences, dialogues (cf. Job), stories (cf. Joseph), fables, proverbs and aphorisms, parables and riddles.[46] Many of these were easy to memorize, since they were characterized by key words, alliterations, acrostics, numerical series, and so forth.

---

"Sagesse et religion chez Ben Sira," ibid., 83–98; Whybray, "The Identification and Use of Quotations in Ecclesiastes," *Congress Volume: Vienna 1980* (ed. J. A. Emerton; VTSup 32; Leiden: Brill, 1981) 435–51.

43. See my "Sagesse et école," 271–72.

44. Proper behavior was one of the aims of education in the schools (see W. Richter, *Recht und Ethos: Versuch einer Ortung des weisheitliches Mahnspruches* [Studien zum Alten und Neuen Testament 15; Munich: Kösel, 1966]).

45. See P. Nel, "Authority in the Wisdom Admonitions," ZAW 93 (1981) 418–26.

46. On wisdom sentences see J. L. Crenshaw, "Wisdom and Authority: Sapiential Rhetoric and Its Warrants," *Congress Volume: Vienna 1980* (ed. J. A. Emerton; VTSup 32; Leiden: Brill, 1981) 10–29. On stories see H.-P. Müller, "Die Weisheitliche Lehrerzählung im A. T. und seiner Umwelt," *Die Welt des Orients* 9 (1977) 77–98; on the Joseph story see G. von Rad, "The Joseph Narrative and Ancient Wisdom," *The Problem of the Hexateuch and Other Essays* (Edinburgh/London: Oliver and Boyd, 1965) 292–300 (repr. in *SAIW* 439–47). On fables see E. Lipiński, "Ancient Types of Wisdom Literature in Biblical Narrative," *Essays on the Bible and the Ancient World* (ed. A. Rofé and

Thus far I have considered mainly the royal schools during the First Temple period. I shall put aside prophetic teaching, which was on occasion addressed to a general audience in a public place and at other times was intended for a small group of disciples in a type of philosophical or religious school,[47] and now turn to consider the problem of the relation of sages to the temple.

## THE SAGE IN THE TEMPLE

The exact location of the royal school(s) in Jerusalem is not known. It may well have been located within the royal palace or, since the temple was a royal institution, in an outbuilding or corner of the temple. The association of schools, libraries, and temples is well attested in Egypt,[48] and the famous discovery of the "book of the law/instruction" (*sēper hattôrâ*: 2 Kgs 22:8, 11) in the "house of the Lord" by the high priest Hilkiah (2 Kgs 22:23) could well hint at such a library in a room of the Jerusalem temple where archives and literary texts would be stored.[49] If the general assumption is correct that this book of the instruction was an early form of Deuteronomy, one may well think that books kept in this bookcase were connected not only with the temple and the priestly tradition, but also more generally with the entire Israelite literary tradition, and more specifically, in this case, with the juridical tradition. Indeed the deuteronomic tradition was connected explicitly with wisdom, since knowledge and practice of this book "will display your *wisdom* and understanding to other peoples. When they hear about these statutes, they will say, 'What a *wise* and understanding people this great nation is!'" (Deut 4:6).

The relation between Deuteronomy, the deuteronomic school, and wisdom literature has been carefully studied by M. Weinfeld. According to him, "The concept of education, so pronounced in Deuteronomy, also derives from the ideology of the sapiential scribes who served as

---

V. Zakovitch; Jerusalem: Rubenstein, 1983), 3:39–55. On proverbs and aphorisms see J. G. Williams, *Those Who Ponder Proverbs: Aphoristic Thinking and Biblical Literature* (Sheffield: Almond, 1981). On riddles see J. L. Crenshaw, "Questions, dictons et épreuves impossibles," *La sagesse de l'Ancien Testament* (ed. M. Gilbert; BETL 51; Gembloux: Duculot, 1979) 96–111.

47. On the prophetic schools, see B. Lang, *Wie wird man Prophet in Israel?* (Dusseldorf: Patmos, 1980) 31–58; and my *Les écoles*, 50–52.

48. See G. Burkard, "Bibliotheken im alten Ägypten," *Bibliothek* 4 (1980) 79–115; and my "Ecritures et langues du Moyen-Orient ancien," in A. Barucq et al., *Ecrits de l'Orient ancien et sources bibliques* (Petite Bibliothèque des Sciences Bibliques: Ancien Testament 2; Paris: Desclée, 1986) 9–57, esp. 38–41.

49. See V. Burr, *Bibliothekarische Notizen zum Alten Testament* (Bonn: Bouvier, 1969) 20.

the nation's teachers and educators: it is no coincidence that the verb
למד occurs only in Deuteronomy and in no other Pentateuchal book."[50]
Literary analysis of the text of Deuteronomy suggests the same setting
as the wisdom Book of Proverbs: the royal school. Weinfeld argues,

> The authors of Deuteronomy and the deuteronomic school must be sought
> for, then, among circles which held public office, among persons who had
> at their command a vast reservoir of literary material, who had developed
> and were capable of developing a literary technique of their own, those
> experienced in literary composition, and skilled with the pen and the
> book: these authors must consequently have been the *sōferim-ḥakamim*."[51]

These teachers were especially responsible for the educational formation of the king's sons. It is no wonder, then, that according to them the
king must "make a copy of this instruction/law in a book from the one
by the levitical priests. And it will be by him and he will read it all his
life, so that he may learn [*yilmad*] to fear the Lord his God and keep all
the words of this law and observe these statues" (Deut 17:18–19; my
trans.).

I will now try to be more precise about the sages, Deuteronomy,
and the temple. In the story of the discovery of the book of the
instruction/law (2 Kings 22), the leading part seems to have been
played by "Shaphan son of Azaliah, son of Meshullam, the scribe
[*sôpēr*]." He is sent by King Josiah to the temple (v 3), receives the
message and the book from Hilkiah the high priest (v 8), reads the book
to the king (v 10), and goes to consult Huldah the prophetess (v 14).
What is remarkable is that later members of the family of Shaphan also
seem to have played an important role in regard to another book, the
one containing the oracles of Jeremiah: "Baruch read Jeremiah's words
in the Temple of the Lord, in the room [*liškâ*] of Gemaryah son of
Shaphan the scribe, in the upper court at the entrance to the new gate
of the Lord's house in the hearing of all the people" (Jer 36:10).
Whatever the precise meaning of the word *liškâ*, which could well have
indicated a room open on one side with benches along the other three
walls (Koehler-Baumgartner 2:309), this was clearly a place convenient
for public reading within the temple enclosure. One may note that, later
on, Jeremiah's scroll was temporarily deposited in another room of the
same type: the *liškâ* of Elishama the scribe (Jer 36:20). The two stories
of the book of the *tôrâ* and the book of Jeremiah show the importance
of the scribes of the Shaphan family who were probably the "leading

50. M. Weinfeld, *Deuteronomy and the Deuternomic School* (Oxford: Clarendon,
1972) 189.
51. Ibid., 177–78.

exponents" of the deuteronomic school.[52] At the same time, these accounts reveal that the appearance of these two books seems connected
with the Jerusalem temple, more precisely with certain rooms (*liškôt*)
of the temple associated with the office of scribe (*sôpēr*). One may
wonder whether the activity of the scribes in these rooms was not, at
least in part, teaching.

However, even if there may have been some connection between
the wisdom teachers and the temple, because they could teach within
the temple enclosure, a literary analysis of the deuteronomic texts and
of the priestly traditions in the Bible shows clearly that these are "two
literary schools representing two ideological currents, the provenance of
one being the temple (P), and the provenance of the second the royal
court (D)."[53] The differences between these two ideological stances
have sometimes been considered to be religious teaching versus secular
teaching, but this is contradicted by the texts. In Israel, as in the other
ancient Near Eastern countries, wisdom is not a-religious. On the contrary, religious behavior ("the fear of the Lord") played the leading role
in traditional wisdom:

> The beginning of wisdom is the fear of the Lord,
>     and knowledge of the Holy One is understanding. (Prov 9:10)
>
> The fear of the Lord is a fountain of life. (Prov 14:27)
>
> The fear of the Lord is training in wisdom. (Prov 15:33)
>
> The fear of the Lord is wisdom. (Job 28:28)

In addition, the wisdom tradition is not anticultic. As has been well
demonstrated by L. G. Perdue, if the wisdom texts contain a "warning
against cultic involvement in the fertility religions" and criticisms "of a
popular misunderstanding of cultic ritual that would involve the magical conception of sacrifice," they seem generally to accept "cultic religion as an essential and important part of both Israel's religious heritage
and the wise man's own religious devotion."[54]

The difference between the wisdom tradition and the priestly
school is rather a matter of the degree of specific details about cultic
organization and ritual. The wisdom teacher was not involved in the
details of cultic rituals and sacrifices, whereas, in the priestly school, the
student had to learn the specific features of rituals, feasts, rules pertaining to clean and unclean, and temple maintenance.[55]

---

52. Ibid., 160.
53. Ibid., 184.
54. L. G. Perdue, *Wisdom and Cult* (SBLDS 30; Missoula, MT: Scholars Press,
1977) 155, 165, 211.
55. See my *Les écoles*, 68–70.

This priestly tradition was mainly oriented to the needs of cultic functionaries. The priestly texts are also very clearly didactic in style, even when they narrate stories,[56] taking the form, more or less, of a handbook with stereotypical phrases. However, these texts are not a reflection on the moral and human life. Wisdom is certainly not their main concern. Rather they are more interested in the practical activities and tasks of the priests and levites. The word "wisdom" (ḥokmâ) appears only in Exod 28:3, 31:6, and 36:1-2 with the meaning of technical knowledge and experience.

What of the Psalms, which are generally considered official prayers sung in the temple? They seem to reflect the variety of traditions in ancient Israel, and some of them give evidence that wisdom was also present in the temple. Actually several psalms, both prayers and meditations, have been classified as "wisdom psalms" by various scholars. One may consider at least the following to be wisdom psalms: 1, 19A, 19B, 32, 34, 37, 49, 73, 78, 112, 119, and 127.[57] These psalms are didactic in style and some are acrostics (cf. Psalms 9-10, 25, 34, 37, 111, 112, 119, and 145). Their main topic is the "instruction" (tôrâ) of the Lord, and they proclaim the happiness (ʾašrê) of the just:

> Happy [ʾašrê] is the man who does not follow the counsels of the wicked . . . ,
> but whose pleasure is in the instruction of the Lord,
>> and who meditates on his instruction night and day. (Ps 1:1-2)

> The instruction of the Lord is perfect and revives the soul,
>> the testimony of the Lord never fails and makes the simple wise. (Ps 19:8)

> My mouth speaks wise words [ḥokmôt],
>> and the meditations of my heart are full of understanding. (Ps 49:4)

> The beginning of wisdom is the fear of the Lord. (Ps 111:10; cf. Prov 9:10)

It is clear these psalms were written by learned people, by skilled scribes concerned with teaching, but the setting is difficult to determine: "It is possible that they were written by temple scribes and sages

---

56. See S. E. McEvenue, *The Narrative Style of the Priestly Writer* (Analecta Biblica 50; Rome: Pontifical Biblical Institute, 1971); J. F. X. Sheehan, "The Pre-P Narrative: A Children's Recital?" *Scripture in History and Theology: Essays in Honor of J. Coert Rylaarsdam* (ed. A. L. Merrill and T. W. Overholt; Pittsburgh Theological Monograph Series 17; Pittsburgh: Pickwick, 1977) 25-46.

57. Perdue, *Wisdom and Cult*, 261-323; J. F. Ross, "Psalm 73," *IW* 161-75; J. P. M. van der Ploeg, "Le Psaume 119 et la sagesse," *La sagesse de l'Ancien Testament* (ed. M. Gilbert; BETL 51; Gembloux: Duculot, 1979) 82-87; and my *Les écoles*, 44. Cf. also J. L. Mays, "The Place of the Torah Psalms in the Psalter," *JBL* 106 (1987) 3-12; A. Hurwitz, "Wisdom Vocabulary in the Hebrew Psalter: A Contribution to the Study of 'Wisdom Psalms,'" *VT* 38 (1988) 41-51.

functioning in the temple school."[58] But one must take into account the possibility that temple school does not necessarily mean priestly school, but could also indicate a royal or wisdom school. Actually, Ben Sira refers to a wisdom student praying in front of the temple: "In my prayer in front of the sanctuary [*lipnê hêkāl*], I asked for her (wisdom)" (Sir 51:14; cf. 1 Kgs 3:4–14).

If the Jerusalem temple very probably played an important role in the formation and transmission of the wisdom tradition during the period of the First Temple (very likely in connection with some kind of library), it is all the more true during the period of the Second Temple when there was no king and no royal school.[59] This period witnessed a fusion of the royal school tradition with that of the priestly school in the development of a single, national tradition. This is shown by the mission of Ezra to enforce the law of Moses (Ezra 7:6), also characterized as the "law of God" and the "law of the king" (Ezra 7:26). Actually, Ezra is presented as having devoted himself "to the study [*lidroš*] and observance of the instruction of the Lord and to teaching [*lĕlammēd*] statutes and ordinances in Israel" (Ezra 7:10). The temple became the national and religious center for all Jews, those in Judea as well as those of the Diaspora. The priestly tradition became part of the general Israelite wisdom tradition. So, for instance, after singing "the praises of the faithful men, the ancestors in their generations" (Sir 44:1), Ben Sira of Jerusalem (Sir 50:27) finishes his teaching with enthusiastic praise of "the high priest Simon son of Onias" (50:1–21).

By the time of Ben Sira the Jerusalem temple was not only the cultic center of the Jewish nation, it was also the main center of Jewish teaching, probably in connection with a temple library.[60] The rabbinic tradition gives many indications that, before 70 C.E., Jerusalem was famous for the number and level of its schools,[61] and the New Testament suggests that the temple was a traditional place of teaching for many Jewish masters (*didaskaloi*), including Jesus himself (Luke 2:46–52, 19:47, 20:1, 22:53; cf. Acts 5:42, etc.).

## CONCLUSION

The weight of evidence suggests that schools were the setting of the wisdom texts and more precisely of the wisdom books in the Bible.

58. Perdue, *Wisdom and Cult*, 268.

59. Hermisson, *Studien zur israelitischen Spruchweisheit*, 129–33.

60. See A. van der Kooij, *Die alten Textzeugen des Jesajabuches* (OBO 35; Göttingen: Vandenhoeck und Ruprecht, 1981) 332–35; and M. A. Friedman, "Publication of a Book by Depositing It in a Sanctuary," *Lešonénu* 48/49 (1983–84) 49–52.

61. See F. Hüttenmeister and G. Reeg, *Die antiken Synagogen in Israel*, vol. 1: *Die jüdischen Synagogen, Lehrhaüser und Gerichtshöfe* (Wiesbaden: Reichert, 1977) 205–14.

These texts were probably written down, read, commented upon, copied, and handed down through successive generations in the context of schools, most probably located in Jerusalem. The teacher in these schools was generally considered to be "the sage" *par excellence*. The teachers' instruction was initially aimed at the education of the children of the leading families connected with the royal palace or temple, but it became increasingly open to popular education. These schools were not cultural ghettoes, but rather were open to Israelite social and political life. Their teachers were often among the leaders or, at least, the leading groups of Israelite society. Even if sages and instructors in traditional wisdom existed outside these schools among family and tribal leaders, for example, and among royal officials who had bene- fitted from instruction in wisdom, it is impossible to understand how the Israelite wisdom tradition was collected and handed down without taking into account the significant role played by sages and scribes functioning in schools.[62]

62. See A. Vanel, "Sagesse," *Supplément au Dictionnaire de la Bible* (Paris: Letouzey, 1986), fasc. 60:4–58, esp. col. 6.

# PART III

---

*The Sage*
*in the Wisdom Literature*
*of the Hebrew Bible*

# THE FEMALE SAGE IN ANCIENT ISRAEL AND IN THE BIBLICAL WISDOM LITERATURE

## Claudia V. Camp

### INTRODUCTION: ISSUES AND METHODS

The attempt to discern the possible presence and nature of the role of female sage in ancient Israel presents a host of problems, compounding those encountered by the seeker after her male counterpart. Given the difficulties of defining wisdom or identifying the wise person, how much more frustrating to rediscover the contributions of women, which seem scarcely discernible in a highly androcentric tradition.[1] A careful sociological and literary analysis can, however, enhance our understanding of the tradition and its tradents.

There are several important theoretical issues and constructs that must be considered at the outset. First, on the reliability of portrayal: how do we know when literary sources are giving a reasonably accurate picture of *historical reality* and when, for reasons ideological or esthetic, this picture has been distorted? The question is particularly pressing in women's studies because so much of the source material has been composed and handed down by men. It comes immediately to the fore in the quest for the female sage because of the dramatically elevated imagery for Woman Wisdom in Proverbs, Sirach, and the Wisdom of Solomon. Although, as I shall suggest, there seems to be some cultural impetus for the emergence of the female wisdom figure from actual wise women (especially in Proverbs), none of the texts

Claudia V. Camp is Associate Professor of Religion at Texas Christian University.

1. On the problems of defining the tradition and identifying its tradents, see, for example, J. L. Crenshaw, "Method in Determining Wisdom Influence upon 'Historical' Literature," *JBL* 88 (1969) 129–42 (repr. in *SAIW* 481–94); and R. N. Whybray, *The Intellectual Tradition in the Old Testament* (BZAW 135; Berlin: de Gruyter, 1974). On the use of proverbs in narrative and prophetic material, see C. Fontaine, *Traditional Sayings in the Old Testament: A Contextual Study* (Bible and Literature 5; Sheffield: Almond, 1982). It is in narrative that we see wise women in action, who appear only poetically in the actual wisdom books.

gives direct or unambiguous information about them and, in the later material, the real women may be reflected in a different way—or lost altogether.

Second, from a sociological perspective, we need to observe the nature and function of *informal and ad hoc roles*, their relative authority and their interrelationship with more formalized roles. This perspective is important for two reasons: (*a*) because the authority of both women and the carriers of "wisdom" is often informal rather than formal; and (*b*) because the rather amorphous role of sage sometimes overlaps with other, more recognizable roles. Related to this is the question of how formal and informal roles function in the two major demographical settings of ancient Israel, the city and the rural villages. In a patrilineal, patrilocal society such as Israel's, we can take as a given that the primary source of a woman's authority will lie in her domestic roles. She may well, however, perform other leadership roles, the acknowledgement of her authority dependent on the credence and authority vested in domesticity in her particular social setting.[2] Cross-cultural, gender-attentive studies have shown fairly consistently that two interrelated factors contribute positively to women's ability to influence larger society: the degree of integration of the public and private spheres, and the degree of decentralization of leadership.[3]

Third, adding the historical perspective to the sociological, we must take account of the *changing nature* of Israel's political and social establishments and the effects of these changes on women and wisdom. It is clear, for example, that wisdom can be found both in premonarchic family and royal court, but its forms and content vary to some degree in these different settings. Similarly, women's roles and authority were affected by the advent of the monarchy.[4] Can we discover intersections in these developments that might tell more about women and wisdom? The sociopolitical configurations that arose after the Exile are,

2. Cf. J. F. Collier, "Women in Politics," *Women, Culture, and Society* (ed. M. Z. Rosaldo and L. Lamphere; Stanford, CA: Stanford University, 1974) 89–96.

3. See, for example, M. Z. Rosaldo, "Women, Culture, and Society: A Theoretical Overview," and L. Lamphere, "Strategies, Cooperation, and Conflict among Women in Domestic Groups," both in *Women, Culture, and Society* (ed. M. Z. Rosaldo and L. Lamphere; Stanford, CA: Stanford University, 1974) 17–42, 97–112; and J. Hackett, "In the Days of Jael: Reclaiming the History of Women in Ancient Israel," and A. C. Klein, "Primordial Purity and Everyday Life: Exalted Female Symbols and the Women of Tibet," both in *Immaculate and Powerful: The Female in Sacred Image and Social Reality* (ed. C. Atkinson et al.; Harvard Women's Studies in Religion; Boston: Beacon, 1985) 15–38, 111–38.

4. C. Meyers, "The Roots of Restriction: Women in Early Israel," *BA* 41 (1978) 101; N. Steinberg, "Gender Roles in the Monarchy" (paper read at the Society of Biblical Literature Annual Meeting, Atlanta, November 1986).

in many ways, even more a matter of conjecture than those of the earlier periods. Yet this is the period in which the wisdom materials as we now have them took their shape. It is also the period in which Woman Wisdom became a prominent figure, so again we must ask concerning the interrelationship between the wisdom tradition and the roles of women within a specific sociohistorical context. Here the second issue raised above becomes relevant. Because the role of wise woman is an informal one, it will be affected differently by social change than more formalized roles are. Because of its informality, it has more flexibility to withstand and endure change (contrast the premier formalized role of monarch, which disappeared under extreme social dislocation); on the other hand, the authority of an informal role is subject to limitation by those with formalized power. Some studies have suggested that the authority accorded to women will be relatively high during periods of communal stress, when demands upon them, both productively and reproductively, are particularly high.[5]

With these considerations in mind, I shall begin by reviewing the texts that are most obviously pertinent to this inquiry, those that actually mention wise women. Then I shall consider the figure of Wisdom personified as a woman in Proverbs, Sirach, and the Wisdom of Solomon, attempting to describe the sociohistorical contexts of these books in such a way as to discern what, if any, relationship this figure may have had to flesh-and-blood wise women.

## WISE WOMEN

The narratives contained in 2 Samuel 14 and 20 tell the tales of two unnamed women, one from Tekoa and one from Abel, who clearly exhibit the qualities of leadership.[6] Analysis of these stories allows the following observations about the female sage:[7]

1. The use of the epithet "wise woman" without any further identifying comments suggests that the role was one known at least to the original audiences of the stories.

5. For example, Meyers, "Roots of Restriction"; and Hackett, "In the Days of Jael."

6. I shall consider here only the two wise woman narratives in 2 Samuel, and not the references in Jer 9:16(17) or Exod 35:25, accepting A. Brenner's distinction between professional sages and women who are skilled in one or another traditional tasks (*The Israelite Woman: Social Role and Literary Type in Biblical Narrative* [Sheffield: JSOT Press, 1985] 44).

7. For a more detailed discussion of these points, see my essay, "The Wise Women of 2 Samuel: A Role Model for Women in Early Israel," *CBQ* 43 (1981) 14–29. Although caution is necessary in deriving sociohistorical data from narrative texts, I believe this article demonstrates that a sufficiently high degree of verisimilitude is operative here to allow confidence in describing this role.

2. Allowing for some possibility that a Judean editor may have
harmonized an originally more diverse picture, the fact that wise
women are said to live in both a northern and a southern city suggests a
commonality of experience between north and south with respect to
this role.

3. The use of the mother-imagery in both of these stories, though
metaphorical, seems to point back indirectly to a certain social reality,
namely, that the authority vested in designated wise women derives
from their primary social role in the education of children and management of the patriarchal household (the bêt-ʾāb).[8]

4. The possibility for female leadership beyond the family level is
suggested by N. K. Gottwald's analysis of the tribe (šēbeṭ) as "an
autonomous association of segmented extended families (bêt-ʾābôt)
grouped in village/neighborhood protective associations (mišpāḥôt) . . .
functionally interlocking through inter-marriage, practices of mutual
aid, common worship, and a levy of troops."[9] In such settings, young
women were the bonding elements between families and often between villages. They were intimate with at least two family groups and
trained, however informally, to function as interfamilial diplomats.[10]
Such factors—combined with the pre- and early monarchic periods'
decentralized leadership and its demands for the contribution of women
to the survival of the community—would have expanded the scope of
the wise mother's potential authority.

5. The use of proverbs (2 Sam 14:14, 20:18) by these women as
part of their negotiating strategy mirrors one of the defining activities of
the sage as seen both in the wisdom literature and in narrative texts
portraying counselors (e.g., 2 Sam 16:23; 17:8, 10–12). From this verbal
acumen, and from the overall skill and authority with which the women
accomplish their sensitive tasks, we should infer a significant degree of
training and experience in positions of leadership.

6. The stories about the wise women provide two of the clearest
representatives of what has been called clan or family wisdom. Their
performances suggest that the distinction between the educative wisdom of the familial patriarchs and matriarchs and the political wisdom
of diplomats is not absolute, nor is politics the exclusive domain of
sages in the royal court. As Carole Fontaine has shown throughout her
*Traditional Sayings in the Old Testament*, we must be alert to inter- and

8. See the article by C. R. Fontaine in this volume for a full discussion of wisdom
in the family setting (pp. 155–64 above).
9. Gottwald, *The Tribes of Yahweh* (Maryknoll, NY: Orbis, 1979) 245–341, quotation at 339.
10. E. Boulding, *The Underside of History* (Boulder, CO: Westview, 1976) 52–56.

intra-tribal negotiation and conflict as possible *Sitze im Leben* for specific sapiential genres.

7. The narrative presentation of the two women shows an overlap with narratives concerning other types of Israelite leaders. The parable enacted by the wise woman of Tekoa parallels that told by the prophet Nathan to David on another occasion (2 Samuel 12). The positioning and verbal strategies of the wise woman of Abel are identical to those used by military leaders in three different incidents (2 Sam 2:18-23, 24-28; 2 Kgs 18:17-36). Although these comparisons may be more the result of literary stylization than historical representation, there is another feature of their roles that cannot be ignored. These women, especially she of Abel, seem to be doing what we would expect elders to do, in particular, representing their people in national political-military situations.[11] It is at least possible that the wise woman of Tekoa has a personal interest in the restoration of Absalom, given his popularity among the people (cf. 2 Sam 15:2-6).[12] As for the wise woman of Abel, although the storyteller focuses on her surrendering Sheba to Joab, there is an elliptical suggestion that her negotiations have the equally important purpose of protecting the rest of the rebel's followers (cf. 2 Sam 20:1, 14, 21-22). She, too, seems to have a discreet hand in national politics.

8. The concerns voiced by the wise women reveal that they were active tradents of the Yahwistic covenantal values of land and inheritance (2 Sam 14:16, 20:19). This latter point should caution against arbitrary division of a so-called secular wisdom tradition from "religious" Yahwism.

These two stories depict a role of "female sage" or wise woman in the early period of Israel's history. We are, however, left with the question of whether or not the role persists in the later eras, as political and religious centralization under the monarchy increased. The question can, of course, only be addressed speculatively, since the sources mostly reflect the experience of the urban elite. Certainly, the needs and lifestyle of the village peasant landholders would not have drastically changed. Thus the role of women in the management of households and rearing of children would have continued to provide them with a base of informal authority. On the other hand, as the work of a number of scholars has demonstrated, the effect of centralization was the removal of power from the hands of the free peasantry, whose ranks

11. Gottwald, *Tribes of Yahweh*, 339.

12. Brenner makes the interesting suggestion that Joab *hired* the woman to play this part (*Israelite Woman*, 35), which would in itself say something about the role of sage, male or female. There are indications in the text, however, that this woman also had her own political reasons for taking the assignment (see my "Wise Women of 2 Samuel," 27).

were reduced by the appropriation of lands by urbanites and the
growth of tenant farming, whose self-determination was limited by
state control of production and establishment of a centralized bureaucracy, and whose organizing ability was diminished by administrative
redistricting for purposes of taxation and *corvée*.[13] Roles such as
"judge," which were once part of the official but probably fairly informal structure of village-tribal authority, now become appointments
made by the king, and laws promote the nuclear family at the expense
of the extended family. Under such conditions, the authority of wise
women would almost certainly be minimized as their base of power is
eroded. Nonetheless, the stories of the wise women of Tekoa and Abel
seemed worth saving, and even embellishing, when the deuteronomistic
historians reworked this material, suggesting a role not forgotten.[14]

## WOMAN WISDOM

The figure of female personified Wisdom appears in Proverbs, Sirach,
and the Wisdom of Solomon. Although the presentations in the later
texts are based on that in Proverbs, there are certain differences that
may also suggest differences in the authors' perceptions of the wisdom
of women.

### Proverbs

Woman Wisdom appears in several poems in Proverbs 1-9: 1:20-
33, 2:1-11, 3:13-18, 4:5-9, 7:1-5, 8:1-36, 9:1-6. (Cf. Prov 3:19-35, where
the depiction of Wisdom falls just short of personification, and 5:15-19,
where love for one's wife is described similarly to love for Wisdom.)
An interpretation of her cannot be separated from the closely related

13. R. Albertz (*Persönliche Frömmigkeit und offiziele Religion* [Stuttgart: Calwer,
1978]), N. Steinberg ("Gender Roles in the Monarchy"), and D. Hopkins ("The Dynamics
of Agriculture in Monarchical Israel," *Society of Biblical Literature 1983 Seminar Papers*
[ed. K. H. Richards; Chico, CA: Scholars Press, 1983] 177-202) all reveal aspects of this
situation from different perspectives. Albertz focuses on the religious dimensions of these
changes by distinguishing between the personal piety of the familial setting and the
official religion of the national cult, which, most noticeably in Deuteronomy, appropriated
the metaphors of familial piety for its own ends. Steinberg's study of the exercise of
centralized political control by means of sexual control, observable in the deuteronomic
laws, reveals another aspect of state dominance of the once autonomous tribal families.
Hopkins does a thorough analysis of the development and effects of state control of
production.
14. The characteristically deuteronomistic combination of the terms "rest" or "resting place" (*nwh*) and "inheritance" (*nhlh*) is ascribed to the wise woman of Tekoa in
2 Sam 14:16-17. Cf. G. Sheppard's discussion of these terms in relationship to Woman
Wisdom in Sirach (*Wisdom as a Hermeneutical Construct* [BZAW 151; Berlin, NY: de
Gruyter, 1980] 38-43).

imagery for the strange woman (Prov 2:16-19; 5:1-14, 20-23; 6:20-35; 7:5-27; 9:13-18) and the woman of worth (Prov 31:10-31). Although there are almost certainly adumbrations of ancient Near Eastern goddesses at work here,[15] the search for the female sage requires instead consideration of allusions to human women in these texts. I have discussed in detail elsewhere a typology of women's roles and images discernible in the Bible that provide a social and literary context for interpreting the Wisdom figure.[16] The question of whether or not we can discover a real-life female sage behind this poetic figure depends in part on our ability to connect this literature with one or more sociohistoric contexts.

Although it would be naïve to imagine that high status or specific roles for women can be directly inferred from the exaltation of Woman Wisdom, the appropriation of such a remarkable symbol does suggest some related social reality.[17] If, as seems likely, the redaction of the Book of Proverbs (if not the initial composition of the Woman Wisdom poems)[18] took place in postexilic Palestine, this time and place provides a point of departure for my investigation. The era was marked in Israel's experience by the need to formulate both social institutions and symbolic representations to replace the fallen monarchy and its royal theology. It is clear that the family and the cult were two of the dominant responses. The synagogue-school also emerged during this period.

We can identify three complex and interrelated ways in which the family bore a heretofore unparalleled weight of meaning. First, the cohesiveness and productivity of the extended family was essential if the newly transplanted community was to survive. Second, the "new" forms of leadership that emerged were to some extent a return to Israel's sociological roots. Whereas the monarchy had taken away power from the decentralized tribal families in its direction of and demands upon their governance and labor, the bêt-ʾābôt now reclaimed these powers. Symbolically also, the family once again replaced the king as the locus of divine blessing among the people of

15. G. Boström, *Proverbiastudien: Die Weisheit und das fremde Weib in Sprüche 1-9* (Lunds Universitets Årsskrift 30.3; Lund: Gleerup, 1935); C. Bauer-Kayatz, *Studien zu Proverbien 1-9* (WMANT 22; Neukirchen-Vluyn: Neukirchener, 1966); and R. Clifford, "Proverbs 9: A Suggested Ugaritic Parallel," *VT* 25 (1975) 298-306.

16. Camp, *Wisdom and the Feminine in the Book of Proverbs* (Bible and Literature 11; Sheffield: JSOT/Almond, 1985) 79-148.

17. I owe much in my effort to interpret this symbol to C. Geertz, *The Interpretation of Cultures* (New York: Basic Books, 1973).

18. Bauer-Kayatz's dating of Proverbs 8 in the Solomonic era is at least possible, if not probable (*Studien zu Proverbien 1-9*, 13-14).

Israel, as, for example, in Second Isaiah's motif of the promise to the barren woman in 49:20-21 and 54:1-3.[19] Finally, the need for identity over against foreign elements pushed the family to the fore on both social and symbolic fronts. A critical issue was that of land claims and inheritance rights, which apparently had been *de facto* appropriated by a combination of peasants who had not been exiled and new foreign inhabitants of the land. The strong emphasis on genealogy in both the Priestly source and in Chronicles bespeaks the tension around this issue, as does Nehemiah's and Ezra's condemnation of marriages to foreign women. Foreign influence in general and foreign marriages in particular also produced the threat of foreign religious practices. Although this was hardly a new problem, the question of who controlled the true and proper worship of Yahweh presented a challenge to both the piety and politics of the period.

The female imagery in Proverbs presents a multifaceted response to these issues. The mother appears repeatedly alongside the father, instructing her offspring in the wisdom of avoiding violent men (Prov 1:8-19), strange women (Prov 6:20-35, 23:22-28, 31:3), and intemperate imbibing (Prov 23:19-21, 31:4-7; cf. Prov 30:11, 17; 20:20; 15:20; 10:1). As counselor to her lover-husband, Woman Wisdom protects him against the several threats of the metaphorical "strange woman," who intimates adultery, foreign worship, and alienation from the community, all conditions that would have been particularly threatening at this time, not only to the individual concerned, but to the community as a whole with its dire need for social—and especially familial—stability. In contrast to Woman Stranger, Woman Wisdom offers wealth, happiness, and the life that comes from Yahweh. In addition, the Wisdom figure assumes many of the symbolic roles of the former monarch, including responsibility for the administration of justice, the control of government, and the ongoing order of the cosmos. Her appearance in both the house and the city gate symbolizes a union of the public and private spheres as the source of social identity, a union that had been disrupted by the monarchy. Here the family household, with the woman at its center, is held up as the defining element of society as a whole.

From this conjunction of social and symbolic concerns evident in female Wisdom, I think we cannot help but infer something about the roles of and attitudes toward women in this period. Chief among them, as always, would be that of wife, mother, and homemaker. Because of the central significance of home and family in the early Persian period,

19. Albertz, *Persönliche Frömmigkeit*, 186; cf. pp. 178-90 for discussion of a variety of ways in which the forms of personal religiosity appear in communal contexts.

however, to be the maker of the home was, in a newly recognizable way, to be the builder of society. Analysis of the wisdom poems in this context reveals that this state of affairs did not go unnoticed by the tradents of the wisdom tradition in particular. Postexilic Israel was, of course, still a patriarchal society with most formal public roles reserved for men. This material suggests, however, that an important informal role of female sage not only existed but was acknowledged as authoritative by the men in charge. The clear impression given by the figure of personified Wisdom is that, like that of the wise women in the pre- and early monarchic periods, the counsel of these women was respected not only in the home but also in the public arena, and that it involved not only "secular" matters but also reflection on what it meant to be a member of the community of Yahweh.

This liminal phase of decentralized and relatively weak social structure did not, of course, endure, as Judaism turned to more centralized, extrafamilial sources of community identity and authority, especially to the Jerusalemite cult. The male priestly theocracy would have functioned with respect to female roles in a manner analogous to the monarchy, reducing their authority not simply by excluding women from formalized positions (which was almost always the case no matter what the circumstances), but by removing authority—both practical and symbolic—from the family households.

Running to some extent counter to this trend was the increasing democratization of the Judean community, with its vesting of authority in the "heads of families."[20] I say "to some extent" because democratization has also, to the degree that it makes official or formal the governing roles of the persons drawn from the general populace, most often excluded women. Moreover, the movement toward formalization tends to lessen the public recognition of informal authority.[21] Further, the growth of the synagogue-school would tend to reinforce the division of the public and private spheres and limit the authority of the mother by removing even basic religious instruction from the home.

It is possible that the portrait of the woman of worth in Prov 31:10–31 reflects a transition period from a time in which the public role of women was acknowledged and affirmed (as suggested in Proverbs 1–9) to one in which women's roles were more severely restricted, as I shall observe below in discussing the Book of Sirach.[22] The concluding poem

20. S. Japhet, "Sheshbazzar and Zerubbabel: Against the Background of the Historical and Religious Tendencies of Ezra-Nehemiah," ZAW 94 (1982) 87–89.

21. Collier, "Women in Politics."

22. A. Wolters has argued that the poem on the woman of worth could not be earlier than the end of the fourth century because it contains within it a bilingual wordplay between the Hebrew ṣôpiyyâ and the Greek sophia in v 27 ("Ṣôpiyyâ [Prov 31:27] as

of Proverbs portrays a middle ground: this woman is a teacher of *hokmâ* and *hesed* (v 26), and her economic activities carry her from home to field to market (vv 14, 16, 24). However, although "her works praise her in the gates" (v 31), it is only her husband who actually sits there (v 23).

In sum, the female imagery in Proverbs most likely reflects a relatively high status for women in society during the Persian period (especially early on), and the possibility of real social influence for women of experience and wisdom. However, once a symbol like Woman Wisdom becomes established in society, it may well persist even when the conditions that nurtured it change. Because this symbol— like all those accepted into the mainstream of religious orthodoxy—was controlled by the male hierarchy, it was possible for it to become as oppressive of women in a later period as it was supportive in the era just considered. I believe we can witness such a shift in the later wisdom literature.

### Sirach

Like the Book of Proverbs, the writing of Jesus ben Sira represents a particular sociohistorical setting and cultural ethos, an early second-century Jerusalem much influenced by Hellenism. Warren Trenchard has done a thorough literary investigation into Ben Sira's attitude toward women.[23] He is certainly correct in evaluating the author's attitude as "negative," but some of his analysis requires further nuancing based on an understanding of the nature of informal authority and the impact of the social background. I would argue that Trenchard has overstated his case on several counts. First, he has discounted the positive valuation of the wife's domestic productivity and spousal counsel (Sir 26:1-4, 13-16; 28:15; 36:24-27; 40:23), both of which are important bases for the authority of the female sage. Second, the phrase *'iššâ mśklt*, a wise or prudent wife (Sir 25:8, 26:1-13; cf. Prov 19:14), certainly implies more than "passive restraint" and the absence of quarreling.[24] The contexts suggest, rather her ability to provide well for her husband and household. Third, as far as the wife's silence is concerned, verbal control, humility, and restraint are virtues of the wise *man* as well (Sir 1:21, 22; 3:17-19; 18:18-20), so this only says that the sage holds women to

---

Hymnic Participle and Play on *Sophia*," *JBL* 104 [1985] 577-87). Although Wolters's conclusion is not inarguable (R. Albertz, personal correspondence), it does suggest at least the possibility of a later date for this editorial finale to Proverbs than I had previously conjectured in *Wisdom and the Feminine*.

23. *Ben Sira's View of Women: A Literary Analysis* (Brown Judaic Studies 38; Chico, CA: Scholars Press, 1982).

24. So Trenchard; ibid., 26-27, 38, 205 n. 187.

similar standards. Fourth, Ben Sira enhances female authority with allusions to the well-known tradition of female personified Wisdom. The good wife is "above pearls," a description applied to Woman Wisdom (Sir 7:19, Prov 3:15). Even the admittedly patriarchal notion that the lucky husband "takes possession" (*qnh*) of his wife (Sir 36:24), receives a somewhat different slant when we realize that it is Woman Wisdom whom both humans and God "possess" in Proverbs (4:5, 8:22). Despite these criticisms, Trenchard's overall assessment stands: the attitude of this book has taken a step backward from Proverbs as far as women are concerned.

The nature of Ben Sira's shift backward bears further attention. What pressures lie behind his shrill protests about women? The threat of idolatry that informs at least one aspect of the strange woman in Proverbs is absent here.[25] This fact bespeaks a conservative, Jerusalemite, temple-oriented piety. Although specifically religious pressure is not yet attested here,[26] the more general cultural threat of Hellenism to men like Ben Sira cannot be denied.[27] Hellenism alone, however, is not sufficient to account for the shift. We must also, within the Hellenistic context, attend to the often neglected impact of patriarchal attitudes toward economic and social control in the family household.

An analysis of the relevant texts shows a strident concern for the husband's control of all aspects of his household affairs. On the most personal level is the matter of women's beauty, a concern not even mentioned in Proverbs. With the exception of one's wife (Sir 36:22; cf. 26:16-18), merely looking upon the beauty of a woman places him in grave danger, whether that woman is one classified as "strange" or the wife of a friend (Sir 9:7-9, 41:21). The injunctions against looking at, "stretching out the elbow with,"[28] or "mixing wine with" a married woman imply severe restrictions on her ability to socialize freely with her husband's male friends. This stands in direct contrast to the freedom in Proverbs with which Woman Wisdom, as lady of the house, "mixes her wine" and sends her maids out on the streets to call people to dine with her (Prov 9:2-5). We should not, however, imagine that Sirach's attempts to restrict the social contact of men and women

25. Trenchard observes that the sage is more concerned about Solomon's concupiscence than about the king's worship of foreign gods (ibid., 89-90).

26. It would not be long until it was, however, once Antiochus IV took the throne in 175 B.C.E.

27. A. A. Di Lella, "Conservative and Progressive Theology: Sirach and Wisdom," *CBQ* 38 (1966) 139-54 (repr. in *SAIW* 401-16).

28. As Trenchard suggests, this phrase may imply a more indecent position than the normal reclining at table (*Ben Sira's View of Women*, 111-12). However, even the usual dining position would be difficult in mixed company, if one were not permitted to look at one's hostess or, at the very least, to notice her beauty.

represent the accepted norm of his day.[29] Indeed, the urgency of his admonitions suggests an effort to control something within the surrounding Hellenistic culture that he considered to be out of hand.

Besides controlling his own sexuality, the wise man must maintain control over his (inordinately lusty) daughters (Sir 7:24-25, 22:3-5, 26:10-12, 42:9-14) and his potentially drunken, jealous, unchaste, and animalistically domineering wife (Sir 26:6-12, 25:14-25). He must, moreover, assert his authority to determine his patrilineage over against his wife's unorthodox(?) efforts to influence its direction by presenting as heir the fruit of her union with another man (Sir 23:22-26). Again rather hyperbolically, these passages suggest that the husband must have the ability to maintain "law and order" within his household, as well as control of its interaction with the outside Hellenistic world.

Finally, Ben Sira reflects how the patriarch's ability to control his and his wife's sexuality becomes intimately related to his management of his other household affairs. Sirach 42:3-7 is worth noting. It presents a list of things a male sage should not be ashamed of, and includes:

> Of sharing the expenses of a business or a journey;
> or of dividing an inheritance or property.
> Of accuracy of scales and balances,
> or of tested measures and weights;
> Of acquiring much or little,
> or of bargaining in dealing with a merchant;
> Of constant training of children,
> or of beating the sides of a disloyal servant;
> Of a seal to keep an erring wife at home,
> or of a lock placed where there are many hands.[30]
> Of numbering every deposit,
> or of recording all that is given or received.
> (Sir 42:3-7)

The foregoing reveals some distinct differences in the authority of women's roles from that evident in the female characters and imagery in 2 Samuel and Proverbs. Some of the reasons for the public recognition of female authority during times of national crisis—specifically the "pioneer periods" of the confederacy and the postexilic restoration— were noted above. To those I might add the fact that neither period was dominated by the centralized worship of the male-run temple. In

29. Cf. E. Schüssler Fiorenza's cautions against assuming prescriptive statements to be descriptive (*In Memory of Her: A Feminist Theological Reconstruction of Christian Origins* [New York: Crossroad, 1983] 89).

30. Trenchard surprisingly doesn't see sexual innuendo here. Cf. Cant 5:4-6, where the imagery of the "lock" contains at least an element of sexual connotation.

Sirach, however, we can see the close association this representative of wisdom had with the cult.[31] This fact, combined with the formalized school setting for teaching wisdom (Sir 51:23), would tend to exclude women from direct contribution to the tradition.[32] Compounding the effects of the formalization and institutionalization of roles was the increasing focus on the authority of written tradition and the glorification of the vocation of scribe (Sir 38:24–39:11). In an evolving oral tradition closely associated with daily life—one of the dominant contexts for wisdom hitherto—there was a strong potential for (at least) the indirect contributions of women. Women are never taught to read and write as extensively as men, however, so this second-century trend could not help but limit their participation.

We must now consider the Hellenistic influences on the Jewish community in Judea as they bear on Ben Sira's view of women and, thus, on what we can discern of the authority of the female sale. Several factors can be observed. One is the extremely urbanized atmosphere of Jerusalem in contrast to the provincial backwater capital it had been at the outset of the Greek era.[33] Urbanization is a factor that has often been noted to decrease women's status, especially "at the level of the petty merchants, scribes, and lower-level administrators."[34] During the Ptolemaic period, moreover, there was a drastic incursion into Judean economic life by representatives of the governing power in Alexandria.[35] It is not improbable that active female participation in trade, evident in Prov 31:10–31, would have been suppressed by this movement, foreign men probably preferring to deal with Judean men, and Judean men probably preferring not to allow such extensive contact between their women and foreigners. The fruits of this economic internationalism were limited, moreover, to the Judean aristocracy. Although there was a dramatic reduction in foreign trade with Simon II's laws

31. Ben Sira's love for the temple even shows up in his description of female beauty in cultic similes (Sir 26:17–18). Although possible association of sages with the cult in the preexilic period should not be ignored (cf. L. Perdue, *Wisdom and Cult* [SBLDS 30; Missoula, MT: Scholars Press, 1977] 267), the material from that period focuses more on courtly wisdom. G. Sheppard has elicited one very clear picture of the cult-related work of the postexilic sages in his discussion of the sapiential editing of the Book of Psalms (*Wisdom as a Hermeneutical Construct*, 136–43).

32. Interestingly enough, there is talmudic evidence for female teachers and students in schools (L. Epstein, *Sex Laws and Customs in Judaism* [New York: Ktav, 1969] 83–88), as well as inscriptional and literary evidence for women leaders in the synagogue (B. J. Brooten, *Women Leaders in the Ancient Synagogue* [Brown Judaic Studies 36; Chico, CA: Scholars Press, 1982]). It is difficult to correlate such data with the attitudes expressed by Ben Sira. The social backgrounds of the various writers demand further study.

33. M. Hengel, *Jews, Greeks, and Barbarians* (Philadelphia: Fortress, 1980) 30.

34. Boulding, *Underside of History*, 212 and passim.

35. Hengel, *Jews, Greeks, and Barbarians*, 23–25.

protecting the purity of Jerusalem,[36] the lot was already cast as far as women were concerned.

Among the Jerusalemite upper-class there developed a fancy for Greek-style education,[37] which would, once again, reduce the influence of maternal training of the young and, hence, reduce the basis for female authority and participation in the handing on of traditional wisdom. If A. Wolters's analysis of Prov 31:10–31 is correct, one purpose of this poem might have been an early effort to counter this trend by upholding the Jewish mother's teaching over against the influence of Greek wisdom.[38] Ben Sira clearly represents a later manifestation of this same conservative Jewish perspective, which overtly resisted Hellenistic influences even as it was infiltrated by them. Given the relative freedom of upper-class women in Alexandria,[39] we might imagine that a similar social liberalism prevailed among the Hellenized leadership of Jerusalem.[40] This was precisely the group that Ben Sira opposed. It is not unlikely, then, that his oft-expressed concern to limit social contact of men and women and to maintain control over the women in his charge stem from these circumstances.[41]

This sage addresses an educated, well-to-do, but—as far as political, economic, and social matters are concerned—persistently threatened audience. As is so often the case, those who are relatively powerless in a given situation both fear the powerful and aspire to be like them. One typical way of acting out this dilemma is to take control where one can and lord it over those to whom it is given to lord, and often this means women. In addition to this psychology of powerlessness, Sirach also reflects the very accurate perception that, given the assimilating tendencies of much of the Jewish leadership, the family was the last bastion of defense against the pressures of Hellenization. Thus, the situation of Jerusalem Jews in the second century B.C.E. was

36. Ibid., 43–44.

37. Even though the Jerusalem gymnasium was not built until 175 B.C., Hengel makes the case that a Greek elementary school must have been in existence much earlier (*Judaism and Hellenism* [Philadelphia: Fortress, 1974], 1.76).

38. "Ṣôpiyyâ," 556.

39. S. B. Pomeroy, *Goddesses, Whores, Wives, and Slaves: Women in Classical Antiquity* (New York: Schocken, 1975) 125–29, 148; and (with emphasis on the *relative*) F. T. Griffiths, "Home before Lunch: The Emancipated Woman in Theocritus," *Reflections of Women in Antiquity* (ed. H. P. Foley; New York: Gordon and Breach, 1981) 247–74.

40. Hengel cites rabbinic evidence for mixed marriages and even "free love" (*Jews, Greeks, and Barbarians*, 114).

41. Epstein suggests that one reason for the Maccabean revolt was the imposition of the *jus primae noctis* by the Greek rulers, under which the resident government official had the right to the first night with virgin brides (*Sex Laws and Customs*, 157). Although Ben Sira does not refer to this custom directly, one wonders if some of his concern for the father's control of his daughters' sexuality derives from it.

wrought with negative influences as far as the public authority of women is concerned. Although their prudence continued to be recognized and treasured in the domestic setting, it was not readily translated into public authority and, even in the home, they were often treated with suspicion by their husbands.

The use of female imagery for Wisdom is, then, all the more surprising. Unlike in Proverbs, were the love and authority shown to Woman Wisdom is paralleled by that granted to one's wife, "Ben Sira's glowing regard for dame Wisdom stands in astounding contrast to his reflections on women in the flesh." [42] I think this fact can be explained in the following manner. First, we must recognize that the female Wisdom figure already existed, and was apparently rather widely accepted, in the sage's tradition. Had this not been the case, it seems unlikely he would have invented it. It is widely recognized in women's studies, however, that idealized female imagery does not always support women's equality. Indeed, the higher the pedestal and the further removed from the life of real women, the more likely such an image may be used to repress women through negative comparison. In Proverbs, in spite of Woman Wisdom's exaltation in some passages, she nonetheless remained imagistically connected to the human women of Israel's social and literary experience.[43] This is not the case in Sirach, where Wisdom becomes identified with Torah. This sort of abstraction by itself would probably have been sufficient to break the connection between women and Woman Wisdom. It is, however, further reinforced by the fact that the study and teaching of Torah have been removed from the domestic domain, where the wife and mother shares that responsibility with her mate, and placed in the institution of the school. Unlike Proverbs, Ben Sira never presents the mother as a purveyor of instruction. In this arena, as in others, a split has occurred between the public and private aspects of social life, inhibiting the capacity of women's informal authority, which is centered in the home, to be publicly expressed. Without doubt, there were as many wise women during the lifetime of Ben Sira and his grandson as there ever were. The "role" of "female sage" has, however, been severely constricted.

## Wisdom of Solomon

Whether the Wisdom of Solomon is to be dated between 37 and 41 c.e.,[44] or in the preceding century,[45] there is agreement that its

---

42. Trenchard, *Ben Sira's View of Women*, 253 n. 206.

43. See my *Wisdom and the Feminine*, 79-148.

44. D. Winston, *The Wisdom of Solomon* (AB 43; Garden City, NY: Doubleday, 1979) 23.

45. Most recently, J. M. Reese, *The Book of Wisdom, Song of Songs* (Old Testament Message 20; Wilmington, DE: Michael Glazier, 1983) 17.

cultural context is the educated Jewish circles of Alexandria and that its purpose is to persuade members of these circles to remain true to their ancestral faith. This purpose is accomplished, in part, by the author's borrowing of genre, language, style, and science from the Hellenistic environment. The figure of female personified Wisdom is developed here with a depth and consistency unparalleled in the other material considered. Unfortunately, the extensiveness with which the sage treats Woman Wisdom is matched by an equally large void of consideration of real women. We may, however, find glimmerings of light on the path to the female sage through study of this work alongside other data on attitudes toward and behaviors of women in the larger cultural context.

As noted above, the Hellenistic period was one in which changing standards clashed with conservative exhortations urging the retaining of traditional female roles.[46] The period is famous for, among other things, its powerful and ambitious queens, a lineage that stretches down to Cleopatra VII (ca. 51–30 B.C.E.), who challenged Octavian and the Romans from her base in Alexandria until the time of her defeat and suicide in 30 B.C.E. It is not impossible that the Wisdom of Solomon was written during her reign or, at the latest, within the next two generations when her memory would have been fresh.

Although one cannot make generalizations about the life of all women based on that of royalty, "the competent women visible in Hellenistic courts were one of the positive influences of this period toward increasing the prestige of nonroyal but upper-class women."[47] In areas newly Hellenized, as opposed to the Greek mainland, developments in private law favoring women are more obvious. Evidence documenting women's participation in economic and other contractual situations is copious, especially in Egypt, where native Egyptian women had even more control over their own affairs than did Greek women. The Alexandrian Jewish community, however, their own tradition to the contrary, seems to have adopted the more restrictive practices of the Greek rulers regarding a woman's need for a guardian to represent her in legal affairs.[48] There was, furthermore, an expansion of women's rights in marriage, a decrease in the father's authority over his married daughters, and, in general, a loosening of strict social controls on women by their husband and father. Egyptian papyri also reveal that some women were able to sign their names to contracts during the Hellenistic and Roman periods, suggesting greater availability of educa-

46. For an excellent summary of women's experiences in this era see Pomeroy, *Goddesses, Whores, Wives, and Slaves,* 120–49.

47. Ibid., 125.

48. Pomeroy, "Women in Roman Egypt," in *Reflections of Women in Antiquity* (ed. H. P. Foley; New York: Gordon and Breach, 1981) 316.

tion for women. The worship of the goddess Isis also had a strong resurgence during this time.

On the other hand, Stoicism, the most popular philosophy of the era, countered these trends with emphasis on traditional roles for women, a notion that was incorporated into the Roman view of marriage and family and "elevated to the level of moral, religious, and patriotic duty."[49] Sarah Pomeroy quotes extensively from one of several extant texts of the smaller sect of Neopythagoreans on proper female behavior:

> We must deem the harmonious woman to be one who is well endowed with wisdom and self-restraint. For her soul must be very wise indeed when it comes to virtue so that she will be just and courageous [*lit.* manly], while being sensible and beautified with self-sufficiency, despising empty opinion. . . .[50]

The text goes on to enjoin the woman against adultery and conspicuous consumption of expensive and stylish goods ("The beauty that comes from wisdom and not from these things brings pleasure to women who are well born") and to agree with her husband in all things. The description of the good wife sounds remarkably like those in Sirach (cf., e.g., the translator's use of *andreia* ['manly'] in Sir 28:15), and the virtues named are almost identical with those of Woman Wisdom's "children" in the Wisdom of Solomon (cf. 8:7).

In Wis 6:12–10:21, the author writes under the persona of "Solomon" in describing his relationship with Wisdom. A large portion of this section conveys a sense of the mystical[51] and, it may seem, of mystification as well. The sage has addressed himself to kings (Wis 1:1) and here pretends to be a king, a lofty pretense indeed, given the political status of Jews in Greco-Roman Alexandria.[52] Wisdom herself appears in a goddess's garb, is described by means of a form akin to the well-known Isis-aretologies,[53] and is ascribed functions identical to Yahweh's. The union of "king" and "goddess" is described in terms of mystical sexual union (Wis 8:2–3, 16).[54]

49. Pomeroy, *Goddesses, Whores, Wives, and Slaves*, 132.

50. Ibid., 134.

51. Cf. Winston, *Wisdom of Solomon*, 41, 64, and also his essay in this volume (pp. 383–97 below).

52. If Winston's first-century-c.e. dating is correct, this status was lower than ever, with anti-Jewish riots and a proclamation by the Roman prefect declaring Jews "aliens and foreigners" in Alexandria (*Wisdom of Solomon*, 23).

53. J. M. Reese, *Hellenistic Influences on the Book of Wisdom and Its Consequences* (Analecta Biblica 41; Rome: Biblical Institute, 1970) 42–49.

54. Reese, *Book of Wisdom*, 93, 97.

While this exaltation of female Wisdom superficially suggests a
high status for women, a closer look shows the opposite. The quest for
Woman Wisdom seems, rather, to turn the sage's focus away from
home and family, resulting in the devaluation of this arena. J. M. Reese
describes the effect of the instruction to fix one's thoughts on the vigilant
pursuit of Wisdom in the following way:

> An implicit contrast lies under the surface, namely, to those who are tied
> down to the cares of raising a family and providing for physical needs (see
> Sir 42:9). Those material tasks create a burden, but Lady Wisdom's com-
> fort makes her pursuers *"free from care"* as she *"graciously"* supplies their
> needs.[55]

The fundamental metaphor for Wisdom is no longer the wise woman of
the house and street, as it is in Proverbs, but rather the sublime "throne
partner" of the king (Wis 6:14), who is God's "throne partner" (Wis 9:4)
as well. Fortunately, after a hard day's work, the tired monarch can say,

> When I enter my house, I shall find rest with her,
>     for companionship with her has no bitterness,
> and life with her has no pain,
>     but gladness and joy.
>
>                                         (Wis 8:16)

No problem with contentious women for this sage! The children of this
union, moreover, will not cause the sage to lose sleep, as Ben Sira did
over his daughters, for the fruit of Wisdom's birthpains[56] will be none
other than the virtues of self-control, prudence, justice, and courage
(Wis 8:7). Real women are mentioned only in the eschatological adulation of those who remain childless rather than transgressing the marriage bed (Wis 3:13; cf. Sir 23:22–26).

In sum, then, the long and richly textured intertwining of wisdom
thought with the real life of men and women in society is abandoned
by this writer in favor of mystical speculation. One might make the case
that it was precisely mystical speculation that was required by the
society of that day. Be that as it may, this orientation removes itself
from the daily life arena of commonsense wisdom, which is the typical
woman's main hope for authority in a patriarchal society and her most
important contribution to the wisdom tradition.

55. Ibid., 65. The italicized words are from the text of Wis 6:15–16.
56. On the sexual imagery in this verse, see ibid., 95.

## CONCLUSIONS

At the outset of this study, I raised the question of whether a quest for the female sage could contribute to our understanding of the wisdom tradition and its tradents as a whole. Although direct information is scanty, the attempt to analyze it using the "glue" of certain sociological constructs does provide some insight, particularly with respect to the interrelationship of what scholarship has recognized as the three major loci of wisdom: the family, the court, and the school.[57] Consistent throughout all periods of Israel's history is the presence of the family, and there can be no doubt that this was always an important context for the preservation and handing on of social mores. What we can observe in the wise women of Tekoa and Abel, however, is that the authority that derives from effective familial leadership can be translated in the setting of the larger community (the *mišpāḥâ* or even the *šēbeṭ*) into political—and even military—wisdom that one would otherwise associate with the royal court. These women are also adept *ad hoc* theologians, able to apply their understanding of the will of God to the situation of the moment.[58] "Wisdom theology" is not, then, reducible to the later speculative wisdom of the schools. This conjunction of political, theological, and daily-life wisdom, produced by women as well as men, is only possible in a setting similar to that of the wise women of 2 Samuel, in other words, in a setting in which authority is to some extent diffuse and roles are sufficiently informal as to allow for an overlapping of functions. My analysis would suggest that the appearance of a separation into different types of wisdom results from the fact that these texts have come down from persons working in rather different settings of centralized authority and formalized role definitions. Direct data from the premonarchic and Persian periods are precisely what is missing to round out the picture.

The authority of women and the integration of wisdom suffer similar fates. With the centralization of power and the formalization of roles, the informal, family-based authority of women has no public outlet, while wisdom can take on either an amorally political or a speculatively bookish cast, depending on which group is in charge. The memory of the connection of powerful, politicized, and faithful women with the tradition is not lost entirely, but its transformation into the idealized figure of Woman Wisdom ultimately ensures that it will remain just that—a memory.

57. Crenshaw, "Method in Determining Wisdom Influence," 130.
58. Cf. Fontaine, *Traditional Sayings in the Old Testament*, 101–7, 125–27.

# THE SAGE IN PROVERBS

## James L. Crenshaw

### THE THREE MAIN CONTEXTS
### OF ISRAELITE LEARNING

The Book of Proverbs expresses the views of countless individuals ranging from simple rural folk to a Queen Mother. These impressions about life's deep secrets and transparent truths have different authors and distinct audiences. Parents tutor their children, often drawing on popular lore from past generations to enable youngsters to succeed. Teachers instruct their students in the ways of the world, particularly in the art of steering the ship of state through treacherous waters. The two fundamental settings, family and school, invite distinct forms of pedagogy.[1] Mothers and fathers appeal to the collective learning of the larger family, and render their fresh discoveries in the form of truth statements, often called *sentences*. By contrast, professional teachers opt for longer *instructions* that have their own rationale built into the imperative—specifically exhortations and warnings—each with supporting arguments.[2] The meaning of sage differed, depending on whether the context of discussion was the family or school.

Despite scant evidence for a third context—the royal court, together with a school that fostered its interest—a case can be made for linking this educational establishment with the subsequent scribal school, for the collapse of the Monarchy in 587 B.C.E. left all surviving teachers and students without a royal patron and notably altered the pattern of their education. No adequate analysis of the sage in Proverbs will ignore these competing groups. Indeed, diversity in viewpoint, style, genre, and intention confirms suspicion that education in ancient Israel occurred in various settings and had multiple goals.

James L. Crenshaw is Professor of Old Testament at the Divinity School, Duke University.

1. W. McKane, *Proverbs* (OTL; Philadelphia: Westminster, 1970), uses the distinction between instruction and sentence to great advantage. His analysis derives from thorough examination of both forms in Egyptian wisdom, as well as study of Babylonian and Assyrian instructions and sentences.

2. In some instances sentences are embedded in instructions, thus bringing into question the neat distinction between the two (cf. Prov 1:17, 6:27–28, and 9:17).

## THE GOALS OF LEARNING

The introductions to two collections of instructions (Prov 1-9, 22:17-24:22) offer direct evidence relating to a technical understanding of a sage. The first serves as orientation for the whole book, although specifically focusing on chap. 1-9. It reads:

> To know wisdom and discipline,
>    to understand perceptive words,
> to receive instruction and astuteness,
>    righteousness, justice, and fairness;
> to give prudence to the simple,
>    knowledge and discretion to the youth—
> the sage may hear and increase learning,
>    and the discerning one may get skill,
> to grasp a proverb and an allusion,
>    the words of sages and their riddles.
>
> (Prov 1:1-6)

The second introduction has fewer technical terms and concentrates on the practical advantages of an education.

> Orient your ear and listen,
>    and put your mind to my knowledge;
> If you retain them [words of the wise][3] in your innermost being,
>    they will bring pleasure;
>    if they are wholly established on your lips.
> To let your trust be in the Lord,
>    I have declared them to you today, yes to you.
> Have I not written for you thirty[4]—
>    counsel and knowledge,
> To make known to you correct and reliable observations
>    for responding to those who sent you?
>
> (Prov 22:17-21)

The religious dimension, which came after the conclusion of Prov 1:1-6 and invites speculation among modern interpreters that it did not belong to the original,[5] appears in the center of the second introduction.

3. "Mit alten Auslegern wird *dibrê ḥăkāmîm* als Überschrift zu verstehen sein"; so O. Plöger, *Sprüche Salomos (Proverbia)* (BKAT 17; Neukirchen-Vluyn: Neukirchener, 1983) 262. The Septuagint opens the section with *logois sophōn paraballe son ous* (v 17).

4. JPSV refuses to follow recent scholarship in translating the rare Hebrew word *šališiwm* (!) on the basis of the thirty chapters in the Egyptian "Instruction of Amenemopet," with which the section introduced by this prologue has much in common.

5. Theories about a secular wisdom antedating religious sentences and instructions have generally appealed to a number of neutral statements in the Book of Proverbs. Similar traditional sayings exist outside wisdom literature and have been studied recently

Nevertheless, the two assertions of faith differ immensely, for Prov 1:7 emphasizes piety as the first principle or ultimate end of learning ("The fear of the Lord is the beginning [chief ingredient?] of knowledge; / ignorant persons despise wisdom and discipline"). The two introductions differ in other significant respects as well; the first one addresses both novices and mature thinkers, seeking to offer appropriate educational material for each group. The second introduction implies that the instruction has a single purpose, to prepare messengers to represent wealthy clients effectively. Whereas the images of the second introduction derive primarily from human anatomy (ears, heart, belly, lips), those of Prov 1:1–6 consist of intellectual abstractions that seem to have special nuances recognizable only to initiates.

A third instruction makes up Prov 31:1–9, but it lacks a specific comment about the goal of learning. The content of the instruction leaves little doubt about the audience and desired result. A mother offers counsel to her son, but she is no ordinary woman and he is no commoner. The Queen Mother instructs a son who is destined to occupy the throne in Massa, a Transjordanian region.[6] She wishes to help him escape the clutches of wicked women[7] and to avoid the baneful effects of excessive drinking.[8] Curiously, she offers no rationale for the warning about notorious women, a topic so dear to the wise in some circles.[9] Instead, she concentrates solely on the judicial responsibility of kings. In her view, wine enables society's castaways (and perhaps condemned criminals) to forget their misery. A king's duty is to speak on behalf of citizens whose lowly estate renders them mute, hence his mind must be clear and his tongue able. Such instruction

---

by C. Fontaine, *Traditional Sayings in the Old Testament* (Bible and Literature 5; Sheffield: Almond, 1982). On secular proverbs, see F. M. Wilson, "Sacred and Profane? The Yahwistic Redaction of Proverbs Reconsidered," *The Listening Heart* (ed. K. G. Hoglund et al.; JSOTSup 58; Sheffield: JSOT Press, 1987) 313–34.

6. This is the only wisdom instruction that is attributed to a woman, but C. V. Camp, in her *Wisdom and the Feminine in the Book of Proverbs* (Bible and Literature 11; Sheffield: Almond, 1985) and "Woman Wisdom as Root Metaphor: A Theological Consideration," *The Listening Heart* (ed. K. G. Hoglund et al.; JSOTSup 58; Sheffield: JSOT Press, 1987) 45–76, has argued for extensive feminine wisdom in ancient Israelite society.

7. B. Lang, *Wisdom and the Book of Proverbs: An Israelite Goddess Redefined* (New York: Pilgrim, 1986), postulates the existence of a goddess in the popular religion of ancient Israelites. If his hypothesis has merit, the struggle against the foreign seductress assumes new dimensions.

8. Although the text lacks an adjective indicating that excessive drinking is being discussed, scholars note that such an attitude as total abstinence hardly suits a court setting.

9. As early as the "Instruction of Ani" a warning against the foreign woman appears. It is tempting to wonder whether this fascination with the dangerous woman in Israel helped foster misogyny in later sages such as Ben Sira.

arises from an exalted concept of the royal office,[10] one easier to achieve in the abstract than in concrete situations of daily existence. The rich rhetoric in this brief unit may derive from an acknowledged discrepancy between the ideal and the actual.

## THE FORMAL SETTING OF LEARNING—
## PRAGMATIC, SECULAR, AND RELIGIOUS

By nature instructions presuppose a formal educational setting, either a royal or a scribal school. Each one has a distinctive purpose, but the two overlap at important points. The essential task of royal schools coincided with the interests of the state. Diplomacy depended on skilled linguists who could read documents in foreign languages and communicate with official representatives of various heads of state. The domestic economy also relied on trained personnel who recorded revenues and kept accurate accounts of commercial transactions. Besides such utilitarian undertakings, exclusively intellectual enterprises may have existed at the royal court, and perhaps exercises in lighter matters such as rhetorical contests for entertaining royalty.[11] The extent of religious indoctrination varied from time to time, depending on the political and spiritual climate.

Scribal schools maintained the earlier commitment to training an elite group of governmental employees, but these places of instruction also began to function more and more in the religious arena. Fundamental questions of existence attracted the attention of teachers and students. Can virtue exist without positive or negative reinforcement?[12] Does life have any meaning?[13] Where does faith belong in the quest for knowledge?[14] Furthermore, pragmatic interests led to concentration on personal growth. How can one escape the clutches of dangerous seductresses? What types of conduct guarantee success and which ones

10. L. Kalugila, *The Wise King* (Coniectanea Biblica, Old Testament Series 15; Lund: Gleerup, 1980).

11. Scholars have devoted too little attention to the lighter side of ancient wisdom, particularly contests in which the sole or primary purpose was entertainment (cf. "The Protests of the Eloquent Peasant" [*ANET* 407-10], which has a serious purpose, and the contest of Darius's guards in 1 Esdras).

12. G. Gutiérrez, *On Job: God-Talk and the Suffering of the Innocent* (Maryknoll, NY: Orbis, 1987), offers fresh insight into the biblical masterpiece about the possibility of disinterested righteousness.

13. I ask this question anew in *Ecclesiastes* (OTL; Philadelphia: Westminster, 1987).

14. Contrasting answers occur in Proverbs 1-9 and in 30:1-14. On the latter sayings of Agur, see my "Clanging Symbols," in the Festschrift for Walter Harrelson (*Justice and the Holy* [ed. D. A. Knight and P. Paris; Philadelphia: Fortress, 1989]).

bring calamity? Above all, do well-intentioned youth have a desirable companion who watches over them and bestows insight on them in times of need? These questions seem to have dominated the thoughts of scribal teachers and students.

In due time, religious instruction seized the lion's share of attention, and professional teachers consciously interpreted sacred traditions. Surrendering to this impulse, Ben Sira actually introduced Israel's religious heritage into the body of wisdom literature.[15] Furthermore, he brought about a virtual symbiosis of priestly and sapiential teachings. No wonder Ben Sira called his professional school a house of exegesis (*beth-hammidrash*). The unknown author of Wisdom of Solomon continued this elucidation of the biblical text, focusing at length on the story of the exodus.[16]

These two educational settings restricted their enrollment to an elite clientele,[17] whether potential courtiers or religious leaders. Did trained teachers ever address themselves to ordinary citizens, thus instituting a democratization of learning? According to the epilogist responsible for the initial comments about Qoheleth in Eccl 12:9-12, the teacher turned to the populace (*hā'ām*) with an unusual message of candor. If this language is not a vague substitute for "students," it implies that Qoheleth reached out to the wider citizenry, offering them the benefits of his private investigations.[18] His teaching lacked any connection with the usual aims of royal or scribal training—the preparation of skilled professionals. Instead, he endeavored to inform the public about life's futility. In Qoheleth's view, chance vitiated all attempts to master one's existence for personal gain and decisively undermined the goal of professional wisdom, despite claims to the contrary by representatives of the spiritual hierarchy (Eccl 8:17).

15. Because of their desire to understand Ben Sira in the light of Hellenistic literature, the strong influence of Yahwism does not come to expression in B. L. Mack, *Wisdom and the Hebrew Epic* (Chicago: University of Chicago, 1985), and T. R. Lee, *Studies in the Form of Sirach 44-50* (SBLDS 75; Atlanta: Scholars Press, 1986).

16. The section from Wis 10:15-19:22 excels in psychological insight and striking imagery, indicating the exceptional generative power of the story about deliverance from bondage.

17. F. Crüsemann, "Die unveränderbare Welt: Überlegungen zur 'Krisis der Weisheit' beim Prediger (Kohelet)," *Der Gott der kleinen Leute* (ed. W. Schottroff and W. Stegemann; Munich: Kaiser, 1979), 1.80-104 (English translation in *The God of the Lowly* [Maryknoll, NY: Orbis, 1984] 57-77), musters arguments in support of an earlier theory that the sages belonged to the privileged class. His case applies more readily to Qoheleth's audience than to their teacher, whose compassionate sentiments are accorded insufficient attention.

18. N. Lohfink, *Kohelet* (Neue Echter Bibel; Stuttgart: Echter, 1980), also understands *hā'ām* in this way.

Astonishingly, the instructions and scribal literature rarely touch on topics whose relevance is limited to professional life. The exception occurs in Sir 38:24–39:11, and its connection with the Egyptian "Satire on the Trades" is well known.[19] Other than Ben Sira, no Israelite scribe mentions a school, although Wis 7:17–22 describes the curriculum in vogue at the time. Particular concerns of the royal court have made no lasting impression on the content of the instructions. The Egyptian instructions likewise seldom call attention to schools,[20] but the existence of these institutions is beyond doubt.[21] Wisdom schools also existed in Mesopotamia, although they served a fundamentally different role in many essentials. Use of analogy from these two countries strengthens the case for schools in Israel, but differences in cultural development and world view suggest caution.[22] This necessity for caution extends to technical vocabulary, whether native to Israel or borrowed from Egypt.[23] Even the Hebrew ḥākām seldom has a technical meaning, a point that has not always been appreciated.[24]

Israelite instructions are profoundly religious. Were they pious from the beginning, or did a later reading of this literature infuse it with religious conviction? In Egypt, a definite development from confident teaching to pious fatalism can be observed, and scholars have argued that Israelite secularism also succumbed to vigorous dogma, conveniently labeled "fear of Yahweh."[25] If this hypothesis prevails, it will undoubtedly influence the understanding of sages. Earlier ones will be characterized as secularists, whereas later sages will be related more closely to religious authorities. Perhaps these professional teachers and students managed to compartmentalize religion and daily existence in the same way folk wisdom did.

19. AEL 1:184–92.

20. E. W. Heaton, Solomon's New Men (New York: Pica, 1974) 108.

21. See the two Egyptian instructions in AEL 2:167–78.

22. See my essays "Education in Ancient Israel," JBL 104 (1985) 601–15, and "The Acquisition of Knowledge in Israelite Wisdom Literature," Word and World 7 (1987) 245–52. See also F. Golka, "Die israelitische Weisheitsschule oder 'des Kaisers neue Kleider,'" VT 33 (1983) 257–70.

23. N. Shupak, "The 'Sitz im Leben' of the Book of Proverbs in the Light of a Comparison of Biblical and Egyptian Wisdom Literature," RB 94 (1987) 98–119, assumes that identical vocabulary implies a similar social context and undervalues the possibility of polygenesis (different cultures may have arrived at the same imagery independently). Nevertheless, the striking affinities in language demand an explanation, possibly the one given by Shupak.

24. R. N. Whybray, The Intellectual Tradition in the Old Testament (BZAW 135; Berlin and New York: de Gruyter, 1974), makes this point with telling force. The word ḥākām refers to various kinds of expertise, even to devious and crafty thinking.

25. McKane, Proverbs, endeavors to distinguish different stages in this process of reinterpreting older proverbs, although the criteria for doing so are highly hypothetical.

## ON THE AUTHORS AND AUDIENCE OF
## THE SENTENCE LITERATURE

What role did sages play in this sentence literature? Answering that question will require close scrutiny of the remaining collections in the Book of Proverbs. The major portion of these popular aphorisms is associated with Solomon and Hezekiah (Prov 10:1–22:16, chaps. 25–29), although a few lack any identification (Prov 24:23–34, 30:15–33, 31:10–31) and one collection derives from an otherwise unknown Agur (Prov 30:1–14).[26] These secondary superscriptions have less to do with origins than use, except for the last one (Prov 31:1).

Two superscriptions use the technical term for the wise (*ḥăkāmîm*). The first one has been accidentally incorporated into the text of the prologue to the collection that somewhat duplicates eleven instructions in Amenemopet ("Orient your ear and listen to *the words of the wise*"; Prov 22:17). The second superscription using technical vocabulary of the wise boldly asserts that "these also are utterances of the wise" (Prov 24:23). Clearly these texts presuppose professional sages in Israelite society as the authors of the advice that follows.

The content and form of these sayings support the attribution to professional teachers, despite an occasional reference to father and mother. The imperatives with motivations belong to the instruction genre, and the type of counsel seems directed toward future governmental employees: behaving wisely at meals, avoiding drunkenness, recognizing the danger posed by harlots, realizing the power of counsel, refusing to act vindictively, fearing God and the king, judging fairly, and perceiving the perils of laziness. This last topic resembles an instruction in Prov 6:6–11, but the form in Prov 24:30–34 is autobiographical or anecdotal. At one point these sayings actually promise gifted persons that they will come to the attention of kings rather than wasting away in obscurity (Prov 22:29).

Like these minor collections of instructions, which consciously attend to the special interests of professional sages, the initial collection in Proverbs 1–9 discusses items that may have pertained to prospective courtiers: the correct attitude toward power and its revenues, proper respect for truth, the advantage of deference, the dangers of sexual license, the pitfalls of laziness, and the importance of wisdom in establishing and governing the inhabited world. On the other hand, nothing in this collection lies outside the realm of ordinary citizens. That point achieves focus in the references to teaching that derives from parents,

---

26. Both this text and Prov 31:1–9 have the Hebrew word *māśśāʾ*, which probably alludes to the place of origin. The word may also contain a pun on the Hebrew word for oracle or burden, at least in the sayings of Agur.

an emphasis that becomes particularly personal on occasion (Prov 4:1–
6—especially v 4). This ambivalence about the real context for these
instructions, home or school, comes mightily to expression in Prov 5:7–
14 where "sons" complain that they disregarded their teachers' instructions and almost came to ruin in the assembled congregation. Here one
could render "sons" by the word "students," for the expression seems to
have taken on a technical meaning.[27] Accordingly, the terms for parents
in the other sections of this collection may connote professional teachers
who functioned *in loco parentis*.

   In sum, Israel's instructions may very well have been written by
professional teachers specifically for potential scribes and courtiers.
These elaborate counsels addressed various topics that appealed to
young men[28] who aspired to work for kings and nobles. In these
collections the wise belong to a privileged class, and the sage stands
apart from ordinary citizens regardless of their intellectual achievement.
Perhaps the Egyptian influence in these instructions relates in some way
to this professionalism. Egyptian sages, too, spoke of a goddess of order
(*ma$^c$at*) who held the symbol of life in one hand and of prosperity in
another. They identified the king's throne with righteousness and wrote
about God's weighing the heart and rewarding the virtuous with a
wreath. They also recognized certain kinds of conduct as an abomination to God, particularly actions that took advantage of the powerless.[29]

## ON THE INTERRELATIONSHIP OF
## PROFESSIONAL SAGES, ASCRIPTIONS OF
## ROYAL AUTHORSHIP, AND POPULAR WISDOM

What place did professional sages occupy in popular wisdom,[30] which
expresses itself in the sentence literature in Prov 10:1–22:16 and chaps.
25–29? Use of the term "popular wisdom" already suggests an answer:
this body of knowledge derives from the populace at large and identifies concerns of general application. Then what do the ascriptions to

   27. The reference to "mother" militates against a technical sense for the word *ʾāb*
(father), but guilds in which parents taught their own sons and others may eventually
have led to a technical meaning of *ʾāb* and *běnî*.
   28. At least two things suggest that Israelite students were exclusively masculine.
First, they are consistently addressed as sons, and, second, they are admonished to remain
faithful to their own wives and to shun foreign women.
   29. G. E. Bryce, *A Legacy of Wisdom* (Lewisburg, PA: Bucknell University, 1979),
gives a comprehensive analysis of Israel's transformation of borrowings from Egypt.
   30. L. Naré, *Proverbes salomoniens et proverbes mossi* (Frankfurt am Main: Peter
Lang, 1986), examines Proverbs 25–29 in the light of African popular wisdom. His insights
often illuminate the biblical text.

Solomon mean, who were Hezekiah's men, and why did someone make this connection between royalty and folk wisdom?

In the Psalter many psalms have the superscription "to David," perhaps in the sense of "pertaining to" rather than "belonging to." Having nothing to do with authorship, the ascription nevertheless identifies the particular psalms as in some way associated with Israel's great king, David. Various traditions linked him with music, making it entirely appropriate to connect his name with the Psalter, whether as patron or as representative of a musical style. A similar phenomenon may have taken place among the sages, who knew the centrality of the pharaohs in Egyptian wisdom and who acknowledged the force of traditions about Solomon's exceptional sagacity.

In their present form, those popular reflections on Solomon's wisdom are wholly immersed in fantasy, although they may rest on authentic memory. The recollections that have the strongest claim to accuracy attribute to him a type of aphorism that rarely appears in the Book of Proverbs. That missing form is nature wisdom, possibly nominal lists (onomastica). The closest thing to such wisdom in the biblical canon occurs in the anonymous supplement to the sayings of Agur. These numerical proverbs draw moral lessons primarily from observing nature (Prov 30:15-33). The literary character of this evidence and its dissimilarity from the actual utterances associated with Solomon in the Book of Proverbs are not easily accommodated to a view of Solomonic authorship or patronage.

Sociological analysis of this king's place in the ancient Near East may lend support to the historicity of the later legends, but the method hardly offers the final answers that some interpreters attribute to it. No amount of special pleading will erase the harsh fact that Solomon's regime was oppressive and blood-letting. Reconciling these practices with "enlightenment" mentality requires considerable mental reservation.[31]

Still, Solomon's diplomacy probably introduced a professional class of the wise into Israelite society. The "men of Hezekiah" may have continued this intellectual tradition, perhaps copying[32] earlier truth statements of popular origin and providing a context for these utterances. In neither case did the wise compose the sayings that appear in the collections attributed to Solomon and associated with Hezekiah's men. Even if a small section of the latter collection actually functions as

31. Surely it is significant that the consistent teachings in biblical proverbs condemn the abuses of power and privilege for which Solomon was known.

32. These men of Hezekiah are called copiers (he'tîqû), not sages (ḥăkāmîm).

a mirror for aspiring rulers (Proverbs 28-29),[33] which is improbable, the vast majority of these truth statements address ordinary citizens. In them the word ḥākām (wise) has a moral connotation and lacks any reference to a profession.

Exceptions to this summary statement do occur. The most notable one concerns the making of war, which ordinarily belonged to kings (Prov 20:18). This observation about the importance of counselors in preparing strategy for a battle may, of course, derive from premonarchic times when family leaders gathered persons of discernment to discuss an approaching skirmish. Nevertheless, the larger context has several statements that exalt kings and allude to righteousness as the foundation of the throne, an idea that also appears in Egyptian wisdom literature.[34] Nowhere in these two collections of truth statements does Egyptian influence shape the expression more notably than in chap. 16, which goes so far as to assert that royal judgments cannot err because God directs the king's thinking (Prov 16:10). Here the ruler's goodness is grounded in the fact that his throne is established by righteousness (ṣĕdāqâ = maʿat), and his approval of integrity is assured (Prov 16:12-13). Although a king's anger is a messenger of death, his favor distills life-giving rain (Prov 16:14-15). Such assertions do not appear to communicate folk wisdom.[35]

This intermingling of popular aphorisms and language from Egyptian courtiers illustrates the complexity of Israelite wisdom literature. No single sociological group was responsible for the sapiential corpus, whether family or royal court. Considerable crossover probably occurred, the same persons belonging to different settings over the years. Consequently, neat divisions of the literature may be more heuristically than historically accurate. Folk wisdom, above all, registers the insights of individuals from the total society.

It follows that many viewpoints surface in these truth assertions. Persons of humble circumstances and individuals of substance observe human nature and draw universal insights from frequent repetition. Some sayings reflect pious presuppositions, others do not take the transcendent realm into account at all. Some focus entirely on domestic situations, others think only of commerce. Some recognize psychological dimensions of various experiences, others seem content to describe what is visible to the naked eye. Moreover, common folk may

---

33. U. Skladny, *Die älttesten Spruchsammlungen in Israel* (Göttingen: Vandenhoeck und Ruprecht, 1962), has defended this hypothesis.

34. H. Brunner, "Gerechtigkeit als Fundament des Thrones," *VT* 8 (1958) 426-28.

35. Do the errors of Hebrew in chaps. 15-16 reinforce suspicion that foreign hands have helped shape this section of the book? Stylistic differences have long been noted as well.

have reflected about kings and the dangers associated with life at
the royal court, while courtiers who owned farms may have talked
about matters related to successful breeding of herds and growing sufficient food for people and animals. That is why subject matter alone
offers a dubious criterion for determining the social setting of a given
aphorism.[36]

A preponderance of evidence still points to popular origin for the
truth statements associated with Solomon and Hezekiah's men. Many of
these utterances may betray literary retouching at the hands of trained
sages,[37] but eloquence was not wholly missing from untutored individuals, as an Egyptian sage acknowledged.[38] In all probability, parents
devoted considerable energy to instructing their children, and the oft-
repeated appeal "my son" points first and foremost to the family context. Numerous sayings are directed to youngsters who faced the perils
of growing up, but other utterances presuppose a married clientele with
responsibilities in the larger society.

## CONCLUDING REMARKS ON THE CONFIDENCE, CHARACTER, AND UNIVERSALISM OF THE SAGES

Regardless of the social context of these utterances, they possessed
astonishing confidence in the power of the intellect. By living according
to the accumulated insights of past generations, individuals guaranteed
prosperity, long life, honor, and well being. For these optimists, the
universe seemed to operate in an orderly manner, rewarding virtue and
punishing vice. Behind this discernible order[39] stood a benevolent
creator whose providential care brought security to those who practiced "fear of the Lord." In their eyes, the wise were righteous and fools
were wicked; hence to be a sage meant adopting a way of life characterized by devout conduct. That was by no means all, for these aphorisms also describe sages as diligent, self-controlled, modest, chaste,
temperate, and respectful. In other words, the wise enabled society to
function successfully. Fools disturbed the calm, necessitating rigorous

---

36. Form critics have always paid attention to social setting, a point that some
interpreters seem to overlook in their excitement over a method in vogue at the moment.

37. H.-J. Hermisson, *Studien zur israelitischen Spruchweisheit* (Neukirchen-Vluyn:
Neukirchener, 1968).

38. "Good speech is more hidden than greenstone, / Yet may be found among
maids at the grindstones" ("Instruction of Ptahhotep"; see *AEL* 1:63).

39. On current debate about the appropriateness of using the concept of order with
reference to biblical wisdom, see my essay "Murphy's Axiom: Every Gnomic Saying
Needs a Balancing Corrective," *The Listening Heart* (ed. K. G. Hoglund et al.; JSOTSup
58; Sheffield: JSOT Press, 1987) 1–17.

measures at the hands of gentler people. Sages therefore recognized the reality of evil, but they believed in their own ability to cope in the face of adversity.

Why did the sages compile the several collections of proverbs? Presumably, instructions arose in an educational context and served as texts in classrooms.[40] Did folk wisdom also function in this setting? Although the wise left no clue about the rationale for the compilation of the Book of Proverbs other than the prologues to chaps. 1–9 and 22:17–24:22, they undoubtedly recognized the educational value of popular wisdom. Precisely when this collecting of proverbs took place remains a mystery, but the initial activity may date from the Solomonic era. This quest to preserve insights from the past probably blossomed under Hezekiah, when political circumstances combined to foster respect for the past and to usher in a sense of urgency that surrounds a people who aspires to greatness against impossible odds. In any event, the collectors added nothing that enables modern scholars to date their work. They may actually have brought the collections together in Josiah's reign or during some later period. Strangely, these later sages respected their predecessors' wish to maintain universal appeal, for they introduced no distinctive feature of Yahwism. That departure from wisdom's usual realm of discourse was left to Ben Sira, a sage quite distinct from those who composed and collected the Book of Proverbs.

40. A. Lemaire, *Les écoles et la formation de la Bible dans l'ancien Israël* (OBO 39; Göttingen: Vandenhoeck und Ruprecht, 1981), makes this point, although with less restraint than the evidence requires. (For a recent review of this subject by Lemaire, see his essay in this volume, "The Sage in School and Temple," pp. 165–81 above.)

# THE SAGE IN THE PSALMS

## Anthony R. Ceresko

One can speak about the relationship of the sage to the psalms, and to the Psalter, from a variety of viewpoints. For example, most commentators admit the presence in the Psalter of a small group of "wisdom psalms," that is, psalms that come from the hand of wisdom writers and that reflect wisdom themes and terminology.[1] Also, a number of other psalms, if not wisdom psalms in the strict sense, suggest at least some influence from wisdom circles.[2] Finally, the Psalter itself is clearly the product of the torah/wisdom teachers, and the final form of this collection of songs bears the stamp of their influence and intent.[3] Thus my title, "The Sage in the Psalms," implies a number of meanings, and I will explore three of them. First, the sage in the Psalms could mean the portrait of the sage, as opposed to the fool, which the psalms themselves present. When one reads the psalms, what does "being wise" seem to imply? One could also understand the sage in the Psalms to mean the sage as author of psalms. In other words, one could examine the wisdom psalms, and the Psalter, looking for answers to questions such as who were these sages and what concerns did they have; what was their purpose in creating the literary productions they have left us. Finally, one could study the Psalter itself, the Book of Psalms, as the product of the sage's work. Thus the compositions therein, once the words by which Israel spoke to God in praise, thanksgiving, and supplication, have now become the Word of God to Israel, the means by

Anthony R. Ceresko, O.S.F.S., is Associate Professor of Old Testament at the University of St. Michael's College, Toronto.

1. R. E. Murphy's article, "A Consideration of the Classification 'Wisdom Psalms,'" *Congress Volume: Bonn 1962* (VTSup 9; Leiden: Brill, 1963) 156–67 (repr. in *SAIW* 456–67), often serves as a starting point in the discussion of wisdom psalms. See also the more recent treatment of J. L. Crenshaw, *Old Testament Wisdom: An Introduction* (Atlanta: John Knox, 1981) 180–85 (note his bibliography on p. 257 n. 8), and the cautions of G. T. Sheppard, *Wisdom as a Hermeneutical Construct: A Study in the Sapientializing of the Old Testament* (BZAW 151; Berlin/New York: de Gruyter, 1980) 12.

2. Murphy, "Consideration of the Classification 'Wisdom Psalms,'" 165–67.

3. Cf. G. H. Wilson, *The Editing of the Hebrew Psalter* (SBLDS 76; Chico, CA: Scholars Press, 1985).

217

which God reveals himself and his will to his people, especially to those trained and able to use the Book faithfully and wisely.

## THE SAGE AS PICTURED BY THE PSALMS AND THE PSALTER: ONE WHO PRAYS AND WHO OBSERVES THE TORAH

To associate certain psalms, or even the Psalter itself, with the wisdom movement in ancient Israel is to imply a connection with teaching and learning. This may at first appear problematic since the psalms, by definition, are principally prayers and are associated first and foremost with the temple and worship rather than the school. However, as some authors have pointed out, the liturgy itself offers occasions for teaching,[4] and it is precisely at this point of common concern, the didactic, that an important link between the psalms and wisdom is established. The most obvious moment is the "testimony" or "confession" element of the Thanksgiving Psalm when the psalmist recounts an experience of deliverance and, on the basis of that experience of God's protection and benevolence, proceeds to exhort the congregation to trust in God's promise of help:

> Thus the testimony to some extent assumes the nature of an *admonition*, whether it calls the person blessed, who confesses his sins and obtains forgiveness and is healed from illness and impurity, or straightway invites others to follow the example of the worshipper (Ps. xxxi 24, xxxii 6 f., xxxiv 6 ff., cxxiv 8).—Here the style and ideas of the "poetry of wisdom" are likely to have made themselves felt; for even the latter has for its object exhortative religious and moral instruction, where the teacher (father) often refers to his own experience as a guarantee of the truth of his words.[5]

Common to both the psalms and the wisdom movement is also the ideological function of "world-building." One of the points of origin of the wisdom movement was the socialization process that took place within Israel and indeed is a process fundamental to every society and culture. In ancient Israel, it was in the context of the family/clan and school that this process took place of "taking over the world in which

---

4. E.g., R. E. Murphy, *The Psalms, Job* (Proclamation Commentaries; Philadelphia: Fortress, 1977) 34.

5. S. Mowinckel, "Psalms and Wisdom," *WIANE* 213–14. See also Murphy, "Consideration of the Classification 'Wisdom Psalms,'" 161; and J. K. Kuntz, "The Canonical Wisdom Psalms of Ancient Israel—Their Rhetorical, Thematic, and Formal Dimensions," *Rhetorical Criticism: Essays in Honor of James Muilenburg* (ed. J. J. Jackson and M. Kessler; Pittsburgh: Pickwick, 1974) 190.

others already lived" and of apprehending "the world as a meaningful and social reality."[6] Both the origins and the products of Israel's wisdom movement are associated with this process of socialization or "world-building" for the young.

If the wisdom movement involved itself in the handing on of the knowledge and values of the community ("the world" in which that community lived) to the next generation, the cult, with its sacred songs (the psalms) functioned to maintain, reshape, and celebrate that world. The wisdom school and the psalmist intersect in their common enterprise of maintaining and/or reshaping this world inhabited by the community of Israel, particularly in the question of the individual and his or her role, comportment, and place in this world.[7] The picture of the "pious" and wise individual—and the foil, the wicked and foolish one—is communicated both directly and indirectly in the poems produced by the wisdom psalmists. From them we can piece together the picture of the ideal Israelite that the authors of the wisdom psalms wished to present, and the words, actions, and attitudes that could truly be characterized as "wise."

J. K. Kuntz lists a number of miscellaneous counsels that, taken together, present a quite concrete description of everyday actions and attitudes of the wise person as portrayed in the psalms:

> Psalmic wisdom recommends that man be mindful of the company that he keeps (1:1) and prudent in his speech (34:14). He should desist from anger (37:8) and quest for peace (34:15; 37:37), living in true harmony with his brothers (Psalm 133). In his dealings he is expected to manifest signs of meekness (37:11; cf. 49:13, 21), generosity (112:5, 9), and integrity (62:11, 112:5). Moreover, he is admonished to wait upon Yahweh in a spirit of trust (32:10; 37:3, 5, 7, 34; 62:9) and confer with the deity in all that he undertakes (127:1-2). As a recompense for his devotion to Yahweh, he may look forward to a large and prosperous family (128:1-4). Finally, he is commanded to shun evil and do good (34:15; 37:3, 27).[8]

6. P. L. Berger and T. Luckmann, *The Social Construction of Reality: A Treatise in the Sociology of Knowledge* (Garden City, NY: Doubleday, 1966) 130; cf. J. H. Hayes, *An Introduction to Old Testament Study* (Nashville: Abingdon, 1979) 325-29.

7. A. Robert, for example, comments that in Psalm 119 "it is the individual who is in focus, and no longer the nation"; "Le psaume CXIX et les Sapientiaux," *RB* 48 (1939) 19.

8. Kuntz, "Canonical Wisdom Psalms," 215. One could elaborate this picture, especially from the frequent description of "the contrasting life styles of the righteous and the wicked" in psalmic wisdom. Psalm 37 is particularly important in this regard; cf. Kuntz, "Canonical Wisdom Psalms," 213-14; and H. Gunkel, *Einleitung in die Psalmen: Die Gattungen der religiösen Lyrik Israels* (3d ed.; Göttingen: Vandenhoeck und Ruprecht, 1975) 392. By way of contrast, Ps 10:3-11 offers a "remarkably detailed description of the godless man," although Kuntz does not attribute wisdom links to the passage ("Canonical Wisdom Psalms," 205).

However, one could parallel almost all of these traits in the Book of
Proverbs, for example. When one examines psalmic wisdom, one must
recognize two further dimensions to the picture of the sage—veneration
of the torah and devotedness to prayer. These are apparent as much
from the spirit and shape of the Psalter itself as from individual wisdom
or wisdom-influenced psalms. For although a small minority of individual psalms are specifically linked with the sages, the Psalter as such is
a product of the postexilic community when the sage had become the
scholar-sage or "scribe."[9] For the latter, wisdom had become identified
with the torah and the wise individual was thus one whose "delight is in
the law [tôrâ] of the LORD, and on his law he meditates day and night"
(Ps 1:2 RSV).[10] Also, since many of these scribes were priests, the interest
in the cult, and especially prayer, had become more central.[11]

Certain psalms (e.g., Psalms 1 and 119), then, and particularly the
whole collection, the Psalter, taken together, image the wise individual
as one who venerates the *torah*:

> In all instances the sage manifests his willingness to subordinate himself to
> the divine will. . . . His task is to comprehend that will as it is revealed in
> the written Torah and his joy is to experience unmitigated delight in his
> thorough knowledge of the law.[12]

Thus, "a spirituality of the Torah has been inserted into the framework
of the psalter as a whole, and is one of the foremost guidelines of
interpretation of the book, a real key to its understanding."[13] One
example of the redactional activity that has given this slant to the Psalter

9. S. Mowinckel, *The Psalms in Israel's Worship* (2 vols.; Oxford: Basil Blackwell,
1962), 2:204: "While the earlier small collections [of psalms] came into existence among
the singers, the Psalter as a whole, and probably even the Davidic psalms group I (Pss.
3–41) were collected by the learned, 'the scribes', 'the wise'. Their interest in psalmography along with their interest in the ancient sacred tradition and all matters of religion
led them to create out of the earlier cultic booklets the large Psalter."

10. Thus does J. Reindl, "Weisheitliche Bearbeitung von Psalmen: Ein Beitrag zum
Verständnis der Sammlung des Psalters," *Congress Volume: Vienna 1980* (ed. J. A.
Emerton; VTSup 32; Leiden: Brill, 1981) 340–41, describe the one responsible for the
editing of the Psalter: "He himself belongs among those men who were knowledgeable in
the scriptures and nourished on torah-piety, those who had taken the place of 'the wise' of
former times, and whose ideal image Ben Sira had sketched"; cf. Sir 39:1–11. Note also
J. L. Mays, "The Place of the Torah-Psalms in the Psalter," *JBL* 106 (1987) 11: "Those who
were at work in the final shaping and arrangement of the Psalter were completely
committed to torah as the divinely willed way of life."

11. E.g., D. F. Morgan, *Wisdom in the Old Testament Traditions* (Atlanta: John
Knox, 1981) 120.

12. Kuntz, "Canonical Wisdom Psalms," 212–13, commenting on "the piety which is
indigenous to psalmic wisdom."

13. B. de Pinto, "The Torah and the Psalms," *JBL* 86 (1967) 174.

is the placing of Psalms 1 and 119, called "torah psalms" because of their emphasis on "torah" or "law, instruction," at pivotal points in the collection. G. H. Wilson notes that

> The placement of Ps 1 as an introduction to the whole Psalter . . . offers the *reader* a pair of "hermeneutical spectacles" through which to view the contents. . . . Ps 1 emphasizes individual meditation rather than communal recitation. The pss thus become the source of *each* man's search for the path of obedience to the "Torah of YHWH": the path which leads from death to life.[14]

In addition, the "massive presence" of Psalm 119 dominates and forms the central focus for the final section of the Psalter (Book V), in this way highlighting the centrality of torah meditation and balancing the introductory Psalm 1 whose main theme it shares.[15]

Besides veneration of the torah, the wisdom redactors of the Psalter and authors of the wisdom psalms recognized an interest in and devotion to *prayer* as a further trait of the wise individual.[16] First of all, the authors of these psalms picture themselves as uttering prayers (e.g., Ps 19:15; 32:5; 73:17, 23–25, 28; 119). Second, they exhort the reader or listener to pray—to "magnify the Lord" and "exalt his name" (Ps 34:4), because "this poor man cried, and the Lord heard him, / and saved him out of all his troubles" (Ps 34:7 rsv; see further Ps 32:11; 37:3–5). Finally, the Psalter as a whole is presented by its authors as a book to be used for prayer and praise.[17]

L. G. Perdue has studied the relationship between wisdom and worship and has concluded that psalms associated with wisdom fall into three categories in their connection with the cult: didactic poems that were not originally written for the cult but were included in the Psalter

14. Wilson, *Editing of the Hebrew Psalter*, 143. See also Murphy, "Consideration of the Classification 'Wisdom Psalms,'" 162. L. Perdue, *Wisdom and Cult: A Critical Analysis of the Views of Cult in the Wisdom Literatures of Israel and the Ancient Near East* (SBLDS 30; Missoula, MT: Scholars Press, 1977) 330 n. 39, notes the similar role that Prov 1:1-7 plays for the Book of Proverbs in providing an interpretative context for what follows.

15. Wilson, *Editing of the Hebrew Psalter*, 223. Mays, "Place of the Torah-Psalms," 9, includes Psalm 19 along with Psalms 1 and 119 and states: "It is not difficult to imagine how this unifying point of view [i.e., the centrality of torah], stated as an introduction to the Psalter and reiterated across its breadth, could provide a perspective from which the rest of the Psalter could be understood and read."

16. Mowinckel, for example, comments: "In spite of the didactic character of the 'learned psalmography', . . . it has one essential thing in common with genuine psalmography: these poems are and will be considered as *prayers*"; "Psalms and Wisdom," 208–9. For more on prayer as a wisdom *Gattung* see G. von Rad, *Wisdom in Israel* (Nashville/ New York: Abingdon, 1972) 47–49.

17. Mays, "Place of the Torah-Psalms," 12.

by the editorial work of the postexilic scribes (Psalms 1, 37, 49, 112, 127);[18] other poems that, "while not intended for use as cultic literature, nevertheless, do reflect over cultic rituals and dogmas" (Psalms 32, 34, 73);[19] and psalms written by the wise specifically for use in the cult (Psalms 19A, 19B, 119). That the association of the later wisdom writers with the cult issues in an interest in and production of prayers is, for Perdue, a quite logical process. First of all, the wise quite naturally "exalted prayer as the single most important cultic act" because they "considered themselves to be able creators and gifted speakers of prayers, based on their ability to write artistic poetry and to speak cogently. . . ."[20] Second, prayer was not only proper and acceptable but indeed the preeminent form of worship of the deity, and the prayer of the wise/righteous person won special hearing and had particular efficacy because of their high status in God's eyes: "When the righteous cry for help, the LORD hears, / and delivers them out of all their troubles" (Ps 34:18 RSV; see also Ps 37:39–40).[21]

## THE SAGE AS AUTHOR OF
## PSALMS: WISDOM AND ORDER

One can also approach this topic by asking what one can learn about the sages themselves who wrote these psalms: what concerns did they have and what was their purpose in creating the literary products they have left us. For one thing, they were not motivated simply by esthetic concerns, *ars gratia artis*. Rather, esthetic interest is subordinated to, and in view of, the creation of community—the creation of the "social world" that Israel inhabited. For Israel's imagination primarily "thinks in terms of the reality of community and the ways that community can reorder its public existence in different and liberating ways."[22] This recalls my discussion above concerning the sages' role as world-builders both by involvement in the socialization process, that is, in their role as teachers, as transmitters of Israel's social world to the next generation,

---

18. Perdue, *Wisdom and Cult,* 268. Perdue notes, however: "It is possible that during the liturgy a place was given to the recitation of didactic poetry, intended to instruct the cultic assembly. If this were the case, then the didactic poems could have had a cultic function as well" (p. 327 n. 19).

19. Ibid., 268.

20. Ibid., 312.

21. Ibid.

22. W. Brueggemann, "Imagination as a Mode of Fidelity," *Understanding the Word: Essays in Honor of Bernhard W. Anderson* (ed. J. T. Butler, E. W. Conrad, and B. C. Ollenburger; JSOTSup 37; Sheffield: JSOT Press, 1985) 24.

and through their contact with the cult and the latter's function in maintaining/shaping/transforming that world.[23]

A key element in this world-building process is the concern for "order," a concern central to the wisdom movement in general, as R. E. Murphy, for example, has noted:

> Wisdom attempts to establish or impose a kind of order upon the myriad human experiences that form the raw material of wisdom sayings and upon nature itself. . . . The sayings of the sages flow from experience and put order into the chaotic events that make up human life.[24]

One of the primary sources even for the very concept of order is the stability of nature and humanity's experience of its regularity, daily and seasonally. Israel saw God at work in this stability and regularity, and this experience is a constant theme in Israel's praise of God in the psalms.[25] In the eyes of the wisdom writers, however, nature and the experience of its stability and regularity served mainly as terms of comparison.[26] For example, the generosity of God in the ordering of nature ("He provides food for those who fear him," Ps 111:5) becomes the model for the generous behavior of the one "blessed by Yahweh" in Psalm 112: "He has distributed freely, he has given to the poor" (v 9).[27] Again, the order evident in the prosperity and fruitfulness of "the tree planted by streams of water" (Ps 1:3) and the decline of "the beasts that perish" (Ps 49:13, 21) mirrors for the psalmist the inevitable ends of the

23. W. Brueggemann, *The Message of the Psalms: A Theological Commentary* (Minneapolis: Augsburg, 1984) 26, notes concerning S. Mowinckel's work on "the creative power of public worship": "Such worship is indeed 'world-making.' These psalms become a means whereby the creator is in fact creating the world. That perhaps is one meaning of the saying, 'God creates by Word.' That creative word is spoken in these psalms in the liturgical process, and it is in the world of worship that Israel 're-experiences' and 'redescribes' the safe world over which God presides."

24. R. E. Murphy, "Wisdom and Yahwism," *No Famine in the Land: Studies in Honor of John L. McKenzie* (ed. J. W. Flanagan and A. W. Robinson; Missoula, MT: Scholars Press, 1975) 120.

25. Brueggemann notes, for example: "The most foundational experience of orientation is the daily experience of *life's regularities*, which are experienced as reliable, equitable, and generous. The psalmic community readily affirmed that this experience is ordained and sustained by God"; *Message of the Psalms*, 28. He proceeds to discuss Psalms 145, 104, 33, and 8 in this context.

26. Murphy, "Wisdom and Yahwism," 121.

27. Following Brueggemann, *Message of the Psalms*, 45–47, who notes that "Psalms 111 and 112 may belong together," and thus sees Psalm 111 providing "the theological basis for the moral conviction of 112" (p. 45). See also Mays, "Place of the Torah-Psalms," 10: "Psalms 111 and 112 are a set of two, both in the acrostic form, and clearly composed to complement each other."

wise and the wicked, respectively. In Psalm 19, the "fine-tuned regularity of the universe" (vv 2–7) witnesses to God's power to ensure in turn a well-ordered and beneficent human community through the torah, observed faithfully by those who are wise and loyal (vv 8–15).[28]

The concern with order, especially order within the community, informs the didactic intent of the authors of the wisdom psalms. W. Brueggemann comments, for example, on the pedagogical intent of Psalm 37: "The purpose of such instruction . . . is to instill in the young socially acceptable modes of behavior," since behavior such as this "contributes decisively to the well-being of the entire community."[29] Such instruction presumes that the way society works is good and beneficent, and it warns against trespassing the community's "good order." Thus psalmic wisdom stresses the notion of "retribution," that is, that such behavior is inevitably rewarded and its contrary invariably works ill both for the individual and for the community.[30]

As I mentioned above (pp. 220–21), much of psalmic wisdom reflects the postexilic situation in which wisdom had become closely tied to torah. Psalms 1 and 119 are good examples of this development and, again, it reflects the focus on order. Observance of torah makes one wise and allows one to bring order into one's daily life (e.g., Ps 119:97–104; see also Ps 1:1–3; 37:30–31). Motivation for such observance is further strengthened by the linking of torah with the divine will and its power for order. Through observance of torah one enters into communion with the one who is the source and center of this world's structures and one is able to live an orderly and satisfying life according to his will and purpose (cf. Ps 119:89–93). The ultimate goal, however, is human community. Psalm 19, for example, celebrates the power for order inherent in the divine will and reflected in the stability of nature (vv 2–7). But the psalmist goes on to praise the torah through which that divine will is revealed so that it might become the basis in turn for the order and life of the community.[31]

For psalmic wisdom, one way in which this concern with order expresses itself concretely, indeed, visually, is in its employment of the acrostic.[32] One of the functions of this convention is to underline the

28. R. J. Clifford, "The Hebrew Scriptures and the Theology of Creation," *Theological Studies* 46 (1985) 516. Note also Mays, "Place of the Torah-Psalms," 5.

29. Brueggemann, *Message of the Psalms*, 43.

30. See, e.g., Brueggemann's treatment of Psalm 112 from this perspective; ibid., 45–47.

31. Clifford, "Hebrew Scriptures and the Theology of Creation," 516.

32. For a description of the acrostic device and its use in Hebrew poetry see W. G. E. Watson, *Classical Hebrew Poetry: A Guide to Its Techniques* (JSOTSup 26; Sheffield: JSOT Press, 1984) 190–200; e.g., p. 190: "In an acrostic poem, the first letter of each line follows a certain sequence. Usually, this sequence is alphabetic, so that each line begins with a successive letter of the alphabet."

sense of order and symmetry that the psalmist attempts to bring to the subject matter of the poem. For example, the elaborate acrostic structure of Psalm 119, with its predictable and orderly movement, serves to reinforce the psalm's message "that life is reliable and utterly symmetrical when the torah is honored."[33]

Psalm 34 is a variant of this acrostic pattern. The normal sequence is followed, with successive lines beginning with successive letters of the alphabet (although for some reason the *wāw* line has been omitted). However, a line beginning with the letter *pê* has been added at the end.[34] A. Fitzgerald comments on the possible origins of the latter:

> The convention of adding this final *pe* to the series apparently developed because in this way *lamed* becomes the middle letter of a series of 23 letters (the 22 letters of the alphabet + *pe*), and thus the three consonants of the name of the first letter of the alphabet (*aleph*) are at the beginning, middle, and end of the series.[35]

That this indeed is the poet's intention in adding a final *pê* verse is confirmed by the appearance of an identical pattern in the letters of the first verse of the psalm.[36] If the letters that function simply as *matres lectionis* are excluded,[37] the verse contains twenty-three consonants, the first consonant being *ʾālep*, the twelfth or middle consonant being *lāmed*, and the final one *pê*:

*ʾăbārăkâ ʾet-yhwh bĕkol-ʿēt tāmîd tĕhillātô bĕpî*

ʾb r k   ʾt yhw   b k l   ʿt t   m d t h l   t   b p

ʾ                    L                        P

Besides the order of the initial letters of the successive lines of the psalm following the order of the alphabet, the psalm is partially "framed" as

33. Brueggemann, *Message of the Psalms*, 40.

34. The same phenomenon occurs in Psalm 25.

35. A. Fitzgerald, "Hebrew Poetry," *Jerome Biblical Commentary* (ed. R. E. Brown, J. A. Fitzmyer, and R. E. Murphy; Englewood Cliffs, NJ: Prentice-Hall, 1968), 1:243 (§13:17). See also P. W. Skehan, "The Structure of the Song of Moses in Deuteronomy (Deut. 32:1–43)," *CBQ* 13 (1951) 160 n. 13 (repr. in his *Studies in Israelite Poetry and Wisdom* [CBQMS 1; Washington, DC: Catholic Biblical Association, 1971] 74 n. 13): "By going from *ʾaleph* to *taw* and then adding *pe*, one makes *lamed* the exact middle of the series and sums up the whole alphabet in the name of its first letter." Psalms 25 and 34 thus differ from most acrostic psalms in Hebrew; in the latter, the first, middle, and final letters spell *ʾmt* ('truth').

36. I have discussed this and other examples of "alphabetic thinking" in Psalm 34 in my essay, "The ABCs of Wisdom in Psalm XXXIV," *VT* 35 (1985) 99–104; see esp. p. 104 n. 13.

37. I.e., the final *hēh* of *ʾbrkh* and *yhwh*, the *yôd* in *tmyd*, the final *wāw* of *thltw*, and the final *yôd* of *bpy*; cf. E. Kautzsch, *Gesenius' Hebrew Grammar* (trans. A. E. Cowley; Oxford: Clarendon, 1910), §7.

well by the letters *ᵓālep, lāmed,* and *pê,* which spell out the name of the
first letter of the alphabet (*ᵓālep*), along the right side of the column of
verse and along the top in the first line.[38]

R. E. Murphy and G. von Rad have both noted the implicit
realization among the wisdom writers of the potential of language to
"put order into the chaotic events that make up human life."[39] I would
carry this a step further and ask whether or not the "play" with the
alphabet reflected in the use of the acrostic witnesses to the wisdom
writers' realization of the ordering potential of language specifically in
its *written* form.[40] The poet of Psalm 34 underlines this ordering potential of written language not only by his use of the acrostic but also by
the partial "frame" he creates for the written poem with the letters
*ᵓālep, lāmed,* and *pê.* These latter form the name of the first of the
twenty-two "tools" used by the writer-poet in his attempt to wrest
order and meaning out of the variety and seeming disconnectedness of
everyday life. These three letters—*ᵓālep, lāmed, pê*—also supply the
verb stem *ᵓlp* I 'to learn, teach', which expresses the process by which
one appropriates and hands on those insights one has gained.[41]

38. One is reminded of the guidelines or "frames" drawn by scribes in ancient times
(e.g., on the scrolls discovered at Qumran) to keep the columns of writing or verse
straight; cf. P. W. Skehan, G. W. MacRae, and R. E. Brown, "Texts and Versions," *Jerome
Biblical Commentary* (ed. R. E. Brown, J. A. Fitzmyer, and R. E. Murphy; Englewood
Cliffs, NJ: Prentice-Hall, 1968), 2:563 (§69:13). The recently discovered eighth-century-
B.C.E. inscription on a plaster wall in the cave at Deir Alla in the Wadi Jabbok in Jordan
was written in two columns (the second only partially filled), each framed by a thick red
line; cf. A. Lemaire, "Fragments from the Book of Balaam Found at Deir Alla," *Biblical
Archaeology Review* 11.5 (Sept./Oct. 1985) 31–35.

39. Murphy, "Wisdom and Yahwism," 120. See also G. von Rad, *Old Testament
Theology* (2 vols.; New York: Harper and Row, 1962–65), 1:418: "In every stage of culture
of course man is set the task of mastering life. To this end he needs to know it, and dare
not cease from looking and listening to discover whether in the tangle of events something like conformity to law, an order, cannot be here and there discerned. . . . But the
means of laying hold of and objectifying such orders when once perceived is language."

40. The very use of the acrostic device presumes a literate milieu since such a device
can be appreciated only in written form; its appeal is more to the eye and mind than to
the ear. Cf. N. K. Gottwald, *Studies in the Book of Lamentations* (SBT 14; London: SCM,
1954) 28–29; and W. G. E. Watson, "Trends in the Development of Classical Hebrew
Poetry: A Comparative Study," *UF* 14 (1982) 267. On the relationship between wisdom
and the art of writing, see P. A. Munch, "Die alphabetische Akrostichie in der jüdische
Psalmendichtung," *Zeitschrift der Deutschen Morgenländischen Gesellschaft* 15 (1936)
708–9.

41. The issue of the definition of "wisdom" and "wisdom writings" is much debated;
see, e.g., Crenshaw's "Introduction: On Defining Wisdom," in his *Old Testament Wisdom,*
11–25. In the context of the foregoing discussion of the awareness on the part of these
wisdom writers of the ordering power of language, I would offer the following definition:
wisdom speech is characterized not only by an obvious skill with language but by
evidence of a conscious exploitation of the potential of language to impose order on and
derive meaning from experience and insight (cf. Ps 49:4–5). For example, T. Eagleton,

## THE SAGE AS AUTHOR OF THE PSALTER:
## HUMAN WORDS BECOME WORD OF GOD

In recent years not a few scholars have shifted their attention from the study of individual psalms to the Psalter itself.[42] Previously, the Psalter was looked upon principally as a collection of hymns, the so-called "Hymn Book of the Second Temple,"[43] analogous to our modern hymnals. It was presumed that—apart from evidence that it was a kind of "collection of collections" that had been somewhat artificially divided into five "books" paralleling the five scrolls of the Torah—no unifying principle was necessarily at work; the placement of various hymns was due either to the influence of the earlier collections, or to simple happenstance.

Recent work on the Psalter, however, has brought to light clearer principles of organization, and it is becoming more apparent that what we have in the Book of Psalms is exactly that, a *book*, not a collection of hymns. Thus I will focus on two questions about the work of the sage as author of this Book of Psalms: what kind of book did he understand he was producing and how did he understand the process of authorship.

G. H. Wilson states that "in its 'final form' the Psalter is a book to be *read* rather than to be *performed*; to be *meditated over* rather than to be *recited from*."[44] In other words, the author of the Psalter has produced a text meant to be incorporated into the set of texts that was becoming Israel's "Sacred Scriptures." One important indication of this is the key role that Psalm 1 plays as a "preface" to the Psalter.[45] As I noted above (p. 220), it was during this period (postexilic) that wisdom and torah piety were merging and the *Weisheitslehrer* ('wisdom teacher') was taking on the identity of the *Schriftgelehrter* ('scribe').[46]

---

*The New Left Church* (London: Sheed and Ward, 1966) 65-66, comments on an episode in the Yahwist creation story, a text acknowledged to have connections with the wisdom movement: "In fact, it is by *naming*, that man comes, not to confirm objects in a detached existence, but to bring them within his control, as Adam's naming of the beasts in Genesis [2:19] is an act of kingship over them—an affirmation of himself as a linguistic, and therefore human, animal." (Cf. L. Alonso-Schökel, "Sapiential and Covenant Themes in Genesis 2-3," *Theology Digest* 13 [1965] 3-10; repr. in *SAIW* 468-80.)

42. Wilson's dissertation (*Editing of the Hebrew Psalter*) is a good example of this kind of shift.

43. E.g., B. W. Anderson, *Understanding the Old Testament* (4th ed.; Englewood Cliffs, NJ: Prentice-Hall, 1986) 544. But note his more nuanced approach in *Out of the Depths: The Psalms Speak for Us Today* (rev. ed.; Philadelphia: Westminster, 1983) 23. See also Wilson, *Editing of the Hebrew Psalter*, 206-7.

44. Wilson, *Editing of the Hebrew Psalter*, 207.

45. On the "introductory" role also of Psalm 2, see ibid., 173, 207-11; Mays, "Place of the Torah-Psalms," 10; and B. S. Childs, *Introduction to the Old Testament as Scripture* (Philadelphia: Fortress, 1979) 516.

46. See Reindl, "Weisheitliche Bearbeitung von Psalmen," 338-39.

With the placement of Psalm 1 at the head of the collection, the sage, now in his incarnation as scribe, has turned this collection of hymns finally into a text to be studied and meditated:

> The effect of the editorial fixation of the first ps as an introduction to the whole Psalter is subtly to alter how the reader views and appropriates the pss collected there. The emphasis is now on meditation rather than cultic performance; private, individual use over public, communal participation. In a strange transformation, Israel's words of response to her God have now become the Word of God to Israel.[47]

The profile of the sage that emerges when one views him as author of the Psalter, then, is the profile of one who looks upon this book that has come from his hand as "Scripture," as "Word of God." A. Robert, in commenting on Psalm 119, a psalm that captures well the spirit of this "late" wisdom, notes

> It is through the sacred text that the soul enters into communion with the thoughts and wishes of God, and yields to the divine pedagogy in a regular and ongoing way. . . . It is through reading that God reveals himself, and no longer through listening, since the era of the prophets has ended; or rather, reading is the only way by which one can henceforth enter into communication with Moses and the prophets.[48]

If the sage saw his work as finally worthy of the label "Word of God," what was his warrant for such an assertion? I would suggest that the answer lies in the sage's understanding of the very act of authorship. B. L. Mack, in his study of Ben Sira's "Hymn in Praise of the Fathers" (chaps. 44–50) examines a text produced by one of those scholar-sages or "scribes."[49] Mack's conclusions about the attitude of this scribe come close to what may well have been the mind of the scribe(s) responsible for the Psalter.

In a chapter entitled "Writing: The Glory of the Scholar Sage,"[50] Mack argues that Ben Sira gives a portrait of the scholar-sage in his poem in praise of the scribal profession (Sir 39:1–11). The portrait owes a heavy debt to Hellenism both in its express combination of scholar-

47. Wilson, *Editing of the Hebrew Psalter*, 206; see also Childs, *Introduction to the Old Testament as Scripture*, 513–14. Reindl, "Weisheitliche Bearbeitung von Psalmen," 339 (quoting H.-J. Kraus, *Die Psalmen* [5th ed.; Neukirchen-Vluyn: Neukirchener, 1978] 136) notes: "In our context, 'the notion of *twrh* [torah] includes in every case and indeed even in first place the scroll of the Psalms.'"

48. Robert, "Le psaume CXIX et les Sapientiaux," 16–17.

49. B. L. Mack, *Wisdom and the Hebrew Epic: Ben Sira's Hymn in Praise of the Fathers* (Chicago: University of Chicago, 1985).

50. Ibid., 89–107.

ship, authorship, and the offering of instruction, as well as in its evidence of the scholar-sage's self-consciousness about his social role within the educational institutions of Judaism.[51] Although first and foremost among the texts the scholar-sage studies is "the law of the Most High" (Sir 39:1a), his sources range much wider,[52] and all of them are read as "wisdom texts," that is, all of them are understood as capable of disclosing knowledge and insight. The texts . . .

> form a canon of disparate genres held together by the scholar's common investment in them. He will study them to win a single vision. That single vision, moreover, will encompass the deep structure of things that orders all reality from God and his world of creation to human good and evil. If he succeeds, he will have overcome. No longer is he exegete and scholar merely, interpreting the texts of others. He will make those words, those texts, his own and find a voice for himself as author.[53]

Peculiar to the Jewish sage's understanding of the authorship process is the context of prayer within which it takes place. That context of prayer, that context of communion with the deity, gives particular value to the product of the process. That "single vision" that he has won by his scholarship is characterized as a gift from God comparable to the inspired insight of the prophet and analogous to the Hellenistic view of poetic inspiration.[54] This is the significance for Mack of the central section (39:5-6) in Ben Sira's "Praise of the Scholar-Sage" (39:1-11) and the specific sequence of the three speech acts recorded therein:

> The first (speech act) is the prayer for mercy; the second is the speaking of wisdom itself ("in double measure"); the third is thanksgiving. This means that the prayer for mercy and the prayer of thanksgiving frame the moment of inspiration. Wisdom speech is therefore divinely inspired, as speech that is possible only in the context of prayer.[55]

Wilson's "strange transformation" that the Psalter has undergone at the hands of the scribal editors—that "Israel's words of response to her God have now become the Word of God to Israel"[56]—turns out not to be so strange after all. If one may compare the self-consciousness of Ben Sira

---

51. Ibid., 102.

52. Cf. Sir 39:1b-4; e.g., "the wisdom of all the ancients," "prophecies," "the discourse of notable men," "the subtleties of parables," "the hidden meanings of proverbs," "the obscurities of parables" (rsv).

53. Mack, *Wisdom and the Hebrew Epic*, 96.

54. Ibid., 98-99.

55. Ibid., 98.

56. See above, pp. 227-28.

as Mack describes it and the self-consciousness of the author(s) of the Psalter, one can see that this is not simply a collection or compilation of liturgical texts but a unity intentionally greater than the sum of its parts. We have a book; not only that, we have a wisdom book;[57] and further, an "inspired" wisdom book, the work of a scholar-sage(s), if not yet fully self-conscious of his (their) role as author, at least on the way. And, following my characterization of the sage pictured by the psalms as "one who prays," what would be more fitting an object of the scholar-sage's authorial skill than a collection of Israel's prayers?

## CONCLUSION

Among the various aspects of the sage's profile that have emerged, the following have been highlighted: the veneration of torah, the interest in prayer, the concern with order, the focus on writing, reading, and the written word as a medium of God's revelation, and the sage's self-consciousness as author. One note of caution should be sounded. The texts I have drawn upon for these elements of a profile of the sage in the psalms span hundreds of years. Taken together these elements do not necessarily represent the portrait of a single person during one particular time period. The closest one could come to a composite of the aspects described above would be the scholar-sage or scribe of the postexilic period. However, I would venture to guess that at least some of those who practice the craft today would recognize as desirable for themselves most, if not all (*mutatis mutandi*), of these very qualities.

57. Cf. Mack, *Wisdom and the Hebrew Epic*, 225 n. 9: "The authority of the Jewish scriptures for Ben Sira is a function of their capacity to be read as wisdom texts."

# JOB AS A SAGE

## Samuel Terrien

Was Job a sage? The folktale represents him as "the greatest of all the Orientals" (1:3), but not as a master of wisdom. He was a pious foreigner who worshiped Yahweh. The poetic dialogue ascribes to him a number of phrases and developments that bear the characteristics of the wisdom literature—in language, style, and attitude toward existence. However, Job also speaks as a psalmist and as a prophet. Did the poet represent him as a sage? And if so, what kind of a sage?

In order to consider this question, it is proposed to examine the following topics: (1) the presence of the words for wisdom and wise people, (2) the use of the sapiential forms of speech, (3) the allusions to wisdom themes, (4) the poet's reaction to conventional wisdom theology, and (5) the sources of theological knowledge.

### REFERENCE TO WISDOM AND THE WISE

Job did not mention the word *wisdom* before the end of the first cycle of discussion, when he apparently answered not only Zophar but all three comforters, whom he addressed in the plural:

> Truly you are the people,[1]
> And wisdom will die with you. (12:2)

This sarcastic rejoinder implies that his adversaries belong to the majority, while he is a solitary dissenter and a nonconformist. More important for the purpose of this inquiry, it also indicates that for him

Samuel Terrien is Emeritus Davenport Professor of Hebrew and Cognate Languages at Union Theological Seminary (New York) and Emeritus Adjunct Professor of Religion at Columbia University.

1. Interpretation of the word *ʿam* 'people' as "upperclass landowners" or "gentry" (M. H. Pope, *Job* [AB 15; Garden City, NY: Doubleday, 1965] 89), or "the strong ones" (M. Dahood, *Psalms I: 1–50* [AB 16; Garden City, NY: Doubleday, 1965] 112–13, by comparison with *ʿmm* in Ps 18:28) is unwarranted. The MT is supported by the ancient versions.

wisdom is not a monolithic body of opinion, belief, or procedure. It allows for a variety of viewpoints and a diversity of trends.

Job ironically returns to the same idea when he quotes a maxim[2] that is apparently shared by the majority:

> Wisdom resides with elderly men,
> And understanding belongs to senior citizens.   (12:12)

Translators show that this proverb does not represent Job's opinion. They insert such formulas as "some say," or they turn declarative sentences into interrogatives. Either device is justified by the immediately following bicolon:

> With [God] dwell wisdom and heroic power,
> To him belong counsel and discernment.   (12:13)

This time, Job goes beyond his earlier opinion concerning the pluralistic aspect of wisdom (12:2). He asserts in effect that wisdom does not even dwell with the elder members of society. Wisdom is exclusively divine. Together with the technical qualities attending it, such as understanding, counsel, discernment, and especially heroic power—these specific virtues only render wisdom effective.

To be sure, Oriental poetry in general and rhetorical forms of Hebraic thinking in particular use blunt contrasts and antonyms. It is thus precarious to affirm—as in the "Hymn to Wisdom" (Job 28:1–27) at the start of his summation—that for Job wisdom is solely the possession of God and completely escapes the human quest. Nevertheless, the speaker establishes a clear distinction between human wisdom and divine wisdom. The former is illusive. The latter alone has "power" (gĕbûrâ), which is akin to the nobility of a hero (gibbôr).

At last, Job's sardonic reply to Bildad goes to the ultimate of sapiential negativity. He implicitly confesses his own "wisdomlessness."

> How well thou givest help to a powerless man,
> And succor to the arm devoid of vigor!
> How well thou advisest a man without wisdom
> And dispensest the gift of savoir faire!   (26:2–3)

Toward the end of the discussion, Job perceives the hopelessness of ever coming to an agreement with his interlocutors. They think he has no wisdom, just as he believes that they have none (cf. 13:5). He also seems to acknowledge that they are correct in asserting that he lacks

---

2. R. Gordis, "Quotations as a Literary Usage in Biblical, Oriental, and Rabbinic Literature," *HUCA* 22 (1949–50) 209–10.

savoir faire (*tūšîyyâ*). The word designates the pragmatic intelligence that guarantees lasting success, the practical know-how of an all-around personality.

## RHETORICAL FORMS OF WISDOM

The proverb is the most typical form of wisdom speech. The friends of Job are thoroughly at ease with it. Job himself quotes proverbs sparingly, as if he were reluctantly compelled to do so only in order to defend his position.

> Does the wild ass bray in the midst of grass,
>   Or the ox low in the proximity of his fodder?   (6:5)

Like most other maxims, the few that Job quotes represent distilled observations of nature, especially the life of plants and of animals. They may also reflect the experience of the human senses.

> Does one eat insipid food without salt?
>   Has the slimy juice of the purslane any taste?   (6:6)

Proverbs in the Joban speeches are always introduced to counter an indirect hint of his guilt. In the above instance, Job manages a double retort to Eliphaz, who has hurled at him irrelevant words and also reproached him for having complained in a manner not befitting the dignity of a sage.

More specifically, proverbs come appropriately whenever the suffering hero strikes at his main target, which is the dogma of individual retribution.

> Torrents from melting snows are soon swallowed up by
> drought and heat;
>   Likewise, Sheol engulfs those who have sinned.   (24:19)

The quotation represents the point of view that Job repudiates. Translators are thus inclined to insert an explanatory phrase, "you say."

Other maxims reflect the elegant manners, however less than candid, with which sapiential debates are conducted. Indirection is therefore the device of civilized discussion.

> The ear appreciates words,
>   As the palate savors tasty dishes.   (12:11)

In view of the scarcity of actual proverbs in the ten speeches of Job, it may be concluded that it is not his favorite debating style to employ such devices.

Rather, the abrupt question, implying denial of self-involvement, is Job's preferred method of response to unjustified attacks.

> Have I ever said, "Make me a gift"?   (6:22)

The interrogative of self-exculpation conceals a countercharge:

> In what have I failed?   (6:24)

And this is often followed by a direct challenge to answer, with a sharp command in the imperative:

> Enlighten me! . . . Show me!   (6:24)

At other times, on account of his need for self-defense, he chooses the technical vocabulary of debate.[3]

> What do you prove with your critique?
> Do you pretend you can criticize my words?   (6:25b–26a)

Various verbal forms of the hiphil of *ykh* designate a rebuke or an attempt to demolish an argument. In the niphal, the verb means 'to reason' (Isa 1:18, Job 23:7); it appears also in the hithpael to introduce the controversy between Yahweh and Israel (Mic 6:2); and it is used synonymously with the common word (*rîb*) for judiciary controversy (Mic 6:1; cf. Job 10:2).

Because Job is neither impressed by the friends' debating skill nor convinced by their reasoning, a quasi-proverbial interrogation comes to his mind. He compares to the gustatory sense—implicitly infallible—his conviction of innocence, which he knows to be unchallengeable.

> Is not my palate able to discern distress?   (6:30b)

Job fully recognizes, of course, that the *māšāl*, proverb, is the most characteristic form of wisdom discourse. The semantic field of the word is, however, extremely wide. While he quotes proverbs, he does not name them as such. Yet, he uses the word *māšāl* in the specific sense of 'fable, byword, parable, or slogan', thereby acknowledging in mockery the rhetorical habits of the wise.

> [God] has made me a public fable,
> And I have become a place of curse.   (17:6)

---

3. G. von Rad calls the dialogue a series of "conversations" and denies that they constitute "contentious debates," but he repeatedly refers to the speeches of Job and his friends as "debate" (*Wisdom in Israel* [Nashville: Abingdon, 1972] 209–14).

In this parallel bicolon, Job likens the *māšāl* 'fable' to *tōphet* 'dump, place of refuse', literally, 'site for spitting', in the ritual sense, which is reminiscent of the magical act of cursing. Tophet was the name given to the Valley of the Sons of Hinnon (Aramaic, *Gehenna*), where kings of Judah, especially during the dark days of Assyrian domination, had sacrificed to Melek, by fire, their sons and daughters (2 Kgs 23:10).

For Job to equate *māšāl* and *tōphet* constitutes the most shocking expostulation of sarcastic humor. He declares himself in effect to be the incarnation of both wisdom and abomination. People may believe he is the supreme exemplar of wisdom because they conclude that his misery is a punishment for his secret crimes and his suffering produces wisdom. On the contrary, Job maintains that he is a public fable because he represents a personification of "non-wisdom." He has become the divine caprice made flesh. By borrowing the sapiential form of speech par excellence, and by applying it to himself, he presents his own being as the living exhibit of chaos in the universe.

## SAPIENTIAL THEMES

In spite of his reluctance to speak as though he were a representative of conventional wisdom, Job alludes to many themes current among the Near Eastern sages of his time.

Like the Egyptian wise, he was aware of embryology and obstetrics (3:11, 10:10-12; cf. Ps 139:13-16, which was written by the Joban poet or by a member of his circle).[4]

He was conversant with cosmology and referred to the phenomena of nature—mountain erosion (9:5), earthquakes (9:6), eclipses (9:7), constellations (9:9). Significantly, he mentioned not only the Great Bear, Orion, and the Pleiades, but also the Chambers of the South, which could be seen only from tropical latitudes. He did not deify these cosmic elements but presented them only as parts of a sapiential theology of creation, which affirmed the power of a single deity (9:4-5).

Cosmic creation was inseparable from personal creation. The theme of cosmology was intricately related to that of embryology and of obstetrics, for each one was dominated by the awareness of artistic creativity. The artisan potter is forever bound to the clay he has molded. Thus Job's complete trust was trust in a God of love, although the word

4. It is possible that the enigmatic sentence, "I have escaped with the skin of my teeth" (19:20b), is not just a proverbial expression but reveals the poet's knowledge of ancient dentistry and pediatrics. Egyptian anatomists might well have known that milk teeth are covered with a skin-like membrane, called today "Nasmyth's membrane," which protects from lactic acids. According to this conjecture, Job claimed that he was as innocent as a suckling infant. This interpretation fits the context.

*love* is never used. This trust was the source of both his hope and his despair (10:8–12). How could the divine artist forget his handiwork? Yet, it is this God who persecutes him.

> Thy hands, they have embraced me;
>> Together they have fashioned me in all my parts,
>> And it is thou who hast engulfed me.
> Remember! Thou hast molded me like clay;
>> Yet thou sendest me back to the dust!    (10:8–9)

The theme of esthetic involvement on the part of God has prevented the hero from accepting the traditional dogma of retribution. His fate proves not his guilt but the contradiction of love and power. This contradiction renders theodicy impossible.

Although the language is still loaded with an imagery that survives from a mythopoetic past, Job never looks upon nature, with its seasonal cycles, as the theater of cosmic love and hatred acted out by anthropomorphic gods. He may allude to Mesopotamian, Egyptian, and Ugaritic myths (7:12, 26:12–13), but he repudiates the validity of the theomachic rituals, for these qualify a theology of transcendence by confusing nature and God. This is the reason for his declaring that Sheol stands within the range of divine omnipresence: "Sheol is naked before God" (26:6a; cf. Prov 15:11; Ps 139:8, 11–12). At once he adds what appears to be a nonsequitur, but it is actually a theological truth.

> It is he who stretches out the Arctic over the Void [*tōhû*],
>> And suspends the earth over the "What-is-it?"    (26:7)

In sapiential theology, creation is not the result of a victory over a so-called primal or preexisting ocean. Omnipresence is inseparable from omnipotence.

Job knows he is going to die soon, but his obsession with the prospect of death is paradoxically divided between dread and desire. As in the Egyptian and Babylonian dialogues on the weariness of existence, he repeatedly dwells upon the motif of extinction. His references to "nought," "nothingness," and "nonbeing" display the ability to exteriorize in concrete words his preoccupation with abstract thinking. In his opening soliloquy, he wishes that the nought of an eclipse might have dropped the day of his birth from the calendar, so that he would not have "come into being" (3:16). He moans over the nothingness of the healing help he has expected from his friends (6:13). He compares their betrayal to the sudden nonexistence of torrents (6:15). He concludes from the friends' failure that their therapeutic mission has been all along a radical nonbeing.

Do you exist? No!    (6:21)

He knows that God will soon murder him, yet, he cannot believe that this same God is lacking love for him. After his death, God will search for him with longing, just as night-guards look for a trace of dawn. But Job turns this belated, divine move into an occasion for black humor.

Thou wilt look for me in the dark, but I shall not be!    (7:21)

God's discovery of Job's nonbeing will be Job's ultimate joke on a frustrated divinity.

While rhetorical forms of debate occur throughout the dialogue, the theme of controversy appears consistently not between Job and his friends, but between Job and his God. The hero argues with them because they claim that they speak for God (13:7). The controversy attempts to match infinity with finitude. Job is unjustly accused, but God, who initiates the contention (10:2), escapes the rigors of the law.

If it is a question of jurisprudence, who will summon him?    (9:19b)

By implication, Job compares him to the corrupt princes of the royal courts who irresponsibly abuse the privilege of their diplomatic immunity and are able to avoid the legal suits slapped upon them by common mortals.

God is not a man like me that I might enter a plea,
    Or that we might appear together in a court of law.    (9:32)

Nevertheless, if a trial could be set, skilful lawyers or judges would distort the defense.

Although I am innocent, my own mouth would condemn me.
    I am blameless, but [my words] would prove me guilty.    (9:20)

This theme of the divine-human controversy becomes one of the channels through which Job develops his theological thinking. He introduces the motif of a being intermediary between remoteness and proximate reality. This being appears three times in three different forms: first, Job dreams of a conciliator (9:33) who would "lay his hands upon us both." This being is then far more than an umpire who simply makes a decision; he is the "go-between" (môkîah) who would "lay his hands upon us both" and bring us to some harmonious and intimate understanding of each other. The wish, however, belongs to the realm of fantasy and is soon abandoned. It is later revived in a new form. Second, a witness in heaven is expected by the sufferer (16:19). It is someone who will vouch for his integrity, but this expectation is other-worldly, since Job will have been slain by God himself and his blood spilled on the ground, before the heavenly witness will intervene in his favor (16:18–21). It is clear that the witness is not God (*contra* the opinion of several exegetes), for his function is to "defend man against God" (16:21). Third, a vindicator will at last intervene (19:25). Through his office, Job "within [his] own flesh" will be able to "see God," and "not as a stranger" (19:27). Apart from these few words, the text is beyond restoration, but the distinction between the vindicator (*gōʾēl*) and God is undeniable. Whether the statement constitutes one of the first hints of a belief in an afterlife remains open to doubt. The issue at stake, however, is Job's legal recognition of his honor, even after death. Perhaps he is merely satisfied to know that future generations of human-kind, reading his inscription on the rock of a cliff (19:23–24), will recognize his integrity.

The theme of the controversy between man and God reflects covenant ritual and civil jurisprudence. In all likelihood, it is inspired by the mores of the royal court, in which sages operated and argued concerning social ethics. It is this sapiential teaching of morality, going beyond the strict requirements of the law codes, which is mirrored in Job's final discourse (29:1–31:40). This discourse presents many affinities with behavioral wisdom.

The review of past happiness (29:1–25) leads directly into a lament over the present misfortune (30:1–24), and the whole plea for innocence reaches a climax with the oaths of clearance (30:25–31:34). These in turn yield a portrait of the ideal sage.[5] This majestically constructed speech of seven strophes,[6] concluded by a final summation (31:35–40), affirms in sapiential terms the relationship between moral character and human destiny. Nevertheless, Job also declares that divine retribution does not always follow the aberrations of behavior. Once more, he mocks the divine spy who scrutinizes the traces of his steps in the sands of the desert (31:4).

Even the dialogue between Yahweh and Job, which should belong to the ineffable realm of the theophany or of the prophetic vision, is couched in the juridical style of the controversy.[7]

5. G. Fohrer, "The Righteous Man in Job 31," *Essays in Old Testament Ethics: J. Philip Hyatt In Memoriam* (ed. J. T. Willis and J. L. Crenshaw; New York: Ktav, 1974) 1–22.

6. Many critics differ on the strophic structure. See A. R. Ceresko, *Job 29–31 in the Light of Northwest Semitic* (Rome: Biblical Institute, 1980) 100–104. Linguistic conjectures based on Ugaritic should be viewed with sharp circumspection.

7. B. Gemser, "The *rîb*- or Controversy-Pattern in Hebrew Mentality," *WIANE* 120–37.

> Will he concede, he who argues with the Almighty?
> Will the accuser of God make a retort?    (40:2)

And even after Job refuses to speak, Yahweh returns to the challenge in legal terms.

> Wilt thou annul my justice
> And condemn me in order to justify thyself ?    (40:8)

This question provides the key to the poem as a whole. Some exegetes are inclined to conclude that the entire book echoes the controversy pattern.


## MASTER OF UNCONVENTIONAL WISDOM

On account of the linguistic, stylistic, rhetorical, and thematic elements that point to wisdom, is it legitimate to speak of Job as a sage?

To a large extent, the answer to this question depends upon the determination of the poet's purpose in the light of the life-situation that he confronted. No literary critic would analyze the character of Hamlet, for example, without seeking information on Shakespeare's *Sitz im Leben.*

Many commentators describe the Joban poet as a master of wisdom who taught young intellectuals in the nascent Judaism of early Persian times (fifth century B.C.E.). Such a master would, of course, have been surrounded by disciples, who at various dates transcribed, enlarged, censored, and generally edited the original *opus* into its present form.[8]

A few scholars suggest that the poet belonged to the North Israelite Diaspora of the seventh or early sixth century B.C.E.[9] More probably, the Dialogue and the Discourses of Yahweh emerged orally in the Babylonian Diaspora of the Jerusalemites during the sixth century B.C.E. (ca. 585–570). Many arguments support this hypothesis.[10] If the Joban dialogue is dated between Ezekiel and Second Isaiah, it is possible to explain the absence of any allusion to the major themes of the Hebrew

8. J. Vermeylen, *Job, ses amis et son Dieu: La légende de Job et ses relectures postexiliques* (Leiden: Brill, 1986) 72–79.

9. D. N. Freedman, "Orthographic Peculiarities in the Book of Job," *Eretz-Israel* 9 (1969) 43–44.

10. For a long time scholars have favored the anteriority of Job over Second Isaiah (e.g., Kleinert, Cheyne, Dillmann, König, Baudissin, Naish, Gunkel, Pfeiffer, et al.). See S. Terrien, "Quelques remarques sur les affinités de Job avec le Deutéro-Esaïe," *Volume du Congrès: Genève 1965* (VTSup 15; Leiden: Brill, 1966) 295–310. For an alternative position on the date of Job, see the essay in this volume by R. Albertz, "The Sage and Pious Wisdom in the Book of Job: The Friends' Perspective," pp. 243–61.

religion, such as election, covenant, law, Zion omphalos-myth, temple, cult, and the day of Yahweh. The Joban poet was thoroughly acquainted with the literature of ancient Israel, but he lived in the midst of a cultural and cultic vacuum that fits neither the last days of the Kingdom of Judah in the sixth century B.C.E. nor the early days of the Restoration in the fifth and fourth centuries. The *Sitz im Leben* of the Joban dialogue is most likely that of the first generation of the Exile, between 585 and 570 B.C.E. It is, however, difficult to describe accurately the religious mood of this period.[11]

Those who survived the final siege of Jerusalem (589–587 B.C.E.), with the usual consequences of a military defeat (famine, epidemics, fire, and massacres), and who, furthermore, endured the brutality of their guards as well as the hardships of a long march toward Lower Mesopotamia, confronted the humid heat of the marshlands[12] infested with insects and probably also with malaria. The uprooted Judahites (a political entity) became the Jews (a religious community). Initially overcome by guilt and despair, they eventually rallied to their faith in Yahweh. Deprived of Holy Space, they preserved Holy Times. Unable to maintain sacrificial worship, they chanted the traditions of the fathers and sang hymns and laments (Psalm 137). As they celebrated the *Rosh Hashana* in a new form, perhaps for the first time (Ezek 40:1), they adored in a foreign land the Lord of the Universe.

With the prophet Ezekiel, the Joban poet was in all probability the most potent initiator of hope in the midst of religious defeatism. What could the people do without a sanctuary? The poet proposed a para-cultic drama, its speeches to be chanted and "acted out" by several participants playing the roles of Job, his friends, and Yahweh.[13] He presented the enigma of suffering in a way that repudiated the dogma of individual and collective retribution,[14] and lifted those first Jews out of their syndrome of guilt and revolt (cf. Ezek 18:1–9, 19–20, 25–29;

11. P. R. Ackroyd, *Exile and Restoration: A Study of Hebrew Thought of the Sixth Century B.C.* (London: SCM, 1968) 31–38.

12. The sedimentary plain where the Judahites were settled was an irrigated marshland situated between the lower valleys of the Tigris and Euphrates. In many ways, it was similar to the present marshlands that in recent centuries have filled the northern tip of the Persian Gulf. See W. Thesiger, *The Marsh Arabs* (London: Longmans, 1964).

13. See S. Terrien, "Le poème de Job: drame para-rituel du Nouvel-An?" *Congress Volume: Rome 1968* (VTSup 17; Leiden: Brill, 1969) 220–35; L. Alonso-Schökel, "Toward a Dramatic Reading of the Book of Job," *Semeia* 7 (1977) 45–61.

14. See von Rad's comments on Job and the Deuteronomic History and Solomon's Prayer (*Wisdom in Israel*, 212–13). Side by side with Deuteronomistic History, proverbs are the vehicle, par excellence, of the doctrine of retribution. See J. L. Crenshaw, "Prolegomenon," in *SAIW* 15.

Lam 2:1-9). Job, the ancient hero of "pure religion" in a folktale that everyone knew by heart, became the symbol of the sufferer who rebels against a seemingly tyrannical or capricious deity. In the end, however, he "sees" God, who grants him a direct, personal, and almost ineffable awareness of communion (42:1-6). Invited to evoke the mythological figures of Behemoth and Leviathan,[15] Job learns that God faces the forces of cosmic evil. That same God neither condemns him, nor proclaims his honor. Job does not "repent" (a mistranslation)[16] of ethical crimes he has not committed, but he strikes into the abyss of nonbeing and thereby confesses his sin of theological hubris (42:6).[17]

Was Job, then, represented as a sage? He objected to the traditional teaching of the wise on rewards and punishments (Prov 10:3, 29; 12:2; 16:3, 7; 17:3; 21:2; 25:21-22; 29:26). While the poet was certainly a member of the sapiential world, his hero was more a fool than a sage.

## SOURCES OF JOB'S KNOWLEDGE

Just as Hosea's adversaries had said of him, "The prophet is a fool" (Hos 9:7), so also Eliphaz intimated that Job belonged to the same category when he remarked insidiously,

> I have seen the fool dig his own roots,
> But in an instant I had to curse his home.   (Job 5:3)

The word *nābāl* and its synonyms possess a wide range of meanings, from obscenity to religious heresy.[18] In the eyes of conventional sages, Job devalued righteousness and undermined religion. Their religious epistemology was based on a respect for tradition confirmed by experience. It is true that Eliphaz invoked the revelation of a ghost (Job 4:12-16), and Elihu appealed to the inspiration of the Almighty (32:8), but they alluded to momentary illumination, and these allusions are

15. See S. Terrien, "The Yahweh Speeches and Job's Responses," *Review and Expositor* 48 (1971) 497-509; O. Keel, "Einige Deutungen der Gottesreden," in his *Jahwes Entgegnung an Ijob* (Forschungen zur Religion und Literatur des Alten und Neuen Testaments 121; Göttingen: Vandenhoeck und Ruprecht, 1978) 44-51; and V. Kubina, *Die Gottesreden im Buche Hiob: Ein Beitrag zur Diskussion um die Einheit von Hiob 38,1-42,6* (Freiburg: Herder, 1979) 160-68.

16. Instead of the verb *šûb* 'to repent', the poet uses here the niphal form of another verb, *niḥam*, meaning 'to feel deep sorrow and compassion'; see S. Terrien, *Job* (Commentaire de l'Ancien Testament 13; Neuchâtel: Delachaux et Niestlé, 1963) 270.

17. Ibid., 269-71; Vermeylen, *Job*, 54-55.

18. T. Donald, "The Semantic Field of 'Folly' in Proverbs, Job, Psalms, and Ecclesiastes," *VT* 13 (1963) 286; G. Gerleman, "Der Nicht-Mensch: Erwägungen der hebräischen Wurzel NBL," *VT* 25 (1975) 240.

couched in detached, almost abstract terms. On the contrary, Job not only challenged the divine enemy to a debate but he also repeatedly turned this challenge into passionate pleas for communion with a God who would never forget the creature whom he had molded artistically, and therefore lovingly, out of mortal dust. Job's faith in a personal creator passed through eclipses of doubt but it remained the basis of his theological epistemology. When at last Yahweh spoke to him out of the whirlwind and offered him the opportunity to engage in the debate so long desired, Job desisted, for he had learned the immense difference between sapiential hearsay and prophetic seeing (42:6).[19] The God from whom he had expected vindication of his honor and therefore justification had been bequeathed to him by the tradition of the wise. His new knowledge reflected a sensual experience of divinity. The sage became a prophet.

Aware of a transcendence, which for his sake comported personal immanence, he renounced wrestling with infinity. The loss of his arrogance resulted from his refusal to judge the divine, not—as it has often been maintained—from an abject submission to a capricious and immoral omnipotence.[20] It was the beginning for the recipiency of an unexpected grace. Indirectness made room for immediacy.

How far might the exegete press a differentiation between the poet and his hero? The Joban poet, belonging to the sapiential world, was a sage and, therefore, a *littérateur* in the good sense of the word. A debtor to the psalmists of lament,[21] he appropriated their language only to renew it through his own agonies. As Bernard Duhm put it, "He wrote with his own blood."[22] Too great a differentiation should be avoided. The hero is the poet's double, and thus a sage, but, as it was implied above, a sage who had learned from Jeremiah and Ezekiel how to look through his own suffering at the misery of the deportees. He discovered that the God who concealed himself in history revealed his ultimate purpose of universality of creation.

19. A. Gelin, "Voir Dieu dans l'Ancien Testament," *Bible et Vie Chrétienne* 23 (1958) 3–12; G. Fohrer, "Nun aber hat mein Auge dich geschaut: Der innere Aufbau des Buches Hiob," *Theologische Zeitschrift* 15 (1959) 1–21.

20. D. Cox, *The Triumph of Impotence: Job and the Tradition of the Absurd* (Rome: Università Gregoriana, 1978) 152–57.

21. C. Westermann, *The Structure of the Book of Job: A Form-Critical Analysis* (Philadelphia: Fortress, 1981) 31–70.

22. B. Duhm, *Das Buch Hiob erklärt* (Freiburg im Breisgau: Mohr/Siebeck, 1897) ix.

# THE SAGE AND PIOUS WISDOM
# IN THE BOOK OF JOB:
# THE FRIENDS' PERSPECTIVE

## Rainer Albertz

### Translated by Leo G. Perdue

Whether the friends in the Book of Job represent a type of sage, and, if so, how that representation is to be understood are debated issues in scholarly research. One would be pleased to see the friends as representatives of a professional class of sages[1] who drive the suffering Job to despair with their dogmatic, inflexible instruction. However, in opposing this interpretation, R. N. Whybray has asserted that "the dialogue in Job is represented as taking place not between 'learned men' belonging to a professional class, but between a (once) wealthy landowner and his friends: that is, between educated farmers."[2]

## THE "WISE" IN THE BOOK OF JOB AND
## THE EDUCATIONAL IDEAL OF THE FRIENDS

The exegetical data initially appear to support Whybray's contention. In comparison to Proverbs and Qoheleth, the adjective *ḥākām* 'wise' occurs quite seldom (only eight times) in the rather sizable Book of Job (5:13; 9:4; 15:2, 18; 17:10; 34:2, 34; 37:24). If one sets aside the occasion where God is characterized as wise, there are only five places where *ḥākām* appears as a substantive (5:13; 15:2, 18; 17:10; 34:2) and two others where it functions as an adjective (34:34; 37:24). Even if one takes into consideration such related synonyms as *ʿārûm* 'shrewd, cunning' (5:13, 15:5), *maśkîl* 'the skilled, the prudent' (22:2), *yōdĕʿîm* 'the knowing one' (34:2), and *ʾănašê lēbāb* 'people of understanding' (34:10,

Rainer Albertz is Professor for Bible Exegesis and Theology at Universität-Gesamthochschule, Siegen, West Germany.

1. Thus V. Maag, *Hiob: Wandlung und Verarbeitung des Problems in Novelle, Dialogdichtung und Spätfassungen* (Forschungen zur Religion und Literatur des Alten und Neuen Testaments 128; Göttingen: Vandenhoeck und Ruprecht, 1982) 125.
2. R. N. Whybray, *The Intellectual Tradition in the Old Testament* (BZAW 135; Berlin: de Gruyter, 1974) 65.

34), it is difficult to speak of a consistent use of terms that would point to a "class of sages" or to a particular professional group. Only once are the friends of Job designated as wise (34:2), and even this occurs in the speeches of Elihu, which comprise a later addition (34:10). Consequently, on the basis of this initial overview of the exegetical data, one must support the position that Eliphaz, Bildad, and Zophar are not presented as representatives of a class. This means they are not represented as wisdom teachers, but rather as friends of Job (the situation is somewhat different with Elihu, as I shall show).[3]

Even so, one should not stop with this negative finding. In examining the evidence more carefully, it becomes evident that the friends do conform rather closely to the sapiential ideal of education. When Eliphaz remonstrates against Job with his statement in 15:2-3, he places in view an ideal type of sage:

> Should a wise man utter windy knowledge,
>    and fill himself with the east wind?
> Should he instruct with unprofitable words,
>    with speech that is useless?

One who wishes to conform to this ideal is faced with a required type of conduct. For Eliphaz, one who desires to satisfy the requirements of this ideal of education cannot simply shout out his words, as Job has done, but must consider their meaning and purpose. It is important in this context that Eliphaz addresses Job with an ideal of learning that they hold in common. The sage as a normative type of educated person is not something that distinguishes the friends from Job, but rather provides the basis for a common perspective.[4]

The commitment to this ideal of learning does not result from a momentary decision, but takes shape within a longstanding tradition:

3. One rather has the impression that Elihu is a professional sage. He feels he is superior to the traditional bearers of the wisdom tradition, the elders (33:6-7), and he tries the case of Job before a forum of sages (34:2-4) who pronounce a negative judgment against Job and dispute his "wisdom" by means of a formal refutation of his "theses" (34:5, 9). This could point to a circle of sages who busy themselves in a methodical manner with the case of Job. When Whybray argues against this view by noting that Elihu's calling is based on divine inspiration, an idea that goes beyond the horizon of traditional wisdom, he overlooks the fact that such an ideal description of the professional sage is also found in Sirach 38-39 (cf. esp. 39:6).

4. Cf. the opposite case in Job 17:10 where Job reproaches the friends for not being able to satisfy his requirements for a sage. The verse is possibly part of an addition (cf. G. Fohrer, *Das Buch Hiob* [Kommentar zum Alten Testament 16; Gütersloh: G. Mohn, 1963] 281). G. von Rad has argued that ḥākām in the dialogues of Job is mainly a designation for a type of person, not a social profession (*Wisdom in Israel* [Nashville: Abingdon, 1972] 20-21).

> I will make you aware, hear me!
>   What I have experienced I will declare unto you.
> What the wise (have repeatedly) imparted,[5]
>   that which their fathers did not withhold from them,[6]
> To whom alone the land was given,
>   and no stranger dwelt in their midst.   (15:17–19)

At this point Eliphaz asserts that his experiences have increased authority, because they are in line with the utterances of the sages of the preexilic period. The term wise at this juncture in the dialogue does not designate a type of person, but rather clearly designates a social group.[7] However the place and function of these sages is to be construed,[8] at least from a retrospective look at the preexilic period, they appear as a specific group that transmitted a particular tradition that could be drawn on by those at the time of the Joban poetry who felt they should conform to a particular ideal of education.

While the Joban poet has Eliphaz describe the transmitted wisdom tradition in a remarkable way, this passage has not received satisfactory attention by scholars to the present time.[9] When he says in v 19 that the land at that time still belonged only to the fathers and had not yet been traversed by strangers, then he obviously contrasts the ideal picture of a closed and homogeneous society in which the early sages were active with the social circumstances of his own period when foreigners had an effect in significant ways on the various spheres of the Jewish community.[10] In this manner the author of the poetry fully disregards the fact that Eliphaz in the earlier Joban narrative came from Tema and

---

5. The imperfect *yaggîdû*, located beside the perfect *kihădû*, has an iterative function.

6. Read *mēhem ʾăbôtām*.

7. One tends to waver between the two options in the cases present in the speeches of Elihu (Job 34:2, 34). To be evaluated differently is the negative use of the term "wise" in 5:13 (cf. below, pp. 246–47).

8. Whybray (*Intellectual Tradition*, 46) undertakes to do this. However, his assertion that Job 15:18–19 does not have a particular wisdom tradition in mind, since "'wisdom' of this kind has always been the property of the nation of Israel as a whole" (p. 54), is a case of *petitio principii* rather than the assertion of the text itself.

9. As far as I can determine, only S. Terrien, *Job* (Commentaire de l'Ancien Testament 13; Neuchâtel: Delachaux et Niestlé, 1963) 128, has clearly brought out that Eliphaz is representing a thesis that sees the tradition as nationalistic and in opposition to the true international nature of ancient Near Eastern wisdom literature. Indeed, Terrien continues: "Le poète s'amuse à faire parler un sage, étranger à l'alliance yahviste, comme s'il était un représentant du nationalisme religieux à tendance xénophobe." Subsequently, this view of Eliphaz is shown to be by no means legitimate.

10. See the descriptions in Ezra 4–7; Neh 4:1–5; 5:17; 6:1–9; 13:4–9, 15–21, 23–27.

was himself a foreigner.[11] The wisdom tradition to which Eliphaz is made to call upon is not an international tradition, but rather an emphatically national, Israelite one.

The allusion to a homogeneous society in which the earlier Israelite wisdom tradition originated has the function in this context of stressing its integrity over against current affairs. If the earlier sages in such ideal, social circumstances came to certain convictions, for example, that the wicked person and the evildoer can support their existence only with great anxiety (15:20), then these convictions are even more valid in the present situation! This conception of a wisdom tradition being passed down and possessing a national identity allows one to assume that during the postexilic period, after the loss of both an exclusive territory for settlement and political independence, the sapiential ideal of education probably required the creation of an identity in the Jewish community, which, because of social and political circumstances, was increasingly difficult to accomplish.

This assumption is defended by the third important place in which the word *ḥākām* occurs in the speeches of the friends. In his first speech, Eliphaz praises God as one

> Who destroys the plans of the shrewd [*ʿărûmîm*],
>   so that their plans cannot come to fruition,
> who seizes the wise [*ḥăkāmîm*] in their craftiness [*ʿormâ*],
>   so that the plan of the cunning ones is overturned.   (5:12–13)

In this parallelism, the terms *ḥākām* and *ʿārûm* receive a negative connotation by reason of their association with the niphal *pātal* 'cunning ones'. The term *ʿārûm* is generally used in a negative fashion in the Book of Job (as over against its use in Proverbs).[12] If *ḥākām* may occasionally designate a type of "cleverness" in the Old Testament that is not entirely legitimate,[13] then Job 5:13 would be different in designating in a negative manner an entire group. This usage becomes even more striking if one asks which group is meant by this designation. The answer is derived from the following verses: the cunning wise person whose deeds God frustrates are the strong (*ḥzq*, v 15) who have the

---

11. When F. Horst, *Hiob* (3d ed.; BKAT 16; Neukirchen-Vluyn: Neukirchener, 1974), 1.228, on the basis of the foreign origins of Eliphaz concludes that "pre- and post-exilic circumstances in Israel are not alluded to," but rather a "bedouin ideal," then the association that Jewish readers of the book must have drawn while reading a statement like Job 15:19 is completely mistaken. Job also embodies an ideal type in Jewish society, in spite of his foreign origins.

12. See Job 15:15 in distinction to Prov 12:16, 23; 13:6; 14:8, 15, 18; 22:3; 27:13.

13. So, for example, 2 Sam 13:4; cf. B. Lang, *Wisdom and the Book of Proverbs: An Israelite Goddess Redefined* (New York: Pilgrim, 1986) 14–15.

poor (*ebyôn*) and lowly (*dal*, v 16) in their power. As may be determined from other places in Job, they are quite simply the wicked (cf.
Job 20:19; 22:5–9; 24:3, 9; 29:16–17).

This means that *ḥākām* refers not only to Job and the friends in
regard to a positive ideal of learning, but also refers to two groups in
diametrical opposition to one another. The group in this book that
receives the negative designations of "wicked," "fools," and "oppressors"[14] may also in some sense be named the *ḥākām*. Of course, one
should take into consideration the possibility of a bitter, ironic meaning,
for example, the wicked only imagine themselves to be wise when their
machinations are successfully carried out by sly and cunning effort.
Even so, one may readily deduce from the use of this language that the
two groups, one represented by Job and the friends and another portrayed as the wicked, are debating what true wisdom is.

Socially speaking one could quite obviously make use of wisdom's
observations and rules of life in ways entirely different than had been
done by Job and his friends. Indeed, if one considers the utilitarian
character of older wisdom and the fact that the wicked in Job are
depicted as those who are manifestly successful (Job 21), then one may
only assume that the so-called wicked consider themselves to be those
who are truly wise. While Job's own experiences shatter the sapiential
ideal of learning, it is the one tirelessly held up to him by the friends.
Nevertheless, it is far from being universally accepted by the society as
a whole. Debated by at least two groups, this ideal of education is not
in a position to shape a widespread, comprehensive identity for all
people in the early postexilic Jewish community.

## SOCIOLOGICAL BACKGROUND OF THE FRIENDS

A preliminary survey of the exegetical data has demonstrated that the
three friends in the Book of Job are neither teachers of wisdom nor
representatives of school wisdom. Even so, based on one particular
viewing of the tradition, they may still submit to an ideal of learning
that, although it claims universal validity, still must be considered as
specific to a particular group. Subsequently, the question is which
group originated this ideal of education represented by the friends.
There are no clear indications as to which group the friends of Job may
have belonged. The stereotypical particulars regarding their foreign

14. For an assemblage of these ideas, see E. Würthwein, "Gott und Mensch in
Dialog und Gottesreden des Buches Hiob" (Inaugural diss., Tübingen, 1938; published
in *Wort und Existenz: Studien zum Alten Testament* [Göttingen: Vandenhoeck und
Ruprecht, 1970] 217–95, esp. 228–29). Würthwein (p. 229 n. 16) notes the striking use of
language in Job 5:12–13, but he makes no attempt at an explanation.

origins[15] belong to the earlier material taken into the Joban tradition and play no further role in the poetry. They and Job, also a foreigner, ultimately represent for the poet and his audience an indigenous group.

We have seen that, according to the description of the poetry, Job has previously adhered to the ideal of learning set forth by his friends (15:2; cf. also 4:3–5, 16:4–5, and 30:25). However, at least for Job, the poetry makes available a full array of sociologically valuable data. He appears in the narrative as a rich and pious property owner (1:2–5, 42:12). The poetic dialogues portray him as a rich, highly regarded, urban aristocrat with public functions in the community (19:13–16; chap. 29; 30:1, 28). His piety demonstrates above all else that he used without reservation his position and possessions to improve the life of impoverished groups in the population (29:12–17; chap. 31).[16] In this manner he participated in an ongoing defensive battle against another segment of the ruling class that prospered by means of cleverly exploiting their social standing, without regard for the devastating damage that would result for the lower strata of the population (29:17, 20:19, 22:5–9).[17] Accordingly, it is likely that the ideal of education that the friends repeatedly set forth was cultivated by this pious group of the aristocracy in the early postexilic Jewish community. Their ideal stood in sharp contrast to the philosophy of life, itself probably sapiential in orientation, followed by other groups of the upper class who are characterized in the Book of Job as the wicked. The impoverished lower-class groups, however, probably did not follow this ideal, for they were far more strongly eschatological in their orientation to life and awaited their redemption by means of a great social upheaval to be occasioned by God.[18] The total absence of the late prophetic views of the future in the thought of Job and his friends demonstrates once more that their conceptual horizon is limited to a specific social class.[19]

15. For a recent discussion, see Maag, *Hiob*, 14–15.

16. I have established this point in a more substantial fashion in my essay "Der sozialgeschichtliche Hintergrund des Hiobbuches und der 'Babylonischen Theodizee,'" *Die Botschaft und die Boten* (ed. J. Jeremias and L. Perlitt; H. W. Wolff Festschrift; Neukirchen-Vluyn: Neukirchener, 1981) 349–72, esp. 358–59.

17. Ibid., 362–63.

18. See such prophetic texts as Isa 29:17–24, 66:5, etc. For more on the probable postexilic background of the Book of Job, see ibid., 364–68. For an alternative position on the date of Job see the essay in this volume by S. Terrien, "Job as a Sage," pp. 231–42 above.

19. Interesting in this regard is a text like Isa 58:5–9a, which has an ideal of piety very similar to the one presented in Job 22:5–9 and 31:13–23. In v 8 the great national promises of Deutero- and Trito-Isaiah (52:12, 60:1) are given a new interpretation by applying them to the pious rich. Such individual promises are also found in Job (5:19–26, 8:21–22, 11:15–19, 22:26–28). See my essay "Die 'Antrittspredigt' Jesu im Lukasevangelium auf ihrem alttestamentlichen Hintergrund," *Zeitschrift für die neutestamentliche Wissenschaft* 74 (1983) 182–206, esp. 191–92.

## THE DUAL FUNCTIONS OF THE SAGES

I shall now attempt to characterize more specifically the ideal of learning articulated by the pious circles of the upper class by first asking what functions were expected of and assigned to those who felt they were obliged to follow it. Initially, one may point to a broadly conceived *educational* function of the sages: they advise ( $y^c$ṣ; 26:3; cf. $^c$eṣâ in 29:21), teach ( *yrh* hiphil; 6:24, 8:10), transmit knowledge ( *yd$^c$*, *bîn*; 6:24, 26:3, 28:11), and give guidance, educate, and instruct ( *ysr* hiphil, *ykḥ* hiphil; 4:3; cf. *mûsâr* in 20:3, 6:25–26, 15:2, 19:5, 32:12; cf. *tôkaḥat* in 13:6). The wise person desires and ought to offer help and provide guidance to others who are undergoing difficulties. This pedagogical purpose is more or less explicit in all the stages of the Israelite wisdom tradition, beginning with the folk proverb. This is typically found in the ideal of learning represented by the entire wisdom tradition, not only the Book of Job. However, the purpose receives special emphasis in Job and Proverbs 1–9.

Striking and, at least for the Book of Job, quite typical is a second function of the wise, namely that of *the pastor* who provides consolation (*nḥm*; 16:2, 31:24), strength (*ḥzq* piel, *$^{3}$mṣ* piel, *qûm* hiphil; 4:3–4, 21:34), help (*$^c$zr*, *yš$^c$* hiphil; 26:2), and healing (*rp$^{3}$*; 13:4). With these terms the educational function of the friends takes on a pastoral dimension possessing a clearly religious undertone.[20] One may choose to think that this function derives from the poetry, which has been interpreted as a "Dialogue of Consolation."[21] However, such an explanation is not sufficient. The poet of Job makes it clear that the friends' effort to console Job is not an exceptional case. In his first speech, Eliphaz reminds Job of his own previous instructions of consolation:

> Behold, you have [even yourself] instructed many [ *ysr* piel],
>     and weak hands repeatedly strengthened [*ḥzq* piel].
> Your words have lifted up [ *qûm* hiphil] those who stumbled,
>     and weak knees you have made strong [*$^{3}$mṣ* piel].
> But now that it has come upon you,
>     will you become weak yourself?
> Since it touches you,
>     will you also become dismayed?   (4:3–5)

---

20. Every verb mentioned here either has its established place in the genres of the personal cult (lament of the individual, thanksgiving, and oracle of salvation) or is found in theophoric personal names with God as their subject; cf. my *Persönliche Frömmigkeit und offizielle Religion: Religionsinterner Pluralismus in Israel und Babylon* (Calwer Theologische Monographien A9; Stuttgart: Calwer, 1978) 61–62.

21. C. Westermann especially has advocated this position; see *The Structure of the Book of Job* (Philadelphia: Fortress, 1981) 8–10.

These sentences attempt to enable Job, who in chap. 3 had become weary of life, to recall his earlier, robust existence. However, they are not merely a psychological strategy, as Job's own description later indicates:

> Or did I not weep for him who [bore] the harshness of the day?
> Did I not grieve over the poor? (30:25)

> I smiled on them, so that they gained confidence,[22]
> The light of my countenance they did not cast down. (29:24)

Job engaged in compassionate and restorative efforts on behalf of those who were being destroyed by "the harshness of the day." He stood by his friends in order to help in an instructive and consoling way the victims of the crisis of his time to come to grips with their difficult situation. By contrast, when fate has dealt Job a blow, threatening him with illness, loss of status, and isolation from the community, the pastoral explanations that he had imparted previously to his friends have now lost their power to convict. Indeed, they only magnify his pain, since he is now the one who hears them from his friends. Of course, as the Joban poet describes it, the consoling help that the friends wish to give to Job fails. Nevertheless, the poet expresses in the entire scope of his writing a pastoral desire to bring out of their despair Job and other members of the pious aristocracy who had suffered misfortune's blow and grown weary of life.[23] This presupposes there is a pastoral dimension to wisdom in the group in which and for which the poet writes.

This pastoral dimension probably originated with the social crisis experienced by the Jewish community in the early postexilic era. Elsewhere I have described the rather far-reaching social upheavals that characterized this situation.[24] It fell to the sages in this crisis to provide the sufferers with instructive, consoling, and meaningful models of explanation that could open up for them a perspective on the future.

---

22. Delete *lōʾ* at beginning of this clause.

23. This pastoral intent of the Book of Job is frequently passed by. It is immediately recognizable, however, when one compares the stance of Job in the beginning (chap. 3) with that in the concluding lament (chaps. 29–31). The one who is tired of life (3:11–26, 6:8–23, 7:21b, 10:18–22) wishes now to live once again (29:2–25). For more details see my essay "Der sozialgeschichtliche Hintergrund," 370–71.

24. For an examination of the social crisis in the Persian period, see ibid., 364–68; see also H. G. Kippenberg, *Religion und Klassenbildung im antiken Judäa: Eine religions-soziologische Studie zum Verhältnis von Tradition und gesellschaftlicher Entwicklung* (Studien zur Umwelt des Neuen Testaments 14; Göttingen: Vandenhoeck und Ruprecht, 1978); and W. Schottroff, "Arbeit und sozialer Konflikt im nachexilischen Juda," *Mitarbeiter der Schöpfung* (ed. L. Schottroff and W. Schottroff; Munich: Kaiser, 1983) 104–8.

## THE SOURCES OF WISDOM:
### EXPERIENCE, ANTIQUITY, REVELATION

A second, specific approach is to examine the sources from which the friends drew their sayings. First of all, the friends point to their own experiences ($r^ʾh$, $ḥzh$, $šm^ʿ$; 4:8, 15:17, 5:27b), which should also provide the basis for Job's reflections ($zkr$; 4:7). They bring together their own inquiry ($ḥqr$; 5:27a, 8:8) and critical examination ($bḥn$; 12:11, 34:3-4) in order to evaluate experiences and discover those things that promote human life. Yet, this basis, which was common to all wisdom from folk proverbs to Qoheleth, had lost its power of conviction for the groups being addressed. Job can contrast his own very different experiences ($r^ʾh$, $šm^ʿ$; 13:1) with those of the friends (21:17), thereby placing the reality of what they affirm into question. He can also point to the experiences of travelers, which correctly contradict those of the friends (21:29-30). It is therefore no wonder that Eliphaz must confirm his experience with a proverb in 4:8 and a presumably ancient wisdom tradition in 15:17-20.

Along with the fundamental basis of experience, the friends regarded the ancients as the special bearers of wisdom (15:10). Yet Job even placed in question this traditional view (12:12),[25] and Elihu, who is introduced later, also speaks vehemently against it (32:4, 7, 9). When Job disputes the validity of their experience, the friends occasionally take up proverbs[26] and call upon honored tradition (8:8, 15:18, 20:4). In Job 8:9 the author may even have formulated his own existentially depressing evaluation in the statement that the experiences of his own transitory generation are not sufficient to provide orientation for the future. And it is probable that the Book of Proverbs obtained its present form in the early postexilic period. This may have been occasioned by the general turning back to tradition, evidenced by the speeches of the friends in the Book of Job. Behind this turning to tradition stands the loss of the plausibility of experience and the pressure for legitimation, both seriously affecting the pious upper class.

How great this pressure of legitimation must have become may be recognized in the friends calling upon a third source for their insights to supplement experience and tradition. This source, which went beyond the traditional horizons of understanding of old wisdom, was divine revelation. Shaped in an almost stylized form, this motif is present in the first speech of Eliphaz (4:12-21). It is also found in a shorter form in the Elihu speeches (33:14-18, 36:7-12), where it is already generalized

---

25. Add $lō^ʾ$ (cf. Fohrer, *Hiob*, 237).

26. Job 4:8, 5:2, 8:11, 11:12, and 5:17 (a beatitude). For other places, see Maag, *Hiob*, 129.

for didactic purposes. Moreover, it is certainly not a special insight that Eliphaz has obtained through divine revelation. The general sinfulness and vanity of human existence as over against God (4:17–21) was inserted into other sections of the dialogue as an entirely normal human insight (15:14–16, 25:2–6). The use of revelation is only another means to legitimate and underline the insight. This also holds in the final analysis for the theophany, which contains the lengthy speech of God at the conclusion (chaps. 38–39; cf. 11:5–6).

If the claim of partaking in supernatural knowledge is still hotly contested in the original Joban poetry (15:7–16, 26:4), this is not the case in the somewhat later Elihu speeches, which trace all authentic, sapiential knowledge back to a divine inspiration that originates in the creation of human beings (32:8, 18).[27] Moreover, Elihu openly places his claim of inspiration by the spirit of his creator in opposition to the experiences of the ancients (32:7, 9). Simple experience is no longer sufficient to authenticate the validity of sapiential teaching.[28]

Consequently, it is clear that the purpose of the Book of Job is to provide an increasingly theological foundation for sapiential knowledge. This probably relates to the need to offer the pious segment of the Jewish aristocracy a clear orientation during a period of social crisis in the early postexilic period. Social experience tended to support the wicked, that is, that portion of the aristocracy which, with clever and self-serving interpretation of sapiential maxims, was openly and outspokenly successful (chap. 21). The religious dimension and theological grounding of the sapiential way of life advocated by the friends point to the desire of one group of tradents to build a theological wall around wisdom, thereby defending it from abuse by the wicked.

## PIOUS WISDOM'S PHILOSOPHY OF LIFE

The conscious religious shaping of wisdom becomes even more apparent if we attempt in a third step to describe the contents of the ideal of learning that the friends of Job set forth. One may correctly designate this ideal as "pious wisdom." This is already demonstrated by the wide use of religious language, for example, such ideas as *mibṭāḥ/kesel* 'trust' (4:6, 8:14, 31:24) and *tiqwâ* 'hope' (4:6; 8:13; 11:18, 20; cf. also *mānôs* 'refuge' in 11:20), which are already at home in the confession of confidence in the lament of the individual and accordingly in personal

27. Zophar is already on the way to this view in Job 20:3. At the time of Ben Sira it clearly belonged to a well-established repertoire of sapiential teachings (Sir 39:6).

28. This new situation is not appreciated by Whybray, *Intellectual Tradition*, 66.

piety.[29] In addition, it becomes clear in the use of such religious forms as the conditional promise (5:19-26; 8:6b-7, 21-22; 11:15-19; 22:21, 26-28) and the reflection on such religious processes as prayer (5:1-2, 8, 17-18; 8:5-7; 11:13-19; 22:21-28; 35:9-16). Throughout the Book of Job one may trace the effort to combine learning with piety.

The apologetic purpose of this synthesis becomes apparent, for example, in the accusation that Eliphaz raises against Job:

> You destroy even piety [yir²â]
>   and diminish meditation before God.
> Indeed, your sins instruct your mouth,
>   and you avail yourself of the speech of the crafty [°ărûmîm].
> Your own mouth pronounces you guilty [rš° hiphil], not I,
>   and your own lips testify against you.   (15:4-6)

With his wild charges against God, including the accusation of caprice, Job has severed himself from pious wisdom's position of being patiently reflective (śîaḥ; in the sense of 'devotion, meditation'; see also Ps 119:97, 99) before God, and instead, has given himself over to the cause of the false sages, the "crafty," who think they are able to conduct their lives either without or even against God (cf. 21:15). In spite of glaring social injustice, it is the desire of the friends to defend God from accusations, and piety from any possible attack.[30]

The manner in which the way of life and piety are connected is most apparent in those places where the traditional formulation of the confession of confidence is taken up and characteristically modified. In his first speech, when he still wishes to console Job, Eliphaz seeks to

---

29. See Ps 22:10, 71:5, 62:6; Lam 3:14; and many other places. For a discussion of the idea of "personal piety" as a category of religion, connected to the intimate circles of life and which should be differentiated from the "official religion" of the entire society, see my *Persönliche Frömmigkeit*, 23-24, in which I did not realize that this is also present in the Book of Proverbs. This has been demonstrated in various ways; see B. Lang, *Die weisheitliche Lehrrede* (Stuttgarter Bibelstudien 54; Stuttgart: KBW, 1972) 72-73; and C. V. Camp, whose work is explicitly connected to my thesis, *Wisdom and the Feminine in the Book of Proverbs* (Bible and Literature 2; Sheffield: Almond, 1985) 247-48. The relationship between wisdom texts and the "lament-thanksgiving cycle" indicated by L. G. Perdue points in the same direction (*Wisdom and Cult* [SBLDS 30; Missoula, MT: Scholars Press, 1977] 199-204). However, I would differentiate between the official cult and the more intimate private religion. Terminological connections to the confession of confidence are found also in Prov 2:7, 14:26, 22:19, 23:17-19, 30:5. Accordingly, these are not a new creation of the Joban poet, though he does integrate them in a more systematic fashion. In pious wisdom, which takes a somewhat different form in Proverbs 1-9, personal religion is transformed into theology.

30. Cf. Job 8:3, 20; 11:6; and with special vehemence Elihu in 33:12; 34:10, 12, 17, 29, 31-33; 35:15-16; 36:3, 5-6.

mediate hope for a speedy solution to his plight with the following
formulation:

> Is not your piety [*yir'â*] your trust [*kesel*],
>      and your hope [*tiqwâ*] the perfection of your way of life.   (4:6)

In the confession of confidence, God himself stood in the place of piety
and the perfect way of life. He is the ground of hope and trust in the
laments of the individual, the one on whom the worshiper depends in
his or her need.[31] Now it would certainly do pious wisdom an injustice,
if one were to impute to it the intention to replace God with religious
and meritorious deeds. Rather, what is meant is the belief that dedication to God and an active determination to satisfy his overall demands
may establish the basis on which God's inclining toward the penitent
may fully and rightly be expected. According to Eliphaz, Job may have
the legitimate hope that God will pay heed to his distress, since he has
complied with his religious and social obligations (cf. Job's lengthy
confession of innocence in chap. 31). The position that the modified
confession of confidence (4:6) opposes is formulated clearly in Bildad's
statement about the wicked:

> Such is the end[32] of all those who forget God,
>      and thus is lost the hope of the godless.
> His confidence [*kesel*] is gossamer,[33]
>      and a spider's web is his trust [*mibṭāḥ*].
> He leans [*š˓n* niphal] against his house,
>      still he cannot continue to stand.
> He holds on to it,
>      but he does not endure.   (8:13–15)

The wicked, who behave in a most unsociable manner (20:19, 22:5–9)
and think they are able to call in their markers of obligation from God,
have nothing upon which they are able to base their confidence and
trust. Indeed, they believe they are able to protect themselves on the
basis of their possessions and the prestige of their family.[34] However,

---

31. Cf. Ps 22:10–12, 71:5. The variation makes clear that the reflective philosophy of
life advocated by pious wisdom must be demarcated from "normal" personal piety, even
when it expresses an entirely obvious belief in retribution, especially in regard to everyday wishes; cf. 1 Sam 24:20, 26:23–25; 2 Sam 2:5–7; Ruth 1:8–9, 2:12; Neh 5:19; 6:14; 13:14,
22, 31; and my essay "Gebet II: Altes Testament," *Theologische Realenzyklopädie* (Berlin:
de Gruyter, 1983), 12:34–42, esp. 37.

32. Read *'aḥărît* with the LXX.

33. Read *qiššure qayiṭ*, Fohrer, *Hiob*, 185.

34. In regard to *š˓n*, cf. *miš˓enet* 'support, staff' (Ps 23:4) in the language of the
confession of confidence. Also see the verb in Isa 31:1 and the synonym *smk* niphal in Ps
71:6. The wicked thought they could support their way of life on the basis of the ancient
proverbial wisdom (Prov 10:15, 13:8, 14:20a, 19:4).

that is a dangerous illusion, a "spider's web," that quickly tears apart. Over against this, Job confesses that he had not yielded to this misleading illusion of the wicked:

> If I had made gold my confidence [*kesel*],
>   and to gold had said, "My trust [*mibṭāḥ*]!"
> If I had rejoiced, because my wealth increased,
>   and my hand had obtained great riches. . . .
> This would also be an iniquity that should be brought before the judge,
>   for I would have denied God above.   (31:24-25, 28)

The wicked have made wealth their ultimate ground of life and consequently have forgotten or denied God.[35] Therefore, their lot is to fall under the judgment of God. Against such an approach to life, which is apparent above all in the unsocial behavior of the wicked, the pious group of the aristocracy set forth their own philosophy of life. For them God opens up a future only for a way of life that is under his direction, meaning in particular the recognition of social obligations deriving from the ownership of possessions.

One may object that this view rationalizes the relationship of trust with God in inadmissible ways and dangerously limits the mercy of God. And certainly this theology misleads Job into thinking that a person has a quasi-juridical claim to both a future and good fortune on the basis of deeds of merit.[36] Indeed, one must consider the fact that it becomes the task of pious wisdom, in its efforts to avoid the way of life undertaken by the wicked, to guard against the danger of "cheap grace." The effort to assure oneself of divine grace by religious or cultic means should be eliminated. Piety and the conduct of life should be bound together in an inseparable unity.

The same desire for the integration of piety and conduct should also be clear in the interpretation of prayer that the friends represent. On the one hand, favorable divine response to prayer generally is bound to the moral character of the worshiper:

> If you yourself will seek God,
>   and to Shaddai plead [for grace],
> If you are pure and upright,
>   surely then he will watch over you.   (8:5-6)

> He delivers the guiltless man,[37]
>   he is saved on account of the purity of his hands.[38]   (22:30)

---

35. It is clear from Ps 62:9-11 that the alternative of trusting in God or in riches took on the character of a *status confessionis* in the postexilic community.

36. Job 13:13-19, chap. 23, 31:35-37. The speech of God also shows that the Joban poet condemned this understanding.

37. Read *îš*.

38. Read *kappāyw*. See also 11:13-15, 22:23.

Even here, one may not understand the condition to mean that the moral qualification of a person automatically procures God's attention and salvation. Rather it is a presupposition that makes the hearing of the prayer possible in the first place. Where morality is absent, as it is with the wicked, God's hearing of prayer is eliminated.

On the other hand, the friends distinguish between legitimate and illegitimate prayer. To Eliphaz the wild protest that expressed Job's pain in chap. 3 is illegitimate. Consequently, Job will neither be heard nor find an intercessor in heaven (5:1). Eliphaz compares such a false prayer with the behavior of the fool whose discontent and zeal finally destroy him (5:2–5). When Eliphaz subsequently gives advice to Job to pray to God (5:8), he has a different kind of prayer in mind:

> Behold, happy is the man whom God reproves,
>   and the discipline of the Almighty do not refuse.
> For God is the one who causes pain, but also the one who binds,
>   he wounds, but his hands also heal.   (5:17–18)

This concerns a prayer in which Job should accept his suffering as a measure of divine education, taking responsibility for his guilt in spite of his own merits, and in the confession of his own inadequacy ask for forgiveness. There is no place for an accusation or charge against God in this understanding of prayer. Legitimate prayer is possible in the view of pious wisdom only when it accompanies a patient demeanor, one that does not attempt to pressure God, but rather trusts that the one who wounds for disciplinary reasons will also heal.[39]

In the same way that the friends make moral qualification the necessary presupposition of a proper relationship with God, they avoid with their interpretation of prayer the possibility of attempting to use their own piety as a weapon against God. They apply a harsh doctrine of retribution only against the wicked. By contrast, in regard to the pious members of their own group, they make it very clear they wish to avoid any literal, religious conception of retribution. Only by living humbly before God, leaving to his charge one's own destiny, may one continue to experience the security and utility of a sapiential way of life.

---

39. Cf. Job 22:21 and in more detail 35:9–16 (Elihu). Elihu contends that the cries of the masses resulting from the power of the oppressor (v 9) shall not be heard by God (vv 12–14). They are not heard "on account of the arrogance of the wicked." Elihu compares such an arrogant lament with the behavior of animals. Against this he contrasts the possibility, chosen by very few, of turning in trust toward the creator, who makes it possible to sing praises even in situations of distress (v 10). The author of the narrative frame has already gone one step further. For him true piety is expressed when one can praise God even when in need (1:2, 2:10). The lament, (*tĕpillâ*) is for him in general something scandalous (*tiplâ*; 1:22) or, in other words, sinful. Such views have permeated Christian piety, but they are very unusual for the Hebrew Bible.

## MODELS FOR THE CRISIS OF
## THE EARLY POSTEXILIC PERIOD

The group of the Jewish aristocracy behind pious wisdom, then, rejected the application of a rigid doctrine of retribution to the pious and was faced with the challenge in its time as to what helpful models it could offer to its members with respect to piety and philosophy of life. In this critical situation, the members of the pious aristocracy must have come to the bitter realization that their confident, religious way of life, which was expressed particularly in a high degree of social involvement on behalf of the impoverished lower class, did not produce a direct payoff. They also were threatened by the loss of social position and isolation.[40] The other group of aristocrats, concerned only with their own advantage and not bothered by religious obligations in their business dealings, drove the lower class into poverty and dependency, prospered economically, and took for themselves prominent social positions (cf. 21:7-13, 23-24, 28-33; 22:8; 34:23-30). Under these social conditions, the questioning of the utility of piety broke open with considerable force. Such questioning is also seen in other, contemporary sources.[41] Considerations of utility certainly have always played an important role in the wisdom tradition.[42] With the synthesis accomplished by pious wisdom as the background, these considerations must have developed into a rather significant religious temptation. Not only were fixed, rational principles of behavior at stake, but also the total relationship of the individual with God.

The wicked, who protected themselves against religious obligations in the social sphere of life, could simply deny that piety had any useful purpose (21:15).[43] The bearers of pious wisdom could not do this, for they did not wish to betray their philosophy of life. They could only seek to reinterpret the questioning. The author of the Joban narrative, which also emanates from the circles of pious wisdom in the early postexilic period, does just this.[44] He interprets the loss of social status

40. See Job 30:1, 15, 28; 8:22; 11:19; 19:9, 13-20; 21:25-26; and my essay "Der sozialgeschichtliche Hintergrund," 361-62.

41. Very clearly in Mal 3:14-15 and Ps 73:13. For the chronological and social setting of the Psalm, see H. Irsigler, *Psalm 73—Monolog eines Weisen* (Arbeiten zu Text und Sprache im Alten Testament 20; St. Ottilien: EOS, 1984), esp. 366-67.

42. Cf. Prov 13:14, 16:16, 21:22, 24:5. For Qoheleth it becomes the most decisive question (2:11, 13, 15; 3:9; and often).

43. Placing Job in the company of the wicked (34:8), Elihu has also contended that Job has denied the question of the utility of piety (34:9, 35:3).

44. Since I cannot go into detail in regard to this position, I will offer only several indications. Job 1-2 and 42:7-17 are not a folktale, but rather a highly theological didactic narrative, which stands very close in its intention to the theology of the friends in the Dialogue. Further, in addition to the language, the figure of the Satan also speaks for an

experienced by Job as divine testing designed to determine if Job's piety is based only on considerations of utility, or if he could also serve God "for naught" (*ḥinnām*; 1:9). Will he continue in humility to hold fast to God even after the loss of his riches and health, giving up, at least for a time, a just reward for his piety?

The author of the poetic dialogues allows Eliphaz to reveal the impropriety of such questioning:

> Can a man be profitable to God?
> No, the wise person is profitable only to himself.[45]
> Is it a concern of Shaddai, if you are religious,
> or a gain, if you make your ways perfect? (22:2–3)

While Eliphaz enters into the question of the utility of piety to God, he points to its impossible implications. Namely, it implies the idea that each time the pious person does something good, God would be ob-ligated to reciprocate *quid pro quo*. However, God refuses to be drawn into such vulgar dealings, for his actions are not placed at humanity's disposal. The sages alone may profit from their own good deeds, though they also provide them the chance to escape the certainty of punishment directed against the wicked by divine judgment. Thus this statement by Eliphaz needs to be understood in the context of the entirety of the poetic dialogues.

On the positive side, the author of the poetic dialogues has the friends offer three models of understanding to help the suffering mem-bers of the pious aristocracy go beyond the obvious lack of advantage provided by their piety. First, they stress with great frequency the view that the fortune of the wicked will not long continue, but rather they will soon suffer a terrible fate corresponding to their unsociable be-havior (cf. 4:7–11; 5:3–5, 12–14; 8:12–19; 11:20; 15:20–27; 18:5–21; 21:6–29). This harsh doctrine of retribution is certainly only a theoretical postulate, which Job is able to contradict rather easily (chap. 21). Nevertheless, one may see in this postulate the resistance of the pious upper class who were unable to come to terms with the unjust social conditions of their time.

Second, the friends interpreted the suffering of the pious as divine discipline.[46] In this way they sought to come to a rational understanding and to establish a positive interpretation of the fully perplexing disasters

---

early postexilic setting (cf. Zech 3:1–2). The origin of the narrative in the upper class may be argued on the basis of the characterizing of Job as a wealthy owner of property. Likewise Job's praise of God in 1:21 and 2:10 can only issue from one whom God had blessed with riches!

45. Read *ʿālāyw*.

46. Job 5:17 has *ykḥ* hiphil and *mûsar*; *tôrâ* occurs in 22:22.

handed them by fate, disasters they had to endure in spite of their great deeds of merit. Since God delivers the pious from suffering, he has not withdrawn from them.[47] But God has in view for the pious something very important: he wishes to move them further along the path of piety (see the paradoxical beatitude in 5:17). Therefore, everything depends on one's being prepared to accept and to learn from the discipline of God. There is the justified hope that this suffering, as is true of every act of discipline, will last only for a limited time and will soon be brought to an end by God (cf. the limited promises in 5:19–26; 8:6b–7, 21–22; 11:15–19; 22:21, 26–28). In this manner the tradents of the pious wisdom tradition sought to cope with the harsh blow dealt to their philosophy of life by describing their relationship to God in terms of pedagogy.[48]

Finally, the friends reach back to the insight of creaturely sinfulness and the worthlessness of human nature, which widely separates people from God.[49] This explanation opposes the widely disseminated, optimistic, pious ideal of education, and serves to eliminate any notion of accusing God. Regardless of how great their own merits may be, they are never sufficient to make people appear just and pure before God (4:17). Consequently, no one from the circles of the pious aristocracy is justified in bringing an indictment against God, as Job has done in demanding just payment for his deeds of merit (chap. 13, 31:35–37). On the contrary, they must humbly acknowledge the justice of God who continues to educate the pious through painful experiences of misfortune.

## THE THEOLOGY OF THE JOBAN SAGES—AN EVALUATION

The philosophy of life represented by the pious friends in the Book of Job and developed by segments of the aristocracy of early Judaism

47. Also in personal piety the distress of the individual may be interpreted as the abandonment of God (see Ps 22:2, 71:11, and often; cf. my *Persönliche Frömmigkeit*, 38–39).

48. The significance of illness as an educational action of God is found also in Prov 3:11–12. This type of explanation is taken up in a rather extensive way by Elihu. He uses it, not only in relationship to illness (33:19–28), but also in relationship both to political events (e.g., the overturning of the powerful; 36:7–12) and to social suffering (36:15). One may here see how a general theological theory of explanation not unproblematically derives from a pastoral type of explanation. God is regularly made a teacher (*môreh*) by Elihu (e.g., 36:22).

49. There probably is a precedent for this insight from the religious world of ideas, namely the lament over the transitoriness of life in the confession of guilt (cf. Ps 39:6–7, 12; 51:7; 143:2; 144:3–4; and often). Moreover, it is the same insight that is offered to and eventually consoles the sufferer in the so-called "Sumerian Job" (ca. 2000 B.C.E.). He humbly subjects himself once more to his God (*ANET* 590, lines 101–2). It is introduced here as an ancient insight of the sages.

becomes a very impressive theology. One may describe it as a conscious synthesis of the sapiential mastering of life and piety, or as
reason's permeation of personal piety, fashioned by the perspective of
the upper class. Subsequently, there is a total absence of explicit
Israelite nationalism and the prophetic-eschatological horizon of expectations. Even so, this theology does not escape the influence of the
national, salvific traditions of Israel. The seriousness of seeking to anchor the religious dimension of existence in the everyday conduct of life
and to actualize a high degree of social feeling, piety, and justice, above
all for the poor, shows points of contact especially with the concerns of
the deuteronomic reform movement, which before the Exile was also
borne to a great extent by the members of the aristocracy.[50] These
points of contact are not accidental. After the death of Josiah in 609
B.C.E., the question of the realization of the social legislation of Deuteronomy led for the first time to a division of the aristocracy into a
"pious" and an "impious" group,[51] which continued into the postexilic
period. Thus, it is understandable that, beginning with the late preexilic
period, the segment of the aristocracy that was knowingly obedient to
the concerns of the deuteronomic reform in public life also created a
philosophy of life for its private sphere. This resulted in a synthesis of
personal piety and a sapiential mastering of life, which had similar ends.
This provided a conscious alternative to the conduct of life led by
another segment of the aristocracy, which denied especially social obligations and either separated piety from a purely success-oriented use
of sapiential maxims or gave piety up altogether.

In the disruption caused by the social upheaval that provides the
background for the Book of Job, the philosophy of life advocated by
pious sages fell into crisis. However, this did not occur, as is frequently
said, because the sages were too dogmatically torpid, but rather because they could not deny the fact that many of their members, in spite
of and perhaps even because of their pious, social involvement fell into
misfortune. The result was that this philosophy of life was itself placed
into question because of social developments. Nevertheless, they were
in the position to react in ready fashion to these challenges, as the Book
of Job in its various parts (narrative frame, poetic dialogues, Elihu
speeches, and chap. 28) demonstrates. The rationalizing models of

50. I can only mention this here. This thesis is amply demonstrated in my "Reli-
gionsgeschichte Israels in vorexilischer Zeit," *Die Bibel: Das Alte Testament in Bildern
erzählt* (ed. E. Lessing; Munich: Bertelsmann, 1987) 285–360, esp. 346–49. For the
sapiential features of Deuteronomy, see M. Weinfeld, *Deuteronomy and the Deuteronomic
School* (Oxford: Clarendon, 1972).

51. See Jer 5:26, where for the first time the rich who oppress the poor are given the
title *rĕšāˁîm* 'wicked, godless'.

explanation (testing, discipline, etc.), which they offered to their members who had fallen into poverty and distress, are characterized by lofty religious and ethical requirements. Certainly, the author of the dialogues makes clear that these lofty requirements frequently demanded too much of the afflicted. And thus he places beside the narrative's concept of a ministry that leads to pious self-denial his dialogical concept that forces the position of pious wisdom to come face to face with the despairing laments of the one who is afflicted. In a realistic manner, he discovers that the teaching of wisdom, while it may still be theologically correct, does not reach Job in his suffering. In addition, he also makes clear the dangers that accompany the rationalization of personal piety. It seduces Job into coming to the understandable, but fully impossible notion that he can call God to task and can carry through in legal fashion his demand for good fortune on the basis of his merits. And it seduces the friends into condemning Job as a wicked man on account of his break with a humble manner of life. However, these are the dangers that underlie not only the theology of the friends, but also any theology that seeks to penetrate and explain the living relationship of God and humanity in a rational manner.

# THE SAGE IN ECCLESIASTES
# AND QOHELETH THE SAGE

## Roland E. Murphy

How many sages are there in the Book of Ecclesiastes? Already in the patristic period, different "voices" in the book were heard; for example, Gregory the Great saw Solomon dialoguing with a fool or a knave. Especially since the work of C. Siegfried (1898), it became fashionable to distinguish (among other glossators) the contribution of a ḥākām, or 'sage', to the work of the original author, Qoheleth. Siegfried allotted the following verses to the sage: 2:13-14a; 4:5; 6:8-9a; 7:11, 12, 19; 8:1; 9:13-18; 10:1-3, 12-15.[1] The perceptive commentary of E. Podechard followed the lead of Siegfried in recognizing several hands at work in the text.[2] For Podechard, 1:2, 7:27-28, and 12:8-12 were ascribed to a student of Qoheleth, whom he called the epilogist; of course, as a student, this person was thereby also a ḥākām. But another ḥākām was also at work. Podechard explicitly acknowledged that "he" might be more than one person, but in any case a wisdom other than that of Qoheleth was to be found in several insertions: 4:5, 9-12; 5:2, 6a; 6:7; 7:1-12, 18-22; 8:1-2a, 3-4; 9:17; 10:4, 10-14a, 15-20; 11:1-4, 6. The atomizing thrust of this analysis has been considerably toned down by later scholars till it is only faintly present in K. Galling and W. Zimmerli,[3] who are not concerned about the precise identity of the alleged glossator (whether a ḥākām or a ḥăsîd, etc.).

Roland E. Murphy, O. Carm., is G. W. Ivey Emeritus Professor of Biblical Studies at Duke University.

1. C. Siegfried, *Prediger und Hoheslied* (Göttingen: Vandenhoeck und Ruprecht, 1898).
   2. E. Podechard, *L'Ecclésiaste* (Etudes Bibliques; Paris: Gabalda, 1912).
   3. K. Galling, "Der Prediger," *Die fünf Megilloth* (2d ed.; Handbuch zum Alten Testament 18; Tübingen: Mohr/Siebeck, 1969) 73-125; W. Zimmerli, "Das Buch des Predigers Salomo," *Sprüche/Prediger* (Das Alte Testament Deutsch 16/1; Göttingen: Vandenhoeck und Ruprecht, 1962) 123-351.

## THE EPILOGIST

For the purposes of this essay, 1:2–12:8, surrounded as it is by an inclusion (*hbl hblym*), is the work of one sage, Qoheleth. No claim is made that he is the "author" of the various proverbial sayings strewn throughout the book (esp. chaps. 7 and 10); he could have been working with traditional material. But this major portion of the book is his work.

The epilogue, 12:9–14, is written *about* Qoheleth and is clearly the work of another person (some would say persons). We know nothing more about him other than his views on Qoheleth and his work. The superscription (1:1) may possibly derive from him, or from a third hand, but it is not important for the purpose of this essay.

It is helpful to begin with the assessment of Qoheleth's work in the epilogue. Several important points emerge from this passage. (1) The epilogist calls Qoheleth a *ḥākām*, who taught the people knowledge and who was concerned with *mĕšālîm* and "words." (2) The reverent attitude of the epilogist toward the "words of the wise" (12:11) suggests that he himself probably belonged to the class of sages. (3) In the same verse the epilogist suggests on the face of it that Qoheleth was a sage of a special sort in the observation: "The words of the sages are as prods, and [those of] the masters of the collections are like fixed nails."[4] (4) For my purpose here, it makes little difference if 12:13–14 is to be attributed to still another sage. It surely reflects a sapiential point of view, emphasizing (*a*) more books, in addition to those already available and obviously the work at hand (Ecclesiastes), are unnecessary, (b) fear of the Lord and the commandments, and (*c*) divine judgment.

In modern times the epilogue has often been interpreted, at least in vv 13–14, as a put-down of Qoheleth, an effort to soften the impact of the book and bring it into line with orthodoxy (so, in varying degrees, the views of commentators such as Galling and Zimmerli). This interpretation is unnecessary and even gratuitous. If the epilogist were really concerned, and wished to *correct* the book in line with "orthodox" wisdom, his was an outstanding failure. Indeed, it can be argued that the epilogue is far from a corrective, that it constitutes an endorsement of the work as being a kind of final statement of the wisdom tradition, to which no more need be added. This seems to be the correct interpretation of *wĕyōtēr mēhēmmâ* in 12:12, which is to be understood

---

4. For a recent discussion of these phrases, see Michael Fishbane, *Biblical Interpretation in Ancient Israel* (Oxford: Clarendon, 1985) 29–32, and the next note. The translation of 12:11 is Fishbane's (p. 29).

as saying: anything beyond these (words of the wise, Ecclesiastes included) are not to be regarded ("my son, beware!").[5]

The assessment of the message of Ecclesiastes in 12:13–14 is rightly
termed a "thematizing" by K. Galling and G. Sheppard, and it differs
from the thematizing of "vanity of vanities" in 12:8. Both of these are
oversimplified interpretations of the book. The skeptical (and certainly
more prominent) side of Qoheleth appears in 12:8, and it makes use of
his favorite word (some thirty-seven times *hbl* occurs). A conservative
aspect appears in 12:13–14. Qoheleth would hardly have put it this way!
He would never have associated fear of God and keeping the commandments. Although fear of God is a concern for him (3:14, 5:6, 7:18,
8:12–13), he never refers to the commandments. As Sheppard has
pointed out, vv 13–14 are "a synopsis of wisdom in terms broader than
Qoheleth"; and they "express an ideology of wisdom like that in
Sirach."[6] This is a very significant fact. Qoheleth was not as shocking
for the ancients as he is for the moderns. Within a relatively short time
of his death he is accepted as a *ḥākām*, whose message can be fitted in
with the identification of law and wisdom so spectacularly recorded in
Sirach 24. It is a testimony to the resilience of biblical wisdom that
neither Job nor Ecclesiastes ever became a stumbling stone.

## QOHELETH, THE SAGE

### Language

The most obvious signs that Qoheleth belongs to the wisdom
tradition are his use of the language and literary forms typical of that
movement, and his treatment of a broad range of characteristic topoi,
the commonplaces of ancient wisdom. In terms of language, the usage
of the root *ḥkm* ('wise') is at least indicative of a preoccupation with

---

5. In *Biblical Interpretation in Ancient Israel* (pp. 29–32) M. Fishbane has pointed
out that 12:9–12 fits into a "colophonic pattern," that draws from a "conventional stock of
ancient Near Eastern scribal practices and vocabulary" (pp. 30, 31). The verbs of v 9 (*ʾzn*,
*ḥqr*, *tqn*) are rendered as 'order', 'examine', 'fix (or edit)', and this vocabulary is similar to
Mesopotamian colophons ('write, compose, and collate'; 'write, check, and collate', etc.).
The "making" of many books seems to have a parallel in the Akkadian verb, *uppušu*
('compose, copy'), which comes from the stem *epēšu* (Hebrew *ʿśh*). The verb *tqn* in v 12
means to 'correct', but comes to have the meaning 'edit' in contemporary Aramaic and
eventually in rabbinic Hebrew.

6. G. Sheppard, *Wisdom as a Hermeneutical Construct* (BZAW 151; Berlin de
Gruyter, 1980) 126.

wisdom, especially when it appears so frequently in the book.[7] The frequency of the root is not as important as its significant usage, that is, when Qoheleth admits that his goal, unattained, was wisdom (7:23–24), or denies that the wise man can understand God's work (8:17), or reflects on the vulnerability of wisdom (9:16–10:1), or describes how his testing of life's pleasures was conducted with wisdom (2:3, 9). Wisdom is at the forefront of his entire enterprise.

## Range of Concerns

A substantial concern of the sages is: What is good (*ṭôb*) for humans? Qoheleth highlights this in his experiment in 2:3, to "understand what is best for humans to do under the heavens during the limited days of their lives." Good is not necessarily opposed to evil (although the latter nuance may not be absent). The "good" can be a positive recommendation in favor of a given line of conduct, or it may be a comparison ('better than', *ṭôb min*) that favors one thing over another. The term itself is not the only indicator of what is good (or better) to do. Substituting for good/evil is the phrase *māh* (or *ʾên*) *yitrôn* ('what profit?': 1:3; 2:11, 13; 3:9; 5:15; 10:11) or 'troublesome business' (*ʿinyān*, or *ʿinyān rāʿ*: 1:13, 2:23, 3:10, 4:8, 5:13, 8:16), or the ubiquitous *hebel*. In 2:13 *yitrôn* is parallel to, and hence the equivalent of, *ṭôb*. In 2:11 (cf. 2:15) *ʾên yitrôn* ('no profit') is parallel to *hbl*, or 'vanity'.

Qoheleth uses the common literary forms that are the stock in trade of the Hebrew sage: the saying and the admonition.[8] In addition, he adds his own particular reflections, introduced by set phrases, such as "I said in my heart" (1:16–17; 2:1, 15; 3:17), etc. Rhetorical questions abound (six of these in chap. 2 alone). O. Loretz has drawn up a list of seventy-one topoi or commonplaces treated in Ecclesiastes and other wisdom books.[9] One does not have to agree with all these instances, and even perhaps others could be added. But the list is significant for the understanding of Qoheleth the sage. He brackets out traditional items such as promises and exodus and covenant, and hews strictly to the realm of experience: the troubles but also the enjoyment of life, the ephemerality of human existence, time, diligence, appetite, greed, the

7. See the list of occurrences in O. Loretz, *Qohelet und der Alte Orient* (Freiburg: Herder, 1964) 167–68; he has drawn up convenient lists of twenty-seven "favorite" words of Qoheleth on pp. 167–73 and records the astonishing fact that these words constitute one-fifth of Qoheleth's vocabulary!

8. For details on the literary forms, see "Ecclesiastes" in my *Wisdom Literature* (Forms of Old Testament Literature 13; Grand Rapids: Eerdmans, 1981) 125–49, and also 4–6, 63–67.

9. Loretz, *Qohelet*, 196–208.

righteous/wicked contrast, speech, woman, and royalty. The entire work is a dense concentration on wisdom concerns.

## Wisdom Sayings

A large number of typical wisdom sayings occurs throughout the book.[10] One cannot determine whether these are original or derived, but they at least illustrate Qoheleth, the "wise man," at work with the tools of his trade. The more important issue is the manner in which he employs them, the measure of approval that he grants or denies. Here only the broad possibilities can be indicated, for the correct exegesis of certain passages is difficult to ascertain.

It is clear that 2:14 ("the wise man has eyes in his head, but the fool walks in darkness") ultimately counts little with Qoheleth because he immediately follows with the question of *yitrôn*, or 'profit'. Since both the wise and the fool are equal in death (2:14b–16), the saying loses its claim on him. The interpretation of the sayings in 7:1–12 is difficult. Either the sayings are affirmed by Qoheleth or they are dialectically related to each other in opposition. Does the phrase, "this also is vanity" (7:6) indicate a rejection of all the sayings in vv 1–6 in favor of the sayings in vv 7–12? (so A. G. Wright)?[11] Or is there a dialectic going on within the collection (so N. Lohfink),[12] whereby one is modified by the other? Thus, if 7:1a is a traditional saying about the advantages of a good name, 7:1b–4 counters this with the idea that nothing can be said about a good name until the person has died. Similarly, the superiority of the wise man's speech (7:5–6) is limited by the fact that oppression can make him a fool (7:7). The ambiguity that attaches to 7:1–12 appears also in 9:18–10:11(20?). It is difficult to assess the validity Qoheleth attaches to several of these sayings. But in the wisdom tradition this should not be surprising. Variations, and hence differences of opinion, appear in the various collections in Proverbs 10–31. They have the appearance of safe and conservative advice handed down by tradition, and the monotonous sequence contributes to their placid air. But what was their prehistory before being collected and arranged? Surely there was a sense of discovery, the realization of a new insight, even the awareness of contradictory aspects (on answering a fool according to his folly, Prov 26:4–5). The sages before Qoheleth were not as simple-minded as many moderns are inclined to think; nonetheless in Qoheleth

10. Though not all would agree on the exact number, the presence of sayings is undeniable. Among them may be counted the following: 1:13b, 15, 18; 2:14a; 4:4–5; 5:2; 6:9a?; 7:1–12; 8:1; 9:18–10:4; 10:8–9, 12–13; 11:1–2(6?).

11. A. G. Wright, "The Riddle of the Sphinx: The Structure of the Book of Qoheleth," *CBQ* 30 (1968) 313–34; cf. p. 330 (repr. in *SAIW* 245–66).

12. N. Lohfink, *Kohelet* (Neue Echter Bibel; Würzburg: Echter, 1980) 48ff.

we encounter a sage whose exciting dialectic surpasses the more static traditionalism of earlier makers of sentences.[13]

## Selective Appropriation of Traditions on Death

A typical example of the way in which Qoheleth agrees and disagrees with the tradition is his handling of Death/Sheol, the enemies of human existence.[14] His definition of Sheol is classic, and even goes beyond the usual description: no activity, no calculating, no knowledge, no wisdom (9:10b). Sheol is the epitome of nonlife, the total absence of the type of life to which Qoheleth had dedicated himself. Hence his recommendation to live vigorously while this is possible (9:10a). In this respect he shares the wisdom tradition, which proclaimed the message of life (in the here and now). It also calmly accepted with the rest of the Old Testament the inevitability of death (e.g., Ps 90:3-10). But Qoheleth radicalizes Death/Sheol in his reflections. Death emerges as a kind of devastating "final solution" to the proud claims of human wisdom. It is his ultimate argument: "How is it that the wise man dies as well as the fool!" (2:16)—perhaps the greatest display of emotion in his book. Death is the *miqreh*, or 'happening' that comes to wise and foolish alike (2:14-16); it is the *miqreh* common to beasts and humans (3:18-21). Because of the way things turn out, it can even be preferable to life ("Therefore I loathed life," 2:17—how contrary to the kerygma of wisdom!—cf. 4:2, 6:3-4). In that dialectic style that is his trademark, he can say that a live dog is better than a dead lion (9:4), but he seems to empty this saying of any meaning by the satirical remark in the following verse that although the dead know nothing, the living know . . . that they are to die! The association of old age and ultimate death is portrayed in the famous "allegory" (at least for 8:3-4a) in 8:1-7. Here again the motivation is to live with zest while the opportunity is present (11:7-10; cf. 9:10a).

The typical "immortality" in the Old Testament consisted in one's progeny that perpetuated one's self, one's name (cf. Prov 10:7, "The memory of the just is a blessing"; cf. also Ps 112:6). The remembrance of the just functioned as a consolation for human mortality. Qoheleth flatly denies this. The reason lies in a frequently repeated claim: there is simply no remembrance of the past (1:11, 2:16, 9:5). This forthright denial is a puzzling aspect of his thought because it seems so gratuitous. He adds no qualification; he does not go on to say in this context that

13. G. von Rad was the first to point out that the sages did not lack an awareness of their own limitations; cf. *Wisdom in Israel* (Nashville: Abingdon, 1972) 97-110.

14. Cf. A. Schoors, "Koheleth, A Perspective of Life after Death?" *Ephemerides Theologicae Lovanienses* 61 (1985) 295-303.

remembrance is inadequate, or that it is destined ultimately to die away.[15] Thus the sage seems to be taken up by the importance of the present (what is, is; cf. 1:9, 3:15), and by the ignorance of what is to come (3:22, 6:12, 8:7).

## The Mystery of God

The "otherness," or mystery, of God is brought out in many ways in the Bible. One cannot see God and go on living (Exod 33:20, Judg 13:22), even if paradoxically many do continue to live! The dangerous presence of the divine must be met with some kind of protection: the hand of God shields Moses in the cave (Exod 33:22), Elijah covers his face with his cloak after the Lord appears in the "sound of thin silence" (1 Kgs 19:13). This biblical viewpoint is reflected in Qoheleth's use of the traditional concept of the "fear of God" (in the sense of awe before the numinous) in 3:14 and 5:6.[16] It is at the basis of his no-nonsense remarks about prayer and promising in God's presence: "God is in heaven and you are on earth; therefore let your words be few" (4:17 [MT 5:1]). But most of all the distance between God and humans appears in the mystery of the divine ma⁽ăśeh, or 'work of God'.

This phrase has a specific coloring in most of the Old Testament. It refers to the created things that are the "work" of the divine hands (Ps 19:2, Job 34:19; cf. Job 10:3–11). All the "works" of creation are associated with divine wisdom in Ps 104:24 (cf. 139:14). The work(s) of God are celebrated as an object of praise in the psalms (66:3; 92:6; 111:2, 7; 118:17). Such connotations are absent in the usage of Qoheleth the sage.

He repeatedly and explicitly describes the work of God as unknowable. God has prevented humans (through that murky hā⁽ōlām placed in their hearts) from discovering (mṣ⁾) his ma⁽ăśeh (3:11). One cannot discover (mṣ⁾) the "work [of God] that is done under the sun" (8:17). He invites the reader to consider the work of God, but immediately characterizes it as something God has made crooked, which no one can straighten out (7:13). The work of God is as unknowable as the mystery of gestation, the "path of the rûaḥ," in the womb (11:5).

15. For a possible explanation, see J. G. Gammie, "Stoicism and Anti-Stoicism in Qoheleth," *Hebrew Annual Review* 9 (1985) 169–87. Gammie posits that throughout Qoheleth is in dialogue with Stoicism and that Qoheleth's assertions on the lack of remembrance after death may have been made in direct opposition to Stoic optimism (p. 182).

16. For a discussion of this topic, and for full references, see my treatment, "Qohelet's 'Quarrel' with the Fathers," *From Faith to Faith* (D. G. Miller Festschrift; ed. D. Y. Hadidian; Pittsburgh Theological Monograph Series 31; Pittsburgh: Pickwick, 1979) 235–45.

Qoheleth is neither the first person nor the first sage in the Old Testament to run headlong into the mystery of God. There is quite a precedent for this, from the incredible "testing" of father Abraham in Genesis 22, through the questions of Habakkuk, to the declaration of Job in chap. 23 and the speeches of the Lord in Job 38–41. But Qoheleth is constantly coming back to the issue. It lies behind the problem of the fate of the wise/foolish and righteous/wicked.

## The Justice of God

If humans cannot make sense of what God is doing, it is not to be expected that the traditional understanding of divine "justice" will make sense. Qoheleth easily points out the painful discrepancies in the treatment of the good and the evil: 3:16–18, 7:15, 8:10–14, 9:1–3. This does not mean that he denies divine judgment (3:17, 11:9b—not to be eliminated as glosses). As an Israelite he could not escape the *fact* of divine judgment, but he was entitled to question its working.

This attitude is unemotional, as usual, but a controlled wrath seems to appear in the repetition that there is "none to comfort" the oppressed (4:1). A bitter cynicism marks Qoh 5:7: oppression need not shock when one contemplates the hierarchical order of society, one level watching another. What good can be expected in such a setup? Although it has been inferred that the sage Qoheleth was a well-to-do bourgeois of Jerusalem, it is difficult to find data in the book to support this claim. He is surely not the typical defender of the status quo. There is a fearsome ring to his word about the implacability of the hand, or power, of God in 9:1. It is impossible to tell whether God loves or hates a person because there is the same *miqreh* for all, both good and evil (9:2–3). The divine tempo and the human tempo (cf. 3:1–11) are along different lines: "A time of calamity comes to all alike. Man no more knows his own time than fish taken in the fatal net, or birds trapped in the snare; like these the children of men are caught when the evil time falls suddenly upon them" (9:11–12).

## Joy as a Muted, But Not Dominant, Theme of the Sage

Despite the dour and pessimistic sayings that abound in Ecclesiastes, there is a clear indication of a zest for life. This is most remarkably expressed in 11:9, "Rejoice, O young man, while you are young and let your heart be glad in the days of your youth . . ." (see also 9:10). In addition, there are the many passages that encourage the enjoyment of the good life, eating and drinking, etc. (2:24–25; 3:12–13, 22; 5:17–19; 8:15; 9:7–10). It is erroneous to conceive of Qoheleth as urging hedonism, epicureanism, etc.—charges that have been made in the past.[17]

17. For a balanced critique of recent literature on the subject, see O. Kaiser, *Der Mensch unter dem Schicksal* (BZAW 161; Berlin: de Gruyter, 1983) 135–53.

But it is also doubtful if this perspective constitutes a major emphasis, a kind of "message of Qoheleth." R. Gordis maintains that for Qoheleth "joy is God's categorical imperative for man," and that "the basic theme of the book was *simḥah*, the enjoyment of life."[18]

This interpretation of Ecclesiastes has found some support, but it remains highly questionable. Qoheleth's emphasis on the enjoyment of life remains severely limited. It is uttered in the perspective of Sheol and the nothingness to come, in the perspective of the arbitrariness of a God who "gives" (2:24, 3:13, 5:18-19, 8:15) such delights, but at the sovereign divine pleasure. It is difficult to maintain that enjoyment is the message of the book when the sage has so strongly modified it by the perspective of Sheol and the mysterious divine will.

## THE CONTRIBUTION OF QOHELETH
## THE SAGE TO TRADITIONAL WISDOM

The "crisis of wisdom" has become a popular phrase to designate the effect of Job and Ecclesiastes on the wisdom movement.[19] But it seems too glib. It disregards the thematizing of Qoh 12:13-14; this viewpoint of the epilogist is important because it shows an assessment from people who were closer in time to him than we are. It must also be said that Qoheleth certainly pushed wisdom beyond her previous depths. He was a sage who admitted that his effort to attain wisdom did not succeed (7:23, 8:17), that the accumulated wisdom of Israel had manifold shortcomings, a sage who considered life a vanity not worth living. But folly was never an option for him. His own wisdom consisted in seeing deeper and further than the traditional wisdom, in purifying it, even to such an extent that it did not appear to be viable. But in style he remained faithful to the tradition of the sages.

The serenity of the views of Ben Sira and the Wisdom of Solomon (and perhaps Proverbs 1-9?), which follow Qoheleth in the wisdom movement, deserves to be pondered. Qoheleth the sage broke open new directions, even shaking wisdom to her foundations. The verdict of futility (*hbl*) was applied directly to life (2:17, 4:2, 9:4), and the mystery of God's doing was revealed with starkness. But Qoheleth was given a niche in the wisdom movement; it was seen that he was keeping wisdom honest.

18. R. Gordis, *Koheleth—The Man and His World* (3d ed.; New York: Schocken, 1968) 129, 131.

19. For references see my "Qohelet's 'Quarrel' with the Fathers," 244 n. 2.

# PART IV

The Sage
in Other Biblical Texts

# THE SAGE IN THE
# PENTATEUCH: SOUNDINGS

## Tikva Frymer-Kensky

At first sight, a study of the sage in the Pentateuch would appear to be swiftly accomplished because of the paucity of the data. Professional sages do not abound in these books, and the term *ḥākām* 'sage' is rare. Among Pharaoh's advisors are professional wise men, *ḥartūmmê miṣrayîm*, (Gen 41:8, Exod 7:11), but there is no such technical office described for Israel.[1] Even wise as an adjective is not common: Abraham, Isaac, Jacob, and their wives possess many good qualities, but they are not called wise, neither is Moses, nor Aaron, nor Miriam. Nevertheless, a close examination of the pentateuchal tradition reveals some significant aspects of the sage in ancient Israel.

## GENESIS AND EXODUS: THE FEMALE AS
## SAGE—EVE, SARAH, REBEKAH, RACHEL, ZIPPORAH

Even though Joseph is the only one designated as sage, others in the pentateuchal narratives exemplify elements normally associated with the sage. The very definition of sage involves knowledge, culture, and wisdom. A meaning seen from the Primeval History (Genesis 1–11), which intertwines a major philosophical treatment of cultural wisdom with its narrative of other basic elements of human existence. At the creation of Adam (*ʾādām*, lit. humankind), the earth creature (*hāʾādām*) exists in such a simple and uncultured form that God could entertain the notion that an animal might be a fit companion for him (Gen 2:18–19).[2] Eve (*ḥawwâ*, lit. life) changed this. Convinced by the serpent that she

Tikva Frymer-Kensky is Director of Biblical Studies at Reconstructionist Rabbinical College, Philadelphia.

1. The *ḥartumîm* of Exod 8:7, 19 [MT 8:3, 15] and 9:11 is probably a more inclusive term, i.e., the "wise" of Egypt were to be numbered among them.

2. See P. Trible, *God and the Rhetoric of Sexuality* (Overtures to Biblical Theology 2; Philadelphia: Fortress, 1978) 12–17, 78–81, for a defense of the reading of *ʾadam* as "humankind" and of *hāʾādām* as 'earth creature'.

could become knowledgeable and godlike by eating the fruit of the tree of knowledge, she acquired the knowledge of things: cultural knowledge. Eve wrested knowledge from the realm of the divine and thus transformed the world.

Eve has often been associated with Pandora in Western tradition, but she is better compared to Prometheus, the bringer of culture (fire) for humanity, who was punished by the gods. When Adam and Eve ate the fruit of knowledge, "their eyes were opened" and they not only realized that they were naked (a category they had not perceived in their childlike simplicity), but they were able to sew themselves loincloths out of the available fig leaves. The liminal Edenic "natural" state had disappeared and humanity had embarked on its cultural existence. Just as women are the recognized mediators between nature and culture—transforming the raw into the edible, the grass into baskets, the fleece and the flax into yarn and then into clothes, and the babies into social beings—so too the first woman effected the change between "natural" simple beings and cultural humanity. And just as the mother is the earliest figure of wisdom to the child, in the biblical account, woman was the initiating agent and conveyer of the very beginnings of human wisdom.[3]

A second aspect of female sages in the Pentateuch may be considered. Having no direct authority of their own, they—on their own initiative—have the power to effect results through their knowledge and their willingness to act upon their knowledge, either through petition and argument or, failing that, through independent action. In the Pentateuch, such a role is usually filled by women, notably by Sarah, Rebekah, and Rachel. The direct power to act resided in the male authority figure, and women in a patriarchal household were limited in what they could do directly. Nevertheless, this limitation did not make them afraid or unwilling to try to achieve their goals. If the man in power was likely to listen, the wife could argue directly and forcefully. Sarah suggested Hagar as a surrogate to Abraham, and then came to tell Abraham to emancipate and send away Hagar and Ishmael, and convinced him (with the help of God). Similarly, Rebekah persuaded Isaac to send Jacob back to Mesopotamia for a wife, and Rachel convinced Jacob to take Bilhah as her surrogate.

---

3. Women continued to be associated with wisdom both as wise (e.g., the wise woman of Tekoa, the wise woman of Abel, Abigail, the capable wife of Prov 31:10–31) and as the very model of personified Wisdom (Proverbs 1-9, Sirach 24, Wisdom of Solomon 7-9). For a study of wisdom and women, see C. R. Fontaine, *Wisdom and the Feminine in the Book of Proverbs* (Bible and Literature 11; Shefield: Almond, 1982), and my forthcoming book, *In the Wake of Goddesses*.

There is a particular tone to these petitions by the matriarchs. They do not plead, and do not address their husbands in the language of obedience or submission. On the contrary, they are uppity women who use a characteristic form of biblical rhetoric, the guilt-producing opening attack. Thus Sarai said, "The wrong done me is your fault! I myself gave my maid into your bosom; now that she sees that she is pregnant, I am lowered in her esteem. The Lord decide between you and me" (Gen 16:5). So too, when Rebekah wanted Isaac to send Jacob to Aram-Naharaim, she emphasized (and perhaps exaggerated) her own mood: "I am disgusted with my life because of the Hittite women. If Jacob marries a Hittite woman like these, from among the native women, what good will life be to me?" (Gen 27:46). A similar argument is used by Rachel in an often misunderstood passage. Rachel stated, "Give me children or I shall die!" And Jacob, reacting badly to the rhetoric, responded sharply, "Can I take the place of God, who has denied you fruit of the womb?" (Gen 30:1–2). But Rachel has just been introducing her real request, which is that Jacob take Bilhah as consort. After all, Jacob already had four sons and was not actively seeking more, and it was more to Rachel's advantage that Jacob take Bilhah than to Jacob's, for when the baby was born, Rachel declared, "He has heeded my plea and given me a son" (Gen 30:6).

This guilt-producing rhetoric is not simply characteristic of the "Jewish mother"! In fact, it is an essential method of biblical argumentation, one used by women other than mothers, and by such great male authority figures as Moses and Samuel.[4] But it is significant that there are not two separate ways of discourse for men and women, and that women do not have to adopt a subordinate posture in their speech. The women of Israel, including the paradigmatic matriarchs, speak as knowledgeable authorities.

They not only speak, they take action. When petition would be useless, as in the case of Isaac's blessing, Rebekah does not resort to it, but rather acts to circumvent Isaac's authority by manipulating him into doing her bidding. Much has been written about Rebekah's trickery of Isaac.[5] Trickery in the Bible is not a female prerogative: it is used by

4. For analysis and details see my forthcoming book, *In the Wake of Goddesses*.

5. See C. G. Allen, "On Me Be the Curse, My Son!" *Encounter with the Text: Form and History in the Hebrew Bible* (ed. M. J. Buss; Philadelphia: Fortress, 1979) 159–72; E. Fuchs, "Who is Hiding the Truth? Deceptive Women and Biblical Androcentrism," *Feminist Perspectives on Biblical Scholarship* (ed. A. Y. Collins; Chico, CA: Scholars Press, 1985) 137–144; and the many articles in *Reasoning with the Foxes: Female Wit in a World of Male Power* (ed. J. C. Exum and J. W. H. Bos; Semeia 42; Atlanta: Scholars Press, 1988).

many male figures, and is not only justified by their (sometimes temporary) underdog status, but is glorified in as an example of their ability to succeed by their wits. We need not discuss the culpability of Rebekah (a question that does not seem to be inherent in the biblical story). However, it is clear that the deception of Rebekah is in accord with the divine plan. According to the narrative, Rebekah had long before received a divine oracle that her younger would rule her elder son, and she acts in the light of this knowledge to ensure the divine will. Her skills at argumentation, her initiative in action, and her prior knowledge all conform to the picture normally associated with a sage.

These sagelike matriarchs are not "alone among all women," but are paradigmatic, for there are other pentateuchal women who have some elements of knowledge and action. Moses twice owes his life to women who knew what to do and did it: his mother who saved him from Pharaoh by conceiving the plan to float him in the basket, and his wife Zipporah who saved him from God by swiftly circumcising their son. Other women with such attributes can be mentioned: Shiphrah and Puah who knew how to circumvent Pharaoh's orders, and Miriam who composed song and dance in honor of God. I do not mean to belabor the point or to consider all women as sages, but rather to point to those characteristics that women have in common with sages and to point out that at least part of the reason that they have similar characteristics is that they play similar roles: like women, male sages have an ancillary position to the holder of direct power. They do not have the power to determine events directly, but rather influence the direction of events through their intelligence and persuasive power.

## GENESIS: THE SOURCES OF CULTURE AND KNOWLEDGE IN THE PRIMEVAL HISTORY

According to Genesis, once Eve had initiated the change from the "natural" state to cultural existence, our world became transformed. Two fundamental aspects of culture developed immediately: humans had to work, and their relationships became institutionalized in a hierarchical cultural order in which woman became subordinate to man. Eve, like Prometheus, suffered in the cultural transformation. The Primeval History then relates the unfolding of other aspects of human existence: shepherding, farming, sacrifice, the founding of cities, pastoral nomadism, metal smithing, music, viticulture, and politics. None of these aspects of civilization is said to have been given by God or effected through divine revelation. Rather, they are the achievements of humanity. The fact that most of these achievements are noted in the geneologies serves to underscore the fact that the development of human culture was a natural multiplicative process. This idea in Genesis is in marked contrast to Mesopotamian tradition about the origin of civilization. Kingship, in the Sumerian King List, "came down from heaven." Moreover, in Sumer, the aspects of civilization were abstracted in the mysterious *me*, held first by Enki and then by Inanna.[6] Mesopotamia also had a myth of the *apkallu*, primeval fishlike beings who arose from the sea to give the cultural arts to humanity.[7] In the Bible, on the other hand, there is no tradition about God granting this civilization to humankind.[8] Even the special divine instruction to which Noah is privy does not give him new cultural knowledge or make him exceedingly wise.

The name of the Babylonian hero of the Flood, Atra-ḫasīs, means 'exceedingly wise', but Noah's outstanding characteristic is different: he is "righteous in his generation" (Gen 7:1). Noah, of course, is not ignorant. He is privy to divine instruction (which, itself, makes him a kind of sage)[9] and after the Flood he has the knowledge to plant a vineyard. But his wisdom is neither the cause of his having been chosen as the saved and savior of humankind, nor is it the agency by which he is able to accomplish his role. Noah—and Lot, too—is impelled to be a savior by divine agency, which directs him exactly as to what his actions should be.

The Primeval History closes with the story of the Tower of Babel (chap. 11), a myth that describes how God sought to set limits on humanity's potential for cultural development. People have come to Shinar (Sumer), have learned how to build from baked bricks, and seek to build a great city with a ziggurat (a meeting place for the divine and human). God's reaction is to think, "If, as one people with one language for all, this is how they have begun to act, then nothing that they may propose to do will be out of their reach" (Gen 11:6), and he thwarted the people by scattering them and confounding their speech. Humanity's knowledge and power had begun to reach the world of the

6. For a discussion of the *me* (divine laws and regulations), see G. Farber-Flugge, *Der Mythos "Inanna und Enki" unter besonderer Berucksichtigung der Liste der 'me'* (Studia Pohl 10; Rome: Pontifical Biblical Institute, 1973). See also the discussion in this volume by Samuel Noah Kramer in his essay, "The Sage in Sumerian Literature: A Composite Portrait," pp. 31–44 above.

7. See B. Foster, "Wisdom and the Gods in Ancient Mesopotamia," *Or*, n.s. 43 (1974) 344–54. On the *apkallu* see also the essays in this volume by Rivkah Harris, "The Female 'Sage' in Mesopotamian Literature," pp. 3–17 above, and Ronald Sweet, "The Sage in Mesopotamian Palaces and Royal Courts," pp. 99–107 above.

8. The situation is quite different, of course, in the pseudepigraphic literature on Gen 6:1–4.

9. On the antediluvian fathers as sages, see the essay in this volume by Loren R. Mack-Fisher, "The Scribe (and Sage) in the Royal Court at Ugarit," pp. 109–15 above.

gods—and this the Lord acted to prevent. But before (and after) the Tower of Babel, humanity had invented and developed its culture on its own.

## GENESIS: JOSEPH AS SAGE

The only pentateuchal hero to be called *ḥākām* 'wise' is Joseph. When Joseph interpreted Pharaoh's dream, he suggested that Pharaoh find a wise man to oversee the collection of food in anticipation of the lean years facing Egypt. Pharaoh acknowledged Joseph's divine inspiration, and declared that no one was as wise as Joseph. It is noteworthy that the designation is made by Pharaoh. Within Israel's own system of values (as embodied in the Pentateuch), wisdom and knowledge are not held up as attributes to be emulated.

Joseph, who like Noah and Lot also functions as a savior, is significantly different from both. Even though God has revealed the coming of the famine to him, it is Joseph himself who conceives of the plan to stockpile grain in central granaries. It is this independent wisdom that earns him the designation of sage.

## DEUTERONOMY AND EXODUS:
## LEARNING AND WISDOM

A spirit different from the other books in the Pentateuch seems to animate Deuteronomy. This difference may be brought out by comparing Deuteronomy and Exodus. Deuteronomy contains *intellectual* language.[10] People are instructed, they are to learn, to know, to remember, to teach. Deuteronomy stresses the cognitive warning against forgetting the law, and not remembering God.

In Deuteronomy, the word wise has a special resonance. Where as Exod 23:8 states that bribes blind the discerning ( *piqḥîm*), Deut 16:19 declares that bribes blind the eyes of the wise (*ḥăkāmîm*). So too, whereas in Exodus when Moses appointed judges to settle the ordinary judicial disputes of the people he chooses *ʾanšê-ḥayil* (Exod 18:25), in Deut 1:12-13 he has the people choose tribal leaders who were 'wise, discerning, and experienced' (*ḥăkāmîm ûnĕbōnîm wîduʿîm*) to be administrators and magistrates. The intellectual capacity of being wise, in Deuteronomy, determines the ability to be a judge. This emphasis on wise men or sages in Deuteronomy reminds us that it was the wise men of the time of Jeremiah who claimed to have the "Torah of the Lord" (Jer 8:8).

10. This is also in marked contrast to the *volitional* language of Leviticus (cf., e.g., Lev 26:24, 21); see also my discussion in the next section below (pp. 285–86).

The intellectual tone of Deuteronomy is consistent, and probably indicates that Deuteronomy was written by people who defined themselves by their intellectual capacities and activity. Moshe Weinfeld has argued for a scribal-professional origin of Deuteronomy. Pointing to the new emphasis on wisdom and wise men in the seventh century, he suggests that in the time of Jeremiah there existed a circle of ḥăkāmîm sopĕrîm who were occupied with the composition of Torah literature.[11] The Book of Isaiah indicates the emergence of wise men in the time of Hezekiah, who should be considered the original patron of this wisdom movement, which concentrated on writing religious literature.[12] Ultimately, this movement culminated in the Josianic period with the writing of Deuteronomy.

The preoccupation with writing and with teaching in Deuteronomy, and its generally didactic tone, certainly indicate that the authors were professionals who thought about religious transmission in intellectual-educational terms. There is no reason to doubt Weinfeld's idea about the milieu in which Deuteronomy was composed. However, it is also important to realize that this group's ideas about knowledge, as reflected in Deuteronomy, were not radical, and did not differ markedly from the ideas about knowledge found elsewhere in the Pentateuch, particularly in Exodus. There is certainly a difference in emphasis, but not really in substance. Deuteronomy's characterization of apostasy as "forgetting" God, or lack of faith as a mark of foolishness, is not a revolutionary perspective. In the much older poem preserved in Deuteronomy 32, Israel is described as a folk void of sense, for:

> Were they wise, they would think upon this,
> Gain insight into their future:
> "How could one have routed a thousand,
> Or two put ten thousand to flight,
> Unless their Rock had sold them,
> The LORD had given them up?"
>
> (Deut 32:29–30 JPSV)

This statement is closely paralleled by Deut 8:14–18: it was a failure of wisdom and knowledge to think that Israel could possibly have accomplished what it had on its own.

11. M. Weinfeld, *Deuteronomy and the Deuteronomic School* (Oxford: Clarendon, 1971) 158–62.

12. Ibid., 161–62; for important corroborative essays commended by Weinfeld, see R. B. Y. Scott, "Solomon and the Beginnings of Wisdom in Israel," *WIANE* 262–79 (repr. in *SAIW* 84–101); and J. Fichtner, "Jesaja unter den Weisen," *Theologische Literaturzeitung* 74 (1949) 75–80 (repr. in *Gottes Weisheit* [Arbeiten zur Theologie 2.3; Stuttgart: Calwer, 1965] 18–26; trans. as "Isaiah among the Wise," *SAIW* 429–38).

Even the appointment of Judges alluded to above is not radically different between Exodus and Deuteronomy. The phrase *anšê ḥayîl* is often translated as 'valiant men' or 'noblemen'. However, in light of the use of *ʾēšet ḥayîl* in Prov 31:10 to describe a wife who is the very personification of earthly practical wisdom, *anšê ḥayîl* is best translated as 'capable men' (as indeed in JPSV). There is no radical break between an Exodus tradition that elevated its soldiers or wealthy men or noblemen to be judges, and a deuteronomic tradition that elevated its wise men. On the contrary, in both traditions men are chosen for their ability, but this ability is particularly stressed as wisdom in Deuteronomy.

In Deuteronomy, there are three major lessons, three major data that are to be learned, studied, and taught. The first is the laws. These Deuteronomy holds to have been given by God to Moses (5:28) and by Moses to the people (5:28; 4:1, 5, 14). These laws are complete: one should not add or subtract from them (13:1). The purpose of learning them is to observe them (4:1-6), and they are to be copied and studied and transmitted to the children (4:9; 6:7, 20; 11:19; 31:12-13). The second item of information to be learned is the "fact" of God, his might and his relationship to Israel: that the Lord alone is God (4:34, 35, 39; 7:9), that none but the Lord crosses at the head of Israel (9:3), that God grants the land not because of the virtue of Israel (9:6), and that God disciplines Israel as a father his child (8:5). The third datum of knowledge is the sacred history that the people themselves have experienced (11:2-7), a sacred history that is to be remembered and transmitted (8:2, 11; 9:7; 15:15; 16:12; 24:18, 22).

None of this is esoteric knowledge. On the contrary, it is highly accessible:

> Surely, this instruction [*miṣwâ*] which I command you this day is not too baffling for you, nor is it beyond reach. It is not in the heavens, that you should say, "Who among us can go up to the heavens and get it for us and impart it to us, that we may observe it?" Neither is it beyond the sea, that you should say, "Who among us can cross to the other side of the sea and get it for us and impart it to us, that we may observe it?" No, the thing is very close to you, in your mouth and in your heart, to observe it. (Deut 30:11-14 JPSV, slightly changed)

In addition, this is not professional knowledge—all the people are expected to know these data and everyone is expected to teach the children. The great wisdom of Israel lies not in its sages, nor in its accumulation of worldly or speculative wisdom, but rather in its laws and the observance of them: "For that will be proof of your wisdom and discernment to other peoples, who on hearing of all these laws will say, 'Surely, that is a great nation of wise and discerning people'" (Deut 4:6). Even though Deuteronomy may have been written by intellectuals, scribes, and teachers, they are not concerned to set up a special class of the knowledgeable, a special profession of the sage: on the contrary, the whole people is to be a nation of wise and discerning people.

This is not to say that there are no gradations in knowledge. Moses chose "wise men" to appoint as judges. Judges needed wisdom, for they were to make thorough investigations (Deut 19:18). Only when a case was too baffling for them were they to come to the place God had chosen and appear before the priests or the magistrate in charge at the time to await and carry out their verdict (Deut 17:8-13). But the knowledge of these wise men—their wisdom—is not qualitatively different from that enjoined on all Israel. Wise men were not to guard their knowledge of the laws as a mark of their special nature or position, but were to teach and impart. Even this act of teaching was not confined to the wise, for every person who heard the laws or experienced the history was to teach the children. The only legitimate special or secret knowledge was that of prophets, to whom God might impart a special revelation. But even this was very limited knowledge. Should a prophet contradict Israel's collective wisdom by exhorting them to worship other gods, then, despite any mantic ability by which he might prove his words, he was to be put to death (Deut 13:2-6). The words of any prophet had to be proved by events: if a prophet's predictions did not come true, the word had not been spoken by the Lord (Deut 18:15-22). Deuteronomy does not deny that there can be other kinds of gnomic knowledge, but these were not legitimate for Israel, for the Lord did not assign soothsayers and augurs to Israel (Deut 18:14).

Deuteronomy's ideas about learning can be paralleled in Exodus. The two books have the same idea about the *content* of Israel's knowledge: they hold that the laws were given by revelation, handed to Moses by God for delivery to the people (Exod 18:20, 24:12); they both state that the central fact to be known from the actions of God is the fact of the Lord (Exod 7:4-5; see also the plague narratives 7:17; 8:6, 18; 9:14, 16, 29; 10:2); and both hold that the experience of God's acts should lead to obedience (Exod 19:4). Deuteronomy and Exodus also share the same sense of the *process* by which one learns, understanding that they learn by experience, by recitation and learning, by writing and reading, and by inductive "tests."

Deuteronomy and Exodus consider experience to be the most direct and effective mode of learning, in particular the experience of the signs and wonders of God. Exodus stresses the importance of experiential learning in the plague narratives, for in them God set out to teach

Egypt that he was God, and that he was with Israel. Israel too, was to
learn that the Lord was their God through its experience of manna
(Exod 16:2) and through God's living in the tent of meeting (Exod
29:44–46). Deuteronomy also stresses the immediate and direct knowledge of those who experienced the deeds of God. The people of the
generation of the Exodus had seen the lesson of the Lord (Deut 11:2)
and they "have been shown to know that the LORD alone is God" (Deut
4:35). Through experiencing hunger and manna they were taught that
man (*hā'ādām*) does not live on bread alone (Deut 8:3). God is known
because of these experiences; other gods have not been so known (Deut
11:28; 13:3, 13).[13]

Knowledge cannot always be learned through direct experience,
and both Exodus and Deuteronomy point to the importance of learning
through hearing. Exodus presents the person of Jethro, a wise man and
sage counselor (though not so called). Through hearing about God's
delivery of Israel, Jethro has come to his knowledge of God: "Now I
know that the LORD is greater than all gods" (Exod 18:11). Even God
learns through seeing and hearing: "I have seen the plight of my
people . . . I have heard their outcry . . . indeed I know their sufferings"
(Exod 3:7). The transmission of Israel's knowledge intergenerationally
to those who have not had the direct experience of God is a particular
concern of Deuteronomy, which stresses the knowledge that comes
from hearing, and provides for the seventh-year assembly in which the
people and the children will learn the Lord and the laws (Deut 31:12).[14]

Deuteronomy and Exodus also both bear witness to Israel's understanding of "the scientific method," the setting up of experiments for
"inductive reasoning." Massah and Meribah are so called because the
Israelites contested and "tried the LORD, saying 'Is the LORD present
among us or not?'" (Exod 17:4–7). In Deuteronomy, God sets up tests
for Israel: "And remember the long way the LORD your God has made
you travel . . . that he might test you by hardships to learn [*lāda'at*]
what was in your hearts, whether you would keep his commandments
or not" (Deut 8:2); so too, a prophet who proves his exhortations to
worship other gods by magical portents is only an instance of God
testing the people (Deut 13:2–6). This idea that God tests the people is
also found in the prophetic writings, and is part of this general theory of
knowledge in which one can learn by setting up a controlled experiment. In this way the Philistines tested whether the ark of the Lord had

13. A similar idea of knowledge coming about through direct experience is found in
relation to the dreadful diseases of Egypt (Deut 7:15; 8:3, 16).

14. As with experiential knowledge, not only the divine message can be learned by
hearing: Israel "knows" the Anakites, even though they haven't seen them, for they have
heard it said, "Who can stand up to the children of Anak?" (Deut 9:2).

caused their plagues by seeing whether the new cart went to Beth-shemesh (1 Sam 6:7–9).

This does not mean that the conceptions of learning in Deuteronomy and Exodus are identical. Deuteronomy stresses writing as a means of ensuring remembrance and tradition (cf., e.g., Deut 31:22), whereas in Exodus the story of Amalek is to be written in a document as a reminder precisely because the memory of Amalek will disappear (Exod 17:14). Exodus is interested in ritual as a way of remembering the past; the Passover and Matzot in particular are the ways to remember the Exodus (Exod 12:14, 13:3). Deuteronomy is much more interested in study and recitation, and the word *lmd* is prominent there. But these differences are relatively minor, and there is no great, essential difference in their idea about what the nature of Israel's wisdom should be and how one acquires knowledge.

## LEVITICUS AND NUMBERS: THE
## SAGE AND SPECIALIZED KNOWLEDGE

Even though Deuteronomy's new, probably professional, emphasis on wisdom is not a radical departure from older Israelite traditions, it was not the only way of looking upon Israel's abilities and responsibilities. A quite different emphasis is found in Leviticus and Numbers. There are two occasions in the Pentateuch in which Moses is depicted as being unable or unwilling to bear the people alone. In Deut 1:9–18, the response to this complaint is the appointment of wise men as judges; in Num 11:14–25, God had Moses choose elders to whom he would impart some of the prophetic spirit. The word wise, or sage, does not appear at all in Leviticus and Numbers. Nor are the people exhorted to know or not to forget God or the law. Rather, the emphasis is on *volition*, on willful acceptance or defiance.

The nonintellectual language of Leviticus and the priestly portions of Numbers is particularly interesting in that the priest himself represented a special type of professional sage. One ordinarily thinks of a priest as a functionary, but he was also the master of specialized knowledge and was called upon to function as expert authority. He was the guardian of the rules and mechanics of the sacrificial system. His knowledge was assumed to be specific and immediately relevant to human life. To cite but one telling example, he was expected to determine whether scaly afflictions were leprosy and whether leprosy had been cured (Lev 13:9–17). Above all, however, the priest was the determinant of holy and profane, pure and impure—crucial distinctions in Israelite thought and practice. To be a priest was to master knowledge unknown to the rest of the population.

Despite the specialized knowledge involved in being a priest, the study required to acquire this knowledge, and the intellectual acumen demanded to keep the technical information straight, the priestly tradition does not speak of wisdom, study, or priestly schools. It does not tell about the training of a priest or the teaching of children. All of this is taken for granted, presumably because it was all known to the priests who were studying and transmitting this tradition. These most characteristic sages of Israel do not present themselves as wise, nor do they exhort Israel to be so. Holiness, faithfulness, and purity are the ideals of these books, and knowledge is just a way to find out how to be pure and holy.

## THE PENTATEUCH: EXTRAORDINARY GIFTS AND THEIR SOURCE

From the pentateuchal perspective, knowledge, human culture, and wisdom developed autonomously. But those cultural elements that define Israel among the nations were God-given. First among these is law, which God originally introduced (Genesis 9) in order to keep humanity from causing God to destroy the world again. This idea that the law is divinely revealed is consistent through the Pentateuch and, indeed, in the Bible. Moreover, Israel's sabbaths and festivals, the tabernacle, the priesthood, the sacrificial system, and the institution of prophecy—all these are presented in the Pentateuch as given and decreed by God.[15] The tabernacle and priesthood were considered so holy, so divine in origin, that even the skill and knowledge needed to build the tabernacle and its accoutrements were considered specifically granted by God to Bezalel, Oholiab, and the others who worked on the tabernacle with them as a "divine spirit of skill, ability, and knowledge in every craft" (Exod 31:2-4; see also Exod 35:30-31, 34; 36:1, 4, 8). The same divinely endowed skill was granted the fashioners of Aaron's garments (Exod 28:3).

## CONCLUSION: A STILL WIDER DESIGNATION

Despite its great diversity, the Pentateuch presents a remarkably integrated view of sagacity. The wisdom to devise plans—as the wise Joseph did—and to outsmart Pharaoh and other human beings are human characteristics. Discernment and cultural knowledge have been human attributes since the actions of Eve. Sages (which term includes

15. Elsewhere in the Bible the fact of Davidic dynastic rule is also presented as divinely ordained.

wise women) utilize such knowledge and discernment to influence the course of human events. But the special holy characteristics of Israel have been taught by God. The priests may be the guardians and specialists of this divine knowledge, but it is not limited to them. On the contrary, these special teachings, according to Deuteronomy, set off Israel as a wise and discerning people. They that follow the Lord are not only a nation of priests and a holy people, they are called to be *a nation of sages.*

# THE SAGE IN
# THE DEUTERONOMISTIC HISTORY

## P. Kyle McCarter Jr.

### SOLOMON'S SAGACITY—
### A LIMITED ACHIEVEMENT

Solomon, the paragon of the Israelite sage, is a central figure in the
Deuteronomistic History, where he is praised as the wisest man who
ever lived.

> God gave Solomon wisdom and very great understanding and a mind
> broader than the sand on the shore of the sea. Solomon's wisdom was
> greater than that of all the people of the East and greater than all the
> wisdom of Egypt. He was wiser than any man—wiser than Ethan the
> Ezrahite, or Heman, or Chalcol and Darda, the sons of Mahol.[1] His fame
> spread to all the surrounding nations. He uttered 3,000 proverbs, and his
> songs numbered 1,005. He spoke about the trees, from the cedar in
> Lebanon to the hyssop that grows on the wall. He spoke about animals,
> birds, reptiles, and fishes. They came from all the peoples to listen to
> Solomon's wisdom—from all the kings of the earth who had heard of his
> wisdom. (1 Kgs 4:29–34 [MT 5:9–14])

Solomon's 'wise and understanding heart' was a special gift from
Yahweh (1 Kgs 3:12; cf. 5:9, 26). Because of this gift, he ruled so well

P. Kyle McCarter Jr. is William Foxwell Albright Professor of Biblical and Ancient Near
Eastern Studies, and Acting Associate Dean of the School of Arts and Sciences at Johns
Hopkins University.

1. These four wise men—Ethan, Heman, Chalcol, and Darda—were great, non-
Israelite sages of the past. Thus Ethan is called *hāʾezrāḥî* 'the Ezrahite', that is, 'the
aborigine'. He was, in other words, a pre-Israelite inhabitant of Canaan. (See the observation of Arthur Hertzberg cited by W. F. Albright, *Archaeology and the Religion of Israel*
[5th ed.; Garden City, NY: Anchor/Doubleday, 1969] 122 and 210 n. 95.) According to the
superscription of Psalm 88, Heman was also an Ezrahite, and the same is probably true of
Chalcol and Darda. By the Chronicler's time, these four Ezrahites had been grafted into
the family tree of the tribe Judah as Zerahites, cousins of the Perezites, from whom the
Davidids were descended (cf. 1 Chr 2:6).

that the people of Judah and Israel prospered (1 Kgs 4:20) and foreigners admired them. Indeed, the Queen of Sheba pronounced them
uniquely blessed (1 Kgs 10:6–9).

Despite its preservation of this tradition about Solomon's wisdom,
however, the Deuteronomistic History does not present a wholly or
even predominantly positive picture of the traditional wisdom of the
sage. On this point, as on many others, the Deuteronomistic view
differs from the view taken in the literary sources of the Deuteronomistic
History. Solomon's wisdom was described in the lost Book of the Acts
of Solomon (1 Kgs 11:41), and it was probably from this book, as well
as from popular tradition, that the Deuteronomistic writers drew their
material about the legendary wisdom of Solomon. As explained below,
however, Deuteronomistic thought did not accept the view that being a
great sage was enough to be a great king, so that Solomon's reign is
presented as a mixture of successes and failures.[2]

## THE SAGE IN THE OLDER SOURCES—
## IN PRAISE OF SHREWDNESS

This cool attitude toward the wisdom of the sage was not present in the
older literary sources of the Deuteronomistic History. The postulate of
wisdom in these materials was that the world has a fixed order within
which events transpire according to consistent and therefore predictable
processes. The glory of the sage is a knowledge of these processes
based on learning and experience. Thus, for example, the "wise woman"
of Abel of Beth-Maacah is functioning as a traditional sage when she
settles a dispute by citing an old proverb (2 Samuel 20).[3]

Wisdom often manifests itself in the older materials as native
cunning, shrewdness, and discernment—the ability, in other words, to
recognize the patterns of human experience and manipulate them ad-
vantageously. The sage who has this ability is valued as a counselor, and
any person of rank would have such counselors ready at hand. Thus the
mother of Sisera, the commander of the army of Canaanite Hazor, has
counselors (ḥakmôt śārôtêhâ 'the wise[st] of her ladies') upon whom she
can call in a time of need (Judg 5:29–30). Similarly, Amnon's friend
Jonadab, who devises the plan for the rape of Tamar (2 Samuel 13), has
this ability to give counsel. In this case it is true that the advice Jonadab

2. A similar view is seen by W. A. Brueggemann in this volume, "The Social
Significance of Solomon as a Patron of Wisdom," who notes: "Solomonic wisdom is
characterized by the Deuteronomist in ironic ways to show that it did not work" (p. 128).

3. Her remarks in 2 Sam 20:18–19 suggest that the town of Abel had a reputation as
a place for settling disputes and receiving good counsel. See my *II Samuel* (AB 9; Garden
City, NY: Doubleday, 1984) 430.

gives is reprehensible from an ethical point of view, but this is beside the point when wisdom is defined as the ability to understand and manipulate the world. The advice enables Amnon to succeed in his objective, demonstrating that Jonadab is, from this ethically blind point of view, "a very wise man" (2 Sam 13:3).

The counseling ability of the sage was routinely called upon at the royal court. The best known of the royal counselors in the Deutero-nomistic History is Ahithophel. His counsel, we are told, was held in the highest regard, "as if the word of God had been consulted" (2 Sam 16:23). The advice he gives Absalom for the conduct of the war against David is militarily sound, and Absalom and his advisers are inclined at first to accept it (2 Sam 17:4). In the course of events, however, Ahitho-phel is outmaneuvered by David and Hushai, whose machinations also belong to the province of traditional wisdom, and Ahithophel's advice is rejected in the end. This shows again that wisdom, traditionally understood, is blind with regard to questions of right and wrong. Trickery, even treachery, operate on both sides of the contest between Ahithophel and Hushai. The single goal of the sage is the success of the project.

Despite the importance of the counsel given by royal advisers, however, it is the king himself, not his wisest counselor, who is the quintessential sage in pre-Deuteronomistic tradition. The stories about Solomon represent the highest development of the tradition of the wise king. Because wisdom is an attribute of the divine in Northwest Semitic tradition, the wisdom of the king is a divine gift, as we have seen, and a godlike quality. "My lord is wise," says the Tekoite woman to David, "like the wisdom of a messenger of God, knowing everything on earth" (2 Sam 14:20; cf. 14:17). As a counselor, the king is "wonderful" (Isa 9:5), that is, endowed with a godlike ability to give counsel.

In the older sources of the Deuteronomistic History, various special skills and talents, being particular types of this knowledge of the world and its secrets, also belong to the category of wisdom. The skilled Tyrian craftsman Hiram is said to have been full of "wisdom, under-standing, and skill" (1 Kgs 7:14), and King Solomon himself is remem-bered as having been an adept craftsman (cf. 1 Kgs 10:16–20). The Tekoite woman who arranges Absalom's return (2 Samuel 14) seems to be an actress, not a sage, since Joab tells her what to say and do;[4] yet her skill qualifies her as a "wise woman" (v 2).

---

4. She does recognizes the godlike wisdom of the king (2 Sam 14:17, 20), though this may be part of the act. See J. Hoftijzer, "David and the Tekoite Woman," *VT* 20 (1970) 419–44, esp. 440–41; T. N. D. Mettinger, *King and Messiah: The Civil and Sacral Legitimation of the Israelite Kings* (Coniectanea Biblica, Old Testament Series 8; Lund: Gleerup, 1976) 242; and my *II Samuel,* 347 (the note on "the king is like an envoy of God").

P. Kyle McCarter Jr.

# WISDOM IN DEUTERONOMISTIC CIRCLES—
## THE TRIUMPH OF TORAH

When one turns to the view of wisdom held in the circles in which the Deuteronomistic History was compiled, one finds an altered picture. In the Deuteronomistic literature, as in the older source materials, wisdom is most often mentioned as a characteristic of good judges and rulers. The men appointed to share Moses' judicial burden, for example, must be "wise and knowledgeable" (Deut 1:13, 15; cf. 16:19), and Moses' successor, Joshua, is filled with "the spirit of wisdom" after Moses lays his hands on him (Deut 34:9). To this extent, the wisdom of Solomon or any other king has the full endorsement of Deuteronomistic thought, and the account of the divine gift of wisdom to Solomon (1 Kgs 3:3–15), which shows clear signs of Deuteronomistic editing (vv. 3, 6, 14), is presented in very positive terms.

What, however, is the source and basis of wisdom in Deuteronomistic thought? In Deut 4:6, Moses says to the people:

> See, I have taught you the statutes and ordinances which Yahweh my god commanded, so that you may practice them within the land where you are about to enter and take possession. You must preserve and practice them, for this will be your wisdom and understanding in the sight of the peoples, who, when they hear all the statutes, will say, "Surely this great nation is a wise and understanding people!"

Wise behavior, in other words, is behavior in accordance with "the statutes and ordinances" commanded by Yahweh.

Here again one encounters the idea that wisdom claims the admiration of foreign peoples, an idea noted in the old stories about Solomon. The people come to admire Solomon's wisdom or, as in the case of the Queen of Sheba, to admire it and proclaim his people fortunate. Nevertheless, the difference between the earlier and later views is more interesting than the similarity. In the Solomonic tradition, wisdom is a direct, charismatic gift, and Solomon's cleverness is the evidence. In Deuteronomistic thought, it is the Torah that is the source of wisdom,[5] and the people's obedience to the Torah is the evidence. In this respect

---

5. Moshe Weinfeld has noted that the view of wisdom expressed in Deut 4:6 is paradoxical, inasmuch as "laws and statutes which were given by God are here regarded as being indicative of the wisdom and understanding of Israel. The verse undoubtedly reflects the difficulties which resulted from the sapiential desire to identify Torah with wisdom. The inherent contradiction was ultimately resolved only by identifying wisdom with Torah, as a result of which both were conceived together as a heavenly element which descended from heaven to take up its abode among the children of Israel (Ben-Sira 24)"; see *Deuteronomy and the Deuteronomic School* (Oxford: Clarendon, 1972) 256.

the Deuteronomistic view of wisdom is very different from—and to some extent even antithetical to—the traditional presentation of wisdom in the literary sources of the Deuteronomistic History. As I have noted, the older view saw the world as a predictable system into which kings and other wise individuals could have insight. Wisdom was the province of the sage, who understood the world through keen observation of life and a thorough education in the wisdom tradition. The Deuteronomistic view sees the world as governed *ad hoc* by Yahweh, whose decisions are neither predictable nor in any way constrained by a cosmic system. Wisdom, then, is an understanding of divine will, and it is available only through special divine revelation, especially Torah and prophetic oracles.

In the circles that produced the Deuteronomistic History, therefore, wisdom was no longer regarded as ethically neutral. There is no place in the Deuteronomistic understanding of the role of the sage for the deplorable advice of Jonadab or the diplomatic trickery of Ahithophel and Hushai. The tradition of royal wisdom has not been suppressed, but it is not shown to lead automatically to good results. The benefits of Solomon's wisdom avail him nothing in the end.[6] Wisdom is now constrained by Torah, and to be a sage is to know the Torah and conform one's life to it.

6. Weinfeld (*Deuteronomy and the Deuteronomic School*, 255) describes the change as follows: "The Deuteronomist no longer conceived of 'wisdom' as meaning cunning, pragmatic talent, or the possession of extraordinary knowledge, but held it to be synonymous with the knowledge and understanding of proper behaviour and with morality."

# THE SAGE IN THE PROPHETIC LITERATURE

## Raymond C. Van Leeuwen

### INTRODUCTION: THE POSING OF THE QUESTION

The problem of the sage in the prophetic corpus may be approached from opposite directions. One may begin with a focus on the final form of the corpus, or one may start with a quest for the original life and literary settings of the various poems and oracles that betray the stamp of wisdom or reveal the presence of a sage. Either approach is fraught with background problems of method, definitions, and presuppositions,[1] and hampered by the limitations of our knowledge concerning both prophecy and wisdom.[2]

If one begins with the canonical form of the MT, it is clear that a wisdom hermeneutic informs the final redaction of the Hebrew Bible. This perspective of torah-wisdom *cum* eschatology links the torah of Moses, the prophets, and the writings. The main evidence for this appears at key junctures in the *Tanak* (Deut 34:9-12, Josh 1:5-9, Mal 4:4-6 [MT 3:22-24],[3] and Psalms 1-2). Ben Sira is a model for such a scribe/sage;[4] he notes that the sage "will be concerned with prophecies"

Raymond C. Van Leeuwen is Associate Professor of Old Testament at Calvin Theological Seminary, Grand Rapids, Michigan.

1. J. L. Crenshaw, "The Influence of the Wise upon Amos," *ZAW* 79 (1967) 42-52; and idem, "Method in Determining Wisdom Influence upon 'Historical' Literature," *JBL* 88 (1969) 129-42 (repr. in *SAIW* 481-94); D. F. Morgan, *Wisdom in the Old Testament Traditions* (Atlanta: John Knox, 1981) 13-29; J. W. Whedbee, *Isaiah and Wisdom* (Nashville: Abingdon, 1971) 21-26; R. N. Whybray, *The Intellectual Tradition in the Old Testament* (BZAW 135; Berlin: de Gruyter, 1974). Whybray, in his essay, "Prophecy and Wisdom," *Israel's Prophetic Tradition: Essays in Honour of Peter R. Ackroyd* (ed. R. Coggins, A. Phillips, and M. Knibb; Cambridge: Cambridge University, 1982) 181-99, provides a history of research into the relation of prophecy and wisdom.

2. R. E. Clements, *Prophecy and Tradition* (Atlanta: John Knox, 1975) 73-86.

3. Note the New Testament expansion: " . . . and the disobedient to the wisdom of the just" (Luke 1:17).

4. J. Reindl, "Weisheitliche Bearbeitung von Psalmen," *Congress Volume: Vienna 1980* (ed. J. A. Emerton; VTSup 32; Leiden: Brill, 1981) 340-41.

(39:1; cf. 44–50 passim). The last verses of Malachi (4:4–6 [MT 3:22–24]) form a bridge to Psalms 1–2,[5] increasingly recognized as the redactional introduction to the Psalter, and thus to the Writings, which embody the wisdom literature proper: Proverbs, Job, Qoheleth. Similarly, the first book of the Twelve, Hosea, concludes with a late wisdom admonition to the reader (14:9 [MT 14:10]), while Isa 1:2–3 opens the Latter Prophets with the divine father's accusation against unwise (*l⁾ htbwnn*), rebellious sons (cf. Jer 4:22).[6]

Thus the latest stage in the redaction/composition of the canon, including the prophetic corpus, was undertaken by literary sages or scribes. But M. Fishbane compellingly argues that similar sapiential scribal activity began in the preexilic era.[7] At earlier stages of composition, matters are complicated by arguments, such as M. Weinfeld's,[8] that Deuteronomy was composed by sages, and that the Former and Latter Prophets both reveal deuteronomistic composition or redaction. In the Latter Prophets, deuteronomistic affinities are most apparent in the prose sections of Jeremiah, but have been argued to exist elsewhere.[9]

5. Psalms 1–2 together form a hermeneutical introduction to the Psalter: "Psalm 2, reread as a vision of the goal of history, puts the torah piety of Psalm 1 in an eschatological context"; so J. L. Mays, "The Place of the Torah-Psalms in the Psalter," *JBL* 106 (1987) 10. Among related psalms, cf. especially Psalms 37 and 119. The verbal and thematic links between Malachi and Psalms 1–2 are to be seen in the context of the aforementioned passages at the borders of the main canonical units. Key motifs include Moses the servant of Yʜwʜ, a coming prophet/Elijah, the law, wisdom, righteous/wicked, fathers/sons (cf. Moses/Joshua), personal or eschatological judgment, and inheritance (or noninheritance) of the earth/land (⁾rṣ; cf. Prov 2:21–22, 10:30; Ps 2:8). I am indebted to John Sailhammer for calling my attention to these redactional connections. See also B. S. Childs, "The Canonical Shape of the Prophetic Literature," *Interpretation* 32 (1978) 51–52. G. H. Wilson, *The Editing of the Hebrew Psalter* (SBLDS 76; Chico, CA: Scholars Press, 1985) 199–228, treats the redactional "seams" that link the five "books" of the Psalter.

6. The origin of this passage is irrelevant to its final role in the canonical text. Whedbee, *Isaiah and Wisdom*, 26–43, sees it as Isaianic; J. Vermeylen, "Le Proto-Isaïe et la sagesse d'Israël," *La Sagesse de l'Ancien Testament* (ed. M. Gilbert; BETL 51; Gembloux: Duculot/Louvain: Leuven University, 1979) 48–49, ascribes it to a deuteronomistic redaction of the exilic age.

7. Fishbane, *Biblical Interpretation in Ancient Israel* (Oxford: Clarendon, 1986) 23–43.

8. Weinfeld, *Deuteronomy and the Deuteronomic School* (Oxford: Clarendon, 1972). C. Brekelmans, "Wisdom Influence in Deuteronomy," *La Sagesse de l'Ancien Testament* (ed. M. Gilbert; BETL 51; Gembloux: Duculot/Louvain: Leuven University, 1979) 28–38, provides helpful critique.

9. W. H. Schmidt, "Die deuteronomistische Redaktion des Amosbuches: Zu den theologischen Unterschieden zwischen dem Prophetenwort und seinem Sammler," *ZAW* 77 (1965) 168–93; J. Vermeylen, *Du prophète Isaïe à l'apocalyptique* (Paris: Gabalda, 1978), 2:519–601, 693–709. J. Blenkinsopp, *A History of Prophecy in Israel* (Philadelphia: Westminster, 1983) 188–93, is appropriately cautious and critical. On the deuteronomistic affinities in Jeremiah, see L. G. Perdue, "Jeremiah in Modern Research: Approaches and

If the danger of a "pan-chokmism" is to be avoided, care must be taken with definitions of wisdom and with inferences drawn from the texts about social milieu.[10] J. L. Crenshaw's distinction between wisdom literature, wisdom tradition, and wisdom thinking was seminal, but concealed within it unresolved problems. Crenshaw suggested that

> It would be less confusing to speak in terms of wisdom literature, *paideia*, and *ḥokmah*. The first would refer to Prov, Qoh, Job, Sir, Wisd of Sol, and Wisdom Pss; *paideia* would suggest the wisdom movement itself, its educational curriculum and pedagogy; *ḥokmah* would indicate a particular stance, an approach to reality.[11]

The idea of "the wisdom movement" is problematic, since it assumes a single tradition institutionalized in a school—a matter of no little debate.[12] But the idea does point to my topic: who might the 'sages' (*ḥkmym*) be, and where in society and history might they dwell? There is a literary wisdom proper to the royal court (cf. Prov 10:1, 25:1), but the existence of wisdom traditions among ordinary folk,[13] rural or urban, requires that we avoid speaking of *the* wisdom tradition, when the reference is actually to one locus of wisdom such as the court. A great body of wisdom, reflecting "a shared approach to reality," was the cultural property of all classes of Israelites.[14] To achieve clarity in this discussion of wisdom, it is prudent to define such an approach in terms of the wisdom literature.

## PROPHETS AND SAGES— LINKS IN THE WISDOM BOOKS

The "original" (as opposed to redactional) sage in the prophetic literature is illusive. According to some scholars, some prophets were themselves sages or at least influenced by wisdom. But the texts make no

---

Issues," *A Prophet to the Nations: Essays in Jeremiah Studies* (ed. L. G. Perdue and B. W. Kovacs; Winona Lake, IN: Eisenbrauns, 1984) 1–32.

10. Perhaps the most widespread error concerning wisdom influence in the prophets is the argument that the 'woe' (*hwy*) oracle is a wisdom form of the clan. A large body of research has demonstrated that the woe oracle is in fact a prophetic adaptation of a funeral cry. Vermeylen, "Proto-Isaïe," 43–44, sums up the discussion and provides bibliography.

11. "Method of Determining Wisdom Influence," 130 n. 4.

12. Most recently, with bibliography, J. L. Crenshaw, "Education in Ancient Israel," *JBL* 104 (1985) 601–15; see also the essay in this volume by A. Lemaire, "The Sage in School and Temple," pp. 165–81 above.

13. C. R. Fontaine, *Traditional Sayings in the Old Testament* (Bible and Literature 5; Sheffield: Almond, 1982). On wisdom traditions among rural people, see E. Gerstenberger, *Wesen und Herkunft des "apodiktischen Rechts"* (WMANT 28; Neukirchen: Neukirchener, 1965).

14. R. E. Murphy, "Wisdom—Theses and Hypotheses," *IW* 39–40.

explicit claim in this regard; such conclusions are inferences drawn from
the texts and are heavily dependent upon presuppositions regarding
wisdom and its history. My judgment is that none of the writing
prophets can be proven to be sages in a technical sense, nor were they
sages prior to their prophetic activity.[15] The *use* of wisdom language,
forms, and ideas known from the wisdom literature proper (Proverbs,
Job, Qoheleth, several psalms) does not prove that the writers or
prophets were sages. It may merely show that they knew such literature
or traditions like it, and that they partook of the general wisdom
thinking common to cultured Israelites.[16] However, it may mean more.
In the case of a prophet like Isaiah, strong verbal and thematic parallels
to proverbs from the court of Hezekiah exist (e.g., Isa 5:21 and Prov

---

15. J. Fichtner, "Jesaja unter den Weisen," *Theologische Literaturzeitung* 74 (1949)
75–80 (repr. in *Gottes Weisheit* [Arbeiten zur Theologie 2.3; Stuttgart: Calwer, 1965] 18–
26; trans. as "Isaiah among the Wise," *SAIW* 429–38), argued that Isaiah had been a wise
man who, as a prophet, came to oppose his former colleagues; cf. R. Anderson, "Was
Isaiah a Scribe?" *JBL* 79 (1960) 57–58. S. Terrien, "Amos and Wisdom," *Israel's Prophetic
Heritage: Essays in Honor of James Muilenburg* (ed. B. W. Anderson and W. Harrelson;
New York: Harper, 1962) 108–15 (repr. in *SAIW* 448–55), was followed by H. W. Wolff,
*Joel und Amos* (BKAT 14/2; Neukirchen-Vluyn: Neukirchener, 1969; trans. as *Joel and
Amos* [Hermeneia; Philadelphia: Fortress, 1977]), who situated Amos in a tradition of
rural "clan wisdom." For critiques, see H. H. Schmid, "Amos: Zur Frage nach der
'geistigen Heimat' des Propheten," *Wort und Dienst* 10 (1969) 85–103 (repr. in *Altorientalische Welt in der alttestamentischen Theologie* [Zurich: Theologischer, 1974] 121–44);
and Crenshaw, "Influence of the Wise upon Amos." Wolff has situated the prophet Micah
similarly: "Micah the Moreshite—The Prophet and His Background," *IW* 77–84. D. E.
Gowan, "Habakkuk and Wisdom," *Perspective* 9 (1968) 157–66; and G. A. Tuttle, "Wisdom and Habakkuk," *Studia Biblica et Theologica* 3 (1973) 3–14, have argued for wisdom
influence on Habakkuk.

16. See W. H. Gispen, *De Wijze in Israël* (Kampen: Kok, 1956). It is a truism that
anyone can use a proverb or wisdom form, but this point is often overlooked. The use of
proverbs, for instance, in diplomatic correspondence (which has affinities with prophetic
communication to the court) is well known. See W. F. Albright, "An Archaic Hebrew
Proverb in an Amarna Letter from Central Palestine," *BASOR* 89 (1943) 29–32; and J. S.
Holladay, "Assyrian Statecraft and the Prophets of Israel," *Harvard Theological Review*
63 (1970) 29–51 (repr. in *Prophecy in Israel* [ed. D. L. Petersen; Issues in Religion and
Theology 10; Philadelphia: Fortress, 1987] 122–43, esp. 129, 140–41 n. 51). This phenomenon is cross cultural and appears in various genres; e.g., on Herodotean use of
proverbs and "proverb-like maxims," see Mabel L. Lang, *Herodotean Narrative and
Discourse* (Cambridge: Harvard University, 1984) 58–67. On the other hand, Whybray's
argument in *Intellectual Tradition in the Old Testament*, 11, that wisdom is "a general
term denoting superior intellectual ability whether innate or acquired, in God, men or
animals" ignores the cultural specificity of *ḥkm*. Whybray says too little with respect to
Isa 31:2 in asserting that this passage means only that "these politicians . . . claimed . . .
superior intelligence" (p. 20). For such intelligence is not some universal "reason" possessed by all humans; rather, the wisdom in question is precisely that enculturated style of
thought most adequately expressed in Proverbs.

26:5, 12, 16; 28:11).[17] It is difficult not to see positive connections between the writers of Proverbs and Isaiah,[18] especially given the tiny social world that both inhabited. That Isaiah used the wisdom of Proverbs to attack courtly wisdom probably means that the sages were not true to their own wisdom, or that there were conflicting factions in the court, some of which, at certain times in his lengthy career, Isaiah attacked. Unfortunately, the limited data leave uncertainty in these matters.

R. N. Whybray's view, however, is too strong:

> It is no longer necessary—and perhaps neither appropriate nor profitable— to look for an "influence" of the wise men or of wisdom literature on the prophets, since whatever similarities may be found between wisdom texts and prophetical texts can be explained in terms of a "shared approach to reality" common to all Israelites, including "wise men" and prophets, in various degrees.[19]

This elevates a legitimate deductive construct (a "shared approach to reality") to an explanatory status that it cannot bear. We possess only the wisdom literature and biblical parallels as evidence for a wisdom approach to reality. Thus Whybray argues mistakenly that "[R. E.] Murphy's concept of a 'shared approach to reality' is so broad as to run the risk of reducing the concept of Israelite wisdom, outside the 'wisdom books' proper, to no more than native common sense such as is to be found generally in human nature."[20] Rather, the elucidation of this shared approach is not possible without reference to the wisdom literature as the criterion that epitomizes Israelite wisdom.

If one minimally defines primary Israelite wisdom as thought and action (whether or not this is expressed in wisdom genres)[21] in conformity with the world view and norms expressed in Proverbs 10–31,[22] and defines "secondary wisdom" as that which reflects Job and Qoheleth,[23]

17. Whedbee, *Isaiah and Wisdom*.

18. Contrary to W. McKane, *Prophets and Wise Men* (2d ed.; London: SCM, 1983) 65–66, Isa 5:21 is not an attack on "old wisdom" per se.

19. Whybray, "Prophecy and Wisdom," 186; see also n. 16 above.

20. Ibid.; see also n. 15 above.

21. A. Dundes, "Folk Ideas as Units of Worldview," *Journal of American Folklore* 84 (1971) 93–103, points out that the expression of world view is not genre specific.

22. Though the dating is uncertain, Proverbs 1–9 and 31 are probably postexilic additions to chaps. 10–30. But they not so much reflect a different world view than chaps. 10–30, as provide a consistent theological elaboration thereof. Cf. G. von Rad, *Wisdom in Israel* (Nashville: Abingdon, 1972) 70, 114.

23. Primary and secondary are not exclusive distinctions; the problems of Qoheleth and Job are anticipated in Proverbs 10–30. For consideration of alternative designations

then wisdom in the prophets will possess a relatively objective criterion. The conclusions drawn from such a criterion will depend upon whether one ascribes to the wisdom literature a peripheral[24] or central status in Israelite culture. Though it cannot here be demonstrated in detail, I would argue the latter option and that the wisdom of the prophetic canon operates primarily in conformity with the world view of Proverbs. Prophetic attacks on false wisdom or sages generally reflect the criteria of Proverbs.[25] It should be noted that the position here taken is contrary to that taken by W. McKane and others who place "sacred" prophecy in opposition to "secular" rational wisdom and who see in the sayings of Proverbs a historical development from secular to religious wisdom.[26] The investigation of wisdom forms and thought in the prophetic and other biblical literature remains worthy of close investigation. There is a particular need now for a comprehensive study of the connections between the secondary wisdom of Job and Qoheleth and the prophets (e.g., Job 3:1–26 and Jer 20:14–18).

In light of the foregoing discussion my task focuses on two questions. First, what is the social role or roles of the sage as portrayed in the prophetic literature? Second, how is the "good" sage to be distinguished from the "bad" sage? These questions are crucial, for these are the questions with which the texts themselves are most concerned. Moreover, the second question parallels that concerning the opposition of true and false prophet and raises similar problems and issues.

---

for primary (as "traditional") and secondary (as "critical" or "skeptical") wisdom literature, see the essays by L. G. Perdue ("Cosmology and the Social Order in Israelite and Jewish Wisdom," pp. 457–78) and J. G. Gammie ("From Prudentialism to Apocalypticism: The House of the Sages amid the Varying Forms of Wisdom," pp. 479–97).

24. H. D. Preuss, "Erwägungen zum theologischen Ort alttestamentlicher Weisheitsliteratur," *Evangelische Theologie* 30 (1970) 393–417; idem, "Das Gottesbild der älteren Weisheit Israels," *Studies in the Religion of Ancient Israel* (VTSup 23; Leiden: Brill, 1972) 117–45.

25. So, for Jeremiah, M. Gilbert, "Jérémie en conflit avec les sages?" *Le Livre de Jérémie* (ed. P.-M. Bogaert; BETL 54; Louvain: Peeters/Leuven University, 1981) 118.

26. McKane's view imposes modern oppositions upon texts to which they are foreign. His introduction (pp. 9–14) to the 1983 edition of *Prophets and Wise Men* reaffirms his earlier (1965) stance. His assertion that the wise "probably drew a distinction between their private lives or their membership of Yahweh's cultus and the public offices which they held" (p. 10) is simply post-Lockean eisegesis. McKane's theory, in the line of Fichtner, Sellin, and Scott, concerning the history of sayings is found in *Proverbs: A New Approach* (OTL; Philadelphia: Westminster, 1970). Amazingly, H. H. Schmid in *Wesen und Geschichte der Weisheit* (BZAW 101; Berlin: Töpelmann, 1966) 144, could already declare that it was "heute unbestritten" that Israel's wisdom, like that of Egypt and Mesopotamia, was religious from the very start. Similar are the positions of G. E. Bryce, *A Legacy of Wisdom: The Egyptian Contribution to the Wisdom of Israel* (Lewisburg, PA: Bucknell University, 1979) 154, 220 n. 3; and von Rad, *Wisdom in Israel*, 53–73, esp. 61. On rational wisdom see the critiques of Clements, *Prophecy and Tradition*, 75–76; and Murphy, "Wisdom—Theses and Hypotheses," 40–41.

The starting point in quest of the historical sage in the prophets must be the contextual use of the terms sage or wise (*hkm*) and related words.[27] The groundwork for such study was laid by R. N. Whybray in *Intellectual Tradition in the Old Testament*, a valuable work flawed by the misleading thesis that *hkm* was never used as a technical term to refer to a professional class. Though *hkm* may not have been a technical term, it *is* used to refer to specialized classes who, according to the prophets, ought to possess a wisdom proper to their office. McKane's judgment remains correct:

> Those who occupied eminent positions in the government of Judah, whether they are called *sōpᵉrīm* or *yōᶜᵃṣīm* or *śārīm*, are certainly *hᵃḵāmīm* and, in particular, it is clear that the *hᵃḵāmīm* against whom the polemic of Isaiah and Jeremiah is directed are, for the most part, eminent statesmen.[28]

The best source of criteria for such courtly wisdom is the Book of Proverbs. For though Proverbs concerns itself with all of life, considerable portions of the book bear the stamp of courtly origin and concern.[29]

## ISAIAH 1–39

Isa 3:1–4 prophesies the removal of the leaders of Jerusalemite society. The list contains the planners and agents of royal policy; in a world-upside-down manner (cf. 3:12; Prov 30:21–23), God will "make boys their princes [*śryhm*]."[30] Included are "the counselor and the skillful [*hkm*] magician and the expert [*nbwn*] in charms." Isaiah's use of *hkm*

---

27. "Unquestionably, the most decisive material for studying the part played by wisdom traditions in the preaching of the prophets remains those passages where explicit reference is made to those who are wise, or who claim to be so, and who make use of a special wisdom"; so Clements, *Prophecy and Tradition*, 82.

28. McKane, *Prophets and Wise Men*, 40–41.

29. "[R. E.] Murphy ["Wisdom—Theses and Hypotheses"] . . . seeks to combine the view of Proverbs as mainly the work of court scribes—a view that no scholar would wish to deny entirely—with the more recent theories that Israelite wisdom was originally at home among the ordinary people" (Whybray, "Prophecy and Wisdom," 185). On a courtly *Sitz* for sections of Proverbs, see B. Kovacs, "Sociological-Structural Constraints upon Wisdom: The Spatial and Temporal Matrix of Proverbs 15:28–22:16" (Ph.D. diss., Vanderbilt University, 1978; repr. Ann Arbor: University Microfilms, 1978); W. L. Humphreys, "The Motif of the Wise Courtier in the Book of Proverbs," *IW* 177–90; and B. Malchow, "A Manual for Future Monarchs," *CBQ* 47 (1985) 238–45.

30. On *śr* see U. Rüterswörden, *Die Beamten der israelitischen Königszeit: Eine Studie zu śr und vergleichbaren Begriffen* (Beiträge zur Wissenschaft vom Alten und Neuen Testament 117/17; Stuttgart: Kohlhammer, 1985). On Prov 30:21–23 see Van Leeuwen, "Prov 30:21–23 and the Biblical World Upside Down," *JBL* 105 (1986) 599–610.

and *nbwn* here is ironic. While the magician[31] appears to have a wisdom proper to his craft, he, the counselor, the diviner, and the prophet are false sources of guidance.

The statesmen proper are the royal counselors (root *yʿṣ*) whose diplomatic plans (*ʿṣh*, Isa 30:1-5, 31:1-3) consistently elevate human wisdom over Yahweh's plan as revealed by the prophet[32] (cf. Prov 19:21 and 21:30-31, which relativize 20:18 and 24:6). Yahweh alone is ultimately wise (Isa 31:2). The judgment of Isa 29:14 applies to such political advisors:[33] "The Wisdom of their wise men shall perish, and the discernment of their discerning men shall be hid."

Isa 5:8-12, 18-24 (to which 10:1-4 is related) seems to refer to a different royal group. The opponents here are not properly speaking "statesmen."[34] Rather they are the wealthy and corrupt agents of the crown who violate the specific wisdom principles for royal legislation (10:1-2; cf. Prov 8:15-16, 31:5, root *ḥqq*) and justice.[35] The judge may not drink lest he corrupt justice (Isa 5:11, 22-23; cf. Prov 31:4-5, 20:1; Qoh 10:16-17; Hos 7:5) and ignore the rights of the poor (Prov 29:4, 7, 14, 26). More generally, he who is "wise in his own eyes" (Isa 5:21) ignores both God and human limits,[36] and violates a fundamental tenant of wisdom as described in a proverb collection stemming from Hezekiah's court (Prov 25:1; 26:5, 12, 16; 28:11; cf. 3:7). Isaiah condemns the sages of the court, with their varied functions, in terms of the wisdom norms that hold for them.[37]

J. Vermeylen demonstrates the close relation of Isa 9:2-7a (MT 9:1-6a) and 11:1-5 (cf. 16:5) to the ancient royal sayings in Proverbs (14:27, 33; 16:10, 12, 13, 16; 20:26, 28; 21:30; 25:5; 29:4, 14) and concludes that these texts reflect the royal theology of the Jerusalem court.[38]

---

31. It is tempting, with Vermeylen ("Proto-Isaïe," 43) and others, to remove the references to "magic/craft" (*ḥrš*) and 'whispering/charms' (*lḥš*). But this is to adjust the text to fit our ignorance. A reference to snake charming here seems unlikely.

32. P. A. H. de Boer, "The Counsellor," *WIANE* 42-71; J. Jensen, "Yahweh's Plan in Isaiah and in the Rest of the Old Testament," *CBQ* 48 (1986) 443-55.

33. See R. E. Clements, *Isaiah 1-39* (Grand Rapids: Eerdmans, 1980) 239; and H. Wildberger, *Jesaja 28-39* (BKAT 10/3; Neukirchen-Vluyn: Neukirchener, 1982) 1122-23. Whybray's arguments (*Intellectual Tradition in the Old Testament* 19) concerning poetry and parallelism are semantically confused and beside the point. That *ḥkm* is not a technical term with only one referent needs no proof; what needs to be explained is Isaiah's use of this term to refer to specific, sometimes professional classes.

34. Cf. McKane, *Prophets and Wise Men*, 65-68.

35. K. Whitelam, *The Just King: Monarchical Judicial Authority in Ancient Israel* (JSOTSup 12; Sheffield: JSOT Press, 1979). On Isa 10:1-2 see Clements, *Isaiah 1-39*, 61.

36. Von Rad, *Wisdom in Israel*, 97-110 (a chapter entitled "Limits of Wisdom").

37. J. Jensen, *The Use of tôrâ by Isaiah: His Debate with the Wisdom Tradition* (CBQMS 3; Washington, DC: Catholic Biblical Association, 1973) 129; Whedbee, *Isaiah and Wisdom*, 126.

38. Vermeylen, "Proto-Isaïe," 45-48.

Whether he is correct in ascribing them to the Josianic era does not matter for my subject.[39] These passages, by describing the ideal Messianic sage, implicitly criticize the failure of present king and courtiers to exercise the wisdom proper to their office.

Two passages deride the false wisdom of foreign courts in planning military exploits without taking Yahweh into account; the Jerusalem court has no monopoly on false wisdom. In Isa 10:13 the king of Assyria, who is only a tool in Yahweh's hand (Isa 10:5), boasts of his wisdom and might. Similarly, the sage courtiers of Egypt (cf. Isa 30:1-15, 31:1-3!) will have their wisdom turned to folly (Isa 19:11-15). Though the dating and ascription of this last passage is disputed,[40] it is nonetheless entirely consistent with the Isaianic focus on the royal court as a locus of false wisdom in conflict with Yahweh's wisdom. In spite of Whybray's argument that a professional class is not in view here,[41] the sages or wise men (vv 11-12) are clearly the counselors (*hkmy y⁽ṣy pr⁽h*) of Pharaoh's court, a class of experts whose stock in trade is wisdom. Courtly sages are not per se false; their failure to heed wisdom's limits and the divine plan (*⁽ṣh*) make them so.

## JEREMIAH

Twice in Jeremiah, *hkm* refers to specialized skills. In Jer 9:17 (MT 9:16) *hkm* refers to the skill of (professional?) mourners (cf. Amos 5:16). In 10:9 it refers to the skill of foreign craftsmen who make idols. But the use of *hkm* here is ironic,[42] for idol worshipers are actually foolish (v 8). The whole passage (Jer 10:1-16)[43] is richly laden with wisdom language. Yahweh, the "King of the nations [*mlk hgwym*]" is contrasted in v 7 with "all the wise ones of the nations [*hkmy hgwym*]," who, contra W. L. Holladay, are best understood as the kings of the nations (cf. Isa 10:13, 19:11b).[44] Not idols, but Yahweh, made the heavens and earth with wisdom and understanding (Jer 10:12 = 51:15).

The bogus wisdom (*hkmh*) or sages of foreign nations are also referred to in Jer 49:7 (twice), 50:35, 51:57. The latter two passages

---

39. So also H. Barth, *Die Jesaja-Worte in der Josiazeit* (WMANT 48; Neukirchen-Vluyn: Neukirchener, 1977).

40. Wildberger, *Jesaja 28-39*, 707, considers it likely Isaianic.

41. Whybray, *Intellectual Tradition in the Old Testament*, 12.

42. W. L. Holladay, *Jeremiah* (Hermeneia; Philadelphia: Fortress, 1986), 1.333.

43. Its authenticity is defended by Holladay, ibid., 321-37.

44. This is the import of the parallel "in all their kingdoms [*bkl mlkwtm*]"; cf. Theodotion's "their kings," which has read *abstractum pro concreto*: so W. McKane, *Jeremiah* (International Critical Commentary; Edinburgh: Clark, 1986), 1.224. McKane mistakenly ascribes the same reading to the Vulgate.

explicitly refer to the royal establishment of Babylon (whether counselors or magician/diviners are intended is not clear),[45] but the wisdom in question concerns political-military strategy, as the contexts show; Jer 49:7 probably refers to the same class in Edom.

Scholarly debate, however, has focused upon the use of ḥkm to describe Jeremiah's countrymen. Is there a class of people called "the wise"? In Jer 4:22 ḥkm is used in a general and ironic way: God's people are wise in doing evil. But the key passages are Jer 8:8 and 18:18. Jer 8:8-9 is best taken to refer to the general wisdom that the people of Judah *ought* to have in light of their possessing the deuteronomic Torah (cf. Deut 4:6).[46] The prophetic expectation that Yahweh's people be wise is apparent in the accusation that they are unwise (l nbwnym) and foolish (Jer 4:22, 5:21).[47] But in his attack on distorted torah-wisdom, Jeremiah has in mind especially the scribes, those cultural leaders (cf. Jer 5:5) "whose perception shapes that of the whole people."[48]

Jer 18:18 is spoken by the opponents of Jeremiah: "The law shall not perish from the priest, nor counsel [ʿṣh] from the wise [ḥkm], nor the word from the prophet." This passage is often compared to Ezek 7:26: "They seek a vision from the prophet, but the law perishes from the priest, and counsel [ʿṣh] from the elders [zqnym]." The continuation to this in v 27 must not be ignored: "The king mourns, the prince is wrapped in despair, and the hands of the people of the land are palsied by terror." It is most likely that both passages refer to counselors of the king whose political strategies Jeremiah and Ezekiel oppose. Thus, the wise correspond to the elders[49] (cf. 1 Kgs 12:6 wyw ʿṣ . . . hzqnym; Prov 20:29, 16:31; Job 15:7-10). Entirely consonant with this picture is Jer 2:8 where a similar tripart description of Jeremiah's opponents is used: the priests who "handle the law" but do not know Yahweh, the "shepherds" (= king and court) who transgress, and the baalite prophets. Thus the sage (ḥkm) of Jer 18:18 seems to refer to a distinct royal class of counselors,[50] in contrast to the wise (ḥkm) scribes and people of Jer

---

45. Whybray, *Intellectual Tradition in the Old Testament*, 16.

46. Ibid., 22-24.

47. Gilbert, "Jérémie en conflit avec les sages?," 106-10, who points out that these verses focus on the failure to respect the wisdom of Yahweh as creator. But torah-wisdom and creation-wisdom are complementary, not mutually exclusive categories, already in the preexilic period.

48. Holladay, *Jeremiah*, 1.283; cf. Fishbane, *Biblical Interpretation*, 33-36.

49. A. Caquot, "Israelite Perceptions of Wisdom and Strength in the Light of the Ras Shamra Texts," *IW* 27.

50. So also Gilbert, "Jérémie en Conflit avec les sages?," 114. The view of M. S. Moore, "Jeremiah's Progressive Paradox," *RB* 93 (1986) 386-414, that Jeremiah's confessions show him more and more to be caught in the views of skeptical sages, who are to be identified with the prophet's opponents, does not commend itself.

8:8–9. But it should be noted that scribes, counselors, priests, prophets, and people with few exceptions are united in their opposition to the prophet. In all these categories there is none so wise as to explain the calamity that befalls the land (Jer 9:12 [MT 9:11]).[51] God's rule in history relativizes the wealth, wisdom, and might (Jer 9:23–24 [MT 9:22–23])[52] of those who exercise civil power. Only the knowledge of Yahweh matters.

Finally, like Isaiah 9 and 11, Jeremiah forsees a time when the present foolish regime (Jer 10:21) will be replaced by shepherds who rule wisely (*dᶜh whśkyl*, Jer 3:15; cf. 23:5). Then the king and his counselors will be true sages.[53]

## OTHER PROPHETIC BOOKS

In Ezekiel, *ḥkm* occurs only within the section on Tyre and Sidon. Two occurrences (Ezek 27:8, 9) refer to the skill of Tyrian seamen. The remaining occurrences (Ezek 28:3, 4, 5, 7, 12, 17) "all refer to the pretended *ḥokmā* of the prince, or king, of Tyre."[54] Noteworthy again is the connection between wisdom and royalty.

The redactional appearance of *ḥkm* in Hos 14:10 was noted above. In Hos 13:13 "an unwise son" does not come forth at the time for birth, a general use of the term in keeping with the wisdom "doctrine of the proper time."[55]

In Second Isaiah *ḥkm* refers to a craftsman's skill in 40:20 (cf. Jer 10:9) and twice (Isa 44:25, 47:10) to the sages of Babylon (cf. Jer 50:35, 51:57) who, by counsel or enchantments, are deluded in their pretensions to lordship over history.

The sages of Obad 8 (cf. Jer 49:7) are most likely the diplomatic elite of the nation (cf. v 7). The reference to the wisdom of Tyre and Sidon in Zech 9:2 seems to refer to skill in gaining wealth through commerce but is also to be compared to Ezekiel 28.

## CONCLUSION

The scholarly discussion of wisdom in the prophetic literature has suffered from vagueness concerning the definition of wisdom. While

51. The passage appears to be postexilic and retrospective.
52. Gilbert, "Jérémie en Conflict avec les sages?," 115–17. Gilbert concludes, from many parallels in Proverbs, that Jeremiah's views are consonant with those "des sages des anciens proverbes." This passage is increasingly seen as authentic; cf. Holladay, *Jeremiah*, 1.316–18.
53. Gilbert, "Jérémie en Conflict avec les sages?," 117–18.
54. Whybray, *Intellectual Tradition in the Old Testament*, 81.
55. Von Rad, *Wisdom in Israel*, 138–43.

wisdom may be described as Israel's world view or "shared approach to reality," its particular forms and themes are best defined in terms of the wisdom literature of ancient Israel. Thus, sages are implicitly present in the prophetic corpus as redactors (cf. Hosea). But the sages (*ḥkmym*) explicitly mentioned in the prophetic texts are almost always opponents of the prophets. Such wise men, as domestic or foreign royal courtiers, stand opposed to the prophets with regard to justice and political guidance. These sages are not false per se but only as they forget the human limits of wisdom (according to criteria from Proverbs) and defy the word of Yahweh's messengers. Thus Whybray's reluctance to admit a technical usage of *ḥkm* to refer to a professional class seems beside the point: courtiers and counselors are expected to be wise. Finally, a comprehensive examination of the parallels among the prophetic literature and secondary wisdom literature (Job, Qoheleth) is yet to be undertaken.

# THE SAGE, THE SCRIBE, AND SCRIBALISM IN THE CHRONICLER'S WORK

## Joseph Blenkinsopp

In explanation of the title, it should be pointed out that the substantive *ḥākām* with the meaning 'sage' occurs nowhere in the Chronicler's work. This, however, does not imply that the author-editor was uninterested in wisdom and the ways in which it could be mediated and acquired. If one wishes to grasp what the books in the Chronicler's work have to say on this matter, inquiry must be directed in the first place to the particular form and function of the scribal office for the emergence and development of which this composition is an irreplaceable source. By "the Chronicler's work" is meant 1 and 2 Chronicles together with Ezra–Nehemiah, constituting a history of Israel from the foundation of the Monarchy—linked genealogically with creation—to the second half of the fifth century B.C.E.[1] Composed probably during

Joseph Blenkinsopp is John A. O'Brien Professor of Biblical Sudies at the University of Notre Dame.

1. The assumption that "the Chronicler," whether understood as an individual or as a plurality sharing the same general outlook, is responsible for the editing and arranging of a great part or all of the material in Ezra–Nehemiah, has been challenged in recent years by several scholars, notably Sarah Japhet ("The Supposed Common Authorship of Chronicles and Ezra–Nehemiah Investigated Anew," *VT* 18 [1968] 330-71) and H. G. M. Williamson (*Israel in the Book of Chronicles* [Cambridge: Cambridge University, 1977] and several subsequent publications). The issue cannot be addressed in detail here, but the following points should be made.

In arguing the case either way, attention must be paid to the extensive use of sources in Ezra–Nehemiah and the quite different situation of the community in the postexilic period, for example, in the matter of marriages with foreign women. Those who argue for separate authorship have made much of the concern for the totality of Israel in Chronicles, a concern they believe to be absent from Ezra–Nehemiah. It is true that the latter concentrates, for obvious historical reasons, on Judah and Benjamin, but the expression "Judah and Benjamin" occurs often in 1-2 Chronicles (1 Chr 12:16, 2 Chr 11:1-3, 10, 12, 23), while Ezra–Nehemiah makes frequent, if sometimes unobtrusive, allusions to the number twelve (e.g., Ezra 2:2; 6:17; 8:3-14, 24, 35). Making all due allowance for the common characteristics of Late Biblical Hebrew, the numerous similarities in vocabulary

the last decades of Persian rule (about the mid-fourth century) it incorporates many sources, principally the so-called Deuteronomistic History
for the period prior to the Babylonian Exile and official correspondence
and personal memoirs for the period subsequent to it. All of these have
been edited and liberally interpolated to bring them into line with the
author-editor's intentions and ideology. Use of the term "author-editor"
is not intended to exclude the possibility of successive editions, though
it may be taken to indicate a basic uniformity of point of view. The
focus, then, of the present study is the scribal office in the work, and to
what extent it corresponds to sociological, political, or religious realities
within the time frame either of the history as recorded or of the
composition of the work.

## THE SCRIBES AS ROYAL OFFICIALS

Following his sources, the author speaks at various points in the history
of Judah of the scribe (sopēr) as a highly placed royal official: Shavsha
and Jonathan under David (1 Chr 18:16; cf. 2 Sam 8:17, 20:25; 1 Chr
27:32), an unnamed official under Joash (2 Chr 24:11; cf. 2 Kgs 12:10-
11), and Shaphan who played a leading role in Josiah's reforms (2 Chr
34:15-21; cf. 2 Kings 22). Earlier sources amply attest to this office for
the entire period of the Monarchy, and it is equally well attested for the
entire Near East.[2] The duties associated with the office were not confined to redacting official documents. Scribes served as advisors to
kings, and one reads of them overseeing the temple treasury (2 Kgs
12:11 = 2 Chr 24:11; cf. Neh 13:13), being sent on important missions
(2 Kgs 19:2-7, 22:14-20), and engaging in negotiations that demanded a
knowledge of foreign languages (2 Kgs 18:18-27). Under the Persians,
who took over much of the administrative apparatus of their predecessors, scribes were employed by the central government (e.g., Esth
3:12, 8:9) as well as at the satrapal and provincial levels.[3] An example
would be the scribe Shimshai who drew up the letter from the chancel-

---

and style remain at least as impressive as those that have enabled almost all scholars to
agree on a priestly stratum in the Pentateuch. Even more impressive are the thematic and
structural parallels: compare, for example, the accounts of the Passovers of Hezekiah
(2 Chronicles 30) and Josiah (2 Chronicles 35) with that of the first repatriates (Ezra 6:19-
22). For these reasons among others, I see no reason to abandon the broad consensus that
has obtained since the work of Leopold Zunz in the early nineteenth century.

2. 2 Sam 8:17, 20:25; 1 Kgs 4:3; 2 Kgs 12:11; 18:18, 37 (cf. Isa 36:3, 22); 19:2 (cf. Isa
37:2); 22:3-12; Jer 36:10, 12, 20-23; 37:15, 20. On the Mesopotamian scribe see H. H.
Schaeder, *Esra der Schreiber* (Tübingen: Mohr, 1940) 39-59.

3. Herodotus 3:128. One of the Elephantine papyri refers to 'scribes of the province'
(*saprē mĕdîntāʾ*); see A. Cowley, *Aramaic Papyri of the Fifth Century B.C.* (Oxford:
Clarendon, 1923; repr. Osnabrück: Otto Zeller, 1967), no. 17, lines 1, 6.

lory in Samaria to the central government (Ezra 4:8–24). The seven counselors of the Persian king (Ezra 7:14–15), elsewhere described as sages (Esth 1:13–14), no doubt belonged to the same category. Their role was not unlike that of the half-legendary and ubiquitous Ahiqar, reputedly court-scholar (*ummānū*) of the Assyrian king Esarhaddon, also described as "a wise and skilful scribe."[4]

## THE SCRIBES AS WRITERS, RECORDERS, AND NOTARIES

Since the need for writing as a specialized skill extended beyond royal chancelleries to other spheres of activity, scribes were also employed, for example, by temple authorities, the army (2 Kgs 25:19 = Jer 52:25; 2 Chr 26:11), and private individuals (e.g., Jeremiah's faithful amanuensis Baruch, Jer 36:26, etc.). The training of scribes presupposes a school system about which, unfortunately, very little is known as far as Israel is concerned. Schools for training scribes, generally attached to temples, are attested in Mesopotamia from the third millennium. Like the youths in the first part of Daniel, who were put through a three-year curriculum (Dan 1:15), students in these institutions were instructed in "the letters and language of the Chaldeans" (Dan 1:4) and much else besides, including mathematics, astronomy, and omen lore.[5] There was a marked tendency for scribes, whether literary specialists or mere scriveners, to belong to guilds presided over by a master-scribe and under the patronage of a deity, for example, Nabu or the goddess Nisaba. These guilds were the transmitters of an intellectual tradition that, to judge by the Babylonian priest Berossus, was still active in the Seleucid era.[6] The scribal office was generally hereditary; Ahiqar, for example, was succeeded by his son Nadin. And there is evidence that scribes took pride in preserving their family genealogies.[7]

4. *Spr ḥkym wmhyr*; see *ANET* 427–30 and J. M. Lindenberger, *The Aramaic Proverbs of Ahiqar* (Baltimore: Johns Hopkins University, 1983); on the adjective *māhîr* (also at Ezra 7:6 and Ps 45:2) see Schaeder, *Esra der Schreiber*, 40, 49–50.

5. On schools for the training of scribes see A. Lemaire, *Les Écoles et la formation de la Bible dans l'Ancien Israël* (Göttingen: Vandenhoeck und Ruprecht, 1981); M. Fishbane, *Biblical Interpretation in Ancient Israel* (Oxford: Clarendon, 1985) 24–32.

6. On scribal education in Babylon see A. Falkenstein, "Die babylonische Schule," *Saeculum* 4 (1953) 125–37; G. R. Driver, *Semitic Writing* (3d ed.; London: Oxford University, 1976) 62–73; on the guild structure see D. E. Weisberg, *Guild Structure and Political Allegiance in Early Achaemenid Mesopotamia* (Baltimore: Johns Hopkins University, 1967); I. Mendelsohn, "Guilds in Babylonia and Assyria," *JAOS* 60 (1940) 68–72; and most recently and conveniently on Berossus, S. M. Burstein, *The Babyloniaca of Berossus* (Malibu, CA: Undena, 1978).

7. Weisberg, *Guild Structure and Political Allegiance*, 79–81; R. N. Whybray, *The Intellectual Tradition in the Old Testament* (BZAW 135; Berlin: de Gruyter, 1974) 38.

In view of the close Babylonian connection, which continued into
the Persian period, it would be surprising if some aspects of Babylonian
scribalism were not reproduced in the province of Judah. One of these
may be the Chronicler's allusion to "the families of scribes dwelling at
Jabez" (1 Chr 2:55).[8] Family (*mišpāḥâ*) would in this instance connote a
guild, and the context in which the allusion occurs testifies that the
practitioners of different *métiers* tended to cluster in distinct locations
(1 Chr 4:14, 21, 23). Like the *sāprayyāʾ* of the Jewish settlement in
Elephantine, these lower-level scribes functioned primarily as notaries,
drawing up and witnessing documents concerning marriage, property,
law suits, and the like.[9]

## LEVITICAL SCRIBES AS INSTRUCTORS OF TORAH

Indications scattered throughout the Chronicler's work suggest that by
the time of writing, and very probably from the early preexilic period,
Levites were beginning to take over some aspects of the scribal function. Thus the Chronicler (or, more probably in this instance, a later
interpolator) has a Levitical scribe recording the twenty-four priestly
courses during David's reign (1 Chr 24:6). He also records that at the
time of Josiah's great religious reform some Levites functioned as
scribes, and the context suggests a religious rather than secular activity
(2 Chr 34:13). This is probably one example of a process by which
several originally distinct functions, for example, those of liturgical
musician and gatekeeper, were absorbed by the Levitical office during
the Persian period.[10]

In this connection I should also note the importance that the Chronicler assigns to the teaching function of Levites. He relates that Jehoshaphat, fifth in succession to David, carried out a thorough judicial reform,
modeled on the deuteronomic law, by appointing magistrates in the

8. The suggested emendation of *sopĕrîm* to *siprîm* (as *Biblia Hebraica Stuttgarten-
sia*), i.e., inhabitants of Kiryat Sepher (Debir), is explained by lack of the definite article,
the unexpected allusion to a trade, and the identification of the families as Kenite,
suggesting a quite different avocation. But trades in specific localities and "families" of
tradesmen occur later on in the lists (1 Chr 4:14, 21, 23), and the emendation is without
support in the versions. In addition to the commentaries see S. Klein, "Die Schreiber-
familien: 1 Chr 2:55," *Monatschrift für Geschichte und Wissenschaft des Judentums* 70
(1926) 410–16; I. Mendelsohn, "Guilds in Ancient Palestine," *BASOR* 80 (1940) 17–21.

9. See the many instances in the Arsham correspondence in G. R. Driver, *Aramaic
Documents of the Fifth Century B.C.* (Oxford: Clarendon, 1957) and, in general, B. Porten,
*Archives from Elephantine* (Berkeley: University of California, 1968) 55–57, 192–97.

10. They are distinguished from Levites in the lists in Ezra–Nehemiah (Ezra 2:40–
41, 70 = Neh 7:43–44, 73; Ezra 7:7; Neh 13:10) but elsewhere the Chronicler assumes their
Levitical status (e.g., 1 Chr 9:33–34, 15:16–22, 23:2–32).

towns and a central judiciary in Jerusalem composed of priests, Levites, and laity (2 Chr 19:4-11; cf. Deut 17:8-13). During the same reign a panel similarly composed went in circuit throughout Judah instructing the people out of a law book that they took with them (2 Chr 17:7-9). He also assigns a teaching role to Levites during Josiah's reform (2 Chr 35:3). Since the existence of Levites as a distinct clerical order of the second rank is not unambiguously attested for the preexilic period,[11] it is clear that in both instances the Chronicler is projecting back into the time of the Monarchy a situation that was well established in his own day. It was therefore to be expected that when he came to describe Ezra's promulgation of the law, he should assign Levites an important role in teaching the people by providing an interpretation of what was being read (Neh 8:7-9).[12]

The conclusion toward which these considerations are leading finds support in the distinctive vocabulary used by the author. A key word, frequently recurring, is the verb *lĕhābîn* (causative of *bîn*), meaning either 'to understand' or 'to impart understanding', that is, 'to teach' (2 Chr 26:5, 35:3; cf. Isa 28:9, 40:14; Ps 119:27; Job 6:24; Dan 8:16, 10:14, 11:33). The participial form *mēbîn*, pl. *mĕbînîm*, referring to a specific skill that can be taught, is used by the author more often than not of Levites, and it includes skill in legal exposition and instruction (1 Chr 15:22, 25:7; 2 Chr 34:12, 35:3; Neh 8:7, 9). The sense of *mēbîn* is close to that of *maśkîl*,[13] which brings to mind the *maśkîlîm* of Daniel who are wise and impart wisdom (Dan 11:33, 35; 12:3, 10) and, somewhat later, the office of *maśkîl* or instructor in the Qumran community (Dan 11:33, 35; 12:3, 10; 1QS 3:13; 9:12, 21; 1QSb 1:1, 3:22, 5:20; 1QH 8:10; CD 12:21, 13:22). G. Vermes has argued persuasively for a connection between this office and the Levitical order as portrayed in the Chronicler's work (2 Chr 30:22, Ezra 8:18, Neh 8:7-8), a conclusion he believes is confirmed by the word *maśkîl*, which occurs in the superscriptions to

11. Allusions to Levites bearing the ark belong to the clearest indications of deuteronomistic editing (Josh 3:3, 1 Sam 6:15, 2 Sam 15:24, 1 Kgs 8:4). In Deuteronomy itself a distinction between priests and Levites is assumed only in the latest strand of the Shechem assembly where the Levites pronounce the curse (Deut 27:14, providing a model for the Qumran assembly, 1QS 2); cf. the quite different allusions in the same passage to Levitical priests (v 9) and the tribe of Levi (v 12).

12. It still seems best to take the pual participle *mĕporāš* in the sense of 'explain', though the syntax remains obscure. *Wayyābînû bammiqrā²* is generally referred to the congregation (e.g., RSV); since, however, *mēbîn bĕ* can be used of a specific skill (e.g., 2 Chr 34:12, Levitical skill in liturgical music; cf. 1 Chr 15:22, 25:7), it may refer to the Levites and their training in interpretative reading.

13. Similar to *lĕhābîn*, *lĕhaśkîl* connotes either being wise or imparting wisdom, i.e., teaching; for the latter sense see 1 Chr 28:19; Neh 9:20; Ps 32:8; Prov 16:23, 21:11; Dan 9:22.

psalms attributed to Levitical authorship.[14] It seems reasonable to conclude, therefore, that though Levites *qua* teachers are not designated
scribes in the Chronicler's work, they embody in effect a new form of
scribalism that emerged in the period of the Second Temple, focusing
on instruction in and interpretation of law.

## EZRA, THE PRIEST AND SCRIBE

A decisive point in the Chronicler's account of the founding of the
theocratic community is the mission of the Babylonian Jew Ezra to
Jerusalem in the seventh year of Artaxerxes, probably the first of that
name.[15] At this point he quotes what purports to be the imperial rescript
or firman authorizing the mission and defining Ezra's tasks and jurisdiction (Ezra 7:12-26). In it Ezra is addressed as priest and scribe of the
law of the God of heaven (*sāpar dātā⁾ dî-⁾ĕlāh šĕmayyā⁾*, Ezra 7:12, 21).
This designation has given rise to much discussion. According to the
interpretation of H. H. Schaeder, advanced more than half a century
ago and widely accepted, scribe (*sāpar*) in this context connotes a high-
level functionary in the Persian imperial service, a sort of commissioner
for Jewish affairs in the province of Judah and the Trans-Euphrates
satrapy in general. It would therefore correspond to an official title,
taken over from Assyrian and Babylonian usage (cf. Akkadian *šāpiru*),
designating the holder as charged with special responsibility for law-
observance within his jurisdiction.[16] In his introduction to the rescript
(Ezra 7:1-11) the Chronicler presents Ezra as both priest and "a scribe
skilled in the law of Moses" and "learned in matters of the commandments of Yahweh and his statutes for Israel" (Ezra 7:6, 11). As such, his
self-appointed task was to study and teach law and, of course, observe
it himself (v 10). Schaeder proposed that the official designation of Ezra
in the rescript suggested to the author a peculiarly Jewish form of the
office, that of expertise and instruction in Torah, further exemplified by
the public reading of the law at which Ezra presided (Nehemiah 8). In
this capacity Ezra marked the beginning of the process leading to
Judaism as we know it, characterized above all by study, teaching, and
observance of Torah.

## THE IMPERIAL DECREE

While Schaeder's view is ingenious and plausible, it relies heavily on the
literal authenticity of the decree, or at least of the description of Ezra

14. G. Vermes, *The Dead Sea Scrolls in English* (Harmondsworth: Penguin, 1962)
23-25.
15. The date is, of course, disputed, and need not concern us here.
16. Schaeder, *Esra der Schreiber*, 39-59.

that it contains. It would be generally recognized that the document was redacted with the help of a Jewish official in the chancellory, perhaps Ezra himself, which would explain the specifically Jewish expressions that it contains without prejudice to authenticity. But it is also possible that it has been subsequently edited in the course of its transmission and incorporation into the history, a view that can be maintained without surrendering its basic historicity. The following indications, probably not exhaustive, suggest that this is the case:

1. The actions mandated in the decree make for a close parallelism with the first return, especially with respect to the return of sacred vessels and the generous public and private subvention provided.
2. Repeated references to offerings freely made, using the verb *hitnaddēb*, reflect a favorite theme of the Chronicler.[17]
3. The deuteronomistic sound of the phrase "the wisdom of God which is in your hand" (Ezra 7:25), parallel with "the law of your God which is in your hand" (v 14), reflects the Chronicler's overall dependence on Deuteronomy in general and the deuteronomic law in particular.
4. The categories Israel, priests, and Levites (Ezra 7:13) correspond to the way in which the Chronicler generally describes the theocratic community.
5. The sacrificial animals are listed in the order that is standard for the Chronicler (cf. 1 Chr 29:21; 2 Chr 29:21, 32; Ezra 6:9, 17; 8:35).
6. Description of the territorial jurisdiction as "Judah and Jerusalem" corresponds to a favorite expression of the Chronicler, occurring in his work about twenty-five times.
7. The command to appoint magistrates and judges is in literal fulfillment of the deuteronomistic provisions for establishing a comprehensive judicial system (Deut 1:16-17, 16:18, 17:8-13) and runs parallel to the author's description of Jehoshaphat's measures in obedience to the same law (2 Chr 19:4-11). A further connection may be between "the matter of Yahweh and the matter of the king" in the same passage (2 Chr 19:11) and "the law of your God and the law of the king" in the rescript (Ezra 7:26). One might also compare the motive for subsidizing the sacrifices, namely, to avert the divine wrath (Ezra 7:23), with the exhortation of Jehoshaphat addressed to the priests and Levites (2 Chr 19:10).

No one of these indications is decisive in itself, but taken together they create a strong presumption in favor of the view that the document has been extensively edited by the Chronicler. And if this is so, the situation may be the reverse of Schaeder's hypothesis. In other words, the description of Ezra in the rescript may derive from the Chronicler's attribution to him of the status of Torah-scribe. This need not be seen as a product of the author's inventive mind, even though he nowhere else associates the scribal office with the law. It seems entirely

17. Apart from Judg 5:2, 9, it occurs elsewhere only in 1 Chr 29:5-17; 2 Chr 17:16; Ezra 1:6, 2:68; Neh 11:2.

plausible, especially in view of the probable Babylonian provenance of the priestly legislation (P), that legal exposition—*midrash halakah*—was being pursued in learned, priestly circles in the Babylonian diaspora and that Ezra, as a prominent figure in those circles, was delegated by the Persian authorities to investigate the situation in Judah. Such a measure would, at any rate, agree with what is known of Persian policy relative to other parts of the empire.[18]

## PRIESTLY SCRIBES AND THE
## INTERPRETATION OF TORAH

It is hardly possible, given the nature of our sources, to be certain that the priestly scribalism exemplified by Ezra existed as a distinct speciali- zation at the time of the mission. Throughout the preexilic period priests had the responsibility for preserving, teaching, and transmitting the laws, and this situation continued after the return (Hos 4:6; Jer 18:18; Ezek 7:26; Deut 17:18; 31:9–13, 24–26; Hag 2:10–13; Zech 7:1–7; Mal 2:6–9). According to Deuteronomy, on which the Chronicler draws so often, the law book was the responsibility of the priests (17:18; 31:9–13, 24–26). They were also charged with its public reading at the feast of Tabernacles (Deut 31:10–11), which is precisely what Ezra did in his capacity as priest and scribe or priest-scribe (Nehemiah 8). For the Chronicler, the office exemplified in the person of Ezra was necessitated by the promulgation of a written law, which is presented for the first time during the reign of Josiah. Deuteronomy itself does not speak of scribes, but an authentic saying of Jeremiah from shortly after that time condemns "handlers of the law" (*tośĕpē hattôrâ*) in a context that associates them with priests (Jer 2:8). Another saying of the same prophet condemns the false pen of the scribes for turning the law into a lie (Jer 8:8–9), which may be taken to imply that a class of legal experts was now engaged not only in writing but interpreting a written law, and that this activity was seen to pose a threat to prophetic authority. There is no definite clue to the identity of these scribes who handled, that is, were skilled in, the law. But since both Deuteronomy and Jeremiah place law firmly within the jurisdiction of the priesthood, it seems reasonable to conclude that this is a specialization of the priestly function created by the need to interpret a written law and hand down decisions based on their interpretations.[19] It is probably along this line

18. For example, the mission of the Egyptian priest and scribe Udjahorresnet during the reign of Darius I; on which see my article "The Mission of Udjahorresnet and Those of Ezra and Nehemiah," *JBL* 106 (1987) 409–21.

19. In addition to the commentaries see my *Prophecy and Canon* (Notre Dame, IN: University of Notre Dame, 1977) 36–39; Whybray, *Intellectual Tradition in the Old Testament*, 22–24.

of development that the twofold office of Ezra as described by the Chronicler should be located.

One can also look ahead from this point in time to the later Second Temple period when the study of Torah was firmly established on the agenda of the Jewish scribe (e.g., Sir 38:24–39:11). No doubt as a result of the universal availability of instruction in the law, attested by the Chronicler, Torah-scribalism gradually emancipated itself from the priesthood, thus conferring on Judaism its character of a lay religion, which it has since maintained.[20]

20. See the remark of E. Bickerman, *From Ezra to the Last of the Maccabees* (New York: Schocken, 1962) 17-18: "The democratization of the instruction in the Law in the fourth century opened the way to the coming of the scribe, and imperceptibly compromised the supremacy of the priest."

# PART V

---

*The Sage
from Before the Close of the Hebrew Canon
to Post-biblical Times*

# THE SAGE IN HELLENISTIC PHILOSOPHICAL LITERATURE (399 B.C.E.–199 C.E.)

## George B. Kerferd

The death of Socrates in 399 B.C.E. may conveniently be taken as something of a turning point in the history of the development of the concept of the sage among the Greeks. Before that date Greek communities tended to accept as sages or wise men those whom they regarded as possessing special talents, whether these showed themselves in certain of the rarer skills (such as knowledge of physical science or things divine, or in the practice of poetry, or in the possession of political skill and wisdom) or in knowledge of other things that were valued as giving a special quality to life. Such people were the objects of both respect and suspicion among ordinary people.[1] During the second half of the fifth century B.C.E. the way was prepared for the changes that occurred in the following century, above all by what it is convenient to call the Sophistic Movement. This was the movement that brought virtually the whole of higher education at Athens into the hands of the Sophists. In their ranks most ordinary Athenians included Socrates himself, even though Plato argued passionately that he should not be so included. A consequence of this development of higher education in the hands of the Sophists was that the purveyors of wisdom, which was what the term *sophist* was widely understood to mean, became not so much special people standing

George B. Kerferd is Emeritus Professor of Greek at the University of Manchester.

Classical references may be traced through the abbreviation lists in *A Greek-English Lexicon* by H. G. Liddell and R. Scott (ed. H. S. Jones et al.; 9th ed.; Oxford: Clarendon, 1940; with *Supplement*, ed. E. A. Barber et al., 1968). For convenience, the volume and page numbers are also given of the English translation in the Loeb Classical Library (LCL), copublished by Harvard University Press and William Heinemann.

1. I have tried to discuss these matters in "The Wise Man in Greece before Plato," *Images of Man in Ancient and Medieval Thought: Studia Gerardo Verbeke* (ed. F. Bossier; Louvain: Leuven University, 1976) 17–28.

outside and apart from the ordinary functions of the societies in which they lived, but rather as an integral part of the educational processes of the city.

The changes that followed were of three kinds. First, teaching at the higher level—higher education—came to be institutionalized in the schools of philosophy and rhetoric, such schools as the Academy, the Lyceum, and the rhetorical schools of teachers such as Isocrates. Second, Plato in his *Republic* developed the concept of the wise man as philosopher in a highly technical sense, that is, as someone possessing a knowledge of the truth—above all, ethical truth or truth about what is the right way for human beings to behave, based on the doctrine of the Platonic Forms constituting ultimate reality, which transcend the derived and inferior truth of the world of phenomenal experience. The concept of the philosopher who is the wise man is henceforward closely allied with the concept of the philosopher as a completely rational thinker. This ideal was incorporated by Aristotle into his concept of God and so of the ultimate end or final cause for each and every human being. So one might say in general that the concept of the wise man must be interpreted from Plato and Aristotle onward in terms of the various systems of philosophy within which the concept is positioned. Inasmuch as the wise man had always been seen as the man who knows, two questions now begin to be posed with a certain technical precision: "What are the things that the wise man knows?"; and, "What is meant by saying that he 'knows' them as distinct from other 'cognitive' relations between the wise man and these same objects?" The answers to these two questions tend more and more to be sought *within* the philosophic systems of each of the various schools in the Hellenistic period. Third, and more generally, the concept of the wise man comes to be identified with the ideal for humans, the perfect man who must be the ultimate objective for human aspirations. This means that any discussion of the sage in the Hellenistic period must deal with two different aspects of the sage: the sage as philosopher, and popular attitudes toward the sage regarded as the ideal for humans, or "ideal type"—to use the terminology of Max Weber. This last leads in turn to what may be called the obverse face of the sage or intellectual in society, involving a rejection of the sage as ideal type either in a love-hate relationship or outright political anti-intellectualism.[2]

## THE SAGE IN STOICISM

The Stoic doctrine of the wise man was famous—indeed notorious— throughout the Hellenistic period. Its challenging and paradoxical char-

2. For discussion see F. L. Vatai, *Intellectuals in Politics in the Greek World from Early Times to the Hellenistic Age* (London: Croom Helm, 1984), chap. 1.

acter was such that accounts of the wise man in other Hellenistic philosophical schools were inevitably deeply influenced by it, not least by rejection of what seemed its more unacceptable features. It may be approached under two headings: first, the position and function of the wise man within the system of Stoic ethics; and, second, the basis and nature of the wisdom in virtue of which he is accepted as being a wise man.

The wise person stands at the culminating point of Stoic ethics, but Stoic ethics in turn can only be understood within the system of Stoic philosophy seen as a unitary whole. For the Stoics, virtue is the perfection of each individual's nature. But early Stoic theory divided humankind sharply into two mutually exclusive classes, the wise and the foolish. Everything in the universe is the product of two fundamental principles: (1) the active principle, which is variously called Nous or Intelligence, God, Seminal Reason (*logos spermatikos*), Creative Fire, and Nature,[3] and (2) the passive or material principle, which is the receptacle for the rational forms and shapes that spring from the active principle. Human beings as part of the universe exhibit the functioning of these same two principles within themselves, and human reason is quite simply the conscious operation of the universal active principle within each particular person. From birth onward, we all have some awareness of our own natures, beginning with an awareness of the physical structure of our bodies. This awareness develops in its range and comprehensiveness with our own development as persons, and this gives an increasing appreciation of actions and activities that are "appropriate" in relation to our natures, and of other actions and activities that are correspondingly inappropriate. Such an increasing appreciation however does not of itself constitute true rationality, and those who are progressing in this way remain for this reason "fools" rather than wise. Likewise the appropriate actions that they come increasingly to prefer cannot be described as virtue—they remain under the general heading of vices, just as lines that are more or less curved or crooked are all in no sense straight lines. The transition from folly to wisdom, when it occurs, has the character of a complete and sudden conversion. Such a conversion is in fact rare, but some historical examples were usually admitted by the Stoics, and it remains always the most desirable end for all human action, namely, that one should become a wise person—the only person capable of truly right actions. These actions will also be appropriate actions, but with an added feature in that the wise person knows and understands fully what it is that makes them right actions and not merely appropriate actions.

3. See, e.g., Diogenes Laertius, *Lives of the Philosophers* 7:134–39 (LCL 185: 238–45), and for discussion David E. Hahm, *The Origins of Stoic Cosmology* (Columbus: Ohio State University, 1977), chap. 4 ("Cosmology").

What then is it that the wise person knows? It is sometimes said that the wise person simply knows everything, that is, he or she is omniscient. I have argued elsewhere against this view,[4] and in favor of a more restricted understanding, namely an understanding of the one divine active principle or *Logos* in the universe. In terms of actions this means that the wise person, and the wise person alone, understands (and knows) *why* a right action is right, namely, because of its rationality. This in turn is to be understood as meaning that right action is seen as right because it is *seen* to accord with reason.

If I am right, this remained the basic Stoic view of the nature of wisdom and the wise person throughout the history of Stoicism, with one possible concession, namely, that progress *toward* virtue did come to be seen (e.g., by Panaetius) as involving an increasing expression of reason in control of the passions, and so as deserving of approval and, indeed, admiration even though it necessarily still fell short of the actual conversion to the full rationality of the wise person.[5]

## THE SAGE IN EPICUREANISM

At first sight the system of Epicurus may seem to constitute a complete antithesis to that of the Stoics. For Epicurus pleasure is the highest good, and it is the standard by which we judge everything that is good. It is a feeling or passion ( *pathos* ) and is one of the three tests of truth, the others being sense-perception and anticipatory concepts. But in a valuable section in Diogenes Laertius's *Lives of the Philosophers* (10:117-21; LCL 185: 643-47), prefixed to Epicurus's *Letter to Menoeceus*, it is made clear that Epicurus did discuss the concept of the wise person, and indeed defined it in relation to the Stoic doctrine itself. According to the Stoic doctrine the wise person suppresses all feelings and acts solely on the basis of reason—the wise person will not pity someone in distress, but will help—*non miserebitur sapiens sed succurret* (Seneca, *De Clementia* 2:6:3; LCL 214: 410-11). For Epicurus also the wise person overcomes, for example, hatred, envy, and contempt by reasoning; but, in an obscure statement (*Lives of the Philosophers* 10:117; LCL 185: 643), he seems to say that while the wise person will be more moved by passions

---

4. "What Does the Wise Man Know?," *The Stoics* (ed. J. M. Rist; Berkeley: University of California, 1978), chap. 5.

5. Panaetius of Rhodes, 2d century B.C.E., is regarded as the founder of what came to be called Middle Stoicism. His ethical doctrines are best known from Cicero, *De Officiis*, books 1-2 (LCL 30: 2-267). Cicero based what he has to say on a nonextant treatise by Panaetius, *On Appropriate Action*. See for discussion M. Van Straaten, *Panétius, sa vie, ses écrits et sa doctrine avec une edition des fragments* (Amsterdam: H. J. Paris, 1946).

this will be no impediment to wisdom. The reference is probably to pleasures and pains regarded as passions to which the wise person will be particularly susceptible, and the word *more* may involve a comparison with the wise person of the Stoics. Stoic in inspiration seems to be the statement that one wise person is not wiser than another (*Lives of the Philosophers* 10:120; LCL 185: 647), and there must be specific rejection of the Stoic view in the statement (in the same paragraph) that acts of wrong doing are not all equal—the Stoics had maintained that they are all equal as being equally wrong.

This is all that seems to have survived from explicit Epicurean discussions of the wise person under the traditional Greek name of *sophos*. But more generally we can surely say with some confidence that for all Epicureans the ideal of the wise person was of course that of the ideal Epicurean philosopher, and all later members of the school regarded this ideal as embodied above all in Epicurus himself. The doctrine of the primacy of pleasure as an ethical principle at the surface level might seem to involve the rejection of the whole tradition of Greek thought stemming from Plato, which was devoted to the need to control or even eliminate the passions in order that people should be controlled and guided by reason. In fact, of course, it is clear that this was not in any sense what Epicurus wished to do—rather he was attempting to vindicate just this same ideal by following a nontraditional route. His analysis of pleasure in his surviving *Letter to Menoeceus* (in *Lives of the Philosophers* 10:128–35; LCL 185: 653–59) was based on the contention that the majority of pleasures, and certainly the most intense physical pleasures, arise from the satisfaction of the most intense desires. But intense desires were regarded by Epicurus as pains. So on a calculus of pleasures the most intense are canceled by the intensity of the pains that precede them, and we are left with a preference for the superior kinds of pleasure, those of the mind, which seem to involve no preceding pains or strong desires, and these are achieved above all by the exercise of the mind on philosophy. Only these, being based on "sober reasoning," avoid disturbance of the soul, and give the ultimate pleasure of freedom from distraction—*ataraxia*. From this it follows that there is something deserving even more honor than philosophy, namely, prudence or practical wisdom—*phronēsis*. Epicurus then proceeds to exalt the person of prudence, the *phronimos*, who has "reasoned out the end ordained by nature." The term *phronimos* had, of course, been used earlier by Aristotle in his *Nicomachean Ethics* for the one who *acts* wisely, as distinct from the *sophos*, and it is probable that Epicurus chose the term deliberately to mark his own departure from the Stoic and Platonic-Aristotelian concept of the *sophos* as the highest ideal for humans. This may indeed be the explanation of

Epicurus's famous advice to a young man: "Set sail and flee from every form of education [*paideia*]" (*Lives of the Philosophers* 10:6; LCL 185: 535)—meaning, perhaps, "Avoid the traditional philosophical and literary education that might lead you to become an Aristotelian, or what would be worse, even a Stoic."

## RESPONSE OF THE SKEPTICS—THE ELUSIVE SAGE

Thus, the wise person, at least for the Stoics, is wise in virtue of acquired knowledge or understanding. This knowledge is certain and infallible, something that has often been taken in the subsequent history of philosophy as an analytic truth about all knowledge. On this view any form of apprehension that is not certain and infallible is by definition not knowledge. The rational basis of personal knowledge means that all behavior by the wise person based on this knowledge is itself rational. It is from this that it was inferred that all that he does is completely self-controlled. Such a way of looking at things inevitably came under attack from the various schools who are grouped generally under the name of Scepticism. First, the distinguishing feature of the position of the Pyrrhonian Sceptics, who were the followers in the Hellenistic period of Pyrrho and Timon, was the denial of the possibility of knowledge—from which it follows that the only right course is *epochē* or suspension of judgment. On the whole the Pyrrhonians preferred simply to deny the existence of any wise person (because of the Stoic doctrines associated with the concept). But if there is such a thing as a wise person, then he or she will be so because of a refusal to assent in all cases and so practicing *epochē* (Sextus Empiricus, *Adversus Mathematicos* 7:156–57; LCL 291: 317–19).

The skepticism of the Academy, first under Arcesilaus, contemporary with Epicurus, and then under Carneades in the second century B.C.E., shared with the Pyrrhonians the requirement for *epochē*. This was emphatically the case with Arcesilaus's attitude to the kind of knowledge assigned to the Stoic sage, and we are expressly told that he regarded such suspension of assent as the only honorable attitude worthy of a wise person (Cicero, *Academica* 2:77; LCL 268: 563–65). Less certainty applies to the question whether this suspension was regarded as applying also to orthodox Platonism within the Academy itself. It is probable that Arcesilaus did intend such an application, and that he preferred not knowledge, but what he called "the reasonable" as the criterion for acting rightly. This means that he equated practical wisdom or *phronēsis* with right actions, those being actions that possess a "reasonable" justification (Sextus Empiricus, *Adversus Mathematicos* 7:157–58; LCL 291: 317–19). The term *reasonable* (*eulogon*) was found already in Stoicism where it was put forward as a device for making distinctions between "appropriate" actions, which lacked the final seal of being "right actions" as performed by the wise person. For Arcesilaus the term applied to all actions that were such as to be preferred.

In the New Academy, under Carneades (second century B.C.E.), this seems to have been developed into a concept of what is usually called "the probable" (*to pithanon*), but which would be less misleading if translated "the persuasive." On this view, sense-impressions— and possibly actions also—can be seen as possessing various degrees of persuasiveness. The whole interpretation of Carneades remains uncertain and controversial.[6] He, like Arcesilaus, certainly rejected the Stoic doctrine of knowledge and favored *epochē*. But he may nonetheless have accepted a criterion of choice between actions that was based on persuasiveness rather than knowledge.

## THE SAGE AMONG THE PERIPATETICS, PYTHAGOREANS, CYNICS, AND LATER SOPHISTS

Four other Hellenistic schools may be mentioned rather more briefly. Not much is known about the Peripatetic philosophers' attitude to the wise person in the period after Theophrastus; the surviving evidence[7] gives mainly details of their treatment of rhetoric, biography, and works of popular moralizing. There seems no evidence that they altered or abandoned the basic Aristotelian position that the wise one is concerned above all with the contemplation of truths that are unchanging. Their concern, however, was not with the *sophos*, but with the behavior of the individual of practical wisdom—the *phronimos*.

The second school is that of the Pythagoreans, of whom virtually nothing is known between Aristoxenus (contemporary of Aristotle) and the first century B.C.E. But then there was a remarkable revival.[8] Throughout the whole history of Pythagoreanism, however, the image of the founder Pythagoras himself remained overwhelmingly predominant. The wise person and the ideal type was consequently the exponent and practitioner of the whole range of Pythagorean philosophy—the number theory, astronomy, musical theory, and above all metempsychosis and

6. See A. A. Long and D. N. Sedley, *The Hellenistic Philosophers* (New York/ Cambridge: Cambridge University, 1987), 1:457–60.

7. See F. Wehrli, *Die Schule des Aristoteles* (2d ed.; 10 vols. and 2 sup. vols.; Basel: Schwabe/SVK, 1967–78).

8. For evidence and discussion of the revival, see H. Thesleff, *An Introduction to the Pythagorean Writings of the Hellenistic Period* (Acta Academiae Aboensis, A/24/3; Åbo: Åbo Akademi, 1961) and idem, *The Pythagorean Texts of the Hellenistic Period* (Acta Academiae Aboensis, A/30/1; Åbo: Åbo Akademi, 1965).

"shamanism."[9] This is of considerable interest for my present purposes as it confronts us with the concept of what has come to be known as the "Divine Man," or *theios aner*, and this seems to bridge two distinguishable types, the intellectual or "idealized *sophos* of philosophy, and the miracle worker of popular (or popularizing) imagination."[10] Many philosophers were concerned to distance themselves as far as possible from this second type by stressing the commitment of the philosopher to reason; see, for example, what Theophrastus had to say in *Characters* about the scorn of the educated person for those who indulged in superstition (§16; LCL 225: 79–83), and Plutarch's treatise *On Superstition*, included in the collection known as the *Moralia* (LCL 222: 451–95). But it is probable that at all periods there was something perceived as common between the two types, and that was a kind of power. The rationality of the wise person could easily be regarded as giving—and so became the expression of—some kind of mysterious power. And the same kind of power, in popular eyes at least, was seen to be present in religious leaders, prophets, magicians, and workers of wonders. For most of the Hellenistic period these two concepts were kept separate and were often seen as mutually opposed. In Neo-Platonism, however, the two ideas were partly fused in the third century C.E., at least in the popular understanding of the personality of the founder, Plotinus.

The Cynics were unified, not to any significant extent by any adherence to a theoretically developed system of philosophy, but by their commitment to a certain way of living. According to Epictetus in his diatribe, "On the Calling of the Cynic" (*Discourses* 3:22; LCL 218: 130–69), this should be seen not in living rough and without material comforts—the traditional view—but in promoting the purity of the rational or ruling element in the soul, and in the recognition that the Cynic has a divine mission to reveal to people how they have gone astray in questions about the things that are good and the things that are bad. Happiness is to be sought within and is independent of externals—a fairly common theme from Socrates through Aristotle and the Stoics. The ideal of wisdom was seen in the practical activities of the practical person (*ho phronimos*) rather than in the theoretical contemplation seen in the traditional sage (*ho sophos*). Such an idealization of the practical person of wisdom came to be identified as the Cynic King.

9. For these topics see W. Burkert, *Lore and Science in Ancient Pythagoreanism* (Cambridge: Harvard University, 1972).

10. See, for this whole question, G. P. Corrington, *The "Divine Man": His Origin and Function in Hellenistic Popular Religion* (New York: P. Lang, 1986); the quotation is from p. 60.

Each period of Greek history had sought to express its own view of the ideal character for a human being in its concept of the hero. In the period of Socrates this ideal became for some that of the wise person. For the Cynic the wise person in this sense came to be identified with the figure of Heracles, and a fairly detailed characterization of such a Cynic Heracles is preserved in Dio Chrysostom's "First Discourse on Kingship" (*Discourses* 1:50–84; LCL 257: 26–47).[11] Heracles had always been one of the most popular heroes in Greek thought, and it is no accident that he was adopted not only by the Cynics, but more generally as a paradigm of divine virtue and the ideal of kingship on so many occasions in the Hellenistic world. Note that Alexander the Great found it convenient to claim descent from Heracles, and that the deluded and half-mad Roman emperor Commodus chose to give expression to his own claim to divinity by dressing as if he himself were Heracles returned to earth, and calling himself *Hercules romanus*. In doing so he was at least in part claiming that he was embodying the Hellenistic ideal of kingship, claims that in his case would lead only to his assassination when just over 30 years of age in 191 C.E.

One of the functions of the wise person had always been that of teacher and professor, and the affiliation of professional teachers of grammar, philosophy, and rhetoric with earlier Sophists and wise people is preserved in the movement known as the Second Sophistic. Under the Roman Empire, from the second century C.E. onward, such teachers achieved in many parts of the Empire a very high reputation. What they taught became the most valued part of higher education, and endowed posts were set up for such teachers at many of the great centers of population. They both sheltered under, and themselves in part contributed to the enhancement of, the high reputation that ordinary people were prepared to give to wise people as the practitioners of wisdom.

Some indications of the popular attitude to wise people may be derived from the writings of the satirist Lucian in the second century C.E. There is first of all the image of the philosopher as a charismatic figure found in the treatise *Demonax* (LCL 14: 141–73). Whether this Demonax was a historical figure or not does not matter for my purpose. According to Lucian his philosophy was kind, gentle, and cheerful, and he was everyone's friend, so that all Athenians admired him and always viewed him as a superior being. Yet as a magistrate he confronted the masses, and acquired from them the same hatred as had accrued to Socrates as a result of his freedom of speech and freedom of action.

11. See R. Höistad, "Cynic Hero and Cynic King: Studies in the Cynic Conception of Man" (Inaugural diss., Uppsala University, 1948), chap. 3.

The other side of the picture is seen in Lucian's *Menippus*. Disillusioned by the unresolved contradictions in the teaching of all human philosophers, he went to the underworld and there inquired of Teiresias what sort of life he considered best. The reply he received was that the life of ordinary people is the best:

> And you will act more wisely if you stop speculating about heavenly bodies and discussing final causes and first causes, spit your scorn at those clever syllogisms, and counting all that sort of thing nonsense, make it always your sole object to put the present to good use and to hasten on your way, laughing a great deal and taking nothing seriously (*Menippus* 21; LCL 162: 107–9).

# THE SAGE IN SELECT HELLENISTIC AND ROMAN LITERARY GENRES
## (PHILOSOPHIC EPISTLES, POLITICAL DISCOURSES, HISTORY, COMEDY, AND ROMANCES)

## Benjamin Fiore

What constitutes the life of the ideal sage (*ho sophos*) or sage in practical affairs (*ho phronimos*) was a matter of intense debate not only among the philosophers but also among writers of a number of other literary genres in the Hellenistic period. With the demise of Persian rule and its replacement by the successors of Alexander, several factors conspired to compel an increasing number of individuals to look beyond the confines of the local village or polis for life's values and direction—the expansion of education and reading, the development of a cosmopolitan culture that cut across lines of political control, the emergence of new philosophies and religions vying for new adherents, and the conscious attempt to apply Greek philosophic concepts in the very shaping of entities larger than the city-state. As Edwyn Bevan put it a number of years ago, with the emergence of the Hellenistic era, the goddess Tyche (Fortune) loomed larger and more potent than the Olympian pantheon of a bygone era.[1] Some philosophers strove to advise people on how to attain happiness in the midst of the turmoil of

Benjamin Fiore, S.J., is Professor of Religious Studies at Canisius College.

Classical references may be traced through the abbreviation lists in *A Greek-English Lexicon* by H. G. Liddell and R. Scott (ed. H. S. Jones et al.; 9th ed.; Oxford: Clarendon, 1940; with *Supplement*, ed. E. A. Barber et al., 1968). For convenience, the volume and page numbers are also given of the English translation in the Loeb Classical Library (LCL), copublished by Harvard University Press and William Heinemann.

1. E. Bevan, "Hellenistic Popular Philosophy," *The Hellenistic Age* (by J. B. Bury et al.; Cambridge: Cambridge University, 1925) 79–81.

the new realities. Other philosophers advised bureaucrats, rulers, and kings on the nature of virtue and proper conduct in public service. Historians interpreted the exploits of great men, the flow of events, and the rise of Hellenistic (and Roman) power in the light of the newly emerging world views. At the same time litterateurs with an eye to the populace altered older forms both to express new insights and to cater to current preoccupations and tastes.

## THE SAGE IN PHILOSOPHIC EPISTLES

The philosophers sought to guide people to happiness (*eudaimonia*) by developing strategies of self-sufficiency (*autarkeia*) and imperturbability (*ataraxia*). The sage who exercised dispassion (*apatheia*) would thus be freed from preoccupation with the vicissitudes of life and from the caprice of the gods or chance. This process necessitated a degree of withdrawal (total for the Epicureans, attitudinal for the Stoics) from civic and social entanglements. The Hellenistic focus on the individual, then, finds expression in the philosophical ideal of the sage. Practical wisdom (*phronēsis*), however, was cultivated as Epicurean and Cynic philosophers turned from physics and metaphysics to ethics.[2]

While the Stoics were primarily responsible for the formation of the typical ideal of the wise person (*ho sophos*) in the Hellenistic period, the Cynics—building upon the teaching of Epicurus[3]—have left in their letters an informative literary record of the process of reaching a definition of the practical sage (*ho phronimos*). Epistles, with their dialogue tone and philophronetic character evoke the face-to-face instructional sessions between teacher and pupil, the public interchange between moralizing preacher and audience, and the admonitions of duties outlined by a superior for subordinates.[4] They were thus particularly well suited for the work of exhortation, since the audience, while participants in the epistolary dialogue, could assume the relatively unthreatening posture of observer, and yet find in the letters matters pertinent to their own situation. The hortatory epistle, one of the letter forms taught in the schools of the Hellenistic period, was adopted by philosophical schools and individual teachers as a means of teaching

2. H. Koester, *History, Culture, and Religion of the Hellenistic Age* (New York/ Berlin: de Gruyter, 1987) 146–47; J. M. Rist, "Are You a Stoic? The Case of Marcus Aurelius," *Jewish and Christian Self-Definition*, vol. 3: *Self-Definition in the Greco-Roman World* (ed. B. F. Meyer and E. P. Sanders; Philadelphia: Fortress, 1983) 23–45; M. Pohlenz, *L'Uomo Greco* (Florence: La Nuova Italia, 1962) 630–53.

3. See G. B. Kerferd's essay in this volume, "The Sage in Hellenistic Philosophical Literature" (pp. 319–28 above), and Koester, *History, Culture, and Religion,* 156.

4. See my book, *The Function of Personal Example in the Socratic and Pastoral Epistles* (Analecta Biblica 105; Rome: Biblical Institute, 1986) 11–12, 42–44.

and maintaining contact among adherents spread across the map of the Hellenistic world. Cicero, Seneca, and Pliny exemplify the practice in the Roman world, as do the Cynic epistles in the Greek world.[5] In fact, the letter itself, a surrogate for the writer's presence and often with references to the writer's attitudes and actions, takes on the function of an example of the teaching it contains (e.g., Seneca, *Epistulae Morales* 71:7; LCL 76: 73).[6] The letter was particularly well suited to Cynic pedagogy, which began with a provocative action or dictum designed to lead the prospective disciple to question one's way of life and then proceeded with an exposition of Cynic principles (*logos*) supported by the living example of the teacher (*bios*). The Cynic letters are constructed around provocative anecdotes and sayings for which they also supply an interpretation and reason. The *bios* of the letter writer, which the letter stands in for, supports the instruction.[7]

The Cynic letters of Socrates and the Socratics is a collection of largely pseudonymous letters that may be dated, respectively, in the first century C.E. (or earlier) and ca. 200 C.E.[8] Though they come from a period following the close of the Hellenistic era, they reflect as well an earlier school setting in their variety of forms, rhetorical devices, philosophical propositions, and arguments, and they represent an effort at presenting the perduring Cynic ideal of practical philosophy within the context of rhetorical education.[9] As such, they disparage other current literary forms as inadequate to the task, like the Platonic dialogues (*Epistles* 15:3, 23:2) and Xenophontic memorabilia (*Epistles* 15:2, 18:2). The letters' Cynic viewpoint about the ideal sage's way to happiness is hammered out in an epistolary debate between proponents of rigorous and mild Cynicism, with the milder view prevailing as more likely to persuade a wider audience. The Cynics of the Hellenistic period, though without an organized doctrinal system, were not anti-intellectual. Nonetheless, they see the elements of a practical ethical idealism (dress, conduct, self-sufficiency, aversion to excess) as more important than a system.[10] Their goals and strategies continued to have an impact far

5. Ibid., 85–87.

6. Ibid., 89.

7. Ibid., 131; and V. E. Emeljanow, "The Letters of Diogenes" (Ph.D. diss., Stanford University, 1968) 21–31.

8. J. Malherbe (ed.), *The Cynic Epistles: A Study Edition* (Society of Biblical Literature Sources for Biblical Studies 12; Missoula, MT: Scholars Press, 1977) 27–29; a Greek text with English translation by S. Stowers and D. R. Worley is found on pp. 217–307. In my following discussion, references to the Cynic "Letters of Socrates" are cited by epistle and section numbers.

9. See my *Function of Personal Example*, 108–13.

10. A. J. Malherbe, "Self-Definition among Epicureans and Cynics," *Jewish and Christian Self-Definition*, vol. 3: *Self-Definition in the Greco-Roman World* (ed. B. F. Meyer and E. P. Sanders; Philadelphia: Fortress, 1983) 46–59.

beyond the Hellenistic period. Thus the emperor Julian (331–363 c.e.) expressed the Cynic strategy when he counseled that change and the process of unlearning vice had to come first, and then came the attempt to live by intelligence and reason alone (Julian, *Orations* 6:201D; LCL 29: 59) and to refrain from what one ought not do because it is "forbidden by reason and the god within us, that is, the mind" (*Orations* 6:196D; LCL 29: 47). The mild Cynic, less proud and aloof than the austere Cynic, is, like the latter, above the common crowd and self-sufficient, rejecting popular values (*Epistle* 6:2–4). But a measure of "hedonism" does not detract from this Cynic's *phronēsis* (*Epistle* 9:3) and the earnest sage (*ho spoudaios/ho phronimos*) can associate with the common crowd (*Epistle* 8) as counselor and guide without harm to oneself since God has been both to the Cynic (*Epistle* 1.2, 10–12). The Cynic can improve society by involvement in the public arena and so need not persist in the abusive frankness (*parrēsia*) and antisocial behavior of the austere Cynic, who challenges individuals from a place at the margins of society.

The Cynic letters thus present the Cynic ideal of the practical sage in the form of an example of a way of life sure to benefit both the individual and society. The ideal shows affinity with Stoic emphasis on the importance of rationality in ethics and on freedom from externals in following the rule of reason in nature and themselves. The Cynic ideal shows an even closer affinity with that of the Epicureans who gather in their own circles of friends to live out the precepts of the sage and founder Epicurus. In common with Epicurus, the Cynics exalted the individual of prudence (*ho phronimos*). In common with the Stoics, they taught that even when the rule of reason has given them some civic or political responsibilities they should fulfil them "as if not" caught up in public entanglements.

## THE SAGE IN POLITICAL DISCOURSES

The popular philosophers worked to help people find a secure home within themselves in a world of economic instability, political change, and religious uncertainty. Despite the collapse of the polis and the close support systems of values and traditions, however, there were still public careers in the Hellenistic cities, and attachment to time-honored civic values centered upon service to the polis persisted. The importance of the "homeland" was expressed by Plutarch (ca. 46–125 c.e.) in his *Life of Demosthenes* 2:2 (LCL 99: 1–79), albeit with a tragic touch: "We inhabit a small city and we remain attached to the homeland so it does not become even smaller." In practical fact, more opportunities to rise in elevated administrative positions were open to more people under the successors of Alexander and the Romans than in the Greek city-states, although lacking was the earlier, natural sense of integration into a totality. Instead of civic virtue and a community-based motivation, there arose a system of professional ethics appropriate to the various categories of service.[11] While philosophers attended to the path to happiness (*eudaimonia*) now that the authority of the polis and the communitarian religion lost significance, earlier writers (such as Isocrates and his school) and later writers (such as Plutarch and Dio Chrysostom) outlined civic duties in their discourses to help train successive generations of public servants in the virtues and obligations of their official positions. Thus the ideal of the philosopher-king found a place in Hellenistic and Roman literature.

At the head of the Hellenistic tradition are the discourses of Isocrates (ca. 436–338 B.C.E.) (*Nicocles* and *To Nicocles*; LCL 209: 38–73, 74–116) and his follower (*To Demonicus*; LCL 209: 2–37), paraenetic works in gnomic form on the virtues of good government and citizenship. Philosophic cultivation of a reverent and virtuous life is urged (*Nicocles* 1–9; LCL 209: 76–81) in order to live well (§2) and fulfil the duties of people who are governed (§10). Practical observations and prescriptions to this effect abound and, despite the discussion of the best form of government (§§10–47), characterize this and the other two discourses. Indeed, intelligent conviction as a supplement to a natural inclination to virtue is advanced as the only sure basis for the virtuous life (§§46–47). The fruitless meanderings of the ignorant (§§10ff., and *Epistle* 9:15; LCL 373: 481) are proof of the benefits of knowledge.

That these are school or instructional texts is suggested by the athletic imagery (*Nicocles* 5), the exhortation to constant striving and advancement (§§4–9), the criticism with a view to greater achievement (§§5–6, 78), and the objects of the exhortation, a young ruler and his successors (§§1–2, 10). In fact, despite the more general audience of the "governed" (§10), the discourse seems to appeal to a more restricted group of persons with appointed tasks (§§48, 50), who oversee royal affairs (§49), have access to wealth and reputation (§§49–50), are heads of households, (§51), engage in public life (§52), give counsel (§51), influence successive generations (§57), enjoy royal privileges (§57), can rise in honor and service (§60), and rule others (§62). The discourse thus translates the ideal of the philosopher-king into the duties of the emerging class of officials and administrators. Nicocles is made to pronounce the prescriptions (§§48ff.), but the good king has already demonstrated by example his own realization of their requirements (§§31–45).[12]

11. Pohlenz, *L'Uomo Greco*, 636–37.
12. A. Burk, *Die Pädagogik des Isokrates als Grundlegung des humanistischen Bildungsideals im Vergleich mit dem zeitgenössischen und den modernen Theorien dargestellt* (Würzburg: Drerup, 1923); and my *Function of Personal Example*, 45–67.

Also meant for a broad range of ruling officials are the discourses *To Nicocles* (§§8, 16, 31), which is considered to be the first of the *principis speculum* tradition, and *To Demonicus* (§37), with a more philosophical *paideia* (§§3-5, 12) and less political than *To Nicocles*. Altogether, the three discourses are a type of manual or brochure, instruction booklets of traditional wisdom (*To Nicocles* 40ff., and *To Demonicus* 54) from which the audience can draw when the occasion calls for it (*To Demonicus* 44).

Successors to the Isocratean works in the Roman period are the "kingship treatises" of Plutarch and Dio Chrysostom (ca. 40-120 C.E.). In Plutarch's *Ad principem ineruditum* (*To an Uneducated Ruler*) philosophy is again offered as a help and protection (779F; LCL 321: 55). Lists of virtues (781A, C; LCL 321: 61-63) and vices (780A, 782C, E; LCL 321: 67-69) replace Isocrates' prescriptions in spelling out what to do and to avoid. These are filled out in examples of attitude and conduct to pursue and avoid (e.g., 779F-80B, 780F-81A; LCL 321: 53-57, 59-61). Plutarch's *Praecepta gerendae reipublicae* (*Precepts of Statecraft*) does offer prescriptions to the young addressee in addition to examples of all sorts (798A-C; LCL 321: 159-61) and lists of virtues and vices. The last mentioned are a characteristic feature of the kingship treatise and well represented in Dio Chrysostom's descriptions of the ideal king (e.g., *Discourses* 1:11-14, 3:29-41, 4:7-10; LCL 257: 7-11, 117-23, 171-73). Dio chooses to describe rather than prescribe (which Isocrates and Plutarch do).[13] The paradigm for future rulers in kingship treatises like Dio's is thus a special case of the depiction in popular philosophy of the ideal sage, and the vices and virtues listed vary with the philosophical orientations of the authors.[14] Political realism also breaks through a description like Plutarch's in *Praecepta gerendae reipublicae* (824E; LCL 321: 293) when he sees a life of harmony and quiet the one advantage for wise people in a subject nation like Greece, both for the intrinsic value of tranquillity and to avoid provoking interference from external forces (also 814A-16A, 823F-24D; LCL 321: 237-49, 289-93).[15] The kingship treatises thus represent the application of the ideal of the philosopher-king to the realities of public life in both

---

13. R. Höistad, "Cynic Hero and Cynic King: Studies in the Cynic Conception of Man" (Inaugural diss., Uppsala University, 1948) 161-62, 184-87, 213-15. See also C. Préaux, "L'image du roi de l'époque hellénistique," *Images of Man in Ancient and Medieval Thought: Studia Gerardo Verbeke* (ed. F. Bossier; Louvain: Leuven University, 1976) 53-75.

14. E. Kamlah, *Die Form der katalogischen Paränese im Neuen Testament* (Wissenschaftliche Untersuchungen zum Neuen Testament 7; Tübingen: Mohr/Siebeck, 1964) 146ff.

15. See my *Function of Personal Example*, 67-77.

the Hellenistic and Roman periods. Time-honored virtues are still extolled and enjoined upon the young official careerists, the measure of
whose success is the degree to which they incorporate and exemplify
the long-standing communal values. The ideal of the sage is presented
as accessible and necessary for a fully satisfactory career as a public
official.

## THE SAGE IN HISTORICAL WRITING

The kingship treatises promoted the ideal of the wise ruler and public
official. Polybius (ca. 200–120 B.C.E.), in his survey of Roman history,
saw the ideal in operation and, for that matter, as the decisive factor in
historical events and the persons who acted with success in them.
Polybius prized the powers of the intellect not just in the subjects of his
history but in himself as well. The historian's task was not simply to
create a narration of the events but a demonstration of a thesis interpreting them. Not a creator of an oratorical encomium that downplays
the negative, the historian had to tell the truth and make judgments
with both praise and blame, and thus prove that the history so recorded
was the logical truth by reasonings (*syllogismoi*) and by a system of
rational connections (2:37:3; LCL 128: 333).[16] In this way, the past can
caution and instruct for the future, and history can be useful (2:61:3,
12:25:3; LCL 128: 391; 159: 381). Polybius shared the Greek conviction
that "man is always equal to himself in his actions and the norms of
conduct remain structurally identical and substantially similar in their
content." One need only know how to discover and investigate them.
Polybius thus aims to give a pragmatic wisdom to Greece and Rome in
his work by elaborating in it a paradigm, the most secure form of
education (1:35:7ff.; LCL 128: 99). He therefore presents a "manual of
ethical and technical duties" and examples of comportment that constitute the most efficacious paradigms of leaders for their successors
(2:56:11–13; LCL 128: 371).[17]

For Polybius the *nous* ('mind') is the supreme faculty, not in Plato's
sense of an intuitive grasp of essences but as discursive reason that
regulates conduct after judgment and knowledge. And so, he looks for
the same qualities in the figures of history as those by which he expects
the historian to operate. He finds two basic character types: (1) those
entirely reasonable who guide themselves by rigorous logic and obtain

16. P. Pédech, *La Méthode historique de Polybe* (Paris: "Les Belles Letters," 1964)
44ff.

17. A. Roveri, *Studi su Polibio* (Bologna: Zanichelli, 1964) 95, 105, 117–19, 135;
Pédech, *La Méthode historique de Polybe*, 50.

results conformed to their reasonings, and (2) those in whom irrational forces disturb the functions of the logical power and who thus fail in their undertakings. Of all his heroes the two Scipios stand out as persons without passion and accident in their character (10:9:3–7, 10:38:3, 21:15:6; LCL 159: 121, 193–95; 160: 263), who act reasonably and intelligently (10:2:6, 11:21:2, 15:7:1; LCL 159: 105, 271, 479), and who rely on reason rather than fortune (10:7:3; LCL 159: 115–17), finding solutions to problematic situations by vigorous calculations (10:5:6, 7:1, 8:8, 35:1; 14:4:4; LCL 159: 111, 115, 119, 189, 441).[18]

Polybius thus presents the exemplary sage as *anēr pragmatikos kai nounechēs* and different from the Socratic/Platonic *kalos k'agathos*. He does not just seek interior perfection by regulating himself according to a transcendent norm but also seeks "the development and a better usage of his natural faculties in public life." In his thesis that the success of great people is due to their reason (10:2:8; LCL 159: 105) he is expressing the historical reality of the philosophical ideal of the sage.[19] He is also using history to urge by example what the kingship treatises do through precept and direct description, though example looms large as a hortatory device in those works as well.


## THE SAGE IN NEW COMEDY

From what has gone before, one would get the impression that the sage and the philosophical route to becoming one were always treated with awe and reverence. For a glimpse at the humorous side, one need only recall the creation by Menippus of Gadara (4th–3d cents. B.C.E.) of the literary tradition of the *spoudogeloion* to which the later Lucian owes a debt, or the "Silloi" ("Lampoons") of the Sceptic Timon of Phlius (born ca. 320–310 B.C.E.), where in mock epic style he exposes the weaknesses and exaggerations of various pundits.[20] New Comedy falls into this irreverent tradition. Its comedic horizons, however, are narrower than those of the satirical romps of older comedians like Aristophanes in that there is increasingly less sexual language and vulgarity, and more chronological and scenic unity, all reflecting a growing inhibition in all the public arts of the period. The local Athenian references (e.g., geographical and political) also give way to allusions proper to the Hellenic

18. Pédech, *La Méthode historique de Polybe*, 211ff.
19. Ibid., 228, 419.
20. Cf. E. A. Barber, "Alexandrian Literature," *The Hellenistic Age* (ed. J. B. Bury et al.; Cambridge: Cambridge University, 1925) 67–75; and A. A. Long, "Timon of Phlius: Pyrrhonist and Satirist," *Proceedings of the Cambridge Philological Society* 204 (1978) 68–91.

world at large and problems of a more universal nature.[21] Worthy sentiments abound in New Comedy, and Greco-Roman moralists, historians, and antiquarians never tire of quoting them. Taken in their contexts, however, the expressions of popular wisdom are as likely to be satirized as endorsed.

Thus the philosophical preoccupation with virtue and moral reputation is cast as remote from the real experiences of life in "Epitrepontes" ("Men at Arbitration") by Menander (ca. 342–292 B.C.E.) when the self-righteous but wayward young husband Charisios comes to realize true virtue and fidelity in his wife whom he falsely suspected of infidelity. In the same play (§§1084–99; LCL 132: 510–12) the slave Onesimus delays the irate father-in-law by engaging in philosophical ruminations on concern for humankind, thus painting philosophy as an idle waste of time. Similarly, the busybody neighbor Chremes in Menander's "Heauton Timoroumenos" (LCL 132: 348–49) passes judgment on situations (§§119–20, 151–57) but does not take his own advice, banal as it is (§§209–10), and is preoccupied with appearance as much as with truth (§§469–89, 572–78). His platitudes on education, while true, assume a satirical color in his mouth (§§151–57, 200–210, 469–89).[22]

In "Rudens," a Roman adaptation of a Greek New Comedy model, by Plautus (d. 184 B.C.E.), the platitudinous moralizing by "people in comedies" is also exposed, in this instance by the figure Gripus who unmasks Daemones' noble sentiments on human greed as irrelevant to his own actions guided as they are by a personal, bourgeois morality (§§1235–45; LCL 260: 413). Likewise, the figure Pseudolus's comments on self-confidence as a counter to Fortune's dominance ("Pseudolus" 678–87; LCL 260: 219–21), while voicing an acknowledged truth, are relativized by their being pronounced in a scene that Fortune alone has made possible.

Thus the poets of New Comedy included heavy doses of moralizing sentiments, which undoubtedly appealed to their audiences. Nonetheless, they exploited these sentiments for humorous effects in the scenic contexts where they are voiced. The sages and their wise utterances are taken with a grain of salt as they appear in far from ideal situations and on the lips of less than exemplary characters. In this way the jaundiced eye of the comic poet turns the moralizing hype of the educational and philosophical establishment to an advantage.

21. R. L. Hunter, *The New Comedy of Greece and Rome* (Cambridge: Cambridge University, 1985) 12–13.
22. Ibid., 99–100, 139–41, 147, 149–50.

## THE SAGE IN HELLENISTIC ROMANCES

The New Comedy has thus shown how not all literary efforts were created to inform and edify. The aim of the former was simply to entertain and in so doing to make sport of hallowed themes.[23] The work of Polybius also demonstrated how Hellenistic authors reveled in erudition. Finally, the Hellenistic romances combine both tendencies and in common with the New Comedy concentrate not on grand, universal, tragic concerns or on the heroic dimensions of human beings, but on more self-centered thoughts and private concerns. Focusing on individuals in love, they parade a great variety of characters through fanciful settings and unusual circumstances. In their narratives they call upon Sophistic rhetoric and encyclopedic learning with increasing frequency as the genre develops. And they do so in connection with the most unlikely characters and situations with playful effect. Learning permeates these novelistic creations. Indeed, Achilles Tatius (fl. 2d cent. C.E.) identifies love as *autodidaktos sophistēs* (a 'self-taught master'; 1:10:1, 5:27:4; LCL 45: 33, 303). He thereby gives a surprising twist to the notion of the sage.[24] The characters of the romances also display great learning, although in incongruous and amusing ways. In fact, the unexpected joining of love themes, sophistic rhetoric, and scholarly learning make adoxography one of the most prominent rhetorical devices exploited in these works, one whereby trivial material is given mock-serious treatment, all to humorous effect.[25] Thus, Achilles Tatius in his *Clitophon and Leucippe* has Cleinias in a soliloquy present a disquisition on the theme "whether to marry" when he realizes that his boyfriend is about to do just that (1:8:1ff.; LCL 45: 25). Elsewhere (§2:8; LCL 45: 69-71) he has Clitophon pronounce a lengthy dissertation (*ecphrasis*) on love's physiology, a topic suggested by the lover's kiss.[26] The latter's ecphrasis on the sexual characteristics of palm trees and other wonders of nature intellectualizes a scene set for seduction (1:16:1; LCL 45: 49), and he derives great satisfaction from his beloved Leucippe's response to his lecture in *Naturwissenschaft*. To add to the humorous incongruity, the audience finds in the ecphrasis a touching lesson on love and fidelity.[27]

23. B. E. Perry, *The Ancient Romances: A Literary-Historical Account of Their Origins* (Berkeley: University of California, 1967) 6-7, 34-35; G. L. Schmeling, *Chariton* (New York: Twayne, 1974) 34-36.

24. G. Anderson, *Eros Sophistes: Ancient Novelists at Play* (Chico, CA: Scholars Press, 1952) 25.

25. Ibid., 7.

26. Ibid., 25-26.

27. G. Anderson, *Ancient Fiction: The Novel in the Graeco-Roman World* (London: Croom Helm, 1984) 49-50; see also T. Hägg, *The Novel in Antiquity* (Berkeley: University of California, 1983) 44-54.

Other romance writers also have their characters exhibit learning. Longus (2d–6th cents. c.e.) in *Daphnis and Chloe* presents Daphnis as knowing more about love than Chloe, but both are naïve rustics (3:22:4–23:5; LCL 69: 161). Nonetheless, like the older and wiser Philetas, who provides a rustic explanation of love (2:3–2:7; LCL 69: 69), they prove more successful in their aims and enjoy a more sympathetic treatment than the characters with more education, like Dorcon (1:15–16, 1:29–30; LCL 69: 31–35, 53–57), the young men from Methymna (2:15–17; LCL 69: 89–91) and the parasite turned sophist (4:17:3–18:1; LCL 69: 215–17). The rustics, in the end, know about love and enjoy its expression, while the sophisticated audience is left to consider the implications of the contrast drawn between the rustics and the learned.[28]

The veneer of education in these works also produced some surprising formulations of the coexistence of love and learning, like the discussion of love by Metiochus at a banquet in the presence of his beloved and a pre-Socratic philosopher where he finds love an "intellectual impulse activated by beauty and aggravated by association" (*Metiochus* 27–29; anon. fr. 2d cent. c.e.).[29] More often, however, reservations like those in *Daphnis and Chloe* are voiced. Similar to the reservations there about wisdom learned in school is the burlesque of Petronius (d. 66 c.e.) in *Cena Trimalchionis*. Here the thoroughly modern student Encolpius, dissatisfied both with the smug world of academe and contemporary society, judges them by his oversophisticated norms (1:1–3:1; LCL 15: 3–7). His learning is contrasted with the old-fashioned but honest education of the freedman (1:8:7, 13–14; LCL 15: 13–15). A trendy but cynical teacher is thrown in (1:3:2; LCL 15: 7) to drive the contrast home.[30]

A somewhat different treatment of learning appears in the romance of Chariton (1st cent. b.c.e.–2d cent. c.e.), *Chaereas and Callirhoe*. In a learned adaptation to an amorous expedition of the speech of Pericles in Thucydides 2:40:1 (LCL 108: 327), Chaereas contemns the Tyrians as employing boastful presumption rather than a prudent mind (7:3:9). The altered classical text is an aspect of the learning in the romances generally. Moreover, the characters of this early, historiographical romance seem to exhibit the qualities of the wise ruler; for example, the Persian king Artaxerxes displays a spirit of moderation, justice, and self-control (5:2:3, 4:8), and Dionysius struggles with his sense of justice, respect for marriage and law, self-control, and prudence in seeking advice (4:6:3–8, 5:8:8–9, 6:3:7–8, 6:4:8).[31] Of course, Dionysius fails to

28. Anderson, *Ancient Fiction*, 50.

29. Published in *Hermes* 30 (1983) 144–50.

30. Ibid., 51.

31. J. Helms, *Character Portrayal in the Romance of Chariton* (The Hague/Paris: Mouton, 1966) 80–86.

maintain his integrity because he succumbs to the blandishments of the unscrupulous eunuch-slave Artaxates, who is interested only in immediate profit and the gratification of desires. He uses flattery and gives the advice he judges his listeners want to hear (6:3:8–9, 6:4:7, 6:7:7). Theron is a similar immoral rascal.[32] The values of the sage are well represented, and with respect, in this romance. In the final analysis, Chariton so projects these values onto his characters that the Persian king Artaxerxes, for example, is less Persian royalty than middle-class Greek.[33]

A rather late romance underlines the independence already noted in the works of this genre with respect to their attitude toward learning and the sage and his values. Thus *The Romance of Alexander the Great* (ca. 300 C.E.) by Pseudo-Callisthenes narrates repeated praises of the wisdom of the young Alexander (§§63, 106, 108, 152, 211, 245), and includes an accolade from his teacher Aristotle for his wisdom and critical judgment (§41).[34] And, to be sure, he acts judiciously in his campaigns and victories, modestly refusing distinctive gifts and superlative praises. He faults others, like Darius, for arrogance and assumption of divine prerogatives (§107), and is credited with understanding the barbarian Persians' stupidity and foolishness (§185). As such, he seems to embody the Polybian ideal.

Just as in the case of his wise father, Egyptian king Nectanebos, however, who ends up relying on magic and astrology, so Alexander's victories are attributed to the un-Polybian factors of fate or providence (§§199, 223) as much as to his own wise actions (§§63, 211, 245). Moreover, shrewdness, decisiveness, and aggressiveness (§§108, 152, 211) are attributes that make his wisdom practical and focused on proximate and tangible goals. The language is redolent of the ideal sage but the narration depicts a man of action rather than a man of learning (despite his call for ten Athenian orators as preceptors and teachers [§146], and his recognition of Aristotle as teacher and guide [§209]). The spirit of the romance, with its fascination with strange people and places and its focus on a hero chosen by fate to be successful in meeting all challenges, rules this work and informs the concept of the sage here.

The sage thus finds a variety of faces in Hellenistic romance literature. Perhaps one might say that, by and large, learning replaces wisdom in this literature for the entertainment of a learned audience.

---

32. Ibid., 89–103.

33. Schmeling, *Chariton*, 33.

34. Paragraph numbers follow A. M. Wolohojian, *The Romance of Alexander the Great* (New York: Columbia University, 1969); the Armenian text was first published by R. Treanc, *The History of Alexander of Macedon* (Venice: Mechitarist Fathers, 1842).

## CONCLUSION

Other aspects of the sage in Hellenistic and Roman literature remain unexplored as this study reaches its close: biography, propagandistic literature, epideictic and panegyric works, satire, and poetic literature generally. The literary genres that have been surveyed indicate the prominence of the practical and ideal sage in Hellenistic and Roman literature and that the treatment of both ranged from reverence to burlesque.

# THE SAGE IN
# THE APOCALYPTIC AND
# PSEUDEPIGRAPHIC LITERATURE

## John J. Collins

In the second volume of his *Old Testament Theology* Gerhard von Rad advanced the controversial thesis that the Jewish apocalyptic literature was the child of wisdom rather than of prophecy.[1] This proposal has been widely criticized and is certainly one-sided,[2] but it has the merit of drawing attention to some hitherto neglected aspects of the apocalyptic books. Not least among these is the fact that the figures to whom the major apocalypses are ascribed, Enoch, Daniel, Ezra, Baruch, are sages or scribes. Daniel came to be regarded as a prophet already in antiquity (Matt 24:15; Josephus, *Antiquities* 10:11:7) but in the Hebrew Bible he is presented as a *maśkîl* and included among the wise men of Babylon (Dan 2:13).[3] There is here a certain blurring of the distinction between sage and prophet, and the apocalyptic sages bear greater resemblance to Ezekiel or Zechariah than to Sirach or Ecclesiastes, but they are sages nonetheless. It may fairly be argued that the earliest apocalypses of Enoch and Daniel mark the emergence of a new ideal of sage in Judaism.

John J. Collins is Professor of Christianity and Judaism in Antiquity at the University of Notre Dame.

1. G. von Rad, *Theologie des Alten Testaments* (5th ed.; Munich: Kaiser, 1968) 316–38. For the English translation of an earlier edition see *Old Testament Theology* (New York: Harper & Row, 1967), 2:301–15.

2. See the recent assessments by M. Knibb, "Prophecy and the Emergence of the Jewish Apocalypses," *Israel's Prophetic Tradition: Essays in Honour of Peter R. Ackroyd* (ed. R. Coggins, A. Phillips, and M. Knibb; Cambridge: Cambridge University, 1982) 165–69; M. E. Stone, "Apocalyptic Literature," *Jewish Writings of the Second Temple Period* (ed. M. E. Stone; Compendia Rerum Iudaicarum ad Novum Testamentum 2.2; Philadelphia: Fortress, 1984) 388–89; and my *The Apocalyptic Imagination* (New York: Crossroad, 1984) 17.

3. See the reflections of K. Koch, "Is Daniel Also among the Prophets?" *Interpretation* 39 (1985) 117–30.

## THE FIGURE OF ENOCH

Since the publication of the Aramaic fragments from Qumran in 1976,[4] it is generally acknowledged that the earliest parts of *1 Enoch* were composed before the Maccabean revolt and that at least their literary sources go back to the third century B.C.E.[5] A certain amount of speculation on the figure of Enoch is presupposed already in the P source in Genesis but not the full legend of Enoch as we find it in *1 Enoch*.[6] The primary narrative about Enoch is found in the first section of the book, commonly called the "Book of the Watchers" (*1 Enoch* 1–36), where Enoch is introduced abruptly in chap. 12:

> And before everything Enoch had been hidden and none of the sons of men knew where he was hidden or where he was, or what had happened. And all his doings were with the Holy Ones and with the Watchers in his days. And I, Enoch, was blessing the Great Lord and the King of Eternity and behold the Watchers called to me, Enoch the scribe, and said to me: "Enoch, scribe of righteousness, go, inform the Watchers of heaven who have left the high heaven. . . ." (*1 Enoch* 12:1–4)

Enoch, then, is introduced initially in the role of scribe, and his function is one of intermediary between the angels in heaven and their fallen brethren on earth. After he has delivered his message, the watchers on earth

> asked me to write out for them the record of a petition that they might receive forgiveness, and to take the record of their petition up to the Lord in heaven. For they themselves were not able from then on to speak, and they did not raise their eyes to heaven out of shame for the sins for which they had been condemned. And then I wrote out the record of their petition and their supplication in regard to their spirits and the deeds of each one of them, and in regard to what they asked, that they should obtain absolution and forbearance. (*1 Enoch* 13:4–6)

Thus far Enoch is apparently modeled on the familiar figure of the scribe, whose skill in writing gives him importance not only in communication but also in legal proceedings. Another skill is attributed to him in the "Book of the Giants," which is not included in the Ethiopic manuscripts of *1 Enoch* but is attested as part of the Enochic writings at

---

4. J. T. Milik, *The Books of Enoch* (Oxford: Clarendon, 1976).

5. M. E. Stone, *Scriptures, Sects, and Visions* (Philadelphia: Fortress, 1980) 27–47. Milik puts the earliest parts of the corpus several centuries earlier.

6. The link between Enoch and the fallen angels is not made in Genesis.

Qumran, in manuscripts from the first century B.C.E.[7] There the giants seek the services of Enoch, "the scribe of distinction," to interpret a dream. The role of dream interpreter provides an interesting association of Enoch with Daniel, and may also be taken to reflect the actual practice of a class of sages in the ancient Near East.

Enoch, however, is no ordinary scribe since he carries communications between heaven and earth. As such he is also a visionary and even has some of the characteristics of a shaman.[8] In *1 Enoch* 13:7-8 he induces a dream by sitting by the waters of Dan, southwest of Hermon, and reading the petition of the watchers until he falls asleep. In 14:9 he ascends to heaven in his vision. If the sage of Ben Sira travels through the lands of foreign nations (Sir 38:4), Enoch travels to the ends of the earth, with an angelic guide, and sees such inaccessible places as the prison of the host of heaven (18:14), the abodes of the dead (chap. 22), the valley of judgment (chap. 27), and the garden of righteousness (chap. 32). From all of this he is necessarily an expert on cosmology. Similarly, in the "Astronomical Book" (*1 Enoch* 72-82) he is an expert on the movements of the stars, not by the fallible process of human observation, but because "Uriel, the holy angel who was with me and is their leader, showed me" (72:1). The sources of his knowledge are succinctly summarized in the "Apocalypse of Weeks" (*1 Enoch* 93:2): "That which appeared to me in the heavenly vision, and I know from the words of the holy angels and understand from the tablets of heaven"— in short, his wisdom is derived from heavenly revelation.

The claims made for Enoch go far beyond the analogies with ancient Near Eastern scribes. To a great extent he is modeled on the mythological figure of Enmeduranki, founder of the *bārû* guild of diviners and omen interpreters.[9] The correspondences are already in evidence in Genesis. Enoch is placed seventh from creation in the P source (Gen 5:21-24). Enmeduranki is the seventh king in several antediluvian king lists. The age of Enoch, 365 years, suggests an association with the solar year. Enmeduranki is favored by the sun god Shamash, who brings him into his presence. Enmeduranki is not the only model for Enoch in Genesis: the translation of Enoch to the divine realm

---

7. K. Beyer, *Die aramäischen Texte vom Toten Meer* (Göttingen: Vandenhoeck und Ruprecht, 1984) 258-68; J. A. Fitzmyer and D. J. Harrington, *A Manual of Palestinian Aramaic Texts* (Rome: Pontifical Biblical Institute, 1978) 68-79.

8. S. Niditch, "The Visionary," *Ideal Figures in Ancient Judaism* (Society of Biblical Literature Septuagint and Cognate Studies 12; Chico, CA: Scholars Press, 1980) 153-79.

9. See especially J. VanderKam, *Enoch and the Growth of an Apocalyptic Tradition* (CBQMS 16; Washington: Catholic Biblical Association, 1984) 23-51. VanderKam also discusses other proposed Mesopotamian models.

corresponds rather to the Mesopotamian flood hero Utnapishtim. Already by the time the Priestly source was written, however, Enoch was being developed as a Jewish counterpart to the primeval heroes of Mesopotamian myth.[10] The most natural *Sitz im Leben* for this development was in the eastern Diaspora.

Genesis gives no hint of the role of Enoch as revealer, which becomes crucially important in *1 Enoch*. This role is, however, illuminated by the analogy with Enmeduranki. A fragmentary cuneiform text describes how the gods Shamash and Adad brought Enmeduranki into their assembly and "showed him how to observe oil on water, a mystery of Anu, [Enlil and Ea], they gave him the tablet of the gods, the liver, a secret of heaven and [underworld]."[11] He then transmitted this knowledge to the *bārû* guild. Enoch too is taken into the heavenly council and shown the tablets of heaven. While the Jewish text does not pick up the Babylonian methods of divination, Enoch corresponds to Enmeduranki insofar as he is a primeval archetypal mediator of revelation.

Like Enmeduranki, Enoch is a mythical figure. The writings attributed to him are pseudepigraphs. The phenomenon of pseudepigraphy was widespread in the Hellenistic period, and is not adequately explained by any one function.[12] The antiquity of Enoch presumably lent authority to the apocalypses, and permitted them to present an overview of history in the guise of prophecy. It is also likely that the pseudonym had social implications. The Babylonian diviners were regarded as "offspring of Enmeduranki." The books of Enoch often speak of a class of the "righteous and chosen" and Enoch, the righteous scribe, must be considered their prototype. We know regrettably little about this Enochic group. We do not know whether they induced dreams or practiced heavenly ascents, but it is at least clear that they thought about these things. It is also clear that they speculated on cosmology and on the movements of the stars, regarded dreams as valid media of revelation and believed that the course of history and eschatology was inscribed on the tablets of heaven. They were, or at least included in their number, scribes who were familiar with a wide range of ancient lore and who wrote books in the name of Enoch. It is attractive to

10. The assimilation of Jewish heroes to pagan prototypes flourished especially in Hellenistic Judaism. See my *Between Athens and Jerusalem: Jewish Identity in the Hellenistic Diaspora* (New York: Crossroad, 1983) 32–43.

11. W. G. Lambert, "Enmeduranki and Related Matters," *JCS* 21 (1967) 132.

12. B. M. Metzger, "Literary Forgeries and Canonical Pseudepigrapha," *JBL* 91 (1972) 3–24; W. Speyer, *Die literarische Fälschung im heidnischen und christlichen Altertum: Ein Versuch ihrer Deutung* (Munich: Beck, 1971); K. von Fritz, *Pseudopythagorica, Lettres de Platon, Littérature Pseudépigraphe Juive* (Entretiens sur l'antiquité classique 18, pseudepigrapha 1; Geneva: Hardt, 1972).

suppose that they regarded Enoch's ascent as a paradigm for their own mystical experiences, but this must, of course, remain a hypothesis.[13] It is noteworthy that belief in reward and punishment after death first appears in Judaism in books attributed to Enoch, who was himself believed to have been taken up alive to God.

Despite the influence of Enmeduranki on the figure of Enoch, the Jewish sages who produced the Enochic literature were by no means diviners of the Babylonian type.[14] Rather they represented a Jewish alternative to the diviners.[15] They also claimed to know divine mysteries and boasted of an ancient prototype who had ascended to heaven. They were influenced by their Babylonian counterparts in some respects— their high regard for dreams, their interest in the stars and in the tablets of heaven. In accordance with Jewish tradition, they rejected most methods of divination and omen-seeking. What one finds in the Enochic apocalypses is ultimately a new phenomenon, which draws motifs and patterns from many sources, both pagan and biblical, but which cannot be adequately understood as the sum of its sources. Apocalyptic wisdom continues to share some assumptions with Babylonian divination, which were also widespread in the Hellenistic world.[16] It is wisdom encoded in mysterious signs, not the straightforward, empirical wisdom of Proverbs and Sirach, and it carries with it the implication that the course of history has been determined on the heavenly tablets.[17] For the decoding of these mysteries, however, the Jewish sages relied not primarily on divinatory techniques but on what they believed to be divine revelation.

## THE FIGURE OF DANIEL

The analogies with Enmeduranki suggest that the figure of Enoch was originally developed in the eastern Diaspora, although the place of

---

13. See M. Himmelfarb, "From Prophecy to Apocalypse: The *Book of the Watchers* and Tours of Heaven," *Jewish Spirituality: From the Bible through the Middle Ages* (ed. A. Green; World Spirituality 13; New York: Crossroad, 1986) 153–54.

14. VanderKam, *Enoch and the Growth of an Apocalyptic Tradition*, 62, notes the dissimilarity between the literature of divination and the apocalypses.

15. Compare the polemic against Babylonian divination in Second Isaiah (Isa 44:25–26, 47:13) and the contrast between Daniel and the wise men of Babylon in Daniel 1–6. See further my essay, "The Place of Apocalypticism in the Religion of Israel," *Ancient Israelite Religion: Essays in Honor of Frank Moore Cross* (ed. P. D. Miller, P. D. Hanson, and S. D. McBride; Philadelphia: Fortress, 1987) 543–44.

16. Compare my remarks in "Jewish Apocalyptic against Its Hellenistic Near Eastern Environment," *BASOR* 220 (1975) 27–36.

17. H.-P. Müller, "Mantische Weisheit und Apokalyptik," *Congress Volume: Uppsala 1971* (VTSup 22; Leiden: Brill, 1972) 268–93, has aptly named this kind of wisdom "mantic wisdom."

composition of the earliest extant Enochic writings remains quite uncertain. One encounters a similar situation in the Book of Daniel. The stories in Daniel 1-6 are explicitly set in Babylon, where Daniel and his companions are trained as professional courtiers. It does not, of course, automatically follow that the stories were composed in Babylon, but the Babylonian setting is most easily explained if at least the underlying tradition originated there.[18] This hypothesis is strengthened by the observation that Babylonian lore is reflected, however inaccurately, in the stories—for example, the legend about Nabonidus in Daniel 4, the name of Belshazzar in Daniel 5.

Unlike Enoch, Daniel is set in postdiluvian history and lives out his career on earth. He can therefore more easily serve as a model to be imitated. He is cast in a quite specific institutional role as courtier. He receives an education in "the letters and language of the Chaldeans" (Dan 1:4) and is thereafter numbered among "the wise men of Babylon" (2:12-13), together with the "magicians, enchanters, sorcerers, and Chaldeans" (2:2). The duties of this class include the interpretation of the king's dreams. When Daniel is successful at this task he is promoted to high administrative office.

There is an obvious parallel between Daniel and the earlier biblical figure of Joseph, but the later stories cannot be explained as a midrash on the Genesis text. Both the Joseph and the Daniel stories belong to a broader genre of court tales, which reflect the similarity in court structures from Egypt to Babylon.[19] While the stories in Daniel 1-6 are obviously legendary, the institutional setting is not incongruous. The argument of W. L. Humphreys that these stories propose "a lifestyle for Diaspora" is convincing, and has been widely accepted.[20]

Within the Babylonian setting, Daniel is distinguished at once by his loyalty to the successive monarchs and his fidelity to Jewish law. Not only is it possible to observe the kosher laws at the royal court, but those who do so outshine their colleagues both in physical appearance and in wisdom. Not only do Daniel and his companions escape punishment for refusing to participate in idolatry, but they ultimately win the respect of the king and promotion in his administration. The stories

18. See further my *Daniel; With an Introduction to Apocalyptic Literature* (Forms of Old Testament Literature 20; Grand Rapids: Eerdmans, 1984) 34-36. For a different approach see J. G. Gammie, "The Classification, Stages of Growth, and Changing Intentions in the Book of Daniel, *JBL* 95 (1976) 196-202, who sets the composition of the tales in Jerusalem in the reign of Ptolemy IV Philopator (221-204 B.C.E.).

19. The genre has most recently been studied by L. Wills, "The Court Legend in Post-Exilic Judaism" (Ph.D. diss., Harvard University, 1987).

20. W. L. Humphreys, "A Life-Style for Diaspora: A Study of the Tales of Esther and Daniel," *JBL* 92 (1973) 211-23.

address the inevitable tension between the particularism of Jewish law and the requirements of serving a pagan ruler and affirm that it can be overcome by the power of God. The message of these tales was most immediately relevant to Jews who worked, in whatever capacity, in the service of foreign governments, and most directly relevant to Jews who served at a royal court. Their relevance was not, of course, restricted to such people. There was also a broader message that true wisdom was founded on fidelity to the God who "gives wisdom to the wise and knowledge to those who have understanding" (2:21). Wisdom comes by revelation from the true God. Prayer and piety are ultimately more important than the technical training of the Chaldeans.

In Dan 1:4, Daniel and his companions are described as *maśkîlîm běkōl ḥokmâ* (RSV: "skilful in all wisdom"). In the last section of the book (11:33, 35; 12:3) *maśkîlîm* is the technical name for the wise Jews who remain faithful at the time of the Maccabean revolt, some of whom are martyred but who are rewarded by exaltation after the resurrection. It is widely recognized that these later chapters (7–12) come from a different situation than the tales in chaps. 1–6. The later chapters clearly focus on the persecution of the Jews by Antiochus Epiphanes in 168–164 B.C.E. While some of the stories in chaps. 1–6 were relevant to that situation, none of them can be shown to have been composed with it in mind. The tales, then, must be regarded as older tradition taken up by the author of chaps. 7–12 in the Maccabean era. The appropriation of the epithet *maśkîlîm* as a label for the heroes of the Maccabean period and the choice of Daniel as pseudonym suggests that the author of chaps. 7–12 wanted to affirm continuity with the heroes of the tales. Comparison and contrast between the two halves of the book provide some interesting insight into the development of the figure of the sage in the Danielic tradition.

While Daniel is presumably still a courtier in chaps. 7–12 he is no longer shown to function in that setting. Rather than interpret dreams and signs for a king, he becomes himself the recipient of revelation, which is interpreted to him by an angel. These chapters are no longer concerned with the problems of a career in foreign service. Instead they are concerned with world history and the survival of the Jewish people. Daniel does not address the Gentile king about these matters, but is caught up in his personal communion with the heavenly world. Ultimately the Book of Daniel holds out the hope that the faithful sages will be elevated to the stars, to join the heavenly host after death.

Martin Buber contrasted the apocalyptic writer with the prophet on the issue of his involvement in this world: "The prophet addresses persons . . . to recognize their situation's demand for decision and to act accordingly. The apocalyptic writer has no audience turned towards him; he speaks into his notebook."[21] One can see how Buber arrived at this assessment if one looks only at the pseudepigraphic figure of Daniel. The apocalyptic writer, however, may be more directly represented in the brief account of the *maśkîlîm* in chap. 11, who do indeed address persons "to recognize their situation's demand for decision and to act accordingly." There does, however, appear to be a change in institutional setting over against the older tales. There is no reason to think that the *maśkîlîm* worked in foreign service. Their mission was to the Jewish public, to make many understand (11:33). They were apparently teachers, but we are unfortunately uninformed about their social organization.

The *maśkîlîm* of Daniel are often identified with the Hasidim who are mentioned in the books of Maccabees.[22] The Hasidim are described as "mighty warriors of Israel" (1 Macc 2:42), supporters of Judas Maccabeus (2 Macc 14:6), who were the first to seek peace when Alcimus became high priest (1 Macc 7:13). They are probably to be identified with the company of scribes (*synagōgē grammateōn*) who came to Alcimus (1 Macc 7:12). Some modern scholars have also credited them with the composition of the Enochic literature. In fact we know very little about these Hasidim. We are given no account of their beliefs, and so do not know whether they were, or included, apocalyptic visionaries. Their militant character is compatible with some of the Enochic literature, but seems incongruent with the *maśkîlîm* of Daniel. It is possible that "Hasidim" was a broad umbrella term that embraced various strands of Jewish resistance at this time, but this is only a possibility. The available evidence does not allow us to fill out our knowledge of the apocalyptic sages by identifying them with the Hasidic scribes.[23]

The nature of the *maśkîlîm* and their wisdom must be inferred from the Book of Daniel itself. As in *1 Enoch* the Danielic sages deal in a wisdom encoded in mysterious signs—typified for Daniel 1-6 by the writing on the wall as well as by Nebuchadnezzar's dreams. In Daniel 7-12 the primary medium of revelation is the symbolic dream. The sage has now become a recipient of dreams, which must be interpreted

21. M. Buber, "Prophecy, Apocalyptic, and the Historical Hour," *Pointing the Way* (New York: Harper, 1957) 200.

22. E.g., M. Hengel, *Judaism and Hellenism* (Philadelphia: Fortress, 1974), 1:175-218; A. LaCocque, *Daniel et son temps* (Geneva: Labor et Fides, 1983) 131-39; English translation as *Daniel in His Time* (Columbia: University of South Carolina, 1988) 27-32.

23. For critiques of the Hasidic hypothesis see P. R. Davies, "Hasidim in the Maccabean Period," *Journal of Jewish Studies* 28 (1977) 127-40; and my "Daniel and His Social World," *Interpretation* 39 (1985) 132-34. See now also the comprehensive study of the Hasidim by J. Kampen, *The Hasideans and the Origin of Pharisaism* (Society of Biblical Literature Septuagint and Cognate Studies 24; Atlanta: Scholars Press, 1988).

by an angel. In Daniel 9 the prophecy of Jeremiah is also interpreted as a mysterious revelation, analogous to the symbolic dream. Just as four beasts can signify four kings in a dream, so seventy years in a biblical prophecy can signify seventy *weeks* of years. This mode of biblical interpretation expounded to the Danielic sage was subsequently developed at length in the Qumran *Pesharim*. The term *pesher* is already used for the interpretation of dreams and of the writing on the wall in Daniel 1–6.[24]

## THE MANTIC SAGE AND
## INTERPRETATION OF SCRIPTURE

Both *1 Enoch* and Daniel have been aptly described as "mantic wisdom."[25] The sage, then, in these works embraces also mantic activities. In both cases the encounter with Babylonian divination seems to have played a part in the development of apocalyptic wisdom, although the Jewish authors were selective in their borrowings and produced an essentially new genre. The emergence of explicit biblical interpretation for the sage in Daniel 9 is a significant milestone in the integration of apocalyptic wisdom into the biblical tradition. The further course of this development is most clearly seen in the Qumran community. The Dead Sea sect preserved multiple copies of Daniel and the early Enochic writings, and has been called an "apocalyptic community" with some justification.[26] The importance of biblical interpretation for that community is evident in the *Pesharim* and various midrashic writings and in the provision for continual study of the Torah in 1QS 6. Two other major pseudepigraphic writings from around the time of Daniel, *Jubilees* and the *Testament of Moses*, are in large part rewritings of the biblical text. Needless to say, these books do not simply reproduce their biblical models, but reinterpret them in the light of other traditions and new circumstances. Both books, however, present their material under the authority of Moses—a far more central figure in Jewish tradition than either Enoch or Daniel—and both portray him as a sage with heightened prophetic powers (*Jub.* 23:23–31, *T. Mos.* 9–10).

24. On the emergence of "mantological exegesis" in Hellenistic Judaism see M. Fishbane, *Biblical Exegesis in Ancient Israel* (Oxford: Clarendon, 1985) 443–524.

25. Müller, "Mantische Weisheit und Apokalyptik." This subject is explored in detail by S. B. Reid, "The Sociological Setting of the Historical Apocalypses of 1 Enoch and the Book of Daniel" (Ph.D. diss., Emory University, 1981).

26. F. M. Cross, *The Ancient Library of Qumran* (Garden City: Doubleday, 1961) 78. See my comments in *Apocalyptic Imagination*, 115–41.

## EZRA AND BARUCH AS VISIONARY SAGES

The tension between the apocalyptic revelation of the mantic or visionary sage and Mosaic authority comes to the fore in the great apocalypses
from the last first century C.E., *2 Baruch* and *4 Ezra*.[27] These works are
separated from Daniel and the early Enochic books by two-and-one-
half centuries and come from a rather different theological milieu. In his
dialogue with the angel, Ezra pointedly does not ask about the exits of
hell or the entrances of Paradise, since he has neither ascended to
heaven nor descended to the abyss (*4 Ezra* 4:7–9). The passage is
reminiscent of the words of Agur in the Book of Proverbs (30:1–4) and
the contrast with Enoch is presumably deliberate.[28] Yet in the end Ezra
accepts the necessity of apocalyptic revelation, in the form of symbolic
visions that explicitly refer back to Daniel (*4 Ezra* 12–13). Like Daniel,
he stimulates visions by fasting, and, without biblical precedent, by
eating the plants of the field (*4 Ezra* 9:26).

The relation of Ezra's revelation to the Mosaic scriptures is explicitly addressed in chap. 14. There God speaks to Ezra from a bush,
as he had spoken to Moses. Ezra laments that the law has been burnt,
and is commissioned by God to reproduce it. He receives inspiration in
the form of fiery liquid and dictates to five scribes for forty days. In this
time they write out not only the twenty-four books of the Hebrew
scriptures but also seventy others, which are reserved for "the wise
among the people. For in them is the spring of understanding, the
fountain of wisdom, and the river of knowledge" (14:46–47). These
secret revelations had also been given to Moses at Mount Sinai (14:4–6),
but the line of transmission had been broken. Ezra receives a new
revelation of the same data. Since the extrabiblical revelation is secret,
there is no record against which it can be checked. The apocalyptic
writers are, in effect, free to advance their own new revelations, while
claiming—and perhaps believing—that they are only reproductions of
the revelation given to Moses and Ezra.

The figure of Baruch differs from that of Ezra in that his community responsibility is emphasized.[29] He addresses the people at regular intervals throughout the book. The people regard him as a "father"
(*2 Baruch* 32:9) and he reassures them that "Israel will not lack a wise
man, nor the tribe of Jacob a son of the Law" (46:4). The primary
function of the wise man is to instruct and admonish the people to

27. See my *Apocalyptic Imagination*, 155–80.
28. See M. Knibb, "Apocalyptic and Wisdom in 4 Ezra," *Journal for the Study of
Judaism* 13 (1983) 56–74.
29. See especially G. Sayler, *Have the Promises Failed?* (SBLDS 72; Chico, CA:
Scholars Press, 1984) 79–85.

observe the Torah (44:2–3, 45:1–2) for "we have nothing now apart from the Mighty One and his Law" (85:3). Despite these assertions, however, Baruch does offer something more than the law. As surely as Ezra, he is a recipient of apocalyptic visions, which put the law in a broader context, informed by eschatological expectations. There is no opposition between the law and these expectations, but the law alone is no longer sufficient for the pastoral needs of the people.

It is instructive at this point to contrast Baruch with another sage who championed the Torah, Ben Sira. Sirach poured scorn on those who trust in dreams: "As one who catches at a shadow and pursues the wind" (Sir 34:2). He allowed the possibility that they might be sent from God as a visitation (34:6) but insisted that "without such deceptions the law will be fulfilled and wisdom is made perfect in truthful lips" (34:8). Baruch's revelations come in visions in his sleep (*2 Baruch* 36:1, 53:1), which are dreams in fact if not in name. While both sages are concerned with the Torah, the understanding they bring to it is very different.

## CONCLUSION—A SUPERIOR WISDOM

Comparison of Enoch and Daniel, on the one hand, and *4 Ezra* and *2 Baruch*, on the other, shows that there are significant variations in the ideal of the visionary sage in the apocalyptic literature. Further nuances could be added by consideration of the full corpus.[30] There are however some consistent features of apocalyptic wisdom that distinguish it from traditional Hebrew wisdom.[31] Most fundamental of these is the claim to have, and reliance upon, a supernatural revelation. Even a sage like Ezra who disavows heavenly ascents, still relies on dreams and visions. Unlike the personified Wisdom of Proverbs and Sirach, Wisdom in *1 Enoch* found no place where she could dwell, and returned to heaven (*1 Enoch* 42:1). Yet the apocalyptic sage is not at a loss, as Qoheleth was, to know what God had done from beginning to end (Qoh 3:11), because he claims to have access to the recesses of wisdom in the heavens, in the person of the pseudonymous visionary.[32] One

30. See my *Apocalyptic Imagination*, passim. The corpus of pseudepigrapha published by J. H. Charlesworth, *The Old Testament Pseudepigrapha* (2 vols.; Garden City, NY: Doubleday, 1983–85), is much more extensive not only because it includes other genres, but also because it contains much later material (some of which may be as late as the ninth century C.E.).

31. See further my "Cosmos and Salvation: Jewish Wisdom and Apocalyptic in the Hellenistic Age," *History of Religions* 17 (1977) 121–42.

32. The psychology of pseudonymity lies beyond the scope of this essay and in any case has hitherto resisted satisfactory explanation. See the inconclusive remarks of C. Rowland, *The Open Heaven: A Study of Apocalyptic in Judaism and Early Christianity* (New York: Crossroad, 1982) 240–47.

finds, then, in the sages of the apocalypses a denial of earthly wisdom, but also a claim to a higher, superior wisdom.

Rabbinic Judaism did not, on the whole, follow this model of wisdom, but reverted to the tradition of Sirach with its combination of the Torah and human ingenuity. The legacy of the apocalyptic tradition was important for early Christianity, however, where Paul could castigate "the wisdom of this world" and yet claim to impart "a secret and hidden wisdom of God" (1 Cor 2:6, 7).

# THE SAGE IN SIRACH

## John G. Gammie†

### INTRODUCTION

The attempt will be made in this essay to assess Ben Sira's understanding of the various roles and functions of the scholar-sage. Writing as he did, shortly after the Greco-Syrians wrested control over Palestine from the Greco-Egyptians, the author of the Book of Sirach permits the modern reader to gain an insight into the way one ancient Jewish intellectual was urging his compatriots to preserve the traditions of their ancestors and at the same time to function as active and influential citizens within their socio-political world ruled by Hellenists. Carefully delineating the kind, and precise points, of accommodation to Hellenism will be one of the major concerns of this essay. Though it was composed after the Battle of Paneas (ca. 198 B.C.E.), the Book of Sirach affords insights in particular to Jewish life and culture that flourished under the Ptolemies for more than a century of their rule.

Three preliminary matters pertaining to text, composition, and classification must be addressed before my inquiry is undertaken. As is well known, roughly a third of the book is not available in Hebrew (the original language). Further, recent study has shown fairly convincingly that one of the extant Hebrew text traditions from about 50–150 C.E. betrays pietistic alterations.[1] Similarly, a younger Greek textual tradition also reflects a decided emphasis on the importance of reverence.[2] The

John G. Gammie was Emma A. Harwell Professor of Biblical Literature at the University of Tulsa.

All translations from Sirach are my own unless otherwise indicated.

1. See H. P. Rüger, *Text und Textform im hebräischen Sirach: Untersuchungen zur Textgeschichte und Textkritik der hebräischen Sirachfragmente aus der Kairoer Geniza* (BZAW 112; Berlin: de Gruyter, 1970).

2. For thorough discussion and clear delineation of the Greek text, which comes from the early church, see J. Ziegler's magisterial work, *Sapientia Iesu Filii Sirach* (Septuaginta Vetus Testamentum Graecum Auctoritate Academiae Scientairum Gottingensis 12/2; 2d ed.; Göttingen: Vandenhoeck und Ruprecht, 1980).

cautious critic thus has to contend not only with two sets of texts—
Greek and Hebrew—but with two subsets as well.[3] Particularly at issue
are chaps. 36 (33) and 51. Because the tone of chap. 36 (33) is so much
harsher than the rest of Sirach, some have called its authenticity into
question;[4] because Sir 50:27-29 contains a colophon that seems to mark
the conclusion of the collection, even though the Greek, Latin, and
Syriac (Peshitta) versions go on to include the hymn of Sir 51:1-12 and
the biographical, acrostic poem of Sir 51:13-30, quite a few scholars are
hesitant to affirm that either part of this chapter goes back to the
original author.[5]

It is common for students of Sirach to point to the poems on
wisdom as being one of the most distinctive aspects of its composition.
In addition to the poems on wisdom at the beginning (Sir 1:1-10),
middle (Sir 24:1-34), and end of the work (Sir 51:13-30), the first half of
the work in particular is characterized by an interspersal of poems on
wisdom: Sir 4:11-19, 6:18-31, and 14:20-15:10. Wolfgang Roth, following the work of Moshe Zevi Segal, has suggested that the opening poem
of wisdom (Sir 1:1-2:18 [sic]) and each one of the other wisdom poems
in part one of the book (chaps. 1-23) introduce a section in which the
major themes are father (ʾāb; 1:1-4:10), shame (bōšet; 4:11-6:17), arrogance (gāôn; 6:18-14:19), and knowledge (daʿat; 14:20-23:27).[6] This
observation is most appealing because, as the discerning reader will
have noted, the successive sections thematically follow the Hebrew
alphabet: ʾaleph, beth, gimel, and daleth. Roth posits a threefold division
of part two of the book (against the fourfold division of Segal), which

3. A convenient, recent summary of all the extant Hebrew manuscripts and their
locations is given by G. Sauer, Jesus Sirach (Jüdische Schriften aus hellenistisch-römischer
Zeit 3/5; Gütersloh: Gerd Mohn, 1981) 485-86. A synopsis of the text-history of Sirach is
given by M. Gilbert in his recent essay, "Wisdom Literature," Jewish Writings of the
Second Temple Period (ed. M. E. Stone; Compendia Rerum Iudaicarum ad Novum
Testamentum 2.2; Assen: Van Gorcum/Philadelphia: Fortress, 1984) 290-92.

4. Gilbert, "Wisdom Literature," 298. As a counter argument, however, see Sir
50:25-26 on the Samaritans, Philistines, and Shechemites for a judgment that could hardly
be called gentle.

5. Ibid., 298-99. See also the fuller discussion on these and other passages in
T. Middendorp, Die Stellung Jesu Ben Siras zwischen Judentem und Hellenismus (Leiden:
Brill, 1973) 112-36. As is well known, a manuscript of the acrostic poem (Sir 51:13-30)
was found at Qumran. See J. A. Sanders, The Dead Sea Psalms Scroll (Ithaca, NY:
Cornell University, 1967) 112-19; idem, The Psalms of Qumran Cave 11 (Discoveries in
the Judaean Desert 4; Oxford: Oxford University, 1965) 79ff.; P. W. Skehan, "The Acrostic
Poem in Sirach 51:13-30," Harvard Theological Review 64 (1971) 387-400. For a defense
of a Siracide authorship of both of these poems, see P. W. Skehan and A. A. Di Lella, The
Wisdom of Jesus Ben Sira (AB 39; New York: Doubleday, 1987) 560-80.

6. W. Roth, "On the Gnomic-Discursive Wisdom of Jesus Ben Sirach," Semeia 17
(1980) 59-79; and M. Z. Segal, Seper Ben Sîraʾ Hašālēm (2d ed.; Jerusalem: Bialik, 1972).

follows this pattern: prologue (24:1-29), autobiographical note (24:30-34), main body (25:1-32:13); prologue (32:14-33:15), autobiographical note (33:16-18), main body (33:19-38:23); prologue (38:24-39:11), autobiographical note (39:12-15), main body (39:16-50:29). Chapter 51 in Roth's reckoning belonged to the first edition of Sirach (chaps. 1-23 and 51). Although Roth's analysis has the merit of uncovering the strategy of placement of the autobiographical notes in part two, it fails to give proper acknowledgment of the most cohesive portion in the entire book, namely, the beautifully constructed encomium entitled "In Praise of the Fathers" (chaps. 44-50).

As Walter Baumgartner pointed out a number of years ago, the predominance of the hortatory, proverbial sentence and the rhythms of synonymous parallelism in the portions of the book prior to "In Praise of the Fathers" militates against the construction of a sustained, progressive development of thought in large units.[7] Notwithstanding, it is possible to identify a number of clusters of sentences devoted to single themes in which the author does exhort in the style of the premonarchic sages, for example: on listening and speaking (4:20-28; 6:32-37; 9:17-18; 19:5-12; 20:1-8, 24-26; 27:4-7; 33:4-6), on etiquette (31:1-31, 32:1-12), on friends and friendship (6:5-17, 19:13-17, 22:19-26, 27:16-21, 28:8-12, 37:1-6), and on women (26:1-18, 36:22-26, 42:9-14). R. B. Y. Scott has suggested the term "small essays" for such thematic clusters, and points, in addition to the sampling I have just identified, to the following: 12:10-18 (on enemies), 14:11-19 (on seizing the opportunity), 23:7-27 (a "lecture" on swearing, vulgar talk, and sexual immorality), 35:1-20 (on acceptable worship), 38:24-39:11 ("on the superiority of the scribal profession"), 16:24-18:14 ("on the works and mercy of God"), and chaps. 44-49 ("In Praise of the Fathers").[8] The latter two passages are not especially happily classified as "small essays"; rather, Sir 16:24-17:14 is better viewed as a hymn on the theme "The Place of Humanity in Creation" and Sir 18:1-14 as a hymn "On the Greatness of the Creator and Limits of Humanity." Recent study has also shown that "In Praise of the Fathers" must be seen as an encomium crafted in conscious emulation of Greek rhetoric.[9] Other hymns are Sir 39:16-35 ("On the

7. W. Baumgartner, "Die literarischen Gattungen in der Weisheit des Jesus Sirach," *ZAW* 34 (1914) 164.

8. R. B. Y. Scott, *The Way of Wisdom in the Old Testament* (New York: Macmillan, 1971) 207.

9. See especially T. R. Lee, *Studies in the Form of Sirach 44-50* (SBLDS 75; Atlanta: Scholars Press, 1986); and B. L. Mack, *Wisdom and the Hebrew Epic: Ben Sira's Praise of the Fathers* (Chicago Studies in the History of Judaism; Chicago: University of Chicago, 1985). Despite his brilliant analysis of the Greek background of Sirach 44-50, Mack's suggestion that it be considered an epic is unconvincing for the simple reason that this

Works and Providence of God"), 42:15-43:33 ("On the Works and
Judgment of God"), as well as the several odes to wisdom mentioned
above (1:1-20, 4:11-19, 6:18-31, 14:20-15:8, 24:1-29). It is his compositions in the lyrical and hymnic genres of which the author seems to be
especially proud (see Sir 39:12-15). Ben Sira also put his hand to
lamentations (e.g., Sir 22:27-23:6, 33:1-13).

Given the variety of subgenres that Ben Sira employs, how may the
entire work be best classified? A number of years ago J. Coert Rylaarsdam suggested that the wisdom literature of the ancient Near East may
be divided into two kinds: prudential admonitions and reflective essays.[10] In a forthcoming study, following the proclivity of the philosophers and historians of rhetoric to divide the major branches of
rhetoric into two main divisions, I have urged that Rylaarsdam's twofold division be retained, but that the subgenre of prudential admonitions may more properly be called parenetic literature. Sirach possesses
a goodly portion of the features of this secondary literary genre: clusters
of admonitions, exhortations, hymns, wisdom poems, historical surveys,
and encomia. Sirach should not be classified as an instruction (a term
especially favored of similar older parenetic works), nor as parenesis
(for Sirach's very fondness of the hymnic and lyrical is foreign to those
works that can easily be so classified, e.g., the Epistle of James), nor as
protreptic (for Sirach lacks the systematic argumentation characteristic
of this genre).[11] Even though the aforementioned are themselves subgenres of the parenetic literature, the broader classification of parenetic
literature suits Sirach best because it does not easily fit into one of the
narrower subgenres. We are now in a position to examine Ben Sira's
understanding of the sage, and will do so under six headings.


## CONFORMITY WITH THE
## PORTRAIT AND WORLD VIEW OF THE IDEAL
## SAGE OF THE MONARCHIAL PERIOD

In his well-known essay on "The Joseph Narrative and Ancient Wisdom" Gerhard von Rad demonstrated how Joseph conformed to the

---

hymnic encomium does not conform to the most basic definition of an epic as a long
narrative poem that treats a single human character of heroic proportions. For a standard
definition of epic, to which it might be expected that works so classified should comply,
see W. F. Thrall and A. Hibbard, *A Handbook to Literature* (ed. C. H. Holman; New
York: Odyssey, 1960) 174-76.

10. J. C. Rylaarsdam, *Revelation in Jewish Wisdom Literature* (Chicago: University
of Chicago, 1946) 4.

11. For further and more detailed substantiation of these characterizations, see my
essay, "Paraenetic Literature: Toward the Morphology of a Secondary Genre," in a
forthcoming issue of *Semeia* under the title *Paraenesis: Form and Act*, ed. L. G. Perdue
and J. G. Gammie.

portrait of the ideal wise person as set forth in Prov 10:1–22:16.[12] In a similar fashion the ideal wise person of Sirach conforms to that of the indisputably older portion of Proverbs. The sage of Sirach will be an advisor to great men or kings (Sir 39:4; cf. Prov 14:35, 25:15), pious and devoted to prayer (Sir 18:27, 39:5; cf. Prov 14:2; 15:29, 33), one who knows how to conceal his thoughts (Sir 8:19, 9:18; cf. Prov 10:19, 12:23) and how to retain secrets (Sir 19:7–12; cf. Prov 25:9–10), one who will shun adultery (Sir 42:12–14; cf. Prov 23:26–28), able to control his appetites (Sir 31:12–21; cf. Prov 20:25–26) and, especially with respect to the imbibing of wine (Sir 31:25–29; cf. Prov 20:1), careful in the selection of friends and counselors (Sir 37:7–15; cf. Prov 13:20) and one who practices generosity and kindness (Sir 4:1–10, 29:8–13; cf. Prov 11:17, 24, 25).

A similar conformity between Sirach and the older portion of Proverbs may be observed in their respective views of God and the world. As Proverbs stresses the omniscience of God (15:11), so does Sirach (42:18, "He searches out the great deep and the human mind" [Goodspeed trans.]; and 39:19, "nothing is hid from his eyes"). As in Proverbs many good things come from the fear of the Lord, such as long life, honor, avoidance of evil, humility, and riches (Prov 10:27, 15:33, 16:6, 22:4), so for Sirach from the fear of the Lord will follow inter alia faith, reward, joy, obedience, adherence to the divine ways, a satiation with the law, and a humbleness of mind (Sir 2:7–9, 15:17). As in Proverbs there is the closest connection between deed and consequence (cf., e.g., 10:25, 30; 11:17, 25; 13:6, etc.) so in Sirach there is the closest connection and a remarkable similarity throughout of the doctrine of retribution (cf. Sir 7:1–3, 29:11–13, 40:12–17, etc.). Indeed, in Sir 14:3–10 Ben Sira profoundly develops the psychological aspects of the doctrine of retribution found in Proverbs when he demonstrates how it is that the soul of the stingy person becomes shriveled.[13]

In only one regard, insofar as I am able to determine, does Sirach seek to reject and distance himself from an aspect of wisdom that had apparently enjoyed a measure of popularity during the monarchical period. The author of this work shows the greatest reserve with respect

12. G. von Rad, *The Problem of the Hexateuch and Other Essays* (Edinburgh and London: Oliver and Boyd, 1966) 292–300 (repr. in *SAIW* 439–47). This essay was first published in German in 1953.

13. J. L. Crenshaw seems to me to be entirely correct in suggesting that one of the advances that Ben Sira makes over the older doctrine of retribution lies in the area of psychology; see *Old Testament Wisdom: An Introduction* (Atlanta: John Knox, 1981) 172. The above-mentioned Sir 14:3–10 is, in my judgment, the most persuasive example of Ben Sira's advancement of the psychological aspect of the doctrine of retribution. It is less clear to me whether Crenshaw is correct in assessing that Ben Sira makes a real advancement of the doctrine in metaphysical terms; the more significant contribution in this regard rests rather with the Wisdom of Solomon (see chaps. 13–19 and esp. chap. 17).

to the esoteric (Sir 3:21–22), oneiromancy (Sir 34:1–8) in particular, and thus respect for mantic wisdom in general. In recent articles H.-P. Müller has called attention to this strand of wisdom, which should be differentiated from pragmatic prudentialism.[14]

## REVERENCE FOR TORAH YET ASSIMILATIONISM

Ben Sira celebrates the Torah and the fear of God. He, nonetheless, also commends for the ideal sage a cosmopolitanism and openness to converse with foreigners, which ruled out for the sage the possibility of adhering to the dietary laws of the Torah. In the era following the Exile, Israel's sages came more and more to venerate the Torah. As is well known, in one of the postexilic wisdom psalms the word torâ (law) or a synonym thereof is to be found in every one of its 176 verses (Psalm 119). Ben Sira shows himself to be very much in this tradition, which celebrates the Torah. Wisdom found its home in

> the book of the covenant of the Most High, the Law [Torah] which Moses commanded for us as a heritage for the synagogues of Jacob.  (Sir 24:23 Greek)

This law Ben Sira seems to hold in the highest veneration, for he says,

> A reverent person inferior in understanding is superior to the one who abounds in prudence yet transgresses the law.  (Sir 19:24 Greek)

Similarly, like the authors of the wisdom psalms Ben Sira taught that the keeping of the commandments was the way to wisdom (Sir 6:37, 23:27). Indeed, in the keeping of the commandments and in the doing of acts of charity one would lay up for one's self a treasury (Sir 29:11–13). All of these affirmations of the law, however, and all of the many other passages that celebrate the fear of the Lord (Sir 1:10–20, 19:20, 2:6–14, 32:24–33:1, 34:13–14, etc.), cannot cover the fact that Ben Sira had stripped from his understanding of the law and commandments all of the food laws and has redefined the place where the line of separation should be drawn between Jew and Gentile. He takes pride that no foreigner (allogenēs) has ever worn the beautiful robes of the priests in the line of Aaron (Sir 45:13), but he has abandoned the line of separa-

---

14. See H.-P. Müller, "Magisch-mantische Weisheit und die Gestalt Daniels," UF 1 (1969) 79–94, and idem, "Mantische Weisheit und Apokalyptik," Congress Volume: Uppsala 1971 (VTSup 22; Leiden: Brill, 1972) 268–93. Recently J. C. VanderKam has astutely observed that the encoded symbols of Mesopotamian divination and of apocalyptic is precisely what "separates them from biblical prophecy"; Enoch and the Growth of an Apocalyptic Tradition (CBQMS 16; Washington, DC: Catholic Biblical Association, 1984) 62. It might be added: and from most, but not all, of Israelite wisdom.

tion insofar as the ingestion of food is concerned. The importance of this shift in the place where the line of separation should be drawn between Jew and Gentile, it seems to me, has been overlooked in recent discussion on Sirach and his so-called anti-Hellenistic stance.

Instead of Ben Sira's elevation of the law as an evidence of his holding fast to Judaism, the very way in which he dismisses the dietary regulations of the law is exceedingly assimilationist.[15] It is most probably due to his secular tasks as scholar, sage, and jurist that the necessity of a more cosmopolitan and assimilationist stance was thrust upon him, for Ben Sira's ideal sage must be ready, he states, to travel:

> He will serve in the midst of the greats and be seen in the presence of leaders; he will travel in the lands of foreign peoples for he has tested the good things and the bad among human beings. (Sir 39:4 Greek)

Pressing the matter even further Ben Sira sets forth rules for conduct so that his traveler-sage will know how to comport himself in foreign lands (Sir 31:1–31, 32:1–13), for example,

> Eat like a man the things set before you. (Sir 31:16a Greek)

> Should they choose you to preside at a feast, become among them as one of them. (Sir 32:1 Greek)

One can hardly imagine any stance further removed from the priestly dietary regulations of Leviticus 11, or from the Holiness Code of Leviticus 17–26 where the injunction to be holy (Lev 19:2) clearly carries with it the notion of remaining separate. The sage that Ben Sira extols champions a Judaism that will not prevent his serving in foreign courts nor ingesting foreign fare. Thus, even though in several regards the Book of Sirach bears similarities with Pharisaic teaching (an openness to scripture apart from the Torah [Sirach 46–49], belief in angels [Sir 42:17, 45:2; cf. 24:2], and divine ordination of the festivals [Sir 47:10]), in the all important criterion of the dietary laws, Ben Sira is decidedly not proto-Pharisaic.

## RELATIONSHIP WITH THE BOOKS OF CHRONICLES

In order to locate the intellectual and spiritual roots of Ben Sira and in order to begin to differentiate the portrait of the sage in the Book of

15. For a most helpful and provocative discussion of the ways in which separatism and assimilationism affected the shape of postexilic Israel, see Morton Smith, *Palestinian Parties and Politics That Shaped the Old Testament* (New York: Columbia University, 1971), esp. chaps. 6–7. For further consideration of the effect that Ben Sira's advocacy of public service for the ideal sage probably had on the way he articulated his affirmation of Israelite traditions, see pp. 363–64 below.

Sirach from others in the canonical and deuterocanonical literature, it is useful to point to the striking similarities between the Book of Sirach and the Books of Chronicles in the following affinities: theology, apparent tolerance of mixed marriages, pride in the temple and temple worship, and openness to foreigners.

## Theology

*Mercy.* In a recent work James L. Crenshaw has observed, "Sirach's emphasis upon God's mercy set him apart from the earlier sages whose legacy he inherited."[16] Even though Crenshaw cites a portion from chap. 51 (therefore a disputed passage) as an example of the theological stress on the divine mercy in Sirach, the observation remains valid because it is true of other parts of the book.

> Human mercy is on one's neighbor,
> But the mercy of the Lord is for all flesh,
> Reproving, disciplining and teaching,
> And bringing it back as a shepherd does with the flock.
> (Sir 18:13 Greek; cf. Sir 2:7–11; 18:5, 11; 47:22)

A similar stress on the divine mercy is found in Chronicles, as is seen especially clearly in the recurring refrain for forgiveness in Solomon's prayer (1 Chr 6:21, 25, 27, 29; see also 2 Chr 30:17–20).

*Omniscience.* Both works similarly place particular stress on the divine knowledge and ability to search out human hearts (compare Sir 15:19, 39:19, 42:18–20 with 1 Chr 28:8–10).

*Wonders.* Both works show a fascination with the divine accomplishments of wonders, miracles, and miraculous deliverances (compare Sir 43:28–33; 48:4–6, 18–21; 50:22–24 with 2 Chr 13:14–17, 20:13–30).[17]

## On Mixed Marriages

H. G. M. Williamson observed a decade ago in his fine study on the Chronicles: "The Chronicler [i.e., the author of 1 and 2 Chronicles] nowhere condemns mixed marriages, but if anything rather condones them."[18] If one relies on the Greek text of Sir 47:19–21 it would appear that Ben Sira did condemn mixed marriages, for following the praise of Solomon (Sir 47:12–18), one reads:

16. Crenshaw, *Old Testament Wisdom*, 173.
17. For a most engaging study of the thaumaturgical dimension of Chronicles, see W. F. Stinespring, "Eschatology in Chronicles," *JBL* 80 (1961) 209–19.
18. H. G. M. Williamson, *Israel in the Books of Chronicles* (Cambridge: Cambridge University, 1977) 61.

Because you laid your loins down with women,
   You diminished your authority [*enexousiasthēs*] by your body;
*You blemished your glory*
   *and polluted your seed*
*So as to bring wrath on your children,*
   To grieve them for your intemperance,
With the result that the Monarchy became divided,
   And a disobedient kingdom started to rule from Ephraim.

The Hebrew text of the Cairo Genizah, however, which is clearly the more original reading, does not condemn the act of intermarriage, but of sexual profligacy. The phrases italicized above read, in Hebrew:

You put a blemish on your glory and defiled your couch [*yṣwʿyk*].

In neither the Hebrew nor the Greek is the noun for 'women' modified by an adjective for 'foreign'. Thus one may reasonably and surely conclude that Ben Sira, like the Chronicler, nowhere condemns intermarriage—for aside from this *crux interpretum* none are present—and chose to bypass the opportunity to do so when the opportunity was readily at hand. Sexual profligacy rather than miscegenation was Solomon's most grievous offense.

## Pride in the Priesthood, the Temple, and Temple Worship

Sirach's elevation of Aaron (Sir 45:6-22), Phineas (Sir 45:23-24), and Simon (II) the high priest (Sir 50:1-24) is so well known as hardly to need demonstration. Similarly, the centrality of the cultus, the presiding priesthood, and the building of the temple under Solomon constitute the capstone of the Chronicler's theology (see esp. 2 Chronicles 1-9).

## Openness to Foreigners

Similarly, both Sirach and the Books of Chronicles express a deep-seated desire not to separate from foreigners, but rather to implore that they might be impressed by the beauty of the temple, the attainments of the people of Israel, and the majesty of their God. I have already noted above (pp. 360-61) Ben Sira's cosmopolitanism, fondness of travel, and desire to have his ideal sage ready to ascend to serve foreign rulers. Though crafted in Hebrew, Ben Sira's entire encomium of Israel's great men is put in the Greek idiom to reinforce as it were for the devout Jew the extent to which one could take pride in the Hebraic heritage as the Greeks did in theirs. The Chronicler, nurtured under the tolerant rule of a Persian overlord, would seem to be the *fons et origo* of both openness to foreigners and pride in the heritage of temple and people. This dual attitude of openness to foreigners and ethnic pride is perhaps best exemplified by the Chronicler in a petition that occurs near the end of Solomon's prayer:

> The foreigner too, the man who does not belong to thy people Israel, but has come from a distant land because of thy great fame and thy strong hand and arm outstretched, when he comes and prays towards this house, hear from heaven thy dwelling and respond to the call which the foreigner makes to thee, so that like thy people Israel all peoples of the earth may know thy fame and fear thee, and learn that this house which I have built bears thy name.   (2 Chr 6:32–33 NEB)

In three out of four of the above affinities—the exception being the elevation of the temple—the Books of Chronicles and Sirach share a theology and sentiment that they share neither with the authors, nor with the figures, of Ezra and Nehemiah. It is all the more remarkable therefore that Ben Sira gives praise to Nehemiah in the course of his encomium (Sir 49:13)—and perhaps not so remarkable that he omits mention of Ezra. It is noteworthy that Nehemiah is praised neither for his social, political, economic, or religious reforms, nor for his theological positions, but rather for his rebuilding of the walls, gates, and houses. In view of the similarities in the social and religious reforms and programs of Ezra and Nehemiah, it seems plausible to suggest that one should see the withholding of praise from Ezra not only as distancing of Ben Sira from Ezra's views, as Burton L. Mack has recently suggested,[19] but perhaps also as a clue in favor of seeing Ben Sira as a layperson rather than a priest.

## BEN SIRA AS LAY JURIST AND SCRIBE

Ben Sira was of a priestly family and therefore may have been himself a priestly scholar-sage. However, present knowledge of the judicial structures of the Hellenistic era (limited though it is), coupled with what

19. Mack, *Wisdom and the Hebrew Epic*, 119. Mack cites two reasons for the distancing: "First, Ben Sira did not share in the exclusivist notion of Jewish identity and ethic reflected in Ezra–Nehemiah. Second, the harsh judgment upon the sins of the fathers and the people and call to repentance and to Torah piety that pervades this literature run counter to Ben Sira's view of Israel's history." Mack also notes that P. Höffken has come to the same conclusion in his article, "Warum schweig Jesus Sirach über Ezra?" *ZAW* 87 (1975) 184–202. J. Blenkinsopp, who is not as inclined as Williamson, Mack, and others to see the disparity between the views of the Books of Chronicles and Ezra–Nehemiah, however, suggests that Ben Sira may have been a (lay?) temple scribe (*Prophecy and Canon: A Contribution to the Study of Jewish Origins* [Notre Dame, IN: University of Notre Dame, 1977] 130, 132). For the standard defense of the view that Ben Sira was a layperson, see G. F. Moore, *Judaism in the First Centuries of the Christian Era* (3 vols.; Cambridge: Harvard University, 1927–30; repr. New York: Schocken, 1971), 1:42.

Ben Sira says directly about the scribe and sage, makes it more likely that he was not an active priest, but rather a lay jurist, one of whose specialties was secular law.

## The Priestly Connection

According to the colophon of the book the full name of its author was Jesus ben Sira ben Eleazar (Sir 50:27). The facts that the author's grandfather was Eleazar and that the author is so devoted to the priestly tradition of Israel make it highly likely that he came from a priestly family. Whether or not Ben Sira was himself a priest, however, is not therewith established. Primarily on the basis of the words on Moses in the "Praise of the Fathers," Mack has recently inferred that Ben Sira, like Moses, was a priest.[20] A closer look at Ben Sira's references to the scribe and sage elsewhere in the book, and especially at his praise of the scribe and scholar in Sir 38:24–39:11, however, cast at least some doubt on the correctness of Mack's conclusion.

## Legal Service

One of the most distinctive functions of the ideal sage described by Ben Sira in Sir 38:24–39:11 is his service as legal counselor to rulers. Ben Sira says of the craftsmen in contrast to the *sōpēr* (Sir 39:24):

> But they will not be sought after for counsel of the people,
>   And in the assembly they will not rise up to high places;
> Nor will they sit on the judge's chair
>   Nor will they devise a legal contract
> Nor manifest erudition and judgment
>   Nor will they be found among rulers.
>
>                              (Sir 38:33 Greek)[21]

Similarly,

> [The sage] will serve among the greatest and appear before those who lead.   (Sir 39:4a Greek)

> The Gentiles will declare his wisdom and the assembly will proclaim his praise.   (Sir 39:10 Greek)

Ben Sira's ideal sage had attained a knowledge of secular, as well as of Israelite, law. And it was because of his expertise in the former that his counsel would be sought and for which he would attain praise outside Israel.

---

20. Mack, *Wisdom and the Hebrew Epic*, 104–6.
21. For the undoubtedly correct reading of the last phrase, see P. W. Skehan, "They shall not be found in parables (Sir 38:33)," *CBQ* 23 (1961) 40.

## Ptolemaic Tribunals

In her valuable social and economic history, *Le monde hellénistique*, Claire Préaux sketches the outlines of the three major tribunals under the Ptolemies:[22] (1) The *dikastērion* was concerned with matters pertaining to Greeks and immigrants of other origin—notably Jewish. It consisted of ten men, one of whom presided, assisted by one who introduced cases upon the request of the *stratēgos* who governed the nome or district. Prior to appearance before the tribunal the introducer sought to effect a conciliation between the litigants. The judges on the *dikastērion* acted as arbitrators and sort of jury. The laws it applied were royal law, law of the city, and equity ("the opinion of the most just"). Little is known of the *koinodikion* ('mixed tribunal') except the name. (2) The tribunal of the *laokritēs* ('country judge') was an Egyptian tribunal and heard cases in the language of the people, Demotic. The judges were taken from the priests, assisted by an "introducer of cases." Again the *stratēgos* was the intermediary in the introduction of cases, only these were cases among Egyptians themselves, dealing with contracts and the like whether in Greek or Egyptian. This tribunal applied the "law of the country." (3) The third tribunal, the tribunal of the *chrēmatistēs* ('circuit-judge'), consisted of three judges and the introducer of cases. It was instituted in the third century, according to the *Letter of Aristeas* (§111), in order to economize and cut down on the length of time country folk would have to spend in Alexandria for a trial. At first it was an itinerant court but in the second century B.C.E. it became permanent in the nomes. The official title of this tribunal indicates their function and importance: they "judge royal, fiscal, and private affairs." Of this tribunal, Préaux suggests, "The importance of the royal revenues in the Egyptian economy makes it certain that this tribunal had a considerable number of cases to hear."[23] In view of what is said about the sage in Sir 39:4 ("The great avail themselves of his services / and he is seen in the presence of rulers. / He travels to foreign countries / and learns at first hand the good or evil of man's lot"), it would seem that Ben Sira had in mind service either on the *dikastērion* in other nomes or on the itinerant *chrēmatistēs* before it became a permanent court in the nomes. Such service as a jurist would hardly suit simultaneous service as a priest in the temple.

## Scribe

The Greek term for scribe (*grammateus*) occurs but twice in the Book of Sirach (10:5 and 38:24); in both instances a Hebrew text is extant. The first is worth citation in full because it well informs the

22. C. Préaux, *Le monde hellénistique* (2 vols.; Paris: Presses Universitaires de France, 1978), 2:277–80, which I have summarized in this paragraph.
23. Ibid., 279.

reader of the kind of person Ben Sira had in mind who might be called a *měḥōqēq* ('commander' [Judg 5:14] or 'scribe'):

> A wise judge makes his people firm
>    and the one who rules brings an understanding of order.
> A judge's litigants [lit. 'smooth talkers', *mlyṣyw*] are like the judge,
>    and a city's inhabitants are like its head.
> A profligate king may ruin his people
>    but a city will grow by the skill of its princes.
> Rule over continents is in the hand of God
>    and he may cause a man to stand over it for a season.
> Rule over every citizen [*gbr*] is in the hand of God
>    and he places his glory in a scribe's [*mḥwqq*] presence.

(Sir 10:1-5)

If the rabbinic tradition of *b. B. Bat.* 21a is to be relied upon, the original Hebrew of Sir 38:24 was *sōpēr*:

> The wisdom of the scribe will multiply wisdom
>    And the one who does not need to contend (with his hands for a living),
>    that one will become wise.

Under the Ptolemies, an oft-mentioned official was the *basilikos grammateus* ('royal scribe') who served as the "right-hand man" of the *stratēgos* and had the duty "to supervise the working of the government machine generally, but especially the statistical reports and records and all fiscal transactions."[24] A district scribe and a village scribe under the Ptolemies were called, respectively, *topogrammateus* and *komogrammateus*.[25] It thus appears to be the case in the Ptolemaic and Seleucid eras, as well as in the Persian era, that the term for scribe—whether the Hebrew *sōpēr*, the Aramaic *sāpar*, or the Greek *grammateus*—was used as an official designation of a governmental official who performed duties of an administrative, financial, or judicial sort. Such is the case of the use of the term in *Words of Ahiqar* (lines 12, 18, 35-36, 42), the Elephantine Papyri (no. 17, lines 1 and 6), Ezra (7:12, 21), and, as seen above, Sirach (38:24, 33).[26] In view of the aforementioned uses of the term (see also p. 365 above), it would seem safe to conclude that for the postexilic era up until the second century B.C.E. the term scribe was a

---

24. E. Bevan, *A History of Egypt under the Ptolemaic Dynasty* (London: Methuen, 1927; repr. as *The House of Ptolemy* [Chicago: Argonaut, 1968]) 143.

25. Ibid., 143-44.

26. On the use in *Words of Ahiqar* and Elephantine Papyri, see A. Cowley, *Aramaic Papyri of the Fifth Century B.C.* (Oxford: Clarendon, 1923), 212-26, 52-53 (the term was also used at Elephantine of 'clerks [of the treasury]'; see papyrus no. 2, lines 12 and 14 [pp. 4-5]). For fuller discussion of the Aramaic *sāpar* in Ezra and its antecedents under the Assyrians and Babylonians, see the essay in this volume by J. Blenkinsopp, "The Sage, the Scribe, and Scribalism in the Chronicler's Work," pp. 307-15.

368 John G. Gammie

governmental title that may have become applied to students of the biblical law derivatively. As Carl Schneider has observed in a brief essay on Hellenistic bureaucracy, the extraordinary use of papyrus undoubtedly demanded also a corresponding number of personnel in the more lowly positions of copyists, clerks, accountants, and female secretaries.[27] Ben Sira's "scribe," however, was no mere clerk.

## THE IDEAL SAGE

Ben Sira's ideal sage was God-fearing; a student of rhetoric, Israelite law, proverbs, and prophecy; and a self-conscious composer who was aware of the extent to which his own writings would outlive him and be a blessing to posterity as well as to his own people.

### The Fear of God

Ben Sira himself was a God-fearing man who taught that the fear of the Lord was the root of wisdom and the ultimate source of human happiness (Sir 1:11–20, 19:20, 34:13–17).[28] Accordingly, his famous descriptive poem on the ideal sage (Sir 38:24–39:11) includes a portion on his rising up early for prayer (Sir 39:5):

> If the great Lord should will, he will be filled with the spirit of understanding.   (Sir 39:6a Greek)

Fear of the Lord thus meant a sense of dependency, for,

> There is but one who is wise, exceedingly awesome and seated upon his throne.   (Sir 1:8 Greek)

### The Study of Rhetoric

Ben Sira's sage would assiduously study the rhetorical masterpieces of the past:

> *He will seek out the wisdom of all the ancients*
> And be occupied with prophecies,
> *He will observe closely the discourse of renowned men*
> And will enter into the intricacies of parables.
> (Sir 39:1–2 Greek)

From the studies of Pautrel, Middendorp, Mack, and Lee, we know that, among the ancients studied by Ben Sira, especially prominent

27. C. Schneider, *Kulturgeschichte des Hellenismus* (2 vols.; Munich: Beck, 1969), 2:107–11.

28. The fullest modern treatment of this theme is J. Haspecker, *Gottesfurcht bei Jesus Sirach: Ihre religiöse Struktur und ihre literarische und doktrinäre Bedeutung* (Analecta Biblica 30; Rome: Pontifical Biblical Institute, 1967).

were the Stoics, Homer, Theognis, and the Greek epideictic literature.[29] The very structure of his own great encomium of the Israelite fathers (chaps. 44–50) betrays a deep indebtedness to the Greek encomia. Thus he counseled:

> Do not neglect the discourse of old men,
>> For they learned it from their fathers.
> For from them you will gain understanding
>> And learn to return an answer in your time of need.
>
> (Sir 8:9 Goodspeed)

## Torah, Proverbs, and Prophecies

In contrast to the craftsmen, the sage is one who by definition

> Improves his mind and concentrates on the law of the Most High.
>
> (Sir 38:34b Greek)

Wisdom, fear of the Lord, and the law are intricately interrelated as the following excerpt shows:

> Happy is the man who meditates on wisdom. . . .
> For he who fears the Lord will do this;
>> And he who holds fast to the law will overtake her.
>
> (Sir 14:20a, 15:1 Greek)

To the young who would attain an education he counsels:

> Be willing to listen to every godly discourse,
> And do not let any wise proverbs escape you.
>
> (Sir 6:35 Goodspeed)

Thus Ben Sira, the composer, seems to place almost equal weight on the study of prophecies and searching out the hidden meanings of proverbs and parables (Sir 39:1b, 2b, 3) as he does on concentration upon the law. With good reason did the grandson of Ben Sira reemphasize in the prologue to his translation that his grandfather had meditated long on the law, the prophets, and the other books. Modern studies on Ben Sira's use of the scripture have underlined the extent to which this is so.[30] Just where Ben Sira himself should be placed in the spectrum between prophet and sage is a matter to which I will turn below (pp. 370–71).

29. See R. Pautrel, "Ben Sira et le stoicisme," *Recherches de Science Religieuse* 51 (1963) 535–49; Middendorp, *Die Stellung Jesu ben Siras*, 7–34; B. Mack, *Wisdom and the Hebrew Epic*, 128–35; and Lee, *Studies in the Form of Sirach 44–50*, 54–245.

30. In addition to the work of Middendorp (*Die Stellung Jesu ben Siras*, 35–91), see J. L. Koole, "Die Bibel des Ben-Sira," *Oudtestamentische Studiën* 14 (1965) 374–96.

## Self-conscious Composer

A number of recent writers have observed the extent to which Ben Sira is unique among the writers of the canonical and deuterocanonical literature, namely, for his deep awareness of the impact of his own writings upon his own and upon, he thought (correctly!), future generations. Elsewhere in the intertestamental period this sense of full consciousness of the impact of one's own endeavors is only equaled in the Thanksgiving Psalms from Qumran. For Ben Sira this self-consciousness is especially apparent in the so-called biographical sections. After having observed how the Law of Moses filled people with wisdom and blessings like the four rivers of the garden of Eden (Sir 24:23-29), he continues:

> I said, "I will water my garden,
> And drench my flower bed."
> And behold, my canal became a river,
> And my river became a sea.
> I will again make instruction dawn like the daybreak,
> And make it shine forth afar.
> I will pour out teaching again like prophecy,
> And leave it behind for endless generations.
> Observe that I have not labored for myself only,
> But for all who seek her out.
>
> (Sir 24:31-34 Goodspeed)

Similar thoughts—but not quite as eloquent—are found in Sir 33:16-18, where Ben Sira rather humbly likens himself to a "grapegatherer." Earlier in his work, in what appears to be an autobiographical note (Sir 18:27-29), Ben Sira seems to focus more on his writing of proverbs:

> Those skilled with words themselves compose and pour forth well-turned proverbs.   (Sir 18:29)

Later in the work, however, just after his disquisition on the scribe, both before (Sir 39:12-15) and after (Sir 39:32-35) his moving hymn that celebrates the goodness of the Creator, he rather has come to focus on his writing of hymns such as the one he had just composed (Sir 39:16-31).


## BEN SIRA AS PROPHET

Even though Ben Sira considered that as an author, sage, and scribe he was in the line of the prophets, he nearly abandons the typical prophetic critique against idolatry of the nations, and considerably mutes the typical prophetic critique of social injustices. In the same way that Ben Sira redefined where the line of separation should be drawn with respect to Jew and Gentile in matters pertaining to the law (see above, p. 369), so he redefined the place where the line of prophetic denunciation of idolatry should be drawn. Ben Sira praises the judges,

> Whose mind did not commit adultery [*exeporneusen*], and who did not turn away from the Lord. (Sir 46:11 Greek)

Nowhere, however, does one find in Sirach a scathing attack on the idolatry of foreigners such as that found in Isaiah of Babylon (Isa 44:12-20) or in Jeremiah (chap. 10). The most natural explanation for this avoidance again is to be found in Ben Sira's commendation of juristic service for the sage in the courts of rulers. Similarly Ben Sira simply avoids denunciations of the structures of foreign violence—as the prophets did not (see, e.g., Amos 1-2). In his ethics he shows himself to be a prudentialist, fairly individualistic, but by no means one who has abandoned the traditional prophetic ethics—simply one who has discretely muted its anti-foreign elements (see Sirach 2, 41:14-42:8). Where then should Ben Sira himself and Ben Sira's understanding of the sage be placed in the continuum of the prophets?

As Joseph Blenkinsopp has convincingly shown in his book *Prophecy and Canon*, throughout the history of Israel the tension between normative order and prophecy constituted a major factor in the emergence of the canon of scripture, and no less so in the postexilic era when prophecy became transformed by priests and scribes.[31] Ben Sira's redefinition of prophecy must thus be seen in the light of the developments of the entire postexilic era and not as some perverse aberration or deviation. In any event, the following judgment of Mack on where Ben Sira should be placed on the continuum between prophet and scribe would also seem to be correct for ethical grounds as well as for the reason stated: "In that Ben Sira himself became conscious about what it means to be an author and understood the process of creative composition to be the result of divine inspiration, his work falls somewhere between that of the prophet and that of the scribe."[32]

---

31. For other studies on the nature of the relationship of Sirach to prophecy, see Middendorp, *Die Stellung Jesu ben Siras*, 62-71; H. Stadelmann, *Ben Sira als Schriftgelehrter: Eine Untersuchung zum Berufsbild des vor-makkabäischen Sōfēr unter Berücksichtigung seines Verhältnisses zu Priester-, Propheten- und Weisheitslehrertum* (Wissenschaftliche Untersuchungen zum Neuen Testament 2/6; Tübingen: Mohr/Siebeck, 1980) 177-270; and Koole, "Die Bibel des Ben-Sira," 378-81. The latter observed: "Just as Israel's history illumines the law, so for Ben Sira it validates the prophets as preachers of the law [*Gesetzesprediger*]" (p. 380, my translation). Stadelmann (p. 215 n. 2) is rightly critical (see pp. 360-61 above) of Koole's finding in Sirach a "Torah-centrism." Middendorp stresses the extent to which Ben Sira understands prophecy after the model of Greek seers who at sites of oracles predicted the future (cf., e.g., 44:3, 38:25).

32. Mack, *Wisdom and the Hebrew Epic*, 126-27.

John G. Gammie

## CONCLUSION

I have outlined above Ben Sira's views on the sage under six headings. By way of summation one may ask what these findings tell about Ben Sira's stance among the competing views of the social order at the end of the third century and the beginning of the second century B.C.E. With respect to Hellenism and strictness of adherence to the laws of the Torah, Ben Sira—and his ideal sage—was a centrist. His use of Hebrew as a vehicle of expression and yet his writing a whole section (chaps. 44–50) in the mode of Hellenistic rhetoric is symptomatic of his centrist position. On the one hand, he rejected the kind of separatism advocated earlier by Ezra and Nehemiah in that he did not renounce intermarriages. On the other hand, he was something of a traditionalist in his adherence to the basic world view of the sage from the monarchial period. His traditionalism, however, did not include an adherence to the dietary laws of the Torah. His elevation of the temple and temple worship, yet openness to foreigners is perhaps closest to the author of 1 and 2 Chronicles. In no way does Ben Sira's openness to foreign culture bring him to reject the Hebraic religion or values in unrestrained embracing of Hellenistic norms of beauty and art. Thus Ben Sira's social universe was not that of Jason who was to acquire the high priesthood within two decades after the demise of Ben Sira's beloved Simon.[33] It might be argued, however, that Ben Sira's failure to speak out forcefully against idolatry, his openness to foreign travel, and obvious attraction to Hellenistic rhetorical models did little to shore up Israel's defenses against a more extreme Hellenization such as that advocated by Jason. In any event, the view of the sage set forth in the Book of Sirach suggests that the author functioned as a self-conscious composer who did not serve as a priest, but as a lay jurist in the Ptolemaic (and possibly Seleucid) court system.

33. For a fine study of the social significance of Ben Sira's praise of Simon, see B. L. Mack, "Wisdom Makes a Difference: Alternatives to 'Messianic' Configurations," *Judaisms and Their Messiahs at the Turn of the Christian Era* (ed. J. Neusner, W. S. Green, and E. S. Frerichs; Cambridge: Cambridge University, 1987) 21–25: "His depiction of Simon as high priest includes functions that, according to Ben Sira, were royal—i.e., benefactions for and defense of Jerusalem (50:1–4). So it appears that Ben Sira understood Second Temple institutions, symbolized in the office of a high priest, to be a sufficient social structure for the realization and cultivation of Jewish identity as a nation" (p. 21).

# THE SAGE IN THE
# LITERATURE OF QUMRAN:
# THE FUNCTIONS OF THE *MAŚKÎL*

## Carol A. Newsom

The documents of the Qumran community are distinctive in many respects, not least because they include texts that, in addition to describing the beliefs of the community, also discuss its structure and organization. Consequently, in asking about the figure of the sage at Qumran, one can examine not only the ideals and values associated with knowledge and insight but also the ways in which these values were embodied in the social structure of the community itself.[1] A full investigation of that topic would require a much longer treatment than is possible here, but some light can be shed on the subject by looking at the figure of the *maśkîl*.[2] To a significant extent the vocabulary and speech forms known

Carol A. Newsom is Associate Professor of Old Testament at Candler School of Theology, Emory University.

1. For more general discussion of wisdom in Qumran literature see A.-M. Denis, *Les thèmes de connaissance dans le Document de Damas* (Studia Hellenistica 15; Louvain: Publications Universitaires, 1967); J. E. Worrell, "Concepts of Wisdom in the Dead Sea Scrolls" (Ph.D. diss., Claremont Graduate School, 1968); and S. J. Tanzer, "The Sages at Qumran: Wisdom in the *Hodayot*" (Ph.D. diss., Harvard University, 1987). In addition, a brief but excellent treatment of wisdom themes in Qumran literature is to be found in M. Hengel, *Judaism and Hellenism* (2 vols.; Philadelphia: Fortress, 1974), 1:218-24. For other soundings on the role of the sage at Qumran, see the essays in this volume by David Winston ("The Sage as Mystic in the Wisdom of Solomon," pp. 383-97) and Michael Fishbane ("From Scribalism to Rabbinism: Perspectives on the Emergence of Classical Judaism," pp. 439-56).

2. Of course the descriptions of roles and functions in the texts are idealized and may not have corresponded to the actual social life of the community. Two other factors make the attempt to describe social roles in the Qumran community difficult. First is the apparent coexistence of communities of the "new covenant" in towns and villages (as described in the *Damascus Document*) alongside a more monastic settlement at Khirbet Qumran. Second is the fact that there must have been changes in the organization of the community over the course of time, changes that are now very difficult to trace. In discussing the *maśkîl* here I am presenting a synthesized picture of the ideal figure that emerges from Qumran documents in existence by the turn of the era. The *maśkîl*, or a figure like him, appears to have been a functionary both in the community at Qumran and in the local village communities.

elsewhere from both aphoristic and mantic wisdom traditions can be
found also at Qumran, but the picture of the sage that emerges in the
various roles of the *maśkîl* is significantly different from both.[3]


## THE FORMATION AND CHARACTER OF COMMUNITY

While the term itself might be translated simply as 'sage', there are
certain contexts in which it is quite clear that the word *maśkîl* refers not
merely to someone who is wise but to someone whose function it is to
make others wise, that is, an 'Instructor' or 'Master'.[4] The clearest
examples are the references to the *maśkîl* in the *Rule of the Community*.
As the introductory heading to the "Treatise on the Two Spirits" says,
"The *maśkîl* shall instruct all the sons of light and shall teach them . . ."
(1QS 3:13).[5] The content of that section, as is well known, concerns the
dualistic and predestinarian beliefs of the Qumran sect, its anthropology,
and pneumatology. Toward the end of the *Rule of the Community* an
entire section is devoted to the "precepts" according to which the
*maśkîl* is to conduct himself (1QS 9:12–10:5). While some of the matters

3. While there are some yet unpublished proverb collections from cave 4, it is
probable that these were not compositions of the Qumran community. It is interesting
that, although a number of the Qumran texts abound in terminology familiar from
aphoristic wisdom (e.g., שכל, בינה, דעת, אמת, ערמה, תושיה), there is a distinct tendency to
avoid the term חכמה. Moreover, the figure of the sage at Qumran is not called a *ḥākām*
but a *maśkîl*. Worrell ("Concepts of Wisdom," 186) has suggested that the Qumran
community avoided the term *ḥākām* because it was already being appropriated by their
Pharisaic opponents. While his suggestion is intriguing, the reasons for the choice of
terminology remain obscure. Tanzer ("Sages at Qumran") has documented the presence
of wisdom themes, vocabulary, and forms (especially the rhetorical question) in a certain
group of the *Hôdāyôt*. Both Tanzer (p. 178) and Worrell (p. 163) note that the referent of
wisdom at Qumran has been particularized to refer to the specific teachings of the sect
and to its sectarian interpretation of Torah.
   Certain vocabulary and themes recall those associated with mantic wisdom, for
example, the repeated references to revelation and the gift of a spirit of knowledge, terms
such as רז, סוד, נסתרות, and the phenomenon of inspired exegesis. But unlike figures such
as Daniel and Enoch, there is no evidence that the sages of Qumran depended on dreams,
visions, and angelophanies as the media of such revelation.
   4. See the discussion of G. Vermes, *The Dead Sea Scrolls in English* (2d ed.;
Harmondsworth: Penguin, 1975) 22–25. Though it is not possible to present the arguments
for each case here, I interpret all of the references to the *maśkîl* in the Qumran literature
as referring to the one who performs the official function of instruction in the community,
that is, to the Instructor or Master. Even if some of the occurrences should be read in the
nontechnical sense, as referring simply to a wise person or sage (rather than the Instructor
or Master), the values and accomplishments associated with the wise person form part of
the ideal that would pertain especially to the leaders of the community.
   5. Ibid., 75. All translations, except where noted, are those of Vermes, *Dead Sea
Scrolls in English*. Where Vermes translates *mśkyl* as 'Master', I have substituted *maśkîl*.

discussed might be obligatory for all members of the community, others pertain to a particular function within the society. In this section the role of the *maśkîl* as teacher is again emphasized. In addition, he is called upon to make judgments about those who are fit to enter the community and to decide when a member should be advanced in the hierarchy of the group. One could say that the functions of the *maśkîl* are concerned with the formation of the community, both through his admission and regulation of members and through his instruction in the knowledge that the community shares in common, yet that separates it from outsiders.

In addition to these functions, the *maśkîl* is associated with another activity that may at first seem surprising. He also has liturgical responsibilities. The section of the *Rule of the Community* describing the precepts of the *maśkîl* concludes with a listing of the times when the *maśkîl* is to bless God (1QS 9:26-10:5). According to the *Manual of Benedictions* (1QSb), the *maśkîl* is also to bless the various groups and leaders of the community. Finally, the individual compositions of the *Sabbath Songs* and the *Songs of the Maśkîl* begin with the headings *lmśkyl*. Although it is not clear exactly how the preposition is to be translated (to? by? for?), the liturgical, angelological, and demonological content of these songs is consistent with the knowledge and functions ascribed elsewhere to the *maśkîl*.

What, one might ask, is the source of the authority for this central figure? Unfortunately, none of the passages that refer to the *maśkîl* discuss the background or qualifications necessary for the exercise of that office. Geza Vermes has made a convincing argument, however, that the *maśkîl* is the same community office that is elsewhere designated as the *mĕbaqqēr* or 'guardian'.[6] According to the *Damascus Document*, the *mĕbaqqēr* is not, or at least need not be, of priestly extraction. His authority does not come from hereditary descent but rather he "shall be . . . one who has mastered all the secrets of men and the languages of all their clans" (CD 14:9-10; Vermes, p. 116). It is knowledge itself, and the community's recognition of his knowledge, that gives the *mĕbaqqēr/maśkîl* his authority. At Qumran knowledge was not seen as a human achievement but always as the gift of God. This was true both for the ordinary member (1QH 4:25) and for the *maśkîl* (1QH 12:11-12).

Above all else, the knowledge with which the *maśkîl* is concerned is the knowledge of "the will of God" (רצון אל), that is, Torah. Discerning and practicing the correct interpretation of Torah is the *raison d'être* for the entire community. As the instructions for the *maśkîl* put it, "He shall conceal the teaching of the Law from men of falsehood, but shall

6. Ibid., 22-23.

impart true knowledge and righteous judgment to those who have chosen the Way" (1QS 9:17–18; Vermes, p. 88). The association of knowledge and Torah is, of course, a well-developed theme in Deuteronomy and in the Book of Sirach. Here, however, the "true knowledge" or "knowledge of truth" that the *maśkîl* is to impart is the particular interpretation of Halakah cultivated in the sect.

While the *maśkîl* is charged with instructing members of the community, he is not, by himself, the source and authority for the correct understanding of the will of God. Such knowledge is described as having been "revealed" and "discovered" (הנמצא/הנגלה) at various times (לפי העתים/לעת בעת; 1QS 9:13). Although there was a tradition of halakic interpretation preserved in the community as a heritage from past teachers (CD 3:13–14, 6:3–11), the process of study and deliberation through which the true interpretation was discovered/revealed continued to be one of the central functions of community life. These occasions are briefly described in the *Rule of the Community*:

> Each man shall sit in his place: the Priests shall sit first, and the elders second, and all the rest of the people according to their rank. And thus shall they be questioned concerning the Law, and concerning any counsel or matter coming before the Congregation, each man bringing his knowledge to the Council of the Community (1QS 6:8–10 [Vermes, p. 81]; cf. 5:3–5).

The process is at once deliberative and hierarchical. Success in this vital matter of discerning the will of God depends on having members who not only possess the appropriate intellectual ability but who have the disposition to work together according to the discipline of the group.

It is in this connection that one can examine another important aspect of the insight required of the *maśkîl* and his function within the sect. The *maśkîl* is the one charged with admitting prospective members to candidacy and with making the hierarchical rankings of the members. According to the *Rule of the Community*, "He shall separate and weigh the sons of righteousness according to their spirit. . . . He shall admit him in accordance with the cleanness of his hands and advance him in accordance with his understanding" 1QS 9:14, 16; Vermes, p. 88). Insight into character was, to be sure, an ability traditionally valued and cultivated by the wise. As developed at Qumran, under the terminology of "spirit," various traits of attitude and behavior were organized according to a dualistic scheme. Presumably, the qualities of spirit that the *maśkîl* looked for in his assessments are those described in the "Treatise on the Two Spirits" as the ways of the spirit of truth and falsehood, respectively (1QS 4:3–6, 9–11).

It would have also been necessary for the members to appropriate for themselves the values and judgments of the *maśkîl*. Just as the *maśkîl* had to have insight into the nature and character of the members of the community, it would have been important for them to understand something about the origin, nature, and destiny of human existence in the world. Even though the search for the true interpretation of the Torah was central to the life of the community, that quest did not take place in a vacuum but in a social and cosmological context. It is in this regard that the so-called "Treatise on the Two Spirits" is important. There it is said that the *maśkîl* "shall instruct all the sons of light and shall teach them the nature of all the children of men according to the kind of spirit which they possess, the signs identifying their works during their lifetime, their visitation for chastisement, and the time of their reward" (1QS 3:13-15; Vermes, p. 75). This instruction thus provides the member with knowledge about his own identity in the context of the divine plan for the world. As members, the individuals know they belong to the children of light as ones destined for salvation. The detailing of the characteristics of the spirits of truth and falsehood undoubtedly provides a guide for the formation of values in the individual community member.

But, as Hermann Lichtenberger has shown, a more specific problem lies at the heart of this discourse. The *Rule of the Community* is also an attempt to analyze and resolve a pressing problem for the community, which understood itself as composed of children of light: Why do the righteous sin?[7] The ancient question of theodicy which so concerned traditional wisdom—Why do the righteous suffer?—is rather easily answered in the dualistic world view of the Qumran sect. They suffer because of the enmity of the powers of falsehood. But why should those who have specifically devoted themselves to doing the will of God and who belong to the spirit of light nevertheless continue to commit sin, iniquity, wickedness, and unlawful deeds (1QS 3:22)? That is the question that posed the greatest threat to the self-understanding of the community and the question for which the *maśkîl* was called upon to provide an answer. The answer contained in the discourse of the *maśkîl*, if not free from all ambiguity, is one of great subtlety and persuasive power. Although the discourse begins with an affirmation of a divine predetermination that has divided human beings into two groups, the children of light and the children of darkness, the latter part

7. H. Lichtenberger, *Studien zum Menschenbild in Texten der Qumrangemeinde* (Studien zur Umwelt des Neuen Testaments 15; Göttingen: Vandenhoeck und Ruprecht, 1980) 129, 136-41.

of the discourse outlines a more complex understanding. All persons participate in both spirits, light and darkness, truth and falsehood, though not in equal portions. Thus even those who have a greater share in the spirit of truth will nevertheless be subject to evil influence. Only through God's eschatological purification will the children of light be eventually freed from that influence. This teaching addresses an important issue for the self-understanding of the individual member of the community and, although the implications are not explicitly drawn, provides a justification for the community's hierarchical structure and its rules of discipline and penance.

One would probably not be mistaken in seeing an implicit didactic function even in the blessings of the *maśkîl*, preserved in 1QSb. This document contains the "words of blessing" that the *maśkîl* was to pronounce over the members of the community, the (eschatological?) high priest, the priests of the community, and the prince of the community (probably also an eschatological figure). Before the actual blessing, each of the sections begins with several lines describing the duties or functions of the person or group to be blessed. Here, as Lichtenberger has noted, there is no discussion of persons as individuals torn between two spirits, as in 1QS 3:15–4:26, or as creatures of dust, as often in the *Thanksgiving Hymns*. Rather, persons are identified, described, and blessed in terms of their role within the community.[8] What one sees here, I believe, is another example of the role of the *maśkîl* in the formation of the community. The individual members of Qumran did not exist simply as individuals. Their identity was fundamentally altered when they were accepted into membership in the community. As it was the *maśkîl* who, through his God-given insight, selected members and assigned them places in the hierarchy of the community, so it was he who had the authority to speak the words of blessing that confirmed their roles and functions.

## TRANSCENDENCE THROUGH KNOWLEDGE AND PROTECTION

As mentioned above, the central focus of the community's quest for knowledge was the discernment of the will of God through proper interpretation of Torah. One of the most fundamental achievements of that quest had been the discernment of the divinely ordained division of time—the division of the day into light and darkness; the division of the year into seasons, months, and weeks in multiples of four, twelve, and seven; and the division of the epochs of creation into weeks of

8. Ibid., 101–5.

years and Jubilee periods. Without a proper understanding of time, one could never do that which God had commanded in the Torah. The subject of time figures in two ways in the instructions for the *maśkîl*. At the beginning of the discourse we read that the *maśkîl* should conduct himself "according to the rule proper to every season" (לתכון עת ועת; 1QS 9:12; Vermes, p. 87). In succeeding lines there are references to what has been "revealed from age to age," "knowledge discovered throughout the ages," and "the precept of the age" (חוק העת). It has been suggested that this is a version of the notion that "the wise man must know, not only *what* to do, but also *when* to do it."[9] That may well be so, though here, as closely similar passages indicate (see 1QS 8:4, 15), the notion refers to the relation between the historical age and the proper fulfillment of the law. The *Book of Jubilees* attests to the successive revelation of the law to the patriarchs and to Moses. But the issue that probably lurks behind this concern for "the precept of the age" is the interpretive tradition that explains why the present temple cult could not be supported (in part because of the observance of the wrong cultic calendar), but how the requirements of the will of God could nevertheless be fulfilled during this "age of wickedness" (see CD 6:11-19; Vermes, p. 103).

The second discussion of the topic of time in the instructions for the *maśkîl* occurs at the end of the unit (1QS 9:26-10:5). There the various divisions of time are enumerated. Significantly, the same topic is taken up in the one composition of the *Thanksgiving Hymns* that is explicitly associated with the *maśkîl* (1QH 12:4-36).[10] It is clear that the heavenly bodies have been placed under divine command to move through the heavens in such a way and with such a motion that they define the various divisions of the calendar. But equally, according to the *Rule of the Community* and the *Thanksgiving Hymns*, the human community has been commanded by an "engraved precept" to mark each of these transitions with praise. Actually, it would be possible to interpret these passages as imposing such an obligation only on the *maśkîl*. I think it more likely, though, that the *maśkîl* is mentioned here as the representative of the community he instructs in its obligations. But whether the mandated acts of praise are carried out by the community as a whole or by someone acting on behalf of the community, the effect is to create an alignment between the divinely ordained

9. P. Wernberg-Møller, *The Manual of Discipline* (Studies on the Texts of the Desert of Judah 1; Leiden: Brill, 1957) 137.

10. Tanzer, "Sages at Qumran," 48, indicates that in H. Stegemann's reconstruction of the *Hôdāyôt*, 1QH 12:4 begins with the heading *lmśkyl*, the same heading that introduces individual compositions in the *Songs of the Sabbath Sacrifice* and the *Songs of the Maśkîl*.

motion of the heavenly bodies and the divinely ordained praise of the human community. It is through his knowledge of these heavenly mysteries that the *maśkîl* shapes the life of the community into harmony with God's eternal will and order.

The coordination of times of worship with the movement of the heavenly bodies, which forms part of the knowledge and responsibility of the *maśkîl*, makes it plausible that he should be associated with another text concerned with liturgy and esoteric knowledge of heavenly matters, the *Songs of the Sabbath Sacrifice*.[11] Each of the thirteen individual compositions of this cycle of songs begins with the heading, "For the *maśkîl* [*lmśkyl*]," followed by the number and date of the Sabbath to which it belongs. While the compositions are themselves acts of praise, they are full of information about the organization of the angelic priesthood, the heavenly sanctuary, and the nature of angelic praise and blessing. In the twelfth song there is an extended description of the divine chariot (*merkābâ*) and its sound of praise, a description that seems to be derived, at least in part, from exegesis of Ezekiel 1 and 10. Since portions of nine copies of the text were found in Qumran caves 4 and 11, it seems unlikely that the heading *lmśkyl* was intended to restrict its readership to the *maśkîl* alone. It seems more probable that the text formed part of the literature for community worship and instruction that belonged to the province of the *maśkîl*. Through the *Sabbath Songs* the Qumran community would have been made privy to a wealth of special knowledge about the heavenly realms. The theme of knowledge is stressed in the songs themselves, with repeated references to wonderful mysteries, angels or spirits of knowledge, etc. As liturgical praxis, the recitation of the *Sabbath Songs* coordinated the praise of the community with that of the angelic worshipers and served as a vehicle of that communion with the angels to which the *Hôdāyôt Thanksgiving Hymns* make repeated reference. The vivid description of the angelic priests and heavenly temple, amounting to a sense of virtual presence in the celestial sanctuary, would have served to reaffirm the Qumran priests' sense of their own identity and validity despite

---

11. The original provenance of this composition is difficult to establish. In my original publication of the document I presented the arguments that favor Qumran authorship; *Songs of the Sabbath Sacrifice: A Critical Edition* (Harvard Semitic Studies 27; Atlanta: Scholars Press, 1985) 1–4. While the document was certainly highly influential at Qumran, it is nevertheless quite possible that, like *Jubilees*, it was composed before the establishment of the sectarian community but adopted by it. See my forthcoming article, "'Sectually Explicit' Literature at Qumran," *Ex Occidente Lux: On the Bible and Its Interpreters* (ed. W. Propp, B. Halpern, and D. N. Freedman; Winona Lake, IN: Eisenbrauns). If it is the case that the *Sabbath Songs* antedate the sectarian community at Qumran, then it is possible that they are responsible for the introduction of the term *maśkîl* into the vocabulary of the community. This possibility, however, must remain a matter of speculation only.

their separation from the Jerusalem temple. The experience of the *Sabbath Songs* was perhaps a foretaste of the common priestly service with the angels, which figures prominently in the *maśkîl*'s blessing of the priests in 1QSb. Here, as elsewhere, the special knowledge of the *maśkîl* is not speculative knowledge for its own sake. Even at its most esoteric such knowledge is functional and serves the formation of character and identity for the member and for the community as a whole.

A final example of this pragmatic use of esoteric knowledge, and one that draws together several of the texts already discussed, is the *Songs of the Maśkîl*. This composition is highly fragmentary, and even the fragments that remain have not yet been fully reconstructed. Still, enough remains to make it clear that the text is literarily dependent both on the *Thanksgiving Hymns* and on the *Sabbath Songs*. Much of the content of these songs consists of praise of God and description of heavenly wonders, including descriptions of the angelic priesthood and heavenly temple drawn from the *Sabbath Songs*. But it is the statement of the use to which such praise and descriptions are put that is particularly interesting. "And as for me, I am a *maśkîl* who makes known the splendor of his beauty, in order to frighten and ter[rify] all the spirits of the angels of destruction and bastard spirits, demons, Lilith, howlers, and s[atyrs . . .]" (4Q510 1 4–5, my trans.; see also 4Q511 35 6–7). Several times in the extant fragments the speaker refers gratefully to the divine gift of knowledge (see 4Q511 18 ii 7–9). That the speaker is the one who holds the office of *maśkîl* and not just one who describes himself as "sage" is made likely by the similarity between the self-description of the speaker in 4Q511 63 iii and the description of the *maśkîl*'s range of knowledge and authority in 1QS 3:13–16 and 9:12–21. The words of the *maśkîl*, powerful though they are, do not pretend to encroach on that which belongs to God alone. The apotropaic power of his songs is "not for an eternal destruction (of the demons) but only for the time of affliction (due to) sin" (4Q510 1 7–8, my trans.; see also 4Q511 35 7–8). The reference here appears to be to the teaching about the period of the dominion of the angel of falsehood, the time when, according to the "Treatise on the Two Spirits," the dark spirit has power to mislead the children of light (1QS 3:21–23, 4:18–20). Even during this time the *maśkîl* is able to draw upon his special knowledge of the heavenly realm and by reciting its wonders offers protection to the community.

## CONCLUSION

There is no doubt that the Qumran community dedicated itself to the search for knowledge: knowledge of the true interpretation of the will of God, the Torah. Conflict with other more dominant groups in Jewish society led, through events that are still obscure, to the establishment of a sectlike community where such knowledge could be pursued in an atmosphere of mutual support and reinforcement. Because of the sectarian social setting, both the kinds of knowledge that were pursued in the Qumran community and the institutional role of its sages took on distinctive forms. To be sure, many of the traditional wisdom concerns, much of its typical vocabulary, and even occasional speech forms can be identified in the Qumran literature. All of it, though, has undergone change through its context in a sectarian community. While all members of the group aspired to insight and knowledge, it was the member known as the *maśkîl* who stood at the head of a hierarchy of knowledge. What the community sought from the one who filled that office was not just a paragon of learning and wisdom. As a community of individuals who had "separated themselves" and "offered themselves freely" to a new purpose, the society required continuous formation of character, both as a group and as individual members. It is in this perspective that the knowledge and responsibilities ascribed to the *maśkîl* form a coherent whole. While the *maśkîl* knew and taught the proper Halakah and calendar, he also had insight into character, into the "spirits" of individuals, a knowledge he used very directly to form the membership of the sect. This knowledge of human nature was set in a comprehensive theology of creation and divine providence, out of which it was possible to explain not only the enmity and falseness of the sect's opponents but also the evident failures of members to fulfill their own ideals. The superior gift of knowledge that God had given to the *maśkîl* made him also the one who could guide the members of the community into the experience of the wonders of the heavenly realm and even show them how such knowledge might be used to protect themselves against the powers of evil until the time when God would put a final end to its dominion.

# THE SAGE AS MYSTIC IN THE WISDOM OF SOLOMON

## David Winston

The author of the Wisdom of Solomon displays a single-minded intensity in his portrayal of the ideal sage and his concentrated pursuit after wisdom. A mildly ascetic Platonic strain pervades his delineation of the proper life-path that ought to be followed, and although he ultimately allows the enjoyment of external goods, they are at best only tolerated as secondary accessions upon a course of action that demands a narrowly exclusive loyalty of its devotees. The vigorous appreciation for life's amenities that characterizes Ben Sira's writing, which does not exclude even a potential hazard such as feminine beauty (Sir 36:22), is here nowhere in sight.[1] The author's Platonism is austere and lacks the subtle playfulness that pervades the dialogues of the founder of the philosophical school that left so great an imprint on him. There is hardly a trace of humor in his admonitory exhortations, nor any echo of Ben Sira's approval of the enjoyment of good food and wine to the accompaniment of tuneful melodies in congenial company.[2] Missing completely is anything like Sirach's bantering advice to the president-elect of a banquet to ensure the enjoyment of his guests by cutting his speeches short and never interrupting the music (30:21-25, 31:27-31, 32:1-6). Yet, as I shall soon show, the portrait of the ideal sage that emerges from the Wisdom of Solomon has considerable affinity with that found in the Wisdom of Ben Sira.

David Winston is Professor of Hellenistic and Judaic Studies at the Graduate Theological Union, Berkeley.

References to classical works in this essay are cross-referenced to the English translations in the Loeb Classical Library (LCL), copublished by Harvard University Press and William Heinemann. All verbatim citations from the Wisdom of Solomon are from my translation and commentary in the Anchor Bible (see n. 3 below).

1. The author of Wisdom of Solomon, or Book of Wisdom, can even say that "it is better to be childless, provided one is virtuous (4:1), since for him, as for Plato (*Symposium* 208E [LCL 166: 199]), it is the life of the soul that is paramount, and if the latter is productive, childlessness is of little moment (cf. 3:13-14).
2. See A. A. Wieder, "Ben Sira and the Praise of Wine," *JQR* 61 (1970-71) 155-66.

## THE SAGE'S ATTRIBUTES

From the author's autobiographical sketches of his encounter with Dame Wisdom a composite portrait of his ideal sage can easily be drawn. Fully trusting in the Lord, wise individuals will not seek to test him, nor will they murmur in their hearts, since the latter cancels out whatever good gift or deed accompanies it (Wis 1:2, 10–11; cf. Deut 6:16, Ps 78:18). Filled with a longing for Wisdom (Wis 8:2), they will prefer her to riches and kingship, although she will eventually grant these gifts too (Wis 7:8–12).[3] Wisdom bestows on sages the four cardinal virtues of self-control, intelligence, justice, and courage (Wis 8:7), a classification that goes back to Plato (*Phaedo* 69C [LCL 36: 241], *Republic* 427E [LCL 237: 347], *Laws* 631C [LCL 187: 25]) and was taken up by Zeno, founder of the Stoic school, who expressed three of them in terms of the fourth, wisdom.[4] She also confers on them a knowledge of the past and the future, of the rules of logic and the resolution of riddles, and ultimately of all natural phenomena (Wis 7:17–22). The latter is lovingly spelled out in elaborate detail as

> [The] unerring knowledge of existent being,
> . . . the structure of the universe and the operation of the elements;
> the beginning, and end, and middle of times,
> the changes of the solstices and the vicissitudes of the seasons;
> the cycles of years and the positions of the stars;
> the natures of living creatures and the tempers of beasts;
> the violent force of spirits and the reasonings of men;
> the species of plants, and the virtues of roots.
>
> (Wis 7:17–20)[5]

3. There is an echo here of the well-known philosophical debate between the Peripatetics and the Stoics as to the relative importance of external goods for the happy life, such as health, beauty, honor, and wealth. The Stoics had stressed the notion that virtue is self-sufficient for happiness and the only good properly speaking (H. F. A. von Arnim, *Stoicorum veterum fragmenta* [4 vols.; Leipzig: Teubner, 1903–24; repr. Stuttgart: Teubner, 1964], 1:187; 3:29–45, 49–67). The Peripatetic view of the triple good (i.e., external, bodily, psychic; see Aristotle, *Nicomachean Ethics* 1098b [1:8:2; LCL 73:37]; "*Art*" *of Rhetoric* 1360b [1:5:1–5; LCL 193: 47–49]; Cicero, *Aims of Good and Evil* 5:84 [LCL 40: 487–89]) was explicitly attacked by Philo, who found it symbolized in scripture by Joseph's coat of many colors (*The Worse Attacks the Better* 6–9; LCL 227: 205–9). It may be noted that "P[apyrus] Insinger's emphasis is on the need to obtain a minimum for a livelihood, to make it last by living frugally, and not to hanker after wealth"; so M. Lichtheim, *Late Egyptian Wisdom Literature in the International Context* (OBO 52; Freiburg, Switzerland: Universitätsverlag/Göttingen: Vandenhoeck und Ruprecht, 1983) 153. For a fuller discussion, see my commentary, *The Wisdom of Solomon* (AB 43; Garden City, NY: Doubleday, 1979) 31–32.

4. Von Arnim, *Stoicorum veterum fragmenta*, 3:255–61.

5. Cf. Aeschylus, *Prometheus Bound* 436–506 (LCL 145: 255–59), and the striking parallel in Pseudo-Plato, *Axiochus* 370B (J. P. Hershbell, *Pseudo-Plato, Axiochus* [Chico:

The sage will thus enjoy repute among the masses and honor among the elders, in spite of youth (Wis 8:10). Admired and honored by rulers, who will seek the sage's advice, the sage will, in fact, join their ranks as governor of peoples and nations (Wis 8:11–12, 14; 6:20; 10:14). The sage will secure wealth and great renown, will be courageous in war, and will exercise the mastery of elocutionary skill (Wis 8:5, 12, 15, 18). Realizing that wisdom is an inexhaustible treasure for humanity, the sage will freely and unstintingly share it with others (Wis 6:23, 7:13).[6] The sage is the stability of the people, and in the ensemble such individuals constitute the salvation of the world (Wis 6:24; cf. 9:18).[7] Finally, becoming a friend and prophet of God and learning the divine pleasure, the sage will have rest, cheer, and joy, and above all the supreme gift of immortality (Wis 7:14, 8:16).[8] In short, occupying the highest rungs of society, the sage will be a leader both at home and abroad, exercising compassion and humanity (Wis 12:19; cf. 1:6, 7:23), and administering the world in holiness and righteousness (Wis 9:3).

A brief comparison with several Jewish writings that exhibit an emphasis on wisdom similar to that in this book will help illuminate the latter's distinctive character. Aside from the books of Proverbs, Job, and Ben Sira, which have clearly influenced this author's portrayal of Wisdom as a female cosmic figure, another important source of inspiration for him was the strong emphasis on wisdom in *1 Enoch*, although that book's insistence on wisdom's supernatural character has been adapted by him to a Platonist philosophical perspective. In the so-called "Apocalypse of Weeks" (chaps. 91–93), Enoch is described as "a skilled scribe and wisest of men" (92:1), and at the close of the seventh "week," we are told that the elect "shall be given sevenfold wisdom and

---

Scholars Press, 1981] 45), where it is argued that it is only through a divine breath in an individual's soul that such knowledge can be attained, and in the light of which immortality is assured.

6. Cf. Philo, *Every Good Man Is Free* 13–14 (LCL 363: 17–19); Pseudo-Aristotle, *On the Cosmos* 391a17 (LCL 400: 347); and Xenophon, *Symposium* 4:43 (LCL 168: 431). In the Pseudo-Platonic *Epinomis*, a protreptic to the purer and happier life, the author similarly states: "For I have sought this wisdom high and low [*anō kai katō*], and so far as it has been revealed to me I will try to render it plain to you" (989A; LCL 201: 477).

7. For the ideal of *eustatheia*, or inner calm and stability, see my commentary, *Wisdom of Solomon*, 160.

8. According to the Isis Aretalogy (Papyrus Oxyrhynchus XI.1380), Isis was especially the goddess of immortality, which she conferred upon her husband and brother Osiris and her son Horus. The author of Wisdom skillfully adapted the Isis aretalogies for his description of Sophia; see ibid., 37. In addition to the literature cited there, see J. S. Kloppenborg, "Isis and Sophia in the Book of Wisdom," *Harvard Theological Review* 75 (1982) 57–84. For Philo's doctrine of immortality see *On Flight and Finding* 97 (LCL 275: 63), *On Abraham* 27 (LCL 289: 17–19), *On the Posterity and Exile of Cain* 23 (LCL 227: 341).

knowledge" (93:10; cf. 91:10, 5:8, 104:12). As to Enoch's eschatological knowledge, it is emphatically stated that it was shown to him in a heavenly vision, that it was an angelic message, and that he had read it from the tablets of heaven (93:2; cf. 103:2–4, 106:19). The "Book of the Watchers" contains a comprehensive picture of the cosmos (chap. 18), but here Enoch's knowledge is based on two cosmic voyages, the second of which culminates in a voyage around the world (chaps. 33–36). In the "Astronomical Book" (chaps. 72–82), it is the angel Uriel who is his source of knowledge. The esoteric nature of Enoch's knowledge is further underlined by his claim that his experience was unique: "And I, Enoch, alone saw the sight, the ends of everything; and no man has seen what I have seen" (19:3; cf. 60:10ff.). In any case, the encyclopedic range of Enoch's knowledge is reminiscent of the similar scope of the sage's knowledge in the Wisdom of Solomon (7:17–22), though the scientific character of the latter is sharply opposed to the mythical and fantastic nature of the former.[9]

Although there is a similar emphasis on knowledge and insight in the Dead Sea Scrolls, with the phrase "I know" and a large number of knowledge synonyms occurring in them very frequently, God's creative wisdom (cf. 1QH 1:14, 20) is never there personified or hypostatized.[10] Moreover, in spite of the fact that the scrolls indicate humans come close to God in relation to wisdom and insight, the Book of Wisdom knows nothing of an esoteric reading of scripture divinely revealed to the elect, as in the Qumran *Pesharim*. The esoteric character of the mystical knowledge vouchsafed to the Qumranites is clearly articulated in the following lines from the *Rule of the Community*: "My eyes have gazed on that which is eternal, on wisdom concealed from men, on knowledge and wise design (hidden) from the sons of men" (1QS 5–6).[11] It is a revelation of the supernal realms and their divine mysteries, and of God's ultimate plan for human salvation, for which the Qumran psalmist is effusive in expressing thanks.

A much closer connection exists between the Wisdom of Solomon and Philo of Alexandria, whose conception of the sage and his relationship to Wisdom is very similar indeed. Both describe *Sophia* (Wisdom)

---

9. See J. C. VanderKam, *Enoch and the Growth of an Apocalyptic Tradition* (CBQMS 16; Washington, DC: Catholic Biblical Association, 1984) 135–40, 148–51; and I. Gruenwald, *Apocalyptic and Merkavah Mysticism* (Arbeiten zur Geschichte des antiken Judentums und des Urchristentums 14; Leiden: Brill, 1980) 3–25. For other similarities between *1 Enoch* and Wisdom of Solomon, see C. Larcher, *Études sur le Livre de la Sagesse* (Paris: Gabalda, 1969) 103–12.

10. See M. Küchler, *Frühjüdische Weisheitstraditionen* (OBO 26; Freiburg, Switzerland: Universitätsverlag/Göttingen: Vandenhoeck und Ruprecht, 1979) 88–113, esp. 94; and W. L. Lipscomb and J. A. Sanders, "Wisdom at Qumran," *IW* 277–85.

11. G. Vermes, *The Dead Sea Scrolls in English* (2d ed.; Harmondsworth: Penguin, 1975) 92.

as an effulgence of God's glory and his agent in creation, whose brightness is more radiant than the sun (Wis 7:25–26, 8:4, 9:1–2, 6:12, 7:29; Philo, *On the Creation of the World* 30 [LCL 226: 23–24], *On the Migration of Abraham* 40 [LCL 261: 155]). Both employ erotic imagery in connection with her pursuit, calling her bride or spouse, and speaking of living with her (*symbioun*) and enjoying kinship (*syngeneia*) with her (Wis 8:2–3, 16–17; Philo, *On Mating with the Preliminary Studies* 74 [LCL 261: 495], *On the Contemplative Life* 68 [LCL 363: 155], and *On the Special Laws* 4:14 [LCL 341: 17]). Wisdom anticipates those who desire her, and those who seek her will not weary (Wis 6:13–14; Philo, *On Mating with the Preliminary Studies* 122–23 [LCL 261: 521], *On the Unchangeableness of God* 160 [LCL 247–91]). Without her, humanity is nothing, and all their words and thoughts are in God's hands (Wis 9:6, 7:16; Philo, *On the Posterity and Exile of Cain* 136 [LCL 227: 407], *On the Cherubim* 71 [LCL 227: 51–53]). Humans must make their souls a proper abode for her, but the godless, inviting death, conclude a pact with the latter (Wis 1:4, 16; Philo, *On Dreams* 1:149 [LCL 275: 375–77], *Who Is the Heir of Things Divine?* 45 [LCL 261: 305–7]). The doctrine of immortality plays a central role in both. The wise live forever, whereas the godless are spiritually dead even while physically alive (Wis 5:15, 1:11, 3:24; Philo, *On Joseph* 264 [LCL 289: 267–69], *The Worse Attacks the Better* 49 [LCL 227: 235–37]). Wisdom must be sought for her own sake, though external goods will follow in due course (Wis 7:7–11; Philo, *Who is the Heir of Things Divine?* 285–86 [LCL 261: 429–31]). Finally, without natural endowments the mind cannot be brought to its fullness, but training with *Sophia* is nonetheless indispensable (Wis 8:18; Philo, *On Abraham* 52–53 [LCL 289: 31]).[12]

I have already referred to the close affinity between the Book of Wisdom's ideal sage and that of Ben Sira, and now identify the points of contact between them. Wisdom requires strenuous efforts on the part of her would-be devotees (Sir 51:19, 14:20–27), but is swift to anticipate their quest (Sir 15:2). She demands of her followers purity of soul, and holds aloof from fraudulence and arrogance (Sir 15:8, 51:20). She promotes the sage above one's neighbors, granting eloquence and crowning with honor (Sir 15:5–6). Although Ben Sira teaches no doctrine of immortality, he promises the sage that memory of the sage will not die (Sir 39:9). The wise person penetrates the intricacies of parables and knows his or her way among riddles (Sir 39:2–3). Since concealed treasure is of no profit, the sage willingly imparts wisdom to others (Sir 20:30–31), serves rulers and travels widely (Sir 39:4), and is in demand at public discussions (Sir 38:33). Finally, upon attaining wisdom the sage finds rest and joy (Sir 6:28, 51:27).

12. For a more detailed discussion with fuller references, see my commentary, *Wisdom of Solomon*, 59–62.

There are, however, several important differences. The central goal of immortality is missing in Ben Sira, as is also the attainment of mystical intimacy with God and prophecy. Perhaps even more significant is the distinction between their respective conceptions of human knowledge. Whereas the wisdom goal of the Book of Wisdom is one of encyclopedic scope and unlimited range, Ben Sira has a considerably more restricted view of the kind of knowledge that is attainable by humans. In a well-known passage he offers the following advice:

> Seek not (to understand) what is too wonderful for thee,
>     And search not out that which is hid from thee.
> Meditate upon that which thou must [or, art permitted to] grasp,
>     And be not occupied with that which is hid.
> Have naught to do with that which is beyond thee,
>     For more hath been shown to thee than thou canst understand.
> For many are the conceits of the sons of men,
>     And evil imaginations lead astray.
>
> (Sir 3:21–24; cf. 18:6–7)[13]

It may well be that in these verses he is referring only to cosmogonic and extraterrestrial speculations, but even if this should be the case, his attitude would still sharply diverge from the audacious and uninhibited confidence that marks the author of the Wisdom of Solomon, who speaks unhesitatingly of his "unerring knowledge of existent being" (7:17). Moreover, in contrast to Ben Sira who alludes to human inability to count "the days of unending time" (1:2), the author of the Book of Wisdom knows "the beginning, and end, and middle of times" (7:17), a phrase with a distinctively cosmogonic ring and one deriving from the Orphic theogony.[14] It may be further noted that Ben Sira refers to Wisdom submitting her disciples to the test before revealing her secrets to them (Sir 4:17–19),[15] whereas in the Wisdom of Solomon there is no

13. Translated by G. H. Box and W. O. E. Oesterley in R. H. Charles (ed.), *The Apocrypha and Pseudepigrapha of the Old Testament* (2 vols.; Oxford: Clarendon, 1913), 1:326. On the phrase "must grasp" in line 22, cf. *1 Enoch* 93:11–14, *4 Ezra* 4, *Test. Job* 38:3–4. Wis 9:13–18 expresses similar sentiments, but only in reference to the human condition when it is bereft of divine wisdom, i.e., when individuals fail to activate their higher intuitive intellect.

14. O. Kern, *Orphicorum fragmenta* (Berlin: Weidmann, 1922) 91, 201. The same Orphic verse is quoted in the fourth-century-B.C.E. Derveni papyrus, and it recurs in the Hellenistic Jewish-Orphic poem. See my commentary, *Wisdom of Solomon*, 173–74.

15. Cf. Philo, *On Mating with the Preliminary Studies* 124 (LCL 261: 521). A somewhat similar notion is contained in the beautiful parable in the *Zohar* (2:99a–b); see G. G. Scholem, *On the Kabbalah and Its Symbolism* (New York: Schocken Books, 1965) 55–56. There is indeed a striking account of the persecution of the righteous person at the hands of the wicked (Wis 2:12–20) and one's ultimate vindication (Wis 5:1–23), but this is quite different from Wisdom's own testing of those who seek her.

hint of any test whatever. In short, the author of the Book of Wisdom appears to be undaunted in his total commitment to the pursuit of the philosophy and science of his age with all its challenges, whereas Sirach's goal in this sphere is more modestly conceived.

## THE SPIRITUAL ODYSSEY BY WHICH
## THE ASPIRANT BECOMES A SAGE

In sketching his own spiritual odyssey, the author of the Book of Wisdom confesses to a passion for *Sophia* that had gripped him from his early youth and had led him to the determination to cast his lot with her forever. There is no impression here of a mere literary artifice (although a number of literary models exist; see below); the reader is clearly in the presence of a genuine religious experience that has enveloped the author's mind and soul and has filled them with the divine presence:

> Her I loved and sought out from my youth,
> and longed to make her my bride,
> and I became a lover of her beauty.
> She magnifies her noble birth by enjoying intimacy with God,
> and the Master of All loved her.
> . . . . . . . . . . . . . . . . . . . . .
> I determined, then, to take her to live with me.
>
> (Wis 8:2–3, 9)

The author's unbridled love for Wisdom is even more vividly reflected in his magnificent fivefold description of her essence, in which she is conceived as an eternal emanation of God's power and glory. Here his language becomes luminous and almost lyrical and the reader is quickly borne aloft on the surging waves of the author's mystical passion:

> She is an exhalation from the power of God,
> a pure effluence from the glory of the Almighty;
> therefore nothing tainted insinuates itself into her.
> She is an effulgence of everlasting light,
> an unblemished mirror of the active power of God,
> and an image of his goodness.
> . . . . . . . . . . . . . . . . . . .
> She is fairer than the sun
> and surpasses every constellation;
> compared to the light of day she is found more radiant;
> for day is superseded by night,
> but over Wisdom no evil can prevail.
>
> (Wis 7:25–26, 29–30)

In addition to the concluding poem of Ben Sira (51:13–22), where one finds an artful use of erotic imagery to describe that author's ardent pursuit of Wisdom, there are several Greek models for the personification of Virtue/Wisdom as a beautiful maiden. In the famous parable known as the "Choice of Heracles" and later adapted by Philo (*On the Sacrifices of Abel and Cain* 21–29; LCL 227: 109–15), the Sophist Prodicus of Ceos had personified virtue as a fair maiden of high bearing who invited Heracles to choose her (Xenophon, *Memorabilia* 2:1:21–33; LCL 168: 95–103). There is also a eulogy that Aristotle wrote after the death of his friend Hermias, cast in the form of a hymn to Arete, Virtue. It begins as follows:

> Aretē, bringer of toil to the race of mortals, the fairest quarry in life, for the sake of thy maiden beauty is death itself a fate to be prized in Hellas, or the suffering of labours continued and endless. Such imperishable reward dost thou implant in the mind, reward above gold or ancestry or soft-eyed sleep.[16]

Moreover, in *On Mating with the Preliminary Studies*, Philo develops an allegory in which Abraham, the soul, is married to Sarah, who symbolizes Wisdom. The union, however, is unproductive, because the soul is not at first ripe for it, and Sarah is barren. She therefore sends the soul to mate with Hagar the Egyptian, who stands for the preliminary training of the Encyclical or School studies.[17] In time, however, Sarah

16. Translation from W. K. C. Guthrie, *A History of Greek Philosophy* (Cambridge: Cambridge University, 1981), 6:32. For the text see D. L. Page, *Poetae melici graeci* (Oxford; Clarendon, 1962) 444 (or Diogenes Laertius, *Lives of Eminent Philosophers* 5:7 [LCL 184: 451]; or Athenaeus, *The Deipnosophists* 15:696 [LCL 345: 231]). For commentary see J. Crossett, "Aristotle as a Poet: *The Hymn to Hermeias*," *Philological Quarterly* 46 (1967) 145–55; and Guthrie, *History of Greek Philosophy*, 6:31–34. Chrysippus is reported to have said that Justice was usually represented by the painters and orators of old as "of maidenly form and bearing, with a stern and fearsome countenance, a keen glance of the eye, and a dignity and solemnity which was neither mean nor cruel, but awe-inspiring" (Aulius Gellius, *Altic Nights* 14:4:2; LCL 212: 37). It may be noted that Homer had already personified death, sleep, fear, justice, rumor, fate, and prayers.

17. Plato had already argued that arithmetic, geometry, astronomy, and harmonics were useful for preparing the guardians for dialectic or pure philosophical reasoning (*Republic* 524D–31C; LCL 237: 159–95). By the Middle Ages seven liberal arts and sciences were recognized: the trivium, composed of grammar, rhetoric, and dialectic, and the quadrivium, composed of geometry, arithmetic, music, and astronomy. In one context or another, Philo mentions all these studies, but he "never gives a definitive enumeration of the disciplines which he included in the encyclia"; so A. Mendelson, *Secular Education in Philo of Alexandria* (Cincinnati: Hebrew Union College, 1982) 4. Although the School studies were rejected by the Epicureans and Cynics, and were an object of debate among the early Stoics, in Philo's time the Stoic view of them was probably that expressed by Seneca, that they were indispensable to philosophy (*Epistulae Morales* 88:25; LCL 76: 363).

can bear a child to Abraham, and then Hagar and Ishmael must be cast out. The allegory goes back to Bion of Borysthenes (ca. 325–255 B.C.E.), who is quoted by Pseudo-Plutarch (*Education of Children* 7D; LCL 197: 35) as saying that those who, unable to win philosophy, wear themselves out in preliminary learning are like the suitors of Penelope, who when they could not win the mistress contented themselves with the maids.[18]

## WISDOM IMMANENT AND TRANSCENDENT

In his all-consuming search for Wisdom, the author addresses a very moving prayer to his Lord with the earnest request that the divine throne-companion be graciously dispatched to him from the holy heavens above, so that she may labor at his side and enable him to learn the divine pleasure (Wis 9:1–6, 9–10).[19] It is evident that prayer for the author of the Wisdom of Solomon is in no way meant to serve as a substitute for the great effort and stringent training needed in order to attain wisdom. Indeed, far from being perceived as a supernatural modality, turning in prayer to God is seen as nothing but the reflex of God's turning to humans. The mysterious Muslim sage Khadir (or Khidr) put it well:

> Thy calling Allah! was my "Here am I,"
> Thy yearning pain My messenger to thee.[20]

It is clear that training, instruction, and predawn vigilance are prerequisites for the attainment of wisdom (Wis 6:17, 8:18, 6:14–15). A similar emphasis on the need for prayer is found in Ben Sira, who relates that while still young he sought wisdom in prayer before the temple (Sir 51:13–14; cf. 37:15), and yet insists on formal instruction (Sir 51:16–17,

---

18. For the use of sexual imagery in describing the intellectual quest, cf. Plato, *Republic* 490B (LCL 276: 29); and for Philo's skillful adaptation of the Greek allegory, see Y. Amir, "The Transference of Greek Allegories to Biblical Motifs in Philo," *Nourished with Peace: Studies in Hellenistic Judaism in memory of Samuel Sandmel* (ed. F. E. Greenspahn, E. Hilgert, and B. L. Mack; Chico, CA: Scholars Press, 1984) 15–25. For further discussion see my commentary, *Wisdom of Solomon*, 193.

19. A similar note is struck in Cleanthes' *Hymn to Zeus*: "O Zeus, all-bountiful, . . . / rescue mankind from wretched / Ignorance, scatter darkness from their minds, / Give them that wisdom by which Thou dost steer / All things in justice. . . ." Translated by F. H. Sandbach, *The Stoics* (Cambridge: Cambridge University, 1975) 111.

20. See R. A. Nicholson, *The Mystics of Islam* (London: Routledge and Kegan Paul, 1963) 113; cf. A. Schimmel, *Mystical Dimensions in Islam* (Chapel Hill: University of North Carolina, 1975) 81, 165–66: "I call Thee," sang Hallaj, "no, Thou callest me unto Thee!" (*Diwan*, qasida no. 1, v. 2). For Wisdom as both immanent and transcendent, see my commentary, *Wisdom of Solomon*, 41.

39:1–3, 6:35–37). The significance of prayer for the attainment of wisdom lies in the sage's firm conviction that all human accomplishments are in reality only the obverse side of effective divine action, and that the fundamental error that must be avoided above all is the self-conceit of one who thinks that human power is completely autonomous. Philo encapsulates this sentiment in his own characteristic way: "But I could not exercise it [virtue], shouldest thou not send down the seeds from heaven to cause her to be pregnant" (*The Worse Attacks the Better* 60; LCL 227: 243).

The helplessness of the human condition in the absence of divine wisdom is strongly emphasized by the author of the Book of Wisdom. It was a notion widely held in the wisdom literature of the ancient Near East, but it is given a Platonic twist in the Wisdom of Solomon and is skillfully integrated into its basic philosophical world view:

> For what man can comprehend the plan of God,
> or who can grasp what the Lord wills?
> The reasonings of mortals are wretched,
> and our devices precarious;
> for a perishable body weighs down the soul,
> and this tent of clay encumbers a mind full of cares.
> We barely make inferences concerning what is on earth,
> and laboriously discover what is at hand;
> who, then, has tracked out what is in the heavens?
> Who was privy to your design, unless you gave him Wisdom,
> and sent your holy spirit from on high?
> Thus it was that the paths of earthlings were set aright,
> and men were taught what pleases you,
> and were saved by Wisdom.
>
> (Wis 9:13–18)

The same idea is eloquently expressed in 1QH 4:30–32 in almost the same language:

> Righteousness, I know, is not of man,
>     nor is perfection of way of the son of man:
> to the Most High God belong all righteous deeds.
> The way of man is not established [*lôʾ tikkôn*]
>     except by the spirit which God created for him
>     to make perfect a way for the children of men.[21]

---

21. See D. Flusser, "The Dualism of Flesh and Spirit in the Dead Sea Scrolls," *Tarbiz* 27 (1985) 158–65 [Hebrew]; this translation of 1QH is from Vermes, *Dead Sea Scrolls in English*, 163.

In its Platonic context this stark recognition of human limitations leads neither to a sense of moral impotence nor to an abject reliance on a supernatural intervention of divine power to adjust the imbalance.[22] From the perspective of the Platonist understanding of reality, the human intellect, far from being eclipsed by divine action, is itself only an extension of it, its earthly image and expression. Hence, the negative intent of the Babylonian wisdom poet's question—"Where have mortals learnt the way of a god?"[23]—is transformed into the positive notion that all one need do is recognize the divine element already lurking within, and by acknowledging its potency allow it to become effectual. The *deus ex machina* has become the God within. The somber plaint of Agur's words, "Who has ascended heaven and come down?" (Prov 30:4; cf. Ps 115:16), yields to the bold confidence of the Platonist mystic who glories in the heavenly gift of reason.

## PURGATION

It is clear from various statements of the author that the aspirant after Wisdom will not attain this goal without first purging oneself of certain fundamental flaws and diverse layers of psychic debris that darken the mind and separate one from the ultimate object of desire. The spiritual quest requires replacing doubleheartedness with a singleness of heart, or learning how to be simple (Wis 1:1).[24] This involves ridding oneself of fraudulence, cunning stratagems, and all forms of injustice (Wis 1:4-5). It also requires a trusting heart that does not seek to test the Lord, and avoids every trace of murmuring against him, even while obeying his commandments (Wis 1:2, 10-11). One must become holy by observing God's holy ordinances in holiness (Wis 6:10). The author further warns

22. For the Platonic background see my commentary, *Wisdom of Solomon*, 41 and 207-9.

23. *Ludlul Bēl Nēmeqi* 38; see W. G. Lambert, *Babylonian Wisdom Literature* (Oxford: Clarendon, 1960) 41.

24. For doubleheartedness see Ps 12:3 (*bĕlēb walēb*), Sir 1:28. "Study to be simple," wrote Marcus Aurelius; "a moment and thou wilt be dead; and not even yet art thou simple" (4:26, 37; LCL 58: 83, 89). The fundamental virtue in the *Testaments of the Twelve Patriarchs* is *haplotēs* 'simplicity' and it is an equally important theme in Philo (*On the Creation of the World* 156 [LCL 226: 123-25], *On the Migration of Abraham* 153 [LCL 261: 221], *On Noah's Work as a Planter* 44-45 [LCL 247: 235-37], *On Mating with the Preliminary Studies* 36 [LCL 261: 477], and *Questions and Answers on Genesis* 4:165 [LCL 380: 450-51]). See my commentary, *Wisdom of Solomon*, 101. The term "wholeheartedness" (*lēb šalēm*) is one of the basic expressions of deuteronomic historiography (1 Kgs 8:61, 11:4, etc.) and was afterward adopted by the Chronicler; see M. Weinfeld, *Deuteronomy and the Deuteronomic School* (Oxford: Clarendon, 1972) 269.

against the enticements of momentary pleasures,[25] such as those of wine, perfumes, spring blossoms, reveling, and especially illicit sex: "For . . . the giddy distraction of desire perverts the guileless mind" (Wis 2:6-9, 3:13-4:6; quotation from 4:12). He further inveighs against blasphemy, arrogance, wealth, and false posturing (Wis 5:8). Above all, however, he points the finger at idolatry, which is born out of a mindless ignorance of God, as being the source of all moral corruption. Following what seems to have been a common Jewish-Hellenistic apologetic tradition, both the author of the Book of Wisdom and Philo draw a sharp distinction between the worship of the natural elements or the celestial bodies, and that of manufactured idols or animals, indicating that the offense of the former is less than that of the latter, although neither is to be excused (Wis 13:6-10; Philo, *On the Decalogue* 66 [LCL 320: 39-41]). The utter absurdity of image worship is easily discerned from the fact that it entails the worship of what is soulless or dead by those endowed with soul, and the addressing of prayers to creations inferior to the craftsmen who made them (Wis 15:17, 13:17-19, 14:18-20; Philo, *On the Decalogue* 69 [LCL 320: 41]). The author deftly describes the three kinds of false worship in the form of a climax (*klimax, gradatio*; see Quintilian 9:3:54 [LCL 126: 477]): the nature worshipers are described as mindless, the idolaters as wretched, and the Egyptian animal worshipers as most foolish of all (Wis 13:1, 10; 15:4).[26] The dire results of idolatry are vividly depicted:

> All is confusion—bloody murder, deceitful theft, corruption, treachery, tumult, perjury, . . . soul defilement, interchange of sex roles, irregular marriages, adultery, and debauchery. For the worship of the unspeakable idols is the beginning, cause, and end of every evil. (Wis 14:25-27)

The author thus drives his main point home, that to know God is the sum of righteousness and to recognize his power is the root of immortality (Wis 15:3).

## GOALS OF THE MYSTICAL QUEST

In a six-part *sorites* of chain syllogism, the author argues that the desire for Wisdom leads—through love for her and the keeping of her laws—to immortality and nearness to God, and that it is this intimacy with the divine that is the ultimate source of all human sover-

25. There may be an allusion here to the extreme view of Aristippus of Cyrene (a companion of Socrates), who enjoyed the pleasures that were at hand (*tōn parontōn*), but saw no reason to exert himself to gain pleasures that involved hard work or effort (Diogenes Laertius, *Lives of Eminent Philosophers* 2:66; LCL 184: 195-97).

26. For further detail, see my commentary, *Wisdom of Solomon*, 248-49.

eignty (Wis 6:17-21).[27] He therefore advises ruling monarchs to honor Wisdom if they wish to reign forever, and those desiring to join their ranks must clearly do likewise. It is undoubtedly significant that Wisdom's intimacy with God is described in virtually the same terms as human intimacy with Wisdom, for this almost certainly implies that the true goal of the pursuit of Wisdom is union with the deity itself, which can only be mediated through union with divine Wisdom.[28] Such union with *Sophia* is possible because of one's kinship with her (Wis 8:17), by virtue of possession of a mind permeated with her spirit (7:23-24). The author's highly charged language leaves one with the strong impression that he is very likely alluding to his own experience of union with the Wisdom aspect of God. The road to this mystical climax, however, does not in his view demand any special esoteric procedures or disclosures. He is convinced that it is an experience open to all, and along with his enthusiastic evocation of Wisdom's exquisite beauties he seeks only to outline the various stages that marked his own passionate search for her, that they may serve as a guide for others. To this end he employs a protreptic or exhortatory discourse in which he offers himself as a living paradigm for others to follow. He is thus not particularly concerned with the transmission of proverbial wisdom, concentrating instead on an attempt to persuade his readers not only that it is *Sophia* who brings her own to ultimate serenity and joy, but that she is openly accessible to all:

> Bright and unfading is Wisdom,
> easily beheld by those who love her,
> and found by those who seek her.
> She is first to make herself known to those who desire her;
> he who anticipates the dawn on her behalf will not grow weary,
> for he will find her seated [*paredron*] before his door.
> To set one's mind on her is perfect wisdom,
> and he that is vigilant for her sake will soon be free of care.
> For she herself seeks out those who are worthy of her;
> with gracious good will she appear to them on their path,
> and in every thought comes to meet them.

(Wis 6:12-16)

27. For a detailed discussion of the *sorites*, see ibid., 154-55. To the many examples given there, add Ahiqar Syriac Berlin 165 no. 55 and Ahiqar Slavonic no. 73; see Lichtheim, *Late Egyptian Wisdom Literature*, 14-17.

28. See U. Wilckens, "σοφία, σοφός," *Theological Dictioary of the New Testament* (ed. G. Kittel and G. Friedrich; Grand Rapids: Eerdmans, 1971), 7:499; and my commentary, *Wisdom of Solomon*, 41. There is already an incipient movement in this direction in Prov 8:30-31, where Wisdom indicates that just as she was God's joy, so was her own joy with humankind.

## THE ISIS MYSTERIES AND QUMRAN

In detailing his spiritual odyssey, the author of the Book of Wisdom thus strikes a religious chord new to the Hebrew wisdom writings, echoing a type of religiosity that was characteristic of the contemporary Isis mysteries in the pagan world and the earlier Dead Sea sect within the Jewish world. This new chord consisted in an extraordinary sense of mystical intimacy and feelings of ineffable joy in the individual's experience of God. With regard to the Isis cult one catches a glimpse of this passionate religious intensity in the vivid account given by Apuleius of the conversion of the Ass-Man Lucius. Using deliberately veiled language, Lucius describes the heart of his initiation ceremony in the following words:

> I approached the boundary of death and treading on Proserpine's threshold, I was carried through all the elements, after which I returned. At dead of night I saw the sun flashing with bright effulgence. I approached close to the gods above and the gods below and worshiped them face to face.[29]

He later addresses Queen Isis as follows:

> Thou in truth art the holy and eternal savior of the human race, ever beneficent in helping mortal men, and thou bringest the sweet love of a mother to the trials of the unfortunate. . . . But I am bereft of talent in singing thy praises . . . indeed a thousand mouths and tongues are not enough for the task. . . . Therefore I shall try to do the only thing possible for one who is devoted but indigent; I shall keep forever, stored in my inmost heart, the memory of thy divine countenance and most holy godhead.[30]

Finally, when keenly agitated by the divine command to undergo yet a third initiation, a gracious form enlightens him thus in a prophetic message by night:

> There is no reason for you to be frightened. . . . Be filled with gladsome joy, rather, because the gods so constantly think you worthy, and indeed rejoice that you will achieve three times a boon that is scarcely granted to others even once. From this number deservedly conclude that you will be happy forever.[31]

---

29. *Metamorphoses* 11:23; translated by J. G. Griffiths, *The Isis-book (Metamorphoses, Book XI)/ Apuleius of Madauros* (Leiden: Brill, 1975) 101.

30. Ibid., 102–3; *Metamorphoses* 11:25; cf. Sir 43:27–30.

31. Ibid., 107; *Metamorphoses* 11:29.

As for the Dead Sea Scrolls, the following passage from the *Hôdāyôt* (*Thanksgiving Hymns*) recalls the impassioned language of the author of the Book of Wisdom when he speaks of his beloved *Sophia*:

> I give thanks unto Thee, O Lord,
> for Thou hast freed my soul from the pit
> and drawn me up from the slough of hell
> to the crest of the world.
> So walk I on uplands unbounded
> and know that there is hope
> for that which Thou didst mold out of dust
> to have consort with things eternal.
> For lo, Thou hast taken a spirit
> distorted by sin,
> and purged it of the taint of much transgression,
> and given it a place
> in the host of the holy beings,
> and brought it into communion
> with the sons of heaven.
> Thou hast made a mere man to share
> the lot of the Spirits of Knowledge,
> to praise Thy name in their chorus.
>
> (1QH 3:19-23)[32]

Like the composer of *Hôdāyôt*, the author of the Book of Wisdom experiences the raptures of divine knowledge in his present existence and already enjoys his prize of immortality. On the other hand, as already seen, in contrast both to the Isis mysteries and the Qumran Scrolls, he disdained the path of esotericism, constantly conveying instead the openness of Wisdom's path, which requires neither secret initiations nor entry into the community of a holy elect.

32. T. H. Gaster, *The Dead Sea Scriptures in English* (Garden City, NY: Doubleday, 1956) 138.

# JESUS AS SAGE:
# AN INNOVATING VOICE
# IN COMMON WISDOM

## Bernard Brandon Scott

Unlike the Hebrew Bible, the New Testament does not include a collection of wisdom books. Consequently, there neither is an archetypical genre nor has wisdom been a dominant category of scholarly analysis. Wisdom material is embedded within other genres. At one extreme, the Sermon on the Mount is a wisdom sermon functioning as a single unit within the narrative genre of a gospel. At the other extreme, proverbs are frequently embedded within dialogues (e.g., Luke 9:57–62), frequently with an eschatological or apocalyptic cast. This precipitates a continuing debate on categories in the study of wisdom. For example, almost all interpreters agree that the Gospel of John involves a wisdom theology, but is it Jewish, Hellenistic, or Gnostic wisdom?[1] But perhaps most momentous for the study of wisdom in the New Testament was the rise of apocalyptic in primitive Christianity. The subsequent struggle with the delay of the parousia, and finally, in Adolf Harnack's phrase, "acute . . . hellenizing of Christianity" have obscured the influence of wisdom in the New Testament period.[2] These factors have tended to push wisdom to the background or periphery.

A critical observation, however, tells against this subordination of wisdom. At the root of the synoptic tradition is the common wisdom tradition, at least formally. The most common forms are those of common wisdom—proverbs, beatitudes, and parables. That is the clear

Bernard Brandon Scott is Darbeth Distinguished Professor of New Testament at Phillips Graduate Seminary, Tulsa Center.

1. See the recent survey of G. MacRae, "Gnosticism and the Church of John's Gospel," *Nag Hammadi, Gnosticism, and Early Christianity* (ed. C. W. Hedrick and R. Hodgson; Peabody, MA: Hendrickson, 1986) 84–96. A similar debate is now raging over the *Gospel of Thomas*; see S. L. Davies, *The Gospel of Thomas and Christian Wisdom* (New York: Seabury, 1983).

2. See Harnack's *History of Dogma* (7 vols.; Boston: Roberts, 1897–1900; repr. New York: Dover, 1961), 1:227.

conclusion of Rudolph Bultmann's magisterial analysis of the Logia under the heading "Jesus as the Teacher of Wisdom."[3] Yet the problem remains how to interpret these forms—against which possibilities of the wisdom tradition should one interpret the material?

## THE ESCHATOLOGICAL JESUS

A common assumption is that synoptic wisdom sayings should be interpreted apocalyptically or eschatologically. Nils Dahl's interpretation of the so-called parables of growth is a prime exhibit.[4] Yet the problem with an eschatological interpretation of the wisdom tradition is that the eschatology often is imposed on the parable rather than emerging from it. This can be seen in two aspects. First, C. H. Dodd's noneschatological interpretation of these same parables at least makes the case that another option is available. As Dodd admits, the interpretation does not emerge from the parable.[5] Second, the eschatology obscures other aspects of the parable or even denies them. For example, in the parable of The Mustard Seed, the significance of the mustard shrub in providing shade for the birds in the same way as the great tree of Lebanon is totally bypassed in the eschatological interpretation.[6]

## THE CYNIC JESUS

A second more recent proposal by several scholars moves in the right direction, yet in my judgment fatally misses the point. This group reads the wisdom sayings of Jesus against Cynic traditions. It is now becoming more evident that Mark and the other Synoptics adapted Cynic models for understanding Jesus as teacher.[7] So the question arises as to

3. Bultmann, *The History of the Synoptic Tradition* (New York: Harper and Row, 1963) 69–108, esp. 105–6 and 166.

4. Dahl, "The Parables of Growth," *Studia Theologica* 5 (1951) 132–66; repr. in his *Jesus in the Memory of the Early Church* (Minneapolis: Augsburg, 1976) 141–66. The influence of Dahl's article would be hard to overstate. J. Jeremias, *The Parables of Jesus* (New York: Scribner, 1972), makes several important references to Dahl's article, on pp. 149, 151, 220, 225.

5. Dodd, *The Parables of the Kingdom* (New York: Scribner, 1961) 142; Dahl admits a similar position ("Parables of Growth," 140–41). For him, the debate with the Pharisees over the signs of the kingdom is the key to interpreting the parables of growth.

6. R. Funk, *Jesus as Precursor* (Philadelphia: Fortress, 1975) 19–26; J. D. Crossan, *In Parables* (New York: Harper and Row, 1973); and my *Jesus, Symbol-Maker for the Kingdom* (Philadelphia: Fortress, 1981) 67–73.

7. See V. K. Robbins, *Jesus as Teacher* (Philadelphia: Fortress, 1984).

whether this was an adaptation of non-Cynic material or whether Jesus himself was a teacher of Cynic wisdom. F. Gerald Downing proposes five elements that belong to the Cynic agenda: (1) the model of teacher, (2) the mission and gathering of disciples, (3) the suffering philosopher-teacher, (4) attacking corrupt authorities and the corrupting ethos, and (5) the identification with and belonging to the lower classes.[8] The two elements of the synoptic picture of Jesus that do not fit with this Cynic teacher model are the wonder-working activity and eschatology. Downing readily admits this and hazards a guess that the wonder-working is connected with Jesus' expectation of the kingdom, since in the ancient world wonder-working is prominently identified with kings.[9] But this is somewhat disingenuous, since kingdom is the point of entry for eschatology.[10] For Downing, "the Cynic-sounding tradition of a healer with an eschatological message originates at least for the most part with the individual teacher to whom it is ascribed—Jesus."[11]

Besides the obvious problems with wonder-working and eschatology,[12] there are even more substantial grounds against a Cynic interpretation of Jesus. The primary *forms* of the synoptic and Thomas traditions are forms closely identified with the Jewish wisdom tradition.[13] As an example of a primary Jewish form I would point to the parables and legal sayings. While short narratives have been found in Hellenistic literature, the parable as a form is limited to the Jesus tradition[14] and the rabbinic tradition. The clearest formal parallels to the Jesus parables are still the rabbinic parables. Second, the *content* of these forms is Jewish. The debate issues are Jewish in their interest and background. This is

8. Downing, "The Social Contexts of Jesus the Teacher: Construction or Reconstruction." *New Testament Studies* 33 (1987) 445. See also B. L. Mack, "The Kingdom Sayings in Mark," *Forum* 3/1 (1987) 3–47; unfortunately Mack's *The Myth of Innocence* (Philadelphia: Fortress, 1988) arrived too late for thorough consideration here, although it is a very significant work.

9. Downing, "Social Contexts of Jesus the Teacher," 446.

10. But see Mack, "Kingdom Sayings in Mark," 11–17, who points out that Cynics did use kingdom language.

11. Downing, "Social Contexts of Jesus the Teacher," 448.

12. Downing's effort to explain all the data with the Cynic model may be too ambitious. It is possible that Jesus was eclectic, or that apocalyptic (eschatology) was introduced into the tradition as a result of the resurrection.

13. One must be careful about reconstructing an overly pure Jewish tradition in isolation from Hellenism. There is still a need to develop clearer models for Judaism and Hellenism and their intermingling. Perhaps earlier scholars overstated the difference, while recent ones have blurred the distinction.

14. Parables are found only in the Synoptics, the *Gospel of Thomas*, and the *Apocryphon of James*.

not to deny the significance of the Cynic materials for understanding the development of the gospel traditions.[15] The Cynic parallels, however, appear to have more to do with the rise of literate narrativity in early Christianity and the increasing Hellenization of the tradition. There is no doubt that the Jesus tradition was amenable to Cynic revision and it clearly happened in the early process of writing (composing) the tradition in the Greek language. But the problems with identifying the root of the wisdom tradition with Cynic wisdom remains irresolvable: the forms as well as the content are Jewish.

## TORAH IN A WISDOM SAYING

If the closest formal parallels with the Jesus wisdom tradition are the rabbinic wisdom tradition, there are nonetheless formidable problems with identifying the Jesus wisdom tradition with that preserved in the rabbinic texts. First, Jesus was not a Pharisee, although "teacher" or "rabbi" is the most common title for him in the Synoptics. More important are the questions of dating and historical difference between the Jesus and rabbinic traditions. The rabbinic tradition is a school or scribal tradition. But perhaps the most important difference between the two traditions is the way in which they handle Torah. Torah is the hermeneutical symbol that dominates the rabbinic tradition.[16] For example, the rabbinic parable is used almost exclusively as an element in the exegesis of Torah; no parable in the Jesus tradition is used a similar way.[17] Jesus' relation to Torah is more jaundiced or, perhaps, more distinctive.

An example will illustrate my point. Q 6:27–36 (Luke 6:27–36 || Matt 5:38–42) is a rhetorical complex constructed of originally independent pieces.[18] The rhetorical structure is quite subtle, made up of three imperatives, three balancing rhetorical questions, and a conclusion.

15. The influence of Cynic common wisdom on Jewish wisdom and their similarity (but without dependence) need further clarification.

16. *m. 'Abot* 5:22; see M. Fishbane, "Torah and Tradition," *Tradition and Theology in the Old Testament* (ed. D. A. Knight; Philadelphia: Fortress, 1977) 275–300.

17. R. Johnston, "The Study of Rabbinic Parables: Some Preliminary Observations," *Society of Biblical Literature 1976 Seminar Papers* (Missoula, MT: Scholars Press, 1977) 337–57, clearly lays out the pattern of formal relation of rabbinic parable to exegesis of Torah. D. Stern has followed up on this model with a most interesting study: "Rhetoric and Midrash: The Case of the Mashal," *Prooftexts* 1 (1981) 261–91.

18. Bultmann, *History of the Synoptic Tradition*, 96; J. S. Kloppenborg, *The Formation of Q* (Philadelphia: Fortress, 1987) 173–76.

A       Love your enemies
B       Bless those who curse you
C       Give to everyone who begs from you
A₁      If you love those who love you
B₁      If you do good to those who do good to you
C₁      If you lend to those from whom you hope to receive

These balancing triads create the undergirding structure of the Q peri-cope. As a wisdom speech its function is "to persuade by argument and rhetorical question."[19]

This structure makes it evident that v 29 is an addition. Not only does it provide an example of B ("Bless those who curse you"), but the form is obviously different. The imperatives are formulated in the second-person plural, while the two cases of v 29 are in the second-person singular and follow the form τῷ + participle + imperative.[20] Verse 29 typifies the alternatives facing the interpretation of wisdom. Matthew preserves this verse but without the elaborate rhetorical structure of Q. For Matthew the saying has been preserved in the context of a legal discussion (ἠκούσατε ὅτι ἐρρέθη) and the saying is now a discourse about the *jus talonis* (Exod 21:24-25, Lev 24:50, Deut 19:21). Siegfried Schulz had argued that Q 6:29 was a prophetic, charismatic interpretation of Torah.[21] For evidence he cited the quotation of the *jus talonis* but also the λέγω ὑμῖν formula of Q 6:27. But this argument is not convincing for three reasons: (1) the formula λέγω ὑμῖν can and often is used as a nonprophetic formula and (2) the *jus talonis* occurs as a direct quote only in Matthew.[22] Further, (3) there are clear Hellenistic wisdom parallels for vv 27, 28, and 30.[23] But that is not true for v 29. The problems at this point become tangled. Verse 29 was originally inserted into the Q complex. Yet Luke is not responsible for the current rhetorical structure,[24] and it is uncertain whether Matthew knows the complex in the present Q form. Furthermore when Q 6:29 is compared with Matt 5:39b-40 an interesting correlation appears.

---

19. Kloppenborg, *Formation of Q*, 179.

20. See S. Schulz, *Q: Die Spruchquelle der Evangelisten* (Zurich: Theologischer Verlag, 1972) 121-23; Kloppenborg, *Formation of Q*, 176, is in agreement.

21. Schulz, *Die Spruchquelle der Evangelisten*, 123-24.

22. So Kloppenborg, *Formation of Q*, 179, elaborating upon D. Zeller, *Die weisheitliche Mahnsprüche bei den Synoptikern* (Forschung zur Bibel 17; Würzburg: Echter, 1977) 103-6.

23. Zeller, *Die weisheitliche Mahnsprüche bei den Synoptikern*, 104-6.

24. Kloppenborg, *Formation of Q*, 178, presents a complex argument for the development of the pericope and its attraction to the Beatitudes.

|                    *Q 6:29*                    |              *Matt 5:39b–40*              |
|------------------------------------------------|------------------------------------------|
| τῷ τύπτοντί σε ἐπι τὴν σιαγόνα | ἀλλ᾽ ὅστις σε ῥαπίζει εἰς τὴν δεξιὰν |

τῷ τύπτοντί σε ἐπι τὴν σιαγόνα     ἀλλ᾽ ὅστις σε ῥαπίζει εἰς τὴν δεξιὰν
πάρεχε καὶ τὴν ἄλλην, καὶ ἀπὸ τοῦ     σιαγόνα [σου], στρέψον αὐτῷ καὶ
αἴροντός σου τὸ ἱμάτιον καὶ τὸν     τὴν ἄλλην· καὶ τῷ θέλοντί σοι
χιτῶνα μὴ κωλύσῃς.     κριθῆναι καὶ τὸν χιτῶνά σου λα-
     βεῖν, ἄφες αὐτῷ καὶ τὸ ἱμάτιον·

To the one who strikes you upon     But whoever slaps you on the right
the cheek offer even the other, and     cheek, turn to him even the other.
from the one who takes from you     And to the one who wishes to sue
the coat do not withhold even the     you in court and to take your tunic,
undergarment.     let him have even your coat.

The closest similarity is between the first two phrases of the parallel sentences.[25] The main variations are due to the redactional performance of incorporating an originally separate piece of tradition. Given the similarity concerning the striking on the cheek, the most arresting difference between the Matthean and Q proverbs is that Matthew mentions the *right* cheek. Why is the Matthean text so specific? Does it make any difference? In the context of Q the specification right would be contrary to the generality of the wisdom exhortation and argument. Yet even the second part of the parallel sentence depends on some form of specification for its meaning, either tunic to coat or coat to undergarment. The tendency of the oral tradition is from specific to the general. There is no compelling reason that Matthean redaction would have added right. The Torah text employed for comment does not specify which eye. Thus it would appear that originally the parallel sentence involved the right cheek.

If right cheek is part of the original proverb, what is its purpose? Robert Tannehill has suggested that this is an example of what he terms a focal instance. A focal instance is language so specific and extreme that it subverts its literalness. The specificness and extremeness place the saying "in deliberate tension with a basic pattern of human behavior."[26] The specificness over-narrows or localizes the instance. A focal instance has the exact opposite effect of a legal saying. A legal saying uses specific literal language to clarify a situation,[27] while a focal instance capitalizes on specific language in a nonliteral sense to engage

25. There is a parallel to the second clause in *Gos. Thom.* 95: "If you have money, do not lend it at interest, but give [it] to one from whom you will not get it back."

26. Tannehill, *The Sword of His Mouth* (Semeia Supplements 1; Missoula, MT: Scholars Press/Philadelphia: Fortress, 1975) 72.

27. Ibid., 26.

the imagination of the hearer, to force the hearer to make a decision. By its over-narrow concentration, a focal instance breaks down literalness. If taken literally both proverbs would lead to ridiculous behavior—one who would be black and blue and naked. John Dominic Crossan has amplified Tannehill's argument by arguing that the two aphorisms of the right cheek and the surrendering of one's coat are a parody of case law. For Crossan, "Jesus is not offering case law, however ideal or radical, but he is challenging his legal tradition." [28]

The Tannehill/Crossan argument is important because it allows one to understand the development of the tradition. There was an originating saying dealing with turning the other cheek when struck on the right one. This was a parody, an over-specific case law mocking the *jus talonis*. The focal moment insists that the hearer move beyond the inappropriate literal language to the imaginative language of metaphor to relieve the tension. The saying was then clustered in the oral tradition with another saying about lending. This cluster was later incorporated into both Q and Matthew in somewhat different ways:[29] Matthew exploited the connection to the *jus talonis* and subordinated the saying to a legal context; Q suppressed the specificity and made the statement a generalized wisdom saying incorporating it into a larger wisdom rhetorical unit.

This example of the successive performances of a legal saying clarifies several different ways in which Torah can be exploited within the wisdom tradition. In the rabbinic tradition Torah is the hermeneutical principal that governs the use of wisdom. Torah is wisdom. Matthew uses a wisdom saying of Jesus to radicalize an exegesis of Torah, much as rabbinic parables justify new interpretations of Torah. Q on the other hand suppresses the Torah reference in favor of wisdom. Finally, in the saying of Jesus one hears the parody or subversion of Torah and wisdom.

## THE DISTINCTIVE VOICE

Crossan in his elaboration upon Tannehill made a jump that Tannehill himself did not make. Crossan identified the speaker of the saying as Jesus, because for him this type of parody is typical of Jesus. Implicitly Crossan was relying on the criterion of coherence. Crossan is raising what I would term the question of voice. Voice is the distinctive key of a given performer. It is those combination of factors that allows one to

---

28. Crossan, *Raid on the Articulate* (New York: Harper and Row, 1976) 67-68.
29. Matthew may have broken down the present Q pericope, but since Q has various layers, it is not clear which layer Matthew may be using.

recognize such a performer. Voice is a particularly appropriate metaphor for Jesus, since he is the product of an oral environment. But voice
is an issue in the study even of moderns who leave behind concrete,
literate artifacts. Cynthia Wolff in her brilliant biography and critical
study of Emily Dickinson makes the following pertinent point.

> Emily Dickinson led such an unremarkable, quiet life that few details of
> her day-to-day existence survive. Principally, she must be known through
> her written remains. The extant photograph has the quality of a momento;
> it satisfies a certain curiosity for many readers; however, few feel it has
> captured the real Emily Dickinson. The *real* Emily Dickinson resides in
> the poetry. Life has been supplanted by art.[30]

Wolff notes that the real Emily Dickinson resides *in* the poetry. By
"real" Wolff does not mean historical—the image in the photograph.
Wolff identifies the real Emily Dickinson with what she calls her "voice,"
those distinctive elements that allow one to identify a poem as an Emily
Dickinson poem. Yet this voice produces a paradox. "This is, by no
stretch of the imagination, a body of poetry that might be construed as
a series of lyrics spoken by many different people. . . . It is the enigmatic
'Emily Dickinson' readers suppose themselves to have found in this
poetry, even in the extreme case when Dickinson's supposed speaker is
male."[31] The criteria of the Dickinson voice are all those characteristics
that make up "the enigmatic 'Emily Dickinson.'"

Similarly when Crossan remarks that specifying the right cheek is a
parody of Jewish case law reminiscent of Jesus, he is hearing that
distinctive voice that allows him to distinguish that voice from other
voices in the New Testament, in this case the voice of Jesus from those
of Matthew and Q.

A chief characteristic of Jesus is his identification as a teacher, but
more important is the form-critical observation that at the base of the
early tradition as represented by Q, Thomas, Mark, Matthew, and Luke
is the common Jewish wisdom tradition.[32] Bultmann made such a point
in his analysis of the *mashal* forms in the Synoptics. They belong to "a
popular, unliterary artistic tradition."[33] But to hear the voice of Jesus
one must listen closely, for this common, nonliterary wisdom tradition
provides the background noise or static against which the distinctive
voice is heard.[34]

30. Wolff, *Emily Dickinson* (New York: Knopf, 1986) 163.
31. Ibid., 178.
32. Even Johannine traditions may exhibit such a basis; see B. Lindars, *Behind the Fourth Gospel* (Studies in Creative Criticism 3; London: SPCK, 1971).
33. Bultmann, *History of the Synoptic Tradition*, 166.
34. Stern, "Rhetoric and Midrash," 56, develops the notion of "a kind of ideal thesaurus of stereotyped, traditional elements" so that a parabolist can improvise a

## ANONYMOUS VS. DISTINCTIVE VOICE

James Williams draws a distinction between proverb and aphorism that is important to the issue of voice. He flags as decisive "the difference in principle between a *collective* voice and an *individual* voice."[35] The construct of the voice of Jesus' aphorisms or parables embodies a distinctive, individual voice whose patterns, accents, styles, themes, and even ideology are recognizable. This is to be distinguished from other proverbs and parables whose voice, being "anonymous," is the projection of common wisdom.

The most prominent characteristic of this distinctive voice, to borrow a musical metaphor, is a tendency to play in minor keys. The most obvious example of a minor key, although not usually noticed as such, is the presiding symbol of Jesus' language, the kingdom of God, a relatively infrequent term in the first century.[36] The more dominant themes such as the Day of the Lord, God as King, or even Torah are virtually absent, suppressed, or parodied in the aphorisms and parables of Jesus.

This preference for a minor key is easily exemplified in the parables. The parable of The Land of a Rich Man (Luke 12:16–20, *Gos. Thom.* 63) draws on a common mytheme that pertains to greed, a major problem in a limited-goods society like first-century Palestine.[37] Since wealth is finite, what the rich person possesses (hoards) is not available for distribution. Greed, then, is a denial of community. The Thomas version of this parable represents this major mytheme—the rich man of that parable seeks to use his money to make more money. The voice of the Thomas parable is common wisdom, anonymous. But the Lucan version differs, even though the voice of Luke is also clear.[38] In that parable the problem is not the accumulation of wealth (greed), but its disposal, or rather lack of disposal. This represents a very minor theme in the tradition and discloses the distinctive voice. The harvest that is so great that it necessitates building all new barns is surely a

---

parable for the illustrand under spontaneous conditions. I have elaborated upon this suggestion in *Hear Then the Parable* (Philadelphia: Fortress, 1989).

35. Williams, *Those Who Ponder Proverbs* (Bible and Literature Series 2; Sheffield: Almond, 1981) 80.

36. See J. J. Collins, "The Kingdom of God in the Apocrypha and Pseudepigrapha," *The Kingdom of God in Twentieth Century Interpretation* (Peabody, MA: Hendrickson, 1987) 81–95; and my *Jesus, Symbol-Maker*, 6–11.

37. See Sir 31:6–11: "Many have come to ruin because of gold. . . . Blessed is the rich man who is found blameless. . . . Who is he? We will call him blessed for he has done wonderful things among his people . . . and the assembly will relate his acts of charity." On the theory of limited goods, see B. Malina, *The New Testament World* (Atlanta: John Knox, 1981) 75–90.

38. Luke has clear preference for monologues in his parables; see my *Hear Then the Parable*, chap. 3.

miracle. Yet this miracle is not used wisely as Joseph used Egypt's harvests, for the rich man plans to keep it for his own pleasure. There is no obvious divine intervention to right this wrong. The man simply dies in his sleep. To the villagers he is still a hero who saved the magnificent harvest for them in brand new barns and they will probably say prayers for him in the synagogue.

In the aphoristic parody of case law this same voice can be heard. The *jus talonis* is parodied in terms of the right cheek. As Tannehill observes, if followed literally, the hearer would be black and blue or, in the case of the coat, naked.[39] The parody is off-key. It does not take seriously the responsibility to make a fence around the Torah, as a later generation would have it.

If one can distinguish a distinctive voice from the anonymous voice of common wisdom, nevertheless, that distinctive voice is in jeopardy. Even though these aphorisms and parables come out of and play against common wisdom, in the end common wisdom frequently subverts the dialectic and disguises the voice. This is neither a reinstitution of the negative criterion, nor the search for a unique Jesus under the guise of listening for the distinctive voice. This triumph of common wisdom over the distinctive voice has a foundation not only in the conservative character of oral society[40] but also in the very way in which memory operates. Short-term memory, which lasts only microseconds, is very limited. At most, short-term memory can hold only three to four items. When the capacity of short-term memory is exceeded, one fails miserably. For example, if one were to try to repeat after just a glance the number 8032962632, it would be most difficult. But if the number is broken up into groupings of three or four (803-296-2632), it becomes much easier.[41] Short-term memory employs these groupings and when items are transferred to long-term memory, they remain in the groupings. It is really the groupings that one remembers. Humans do this not only with numbers but with all memories—they group or schematize them. Common wisdom, proverbs, traditional tales, etc., are all ways in which a culture schematizes its wisdom. Humans then use these schematic memories to organize and structure

39. Tannehill, *Sword of His Mouth*, 70.

40. See W. Ong, *Orality and Literacy: The Technologizing of the World* (New York: Methuen, 1982) 41–42. It is also probably based upon the relation between signifier and signified. Since that relation is arbitrary, language is haunted by an instability and so the practice of language is a kind of amnesia in which one forgets the arbitrary relation between signifier and signified and pretends that it is necessary. Linguistically, metaphor is an exploitation of the arbitrary relation.

41. United Parcel Service, a company noted for its extensive use of efficiency studies, instructs its delivery personnel to break all numbers into groups of three so that they will not have to look at the number more than once.

what they remember. F. C. Bartlett in his book *Remembering* showed that people remember even literal events in terms of cultural schemata. Memories introduce elements from cultural schemata that were not in an original event, and similarly suppress some elements of the original event that do not fit in the cultural schemata. In a test performed by Bartlett, his subjects were told an American Indian folktale. When asked to repeat it they always modified it toward those similar stories or schemata from their own culture.[42]

Thus one should expect that Jesus' wisdom sayings would be reclaimed by common wisdom, either internally in subsequent performances of the structure by others or external to the structure in the interpretation. In the parable of A Grain of Mustard Seed, found in both Luke and Matthew (so probably in Q), the seed grows into a tree, an appropriate symbol of the kingdom (a great thing) in common wisdom, while the use of a mustard seed and its growth into a shrub (Mark) is a bit of whimsy that pokes fun at the expectation of a magnificent kingdom. Internal structural shift is also evident in the Beatitudes as they occur in the Synoptics and the *Gospel of Thomas*. The distinctive voice is there and obvious in the presence of a kingdom made up of the poor. This is, of course, paradoxical, for one expects that the poor are blessed because theirs *will be* the kingdom, not *is* the kingdom. But the schemata of common wisdom exert their influence upon performances. Matthew and Luke in their performances of the structure modify it toward their schemata, for Matthew "in spirit" and for Luke by contrasting the beatitude with a woe against the rich, so that both poor and rich are literalized. In both cases the focal moment is lost.

## LEAVENING COMMON WISDOM

Sometimes the schemata assert themselves outside the structure. One of the most unambiguous examples of this occurs with the parable of The Leaven. This parable appears in Matthew and Luke (Q) in almost identical versions and without interpretation.[43] So the interpretation is not derived from redaction, but from how one applies the schemata associated with the parable's terms.

Leaven belongs to conventional language, to an established metaphorical network. That leaven was in the ancient world a symbol for

42. Bartlett, *Remembering* (Cambridge: Cambridge University, 1932) 206. The literature on the empirical limits of memory is vast and is of importance to the topic under discussion.

43. *Gos. Thom.* 96 is an example of internal structural modification—a little leaven becomes big loaves.

moral corruption has long been recognized. A. R. S. Kennedy in his turn-of-the-century article in *Encyclopaedia Biblica* summarized the evidence as follows: "In the view of all antiquity, Semitic and non-Semitic, panary fermentation represented a process of corruption and putrefaction in the mass of the dough."[44] The usage in the Hebrew Bible and the New Testament sustains Kennedy's summary.

The physical characteristics of leaven abet the metaphor for corruption.[45] Leaven is made by storing a piece of bread in a damp, dark place until mold forms. The bread rots and decays, until it ferments, unlike modern yeast which is domesticated.

In the commands for the Feast of the Unleavened Bread, leavened bread must not be eaten and even must be cleansed out of the house: "For seven days no leaven shall be found in your houses; for if any one eats what is leavened, that person should be cut off from the congregation of Israel" (Exod 12:19; see also Exod 13:3, 6–7; Deut 16:3–4). Not only does leaven symbolize impure Israel, conversely, unleavened bread symbolizes holy Israel: "Seven days you shall eat unleavened bread; on the first day you shall put away leaven out of your houses. . . . On the first day you shall hold a holy assembly" (Exod 12:15–16). During the seven days of the feast, a feast of the Lord to be observed forever, unleavened bread replaces leavened bread to symbolize the people's holiness. In Israel there is an equation that leaven equals the unholy, the everyday, and unleavened equals the holy, the sacred, the feast. Leaven and unleavened are physical objects that function as metaphors for and replicate the fundamental division between the sacred and the profane.

This negative association with leaven persists in the New Testament. Twice Paul quotes an otherwise unattested proverb, "A little leaven leavens the whole lump." In Gal 5:9 he uses the proverb to warn that someone is leading the Galatians from the true path by demanding circumcision. The proverb implies that this one is corrupting them, that one person is destroying the good of the group. This analogy of the leaven exactly parallels the proverb, "One rotten apple spoils the whole barrel." In 1 Cor 5:6–8 Paul interweaves the proverb into a more complex rhetorical structure. Boasting, like a little leaven, can corrupt all the good one does. But then leaven suggests its contrary, the feast of unleavened bread: "Cleanse out the old leaven that you may be a new lump, as you really are unleavened." The distinction between leaven as evil and unleavened as holy is implied. The metaphor is somewhat

44. Kennedy, "Leaven," *Encyclopaedia Biblica* (ed. T. K. Cheyne and J. S. Black; London: A. & C. Black, 1902), 3:2754.

45. G. Lackoff and M. Johnson, *Metaphors We Live By* (Chicago: University of Chicago, 1980) 19, argue that every metaphor has a basis in experience and cannot be comprehended apart from that experimental basis.

mixed because old leaven suggests new lump based on the metaphorical structure old/new, but Paul switches to leaven/unleavened as the contrast. This leads naturally then to "For Christ, our paschal lamb, has been sacrificed." Finally, Paul concludes by contrasting the symbols of leaven and unleavened as representing moral states: "Let us, therefore, celebrate the festival, not with the old leaven, the leaven of malice and evil, but with the unleavened bread of sincerity and truth."

The Pauline proverb, like all proverbs, summarizes a piece of common wisdom, that the involvement with even a little evil can corrupt the whole. This same proverbial insight underlies Jesus' warning to the disciples, "Beware of the leaven of the Pharisees." In Mark the warning is combined with a warning against the "leaven of Herod" (Mark 8:15). It follows immediately on the feeding of the four thousand and the Pharisees' request for a sign. In Mark the warning is enigmatic, its specific reference unclear. Matthew and Luke resolve the enigma and clarify the reference. Matthew interprets the leaven to be "the teaching of the Pharisees and Sadducees" (Matt 16:12), and Luke appends an explanation that the leaven is hypocrisy (Luke 12:1), for which he has just condemned the Pharisees (11:37-52). Regardless of application, all three understand leaven to be negative and corrupting. Furthermore, as both Paul and the Synoptics prove, not only is leaven itself a negative metaphor but the action of leavening is likewise viewed negatively, as corrupting.

Despite the overwhelming evidence that leaven is a metaphor for moral corruption and absence of leaven is the metaphor for holiness, traditional interpretation of the parable of The Leaven has ignored the negative aspects.[46] Why? Because the metaphorical structure of the kingdom of God implies holy and good and so conflicts with leaven's metaphorical structure, which implies moral corruption. I. A. Abrahams thoroughly surveyed rabbinic usage and concluded exactly what I have. Yet he exempts the parable of Jesus from the universal negative connotation: "It is probable, however, that the parable also takes account of the result; the leavened mass of humanity, through intrusion of the leaven, attains a superior moral condition, just as the leavened bread is a more perfect food that unleavened."[47] Yet precisely the process of leavening is seen as moral corruption in the ancient world. Only the repeated, though subtle, Christian insistence that leaven is good can explain how a Jew could envision leavened bread as "more perfect

46. This traditional interpretation has also missed the negative associations with "woman," "hid," "until all was leavened." For a treatment of all these factors, see my *Hear Then the Parable*, chap. 15.

47. Abrahams, *Studies in Pharisaism and the Gospels* (Cambridge: Cambridge University, 1917-24; repr. New York: Ktav, 1967), 1:51.

food than unleavened." But in this parable one hears that distinctive voice, a voice at odds with common wisdom. In this case common wisdom did not overpower the voice in the performance of the parable's internal structure but externally in its interpretation. The cultural schemata were imposed from outside.

## COMMON WISDOM SUBVERTED— TESTING AN HYPOTHESIS

The contest between common wisdom (the anonymous voice) and the distinctive voice furnishes a two-edged criterion. On the one hand it says that those sayings that exhibit only common wisdom do not belong to the Jesus corpus. On the other hand, those logia that exhibit the contest with common wisdom, do belong to the corpus. But the issue is not so simple, for often the skill of an interpreter is needed to reconstruct the common wisdom of the period, to be sensitive to the clues contained in a saying that reveal common wisdom or the distinctive voice. Even more, one must imagine how a wisdom saying would function in the matrix of Jesus' language and the language of the period.[48] The issue is not *Sitz im Leben* as conceived by Joachim Jeremias, but reconstructing the linguistic, mythical, and wisdom traditions in which the sayings operate as semantic phenomenon.

Since what I am proposing is an hypothesis, namely that Jesus' distinctive voice is recognized in the way he innovates in the common wisdom tradition by playing in minor keys and using wisdom images against themselves, to test the hypothesis I must show its predictive powers. In pure science this is easy; the hypothesis should predict the outcome of an experiment. But in the historical disciplines this is a more formidable challenge because experiments with unknown responses are more problematic to design. The material is so familiar that I have nothing on which to try afresh my hypothesis. Well, almost nothing new. In the *Gospel of Thomas* there are several parables that have no parallel in the synoptic tradition and until recently have been unknown. The parable of A Women with a Jar (*Gos. Thom.* 97) is a parable without interpretation in Thomas, is enigmatic, and has generated little scholarly discourse. Thus it should present a good test case for my hypothesis. Can one hear a distinctive voice that involves the characteristic interplay with common wisdom, or is the parable a piece of common wisdom? First the parable:

> The kingdom of the [father] is like a certain woman who was carrying a [jar] full of meal. While she was walking [on the] road, still some distance

48. Crossan, *Finding Is the First Act* (Semeia Supplements 9; Philadelphia: Fortress/ Missoula, MT: Scholars Press, 1979), is an excellent example of this reconstructive effort.

from home, the handle of the jar broke and the meal emptied out behind her [on] the road. She did not realize it; she had noticed no accident. When she reached her house, she set the jar down and found it empty.

The parable occurs in the middle of a triptych of parables, The Leaven, The Empty Jar, and The Murderer. The rhetorical pattern is built around a series of contrasts: little leaven/large loaves, full jar/ empty jar, powerful man/weak man. Within these contrasts the middle parable of the woman and her empty jar is an example of failure. Jacques Ménard in his gnostic reading of the parable sees it as exhibiting the remoteness of the redeemer from the foreign earth and points to a passage in the *Gospel of Truth* where spoiled jars are broken "and the master of the house does not suffer loss. Rather [he] is glad because in place of the bad jars there are full ones which are made perfect."[49] This suggestion seems farfetched and not obvious. Perhaps more to the point, it shows that the expectation is that full jars are good and empty (broken) jars are bad. Hugh Montefiore notes that the point in the *Gospel of Thomas* is the imperceptible loss of the meal.[50] The woman is an example of those who do not know wisdom. Since the parable in the *Gospel of Thomas* exemplifies unknowing, the repetitive phrase, "she did not realize it, she had noticed no accident" probably is an addition to fit Thomas's performance and tugs the parable toward common wisdom.

Montefiore further notes that the parable "is as homely as the Parable of the Leaven" and then provides an eschatological interpretation. The parable, he argues, refers to the imperceptible coming of the kingdom until it is suddenly revealed, referring to the parable of A Man Casts Seed (Mark 4:26-29) for a comparable theme. The problem with this interpretation is that Montefiore seems to forget that when the woman gets home the jar is empty! But he is correct to point to the parable of The Leaven, for both it and the parable of A Woman with a Jar employ negative images, and, in a way he does not suspect, the parable is like the parable of A Man Casts Seed because both make a scriptural allusion.

The parable of A Woman with a Jar requires of its hearer two deliberate operations at the discourse level.[51] Initially one observes that the woman arrives home empty handed. How is that like the kingdom? The kingdom is here identified with loss, accident, emptiness, bareness.

49. Ménard, *Le Évangile selon Thomas* (Nag Hammadi Studies 5; Leiden: Brill, 1975) 197-98. This treatment of The Woman with a Jar is highly dependent on my earlier study in *Hear Then the Parable*, chap. 14.

50. H. E. W. Turner and H. Montefiore, *Thomas and the Evangelists* (SBT 35; London: SCM, 1962) 71.

51. See the distinction of S. Chatman, *Story and Discourse* (Ithaca, NY: Cornell University, 1978) 2.

Thus the parable is much like the parable of The Leaven, for it identifies the kingdom with the unclean, not with its expected signified, the clean and whole.

The next operation does not relieve this tension but increases it. The parable echoes the story of the widow of Zarephath (1 Kgs 17:8–15).[52] A famine ravages the land and Elijah is told to go to Zarephath and there "I have commanded a widow to feed you" (v 9). He spots a widow at the city gate and asks for a piece of bread. She replies: "As the Lord your God lives, I have nothing baked, only a handful of meal in a jar, and a little oil in a cruse" (v 12). She had been gathering sticks in order to bake some cakes for her child and herself. Elijah commands her to bring him the first cake: "For thus says the LORD, the God of Israel, 'The jar of meal shall not be spent . . . until the day that the LORD sends rain upon the land'" (v 14). She does as Elijah commands and the prophet, she, and her child ate for many days: "The meal was not spent . . . according to the word of the LORD which he spoke by Elijah" (v 16).

The parable of A Woman with a Jar revokes the story in 1 Kings. Given the significance of Elijah in eschatological speculation and the prominent protection promised widows,[53] this parable's referencing of the Elijah story creates a real scandal. There is no prophet to come to the woman's aid, nor will her jar be filled.[54] The kingdom is not identified with divine intervention, but divine emptiness. Like the parable of The Leaven, this parable attacks and subverts the myth of the appearance of God. Blessed are the poor for theirs is the kingdom of God. God is identified with the unclean. This not only coheres with Jesus' association with the outcast, but parallels the use of a Samaritan as the hero who rescues a Jew in the ditch.

## CONCLUSION

William Beardslee in his pioneering study of synoptic proverbs noted that the function of a proverb was to preserve common wisdom, the insight into typical behavior that makes life liveable, that solves the problems of everyday life.[55] While proverbs are anonymous, without

52. E. Waller, "The Parable of the Leaven: A Sectarian Teaching and the Inclusion of Women," *Union Seminary Quarterly Review* 35 (1979–80) 103, notices the similarity.

53. The triadic formula widow/orphan/foreigner summarizes in the Hebrew Bible those in need of special protection.

54. In the parable In a City There Was a Judge (Luke 18:2–5) the judge comes to the widow's aid not out of any sense of justice but because she is bothering him.

55. Beardslee, "The Uses of the Proverbs in the Synoptic Gospels," *Interpretation* 24 (1970) 67–69.

voice, they do exert a presence, the presence of the community and tradition. Jesus' innovation in the wisdom tradition is the discovery of an individual sage's voice that subverts the voice of commonality. Thus it prevents the proverb or parable or beatitude from providing that presence that resolves the conflicts of life.[56] But the sage's voice is a disappearing artifact. In the end the voice exposes a nonpresence without image. The parable, the proverb, the beatitude imitate in language the no-image God of Israel. The expected divine presence becomes a divine absence. Idolatry, of course, is to give that voice an image, to make the absence a presence, to fill up the woman's jar, to turn the leaven into the holy, to make of the right cheek a rule.[57]

56. This innovating voice likewise attacks the myth of the apocalyptic redeemer.

57. In the course of this essay, I have not attempted to explore the important question of the relation of common wisdom to school wisdom; on the latter see, for example, J. Suggs, *Wisdom, Christology, and Law in Matthew's Gospel* (Cambridge: Harvard University, 1970).

# THE EARLY RABBINIC SAGE

## Steven D. Fraade

From when the dust of the destruction of the Second Temple settled in the late first century C.E. until the early third century, a historically critical period of over one hundred years during which the rabbinic sage movement took root and underwent significant growth and development, there is not a single clearly datable rabbinic source, nor much in the way of extrarabbinic sources relating to those sages.[1] From the early third century on there is a steady succession of rabbinic documents, which constitute the main sources of information about Judaism and Jewish history of that period. Those texts take the form of biblical commentaries (*midrash*) and translations (*targum*), topically arranged collections of rabbinic rules (*mishnah*), and discursive expositions of those rules (*talmud*). Each of these collections incorporates traditions and the literary crystallizations of traditions that predate the time and circumstances of their formation into redacted texts. Many of these incorporated traditions and texts are likely to derive from times anterior to the appearance of the earliest rabbinic documents in the third century. But the process of textual redaction has left such a deep mark on these incorporated traditions and texts that their extraction (not to mention distillation and synthesis) for purposes of historical representation of a time much earlier than their redaction is fraught with difficulties.[2]

Steven D. Fraade is Mark Taper Professor of the History of Judaism at Yale University.

A substantially expanded version of this essay will appear as chapter 3 of my forthcoming book *From Tradition to Commentary: Torah and Its Interpretation in the Midrash Sifre Deuteronomy* (Albany: State University of New York).

1. I speak here principally of literary sources, but for the period of the late first and second centuries C.E. we are also largely at a loss for archeological sources relevant to the rabbinic sage and his institutions.

2. On the general problem of the use of highly rhetoricized rabbinic narrative forms for purposes of historical and biographical reconstruction, especially with regard to the figure of the sage, see Henry Fischel, "Story and History: Observations on Greco-Roman Rhetoric and Pharisaism," *American Oriental Society, Middle West Branch, Semi-Centennial Volume* (ed. Denis Sinor; Bloomington: Indiana University, 1969) 59–88. For a

I begin with these general comments on rabbinic literature since it is at the heart of that vast and complex literature that we find the figure and class of the rabbinic sage (*ḥākām*).[3] In order to construct a picture of that class of sages, it is to that literature—with all its difficulties for historical reconstruction—that one must turn. I say "construct" since the information about the rabbinic sage is not found gathered in any one part of rabbinic literature. Distributed throughout are anecdotal stories about individual sages in their dealings with one another, and occasionally with nonsages, both Jewish and non-Jewish; legal and nonlegal teachings attributed to individually named sages, groups of sages, or the collectivity of sages; statements prescribing attitudes and conduct appropriate to the sage; and discussion of the institutions within which the sages worked or upon which they sought to exert their influence. Several important studies have culled rabbinic literature for these sorts of information out of which to fashion a synthetic, narrative portrayal of the rabbinic sage and his society, in some cases typologically or chronologically differentiated.[4] But in such work of distillation, another,

---

discrete case study, see Robert Goldenberg, "The Deposition of Rabban Gamaliel II: An Examination of the Sources," *Journal of Jewish Studies* 23 (1972) 167–90. On the impossibility of using rabbinic sources to write biographies of individual sages, see William Scott Green, "What's in a Name?—The Problematic of Rabbinic 'Biography,'" *Approaches to Ancient Judaism: Theory and Practice* (ed. W. S. Green; Missoula, MT: Scholars Press, 1978), 1:77–96; idem, "Storytelling and Holy Men: The Case of Ancient Judaism," *Take Judaism for Example: Studies toward the Comparison of Religions* (ed. Jacob Neusner; Chicago: University of Chicago, 1983) 29–43; Jacob Neusner, "The Present State of Rabbinic Biography," *Hommage à Georges Vajda: Études d'histoire et de pensées juives* (ed. Gérard Nahon and Charles Touati; Louvain: Peeters, 1980) 85–91 (with references to Neusner's earlier writings on this question). This set of problems is not unique to the study of ancient Judaism, as can be seen from M. I. Finley, *Ancient History: Evidence and Models* (New York: Viking, 1986), esp. chap. 2, "The Ancient Historian and His Sources."

3. Although several terms are employed in rabbinic literature for the sage, *ḥākām* is the most frequent and inclusive of them, denoting members of the rabbinic class. On the use of the word "class" for the rabbinic sages, see Lee I. Levine, *The Rabbinic Class in Palestine during the Talmudic Period* (Jerusalem: Yad Izhak ben Zvi Institute, 1985) 2 [Hebrew]. The terms *rab* ('master') and *rabbî* (literally, 'my master') are used mainly in direct address, as titles preceding a particular sage's name, or when the master-disciple relationship is specifically being referred to. In inscriptions it is difficult to discern when the term *rabbî* (and its cognates) is a conferred title denoting a member of the rabbinic class and when the term is simply honorific, denoting someone deserving of respect. See Hershel Shanks, "Is the Title 'Rabbi' Anachronistic in the Gospels?" *JQR* 53 (1962–63) 337–45; idem, "Origins of the Title 'Rabbi,'" *JQR* 59 (1968–69) 152–57; E. Lohse, "ῥαββί, ῥαββουνί," *Theological Dictionary of the New Testament* (ed. G. Kittel and G. Friedrich; Grand Rapids: Eerdmans, 1968), 6:961–65; Shaye J. D. Cohen, "Epigraphical Rabbis," *JQR* 72 (1981) 1–17.

4. See in particular the following writings of Ephraim E. Urbach: "Class-Status and Leadership in the World of the Palestinian Sages," *Proceedings of the Israel Academy of Sciences and Humanities* 2 (1968) 38–74; "Talmudic Sage: Character and Authority,"

equally important type of information about the rabbinic sage is often ignored: the discursive practices of those texts, which in and of themselves give, I shall argue, the best expression to who the rabbinic sages were or sought to become (the two often being difficult to differentiate).

## THE "CHAIN OF TRADITION"

The problem with representational portrayals of the rabbinic sage from the evidence of rabbinic literature is not only that they reduce that literature to its discursively denuded contents, but that they assume those contents to be themselves representational, not only of the time when the texts in which they are found were redacted but of the earlier times for which they provide fragmentary accounts. Such portrayals fail to take seriously enough the nature of that literature (and the same may be said, *mutatis mutandis*, of ancient literature more generally) as a medium dedicated *both* to transmission and to transformation: its texts not only transmit received traditions from an earlier time, but simultaneously transform—for purposes of their own place and program in time—what they seek to transmit.

Let me illustrate this point, and at the same time move further into the topic of this essay, with a well-known rabbinic text from *The Sayings of the Fathers*:

> Moses received Torah from Sinai and transmitted it to Joshua, and Joshua to the elders, and the elders to the prophets, and the prophets transmitted it to the men of the Great Assembly. They said three things: Be thorough in judgment, raise up many disciples, and make a fence around the Torah. Simeon the Just [ca. 200 B.C.E.] was among the last of the Great Assembly. He used to say. . . . Antigonus of Soko received [Torah] from Simeon the Just. He used to say. . . . (*m. ʾAbot* 1:1–3)[5]

This "chain of tradition" continues with five pairs of teachers, each of whom adds one or more teachings to what he has received before transmitting the newly transformed Torah to the next link in the chain.

---

*Jewish Society through the Ages* (ed. H. H. Ben-Sasson and S. Ettinger; New York: Schocken, 1969) 116–47; *The Sages: Their Concepts and Beliefs* (2 vols.; Jerusalem: Magnes, 1979), esp. 1:564–648. For more critical approaches, which are therefore more limited in focus, see, for the Babylonian sages, Jacob Neusner, *A History of the Jews in Babylonia* (5 vols.; Leiden: Brill, 1965–70), 4:279–402; idem, *School, Court, Public Administration: Judaism and Its Institutions in Talmudic Babylonia* (Atlanta: Scholars Press, 1987); and for the Palestinian sages, Levine, *The Rabbinic Class in Palestine during the Talmudic Period*.

5. For English translations of the *Sayings of the Fathers*, see Charles Taylor, *Sayings of the Jewish Fathers* (2d ed.; Cambridge: Cambridge University, 1897; repr. New York: Ktav, 1969), or Joseph Hertz, *Sayings of the Fathers* (New York: Behrman, 1945).

The last pair is that of Hillel and Shammai (ca. 30 B.C.E.–10 C.E.), who in turn (despite some kinks in the chain) transmit what they have received and taught to Rabban Johanan ben Zakkai (*Sayings* 2:9), who together with his five students establishes the first specifically rabbinic center for learning at Yavneh (Jamnia).[6]

In this "genealogical" chain, each link (explicitly beginning with the men of the Great Assembly, but implicitly for their predecessors) transforms as it transmits Torah. That which is added at each successive link in the chain is no less Torah than that which precedes it as it takes its place within the cumulative tradition, which is said to originate in the divine revelation at Sinai.[7] Presumably, each teacher (or generation of teachers) taught more than is here explicitly credited to him and thus transformed what he received more complexly than is here schematically expressed. Furthermore, there is no way of verifying whether the named teachers actually said what is credited to them, the attributions themselves being a product of the tradition's complex history of transmission and transformation.

## THE PROTO-RABBINIC SAGES—AN UNCERTAIN LINK

The transformative quality of the opening chapter of *The Sayings of the Fathers* is as much historiographic as it is literary. In historiographic terms the chain set forth in the *Sayings* is most significant for what it omits: the priesthood. Like other rabbinic texts it presumes that proto-rabbinic sages had primary responsibility for the transmission and teaching, not to mention judicial implementation, of Torah texts and traditions during the Second Temple period. Modern scholars have similarly presumed that some time in the third century B.C.E., with the increasing canonization of the Hebrew Scriptures and the hellenization of the priesthood, a new class of *nonpriestly* scribes arose to challenge the authority of the priests as guardians and interpreters of Israel's Scriptures and traditions, even though that authority is repeatedly vested, overall, in the descendants of Levi by Scripture itself. These scholars argue that the priesthood, having become increasingly self-serving, lost touch with the needs and sentiments of the common people, who turned instead for teaching and guidance to the lay scribes and their antipriestly "democratizing" program of extending Torah

6. Much has been written on this passage. See in particular Elias Bickerman, "La chaîne de la tradition Pharisienne," *RB* 59 (1951) 44–54; Moshe D. Herr, "Continuum in the Chain of Torah Transmission," *Zion* 44 (1979) 43–56 [Hebrew].

7. Note the following often cited saying: "Even that which an advanced disciple will some day teach before his master was already said to Moses at Sinai" (*y. Pe'a* 2:6 [17a]).

teaching into everyday life. These lay scribes, it is claimed, were the precursors of the Pharisees and in turn of the rabbinic sages.[8]

As attractive as this picture may be from a postpriestly perspective, it is hardly supported by the extant evidence from the Second Temple (that is, prerabbinic) period. First, there is little evidence for the existence of a broad class or movement of nonpriestly (and certainly not antipriestly) scribes and sages in this period.[9] Second, the extant sources, right up to and shortly following the destruction of the temple, continue to associate the overall authority to preserve, interpret, teach, and legally apply sacred Scriptures with the priesthood, even as that authority shifted between different priestly families and strata and even as that priesthood was split by sectarian schisms. Those groups that rejected the Jerusalem temple and its officiating priesthood as being illegitimate or defiled did not question in principle Israel's priestly "constitution," but rather created alternative priestly structures and ideologies in the hope that one day the Jerusalem temple and priesthood would be transformed along the lines of their alternative priestly programs.[10] Rather than a *split* between priests and scribes, the Second Temple sources show evidence of inner-priestly *shifts* of Torah and legal authority to specialized priestly subgroups, particularly scribes and

8. Some influential works that evidence this view are Viktor Tcherikover, *Hellenistic Civilization and the Jews* (Philadelphia: Jewish Publication Society, 1959) 124–25; Emil Schürer, *The History of the Jewish People in the Age of Jesus Christ* (*175 B.C.-A.D. 135*) (rev. ed.; ed. Geza Vermes et al.; Edinburgh: T. & T. Clark, 1979), 2:322–23; George Foote Moore, *Judaism in the First Centuries of the Christian Era* (3 vols.; Cambridge: Harvard University, 1930), 1:308–9; Elias Bickerman, *From Ezra to the Last of the Maccabees: Foundations of Postbiblical Judaism* (New York: Schocken, 1962) 67–71; Martin Hengel, *Judaism and Hellenism: Studies in Their Encounter in Palestine during the Early Hellenistic Period* (2 vols.; Philadelphia: Fortress, 1974), 1:78–83. More recently, see Isaiah Gafni, "The Historical Background," *The Literature of the Sages, First Part: Oral Tora, Halakha, Mishna, Tosefta, Talmud, External Tractates* (ed. Shmuel Safrai; Compendia Rerum Iudaicarum ad Novum Testamentum 2/3a; Assen/Maastricht: Van Gorcum; Philadelphia: Fortress, 1987) 4; and Shaye J. D. Cohen, *From the Maccabees to the Mishnah* (Library of Early Christianity; Philadelphia: Westminster, 1987) 101–3, 160, 172–73, 218. See my study "Of Priests, Scribes, and Sages in Second Temple Times" (forthcoming, *JBL*) for a more extensive marshalling and analysis of the evidence for the following challenge to that conventional view.

9. I use the terms "priestly" and "priesthood" to refer to members of families that trace their ancestry back to Aaron (including the Levites), whether or not they served as temple functionaries. For a useful survey of the different priestly social strata in Second Temple times, see Menaḥem Stern, "Aspects of Jewish Society: The Priesthood and Other Classes," *The Jewish People in the First Century* (ed. S. Safrai and M. Stern; Compendia Rerum Iudaicarum ad Novum Testamentum 1/2; Assen/ Amsterdam: Van Gorcum; Philadelphia: Fortress, 1976) 561–630.

10. This finds its clearest expression in the Dead Sea Scrolls, but also in the Enochic corpus, both of which are discussed in my "Of Priests, Scribes, and Sages."

Levites (the latter being, in a sense, quasi-priests), with the two often overlapping.[11] However, it is important to stress that despite such shifts and schisms, the extant sources concur that the prophetic authority to interpret and the juridical authority to implement scriptural laws remained principally with the priesthood, however it may have been conceived and distributed at different times and by different groups.[12] There were, however, important exceptions to this pattern, especially at the end of the Second Temple period: the quasi-priestly Pharisees (who are by all accounts the closest antecedents to the rabbinic sage) and individual nonpriestly charismatic teachers (*sophistai*) and their disciple circles. Unfortunately, it is impossible to gauge the extent and impact of either of these developments. It is important, however, not to make of such exceptions the rule.[13]

In light of the preponderance of evidence for the continued paramountcy of the priesthood in matters of Torah preservation, transmission, and adjudication throughout the Second Temple period, how are we to understand the absolute omission of the priesthood from the rabbinic chain of tradition text cited above? One might conclude that while the opening chapter of *The Sayings of the Fathers* is not a correct representation of that period of the history of Torah transmission, it *is* symptomatic of the situation in a time when sages and not priests filled such roles in Israelite society. This text may then be thought of as the creation of such sages who wished retroactively to transform the past from the vantage of an *already* transformed present.[14] But, lacking

11. Note in particular the transference of teaching and administrative roles from the priests to the Levites, and in particular to the Overseer (*měbaqqēr*) at Qumran; see 1QSa 1:22–25; CD 13:2–7, 14:3–18; see my "Of Priests, Scribes, and Sages" for discussion and further evidence. For the New Testament "scribes" as members of the Levite class, see Daniel R. Schwartz, "'Scribes and Pharisees, Hypocrites': Who Were the Scribes?" *Zion* 50 (1985) 121–32 [Hebrew]; and my "Of Priests, Scribes, and Sages" for further discussion.

12. This is not to deny the existence or importance of a lay elite (that is, not specifically priestly) in Second Temple Jewish society, but to argue that its functions are generally not evidenced to be those of Torah teaching and interpretation. At the *local* level a hereditary lay elite is likely to have sat on regional and village courts and councils. Instruction of children, when not conducted by their parents, may have been entrusted, especially by the rich, to professional (lay?) tutors. However, there is little evidence, as is often presumed (see sources cited above, n. 8) that the synagogues were a lay alternative to the temple or that *institutions* of lay education were in place before the destruction of the temple. For further details see my "Of Priests, Scribes, and Sages."

13. Another exception might have been the early followers of Jesus, but we know too little about them to say much (having to depend again on later, retroactively transformative sources).

14. This is the implicit argument of M. D. Herr ("Continuum in the Chain of Torah Transmission"), who understands the shift of Torah teaching from priests to sages to have taken place in early Hellenistic times (third century B.C.E.), and the tradition about the chain of tradition to have come into being some time in the last century B.C.E. or the first century C.E.

external evidence to the contrary, one could just as easily argue that this text at the opening of the *Sayings* was created at a time when the priesthood still filled, or claimed for themselves, such roles, and that the creators of this text, *critical* of that present situation, sought, perhaps in part through the very force of their *discourse,* to transform it.[15] And finally, but not necessarily independent of the preceding possibilities, one might consider this text, and the wider body of rabbinic texts for which it stands, to be transformative in still another way: disciples of sages, through their engaged study and hence interpretation of this text, might be *empowered* to view the very activity of *their* study as part of an unbroken, living chain of Torah and tradition extending back to and deriving from Sinai, with themselves as its latest links.[16]

　　This is by no means to suggest that the above-cited text or rabbinic literature more generally should be dismissed as pseudepigraphic fabrication. Rather it is to caution that the *representational* employment of such a text, not only for periods anterior to the time of its redaction but for that time as well, needs to be conditioned by considerations of the dialectical intertwining of transmission and transformation that is so central to the self-understanding of the rabbinic sages who claimed the status of Torah for their own rhetorical texts of teaching.

## EXTENT OF KNOWLEDGE OF THE PERIOD OF THE TANAAIM (CA. 70–212 c.e.)

This brings me to the line that divides the extant sources for the history of the sage, pre- and post-70 (roughly speaking). For the period between about 70 c.e. and the early third century there are virtually no nonrabbinic sources against which to measure the historical reliability of rabbinic accounts of the lives and teachings of the sages of that time (the tannaim). By contrast, for the period before 70 there is a varied

15. It is often assumed that with the destruction of the temple in 70 c.e. the priesthood's social status and influence suddenly terminated, leaving the Pharisaic sages without serious competition for the roles of religious and political leadership. Several kinds of evidence suggest rather that priestly status and influence continued to be factors in Jewish communal life long after 70 c.e. and that the priesthood's longstanding and scripturally rooted claims to be the authentic guardians, interpreters, and adjudicators of Israel's Scriptures and laws were not so easily set aside. For details, see my *From Tradition to Commentary,* chap. 3, n. 20.

16. The terminology of symptomatic, critical, and transformative, and the conception of their dialogical interplay, is adapted from Dominick LaCapra, *History, Politics, and the Novel* (Ithaca, NY: Cornell University, 1987). For a fuller discussion of the interrelation of historical and literary criticisms in the study of rabbinic literature, see my *From Tradition to Commentary,* chap. 1, as well as my two-part review essay, "Interpreting Midrash 1: Midrash and the History of Judaism." *Prooftexts* 7 (1987) 179–94; "Interpreting Midrash 2: Midrash and Its Literary Contexts," *Prooftexts* 7 (1987) 284–300 (with errata in *Prooftexts* 8 [1988] 159–60).

abundance of materials with which to test the Rabbis' claims to be the
successors to an uninterrupted chain of nonpriestly sages extending
back well into Second Temple times (and ultimately to Sinai), and from
which to fashion (albeit not easily or completely) an alternative picture
of the antecedents to the rabbinic sage.[17]

It is as though one enters a historiographic tunnel shortly after the
destruction of the Second Temple, and does not emerge until the early
third century. "Before" and "after" pictures can be put together (however blurry and partial), but there is much less certainty of how much
of the transformation in Jewish learned circles that occurred within that
tunnel occurred near its beginning (at Yavneh after the destruction of
the temple), around its middle (in the Galilee following the failed Bar
Kochba revolt), or not until its end a century and a half later (with the
ascendancy of R. Judah as Patriarch). It should not be surprising if the
earliest texts of rabbinic transmission and transformation, appearing in
the third century, project some of the most significant transformational
aspects of rabbinic Judaism back onto its "foundational" figures and
their times: R. Akiba, R. Joḥanan b. Zakkai, Hillel, and their presumed
antecedents.[18]

In what follows I shall examine a selection of rabbinic texts that
deal, either explicitly or implicitly, with the rabbinic sage. They are all
drawn from the third-century *Sifre* commentary to the Book of Deuteronomy, the earliest commentary to that book, created shortly after
the emergence of the rabbinic sage from, what might historiographi-
cally be termed, the tannaitic tunnel. This collection is of particular
interest since it is the Book of Deuteronomy that is the most didactic of
the books of the Pentateuch—in its rhetorical style, its narrative framework, and its frequent admonitions to Israel to teach and learn God's
words. But it is also the most explicit of the books of the Pentateuch in

17. This I have done in my aforementioned forthcoming study "Of Priests, Scribes,
and Sages." I do not mean to suggest that Second Temple Jewish sources are without
their transformative effects and that they can be taken as straight historical representations. Each one, depending on its rhetorical genre, intellectual and political purpose, and
social setting, displays a different intermixture of symptomatic, critical, and transformative aspects. However, the very *variety* of these texts' genres, purposes, and perspectives
permits, by juxtaposing and testing their different views against one another, construction
of at least a rough picture of who the Second Temple antecedents to the rabbinic sage are
likely or unlikely to have been.

18. Depictions of what occurred at Yavneh per se, as desirable as these may be,
remain, therefore, highly speculative. For two recent examples, see Shaye J. D. Cohen,
"The Significance of Yavneh: Pharisees, Rabbis, and the End of Sectarianism," *HUCA* 55
(1984) 27–53; and Jacob Neusner, "The Formation of Rabbinic Judaism: Yavneh (Jamnia)
from A.D. 70 to 100," in *Aufstieg und Niedergang der römischen Welt: Principat*, vol. 19:
*Religion* (ed. W. Haase; Berlin: de Gruyter, 1979), 2:3–42.

stressing the role of the priests, here being the descendants of Levi, as the authoritative teachers of God's revelation and as the judicial authorities for the implementation of Israel's covenantal laws (see Deut 17:8–13, 18; 19:7; 21:5; 24:8; 27:9–10; 31:9–11, 25–26; 33:10). The Book of Deuteronomy, thus, presents the early rabbinic exegetes and the redactors of the *Sifre* with numerous opportunities to assert the importance of study of Torah as a central religious obligation, while challenging them to express their claims to be the paramount authorities in matters of Scripture and Jewish law in exegetical engagement with a biblical text that associates that authority with the hereditary priesthood. This is a challenge to advance the rabbinic work of collective self-definition in relation to a scriptural text that, perhaps like social reality, offered some resistance to that work.

My examination of the following texts, therefore, will not seek simply to extract information about the rabbinic sage (as if those texts were linguistically autonomous of the sages who both produced and studied them). Rather, it will seek to engage critically the discursively transformative practices of those texts as the best guides to who the rabbinic sages were and were working to become—successors to the priests, prophets, and elders of earlier times—through the medium of their own self-defining engagement in the work of textual study.

## TWO TYPES OF SAGE AND A DUAL IDENTIFICATION

The scriptural context of Deut 1:13 is Moses' decision to distribute leadership responsibility, especially in judicial matters, to a select group of *lay* tribal leaders (the "elders" elsewhere).[19] According to the lemma, these are to be selected according to three qualities:

> Select from each of your tribes persons who are wise [*ḥăkāmîm*], and discerning [*năbônîm*], and experienced [*yeduʿîm*], and I will appoint them as your heads.

The discussion of this verse in *Sifre Deuteronomy*, between Arios[20] and R. Jose, revolves around the difference between two of these, the

19. Cf. Exod 18:13–26, where Moses shares his authority with a lay leadership at Jethro's recommendation, and Num 11:16–25, where he does so at God's command. The larger context of the *Sifre*'s commentary to this biblical passage is treated in my *From Tradition to Commentary*, chap. 3.

20. Arios is presumably a nonrabbi, if not a non-Jew; see *t. B. Meṣ.* 3:11 (see the edition by Moses Samuel Zuckermandel, *Tosefa, ʿal pi kitve yad Erfurt uVina* [Trier, 1881–82]; repr. as *Tosephta, Based on the Erfurt and Vienna Codices* [Jerusalem: Bamberger and Wahrmann, 1937]) 376. Moshe D. Herr, ("The Historical Significance of the Dialogues between Jewish Sages and Roman Dignitaries," *Studies in Aggadah and*

*ḥākām* and the *nābôn*, now representing not simply two intellectual qualities but two types of intellectuals:

> [A] With regard to this Arios asked R. Jose [ca. 150 c.e.]: "Who is a wise person [*ḥākām*]?" He replied to him: "Whoever maintains [*mĕqayyēm*] his learning." [Arios asked:] "But is this not a discerning person [*nābôn*]?" He replied to him: "'[Persons who are] discerning' has already been mentioned."
> [B] What is the difference between a wise person and a discerning person? A wise person resembles a rich money changer. When someone brings him [money] to examine he examines it, and when no one brings him [money] to examine he takes out his own and examines it. A discerning person resembles a poor money changer. When someone brings him [money] to examine he examines it, and when no one brings him [money] to examine he sits waiting anxiously.[21]

The midrashic passage as a whole (if not R. Jose) clearly favors the *ḥākām* over the *nābôn*. R. Jose defines the *ḥākām* as one who, unlike the *nābôn*, not only learns Torah, that is, acquires a knowledge of it, but maintains it through constant review. What follows (paragraph *B*), the metaphorical comparison of these two types of learned men, may either be seen as R. Jose's further response or as an editorial juxtaposition to the preceding dialogue, the latter being my preference.

The contrast between *ḥākām* and *nābôn* as two different types of scholars is now illustrated through comparison with rich and poor money changers, the preference for the *ḥākām* now becoming manifest, even though the precise difference between the two requires interpretation on the part of the student of the text. Like the rich and poor money changers, the *ḥākām* and the *nābôn* provide a service to those who

*Folk-Literature* (ed. Joseph Heinemann and Dov Noy; Scripta Hierosolymitana 22; Jerusalem: Magnes, 1971) 149, considers Arios to have been a convert, but the evidence is too slim to allow any such identification.

21. *Sifre Deut.* §13 (Finkelstein 22.1–5). The critical edition is S. H. Horovitz, *Siphre ad Deuteronomium* (ed. Louis Finkelstein; Corpus Tannaiticum 3:3:2; Berlin: Jüdischer Kulturbund in Deutschland, 1939; repr. as *Sifre on Deuteronomy* [New York: Jewish Theological Seminary, 1969]); references to *Sifre Deuteronomy* below will include § plus the section ( *pisqaʾ*) number, followed by the page and line numbers from Finkelstein's edition. In this and subsequent passages, the translation is my own, based on a critical evaluation of the textual witnesses, but usually following ms Vatican (and ms London where ms Vatican is not extant). Sometimes, therefore, the text that I provide differs from that of Finkelstein, who is more eclectic in reconstructing the text of the *Sifre*, and from the translations of Reuven Hammer (*Sifre: A Tannaitic Commentary on the Book of Deuteronomy* [New Haven: Yale University, 1986]) and Jacob Neusner (*Sifre to Deuteronomy: An Analytical Translation* [2 vols.; Atlanta: Scholars Press, 1987]), who follow Finkelstein's text. For justifications of my text critical choices and for explanations of my translation choices, see my notes to the same passages in *From Tradition to Commentary*, chap. 3.

come seeking their expertise, most likely in legal matters. But the difference between the two is that the former preoccupies himself with the examination and evaluation of his wealth of acquired rules and traditions whether or not his services are sought. In other words, he spends his time absorbed in study *for its own sake*, and not, like the *nābôn* (poor money changer), only when his expertise is sought for a practical application.

There is in this twofold interpretation of the *ḥākām* a tension (evidenced elsewhere in the *Sifre*, as we shall see): the sage is someone who serves the public, yet who is, ideally at least, constantly engaged in Torah study for its own sake. But there is another, even more important social thrust to this seemingly simple passage with its privileging of the *ḥākām*. While several qualities are mentioned in Scripture as criteria for the selection of men to share leadership with Moses,[22] that which is singled out for favored treatment is the one by which the Rabbis call themselves, as if to suggest that they view themselves as the successors to the anonymous lay leaders (*zĕqēnîm*) who shared the burden and honor of leadership with Moses.

By contrast, the terms *ḥākām* and *nābôn*, frequently connected to each other in Scripture (e.g., Gen 41:31, 39; Deut 4:6; 1 Kgs 3:12) are also differentiated from one another in the *Damascus Document* (CD) of the Dead Sea sectaries, where the *nābôn* and not the *ḥākām* is privileged. There it is said that God raised up the elect community, comprising "from Aaron men of discernment [*nĕbônîm*], and from Israel men of wisdom [*ḥăkāmîm*], and made them hear [His voice]" (CD 6:2-3). Whereas discernment is associated with the priests of the community, who were considered the prophetic conduit through which God made his will and the proper interpretations of prophecies known to the community as a whole, the community's *laity* are characterized by the attribute of wisdom.[23]

This is not to suggest that this *Sifre* passage be read as an anti-sectarian polemic.[24] Rather, against a background in which some associated the authoritative teaching and adjudication of covenantal law

22. In Exod 18:21 four different criteria, being moral rather than intellectual, are suggested by Jethro. According to *Sifre Deut.* §15 (Finkelstein 24.7-8), Moses could only find men with three of the seven qualities suggested to him by Jethro.

23. For *ḥākām* as a term for the sect's laity overall, see 1QSa 1:28, 2:16; CD 6:3; 1QH 1:35. In the Dead Sea Scrolls in general, forms of the root *byn* are much more frequent (by about four times) than those of the root *ḥkm*, whereas in *Sifre Deuteronomy* these proportions are reversed. In the Dead Sea Scrolls the verb *hēbîn* is commonly used to denote the prophetic enlightenment of the community by its priestly leaders and by God. For details see my *From Tradition to Commentary*, chap. 3, n. 140.

24. Held by Chaim Rabin, *The Zadokite Documents* (2d ed.; Oxford: Clarendon, 1958) 21 (note to CD 6:2).

with an inspired priesthood, the *Sifre* text wishes to downplay the *nābôn* in favor of the *ḥākām*, whose genealogy extends back to Moses through the anonymous lay elders, and whose pedagogic and juridical authority is predicated upon his incessant engagement with a wealth of divine texts and traditions for their own sakes. The *ḥākām*, unlike the *nābôn*, according to this formulation, is not simply a privileged *source* of sacred wisdom, but its very *embodiment* through his *life* of Torah study.

The identification of the rabbinic sages with the elders (*zĕqēnîm*) on the one hand, and of the elders with the prophets on the other, is common in rabbinic texts.[25] This dual identification is important since it is the biblical lay elders who both accompany Moses to Mt. Sinai (Exod 24:1, 9) and are assigned leadership and judiciary functions by him. The Rabbis, viewing themselves as the contemporary elders, understand themselves as the inheritors of the authority of the scriptural lay elders— as their descendants in the chain of tradition.

## THE SAGES AS LINKS IN A VERTICAL CHAIN

If the rabbinic sages view themselves as the latest link in the horizontal chain of tradition, they also view themselves as an essential link in the vertical chain that connects Israel to God:

> "[If, then, you heed (*šāmōᶜa tišmĕᶜû*) my commandments] that I command you today" [Deut 11:13]: From whence can you derive that if a person learns [*šāmaᶜ*] a teaching from one of little learning [*qāṭān*] within Israel, he should consider it as if he had learned it from a sage [*ḥākām*]? From the words, "That I command *you* [plural] today." And is not one who learns from a [single] sage like one who learns from [the collectivity of] sages, as it is said, "The words of sages are like goads" [Eccl 12:11]?[26] Just as a goad guides the cow along its furrows so as to bring life to its masters, similarly the words of Torah guide a person's thoughts toward knowledge of God. And is not one who learns from [the collectivity of] sages like one who learns from the Sanhedrin, as it is said, "Masters of assemblies [*ʾăsūppôt*]"? For "assemblies" must refer to the Sanhedrin, as it is said, "Assemble [*ʾespâ*] for me seventy men of the elders of Israel" [Num 11:16]. And is not one who learns from the Sanhedrin like one who learns from Moses, as it is said, "They were given by one shepherd" [Eccl 12:11]? And furthermore it says, "They remembered the ancient days, the

25. For other rabbinic texts, including several in *Sifre Deuteronomy*, that identity elders with sages and associate elders with prophets, see my *From Tradition to Commentary*, chap. 3, nn. 27–31, 47.

26. The transition from the single sage to the collectivity of sages may derive exegetically from the fact that the two verses preceding Eccl 12:11 speak of the teachings of Qoheleth, the single *ḥākām*.

days of Moses [. . . the shepherd of his flock]" [Isa 63:11]. And is not one
who learns from Moses like one who learns from the Mighty One, as it is
said, "They were given by one shepherd"?[27] [And furthermore it says,]
"Give ear, O shepherd of Israel [. . . You who are enthroned on the
cherubim]" [Ps 80:2]. And furthermore it says, "Hear, O Israel, the Lord is
our God, the Lord is one" [Deut 6:4]. (*Sifre Deut.* §41; Finkelstein 86.4–12)

There are, broadly speaking, two parts to this section of commentary. The first interprets the lemma, Deut 11:13, by focusing on the
plural direct object "you" (*ʾetkem*), stressing that it is to *all* of Israel that
Torah is commanded and hence revealed. Therefore, even the non-
learned may have something to teach and may be regarded *as if* a sage,
or as a potential sage.[28] The second part interprets atomistically the
words of Eccl 12:11 so as to link the teaching of the individual sage with
that of the collectivity of sages, and in turn with the authority of the
Sanhedrin,[29] which is identified with the biblical elders, and then with
Moses the single lawgiver, and finally with the one God.

The editorial combination of these two exegeses, the second being
found in other early rabbinic sources independently of any interpretation of Deut 11:13,[30] results in a vertical chain, or hierarchy, that begins
with a single, one might say average, Israelite and ends with a single
God. The distance between these two single figures is filled, or mediated, by the collectivity of sages, who while not being genealogically
distinct from the people, trace their intellectual ancestry back through
the seventy elders of the Sanhedrin (the elders) to Moses. By stressing
on the one hand that *all* of Israel are teachers of Torah, all having been
equally addressed by God, yet on the other that it is the sages in
particular who have inherited the role of the elders (Sanhedrin) to
mediate between Israel and God, the text expresses two views of the
sage that cannot but be in some tension with each other: the sages are of
the people, yet distinct from (and implicitly superior to) them.

27. The single "shepherd" of Eccl 12:11 is interpreted twice, once signifying Moses
and once God.

28. Cf. *m. ʾAbot* 4:1: "Ben Zoma says: Who is wise [*ḥākām*]? One who learns from
every person." For other expressions of an egalitarian Torah ethic, see below, n. 32.

29. It is unclear whether Sanhedrin here refers to an authoritative, national institution
in rabbinic times or to the Sanhedrin of Second Temple times. For the view that such a
body no longer existed in Palestine by the third century C.E., see Levine, *The Rabbinic
Class in Palestine during the Talmudic Period*, 47–52.

30. It is at the point at which these two exegeses are joined that the transition from
single sage to collectivity of sages is exegetically the weakest; see above, n. 26. The
earliest parallel, in *t. Soṭa* 7:9–12 (and *b. Ḥag.* 3a–b with slight variations), contains the
explication of Eccl 12:11 without that of Deut 11:13 and sets it in an entirely different
narrative frame. There the emphasis is not on the sages as a link between Israel and God
but on the idea that, despite the multivocality of contradictory rabbinic teachings and
rulings, they all derive from a single lawgiver and God.

What is striking in this text is the way in which this view gradually and dynamically unfolds through the dialogical dissection, interpretation, and unexpected interrelation of six scriptural verses. It would be a mistake, it seems to me, to collapse the middle of this text so as to reduce its message to the simple statement, "Even if you learn it from a lesser teacher, it is as if it comes from God."[31] For the intermediary position and function of the sages find their expression in the unfolding exegetical discourse by which the text's middle transports its student from the single simple Israelite with which it begins to the single supreme God with which it ends.

## "ALL ARE EQUAL WITH REGARD TO TORAH"

The tension between egalitarian and elitist Torah ethics is even more forcefully expressed in the following piece of commentary:

> [A] Another interpretation of "If, then, you carefully keep [all this commandment]" [Deut 11:22]: Perhaps you might say, "[Leave it to] those who are elders, those who are leaders [gĕdôlîm], those who are prophets." Therefore Scripture teaches, "If, then, you [plural] carefully keep." This teaches that all are equal with regard to Torah. Similarly it says: "Moses commanded us Torah as an inheritance of the congregation of Jacob" [Deut 33:4]. It does not say "priests, Levites, and Israelites," but "congregation of Jacob." And similarly it says: "You stand this day, all of you [before the Lord your God]" [Deut 29:9].
>
> [B] Had it not been for those who arose and preserved Torah in Israel, would not the Torah have been forgotten? Had it not been for Shaphan in his time, Ezra in his time, and R. Akiba in his time, would not the Torah have been forgotten in Israel? For it says, "A teaching [dābār] in its time, how good it is!" [Prov 15:23]. The teaching of one such as this is equal to all the rest together. (Sifre Deut. §48; Finkelstein 112.7–13)

By attending to the plural form of address in the lemma, the commentary stresses that all of Israel, and not a select class of leaders, are enjoined to attend to the Torah. Other verses are adduced to the same effect. Two types of special status are specifically rejected: acquired (elders, leaders, and prophets) and inherited (priests, Levites, and Israelites). Although the sages regard themselves as a distinct and elite class within Israelite society, they draw their disciples from Israelite society as a whole, regardless of genealogical pedigree or social status.[32]

31. This is Hammer's paraphrase (Sifre: A Tannaitic Commentary, 411 n. 19) of Finkelstein's note ad loc.

32. For other expressions of an egalitarian Torah ethic, note the following: "The commoner is equal to the king with regard to words of Torah" (Sifre Deut. §161; Finkelstein 212.5); the Torah is an inheritance to royalty and commoners alike (Sifre Deut.

Notwithstanding the comment that "all are equal with regard to Torah," the next section (paragraph *B*) stresses that certain individuals are "equal to all the rest together" because of their labors to preserve Torah at times when the people as a whole might otherwise have forgotten it. The three individuals mentioned are presented in chronological order, constituting, in a sense, a chain of Torah preservers. They are significant for the fact (according to tradition) that they all lived at times of crisis and restoration, and were either directly or indirectly involved in the *scribal* activity of collecting and editing Torah. Shaphan was the scribe who read to King Josiah the newly discovered "scroll of the Teaching," resulting in Josiah's sweeping reforms (2 Kgs 22:8–20, 2 Chr 34:14–28). Ezra, also a scribe, established the Torah as the constitution for the third generation of the restored community after the Babylonian Exile. R. Akiba, one of the foremost early rabbinic sages and master of disciples, was active during the critical period between the destruction of the temple in 70 C.E. and the Bar Kochba revolt in 135, and is credited with having initiated the editorial compiling of the "oral Torah."[33] While Shaphan held an official position in Josiah's royal court and Ezra was a priest who acted with the authorization of the Persian empire, R. Akiba, as far as we know, enjoyed neither acquired nor hereditary status apart from his learning. By placing R. Akiba on a par with the scribes Shaphan and Ezra, the text implicitly places R. Akiba's status on a par with theirs. Since they were responsible for preserving texts of Scripture and he for collecting and ordering the traditions of the sages, this commentary also equates the status of the latter (of which its text must be seen as part) with the former.

The special status claimed here for Shaphan, Ezra, and R. Akiba derives not from hereditary pedigree, but from their work of preserving Torah in *their* own times. Implicitly, however, they form a scribal chain of authority, by virtue of which they stand apart from and superior to the people as a whole. The rabbinic sage, as represented by R. Akiba, derives from the people with whom he is "equal with regard to Torah." Yet, as one who sustains his learning through constant study and review, he is "equal to all the rest together." The tension between these two rabbinic Torah ethics—egalitarian and elitist—is not resolved

---

§345 on Deut 33:4; Finkelstein 402.6–8); for the Rabbis as a recognizable class within Israel, see *Sifre Deut.* §343 (Finkelstein 400.5–6): "The disciples of the sages can be recognized by the way they walk, by the way they speak, and by the way they dress in the marketplace."

33. For reports of R. Akiba's editorial activity, see *ʾAbot R. Nat.* A 18 (see the edition of Solomon Schechter, *Masekhet Aboth de-rabbi Nathan* [Vienna: C. D. Lippe, 1887; repr. Hildesheim/New York: Olms, 1979] 67); and *y. Šeqal.* 5:1 (48c), as understood by Saul Lieberman, *Hellenism in Jewish Palestine* (New York: Jewish Theological Seminary, 1962) 90–91.

by the commentary, which in juxtaposing them leaves it to the student of the text to struggle with their dialectical implications.

## "OR THE MAGISTRATE IN CHARGE AT THE TIME"

The above chains, like the chain of tradition cited above, conspicuously omit the priesthood, both horizontally as the authorized transmitters of Torah and vertically as the intermediaries between Israel and God. Yet Scripture, and the Book of Deuteronomy in particular, assigns primacy of place to the priesthood in these two regards, and especially in the realm where they join, that is, in effecting of God's will within Israelite society through the implementation of Scripture's system of justice. Deut 17:8–13 prescribes that when a local court is unable to decide a case, it is brought before a centralized tribunal, which is located at the place designated by God and which is comprised of levitical priests and a (lay?) magistrate. In two ways *Sifre Deuteronomy*'s commentary transforms the biblical passage with which it is engaged: (1) It emphasizes that the central tribunal of Deuteronomy is in fact a series of three courts, all of them located in the temple domain. Through the text's repetitive detail, its students are drawn into the very process of progressing and ascending by stages from one to the next of these three courts. It is only upon completing this process that we are told that is from the temple, and from the high court in the Chamber of Hewn Stone in particular, that Torah emanates to *all* of Israel. Thus, the central place of Deuteronomy has been transformed from a place to which difficult cases are brought for adjudication to a place of origin for all Torah teaching. The double verb for ascending is interpreted doubly: not only is the temple the highest place within the land of Israel, but the land of Israel is higher than the rest of the world. The pathos of such a text being created (at least in its present, redacted form) and studied at a time when that temple had long ago been destroyed and its Mount long ago desecrated, with little immediate hope for a reversal of that calamity, is fully experienced only upon arriving at the end of the section. (2) Paradoxically, even as the central court(s) of Deut 17:8–13 are consigned to a presently unrecoverable past, their functions are contemporized (rabbinized). These courts, according to this commentary, do not so much decide between conflicting parties in civil or criminal dispute as between *teachers* who differ in their legal interpretations.

The resolution of these seemingly contradictory exegetical moves comes in the succeeding section ( *pisqaʾ*):

[A] "And you shall appear [*ûbāʾtā*]" [Deut 17:9]: [This is stated so as] to include the [rabbinical] court at Yavneh.

[B] "Before the levitical priests": It is a commandment that the court include priests and Levites.[34] This being the commandment, might we infer that if [a court] lacks priests and Levites it is disqualified? Therefore, Scripture says, "Or the magistrate [*šōpēt*]": Even though it lacks priests and Levites, it is [still] qualified.

[C] "In charge at that time": R. Jose the Galilean said: Might we have thought [that one should go to] a magistrate who is not living in your time? Rather, this refers to a magistrate who is qualified and authorized [to serve] in your time. Thus, one who previously had been related [to one of the parties, and had been disqualified to judge,] but has since ceased to be related, is [now] qualified. Therefore it says, "Do not say, 'How is it that the former days were better than these?'" [Eccl 7:10].

[D] And you shall seek their decision, and they shall declare the verdict in the case. (*Sifre Deut.* §153; Finkelstein 206.10–207.3)

The verb "you shall appear" (literally, "come") following the previous expression, "you shall rise and ascend," could not, from the rabbinic perspective, be a mere repetition. While Deut 17:8 was taken to refer to high courts in Jerusalem on the Temple Mount to which one ascended while the temple stood, Deut 17:9, which does not by itself mention ascending, is taken to refer to (or at least to include) the successor rabbinical court at Yavneh. This court not only is located outside the chosen place on the Temple Mount in Jerusalem, but it does not require the presence of priests or Levites. The magistrate of Deut 17:8–13 is understood in contrast to the preceding "levitical priests" to be a nonpriest, presumably a rabbinic sage, given the earlier reference to Yavneh.[35]

The interpretation of the phrase seemingly unnecessary "in charge at that time" stresses that those who may not have been qualified to judge in the past may now be qualified. The commentary, therefore, argues that changing circumstances have necessitated a shift not only of the central court from Jerusalem to Yavneh (and, by implication, to the successor rabbinic centers), but also a change in the makeup of that court. A citation from Eccl 7:10 acknowledges yet rejects the nostalgic tendency to compare the present (rabbinic) leadership with that of the past. Finally, an interpretation of the conclusion of v 9 (paragraph *D*) once again intellectualizes (rabbinizes) the function of the central court:

34. On "levitical priests" becoming "priests and Levites," see 11QTemp 61:8. Cf. Josephus, *Antiquities* 4:218; and Philo, *On the Special Laws* 4:36 §§188–92.

35. For the *šōpēt* as lay judge (as in Deut 19:17), see S. R. Driver, *A Critical and Exegetical Commentary on Deuteronomy* (International Critical Commentary; 3d ed.; Edinburgh: T. & T. Clark, 1901) 208. However, Philo (*On the Special Laws* 4:36 §§188–92) understands this to be the High Priest, and Josephus (*Antiquities* 4:218) substitutes *gerousia* ('council of elders').

434        Steven D. Fraade

one comes to it not so much to receive a specific legal sentence (*dĕbar hammišpāṭ*) as to learn the fine points of legal argumentation (*diqduqê mišpāṭ*).

The combined impression of these adjoining parts of the commentary is both a sense of deep loss caused by the destruction of the temple with its central judiciary, and, almost conversely, a sense of continuity between that institution and its rabbinic successors. The Torah that once went forth from the Chamber of Hewn Stone now goes forth from "Yavneh." That sense of continuity is exegetically achieved both by portraying the work of the central tribunal of Second Temple times in rabbinic intellectual terms, and by loosening the scriptural requirements for its location (Temple Mount) and makeup (priests) "in that day" (the commentary's present).

## "ATTACH YOURSELVES TO THE SAGES AND THEIR STUDENTS"

The rabbinic sages not only claimed for themselves roles that were formerly assigned to the priesthood, but claimed that the activity of Torah study (*talmûd tôrâ*) was a paramount religious act, indeed an act of worship, not simply equal but superior to that of sacrificial worship.[36] But just as sacrificial worship had been a social practice, conducted under the leadership of the priests in the public arena of the temple (*bêt hammiqdāš*), so too Torah study was to be a social practice, conducted in the company of sages in the public arena of the study house (*bêt hammidrāš*). As a form of worship, study was to be not simply a religious *obligation*, but a religious *experience*, potentially of the highest order:

> [A] "[If, then, you faithfully keep all that I command you, loving the Lord your God, walking in all his ways,] and holding fast to him" [Deut 11:22]: But is it possible for a person to ascend to heaven and to cleave to fire? For has it not been said, "For the Lord your God is a consuming fire" [Deut 4:24], and it says, "His throne was fiery flames" [Dan 7:9]. Rather, attach yourself to the sages and their disciples, and I will account it to you as though you had ascended to heaven to receive it [Torah]—not that you ascended to receive it in peace, but rather as though you waged war in order to receive it. And thus it says, "You went up to the heights taking captives" [Ps 68:19].

36. For study as a religious act among the Dead Sea sectaries as a group, see 1QS 6:6–8, 8:12–16. For the obligation of study as an act of "serving" God, on a level with, if not superior to, sacrificial worship, see *Sifre Deut.* §41 (Finkelstein 87.11–88.13), treated in my *From Tradition to Commentary*, chap. 3.

[B] The expounders of *haggadot* say: If you desire to come to know the one who spoke and the world came into being, study *haggada*, for thereby you will come to know the one who spoke and the world came into being and cling to his ways.

[C] If you do what is required of you, then I too will do what is required of me: "The Lord will dislodge [before you all these nations]" [Deut 11:23]. (*Sifre Deut* §49; Finkelstein 114.14–115.5)

The idea of attaching oneself to God is understood literally, only for this understanding to be rejected as an impossibility. Rather, it is by attaching oneself to the sages and their disciples, that is, by engaging in the study of Torah under the direction of the sages and in the company of their disciples, that this verse can be fulfilled. The commentary appears to be saying, in God's voice, that if you attach yourself to the sages in study of Torah, I will account it to you as if you, like Moses, had ascended to heaven to receive it. And just as Moses, according to rabbinic interpretations of Ps 68:19, had to wage war against the angels in order to reach heaven to receive the Torah, so too Moses' successors when they study Torah are considered to ascend to heaven in struggle and to return with Torah as their captive. The text does not simply state that those who study Torah with the sages are like Israel when they stood at the foot of Mt. Sinai to receive the Torah (which is also described in rabbinic traditions as having been a struggle), but are like Moses himself when he ascended to heaven to acquire the Torah on Israel's behalf.[37]

The teachers of that branch of the rabbinic Torah curriculum to which the present text may be said to belong next raise their voices (paragraph *B*) to claim that it is only through the rabbinically guided study of the scriptural narrative of Israel's sacred history that God the creator can be known. It is at this point that God's voice reenters the discussion, linking the rabbinic interpretation of the scriptural protasis with its adoposis in the next verse: Only when you, Israel, do your part—now understood as joining the sages in the study of Torah—will "the Lord dislodge before you all these nations" (Deut 11:23). Thus, Torah study in the company of the sages is the most realizable route not only to the religious goal of attachment to God, but to the political fulfillment of God's promise to redeem Israel from the rule of the nations.

37. Moses is, in a sense, the Rabbis' rabbi (*mōšeh rabbēnû*), their intellectual progenitor. For details, see my *From Tradition to Commentary*, chap. 3, n. 28. For the equating of intensive Torah study with the receiving of the Torah at Sinai, see *Sifre Deut.* §58 (Finkelstein 124.12–14).

## CONCLUSION

Rabbinic texts, such as the ones examined here, do not so much recount stories about heroic sages as cultivate a culture and society of sages and their disciples by engaging them together in the religious and redemptive practice of Torah study. The sages and disciples who stand both behind and before such texts understood themselves to be preserving and transmitting "words of Torah," which could justify, sustain, and transform, through *rabbinic* mediation, the life of Israel as a holy nation bereft of what had once been its holy center. These sages sought not only to replace that holy center but to establish themselves both as its officiants and exemplars. To succeed in this compound task the rabbinic sages dedicated themselves to the central holy act of Torah study for its own sake even as they increasingly asserted and broadened their practical influence upon public affairs. They had to understand themselves as being of the people while also distinct from and superior to them. They had to claim being the descendants of Moses and the biblical elders while also the successors to Aaron, the priests, and the Levites. It was especially in the continuous and collective practice of transforming Torah (both "written" and "oral") through intensively engaged, multivocal commentary as a religious act, that the sages sought to transform *themselves* into a cohesive society whose own discourse and deeds would make them worthy and capable of transforming, in turn and in time, the practices, structures, and self-understandings of Jewish society more broadly.

# PART VI

*The Symbolic Universe of the Sage*

# FROM SCRIBALISM TO RABBINISM: PERSPECTIVES ON THE EMERGENCE OF CLASSICAL JUDAISM

## Michael Fishbane

For the historian of religions, the rise and fall of forms, along with concomitant changes in thought and action, evoke basic questions for the periodization of religious history. What, for example, is the measure of a genuine innovation or rupture in cultural formation? And what, by contrast, is the mark of a mere revival of transformation of old patterns? Merely to contemplate these changes, or chart their occurrence, will thus conjure forth a host of methodological goblins sufficient to test the mettle of even the most valiant interpreter.

Similar concerns confront the historian of art, as well. The profound meditations on temporal development in Henri Focillon's *The Life of Forms in Art* come especially to mind in this regard.[1] The subtle precision of his arguments challenge routine judgments and hasty hypotheses alike. Nevertheless, the elusive potential of bold intuitions, like Karl Jasper's speculations on an "Axial Age" in the late 1st millennium B.C.E., will always intrigue the cultural historian.[2] While focused on a particular moment in world civilization, Jasper's reflections have broader import. They ponder the occurrence of true transformations in history—of decisive conceptual changes, for example, in the relationship between the transcendental (or cosmic) and the mundane (or human) orders of existence.[3] Such axial developments (or breakthroughs) draw in their wake a flotilla of cultural adjustments. Thus shifts between the transcendental and mundane orders elicit correlative shifts in the relations between myth and revelation or between revelation and reason.

Michael Fishbane is Samuel Lane Professor of Jewish Religious History and Social Ethics at Brandeis University.

1. The second English edition of *Vie des formes* was published in 1948.
2. See *Vom Ursprung und Zeil der Geschichte* (Munich: Piper, 1949) 15–106.
3. On this, cf. the valuable symposium on "Wisdom, Revelation, and Doubt: Perspectives on the First Millennium B.C.," published in the Spring 1975 issue of *Daedalus*.

Diverse patterns of rejection or accommodation result. Invariably, these changes are revealed by the emergence of new types of holy men, sacred texts, and ritual behaviors. Comparative analysis further serves to reveal otherwise obscure configurations in particular cultures, and sets the whole within the full framework of intellectual and religious history.

In an earlier essay called "Israel and the Mothers," I considered several aspects of axial developments in ancient Israelite religion in connection with its primary break (both conceptual and symbolic) from what I there called the *mythic plenum*.[4] As I indicated, this formative rupture was neither final nor complete, and different patterns of mythic retrieval are discernible in later Jewish thought. Nevertheless, a decisive dissociation from mythopoeic forms set Israelite religion on an entirely new course. In the present essay I aim to continue this line of analysis and focus on what may be termed a "secondary break-through" in ancient Israelite religious history. In brief, my concern is to capture something of the axial transformations that mark the onset of classical Judaism. This involves making the movement from a culture based on direct divine revelations to one based on their study and reinterpretation. The principal custodians of the former were the sage-scribes of ancient Israel; the purveyors of the latter, the sage-scholars of early Judaism. For their part, the sage-scribes inscribed divine words and traditions as they came to hand. The sage-scholars, on the other hand, variously extended these divine words and sacred traditions through interpretation. To be sure, these scholars inherited modes of study and interpretation from their forebears; at the same time, they also initiated a new centrality and significance for these modes that is nothing short of decisive—and marks the closure of "ancient Israel" and the onset of "ancient Judaism." It is this cultural arc and transformation that my title ("From Scribalism to Rabbinism") strains to signify.

## THE AXIAL SHIFT IN THE ROLE OF
## THE SAGE WITH THE EMERGENCE OF TORAH PIETY

The historical records of the early postexilic period in ancient Israel have left incontrovertible evidence for the reconstruction of my topic. Two details mentioned in connection with Ezra's return from Babylon in the 5th century B.C.E. are especially pertinent. The first is the almost offhand archival notice concerning the loss of the ʾûrîm and tûmmîm, the ancient priestly devices for mantic practice (Neh 7:65). The second

---

4. See *The Other Side of God* (ed. P. Berger; Garden City, NY: Doubleday, 1981) 28–47.

is the rather explicit account of a national convocation in the year 458 B.C.E., at which time Ezra led the people in a public event of Torah instruction (Neh 8:1–8). Together, these facts signal a shift in the modes of access to divine revelation.

Of central importance is the depiction of Ezra himself. As leader of a delegation of returnees to Zion, he is identified as a priest (Ezra 7:1–5) and called "a diligent scribe in the Torah of Moses, which YHWH, God of Israel, had given" (v 6), "a scribe of the words of the commandments of YHWH, and his laws for Israel" (v 11). Ezra is thus, first and foremost, an authoritative guardian of the written revelations. But he is also a teacher of these divine instructions, for we are told that "Ezra set his heart to investigate [*lidrôš*] the Torah of YHWH, and to do and teach [both] law and ordinance in Israel" (v 10). This is no mere depiction of a routine priestly function of ritual instruction, in the manner of some older pentateuchal accounts (cf. Lev 10:11). It is, rather, an extension and virtual transformation of this role. Special significance thus lies in the fact that the very idiom used to describe Ezra's activity ("*lidrôs* the Torah of YHWH") is a precise reworking of an ancient formula used to indicate oracular activity (cf. "to consult [*lidrōš*] YHWH," 1 Kgs 22:8). Since Ezra's textual task is to seek from the Torah new divine teachings (or explication of older ones) for the present, there is a sense in which exegetical praxis has functionally co-opted older mantic techniques of divine inquiry. This somewhat mantic or inspired dimension of study is underscored by the fact that, in this very context, Ezra is twice described as one who has the "hand of YHWH . . . upon him" (vv 6, 9). Since early times, this expression was a standard way of denoting the force of divine inspiration upon an individual (cf. Ezek 1:3).[5]

The combination of these two factors—the resignification of the verb *lidrôš* and the reuse of the idiom "hand of YHWH"—highlights the chief *novum* of this historical record: Ezra is a priestly scribe who teaches the received, written revelation through his inspired study of it. In the process, the Torah traditions undergo a corresponding refiguration. No dead letter, the ancient divine words become the very means of new instruction through their proper inquiry and interpretation. Ezra is further aided in his task by levitical instructors who bring Torah understanding (*měbînîm*) to the people (Neh 8:7, 9) and convey to them the sense (*śekel*) of the text being studied (v 8; cf. v 13, *lěhaśkîl*).[6]

5. See my discussion in *Biblical Interpretation in Ancient Israel* (Oxford: Clarendon, 1985) 107–119, 245, 263–65.

6. For other postexilic uses of *měbîn* to designate skill in a levitical craft, cf. 1 Chr 15:22, 25:7; and for the use of *hiśkîl* to denote knowledge and instruction by levitical personnel, cf. 1 Chr 28:19.

No further indication of inspired interpretation is applied to these teachers. For this dimension, one must turn to Ps 119:18.

Psalm 119 is a postexilic prayer replete with Torah piety. The psalmist repeatedly requests instruction in the *received* laws (vv 12, 27, 33, 64, 66, 68, 73, 108, 124) and, on one occasion, even used the ancient priestly benediction as a vehicle for petitioning divine grace to guide his understanding of the ancient statutes (v 135).[7] Elsewhere, he prayed: *gal ʿênay wěʾabbîṭâ niplāʾôt mittôrātekā*, "Unveil [thou] my eyes that I may behold wonderful things *from out of* your Torah" (v 18). In light of the preceding requests, this plea for illumined visions must also be understood as a petition for divine aid in the interpretation of scripture.[8] In fact, this request is formulated through a reuse of older mantic terminology—specifically, language known from the traditions of Balaam the seer. Concerning him we read that "YHWH unveiled the eyes of Balaam, and he saw . . . ," *wayěgal yhwh ʾet ʿênê Bilʿām* (Num 22:31). A comparable, contemporary instance marking the transformation of Torah learning occurs in the teachings of Ben Sira. On the one hand, this sage harks back to the terminology of Ezra 7 when he refers to the interpreter of Torah (*dôrēš hattôrâ*, 3:15) as one who "pours out teachings as prophecy" (Sir 24:33). At the same time, an echo of the mantic terminology of Ps 119:18 can also be detected in Ben Sira's admonishment that "many are the mercies of God and he reveals [*yigleh*] his secret to the humble. Search not for what is too wondrous for you [ *pilāʾôt mimmekā ʾal tidrôš*] and investigate not what is hidden from you. Meditate upon what is permitted to you, and deal not with secret things" (Sir 3:20–22).

Both the immediate context of this admonition, as well as early rabbinic citations and discussions of it,[9] suggest that the sage is advised to focus his interpretative skill on the revealed Torah and not to speculate on cosmological or related wonders ( *pilāʾôt*)—as had become fashionable during the Hellenistic period. Indeed, if he is properly pious, this sage may even hope to receive exegetical revelations (*yigleh*) from God. In this way he is the direct spiritual descendent of the psalmist, cited earlier, who also hoped to receive exegetical revelations (*gal*) from God in order to know the wonders (*niplāʾôt*) hidden in the Torah. Both presuppose a new sensibility: one in which scripture has become the vehicle of new revelations, and exegesis the means of new access to the divine will. Thus, complementing the divine revelation

7. See B. Gertner, "Midrashim in the New Testament," *Journal of Semitic Studies* 7 (1962) 276; and my *Biblical Interpretation in Ancient Israel*, 334 n. 50.

8. See my *Biblical Interpretation in Ancient Israel*, 539–40.

9. See *b. Ḥag.* 13a and *Gen. Rab.* 8:2, as well as the minor variations of the lemma cited.

now embodied in a written Torah, the sage seeks from God the grace of an *ongoing revelation* through the words of scripture itself—as mediated *through exegesis.*

## A COMPARABLE SHIFT EXEMPLIFIED BY DANIEL

Alongside the "Law," there are the "Prophets." It is therefore of interest to note a parallel development toward the inspired exegesis of written revelations found in the prophetic genre as well. As Ezra exemplified the axial shift with respect to the Torah, so Daniel may serve as a paradigm with respect to the Prophets.[10] Similar terms for exegetical illumination reinforce this correlation.

It is well known that the traditions about Daniel range from the depiction of a court sage to the purveyor of mantic wisdom. In the oldest records, he and his fellow advisors in the Babylonian court are described as "knowledgeable [*maśkîlîm*] in every wisdom . . . and understanders of [all] knowledge [*mĕbînê* maddāᶜ]" (Dan 1:4). These abilities include skill in the interpretation of dreams. However, Daniel's role as a latter-day Joseph is decisively altered in the final chapters of the book (Daniel 9-12). He is there portrayed as inspired with the true meaning of ancient prophecies—prophecies that he reads and studies to small avail until he merits divine guidance. Thus he reports how "I studied [*bînōtî*] the books" (Dan 9:2) of prophecies in the hopes of knowing the true meaning of Jeremiah's prophecy of seventy years of desolation for Jerusalem (Jer 25:9-11).[11] It would even appear that Daniel's study was connected with types of ascetic practice designed to achieve this very illumination. For in the immediate context of his study, Daniel reports how he engaged in intense prayer, fasting, and abasement (9:3)—and only then, *in the very course* of these acts (vv 20-21a), was he granted a vision of the angel Gabriel flying toward him with the words: "Daniel, I have now come forth to give you understanding [*lĕhaśkîlĕkā bînâ*]" (vv 21b-22), about the text *he had just been studying* (vv 24-25). The likelihood that Daniel was engaged in a ritual praxis for exegetical illumination is reinforced by the words of Gabriel himself, who says (v 23): "At the beginning of your supplication the word [*dābār*, viz., interpretation] came forth, and I have come

---

10. The Book of Daniel, of course, belongs to the Kethubim (Writings), but as will be shown below Daniel looks back to and interprets portions of the Nebiᵓim (Prophets). He therefore functions as a prophetic figure. For a recent discussion, see K. Koch, "Is Daniel Also among the Prophets?" *Interpretation* 39 (1985) 131-43.

11. Cf. my *Biblical Interpretation in Ancient Israel*, 487-95.

to tell you that you have found [divine] favor and [are graced with] the understanding of the word [ûbîn baddābār]."[12]

The axial significance of this description of textual illumination is underscored by the narrator's reuse of an ancient literary convention used to present prophetic commissions. This form now serves to legitimate a receiver of exegetical truth *about* the older prophecies. Thus whereas it was earlier reported that a divine being flew (wayyā⁻āp) toward Isaiah and touched (nāgaᶜ) him on the mouth (Isa 6:6-7), thereby consecrating him to prophecy, we are now told that a divine messenger (an *angelus interpres*, in fact) flew (muᶜāp bîᶜāp) toward Daniel in his vision and touched (nōgēᶜa) him, thereby initiating him into sealed mysteries of older prophecies. If in the first case the inaugural event occurs as part of an ecstasy induced by the awesome holiness of shrinal practice, and results in a commission to speak the living prophetic word, in the case of Daniel the initiation occurs within an ecstatic trance induced by ritual ceremonies in the context of study. The result is no living word but an interpretation of written oracles. Direct prophecy has ceased here, and is replaced by a knowledge of past texts and their resignification for the future.

Given the importance of this transformation, a second instance of the reuse of a prophetic commission may be noted. In this case, traditions from the Book of Ezekiel influence the formulation. One will recall that this prophet had an inaugural vision of the divine throne and its fiery panoply while in Babylon, on the banks of the Chebar Canal (Ezek 1:3-28). The vision is described in rich detail—starting with the lower complexes of the chariot, and climaxing with a vision of one "like a man" enthroned high above and surrounded by flashes of fire and light (vv 26-28). Upon seeing this spectacle, the prophet is unloosed by fear (1:1). He is forthwith supported by God and told not to fear (2:6). Indeed, to counteract his fear of incompetence, the prophet is given to eat the very divine words he must proclaim (Ezek 2:8-3:2). It is perhaps not insignificant for our understanding of late biblical religion that these words are themselves written on a scroll. At any rate, these events conclude with another divine vision and a command that the prophet remain silent (wĕneʾ ĕlamtā) until the Lord will again open his mouth to prophesy (3:25-27).

The features from Ezekiel 1-3, together with the already noted characteristics from Isaiah 6, are reworked in Daniel 10.[13] As in Dan

12. In these instances, *dābār* bears the sense of 'interpretation' or 'explication'. A similar, though generally unrecognized, example of this sense is found in connection with the dreams of Joseph (see Gen 37:8, and especially v 10).

13. See my "Ha-Ot Ba-Miqra," *Shenaton: An Annual for Biblical and Near Eastern Studies* 1 (1975) 224 n. 28 [Hebrew].

9:3, this text also begins with a portrayal of Daniel engaged in intense ascetic practices geared to invoking divine illumination. But now, following the example of Ezekiel, Daniel also received his vision near a bank of water in Babylon (10:4). Moreover, in his trance, Daniel envisions a heavenly figure, of fiery and flashing visage, and falls to the ground in terror (v 9). The being then raised Daniel up, and told him that his supplication was accepted and (exegetical) understanding (of the Jeremiah oracle) would be granted him (vv 11–12, 14). Hearing this, Daniel fell dumb (wĕne°ĕlāmtî, v 15) and shuttered until the divine being told him not to fear. Then one "like a man" touched (wayyigga°) Daniel (v 18) and told him that he would be instructed in the meaning of the prophecies that were "inscribed in a true writing" (v 21). This instruction is found in Daniel 11—a text saturated with reworked passages from the preexilic prophets.

Ecstasy induced in conjunction with the study of old prophecies has thus produced a new type of "prophetic" figure—a pneumatic exegete, guided by divine instruction into the true meaning of ancient oracles. Exegetical revelation has thus replaced the radical *novum* of unmediated divine communication to a prophet. At the same time, such exegetical illumination has become a new mode of access to God for a new type of community—formed around teachers and the texts that they authoritatively interpret. This was the earlier situation with Ezra, too, where the reconstitution of the people around Torah study led to formulations of the true community *on the basis of* exegesis performed by authoritative leaders (cf. Ezra 9, Nehemiah 10). In the case of Daniel, a specific community of interpretation likewise formed. Those in possession of the special exegetical illumination are called "knowers" (maśkîlîm) who "understand" (yābînû) the true application of the prophecies (12:10; cf. 11:33, 35). Like the students of the Law, whose textual inquiry was guided by God and for whom exegesis had become a mode of divine encounter, the illuminates of Prophecy are also divinely guided into the "hidden and sealed" meaning of ancient revelation (Dan 12:9). It is this special understanding that functions for them as a mode of divine sustenance in the awesome and wondrous ( pilā°ôt) times of the end (v 6).

## TORAH STUDY AND THE EMERGENCE OF NEW MODES OF RELIGIOUS EXPERIENCE

Textual strands from late biblical literature may further nuance these observations of axial developments in ancient Israelite religious sensibility. If, on the one hand, the emergence of a scriptural corpus of revelations fostered new modes of access to God's will, instruction developed through the exegetic study of the Torah and the Prophets. Such study contributed to new modes of religious experience. Both features develop and reinforce one another along the trajectory "from scribalism to rabbinism."

The increased importance of the Torah as a corpus of covenantal instructions in the postexilic community is indicated by many factors. Among these is the reuse of old historical notices in order to emphasize the legal piety of bygone kings. For example, the report referring to Asa's campaigns against cultic abominations (1 Kgs 15:11–13) was taken over by the Chronicler (2 Chr 14:1–2, 4) and supplemented by the comment that the king "obeyed the Torah and commandments" (v 3). In other instances, the pivotal role of obedience to the Law is introduced into the narrative. A case in point is Solomon's revision of the unconditional promise of divine grace to David (2 Sam 7:15–16); for in his formulation of it that old divine promise was made conditional upon proper fulfillment of the Law ("No one who will sit on the throne of Israel will be cut off from me *if* your sons heed their ways, to go before me as you went before me"; 1 Kgs 8:25). And in a further reappropriation, this transformation was itself reworked in 2 Chr 6:16. Not content to say that future kings will "go before me," the Chronicler rewrote the older passage to read "to go *in my Torah* as you went before me." In this way, the mediating position of the Torah as the condition of dynastic continuity was underscored.

This attitude toward the Torah also affects the nature and expression of religious experience. A comparison of parallel formulations bears this out. The one type, found in a host of liturgical expressions, reflect concrete hopes for divine nearness and help; the other, principally preserved in Psalm 119, reformulates these desires in accordance with its ideology of the Law and commandments. Thus whereas some psalmists say, "I have set Yhwh [*šiwwîtî yhwh*] before me" (Ps 16:8), or urge Israel to "trust in Yhwh [*beṭaḥ bayhwh*]" (115:9), the author of Psalm 119 proclaims, "I have set your ordinances [*šiwwîtî mišpāṭekā*] before me" (v 30), and avers that "I have trusted in your word [*bāṭaḥtî bidbārekā*]" (v 42). Along the same lines, a threnodist exhorts the needy to "raise your hands [*śěʾî ... kappayik*] to him [*ʾēlāyw*, viz., to God]" (Lam 2:19) in entreaty, while the psalmist piously proclaims that "I have raised my hands [*wěʾeśśāʾ kappay*] to your commandments [*ʾel miṣwôtekā*]" (Ps 119:48). And finally, we read in Deut 4:4 of those "who cleave to Yhwh [*hadděbēqîm bayhwh*]," whereas the late psalmist says, "I have cleaved to your testimonies [*dābaqtî běʿēdôtekā*]" (Ps 119:31).

These expressions of religious ideology and experience in Psalm 119 must not be assumed to reflect a simple or exclusionary development. Certainly, a religious relationship to the Law never supplanted a direct relationship to God. The remarkable clustering of expressions of trust in the Law found in Psalm 119 must rather be attributed to the intense preoccupation of that psalmist with the Torah. In fact, given the fact that this psalm is manifestly an address *to God* it is reasonable to interpret these expressions of cleaving to the Law or trust in the legal instructions as various attempts by the psalmist to proclaim his consummate loyalty to God's Torah. This granted, it is nevertheless clear that Psalm 119 registers a profound shift of religious sensibility: a deepening of religious experience *in and through* the Torah study. It is only within this framework, I think, that one can properly measure such startling expressions as "I have believed [or relied] upon your commandments [*běmiṣwôtêkā he'ĕmāntî*]" (Ps 119:66). The echo of an earlier expression of faith, "And when the Israelites experienced the might that YHWH had wrought in Egypt . . . they believed in YHWH [*wayya'ămînû ba-yhwh*]" (Exod 14:31), resounds over these late words and counterpoints the momentous developments in ancient Israelite religious life taking place in the postexilic age.


## ANCIENT PROPHECIES AND RELIGIOUS EXPERIENCE

Alongside the Law as a primary religious modality, similar trends occur with respect to Prophecy. Of particular interest is a striking revision of an old exhortation by the prophet Isaiah (eighth century B.C.E.). Speaking to King Ahaz during the Syro-Ephraimite aggression, the prophet used old military formulas to encourage the monarch to stand firm. "Do not fear," he exhorted, "and let your heart not weaken" (7:4), for YHWH would not allow the invasion to occur. And then, as a capstone to this charge, he added this spiritual condition: "If you do not believe [*ta'ămînû*, viz., have reliance] you will not endure [*tē'āmēnû*]" (v 9b). The overt intent of this exhortation was to promote trust in YHWH's power; and just this was how the Chronicler understood the idiom centuries later. In connection with a military buildup threatening King Jehoshaphat, the king is told: "Do not fear and be not afraid . . . [for] YHWH will be with you" (2 Chr 20:15, 17); and after this prophetic exhortation Jehoshaphat himself admonished his people with the words: "Believe [*ha'ămînû*] in YHWH, your God, and you will endure [*wětē'āmēnû*]" (v 20). But this is not all. After a reprise of the old words of Isaiah, the historian has the king voice this charge: "Believe [*ha'ămînû*] in his prophets and succeed!" It is thus not solely reliance upon God that will bring salvation and victory; the people must trust in his spokesman as well.

It would be unwarranted to infer from this historiographical formulation that the Chronicler advocates trust or belief in the prophets (and their oracles) independent of God. The explicit words "believe in *his* prophets" contradict such an inference, and underscore the presentation of the prophet as a messenger of God. Nevertheless, the Chronicler's supplementation of Isaiah's language suggests something more: that the prophets have come to represent intermediary figures who serve an exemplary function for the community. At a time when the prophetic traditions were being gathered, it is significant that several strands of postexilic historiography recall the prophetic watchword as God's providential interventions on behalf of his people (cf. 2 Kgs 17:7-17, esp. v 13; Jer 25:1-7, esp. v 4; and Neh 9:29-30). Failure to heed these warnings of repentance resulted in exile. The Chronicler himself repeatedly presents prophetic words as pivotal in the nation's fate.[14] One may therefore consider his admonition in 2 Chr 20:20 as indicative of this overall concern.

Parallel to developments in religious experience due to study of the Law, then, the knowledge and study of written prophecies also came to sponsor correlative modes of religious experience. Traces of this development may also be discerned by tracking reuses of the verb *hakkēh* over six centuries. This verb is used in the prophetic corpus to indicate the act of awaiting the fulfillment of prophecies. Three passages are decisive. The first is Isa 8:17, where the prophet Isaiah says: "So I shall wait for YHWH [*wĕḥikkîtî layhwh*] who is hiding his face from the house of Jacob, and I shall trust in him." This proclamation of hope concludes a series of oracles dealing with the Assyrian menace, and follows an instruction by the prophet to "seal [*ḥătôm*] the oracle" of hope among his disciples (v 16). His purpose was presumably to preserve a record of the divine words, and thus to dramatize their eventual fulfillment. In the interim, the prophet avers that he will await the Lord—the speaker and fulfiller of these promises. His proclamation is thus entirely different from Hab 2:3, where the prophet Habakkuk is told by God to write down an oracle of future salvation (vv 2-3a). An exhortation acknowledging the delayed fulfillment of divine salvation follows this command: "Though it tarries, wait [*hakkeh*] for it; for it will surely come, without delay" (v 3b). Note that the formulation here is to "wait for *it*," that is, for the prophecy's fulfillment—and not for God, the fulfiller of prophecies. Accordingly, the famous passage that immediately follows this exhortation, *wĕṣaddîq bĕ'ĕmûnātô yihyeh*, must surely mean: "And the righteous one will be sustained [rewarded

---

14. See S. Japhet, *Emunot Ve-De'ot Be-Sefer Divrei Ha-Yamin* (Jerusalem: Bialik, 1977) 152-58 [Hebrew]; and my *Biblical Interpretation in Ancient Israel*, 388-92, 401-3.

with life] through his faith in *it*." Faithful waiting for the fulfillment of a (written) oracle is thus the life testimony of the *ṣaddîq*, the righteous one who trusts God's words.[15]

With this formulation of faithful living with prophecies in mind, one can see how old oracles could be interiorized as a dimension of religious experience. One need not conclude that this religious sensibility is original to Habakkuk in order to sense that, in his articulation of it, a shift has taken place. The full measure of this shift is most fully apparent in Daniel 11–12, where both prophetic passages are reused. Thus Habakkuk's prophecy that salvation will "yet" come (Hab 2:3a) is cited in Dan 11:27, 35; Isaiah's notice (Isa 8:17) that a prophecy has been "sealed" up among disciples recurs in Dan 12:4, where the angel Michael instructs Daniel to "seal" (*ḥătōm*) the prophecies for the illuminates (cf. v 9); and the two references to "waiting" for the fulfillment of prophecies are resumed in Daniel's concluding exhortation: "Happy is the one who waits [*hammĕḥakkeh*] and it arrives after 1,345 days" (12:12). Clearly, the faithful waiting for the fulfillment of prophecies is inextricable from the special knowledge that the illuminates (*maśkîlîm*) believe themselves to possess—a knowledge that sustains them during their suffering (11:35, 12:9–10). To be faithful to and believe in the prophecies is thus to believe in their interpretation as mediated by an angelic revelation. It is a situation in which exegesis constitutes the very structure of the religious experience. The result is not so much an expression of emergent "rabbinism" as a mode of "religious scribalism" in one of its remarkable transformations.

## DEVELOPMENTS AT QUMRAN AND AMONG THE PHARISEES

The various trends discussed so far are continued in the literature of the Dead Sea Scrolls and the early Pharisaic sages. For these two communities, the Law and the Prophets constitute literary collections of revelation; and the ongoing interpretation of these divine words, by authoritative teachers, resulted in an ongoing renewal of revelation and the types of religious experience based upon it. I shall adduce here but the tiniest fragment of this evidence—and even then my concern will be to echo or extend motifs and texts considered earlier. As in the earlier discussions, the axial transformations effected by the interpretation of scriptures will be demonstrated through texts that themselves reinterpret earlier passages from the Bible.

15. For a thoughtful reevaluation of this passage, see J. G. Janzen, "Habakkuk 2:2–4 in the Light of Recent Philological Advances," *Harvard Theological Review* 73 (1980) 53–78.

For the sectarian community that produced the Dead Sea Scrolls, the Torah of Moses was their special possession—not because they alone possessed this text, but because they regarded their interpretation of it to be the *only* true interpretation: a special revelation of "hidden things" (*nistārôt*) vouchsafed to them through their founding master, the Teacher of Righteousness. Indeed, it was just this special knowledge (*daʿat*) of the Torah that was believed to guarantee salvation to the members of the sect; and it was also this special knowledge that separated them from the community of Israel as a whole—whose oft proclaimed "evil way" was essentially a *different* interpretation of scripture. Thus transgression was not so much a rejection of God and his teachings per se, as in the rebuke of the prophet Zephaniah against those "who fall way from YHWH and do not beseech him or seek him [*děrāšûhû*]" (1:6). It was much more a rejection of the proper interpretation of that teaching, as is explicitly stated in a passage from the community's *Rule Scroll* (1QS 5:11), which transforms Zephaniah's rebuke to say: "The people of iniquity [are those] who walk in the evil way, for they do not beseech [God] and do not seek him [*děrāšûhû*] through his laws to know [*lādaʿat*] the hidden things [*nistārôt*]."

As possessors of these exegetical secrets, both the community and its teacher could say: "These things I know [*yādaʿtî*] from your knowledge [*bînātêkā*], for you have unveiled [*gālîtā*] my ear to mysterious wonders [*rāzê pelāʾ*]."[16] Surely just this ideological framework illumines the full polemical force of Ben Sira's admonition, cited earlier: "Do not seek out [*tidrôš*] things too wondrous [*pělāʾôt*] for you . . . ; [but rather] know well [*hitbônēn*] what has been permitted to you, and do not deal with hidden things [*nistārôt*]" (Sir 3:21–22). Another critique of "hidden knowledge" can be found in the old *logion* transmitted in the name of Rabbi Eleazar Ha-Modaʾi: "Whosoever desecrates holy things, or contemns the festival seasons, *or reveals* [*měgalleh*] *the interior sense* [*pānîm*] *of the Torah*, or breaks his covenant with Abraham, our father, or shames his colleague—though he has [accumulated the merit of] good deeds, he has no share in the world to come" (*m. ʾAbot* 3:11).[17] While diverse, a strong emphasis of this admonition is the concern with

16. 1QH 1:21, following the edition of the Qumran Hymns by J. Licht, *Megillat Ha-Hodayot* (Jerusalem: Bialik, 1957) [Hebrew]. An echo of Ps 119:18 is further suggested by 1QH 8:19: "[Ho]w could I behold [*ʾabît*] [such things] if you did not unveil my eye [*gālîtā ʿênî*]"; and cf. in the *Rule Scroll*, 1QS 11:3: "And my eye has beheld the wonders of it [*ûbenip-leʾôtâb habîṭāh ʿênî*].'

17. The mishnah is cited according to MS. Kaufmann. Its principal differences from the printed versions is a variation in the idiom used to denote the public embarrassment of a fellow scholar (*ḥābēr*) and its position in the text; in the expression "good deeds" instead of "Torah [viz., the merit of study] and good deeds"; and the absence of the phrase "against the halakha" (on which, see n. 18).

ritual offenses (including failure to perform circumcision, which is the "covenant of Abraham" in rabbinic parlance) and inappropriate demeanor (including improper performance of the ritual praxis of study). Accordingly, the sharp censure of those who reveal improperly the deeper sense of scripture must be understood as directed against those who interpret the Torah "against the *halakha*," as a later glossator of this mishnah has it[18]—which is to say, against the official rabbinic modes of exegesis. Numerous early debates on fixing the festival seasons among early Jewish groups (including strong polemical ripostes within the Dead Sea Scrolls themselves), give ample background to the first part of Rabbi Eleazar's teaching. The contemporary rejection of ritual circumcision in Pauline allegorical exegesis (Rom 2:28–29) suggests that this *logion* also has an anti-Christian component.[19] As Paul was at pains to preach, and the sages believed as well, proper exegesis has a salvific dimension. Whoever interprets scripture incorrectly "has no share in the world to come."

*En route* "from scribalism to rabbinism," exegesis thus makes the decisive claim that it is the very means for redemption. And what holds for the Law, holds for the Prophets as well. Indicative of this in the literature of Qumran is the remarkable interpretation given to Hab 2:3. Convinced that the Teacher of Righteousness (*ṣedeq*) was pneumatically graced with the *true* understanding of the ancient prophecies, and thus even exceeded what the original prophets understood about the application of their words (1QpHab 7:2), the biblical passage is construed with reference to the sectarian community. Just they, "who [properly] observe the Law . . . will God save from the House of Judgment—on account of their tribulation and *their faith in* the Teacher of Righteousness" (8:1–3). Such faith "in" the teacher is, of course, faith in him as a divinely guided medium of "all the mysteries [*rāzê*] of the words of . . . the prophets" (7:5)—"for the mysteries of God [*rāzê ʾēl*] are wondrous [*lĕhaplēh*]" (7:7).

The Teacher is thus the revealer of the true meaning of the Law and the Prophets; and knowledge of both is redemptive. Proper practice of the Law does not obviate prophetic hope in the end-time, nor does the proper understanding of the Prophets cancel practice of the Law. The Law is to be observed while one waits for the final days. Thus, when interpreting the passage from Habakkuk that "it will surely come" and one must "wait for it," the sectarians taught: "The interpretation [of it] concerns the men of truth, those who observe the Law, whose hand

18. The phrase is missing in MSS. Kaufmann and Cambridge, as well as the parallel discussion in ʾAbot de Rabbi Nathan (A.) chap. 26.

19. Cf. the discussion of E. Urbach, *Ḥazal. Pirkei Emunot Ve-Deʿot* (Jerusalem: Magnes, 1969) 265–66 and 265 n. 39 [Hebrew] for earlier literature and explanations.

do not grow slack in the service of the truth, when the last end-time is drawn out for them, for all of God's end-times will come according to their fixed order, as he [the Teacher] decreed for them in the mysteries of his prudence" (7:10–14).

It was presumably the fear that observance of the Law could be abrogated by prophetic enthusiasts that a final coda was added to the prophetic corpus of scripture: "Remember the Torah of Moses, my servant, to whom I commanded at Horeb laws and statutes for all Israel" (Mal 3:22).[20] And it was presumably the revolutionary and antinomian potential of prophecy that induced the early sages to proclaim, despite evidence to the contrary,[21] that "when the last prophets, Haggai, Zechariah, and Malachi died, the holy spirit departed from Israel" (*t. Soṭa* 13:2). A similar concern recurs in the remark that "since the day when the [First] Temple was destroyed prophecy has been taken from the prophets and given to the sages" (*b. Meg.* 17b). It has been wondered whether such comments derive from anti-Christian concerns.[22] However this be, the strong emphasis in the latter statement on the replacement of prophecy by Torah study provides an instructive foil to the depictions of Ezra and Ben Sira. It will be recalled that both of these sage-scribes were described with prophetic terminology. Against the background of the foregoing rabbinic *logia*, such depictions seem to express a neutralization of the prophetic impulse—its scribalization, one might say, and its reemployment in the service of the Law.[23]

## RECAPITULATION:
## THE IMAGE OF THE FONT OF WATERS

By way of review, I recapitulate the range of religious transformations discussed so far through the prism of the image of the font of waters, or well.

### At Qumran

Among the Dead Sea Scrolls, this image plays a central role in the *Damascus Document* (CD). It occurs in the context of an account of

20. Cf. my *Biblical Interpretation in Ancient Israel*, 524 and n. 33.

21. See Josephus, *Antiquities* 18:85–87; 20:97–98, 188; *Jewish War* 2:258–63, 6:288–309. Sometimes Josephus himself assumes a prophetic persona; cf. *Jewish War* 3:399–408, 4:622–29.

22. Cf. N. Glatzer, "A Study of the Talmudic Interpretation of Prophecy," *Review of Religion* 10 (1946) 116, 136.

23. For related observations, see J. Blenkinsopp, *Prophecy and Canon: A Contribution to the Study of Jewish Origins* (Notre Dame, IN: University of Notre Dame) 124–38.

the community's origin, and its distinctive method of Torah study under the inspired leadership of the Teacher of Righteousness. The scriptural vehicle for this presentation is the so-called Song of the Well (Num 21:17b-18)—a poetic evocation that "Israel sang" when they stopped for water at a desert oasis called Be⁾er ("Well"):

> Spring up, O well!—(Greet it with song):
> The well which the chieftains dug,
> Which the leaders of the people opened up
> With the staff and their maces.

In the precise, atomizing way, the components of this biblical unit are serially resignified: "the well [*bĕ⁾ēr*] is the Law" (CD 6:4), "the Staff [*mĕhôqqēq*] is the searcher [*dôrēš*] of the Law" (6:7), and "the leaders of the people are they who have come to dig the well with the staffs that the staff [*mĕhôqqēq*] instituted [*hāqaq*] to walk in them during all the epoch of wickedness" (6:8-10).[24]

Thus in the self-understanding of the community, a new well of Torah has been opened up "with the staff," this being the Teacher of Righteousness. This new well is, in fact, the source of the secret interpretations (*nistārôt*) of the Torah that God himself "has opened for them; and they [the faithful] digged a well for much water, and whosoever despises it [the water of Torah, correctly understood] shall not live" (CD 3:14-17). Accordingly, the follower of this way believes himself sustained by the fountain of true life (the Law) and exults: "I sha[ll praise thee, my Lord, for yo]u have placed me at the font of streams in dry land" (1QH 8:4). A more personal testimony of this conviction is expressed by the community psalmist, who says: "Secret truth you [God] have established in my heart; and well water for those who seek it [*dôrešehā*]" (5:9). Knowledge of the mysteries of the Torah

24. On the one hand, the association between *mĕhôqqēq* and the verb *hāqaq* may have called attention to the exegetical potential of this passage in terms of teaching and legislation. At the same time, there is an old exegetical tradition, already reflected in the Greek translation of the Hebrew *mĕhôqqēq* 'staff' as *grammateus* 'scribe'. This interpretation is the basis for the long paraphrastic comments in the Targumim to Num 21:18. Onqelos, for example, glosses the noun with *sāprayyā⁾* 'scribes'; and in the Fragmentary Targum (MS. Paris) this gloss is further explicated by the remark that these "*sāprayyā⁾* are the scribes [*sāprayyā⁾*] of Israel, Moses and Aaron" (see M. Klein, *The Fragment-Targums of the Pentateuch* [Rome: Pontifical Biblical Institute, 1980], 1:101). This paraphrase thus provides a precise rabbinic counterpoint to the Qumran tradition. Even more remarkable, in this regard, are the targumic glosses to the noun *mĕhôqqēq* in Deut 33:21 (the blessing of Gad): Onqelos has "Moses, the great scribe of Israel"; while the Fragmentary Targum (Klein, p. 116) actually reads "Moses *the prophet*, scribe of Israel"! In this remarkable formulation, the two functions are integrated.

is thus a religious experience: a source of spiritual sustenance in this life and a guarantee of salvation in the judgment to come.[25]

## Early Rabbinic Sources

The Torah is also deemed the saving water of life in early rabbinic sources. Thus an old tannaitic (second century c.e.) tradition allegorically interpreted the reference to "water" in Exod 15:22 as "Torah" (*b. B. Qam.* 82a). In other instances, directly continuous with the Dead Sea Scroll traditions just cited, scholars of the Law are described as a font of waters. Rabbi Eleazar ben Arak (a student of Rabbi Yohanan ben Zakkai) was especially famous for this attribution. For example, in *m. ʾAbot* 2:8 he is summarily called "an overflowing fountain"; whereas in the more expanded formulation of *ʾAbot de Rabbi Nathan* (A) 14 he is called "a rushing stream, an overflowing fountain—whose waters overflow and go outward, to fulfill what is stated [in scripture]: 'Let your fountains burst outward, your rushets of water into the broad places' [Prov 5:16]." At one level, this characterization of Rabbi Eleazar expresses the boundless learning of a sage; and the choice of Prov 5:16 as a prooftext also highlights the value of pedagogy so dear to the tannaitic sages (cf. *Sifre Deuteronomy* 48). At the same time, one senses that this pedagogical elaboration somewhat neutralizes (or socializes) the image. It is therefore instructive to note another (contemporary) instance of this literary *topos* that focuses on the supernatural boon of Torah study. According to Rabbi Meir in *m. ʾAbot* 6:1, inspired wisdom is one of the divine graces granted the devoted student of the Law. He teaches:

> Whoever devotedly studies the Torah for its own sake merits many things; and not only this but [one may even say] that the entire world is found deserving for his sake. He is called beloved companion, who loves the divine presence and loves all creatures, [and] who makes the divine presence glad and makes glad all creatures. And it [i.e., Torah study]

25. A striking parallel to these two *Hôdāyôt* texts, which portray the spiritual power of Torah for the community and the individual through water imagery, is found in Ben Sira's famous "Praise of Wisdom" (Sirach 24). On the one hand, there is a direct comparison of the rivers of Paradise to the wisdom of the Torah, a divine wisdom of inexhaustible profundity (24:23-28). Following this, the speaker attests in personal terms to his own transformation by this knowledge: "I also became as a stream from a river . . . [So] I said [thought] 'Let me water my garden . . .'; and behold! the stream became [for me] a river, and [then] my river became an ocean" (24:30-32). It is significant that the line quoted at the outset, wherein Ben Sira says that "he will pour out wisdom like prophecy" comes *just after* the preceding similes and testimony (24:33). The tannaitic source treated below, which derives from the class ideals of the sages, is a direct inheritor of this religious sensibility inculcated through study.

robes him with humility and fear; enables him to be righteous, pious, upright, and faithful; and keeps him far from sin and near to merit. And people shall benefit from his counsel, discernment, understanding, and fortitude. . . . *And the mysteries [rāzê] of the Torah are revealed [měgallîn] to him, and he becomes like an overflowing fountain and ceaseless torrent*; . . . and it makes him great and lifts him above the entire creation.

The teaching permits a deeper glimpse into the spiritual sensibilities of the sages, and their belief in the transformative powers of devoted study. For them, God's manifold grace flows to those sincerely occupied with Torah—who study it without precondition or presumption. Such pure study is divinely requited by gifts of humility and piety, sage counsel and righteousness, and insights into the very mysteries of the Law. Such a person can only be called a beloved companion, a friend of God and all creatures. To this one is revealed a revelation from the very depths of the revelation, the written Torah. Devoted study of God's Word thus opens up the flood of divine Wisdom, so that one, in turn, may become a font of divine teachings. It is therefore quite likely that this profound religious experience, *of transcendence in and through study*, is also a moment of mystical illumination.[26] One may assume that it was personally known to Rabbi Meir, and that these qualities of an illuminate-sage attracted him to Rabbi Akiba—his student, and himself a reknowned mystic.[27]

Rabbi Meir's *logion* of moral and spiritual transcendence through Torah study is complemented at the end of the next mishnah (*m. ʾAbot* 6:2) by a brief teaching in the same style by Rabbi Joshua ben Levi: "And whoever diligently studies the Torah repeatedly is exalted, as [scripture] says: 'And from Mattanah to Nahaliel, and from Nahaliel to Bamot' [Num 21:19]." From the formulation alone, it is difficult to determine the exact nature of the exaltation—whether mundane privilege merely, or (also or only) some form of spiritual transcendence. Nor will an analysis of the prooftext resolve the ambiguity, since the key term *bamôt* is opaque in this context. Nevertheless, the use of these place-names from the desert itinerary following the Song of the Well

26. For related midrashic sources suggesting a nexus between mystical illumination and Torah study, see M. Idel, "Mysticism," *Contemporary Jewish Religious Thought* (ed. A. Cohen and P. Mendes-Flohr; New York: Scribner, 1987) 644–45.

27. For a consideration of the role of Rabbi Akiba in the famous talmudic story of "Four Who Entered Paradise" (*b. Ḥag.* 14b), and its place in the wider context of early Jewish mysticism, see G. Scholem, *Jewish Gnosticism, Merkabah Mysticism, and Talmudic Tradition* (New York: Jewish Theological Seminary, 1965) chap. 3. Evidence for mystical experience (divine visions) based on textual study of the Song of Songs can be gleaned from ancient midrashic sources; see *"Mishnat Shir Ha-Shirim,"* by S. Lieberman (appendix D in Scholem's book, pp. 118–26).

provides an instructive finale to these observations about the sages'
understanding of Torah and its powers.

One may assume that Rabbi Joshua's attention was drawn to these
toponyms in connection with Torah study for two reasons: first, because
of the widespread exegetical association of water and Torah; and,
second, because of the specific phrase that follows the song: *ûmim-
midbār mattānâ* (v 18). On the one hand, these words may be reasonably construed as an ecstatic conclusion to the song (something like: "A
gift [*mattānâ*] from the desert [*midbār*]!"). At the same time, a contextual perspective supports the assumption that these words resume
the desert itinerary interrupted by the song (thus: the people traveled to
Beʾer [*běʾērâ*], from there to Midbar, from Midbar to Mattan [*mattānâ*;
v 18b], from there to Nahaliel, and on to Bamot [v 19]). The occurrence of this passage as a prooftext *in the context of the rewards of
study*, suggests that Rabbi Joshua combined both readings. As a rabbinic sage, his eye would readily perceive in the first phrase (*ûmim-
midbār mattānâ*), which precedes his prooftext, an allusion to the
"giving [*mattān*] of the Torah" in the desert (*midbār*) of Sinai. This
being so, it would be natural to construe the toponymns in v 19
midrashically. The result is the transformation of a spatial itinerary into
a spiritual one: "And because of the gift [*mattānâ*] of the Law [the
people of Israel] inherited God [i.e., they could say, lit., *naḥălîʾēl*, 'God
is my inheritance']; and because of this inheritance they gained heights
[*bamôt*; lit., 'high places']."

The precise exaltation due to Torah study may remain ambiguous
here, but one can hardly overlook the remarkable assertion that underlies the use of this biblical passage: through Torah one inherits God.
For the sages, as this context teaches, this divine inheritance is the grace
of *the study and interpretation* of Torah. With this bold assertion,
grounded in profound conviction, the development from scribalism to
rabbinism is complete. No mere scribal custodians of the letters of
scripture, the sages know themselves to be the faithful students of
divine truths—truths that may ever burst forth anew from their source,
like a well of living waters. The beloved companion may even hope to
be a conduit of this stream. In such hope, the profound abyss between
revelation and interpretation may be obscured—or transcended.

# COSMOLOGY AND
# THE SOCIAL ORDER
# IN THE WISDOM TRADITION

## Leo G. Perdue

### WISDOM AND THE
### SOCIAL CONSTRUCTION OF REALITY

*Introduction*

The wisdom tradition in ancient Israel is the product of sages from the tribal beginnings of Israel well into the Hellenistic period. From the knowledge produced by the sages, one may reconstruct their understandings of cosmology and the social order, as well as the underlying paradigms that produced and integrated this knowledge.[1] This social knowledge also provides direct, though limited, evidence about the social roles and functions of the sages.

Sociologists delineate two major paradigms for the conceptualization and organization of society: order and conflict.[2] Each represents significant assumptions about the cosmos, human nature, society, and knowledge. The thought of the traditional sages and Qoheleth is framed within a paradigm of order, while the Book of Job develops from a conflict model.

Leo G. Perdue is Professor of Hebrew Bible and Dean of Brite Divinity School, Texas Christian University.

1. See I. Barbour, *Myths, Models, and Paradigms* (New York: Harper and Row, 1974).

2. See W. D. Perdue, *Sociological Theory* (Palo Alto, CA: Mayfield, 1986). The paradigm of order is represented in the following works: E. Durkheim, *The Division of Labor in Society* (New York: Macmillan, 1933); R. K. Merton, *Social Theory and Social Structure* (New York: Free Press, 1968); and T. Parsons, *The Structure of Social Action* (Glencoe, IL: Free Press, 1937). The paradigm of conflict is represented by Karl Marx, *Capital: A Critique of Political Economy* (3 vols.; New York: International Publishers, 1967–85); H. Marcuse, *Reason and Revolution* (New York: Humanities, 1983); and J. Habermas, *Toward a Rational Society* (Boston: Beacon, 1970).

## The Paradigm of Order

In their social construction of reality,[3] the sages developed a paradigm of order (*ṣdq*) that integrated three separate spheres: cosmology, society, and human nature.[4] Ṣedeq refers to the 'righteous order' of the cosmos that is to permeate social institutions, particularly the rule and judicial decisions of kings (Prov 8:15-16, 25:5, 31:9), while *ṣĕdāqâ* 'righteousness' is the behavior of those who both actualize and live in harmony with the righteous order (Prov 10:2; 11:4, 6, 19; 14:34; 21:3). Ṣaddîq refers to the 'righteous person' who either lives in harmony with or acts to shape or sustain the just order of the world. The behavior of the *ṣaddîq* established a sphere of well-being that the community of righteous experiences (Prov 10:3, 16, 20, 21, 24). The wicked (*rāšāᶜ*), by contrast, are those whose actions and speech undermine social order and bring destruction, not only to themselves but to the community as well (Prov 11:5, 13:6, 28:12, 29:2).

These three terms conveyed three distinct meanings to the sages: correctness (*ṣedeq*), righteousness (*ṣĕdāqâ*), and conformity (*ṣaddîq*). Allowing for the mysterious and the inexplicable, the sages perceived cosmic order to have originated at the beginning of creation, to continue to permeate reality, and to be maintained by the justice of divine rule. For something to be *ṣdq* meant to exist in a state of order, correctness, and reliability. The elements of creation acted in accord with their nature. Wise language was correct or proper, that is truthful and reliable (Prov 12:17, 16:13). The various phenomena of creation could be observed to possess a certain regularity in their behavior, and thus provided insight into the constancy of the natural order and its structures of life (e.g., the orderly and life-sustaining behavior of ants in Prov 6:6-8, 30:24-31). The creator instituted and maintained these structures, enabling life to endure. Even so, *ṣedeq* did not mean that the order of the cosmos was static and impervious to change. Rather it was a state that came into being through the creative action of God and continued to be shaped and sustained by the life-giving and righteous actions of God.

Ṣedeq also suggested a moral order operative in the universe, which responded directly to human behavior: wise actions and thoughts led to well-being, while foolish and subversive actions culminated in

3. See P. Berger and T. Luckmann, *The Social Construction of Reality* (Garden City, NY: Doubleday, 1966), who argue that human thought creates a social reality by the process of externalization, internalization, and maintenance.

4. See H. Gese, *Lehre und Wirklichkeit in der alten Weisheit* (Tübingen: Mohr/Siebeck, 1958); H. H. Schmid, *Gerechtigkeit als Weltordnung* (Beitrage zur historischen Theologie 40; Tübingen: Mohr/Siebeck, 1968); and A. Dünner, *Die Gerechtigkeit nach dem Alten Testament* (Schriften zur Rechtslehre und Politik 42; Bonn: H. Bouvier, 1963).

destruction. While *ṣedeq* refers primarily to a state of being, *ṣĕdāqâ* is more linked to action (Prov 21:3).[5] It is that which is done or established (*ʿaśâ*). Thus, the moral order in the world was not closed to the free intervention of God, who acted to insure the well-being of the righteous and the eventual destruction of the wicked who rejected wisdom's call (Prov 10:3; 15:9, 29). In this way the sages maintained the integrity of divine freedom and will.

Because of their conformity to the discipline (*mûsār*) of instruction taught them by wisdom, the righteous lived in harmony with the cosmic order and experienced divine blessing (Prov 10:25, 30). One of the dominant metaphors for life in conformity with the moral order of society and cosmos was finding and walking on the path (*derek*) of righteousness or of life (Prov 11:5, 12:28, 13:6, 21:21). Frequently linked to the behavior of the righteous is "life," understood in a rich variety of ways: longevity, fulfillment, happiness, success, contentment, and health (10:2, 11:4-6, 12:28). Creation language is often used to describe the behavior and results of the righteous. According to the imagery of Prov 10:25, the righteous are established (*sôd*) forever. *Sôd* is a common term in creation texts to describe the creator's establishment of the earth on a firm and solid basis (Prov 3:19-20). Like the pillars of the earth that support the stable order of creation, the righteous do not move and sway (*môṭ*; Prov 10:30). On one hand, to be a *ṣaddîq* 'righteous one' conveyed the understanding of living in harmony with and in subjection to cosmic and social order. On the other hand, to be a *ṣaddîq* meant active participation in shaping cosmic and social order through wise language and actions.[6] These two different understandings of righteousness provided a continuing tension in sapiential ethics.

This paradigm of order served as the hermeneutic by which the sages arranged and interpreted the data, events, and experiences of reality. Knowledge consisted of the search for and observation of the order underlying the cosmos, society, and human nature. Indeed, the sages thought that the knowledge they produced and transmitted provided the basis by which the structures of reality were formed and sustained.

## The Paradigm of Conflict

A second paradigm for the social knowledge of the sages is conflict. This paradigm makes its own assumptions about the cosmos, society,

5. A. Jepsen, "צדק und צדקה im Alten Testament," *Gottes Wort und Gottes Land* (ed. H. Graf Reventlow; H. W. Hertzberg FS; Göttingen: Vandenhoeck und Ruprecht, 1965) 78–89. Jepsen argues that *ṣedeq* refers mainly to the correct order, while *ṣĕdāqâ* indicates more the proper behavior that is related to order.

6. H.-J. Hermisson, *Studien zur israelitischen Spruchweisheit* (WMANT 28; Neukirchen-Vluyn: Neukirchener, 1968).

human nature, and knowledge. In the critical wisdom tradition, especially the Book of Job, divine forces of creation and chaos contended for the domination of the cosmos. Order was not indigenous to the cosmos, but rather was achieved only by the continuing defeat of chaos. Order and the structures of life were not static and enduring, but processes that were ever under threat.

Struggle characterized social life as well, due in part to the perceived propensity of humans for unlicensed passion and selfish desire. Righteousness was not a dominant feature of human nature, though through discipline (*mûsār*), correct and just behavior could be learned and practiced. Wisdom was both the rational process and the moral tradition that limited the destructive capacity of human nature. Through instructions and just institutions, social order could be achieved. Yet these institutions existed without grounding in any cosmic order. And the limits of human knowledge and even divine power were recognized. Mystery and ambiguity made human knowledge a more risky venture. Even so, there was the possibility of informed human participation in the shaping of a social and cosmic order that not only made life possible, but also gave it meaning.

## WISDOM AND EPISTEMOLOGY

### Natural Law and Natural Revelation

The beginning of the quest for knowledge was "the fear of God," that is, the conviction that the structures of life were created and sustained by the just and beneficent rule of God (Prov 1:7, 14:27). Normally eschewing prophetic charisma and priestly theophanies, traditional sages believed true wisdom originated with God and was transmitted to them through their powers of observation, reason, and reflection.[7]

Experience of the world was indirectly an experience of God, at least in the understanding that the just and orderly regulation of nature and the beneficent structures of existence reflected the nature and will of the creator.[8] It was only during occasions of crisis (Job) followed by periods of pessimism (Qoheleth) that significant tensions developed between faith and reason. Even traditional sages believed God transcended the world, residing beyond human perception. It was Woman Wisdom, the "voice" of God in nature and thought, who mediated knowledge to the sages.[9] Faith had to do, not with the existence of God,

7. J. C. Rylaarsdam, *Revelation in Jewish Wisdom Literature* (Chicago: University of Chicago, 1946) 72.

8. G. von Rad, *Wisdom in Israel* (Nashville: Abingdon, 1972) 144–76.

9. R. E. Murphy, "Wisdom and Creation," *JBL* 104 (1985) 3–11.

but rather with the affirmation of the goodness and justice of the creator revealed in the just and beneficent order of creation.

## Wisdom as Reason and Experience

The sages searched for patterns and consistencies in reality. They sought to discover regularity in the variety of natural and social phenomena and to establish their relationships. Even unrelated phenomena were studied to find correlations that would point to the order and interconnectedness of the world (Prov 26:11, 26:20, 30:15–33). Events were thought to connect as well, leading to the development of a principle of causality. This regularity led to a unified construction of reality that established a direct correspondence between what was observed and the rational categories of the mind. Regularity in the world was seen to be consistent with the processes of human perception.

While significance was attached to the validity of individual experience, the collective knowledge of the sages formed an authoritative tradition that was to shape the beliefs and values of both sages and society as a whole. The internalization of this tradition through socialization (teaching in a variety of settings) made it possible for individuals to make their way successfully in the world (Prov 2:1–15). Yet the tradition was to be fluid and open, not static and inflexible, for its teachings had to stand the critical test of new and sometimes disconfirming experiences.

## Wisdom and Torah

While the sages in the period of the First Temple were active within the tribal and especially the royal social traditions, their successors in the Second Temple period were primarily active within the realms of foreign government service and religion, in first the temple and eventually the synagogue. The efforts of Ezra and Ben Sira clearly demonstrate that sages were active in shaping the Torah into the religious and social constitution for Second Temple Judaism. If Erhard Gerstenberger and Moshe Weinfeld are correct, sages may well have contributed significantly to this process of the formulation of legal codes in tribal and monarchic societies in the preexilic period.[10]

The identification of wisdom with the Torah is made by Ben Sira. His elegant hymn of Wisdom's heavenly origins and eventual residence in Israel concludes with the equating of wisdom and the "book of the covenant of the Most High God, the law which Moses commanded us"

---

10. E. Gerstenberger, *Wesen und Herkunft des "apodiktischen Rechts"* (WMANT 20; Neukirchen-Vluyn: Neukirchener, 1965); and Weinfeld, *Deuteronomy and the Deuteronomic School* (Oxford: Clarendon, 1972).

(Sir 24:23). Johann Marböck has demonstrated that Ben Sira was consciously a theologian, standing in the deuteronomic tradition, who constructed a synthesis between popular Greek philosophy and Hebrew wisdom, creation and salvation history, and Torah and wisdom.[11] However, Ben Sira is not the first to establish the identification of wisdom and Torah, for the Psalter includes several "torah psalms" that probably predated his work: Psalms 19 and 119. Composed most probably by postexilic sages, both of these psalms praise the Torah as the source of divine revelation, which provides the wise with both knowledge of God and direction in life. But Ben Sira indicates that the increasing prominence given to the Torah as a source of revelation does not replace creation (cf. Sir 39:1-35). Indeed, creation and Torah are the twin poles for authoritative knowledge, for the wisdom used by God in creating and sustaining the world now resides in nature and the text of the Torah (cf. Psalm 19).

## Beauty

Knowledge of the world was not limited to rational perception, quantifiable experiences, and authoritative traditions. Reality was also a thing of beauty (an "esthesis") that attracted and awed its beholders. The grace and telos of the play of Wisdom (Prov 8:30-31), the majesty and strength of the earth's foundations (Job 38:4-7), and the persuasiveness of fine speech (Prov 16:20-24) were among those things admired for their elegance and form. The sages cultivated beauty particularly in the crafting of language. More than a precept, the saying constructed its own minute esthesis in which the content of reason and experience assumed the shape of elegant form.[12] Far more than rhetorical display or literary embellishment, the artistic shaping of language formed and maintained a world of beauty in which even the creator took delight (Prov 8:30-31).

## Mystery and the Limits of Knowledge

The sages recognized the limits of human knowledge.[13] They freely admitted there were mysteries that eluded human comprehension (Prov 14:12), and, of course, there was the acknowledged sovereignty of God who acted in freedom to direct the courses of nature and history. Thus, even the best-laid plans of human counsel could not guarantee success in a world of limits where God has both the freedom and the power to

11. Marböck, *Weisheit im Wandel: Untersuchungen zur Weisheitstheologie bei Ben Sira* (Bonner biblische Beitrage 37; Bonn: Peter Hanstein, 1971).

12. See my essay, "The Wisdom Sayings of Jesus," *Forum* 2 (1986) 7-8.

13. Von Rad, *Wisdom in Israel*, 97-112.

control events (Prov 16:9; 19:14, 21; 21:30–31). And there were the inevitable contingencies that could adversely affect even the wisest and most moral of sages.

While the sages trusted in the goodness of their creator, they recognized that their understanding of God was quite limited (Prov 25:2). In the final analysis, it was the "fear of God," not knowledge, that was the ultimate grounding of sapiential existence. Yet this same willingness to admit limits to their knowledge led many sages to an openness both to the world and its perception. Examination and testing of tradition and the search for new insights were the epistemological poles that produced a developing body of sapiential knowledge.

## COSMOLOGY IN THE WISDOM TRADITION

### The World as Order

Sapiential cosmology is rooted in a theology of creation.[14] Their observations of nature did not lead the sages to the cosmological argument for the existence of God. And the closest they came to constructing a theogony was the poetic description of the origins of Woman Wisdom in Prov 8:22–31. Rather, the sages began with the origins of creation (Prov 3:19–20, Job 38:1–42:6).

Drawing on a variety of creation myths and their root metaphors, which were prominent in ancient Near Eastern cultures, the traditional sages told of God originating and then using wisdom to create the world.[15] Two metaphors were frequently used by the sages to portray the origins of the world: word and artistry. By the power of the word, God spoke the cosmos into existence and continues to rule by divine decree (Job 38:11–12, Sir 39:12–35). As head of the divine council, God sends the rain to revitalize the earth (Job 5:10, 38:25–30) and he sustains humans (Sir 39:26–27) and other creatures (Job 38:39–39:30). As judge,

14. See R. Albertz, *Weltschöpfung und Menschenschöpfung* (Calwer Theologische Monographien A/3; Stuttgart: Calwer, 1974); P. Doll, *Menschenschöpfung und Weltschöpfung in der alttestamentlichen Weisheit* (Stuttgart: KBW, 1985); H.-J. Hermisson, "Observations on the Creation Theology in Wisdom," *IW* 43–57; R. Knierim, "Cosmos and History in Israel's Theology," *Horizons in Biblical Theology* 3 (1981) 59–123; D. A. Knight, "Cosmogony and Order in the Hebrew Tradition," *Cosmogony and Ethical Order* (ed. R. W. Lovin and F. E. Reynolds; Chicago: University of Chicago, 1985) 133–57; Schmid, *Gerechtigkeit als Weltordnung*; and idem, *Altorientalische Welt in der alttestamentlichen Theologie* (Zurich: Theologischer Verlag, 1974). For a survey of the relationship of cosmology to theology, see *Cosmology and Theology* (ed. D. Tracy and N. Lash; New York: Seabury, 1983).

15. See my essay, "Job's Assault on Creation," *Hebrew Annual Review* 10 (1986) 295–315.

God commands the appearance of dawn, with each new day signaling the re-creation of the world (Job 38:12–15). All authentic law originates with God, whose will is revealed in both the natural order (Psalm 19A) and the Torah (Psalms 19B, 119; Sirach 24).

Elsewhere God is the divine architect who plans and constructs the cosmos in the form of an elegant and well-planned building (Job 38:4–7, Prov 3:19–20). The building is not only functional, but also pleasing in its dimensions, thus eliciting the praise of its beholders (Job 38:4–7). For the priesthood, the building and maintenance of human dwellings, palaces, and temples imitate the mythic construction of reality and maintain the cosmic and social order.[16] For the sages, it is Woman Wisdom who constructs her own palace (school?) and initiates her worship by inviting the unlearned to partake of her feast (Prov 9:1–6). With this metaphor, the sages speak of the origins of their tradition, which forms and sustains both cosmic and social reality.

With each metaphor it is divine wisdom that is identified with the conceptual design, skill, and power in the origination of creation. For the sages, there is no *creatio ex nihilo*, but rather a process of ordering by which preexistent chaos is fashioned and contained by spoken word and skillful act (cf. Wis 11:2). These metaphors convey the belief that the world is orderly, intelligible, and good.

For the sages, the "belief that the natural forces and the moral purposes of the Creator are complementary powers"[17] was expressed in a theory of retribution that was open to various nuances of understanding.[18] In the view of many sages, sapiential act and divine response created a sphere of beneficence in which well-being was experienced by the righteous.[19] The consequences of individual actions directly affected all members of society. Denied access to this sphere fools and sinners suffered the consequences of their actions, yet the well-being of society was also adversely affected. Divine justice punished offenders, yet God's freedom allowed the tempering of judgment with compassion. Other sages, especially the opponents of Job, required far more of their cosmology, demanding a guarantee that the wicked meet their just desserts, while the righteous, though never perfect and ever subject to divine chastisement, would eventually be rewarded. The mechanical understanding of retribution negated mystery and ambiguity, even in regard to God. Its hardened dogmatism led to the crisis of wisdom reflected in the Book of Job.

16. M. Eliade, *Cosmos and History: The Myth of the Eternal Return* (New York: Harper and Row, 1954) 6.

17. O. S. Rankin, *Israel's Wisdom Literature* (Edinburgh: T. & T. Clark, 1936) 38.

18. For a thorough discussion, see K. Koch, "Gibt es ein Vergeltungsdogma im Alten Testament?" *Zeitschrift für Theologie und Kirche* 52 (1955) 1–42.

19. Von Rad, *Wisdom in Israel*, 74–96.

## Cosmic Space

The sages shared the spatial views of reality in the ancient Near East. The bipartite spatial reality is found in the expression "heaven and earth." This duality is represented in two different ways in the ancient Near East: as the union of a primeval, divine pair,[20] and as two distinct spheres for separating divine and human habitation. While the special presence of God on the earth is made possible by sacred spaces (e.g., temples, sacred mountains, springs, and trees), heaven is the particular domain of God and earth the space of human habitation.

The cosmology of the wise follows this second representation of heaven and earth (Prov 3:19-20, 8:22-31; Qoh 1:13, 2:11; Sirach 24). The transcendence and sovereignty of God and divine mystery accompany this cosmology. On occasion, however, human beings when filled with hubris contest divine rule. They seek to replace divine with human rule, though with tragic results (Isaiah 14, Job 3-31). Thus divine law and wisdom become the necessary institutions to subdue human disobedience and to quell the spirit of revolt.

A tripartite cosmology of heaven, earth, and chaos (Psalm 139, Ezek 26:20) or the primeval ocean (Psalm 33) represents a second view of cosmic space shared by the sages.[21] During seasonal struggles, the deity of order overcomes the threat of the chaos monster, and once again ascends the throne to order the world by divine decree. In this cosmology, God is the transcendent sovereign who maintains the structures of existence on the earth. The righteous join with God in repulsing the threats of chaos and its embodiment in the wicked (Job 38:1-42:6).

## Cosmic Time

The mythic constructions of reality contained a dual understanding of time. In one sense, "in the beginning" is a mythic time, an *illud tempus* that collapses past, present, and future into an eternal now. In another sense, myth distinguishes between the time of origins and *creatio continua*, most commonly expressed in the cyclical movements of the seasons. By contrast historical time portrays the linear succession of unrepeatable moments that embrace the steady movement of sequenced events. God's interruptions into human history were the exceptional moments in which heaven's active participation in the affairs of humankind disrupted the normal course of temporal sequence and the events that linear time enfolded. While unrepeatable, the salvific acts of divine redemption, most notably the Exodus, became paradigmatic for God's future interventions that redirected historical reality toward a new and vital course. Thus, in speaking of the return from Exile, the

20. O. Keel, *The Symbolism of the Biblical World* (New York: Seabury, 1978) 31.
21. Ibid., 35-47.

Exodus became the model for prophetic imagination, which redescribed reality by proleptic actualization of an imminent act of new redemption (cf. Isaiah of Babylon). In the cultic celebration and memory of the community, these paradigmatic acts of divine redemption were wedded to the temporal duality of mythic time and the events of divine creation, mythologizing, as it were, not historical time and events, but rather exceptional, salvific interruptions into the world of the ordinary. Eschatology pointed to a culmination of human history, a final "end" to historical moments and successive human events when linear time and sequenced actions will be eventually absorbed into the eternal now.

The sages adopted the dual conceptions of mythic time (Prov 3:10–20, 8:22–31; Job 38:1–42:6) as they spoke of the origins of the world and their traditions that sustained the ongoingness of creation. The study of wisdom, the creative power and order of God in shaping and sustaining the cosmos, succeeded in revitalizing the world and sustaining the structures of life, both in nature and social constructions. However, for preexilic sages, it was not paradigmatic events of divine redemption that were cyclically repeated, but rather the articulation of revealed wisdom in sapiential discourse and the actualization of the tradition by study and action. Word and event helped to revitalize and sustain cosmos and community.

And certainly these sages were aware of historical time and even placed this temporal sphere under the ultimate control of providence (Job 12:13–25). But knowledge of the "times" for the sages meant, not the order of mythic, paradigmatic or linear time, but rather the awareness that there were moments when wise actions were successful in shaping the structures of life and well-being, and other inopportune periods when even the sagest of actions would certainly fail (Prov 27:23–27, Qoh 3:1–8, Sir 4:20).[22] Thus the sages sought to come to a knowledge of the larger temporal order of cosmology and history, for they realized that this more extensive structure provided the context in which individual and communal existence could be secured (Wis 7:15–22). Within this larger order of mythic and linear times, then, there were episodic periods for every event in human existence. While the direction of cosmic and historical times was ultimately under the control of providence, individuals and communities possessed a substantial measure of freedom to participate in the shaping of their own existence. It was the understanding of the totality of temporal reality that the traditional sages sought, Qoheleth negated, and the apocalyptic seers claimed.

22. Von Rad, *Wisdom in Israel*, 138–43; and H. W. Wolff, *Anthropology of the Old Testament* (Philadelphia: Fortress, 1974) 89–92.

By the postexilic era, the sages eventually incorporated into their tradition salvation history and eschatology (Ben Sira and Wisdom). In Ben Sira's grand portrait of realized eschatology, creation, universal human history, and the story and institutions of Israel (including Torah, temple, and wisdom) achieved their cumulative meaning in the Jewish community of the Second Temple (cf. Sirach 24).[23] The Wisdom of Solomon set forth a temporal matrix in which eternal, divine wisdom is the spirit of righteousness permeating the cosmos and taking up residence within righteous souls, providing the ultimate gift of immortality. Yet she is also the trusted guide of the righteous, entering into human history to redeem wise and righteous leaders from the threats of extinction. In this Hellenistic-Jewish text, cosmology, history, and sacred interruptions intersect by means of the nature and functions of divine wisdom.[24]

## Wisdom in the Cosmos

Originating within the language of mythos, a variety of metaphors were appropriated by the sages to authenticate the esthetic and rational discourse of their instructions and sayings. The sapiential tradition was imagined in the form of Woman Wisdom, who mediated between heaven and earth and revealed the proper correlation of human and divine actions contexted within the intersection of mythic, paradigmatic, and episodic times.[25] Originating as the daughter of God and designated as the first and best of all creation (Prov 8:22–32), she revealed to the sages their proper place and function within the cosmic and social order, enabling them to study and live so as to achieve well-being. Wisdom becomes the voice of God in creation, ordering and sustaining the world from the beginning (Genesis 1, Psalm 33) and revealing the character and will of the creator. The cosmos was affirmed as "good," that is, a righteous and beneficent order, revealing many of its mysteries and even its trustworthy creator to those who respond to Wisdom's call.[26] She is also the queen of heaven who orchestrates divine rule by choosing kings and princes to govern the earth (Prov 8:12–21), and offering her followers both life and fortune (Prov 3:15–18).[27]

23. B. L. Mack, *Wisdom and the Hebrew Epic: Ben Sira's Hymn in Praise of the Fathers* (Chicago: University of Chicago, 1986).

24. See J. J. Collins, "Cosmos and Salvation: Jewish Wisdom and Apocalyptic in the Hellenistic Age," *History of Religions* 17 (1977–78) 121–42.

25. For overviews, see B. Lang, *Frau Weisheit* (Düsseldorf: Patmos, 1975); and C. Camp, *Woman Wisdom* (Sheffield: Almond, 1986).

26. Von Rad, *Wisdom in Israel*, 144–76.

27. Cf. the Egyptian goddesses Isis and Maat; see C. Bauer-Kayatz, *Studien zu Proverbien 1–9* (WMANT 22; Neukirchen-Vluyn: Neukirchener, 1966).

Woman Wisdom, who mediated between the heavenly regions and the world of human habitation, finally took up residence among the people of Israel and dwelt within their institutions of temple cult and Mosaic law (Sirach 24). The Wisdom of Solomon even combines the images of the Stoic cosmic soul with the biblical breath of God (Ps 104:27–30) to describe divine Sophia, now a transcendent goddess enthroned next to God, a creative power that renews the vital forces of life, and the redemptress who saves the righteous from death. In this latter text, Wisdom has moved from metaphor to hypostasis, a divine attribute becoming now the consort of God (7:22–8:1).[28]

Elsewhere the metaphor of artistry is used to express the understanding of wisdom. In Job 28, wisdom is a "blueprint" for the cosmos, containing its order, measurements, and weights, though known only to the divine artisan. The building activities of humans, including their construction of mines and canals, do not discover wisdom's character and hidden secrets. In the Wisdom of Solomon, Sophia takes on a more active role by becoming the *technitis* 'artisan' (7:21, 8:6) who has shaped a world of alluring beauty and order, which, like herself, evokes the wonder and praise of those who honor her.

Wisdom, including both the social knowledge produced by the sages and what remained beyond their grasp, held a position second only to God himself. In the sapiential tradition, wisdom was the divine skill used to originate and sustain the cosmos, the mediator between God and the world inhabited by humans, the indwelling spirit that nourished creaturely life, the worldly and divine knowledge whose possession enabled the wise to experience well-being and to live in harmony with God and creation, and the system of values that guided humanity in the quest for the moral life. Moving from personification to hypostasis, wisdom becomes in the Wisdom of Solomon the consort of God, assuming the divine roles of artisan, providential guide, and redemptress.

## Order as Tyranny

Order acquires the dimensions of rigidity and tyranny in Qoheleth. For this sage the cosmos was neither a just order nor an esthesis of elegance and grace. Rather nature's daily movements of sunrise and sunset, the circuitous routes of the wind, and the flow of streams into unfilled seas revealed neither an inherent goodness nor a righteous order. These movements did not elicit the response of wonder and awe, for they were perceived to be monotonous, unendingly repetitious (Qoh 1:4–7).

28. H. Ringgren, *Word and Wisdom* (Lund: H. Ohlssons, 1947).

Confidence in the justice and beneficence of God was replaced by a deep-seated terror and final resignation before an unknowable God whose uncontested decrees determined the fates of human creatures. Indeed, God remains the *deus absconditus*, dwelling within the heavenly regions, separated and removed from human habitation and under- standing of the wise. Even wisdom could not mediate between the two cosmological spheres. "The God" ruled the heavens and the earth with unrivaled power, which did not recognize any human standards for justice. There is a hierarchy of tyrannical order grounded in and su- stained by power alone (Qoh 5:8–9).

While Qoheleth affirms that everything God has created has an appropriate time for existing, he denies that God grants even to sages any comprehension of the larger temporal order in the world: God "has placed darkness [*˓lm*][29] into the minds of humans so that they cannot discover what he does from the beginning to the end" (Qoh 3:11–12). Human beings are also denied the ability to influence the course of cosmic and historical events directed by God in secret (8:17). And they do not know the destiny that God has set for them. Even the knowledge of episodic moments, those occasions when deeds may be successfully undertaken, is denied them. One may only passively respond in joy to the "day of prosperity" created by God and learn from the "day of adversity" that the creator is the sole determiner of human history (7:14).[30]

## The World as Conflict

The experience of the catastrophic dissolution of social and politi- cal order, occasioned by historical disasters, led to the destabilization and ultimately fragmentation of the cultural and religious traditions that this paradigm had produced. To attack the old order and to forge new traditions of meaning required a major paradigm shift for the critical sages. Without new formulations, the fragmentation of old traditions would ultimately result in either the submergence of wisdom's critical stance within an unquestioning naïveté or in the dissolution of the sapiential communities themselves.

The first response was rendered by the opponents of Job who continued to avow God's just administration of the cosmos, denying validity to any accusation brought against divine sovereignty. A hard- ened theory of retribution demanded from its cosmology the impossible contention that the wicked were inevitably punished and the righteous

29. Reading the stem as 'darkness' instead of 'eternity'.
30. See K. Galling, "Das Rätsel der Zeit," *Zeitschrift für Theologie und Kirche* 58 (1961) 1–15.

eventually but certainly rewarded. The second response was made by Job, a sage who comes to develop a model of conflict as a new and compelling paradigm for understanding the nature of God, the cosmos, and human community. Initially for Job, God had become a malevolent power seeking to destroy his own creation and singling out the righteous for particular abuse. However, in the theophany God speaks as a Divine Warrior who describes his active struggle with chaos for kingship over creation. No retributive moral order permeates reality, bringing blessing to the righteous and destruction to the wicked. While death and suffering are an inevitable part of existence, they are not directly linked to immoral behavior. Rather they are constituent features of human experience in the reality God has shaped. Seeking new words to praise the creator, Job learns that human righteousness entails actively participating with God in the struggle against chaos and its various incarnations. Suffering is inevitable and mortality circumscribes human efforts, but the structures of life for creation and human communities are secured only by the struggle for justice.

## THE ETHICAL ORDER IN WISDOM

For the sages, moral reasoning was not isolated, self-contained mental activity, but rather a process that occurred within an integrated system of cosmology, social institutions, and human nature. Actions and words have a meaning that reaches beyond the observable results for the individual agent to have impact on the anthropological, social, and cosmic order originating within primordial beginnings.[31]

Several ethical systems are implicit to the wisdom tradition. An *ethic of results* assumes a benign creator has established a beneficent world whose order must be actualized by righteous and wise deeds and words. The purpose of the sage was to "master" (*māšal*) life, that is, to extend and sustain the life-giving orders of creation and society.[32] The human response to the world and the divine commission is active ordering, not passive submission. This ethic uses the metaphor of king to describe both humanity's place and task of going forth into the world to apprehend, establish, and order reality (Job 29, Prov 8:12–21). The "good" resulting from human effort was not a moral virtue, but rather a "social phenomenon," that is, a life-enhancing power that produced and sustained a communal sphere of righteousness in which well-being was

31. Hermisson (in *Studien zur israelitischen Spruchweisheit*) notes that the saying connects deed and result, thereby creating an order of life.

32. W. Zimmerli, "The Place and Limit of the Wisdom in the Framework of the Old Testament Theology," *SAIW* 314–26.

experienced.[33] The Book of Job alters this ethic by uprooting it from its cosmological grounding. For this wisdom book, justice is not an ontological power innate to the cosmos, which integrates and sustains creation, but rather an active process in which God and humanity struggle against chaos to establish and sustain the structures of life.

Construed by the metaphor of slave, the *ethic of maintenance* contends that the purpose of the moral life is to live in harmony with the cosmic and social order and to submit to established decrees (Job 7:1-4, 14:1-6). People are to accept their place in the social order, whether it is that of slave or royal counselor. This is an ethic of duty and responsibility defined concretely by the role and status one has in the social order. The cosmological grounding of this ethic sees the world as a righteous, but static order, and regards human nature as weak and subject to uncontrolled passions that threaten destruction. In response to this anthropology, this ethic seeks to cultivate virtues, eliminate destructive vices rooted in desire and greed, and urge moral progress toward becoming wise. Wisdom is the redemptive means by which human beings are saved from their own tendencies of self-destruction. In this understanding, the sages seek to discover their place and function in the world and to make their way by recognizing and learning from the sustaining patterns of regularity and life in nature and society, all the while aware of the various contingencies that threaten them. Wisdom enabled one to know when and how to act so as to secure well-being. The goal and meaning of existence is a this-worldly life full of joy and wholeness.[34]

An *ethic of well-being* appears in Qoheleth, linked, not to cosmology, but rather to human nature. The crisis for Qoheleth was the breakdown of the connection between the moral life and cosmology. Rejecting the doctrine of the utter depravity of human nature expressed by the friends (e.g., Job 25:1-6), Qoheleth argues that humans are created upright (*yāšār*), but their actions tend to be evil. Indeed, Qoheleth uses hyperbole to conclude that it is extremely rare to find a righteous person (7:25-29). And Qoheleth speaks of the weakness of human beings, their utter dependency on God for life, and the inevitability of death for all, regardless of their moral character. God is not the beneficent deity who redeems them from sorrow, but rather the despot whose decrees cannot be altered by human response. Indeed the

33. Von Rad, *Wisdom in Israel*, 80. While J. F. Priest is correct in emphasizing wisdom's confidence in the human ability to shape the world in productive ways, he does not adequately develop the theological grounding of sapiential "humanism" succinctly expressed in the rubric, "the fear of God"; "Humanism, Skepticism, and Pessimism in Israel," *Journal of the American Academy of Religion* 36 (1968) 311-26.
34. W. Brueggemann, *In Man We Trust* (Atlanta: John Knox, 1972).

inevitable fate of all humans is death, an eternal oblivion in which there is neither memory of the past nor awareness of the present. Even the pragmatic value of wisdom is greatly diminished, seeing that there is no righteous, enduring cosmic order discernible to human perception. Indeed God and divine action remain hidden and mysterious.

Moral reasoning in Qoheleth is grounded in the desire for "well-being [$tôb$] in human existence." "Good" for Qoheleth is not a virtue, a successful outcome, or a social sphere of well-being. Rather the only "good" to human beings in living is joy ($simhâ$), which may derive from three sources: festive occasions ("eating and drinking"), the intimate relationships with family and friends, and human labor. Joy is both a capacity residing within human nature and an experience that is possible, though not guaranteed. Even the experience of joy is ultimately contingent on the caprice of divine favor.

## THE SOCIAL ORDER IN WISDOM

### Cosmology and the Social Order in Traditional Wisdom

As noted above, two major social paradigms are operative in wisdom literature: order and conflict. For traditional wisdom, social institutions and the roles and behavior subsumed under each are given an ontological status by being rooted in the cosmic order. A righteous and stable society embodies or actualizes the cosmic order originating at the time of creation.[35] The fragmentation of the social order in turn leads to the destabilization and even collapse of the cosmos as chaos returns to destroy creation. This social theory is exemplified by the following numerical saying:

> Under three things the earth quakes [$rāgaz$],
> It is not able to endure four:
> When a slave becomes king,
> When a fool becomes satiated with bread,
> When a despised woman gets a husband,
> And when a maid succeeds her lady.
> (Prov 30:21–23)

$Rāgaz$ 'to quake' often occurs in parallel lines of Hebrew poetry with $rā°aš$ 'to shake'. Both refer to the shaking of the foundations of heaven and earth when chaos threatens to overwhelm the created order (Job 9:6, Isa 13:13). In this saying, the turning upside down of the hierarchical

---

35. H. H. Schmid, "Schöpfung, Gerechtigkeit und Heil," *Zeitschrift für Theologie und Kirche* 70 (1973) 1–19; trans. as "Creation, Righteousness, and Salvation," *Creation in the Old Testament* (ed. B. W. Anderson; Philadelphia: Fortress, 1984) 102–17.

structures of society and the abnormal success of the lowly and the despised bring instability to the cosmic order and threaten it with collapse. Thus the maintenance of the social order, acceptance of the proper roles and functions for each person, and the support of divinely legitimated institutions were necessary for both cosmic and social life to endure.

Implicit to the social tradition of the sages is the view that institutions are the reified structures of communal life that control the way human beings live. They serve to meet basic human needs, preserve the total social system, and control contingencies that threaten corporate life. Of these structures, six are significant: the state and political organizations, economic organizations, law, education, religion, and family. These were thought to precede individual action and choice, being created by God and anchored within the cosmic order of creation. The traditional sages pointed to the cosmic foundation of social institutions, legitimated their existence and character by divine sanction, and described the behavior appropriate to the offices and roles that were their constituent parts. Space restrictions allow only a brief examination of the institutions of kingship and its postexilic successor, the high priesthood.

For the wisdom tradition, the Monarchy (first native and then foreign) was the most important political institution.[36] The Book of Proverbs includes instructions to kings on how to rule, descriptions of proper royal behavior and knowledge, and guidance on proper conduct in the presence of the king. The underlying basis for this political institution is the righteous order that undergirds creation.[37] One saying well illustrates this understanding:

> It is an abomination for kings to practise evil,
>     for the throne is established [ *yikkôn* ] in/by righteousness [*ṣĕdāqâ*].
>
>                                                                     (Prov 16:12)

"Established" (*kûn*) is a term used elsewhere for the divine act of creating and sustaining the cosmic order: Prov 3:19–20, 8:27. The specific meaning of the saying turns on the function of the preposition *bĕ*. If taken as a locative, the saying would indicate that the institution of the

---

36. The sayings in Proverbs pertaining to kingship include 8:14–16; 12:28, 35; 15:22; 16:10–15; 17:7; 19:10, 12; 20:2, 8, 18, 28; 21:1, 22; 22:11, 29; 23:1; 24:5–6, 21–22; 25:1–7, 15; 27:23–27; 28:2, 15–16; 29:2, 4, 12, 14, 26; 30:1–9). For transformations in the sages' understanding of the king, see also the concluding essay in this volume by John G. Gammie, "From Prudentialism to Apocalypticism: The House of the Sages Amid the Varying Forms of Wisdom, pp. 479–97.

37. Schmid, *Gerechtigkeit als Weltordnung*; H. Brunner, "Gerechtigkeit als Fundament des Thrones," *VT* 8 (1958) 426–28.

Monarchy is grounded *in the cosmic order*. If given an instrumental function, then the saying would emphasize that the stability of the throne is secured *by means of* the king's righteous behavior (cf. Prov 20:29 [LXX], 25:5). Both functions of the preposition are probably suggested. Not only is the institution grounded in the cosmic order, but its continuation, and consequently that of society and even creation, depend on the just and proper rule of those who hold the royal office.

Sapiential examination of the office of the high priest is found in Ben Sira's "Hymn in Praise of the Fathers" (chaps. 44–50). The social offices held by the recipients of praise are the fathers, priests, prophets, kings, and judges.[38] Burton L. Mack notes that the presentation of the heroes finds its unity in the office and accomplishments each person performed in relationship to the office held. Both the office and the performance of duties, not personal skill or intelligence, set the heroes apart and bring them honor.

It is the office of the Zadokite high priesthood that receives Ben Sira's greatest adulation, and especially noteworthy for his performance is the high priest Simon II (50:1–21). While Simon's significant social and political achievements are mentioned (temple repairs, fortification of the city, construction of a reservoir, and deliverance of Jerusalem during the Ptolemaic-Seleucid War), it is the high priest's role on the Day of Atonement that receives the most attention. The appearance of Simon is described in almost theophanic terms, and the performance of his sacred duties during this day concludes with the pronouncing of divine blessing that is to secure well-being for the people. Through the proper functioning of this office, the community of the Second Temple, representing the culmination of human history, achieves harmony with God and the cosmos. And divine blessing thereby secures the structures of life.[39]

## *The Social Order in the Critical Wisdom Tradition*

Social institutions receive a very different assessment in Job and Qoheleth. Qoheleth's cosmology denies that there is any righteous order permeating creation. Thus institutions are given a different basis and character. As regards kingship, Qoheleth places the institution (probably a Persian reign is reflected) within a tyrannical model of hierarchical order (8:9). In this power model of rule and governance, each official is overseen by a higher one, reaching eventually the throne of "the God"

38. Ben Sira has a separate section for the office of sage (38:24–39:35), though he does not single out any particular person as worthy of honor. Nevertheless, the sage is the recipient of substantial praise and "his name will live throughout the generations" (39:9).

39. Mack, *Wisdom and the Hebrew Epic*, 84–87.

(5:6-7). Righteousness in any sense is removed from divine and human rule. Indeed both divine and human rulers turn a deaf ear to the cries of the oppressed (4:1-3). The place, power, and quality of human rulers depend on the arbitrary, incalculable decision of a sovereign God who rules in secluded obscurity. Fools may ascend to the throne, and even formerly good kings may become old and foolish (10:5-7, 16-17). Yet kings, like God in heaven, are to be feared, because of the power that they wield (10:20).

In the poetry Job is presented in the guise of an ancient king (chaps. 29-31) who, like many of his Mesopotamian counterparts, has experienced an inexplicable fall from status and power, in addition to his affliction of acute suffering and personal loss of wealth and children.[40] In former times, prior to his fall, Job judged the people at the gates, defended the lowly, and provided hospitality to strangers. Now Job has been humiliated by God and made to suffer the disparagement of the lowest dregs of human society. In reflecting on his fall from king to slave, Job's language moves into mythic discourse in which the metaphor of slave is used to challenge the legitimacy of the metaphor of king in describing humanity's place and function in the cosmic order (Job 7:17-20).[41] In his challenge to divine rule, Job takes on the mythic role of the Primal Man, the first of God's creation and the king who guarded the sacred garden from violation. It is this "prince" who would approach God's throne, issue an indictment detailing divine misrule, and ascend the throne over heaven and earth.

In the Yahweh speeches, not only humanity but also the institution of human rule is removed from any central place in God's creation. Indeed, Yahweh deconstructs all anthropocentric meaning systems that exalt humanity as the king of God's creation. As Divine Warrior God comes to battle mighty Leviathan, and in victory to ascend once again the throne of heaven and earth (40:6-14). It is the power and rule of God that maintains the order of creation and its communities of life. Job as well as all humans are to join with Yahweh in this struggle, but it is the power of God that achieves life-giving justice on the earth, not the weakness of mortal rule. In moving from mythic to descriptive discourse, it is clear that the radical sovereignty of God is affirmed. Human institutions of power and rule, especially that of kingship, are removed from any grounding in the cosmic order. Their legitimation, by implication, derives only from their efforts to join with the creator in the battle with chaos to establish justice.

40. See R. Albertz, "Der sozialgeschichtliche Hintergrund des Hiobbuches und der 'Babylonischen Theodizee,'" *Die Botschaft und die Boten* (ed. J. Jeremias and L. Perlitt; H. W. Wolff FS; Neukirchen-Vluyn: Neukirchener, 1981) 349-72.

41. See my essay, "Job's Assault on Creation."

## THE SOCIAL LOCATIONS OF THE SAGES

### Sages and the Paradigm of Order

The social knowledge produced by traditional sages points to intellectuals who either possessed political power and wealth or were supported by those who did.[42] Certainly the invitation to take up wisdom, which included acquiring the elite skills of reading and writing, demarcated sages and their tradition from everyday Israelite and Jewish society. Farmers, laborers, and artisans may have possessed admirable skills along with the wisdom to perform their tasks well, but they were not among the sages who produced the wisdom tradition. Some of the wisdom teaching may have been universal in appeal and possessed practical benefit for molding the character of human beings in general, but the wisdom tradition was written by and intended for well-educated sages whose intelligence and training prepared them for positions in the administration of the major national institutions of government and temple cult. While some evidence points to the development of a tribal-familial wisdom tradition,[43] the extant literary corpus points mainly to monarchic government in the preexilic period and to the institutions of the temple and eventually the synagogue in the postexilic age as the primary social matrices.

In the preexilic period, the traditional sages occupied a variety of social positions, which included the upper echelons of Israelite society— teachers, rulers, political counselors, and diplomats.[44] However, the great majority of sages most probably belonged to the vast royal bureaucracy responsible for the administration of the kingdom. Being either members of the sociopolitical elite or teachers and bureaucrats

42. B. W. Kovacs is only partially correct in arguing that the sages were close to and admired wealth and power, though they did not possess them; "Is There a Class-Ethic in Proverbs?" *Essays in Old Testament Ethics* (ed. J. Crenshaw and J. Willis; J. P. Hyatt FS; New York: Ktav, 1974) 171–90. Included in the ranks of sages were rulers and counselors who possessed a substantial degree of both; cf. W. McKane, *Prophets and Wise Men* (SBT 44; London: SCM, 1965). R. N. Whybray is correct in emphasizing that sages were intellectuals in Israelite-Jewish society, but he disembodies them when he denies that the term *ḥkm* 'wise, wisdom, sage' is associated with any particular office or role; *The Intellectual Tradition in the Old Testament* (BZAW 135; Berlin: de Gruyter, 1974). Sirach's description is the best evidence that the typical offices held by sages included those of teacher, statesman, and judge (38:24–39:11; cf. 10:1–5).

43. C. Fontaine, *Traditional Sayings in the Old Testament* (Sheffield: Almond, 1982).

44. J. Gaspar, *Social Ideas in the Wisdom Literature of the Old Testament* (Washington: Catholic University of America, 1947) 138–39; and R. Gordis, "The Social Background of Wisdom Literature," *HUCA* 18 (1944) 77–118. Gordis is correct in seeing an aristocratic level in the wisdom corpus, though he overstates his case by attempting to associate all sages with the social elite (see, e.g., the "poor wise man" contrasted with the "great king" in Qoh 9:13–16).

supported by the ruling aristocracy (e.g., as teachers and scribes), the sages were involved in articulating a world view in which the prevailing social system was grounded in the order of the cosmos. The legitimation and maintenance of this social construction was the major function of traditional sages and their wisdom texts.

As proponents of the existing social order, the primary social matrix for wisdom shifts during the period of the Second Temple from the royal administration and bureaucracy to the temple and eventually the synagogue. Ben Sira's well-known comparison of the profession of the sage with other, far less attractive occupations points to sages who required time to study and think, held positions in the local councils, sat on the judge's bench, studied the Torah, prophets, and wisdom of the ancient sages, served great persons, appeared in the presence of rulers, traveled in foreign lands (presumably in foreign diplomacy), and taught the unlearned.[45] While some served in foreign governments, both in high administrative places as well as in the more ordinary positions of the bureaucracy, they still wielded considerable power on the local level (e.g., Ezra).

Prior to the oppressive policies of Antiochus IV, the Jews were allowed enough freedom to establish and follow their own social and religious traditions. From the mixture of Jewish traditions and eventually Hellenic *paideia*, the sages forged a theological foundation for Second Temple Judaism. With the end of monarchic self-rule, the temple and priestly tradition became more closely aligned with that of the sages. For Ben Sira, a teacher in a *bêt midraš* in the city of Jerusalem, the institutions of Torah, temple, and Zadokite priesthood were at the center of a sacred community, not only grounded in the order of creation, but also the culmination of history. Ben Sira represents an accommodation to the political order of Ptolemaic and then Seleucid rule.

Qoheleth's cosmology takes another turn. Order is based on power, wielded by a transcendent God who secretly determines the course of events and establishes rulers, presumably foreign ones, on their thrones. Their rule too is characterized by despotism, without regard to justice (4:1-3). While the assumption of the position of king may only be a part of the fictive reality constructed by Qoheleth's royal testament, an alternative view would be to see him as representing a former ruling aristocracy displaced by foreign rule. Any hope for a new sociopolitical reality is shattered by an inaccessible and despotic God. There is no prophetic critique of the abuse of power in Qoheleth. The abuse of power is a point for despair, but not an impetus for reform. Nor is there

45. See J. G. Gammie's essay in this volume, "The Sage in Sirach," 355-72 above.

the emergence of an apocalyptic community in which the power structure for a new social reality is being shaped in incipient form. Rather, for Qoheleth the response to the prevailing sociopolitical order is fearful submission in which one acknowledges the power of God and foreign king to bring destruction to those foolhardy souls who dare to resist. Even in this critical reflection, Qoheleth's religious pessimism ("the fear of God") supported the current sociopolitical order. The *Gemeinschaften*, labor, and festive occasions are the only possible sources for the one "good" in human existence: the celebration of life.

## Sages and the Paradigm of Conflict

The conflict model of society, articulated in Job, would best derive from the *déclassés* who had formerly held high status and political power (cf. especially Job 1–2 and 29–31 where Job is depicted as an aristocrat in royal terms).[46] A new social order has emerged that denies them access to status and power. Placement of the poetry of Job within the Babylonian Exile or the early postexilic period would probably account for the social reality in which the paradigm of conflict was constructed: a political system has emerged, based on foreign power and domination. God's legal ruling affirms the integrity of the dispossessed and suffering Job and condemns the friends whose world view automatically correlates justice with the emergence of a new sociopolitical reality. The "Speeches from the Whirlwind" emphasize that cosmic and social justice is created only through struggle. Struggle constructs the justice that orders and sustains the world and removes the wicked from the earth. Yet it is the power of God, not that of mortals, that is able to remove corrupt rulers from their thrones (Job 40:11–14). Indeed, Job's restoration to status and position in the Epilogue held out hope to the *déclassés* that God's judgment one day would lead to a new social order. Even so, it is the sovereignty of divine rule, not human kings, that battles for justice, defeats chaos, and re-creates the world.

46. Albertz, "Der sozialgeschichtliche Hintergrund des Hiobbuches."

# FROM PRUDENTIALISM
# TO APOCALYPTICISM
## THE HOUSES OF THE SAGES AMID
## THE VARYING FORMS OF WISDOM

## John G. Gammie†

> Wisdom has built her house,
> she has hewn her seven pillars.
> (Proverbs 9:1)

As squirrels build nests with leaves and twigs for physical protection from the elements, so human beings, with ideas about social and cosmic realities, fashion constructions that afford them intellectual and spiritual shelter from threats of anomie and paralysis. Such, in any event, is the argument of the sociologists of knowledge, which comprises the starting point for the final three essays in this volume.[1] The argument is well founded. One may consult, for example, Henri Frankfort's persuasive demonstration of a generation ago that moderns should marvel not so much at the construction of the pyramids of Egypt or at the hanging gardens of Babylon but rather at the beauty and power of the religious systems of the two great ancient riverine civilizations.[2] In this concluding essay the attempt will be made to show that the varying and varied social constructions of reality erected by ancient Israelite sages in the course of the first millennium B.C.E. are worthy of cautious admiration.

Squirrels' nests vary according to whether they are built in burrows underground, under rocks or logs, or in trees; similarly the houses of the sages varied according to the forms they chose. It is the hope of the

John G. Gammie was Emma A. Harwell Professor of Biblical Literature at the University of Tulsa.

All translations of biblical texts are my own unless otherwise indicated.

1. Cf. P. Berger, *The Sacred Canopy: Elements of a Sociological Theory of Religion* (Garden City, NY: Doubleday, 1967) 3–28.
2. H. Frankfort, *Kingship and the Gods* (Chicago: University of Chicago, 1948) ix and passim.

editors and authors of this volume that its readers will exercise care in making generalizations about the "sage," for a "sage" may denote a scholar, a royal or temple scribe, a particularly wise person, an intellectual, a counselor to kings, an author of a book of wisdom, or a maker of proverbs. Similarly, caution is advisable in undertaking generalizations about the houses the sages built. The researcher should keep in mind not only the varying denotations of "sage," but also the varying types of wisdom in which the sages engaged as well as the varying literary genres that they employed. To this task I now turn.

## THE TYPES OF WISDOM AND ITS MAIN LITERARY FORMS

In the previous essay Leo Perdue distinguished between traditional wisdom (e.g., Proverbs and Sirach) and critical wisdom (e.g., Job and Qoheleth). These two major types of wisdom in turn embody, respectively, "prudentialism" and "skepticism,"[3] and appear, respectively, in two secondary genres, which may properly be called "parenetic literature" and "reflective essays."[4] Parenetic literature, representative of the traditional and prudential side of wisdom, is hortatory and instructive, and, in turn may be divided into two major divisions: instructions (e.g., Proverbs 1–9) and pareneses (e.g., Proverbs 10–31, Sirach). The terms *parenetic literature* and *parenesis* (derived from the Greek *parainein* 'to exhort, advise, counsel') have a venerable usage among students of the Hebrew scriptures.[5] Reflective essays, representative of the critical and skeptical side of wisdom may also be divided into two major divisions:

3. For the use of the term *prudentialism*, I am especially indebted to S. J. De Vries, *The Achievements of Biblical Religion: A Prolegomenon to Old Testament Theology* (Lanham, MD: University Press of America, 1983) 240–41. *Skepticism* is explored in connection with Qoheleth and Job by J. L. Crenshaw, *Old Testament Wisdom: An Introduction* (Atlanta: John Knox, 1981) 191–211. For a recent assessment of the distinctiveness of Israel's traditional wisdom and its relation to Yahwism, see O. Plöger, *Sprüche Salomos (Proverbia)* (BKAT 17; Neukirchen-Vluyn: Neukirchener, 1984) xxx–xxxvii.

4. The basic distinction between these two types goes back to J. C. Rylaarsdam, *Revelation in Jewish Wisdom Literature* (Chicago: University of Chicago, 1946) 4: "This [wisdom] literature, whether in Egypt, Babylon, or Israel, divides itself into two kinds: prudential admonitions, commonly in proverbial form, that may serve the young as directions for a happy and successful life, and reflective essays on the meaning and significance of life, often in a pessimistic vein." Because recent study has shown that "admonitions" is rather a subgenre than a larger, composite or complex form, it seems advisable to utilize instead of Rylaarsdam's "prudential admonitions" the designation *parenetic literature*. For further discussion, see the forthcoming issue of *Semeia*, subtitled "Paraenesis: Act and Form," edited by L. G. Perdue and myself, and especially my essay therein, "Paraenetic Literature: Toward the Morphology of a Secondary Genre."

5. See, e.g., J. Hempel, *Die althebräische Literatur und ihr hellenistisch-judisches Nachleben* (Wildpark-Potsdam: Athenaion, 1930).

disputations (e.g., Job) and reflections (e.g., Qoheleth).[6] One of the purposes of the latter distinctions in my judgment is to help the student of the wisdom literature to keep in mind significant differences within writings in the traditional vein and within writings in the critical vein. Subtle differences obtain, for example, between the skepticism expressed in Job and that in Qoheleth. Similarly, the prudentialism of Proverbs 1-9 differs from that of Proverbs 10-31. Difference in form thus signals difference in content—and in the kind of intellectual houses constructed by the respective sages.

An important subgenre of both the parenetic literature and the reflective essays is the didactic tale. In the Book of Job, for example, a didactic tale serves to frame the poetic dialogues and divine speeches. The prudential or traditional side of Israelite wisdom, however, appears to have been especially fond of the didactic tale as a vehicle of expression (e.g., Jonah, Esther, Daniel 1-6, Judith, Tobit).[7]

Four other types of wisdom may be identified within Israel and the ancient Near East. Including the first two major types outlined above, this provides the following list: (1) prudential or practical, (2) critical or skeptical, (3) juridical, (4) wisdom of nature, (5) theological, and (6) mantic or magical. Four of these types were already identified by James Crenshaw (practical, juridical, "natural" [or nature wisdom], and theological).[8] A bit more may be said now about items 3-6.

As the term suggests, juridical wisdom has to do with law (Latin, *jus, juris*), and in the Hebrew Bible is to be found chiefly in the three wisdom psalms that focus on the *tôrâ*, Psalms 1, 19, and 119. Even though there is a close affinity between this type of wisdom and the practical, it is employed also by critical wisdom, for example, in the Book of Job when the thought patterns of the law court are drawn into use (Job 9, 23, 31).

The wisdom of nature (German, *Naturweisheit*) focuses upon the realm of natural phenomena, such as fauna, flora, birth, survival, and conditions necessary for the sustenance of life, as well as upon patterns and groupings in animate beings and in the inanimate world. In the Hebrew Bible this focus is seen in certain other wisdom psalms such as Psalms 104, 127, and 128, as well as in critical wisdom (Job 38-39; Qoh 1:1-11, 3:1-11).

6. For discussion of these forms, see my essay "Paraenetic Literature."

7. For a discussion of these works as expressive of Israelite wisdom, see esp. R. B. Y. Scott, *The Way of Wisdom in the Old Testament* (New York: Macmillan, 1971) 78-96; see also D. F. Morgan, *Wisdom in the Old Testament Traditions* (Atlanta: John Knox, 1981) 49-50, 123-25.

8. J. L. Crenshaw, "Method in Determining Wisdom Influence upon 'Historical' Literature," *JBL* 88 (1969) 132-34; repr. in *SAIW* 482-84.

When sages wrestle with issues of meaning, purpose, justice, creation, and order they are engaging in theological wisdom. This type, like
the others is largely to be determined by content; like the two minor
types mentioned above, it is not confined to either critical wisdom or
traditional wisdom but is to be found in both, for example, Proverbs
1-9, 30:1-9, and Sirach 1, 24, and 51. Unlike juridical wisdom and the
wisdom of nature, theological wisdom is not a minor type. The engagement with matters pertaining to meaning and purpose in the Book
of Job, Qoheleth, and the Wisdom of Solomon is so extensive that these
works in their entirety may be understood as theological wisdom
coalescent with other types. In the case of the former two works the
theology is employed in the service of critical wisdom; in the case of
the latter of more traditional wisdom. A few of the wisdom psalms
should also be included in this category.[9]

Mantic or magical wisdom has to do with the interpretation of
dreams and hidden signs or omens, with the utterance of spells to inflict
harm on an enemy, or with the formulation of sayings to exorcise an
unwanted spirit. Mantic wisdom was especially popular in Babylonia
with its abundance of omen texts and exorcisms. Scholars have long
since recognized that the "enemy" in a number of the psalms may have

---

9. A number of factors enter into the determination of whether a psalm should be
classified as a wisdom psalm: use of the *ašrê* formula, contrast between the righteous and
ungodly, reference to *yirat yhwh*, employment of the acrostic form, etc. For purposes of
tracing the activity of the sages and their impact on other writers, a broader list of
wisdom psalms is far more useful than the more restricted lists of R. E. Murphy and J. K.
Kuntz. Accordingly, in the overall designation of wisdom psalms I also include those that
H. Gunkel and Murphy acknowledge contain wisdom elements. This broader list is not
indiscriminate or without criteria: to be classified as a wisdom psalm, the psalm must
contain a cluster of formal elements, typical vocabulary, and themes employed by the
traditional wisdom writers. Thus, in my judgment the acrostic psalms 9-10 and 25 may
not be so classified for want of a requisite number of elements. Acrostics in the following
overall list of wisdom psalms are marked with an asterisk: (1) psalms of juridical wisdom
that emphasize the Torah (1, 19, 119*), (2) psalms of natural wisdom that focus on the
created order, offspring, life, and fruitfulness (45, 91, 104, 127, 128, 133, 139, 147),
(3) psalms of theological wisdom that probe matters of right conduct, theodicy, and
retribution (14, 15, 37*, 49, 53[=14], 73, 94), (4) psalms of thanksgiving that emphasize
practical wisdom (32, 34*), and (5) hymns of praise that utilize traditional wisdom themes
(78, 111*, 112*, 145*). For discussion, see Gunkel, *Einleitung in die Psalmen* (3d ed.;
Göttingen: Vandenhoeck und Ruprecht, 1975) 381-97; Murphy, "A Consideration of the
Classification 'Wisdom Psalms,'" *Congress Volume: Bonn 1962* (VTSup 9; Leiden: Brill,
1963) 156-67 (repr. in *SAIW* 456-67); Kuntz, "The Canonical Wisdom Psalms of Ancient
Israel—Their Rhetorical, Thematic, and Formal Dimensions," *Rhetorical Criticism: Essays
in Honor of James Muilenburg* (ed. J. J. Jackson and M. Kessler; Pittsburgh Theological
Monograph Series 1; Pittsburgh: Pickwick, 1974) 186-222; and A. R. Ceresko, "The Sage
in the Psalms," pp. 217-30 above.

been such practitioners of the mantic art.[10] This type of wisdom, however, is clearly a minor one in the Hebrew Bible, but unmistakably present, for example, in the novella (didactic tale) of Joseph (Genesis 37–50) and in the romances (didactic tales) of Daniel 2 and 4, where it is skill in the interpretation of dreams (a mantic art) that is so highly prized by a foreign monarch. In the didactic court tale of Daniel 5, Daniel alone has the power to unlock the mysterious meaning of the handwriting upon the wall. A different sort of mantic wisdom is alluded to in Job's lament of the day of his birth (Job 3:8)—the skill to "rouse up Leviathan." In recent times Hans-Peter Müller has underlined the presence and importance of this type of wisdom in ancient Israel.[11]

A generation ago Robert Gordis demonstrated convincingly that the social location of the sages is to be found among the upper classes.[12] More recently Leo Perdue, drawing upon the social scientific research of A. Van Gennep and V. Turner and others, has shown that the sages in the parenetic literature were concerned to speak to persons about to cross important thresholds in life (e.g., from childhood to adulthood, from being single to marriage, from being childless to having children, from being within the womb to coming out, from life to death, from having been married to becoming a widow or widower, from having been reared in one tribe or group to entry into another).[13] Following along this line, it may be reasonably suggested that the critical wisdom tradition of Israel speaks to recurring life crises: of whether one's basic attitude toward the world should be one of trust or distrust, of autonomy, of self-identity, of intimacy and sexuality; in the middle years one's concern would be creativity or stagnation (depending on whether a new sense of responsibility emerges) and integrity or despair (depending on whether there emerges "the conviction of the moral paternity of one's own soul").[14]

10. See S. Mowinckel, *Psalmenstudien 1: ʾAwän und die individuellen Klagepsalmen* (Oslo: J. Dybwad, 1921).

11. H.-P. Müller, "Magisch-mantische Weisheit und die Gestalt Daniels," *UF* 1 (1969) 79–94, and idem, "Mantische Weisheit und Apokalyptik," *Congress Volume: Uppsala 1971* (VTSup 22; Leiden: Brill, 1972) 268–93.

12. R. Gordis, "The Social Background of Wisdom Literature," *HUCA* 18 (1943–44) 77–118; repr. in his *Poets, Prophets, and Sages* (Bloomington: Indiana University, 1971) 160–97.

13. L. G. Perdue, "Liminality as a Social Setting for Wisdom Instructions," *ZAW* 93 (1981) 114–26.

14. See J. Bruner, *On Knowing: Essays for the Left Hand* (Cambridge: Harvard University/Belknap, 1964) 45–48. The categories of Bruner, an educational psychologist, in turn are taken from E. Erickson, *Childhood and Society* (New York: Norton, 1950). Bruner convincingly shows how modern novelists focus on these several crises.

Having made the above distinctions in types of wisdom and in the literary forms of wisdom, I am now in a position to turn to the question of houses of the sages. In order to give focus to this inquiry, attention will be given to four aspects of the houses of the sages: family, king, nation, and other nations. In the course of the following discussion I will seek to draw out whether some clues may be garnered on the important transition that transpired during the course of the postexilic era from prudentialism to apocalypticism. A "sage" in this essay is taken to be the author of any one of the various types of wisdom works alluded to above.

## FAMILY

The basic family unit for the sages included husband, wife, offspring, relatives, and servants.[15] Major elements in the sapiential ethics of the family from virtually all periods are honor of parents, joy in one's spouse, warnings against adultery, and preferential treatment for the family line through the elder brother.[16] Up until the Hellenistic era the conception of the solidarity of the family played an immensely important role among the biblical sages as a means of handling the threat of a seemingly chaotic universe that would allow the righteous to suffer and the ungodly to prosper. Against the threat of this anomie—that the all-knowing God was apparently lacking in justice—the sages explained that even though an individual person might go for a time unpunished for grievous wrongs, it was certain that his or her offspring would receive due punishment. This sapiential notion is expressed most plainly perhaps in the Decalogue: "I punish the children for the sins of the fathers to the third and fourth generations of those who hate me. But I keep faith with thousands, with those who love me and keep my commandments" (Exod 20:5-6 NEB). But this is found throughout the wisdom literature in several variations: the house of the ungodly will be barren (Prov 21:12, Job 15:34-35), whereas the one who fears God will be richly blessed with offspring (Job 5:24-25; Psalms 127, 128); a son

15. See H. A. Hoffner, "בַּיִת bayith," *Theological Dictionary of the Old Testament* (ed. G. Botterweck and H. Ringgren; Grand Rapids: Eerdmans, 1977), 2:107-16; J. Pedersen, *Israel: Its Life and Culture I-II* (London: Oxford University, 1926) 46-60; I. Mendelsohn, "The Family in the Ancient Near East," *BA* 11 (1948) 24-40; R. de Vaux, *Ancient Israel* (New York: McGraw-Hill, 1961) 19-61. For a helpful comparison of family motifs in Genesis and Ugarit, see C. Westermann, *The Promise to the Fathers* (Philadelphia: Fortress, 1980) 165-86.

16. For references and further discussion on these subjects, see de Vaux, *Ancient Israel*; Pedersen, *Israel: Its Life and Culture I-II*; and C. Fontaine, "The Sage in Family and Tribe," pp. 155-64 above.

may take vengeance on enemies (Sir 30:6); a good name (reputation) is better than riches (Prov 22:1) and will survive long after death, whereas the sinner will not leave such to posterity (Sir 41:11–13).

This powerful construct for the maintenance of the justice of God (theodicy) became weakened in the postexilic era with the rise of individualism (see, e.g., Ezekiel 18 and Qoh 3:19–22) and especially with the notions of the resurrection of the just and unjust (Dan 12:1–4) and of the immortality of the soul (Wis 3:1–9). The family as a societal unit of utmost importance continued to be attested in the narrative forms of wisdom (Esther, Tobit, and the Additions to Daniel), but is all but ignored in those sapiential books where the breakthrough to an unmistakable belief in the afterlife was finally accomplished (cf. Daniel 7–12 and the Wisdom of Solomon). The reason is apparent: once belief emerged in a realm beyond death in which the inequities of the present world would be resolved, the family as an intellectual construct with which to defend theodicy was no longer so urgently needed. The function of the concept of the solidarity of the family to explain the anomaly of the prosperous sinner or the suffering righteous had been supplanted. The way was thus opened up for the sages to celebrate the blessedness of married or unmarried persons who would produce no physical offspring.

Prior to belief in the afterlife, the sages celebrated the blessings of many children and the joys of marriage (Psalms 127, 128; Prov 31:10–31), but afterward, the Hellenistic Jewish sage would rather celebrate the blessings of the childless woman and eunuch (Wis 3:13–4:6). A different house indeed! Like the sages of old (cf. esp. Proverbs 1–9) the author of the Wisdom of Solomon continued to inveigh against the threat to the family of adultery (Wis 3:16–19), but the new commendation of child-lessness for the virtuous is simply unimaginable in the older constructions of the sages. Both the older sages (Proverbs 1–9) and the new (Wisdom of Solomon 7–9) enjoined the pursuit of Lady Wisdom, but the latter alone commended childlessness. This shift in design by the Israelite sages of the intellectual house on the family was to have a significant impact on the daughter religion Christianity, which lasts unto this day.[17]

---

17. The commendation of virtuous childlessness (and virginity) constitutes, of course, an important element in the development of clerical celibacy and monasticism, as well as in the history of sexuality in the West. For making me more alert to these developments I am indebted to a lecture given at the University of Tulsa in March 1985 by Keith Hopkins, Professor of Ancient History at Kings College, Cambridge University, in which Hopkins sought to find the origins of the advocacy of virginity among Christians sub-sequent to Constantine's conversion to Christianity.

For background reading, see M. Foucault, *The History of Sexuality*, vol. 1: *An Introduction* (London: Allen Lane, 1978) 158–59; vol. 2: *The Use of Pleasure* (New York:

## KING

The design of the portions of the house that the sages built with respect to the king underwent a shift equally as radical as the one just examined.

The sages were well aware of the weaknesses, vagaries, and imperfections of human kings. Sages writing in both the traditional and skeptical types did not tire in relating how kings were subject to profligacy (Prov 31:4, Qoh 10:17), folly (Qoh 4:13, 10:6), madness (Job 12:10–23), and mortality (Sir 10:10, Wis 18:11). The sages of all periods also delighted in drawing attention to different aspects of the point-counterpoint between the human kings and the divine sovereign.[18] As a rule this comparison constituted a legitimation of the wisdom and institution of the Monarchy.[19] The ability of the wise king to "sift out the wicked" is compared to the divine searching of every human soul (Prov 20:26–27); the king's heart is unfathomable (Prov 25:3), but "the Lord turns it wherever he wills" (Prov 21:1). It is not only the omniscience of God that the sages celebrate (Prov 15:3, 11; 16:2) but also the

---

Pantheon, 1985) 14, 20–21, 30–32; vol. 3: *Dreaming of One's Pleasures* (New York: Pantheon, 1986) 43, 122, 129, 143; P. Brown, "The Notion of Virginity in the Early Church," *Christian Spirituality: Origins to the Twelfth Century* (ed. B. McGinn and J. Meyendorff; World Spirituality 16; New York: Crossroad, 1985) 427–43; P. Ariès and G. Duby, *A History of Private Life*, vol. 1: *From Pagan Rome to Byzantium* (Cambridge: Harvard University/Belknap, 1987), esp. the chapter by P. Brown, "Late Antiquity" (pp. 235–312); and K. Baus, *History of the Church*, vol. 1: *From the Apostolic Community to Constantine* (New York: Crossroad, 1986) 295–305. For the reference to the work by Foucault I have Prof. Hopkins to thank, and for the reference to the volume by Ariès and Duby, Prof. Callie Williamson of the University of Tulsa.

Biblical scholars, of course, will have particular interest in the role that Wis 3:13–4:6 may have played in the course of Christian thinking. C. Larcher lists commentators who interpreted Wis 3:13–4:6 as a praise of virginity but he—at first—concludes that the text extols not the virgin woman but the barren married woman who has remained faithful; cf. *Le Livre de la Sagesse; ou, La Sagesse de Salomon* (3 vols.; Etudes Bibliques, n.s. 1, 3, 5; Paris; Gabalda, 1983–85), 1:299–311. In the next volume, however, Larcher (or his editor?) appears to reverse the position of vol. 1 and raises the question whether the text does not suggest "the possibility of a voluntary renunciation of procreation in favor of a higher virtue." In effect he sees that the author is rediscovering here "a rather old Greek tradition" of "a more or less direct eulogy of virginity (for the sake of the exaltation of an eminent virtue)"; cf. Plato, *Symposium* 196b–d [LCL 166: 157]; Larcher, *Le Livre de La Sagesse*, 2:314.

18. For the expression that the human kingship provides a counterpoint to the divine kingship, I am indebted to T. E. Fretheim, *Deuteronomic History* (Nashville: Abingdon, 1983) 43.

19. For more references than are given below and more on the ideological dimensions of those sages who wrote on the Solomonic monarchy, see the essay in this volume by W. A. Brueggemann, "The Social Significance of Solomon as a Patron of Wisdom," pp. 117–32 above.

king's ability to fathom things hidden (Prov 25:2). Wisdom, however, belongs to the Lord (Job 12:13) and when he wills, "He takes away their wisdom from the rulers of the nations / and leaves them wandering in a pathless wilderness" (Job 12:24 NEB). Similarly through wisdom do human kings derive their sovereignty and make just laws (Prov 8:15). Both early and late do the sages ascribe a very positive role to the functioning of kings: "Through justice a king causes a land to stand firm" (Prov 29:4a); "As an abundance of sages brings healing to the world, so a prudent king brings about his people's well-being" (Wis 6:24; cf. also Sir 10:1–3).

Perhaps it is because of the high social standing of both the traditional and skeptical sages, and their proximity to regal power, that they are not more critical of royal abuses of power. The sages can hardly be accused of underestimating the consequences of speaking ill of a king (Qoh 10:20) or of taking a course counter to the king's wishes (Qoh 8:2–3). Rather they knew the wrath of the king to be a "messenger of death" (Prov 16:14) and, accordingly, "In the light of the king's countenance is life" (Prov 16:15). Theirs was a prudential realism that describes the effects and source of human rule with a certain dispassion, as the following citation from the Greek of Sirach illustrates:

> A wise ruler will instruct his people
>     and governance by the intelligent will be commanded.
> As a people's leader, so will be its public servants,
>     and as a city's governor, so will be all its inhabitants.
> An unlearned king will destroy his people
>     but a city will be rendered inhabitable by the discernment of those who
>         hold power.
> Authority over a land resides in the hand of the Lord,
>     and in due season he will raise up over it the beneficent.
> Whether a man's journey is prosperous is in the Lord's hand
>     and he will cause his honor to rest on a scribe's visage.   (Sir 10:1–5)

Thus through the utterances of the sages the functioning of kings—and their counselors—was given a place within the divine order.

One of the most fateful developments among the sages turns on the subject of the relatively fleeting rule of human kings in comparison to the perduring eternity of the divine sovereign. The prophetic requirement of justice was acknowledged as indispensable for the security of any monarch (Prov 29:14). Yet increasingly the sages stressed the ephemerality of kings. Thus Sirach notes how the prophet Samuel "showed a king his [coming] demise" (Sir 46:20), and elsewhere tersely comments, "A king today may die tomorrow" (Sir 10:10). The sages were relatively late in addressing God as king; but we see it in a

postexilic wisdom psalm (Ps 145:1) and also at the outset of one of the
hymns in Sirach (Sir 51:1). The latter celebrates the deliverance from
death through the divine rescue, and the former celebrates the divine
goodness and righteousness (Ps 145:7, 17). Both author-sages are confident in the divine response to prayer (Ps 145:19, Sir 51:11–12). It is not
certain whether Sirach himself was the author of the hymn in 51:1–12,[20]
but Sirach draws the contrast between the brief span of the average
human upon earth in comparison to the enduring stars and their maker
(Sir 16:24–17:14) and, as I have noted above, he also underlines the
ephemerality of monarchs. The same comparison is implicit in Psalm
145: "Thy kingdom is an everlasting kingdom, / and thy dominion
stands for all generations" (Ps 145:13). This comparison was not confined
to the traditional sages for it is found among other psalmists (Ps 102:11–
12 [MT 102:12–13]; cf. 103:14–16, 19) as well as among those sages and
their successors who chose to employ the apocalyptic genre (Dan 4:3,
34 [MT 3:33, 4:31]; see also Isa 40:7–8 where the contrast is drawn
between short-lived humanity and the eternity of the divine word).
With the apocalypticist, however, one sees an advance beyond the
pragmatic observations of the more prudential sages, for the scribal
authors of the Book of Daniel,[21] who draw upon sapiential, prophetic,
and priestly traditions, posit that the everlasting kingdom shall be
passed on to "one like a son of man" and to "the people of the saints of
the Most High" (Dan 7:13, 27).[22]

The divine kingdom that among the earlier sages would endure
from generation to generation now for the scribal-sages and authors of
apocalyptic becomes a kingdom that the Most High chooses to transfer
to a heavenly being ("one like a son of man") who is representative of
the people of Israel. The apocalyptic sages who wrote the Book of
Daniel also stressed the mortality of human monarchs (see esp. chaps. 5
and 7) but did not stop short where their prudential predecessors had
done of old. For them, after earthly kingdoms and empires had passed,
at some future date, the Most High would also allow his people ("the
people of the saints of the Most High") to share in the everlasting

20. For the reasons, see T. Middendorp, *Die Stellung Jesu Ben Siras zwischen Judentum und Hellenismus* (Leiden: Brill, 1973) 116–18.

21. For a convincing demonstration of the scribal background of the apocalyptic writers, see J. Z. Smith, "Wisdom and Apocalyptic," *Religious Syncretism in Antiquity* (ed. B. A. Pearson; Missoula, MT: Scholars Press, 1975) 131–56; repr. in *Visionaries and Their Apocalypses* (ed. P. D. Hanson; Issues in Religion and Theology 2; Philadelphia: Fortress, 1983) 101–20.

22. For a convincing demonstration that the "faithful Jews" are the "human counter-parts" of the "one like a son of man," see J. J. Collins, *The Apocalyptic Vision of the Book of Daniel* (Harvard Semitic Monographs 16; Missoula, MT: Scholars Press, 1977) 123–47.

power and sovereignty, which among the older sages belonged to God alone.[23] Thus, once again, the design of a portion of the house that the sages built underwent considerable transformation. It will be worthwhile to pause to assess whether or not there is a common element in the two radical shifts observed in the sages' constructions pertaining to the family and the king.

Both of the transformations that I have chronicled above were accompanied by the emergence of a more vivid eschatology and acceptance of what may be called a temporal dualism. Temporal dualism contrasts the events of the present age ("this age") with those of "the age to come" (cf. 2 Esdr 7:43 [7:113]). Belief in the immortality of the soul (Wisdom of Solomon) and in the resurrection of the dead (Book of Daniel) permitted a radical rethinking in the design of the houses the sages constructed to afford their compeers protection from anomie and attacks that suggested that the cosmos was without divine justice. In the former section I traced how the movement was from celebration of the physical family to celebration of virtuous childlessness; in the present section I have traced how the latter-day successors of the earlier sages moved from prudentialism to apocalypticism.

## NATION AND OTHER NATIONS

To probe the design of the houses of the sages with respect to nation and other nations is to probe their teaching on self-identity, for ethnicity along with occupation (or trade) constituted perhaps the two important elements in the notion of self in antiquity. That the consciousness of other nations was prominent in antiquity is vividly demonstrated in the *Execration Texts* from Egypt, which list by name the nations threatening to Egypt and accompanies each with a formulaic curse, whereas the importance of trades is illustrated by the Egyptian "Satire on the Trades."[24] Ethnicity, religion, and key occupations then as now were

---

23. For a fine survey of the motif of the kingdom of God between 200 B.C.E. and 100 C.E., see J. J. Collins, "The Kingdom of God in the Apocrypha and Pseudepigrapha," *The Kingdom of God in Twentieth-Century Interpretation* (ed. W. Willis; Peabody, MA: Hendrickson, 1987) 81–95. See also in the same volume the essay by B. Viviano, "The Kingdom of God in the Qumran Literature" (pp. 97–107). The other twelve essays in this anthology informatively deal chiefly with New Testament scholarship on the kingdom of God. The classic study on this subject in the scholarship of the Hebrew Bible is M. Buber, *Kingship of God* (3d ed.; New York: Harper and Row, 1967). See now also J. Gray's thorough survey, *The Biblical Doctrine of the Reign of God* (Edinburgh: T. & T. Clark, 1979). Viviano has recently published an excellent survey of the treatment of this subject in theological writings from the New Testament period up to the present, *The Kingdom of God in History* (Good News Studies 27; Wilmington, DE: Michael Glazier, 1988).

24. See *ANET* 328–29 and *AEL* 1:184–92 for English translations of these texts.

often interlinking and overlapping. The early Israelite poems "The Blessing of Jacob" (Genesis 49) and "The Blessing of Moses" (Deuteronomy 33) demonstrate this interlinking and overlapping with respect to the tribes in Israel, but not, of course, with respect to religion that the tribes shared. In contrast to the aforementioned poems, the Israelite sages in the early period did not focus upon the distinctiveness of Israel nor on the differences among the nations and tribes; their concern seemed to be rather to make generalizations that would apply to all nations—including Israel and Judah. In any event, three main stages in the development of the sages' teaching on the nation and nations may be discerned: (1) internationalism, (2) sense of national identity seen in connection with the law, and (3) intensification of sense of national identity. The latter stage exhibits three phases: (*a*) belief that personified wisdom had come to lodge in Israel, (*b*) belief that the prosperity of other national states in the present age would give way to an eternal rule for the people of God in the world to come, and (*c*) stress that the other nations practiced idolatry. This development may be described in the first and last phase (*a*, *c*) as the prophetization of wisdom, for finally with Sirach and the Wisdom of Solomon those doctrines central to the prophets of election, covenant and sacred history became incorporated into the sapiential world view. In the median and final phase also (*b*, *c*) the development may be described as the eschatologization of wisdom. The course of the shifting design in the houses of the sages with respect to nation and the nations may now be traced.

## Internationalism

In an important study, "The Hebrew Sage and Openness to the World," Roland Murphy demonstrated that the internationalism of the sages contains many biblical undergirdings for the current ecumenical movement, which have been, for the most part, passed over.[25] The openness of the sages to learning from other nations is observable in all periods but is particularly apparent in the earliest stage. Generalizations about the nation are made with respect not simply to Israel but to all nations. Even though the sages evolved a marked ethical dualism in which they contrasted the way of the righteous with the way of the ungodly (see esp. Proverbs 10–15 and Psalm 1)[26] in the earlier periods, they did not apply this teaching to contrast Israel with other nations. Rather their comments about the kings and nations applied for them

25. R. E. Murphy, "The Hebrew Sage and Openness to the World," *Christian Action and Openness to the World* (ed. J. Papin; Villanova University Symposium 2–3; Villanova, PA: Villanova University, 1970) 219–44.

26. I have examined this dualism in a number of texts in my essay, "Spatial and Ethical Dualism in Jewish Wisdom and Apocalyptic Literature," *JBL* 93 (1974) 356–75.

with equal strength to all nations—including Israel. Thus: "Righteousness exalts a nation, / but sin is a reproach to any people" (Prov 14:34
RSV). Here the sage and sentence-maker sounds prophetic as the following utterance also attests: "Mercy and truth protect a king, / and he
strengthens his throne with mercy" (Prov 20:28; cf. also 14:31; 16:11, 12;
21:3, 15; 22:8; 24:24). The sages saw for themselves a place in the
governance of nations: "Where there is no shrewd guidance a nation
will fall, / but prosperity is an abundance of counsel" (Prov 11:14; cf.
also 20:18). But there remains also an awareness of the limits of the wise
to effect success: "Neither wisdom nor discernment nor counsel is a
match for the Lord" (Prov 21:30).

A major theological reason for this position of openness is to be
found in the sages' wholehearted espousal of the teaching of the divine
omniscience (cf. Prov 15:3, 11; 16:2). This teaching is not confined to
the older sages and the sentence literature, but is to be found also in the
wisdom psalms (Ps 14:2 [=53:2], 139:7–16) and includes the notion that
God who is all-knowing provides for all (Ps 104:13, 145:15–16).

The impact of this period of the internationalism of the sages can
hardly be overestimated. The pronouncements of the prophets against
the foreign nations (Amos 1–2, Isaiah 13–23, Jeremiah 46–50, Ezekiel
25–31) are but an outgrowth of the conviction that God is the God of
all peoples whose principles of righteousness and mercy apply to all
equally. This conviction articulated by the prophets was clearly nurtured
by the Israelite sages. Similarly, in the postexilic era when the author of
the Books of Chronicles is retelling Israel's history from the perspective
of Judah and Jerusalem, he does so without a harsh or judgmental
attitude on other nations and peoples.[27]

So too, despite advances and refinements, the internationalism of
the sages remains as a beneficial, leavening influence against xenophobia
and ethnocentrism. This may be seen especially clearly when the sages
employed narrative forms. In the Joseph cycle it is not descried when
Joseph ascends to a position of authority in the Egyptian court or
marries the daughter of an Egyptian priest (Gen 41:39–46). In the
romances of Esther and Daniel 1–6, even though certain of the courtiers
are portrayed as nefarious and plotters of evil, the foreign court as a
place of service is not despised. To be sure, in Esther the king ac-
quiesces in a genocidal decree (Esther 3), but in the romances of
Daniel, the king is distressed when the death decree falls on his Judaic
courtier and four times a foreign monarch utters praises of Daniel's

___

27. For a careful tracking of the difference between the Books of Chronicles and
the Books of Ezra and Nehemiah, see esp. H. G. M. Williamson, *Israel in the Books of
Chronicles* (Cambridge: Cambridge University, 1977).

God (Dan 2:20–23, 4:1–3 [MT 3:31–33], 4:34–35 [MT 4:31–32], 6:25–27 [MT 6:26–28]). In the didactic tale of Jonah,[28] the foreign sailors are portrayed as kindly and the king and inhabitants of Nineveh are shown to be objects of the Lord's mercy and therefore of great worth.

## National Identity and the Law

The second stage in the sages' design with respect to nation and foreign nations is reached only after national crisis.[29] The emergence of the law as an object of intense study approaching that of veneration advanced in two phases following the collapse of the national states of Israel and Judah. Already with the publication of Deuteronomy 4–30 (ca. 680 B.C.E.) the authors—possibly scribal sages[30]—perceive national identity with respect to the law:

> For what great nation is there that has a god so near to it as the LORD our God is to us, whenever we call upon him? And what great nation is there, that has statutes and ordinances so righteous as all this law which I set before you this day? (Deut 4:7–8 RSV)

A similar sense of identification in connection with the law is seen in the wisdom psalm, Psalm 78, the author of which concludes that the chief reason for the demise of the northern kingdom rests in the fact that the northern kingdom refused to live by the law (vv 9–11) even

28. For the notion that the Book of Jonah should be seen as a piece of literature that emerged in the sapiential milieu of the *sôd* or council, see P. Trible, "Studies in the Book of Jonah" (Ph.D. diss., Columbia University, 1963).

29. For a pioneering work on the relation of wisdom and law, see J. Blenkinsopp, *Wisdom and Law in the Old Testament: The Ordering of Life in Israel and Early Judaism* (Oxford: Oxford University, 1983). A number of issues that Blenkinsopp begins to examine in this volume merit further exploration.

30. For the arguments, see the essay in this volume by A. Lemaire, "The Sage in School and Temple," pp. 165–81 above; and esp. M. Weinfeld, *Deuteronomy and the Deuteronomic School* (Oxford: Clarendon, 1972) 158–78, 244–319. In addition to the arguments proffered by Lemaire and Weinfeld, it may be noted that because Deuteronomy 5–11 contains a number of exhortations scholars have been inclined to designate this section as "parenetic" (e.g., A. D. H. Mayes and R. P. Merendino). When the terms *parenetic, parenesis,* and *parenetic literature* are further refined, as I have attempted to do in my essay "Paraenetic Literature," not only does Deuteronomy 5–11 qualify as parenetic (because of the preponderance of moral exhortation), but Deuteronomy 12–28 may be classified as parenesis (for it conforms precisely to the most defensible definition of parenesis as "an assemblage of moral precepts"). As may be recalled, in this essay I have taken the sage to be an author of a wisdom book. Because Deuteronomy qualifies, under my reasoning, for classification as parenetic literature—one of the two main subdivisions of the biblical wisdom literature—the authors of Deuteronomy therefore qualify to be designated as sages! See Mayes, *Deuteronomy* (New Century Bible; London: Oliphants, 1979) 30, 35, 36, 46, 48–49; and Merendino, *Das Deuteronomische Gesetz* (Bonn: Peter Hansen, 1969) 11–18, 109–11, etc.

though God had solemnly charged Jacob to teach it to his sons and to keep the commandments (vv 4–8). In view of the rejection of the tent of Joseph and the tribe of Ephraim, "he [the Lord] chose the tribe of Judah and Mount Zion, which he loved" (vv 67–68). It may be noted that for the psalmist, as for Isaiah of Jerusalem and the author of the Books of Chronicles, there is a tendency to think not simply in terms of a single regional entity, Judah, but rather in terms of the city-state as an hendiadys, hence, "Judah and Jerusalem" (Isa 3:1a, 8a; 5:3; 8:14; 2 Chr 10:14; 24:9, 19, 23; 29:8; etc.) or "Judah and Zion" (Ps 78:68).

Thus prior to the fall of Jerusalem in 587/86 B.C.E., both Deuteronomy and Psalm 78 attest to a sense of national self-identity among the sages and their followers as one intimately bound up with the gift of the law. The same remains the case following the fall of Judah and Jerusalem. This is seen especially in the juridical-wisdom psalm, Psalm 119: "I will speak of thy instruction before kings / and will not be ashamed" (v 46 NEB) or, again, "All the wicked of the earth thou dost count as dross [sigîm]; / therefore I love thy testimonies" (v 119 RSV). In the latter verse the implication is plain that the law is to be associated with the pure silver.

Perhaps the most significant development in the construction of that portion of the sages' house on nation and nations is to be found in the theological-wisdom psalm, Psalm 94. A sentiment that is already implicit in the afore-cited verse from Psalm 119 emerges with particular clarity in Psalm 94. The enemies are "the wicked" (rĕšaʿîm), national enemies who "beat down thy people" and "oppress thy chosen nation" (vv 3, 5 NEB). Upon these the psalmist is confident that the Lord will bring down the vengeance and chastisement for which he calls (vv 1–2, 10–11, 23). This psalm is important not only because it illustrates the association between the law and national identity in the mind of a sage ("Blessed is the man whom thou dost chasten, O LORD, / and whom thou dost teach out of thy law"; v 12 RSV) but because it illustrates especially clearly how one of the attitudes toward other nations could be one of deep hostility. Whereas in a psalm of natural-wisdom such as Psalm 139 the sage may declare his hatred of an indefinite group called "the wicked" and call for their destruction and departure from him (vv 19–22), in Psalm 94 the identity of the wicked is not left indefinite, but specified as the nations and their rulers: "He who chastens the nations, does he not chastise?" (v 10a RSV); "Can wicked rulers be allied with thee, / who frame mischief by statute?" (v 20 RSV). In Psalm 94 one sees unmistakably the application of ethical dualism, a hallmark of the sages, to the national level. This new element in the design of the sages' house does not, as I have shown, replace the internationalism of the sages, but rather stands side by side and in tension with it. Within the construction of the sages on nation and the nations is to be found both an openness to other nations *and* a xenophobia, a tolerance *and* a suspicion, a benevolence *and* an ill will. Self-identity gained upon close association with the law does not necessitate hostility to other nations, but self-identity gained upon designation of other nations as "the wicked" is a self-identity gained at a price.

## *Intensification of National Self-Identity*

The ambivalence of the second stage in the sages' constructs on nation and other nations carries through to the third stage in all three of its phases. Thus in the first phase—belief that personified wisdom had come to lodge in Israel—with the Wisdom of Jesus ben Sira, there is a remarkable openness to travel to other nations (Sir 39:4), a confidence that "the nations will declare his [God's] wisdom" (Sir 39:10), and a full-fledged encomium of the Hebrew people in the style of the typical Greek panegyric of the epideictic literature, which nowhere denigrates other nations (Sirach 44–50).[31] As was the case in the second stage, the notion of election is embraced ("For every nation he appointed a ruler, / but chose Israel to be his own possession"; Sir 17:17 NEB). In this third stage the sense of election is intensified with the introduction of wisdom personified—yet, again, without any disparagement of other nations. In the following citation Wisdom is speaking—and, as if she possessed extraordinary power as well as personal attributes:

> I ruled as master [*ektēsamēn*] over the waves of the sea,
>    over all the earth and over every people and nation.

> I took root in a people glorified,
>    in the Lord's appointed lot, even his inheritance.

> Those who have eaten of me will hunger for more,
>    and those who have drunk of me will thirst for more.

> All these things are the book of the covenant of the Most High God,
>    the law that Moses commanded for us,
>    an inheritance for the synagogues of Jacob.

> (Sir 24:6, 12, 21, 23)

As a counterpoint to this outlook on Israel as a nation among nations specially chosen for the dwelling place of Wisdom, without disparagements of other peoples, are the verses just before the colophon:

---

31. On the Greek background and form of "In Praise of the Fathers," see esp. B. L. Mack, *Wisdom and the Hebrew Epic: Ben Sira's Hymn in Praise of the Fathers* (Chicago: University of Chicago, 1985) 128–37; and T. R. Lee, *Studies in the Form of Sirach 44–50* (SBLDS 75; Atlanta: Scholars Press, 1986) 81–84.

> With two nations my soul is vexed,
> and with a third that is no nation:
> those who sit on the Mount Seir, the Philistines,
> and the foolish people who dwell in Shechem.
>
> (Sir 50:25-26)

An exceedingly nationalistic prayer is to be found in Sirach 36:1-17, but a close examination reveals that it probably does not come from the hand of the original sage-author who composed the rest of the book.[32]

The second phase in the intensification of the sages' teaching on nation and nations—belief that the prosperity of other national states in the present age would give way to an eternal rule for the people of God in the world to come—has already, in part, been anticipated above in the section on the king. The sage-authors of apocalyptic rehearse the latter part of Israel's sacred history (Dan 9:4-19), and also conjoin to their contrast between the nation (Israel) and other nations, a temporal dualism. Following the rule of the successive world empires will come the rule of the one like a son of man, even the rule of the people of the saints of the Most High (Dan 7:13-14, 27). Herein one sees a remarkable transformation of a time-honored contrast among the sages of the righteous with the ungodly. The transformation has taken place in two steps: (1) the contrast between the righteous and ungodly was cast onto a larger screen having to do not simply with individuals but with nations, and (2) the contrast is cast onto a yet more remote screen of the end time. As successive generations of sages moved from prudentialism to apocalypticism a familiar construct of wisdom became first nationalized and then eschatologized.

The third phase in the intensification of the sages' teaching on nation and nations—stress upon the idolatry of other nations—adds to the eschatological dimension a further specification on the folly of the other nations. The nationalized contrast between righteous and ungodly remains intact, as does its eschatologization, for "the souls of the righteous are in the hand of God and torment will not touch them" (Wis 3:1); whereas at God's coming the godless will be punished (Wis 3:10) and the righteous will be to them like flames to stubble (3:7). Indeed, of the righteous it is said:

> They will judge the nations and will rule over the peoples;
> and the Lord will be their king for ever and ever.
>
> (Wis 3:8)

---

32. For the arguments see Middendorp, *Die Stellung Jesu Ben Siras*, 125-32. For a contrary view, see P. W. Skehan and A. A. Di Lella, *The Wisdom of Ben Sira* (AB 39; Garden City, NY: Doubleday, 1987) 420-23.

The Wisdom of Solomon, however, advances beyond both Sirach and Daniel in one important regard, namely, in the degree to which it analyzes the root of the offense of the nations in the sight of the divine. The sage and apocalyptic writer of the visions of Daniel had inherited the tales that underlined the idolatry of Israel's captors (Daniel 3; 5:23) and did not tire pointing to the sacrilege of the tyrant Antiochus IV Epiphanes (Dan 7:25, 8:10–12, 11:31–39). With less assiduity than the authors of Daniel, but nonetheless plainly, Sirach notes how some of the fathers rejected idolatry (Sir 46:11). But the sage and author of the Wisdom of Solomon piles one description after another of the folly and depth of degradation and evil that emanate from the making of idols (Wis 11:15–15:19) and then turns to contrasting the kindness God has shown to his own people with the punishments and judgments he poured forth on the idolaters in Egypt (Wis 15:1–19:22). In all these recriminations the author of the Wisdom of Solomon shows himself to be a spiritual successor of Isaiah of Babylon and Jeremiah (cf. Isa 44:12–20; Jer 2:13, 19, 25, 28; 10:1–25). Therefore, it is all the more correct to speak of the prophetization of wisdom in this third phase of the third stage in the development of the sages' construct of nation and nations, for to the doctrine of election and sacred history of the prior two phases, the sage-author of the Wisdom of Solomon has added two extended meditations in the vein of the prophetic indictments of idolatry. This indictment is perhaps best summarized in the following verse:

> For the worship of idols, whose names it is wrong even to mention, is the beginning, cause, and end of every evil.   (Wis 14:27 NEB)[33]

## CONCLUSION

Thus, in each portion of the houses of the sages under examination (namely those pertaining to family, king, nation and other nations)

---

33. Scholarly judgment on the date and provenance of the Wisdom of Solomon vary considerably. Thus D. Winston argues for a provenance in Alexandria during the reign of Gaius Caligula (ca. 37–41 C.E.) (*The Wisdom of Solomon* [AB 43; Garden City, NY: Doubleday, 1979] 20–25); Larcher prefers a setting in Palestine between 31 and 10 B.C.E. (*Le Livre de la Sagesse ou La Sagesse de Salomon*, 1:125–61); and D. Georgi posits a Syrian provenance between 130 and 100 B.C.E. (*Weisheit Salomos* [Jüdische Schriften aus hellenistisch-römischer Zeit 3/4; Gütersloh: Gerd Mohn, 1980] 395–97)! Because the author distances himself to such a great extent from the Egyptian idolaters he condemns, it is hardly convincing to me that the author could have been a member of the Jewish community in Alexandria that had prospered and flourished there, in part, because it sought to reach out to non-Jewish groups and identify points of common theological conviction (on which see n. 35). On the other hand, the rivalry between the Seleucids (Greco-Syrians) and Ptolemies (Greco-Egyptians) is well known. In any event, one's assessment of the author's daring and depth of alienation from his immediate surroundings will vary considerably depending on which provenance one accepts.

significant transformations took place in the course of the first millennium B.C.E. The introduction of the notion of the world-to-come was apparently responsible for the most radical shifts in the design of the houses of the sages: from high evaluation of the productivity of offspring (Proverbs, wisdom Psalms) to an exaltation of righteous childlessness (Wisdom of Solomon); from a contrast between the eternity of the divine kingdom and the ephemerality of successive human generations (Psalm 145; cf. Psalm 49) to a contrast between ephemerality of other human kingdoms and the sharing of the people of God in the kingdom of the Most High (Daniel 7); and from an internationalism that viewed Israel as one nation among others, governed by the same omniscient God who required justice and brought about retribution (Proverbs), to a greater particularism (Sirach, Wisdom of Solomon). Another radical shift in the design of the houses of the sages was apparently brought about by the collapse of the national state in the northern kingdom and then in Judah: it was the shift away from a relative lack of concern with respect to national self-identity (seen in both the older works of traditional wisdom as well as in some later skeptical works) to a sense of national self-identity closely associated with the law (Deuteronomy; Psalms 78, 119; Sirach). In the first radical shift noted above I suggested that the phase *eschatologization of wisdom* was appropriate; the second shift might be called the *"torahization" of wisdom*,[34] and in yet another shift I observed a *"prophetization" of wisdom*, with the reincorporation of the prophetic doctrines of election and sacred history (Sirach) and severe strictures against idolatry (Wisdom of Solomon).

Particularly in that portion of the social construction of reality pertaining to nation and other nations did I note that an ambivalence and tension obtains in the second and third stages: a particularistic spirit stands in tension with a universalistic spirit. The latter, which finds expression among the sages of all periods, is a spirit that particularly commends itself in an ecumenical age where representatives of diverse religious traditions seek to be open about common elements in religions and cultures other than their own.[35] Despite necessary particularistic elements in all religious traditions the sages may function—should they choose—not only as builders of houses but also as builders of bridges.

34. The term is not my invention.
35. See esp. Murphy, "The Hebrew Sage and Openness to the World." See also my essay on the Alexandrian sapiential work, *The Letter of Aristeas* (ca. 150 B.C.E.), in which I show how, despite its literary shortcomings, this work nonetheless displays an uncanny ability to affirm elements in its own religious tradition that it shared with other religious traditions; "The Hellenization of Jewish Wisdom in the Letter of Aristeas," *Proceedings of the Ninth World Congress of Jewish Studies* (Division A: The Period of the Bible; Jerusalem: World Congress of Jewish Studies, 1986) 207–14.

# SELECT BIBLIOGRAPHY

## 1. HISTORICAL BACKGROUND OF ISRAEL AND THE ANCIENT NEAR EAST

Bevan, Edwyn R. *A History of Egypt under the Ptolemaic Dynasty.* London: Methuen, 1927. Reprinted as *The House of Ptolemy.* Chicago: Argonaut, 1968.
———. *The House of Seleucus.* 2 vols. London: Arnold, 1902. Reprinted New York: Barnes & Noble, 1966.

Bickerman, Elias J. *Institutions des Séleucides.* Bibliothèque Archéologique et Historique 26. Paris: Geuthner, 1938.

Boyce, Mary. *A History of Zoroastrianism.* Volume 1: *The Early Period.* Handbuch der Orientalistik 1.8.1.2.2a. Leiden: Brill, 1975.

———. *Textual Sources for the Study of Zoroastrianism.* Totowa, New Jersey: Barnes & Noble/Manchester: Manchester University Press, 1984.

Fraser, Peter M. *Ptolemaic Alexandria.* 3 vols. Oxford: Clarendon, 1972.

Heaton, Eric W. *The Hebrew Kingdoms.* The New Clarendon Bible: Old Testament 3. London: Oxford University Press, 1968.

Hengel, Martin. *Judaism and Hellenism: Studies in Their Encounter in Palestine during the Early Hellenistic Period.* 2 vols. Translated by John Bowden. Philadelphia: Fortress/London: SCM, 1974.

Jacobsen, Thorkild. *The Treasures of Darkness: A History of Mesopotamian Religion.* New Haven: Yale University Press, 1976.

Kramer, Samuel N. *The Sumerians: Their History, Culture, and Character.* Chicago: University of Chicago Press, 1963.

Oppenheim, A. Leo. *Ancient Mesopotamia: Portrait of a Dead Civilization.* Revised edition. Completed by Erica Reiner. Chicago: University of Chicago Press, 1977.

Préaux, Claire. *Le Monde Hellénistique: La Grèce et l'Orient (323–146 av. J.-C.).* 2 vols. Nouvelle Clio 6. Paris: Presses Universitaire de France, 1978.

Russell, James R. *Zoroastrianism in Armenia.* Harvard Iranian Series 5. Cambridge: Harvard University Press, 1987.

Tcherikover, Victor [Avigdor]. *Hellenistic Civilization and the Jews.* Translated by S. Applebaum. Philadelphia: Jewish Publication Society, 1959. Reprinted New York: Atheneum, 1970.

## 2. TEXTS AND TRANSLATIONS

Fisher, Loren R. (editor). *Ras Shamra Parallels: The Texts from Ugarit and the Hebrew Bible.* Volume 2. Analecta Orientalia 50. Rome: Pontifical Biblical Institute, 1975.

Gordon, Edmund I. *Sumerian Proverbs: Glimpses of Everyday Life in Ancient Mesopotamia*. Philadelphia: The University Museum, University of Pennsylvania, 1959.

Klein, Jacob. *The Royal Hymns of Shulgi, King of Ur: Man's Quest for Immortal Fame*. Transactions of the American Philosophical Society 71/7. Philadelphia: American Philosophical Society, 1981.

Lambert, Wilfred G. *Babylonian Wisdom Literature*. Oxford: Clarendon, 1960.

Lichtheim, Miriam. *Ancient Egyptian Literature*. 3 vols. Berkeley/Los Angeles: University of California Press, 1973–1980.

Pritchard, James B. (editor). *Ancient Near Eastern Texts Relating to the Old Testament*. 3d edition. Princeton: Princeton University Press, 1969.

Schaeffer, Claude F. A. (editor). *Ugaritica*. Volume 5. Mission de Ras Shamra 16. Paris: Imprimerie Nationale/Geuthner, 1968.

_____. *Ugaritica*. Volume 6. Mission de Ras Shamra 17. Paris: Geuthner, 1969.

Shaked, Shaul. *The Wisdom of the Sasanian Sages (Denkard VI)*. Boulder, Colorado: Westview, 1979.

Simpson, William K. *The Literature of Ancient Egypt: An Anthology of Stories, Instructions, and Poetry*. 2d edition. New Haven: Yale University Press, 1973.

## 3. INTRODUCTIONS TO ISRAELITE WISDOM *

Bauer-Kayatz, Christa. *Einführung in die alttestamentliche Weisheit*. Biblische Studien 55. Neukirchen-Vluyn: Neukirchener Verlag, 1969.

Baumgartner, Walter A. The Wisdom Literature. Pp. 210–37 in *The Old Testament and Modern Study*. Edited by Harold H. Rowley. Oxford: Clarendon, 1951.

Crenshaw, James L. *Old Testament Wisdom: An Introduction*. Atlanta: John Knox/London: SCM, 1981.

_____. Wisdom. Pp. 225–64 in *Old Testament Form Criticism*. Edited by John H. Hayes. San Antonio: Trinity University Press, 1974.

_____. The Wisdom Literature. Pp. 369–407 in *The Hebrew Bible and Its Modern Interpreters*. Edited by Douglas A. Knight and Gene M. Tucker. Philadelphia: Fortress/Chico, California: Scholars Press, 1985.

Dubarle, André M. *Les Sages d'Israël*. Lectio Divina 1. Paris: Cerf, 1946.

Duesberg, Hilaire, and Irénée Fransen. *Les Scribes Inspirés: Introduction aux Livres Sapientiaux de la Bible*. Revised edition. Marsedsous, Belgium: Marsedsous, 1966.

Emerton, J. A. Wisdom. Pp. 214–37 in *Tradition and Interpretation*. Edited by George W. Anderson. Oxford: Clarendon, 1979.

Fichtner, Johannes. *Die altorientalische Weisheit in ihrer israelitisch-jüdischen Ausprägung: Eine Studie zur Nationalisierung der Weisheit in Israel*. Beiheft zur Zeitschrift für die Alttestamentliche Wissenschaft 62. Giessen: Töpelmann, 1933.

Gese, Hartmut. *Lehre und Wirklichkeit in der alten Weisheit: Studien zu den Sprüchen Salomos und zu dem Buche Hiob*. Tübingen: Mohr (Siebeck), 1958.

* Many of the works in this section contain bibliographies on Israelite wisdom.

Murphy, Roland E.    Hebrew Wisdom. *Journal of the American Oriental Society*
101 (1981) 21–34.

_____. *Wisdom Literature: Job, Proverbs, Ruth, Canticles, Ecclesiastes, and
Esther*. Forms of the Old Testament Literature 13. Grand Rapids: Eerdmans,
1981.

von Rad, Gerhard. *Wisdom in Israel*. Translated by James D. Martin. Nashville:
Abingdon/London: SCM, 1972.

Rankin, Oliver S. *Israel's Wisdom Literature: Its Bearing on Theology and the
History of Religion*. Edinburgh: T. & T. Clark, 1936.

Rylaarsdam, J. Coert. *Revelation in Jewish Wisdom Literature*. Chicago: University of Chicago Press, 1946.

Schmid, Hans H. *Wesen und Geschichte der Weisheit: Eine Untersuchung zur
altorientalischen und israelitischen Weisheitliteratur*. Beiheft zur Zeitschrift für
die Alttestamentliche Wissenschaft 101. Berlin: Töpelmann, 1966.

Scott, Robert B. Y. *The Way of Wisdom in the Old Testament*. New York:
Macmillan, 1971.

Vanel, A.    Sagesse. Fasc. 60: cols. 4–58 in *Supplément au Dictionnaire de la
Bible*. Paris: Letouzey, 1986.

Whybray, Roger N.    The Social World of the Wisdom Writers. Pp. 227–50 in
*The World of Ancient Israel: Sociological, Anthropological and Political Per-
spectives*. Edited by Ronald E. Clements. Cambridge: Cambridge University
Press, 1989.

## 4. ANTHOLOGIES OF ESSAYS ON ISRAELITE WISDOM

Crenshaw, James L. (editor). *Studies in Ancient Israelite Wisdom*. New York:
Ktav, 1976.

Gammie, John G., Walter A. Brueggemann, W. Lee Humphreys, and James M.
Ward (editors). *Israelite Wisdom: Theological and Literary Essays in Honor
of Samuel Terrien*. Missoula, Montana: Scholars Press for Union Theological
Seminary, 1978.

Gilbert, Maurice (editor). *La Sagesse de l'Ancien Testament*. Bibliotheca Ephemeridum Theologicarum Lovaniensium 51. Gembloux: Duculot/Louvain:
Leuven University Press, 1979.

Noth, Martin, and D. Winton Thomas (editors). *Wisdom in Israel and in the
Ancient Near East: Presented to Professor Harold Henry Rowley*. Vetus Testamentum Supplement 3. Leiden: Brill, 1955.

Skehan, Patrick W. *Studies in Israelite Poetry and Wisdom*. Catholic Biblical
Quarterly Monograph Series 1. Washington, DC: Catholic Biblical Association, 1971.

Wilken, Robert L. (editor). *Aspects of Wisdom in Judaism and Early Christianity*. Notre Dame: University of Notre Dame Press, 1975.

## 5. EDUCATION, THE TEMPLE, SCHOOLS, AND SCRIBES

Begrich, Joachim. *Sōfēr und mazkir*: Ein Beitrag zur inneren Geschichte des
davidisch-salomonischen Grossreiches und des Königsreiches Juda. *Zeitschrift
für die Alttestamentliche Wissenschaft* 58 (1940–1941) 1–29.

Boecker, Hans J.  Erwägungen zum Amt des Mazkir. *Theologische Zeitschrift* 17 (1961) 212-16.

Brunner, Hellmut.  *Altägyptische Erziehung.* Wiesbaden: Harrassowitz, 1957.

Civil, Miguel.  Sur les "Livres d'Écolier" a l'Époque Paléo-Babylonienne. Pp. 67-78 in *Miscellanea Babylonica: Mélanges offerts à Maurice Birot.* Edited by Jean-Marie Durand and Jean-Robert Kupper. Paris: ERC, 1985.

Cody, Aelred.  Le Titre Égyptien et le Nom Propre du Scribe de David. *Revue Biblique* 72 (1965) 381-93.

Crenshaw, James L.  Education in Ancient Israel. *Journal of Biblical Literature* 104 (1985) 601-15.

Demsky, Aaron.  Education (Jewish). Vol. 6: cols. 381-98 in *Encyclopaedia Judaica.* Jerusalem: Keter, 1971.

――――.  Scribe. Vol. 14: cols. 1041-43 in *Encyclopaedia Judaica.* Jerusalem: Keter, 1971.

Dürr, Lorenz.  *Das Erziehungswesen im Alten Testament und in antiken Orient.* Mitteilungen der Vorderasiatisch-Ägyptischen Gesellschaft 36/2. Leipzig: Hinrich, 1932.

Falkenstein, Adam.  Die babylonische Schule. *Saeculum* 4 (1953) 125-37.

Golka, Friedemann W.  Die israelitische Weisheitsschule oder "des Kaisers neue Kleider." *Vetus Testamentum* 33 (1983) 257-70.

Haran, Menahem.  On the Diffusion of Literacy and Schools in Ancient Israel. Pp. 81-95 in *Congress Volume: Jerusalem 1986.* Edited by J. A. Emerton. Vetus Testamentum Supplement 40. Leiden: Brill, 1988.

――――.  *Temples and Temple-Service in Ancient Israel: An Inquiry into Biblical Cult Phenomena and the Historical Setting of the Priestly School.* Oxford: Clarendon, 1978. Reprinted Winona Lake, Indiana: Eisenbrauns, 1985.

Klostermann, August.  Schulwesen im alten Israel. Pp. 193-232 in *Theologische Studien: Theodor Zahn.* By Nathanael Bonwetsch et al. Leipzig: Deichert (Böhme), 1908.

Lang, Bernhard.  Schule und Unterricht im alten Israel. Pp. 186-201 in *La Sagesse de l'Ancien Testament.* Edited by Maurice Gilbert. Bibliotheca Ephemeridum Theologicarum Lovaniensium 51. Gembloux: Duculot/Louvain: Leuven University Press, 1979.

Lemaire, André.  *Les Écoles et la Formation de la Bible dans l'Ancien Israël.* Orbis Biblicus et Orientalis 39. Göttingen: Vandenhoeck & Ruprecht/Freiburg: Universitätsverlag, 1981.

――――.  Sagesse et Écoles. *Vetus Testamentum* 34 (1984) 270-81.

Marrou, Henri I.  *A History of Education in Antiquity.* Translated by George Lamb. London: Sheed & Ward, 1956. Reprinted Madison: University of Wisconsin Press, 1982.

Mendelson, Alan.  *Secular Education in Philo of Alexandria.* Cincinnati: Hebrew Union College, 1982.

Nilsson, Martin P.  *Die hellenistische Schule.* Munich: Beck, 1955.

Perdue, Leo G.  *Wisdom and Cult: A Critical Analysis of the Views of Cult in the Wisdom Literature of Israel and the Ancient Near East.* Society of Biblical Literature Dissertation Series 30. Missoula, Montana: Scholars Press, 1977.

Puech, Emile. Les Écoles dans l'Israël Préexilique: Données Épigraphiques. Pp. 189–203 in *Congress Volume: Jerusalem 1986*. Edited by J. A. Emerton. Vetus Testamentum Supplement 40. Leiden: Brill, 1988.

Rainey, Anson F. The Scribe at Ugarit: His Position and Influence. *Proceedings of the Israel Academy of Sciences and Humanities* 3 (1969) 126–47.

Schaeder, Hans H. *Esra der Schreiber*. Beiträge zur Historischen Theologie 5. Tübingen: Mohr, 1940.

Sjöberg, Åke W. The Old Babylonian Eduba. Pp. 159–79 in *Sumerological Studies in Honor of Thorkild Jacobsen*. Assyriological Studies 20. Chicago: The Oriental Institute of the University of Chicago, 1975.

———. Der Vater und sein Missratener Sohn. *Journal of Cuneiform Studies* 25 (1973) 105–69.

Vanstiphout, H. L. J. How Did They Learn Sumerian? *Journal of Cuneiform Studies* 31 (1979) 118–26.

Williams, Ronald J. Scribal Training in Ancient Egypt. *Journal of the American Oriental Society* 92 (1972) 214–21.

## 6. WISDOM LITERATURE OF ANTIQUITY

Bolle, Sara D. *Wisdom in Akkadian Literature: Expression, Instruction, Dialogue*. Ph.D. diss., University of California (Los Angeles), 1982.

Boyce, Mary. Middle Persian Literature 5: Wisdom literature. Pp. 51–55 in *Literatur*, by I. Gershevitch, Mary Boyce, et al. Handbuch der Orientalistik 1.4.2.1. Leiden: Brill, 1968.

Bryce, Glendon E. *A Legacy of Wisdom: The Egyptian Contribution to the Wisdom of Israel*. Lewisburg, Pennsylvania: Bucknell University Press, 1979.

Burgess, Theodore C. *Epideictic Literature*. Chicago: University of Chicago Press, 1902. Preprinted from *Studies in Classical Philology* 3:89–261

Cazelles, Henri. Les Nouvelles Études sur Sumer (Alster) et Mari (Marzal) nous aident-elles à situer les Origines de la Sagesse Israëlite? Pp. 17–27 in *La Sagesse de l'Ancien Testament*. Edited by Maurice Gilbert. Bibliotheca Ephemeridum Theologicarum Lovaniensium 51. Gembloux: Duculot/Louvain: Leuven University Press, 1979.

Fecht, Gerhard. *Der Habgierige und die Maat in der Lehre des Ptahhotpe (5. und 19. Maxime)*. Abhandlungen des Deutschen Achäologischen Instituts Kairo 1. Glückstadt: Augustin, 1958.

Foster, Benjamin R. Wisdom and the Gods in Ancient Mesopotamia. *Orientalia* 43 (1974) 344–54.

Lichtheim, Miriam. *Late Egyptian Wisdom Literature in the International Context: A Study of Demotic Instructions*. Orbis Biblicus et Orientalis 52. Göttingen: Vandenhoeck & Ruprecht/Freiburg: Universitätsverlag, 1983.

Posener, Georges. *L'Enseignement Loyaliste: Sagesse Égyptienne du Moyen Empire*. Hautes Études Orientales 5. Geneva: Droz/Paris: Champion, 1976.

Reiner, Erica. The Etiological Myth of the "Seven Sages." *Orientalia* 30 (1961) 1–11.

*Les Sagesses du Proche-Orient Ancien: Colloque de Strasbourg, 17–19 mai, 1962*. Paris: Presses Universitaires de France, 1963.

Schmid, Hans H. *Altorientalische Welt in der alttestamentlichen Theologie.* Zurich: Theologischer Verlag, 1974.

Schwartz, Benjamin I. (guest editor). Wisdom, Revelation, and Doubt: Perspectives on the First Millennium B.C. Spring 1975 issue of *Daedalus.*

Walcot, Peter. *Hesiod and the Near East.* Cardiff: University of Wales Press, 1966.


## 7. ROYAL ADMINISTRATION AND ROYAL OFFICES

Ahlström, Gösta W. *Royal Administration and National Religion in Ancient Palestine.* Studies in the History of the Ancient near East 1. Leiden: Brill, 1982.

de Boer, Pieter A. H. The Counsellor. Pp. 42–71 in *Wisdom in Israel and in the Ancient Near East: Presented to Professor Harold Henry Rowley.* Edited by Martin Noth and D. Winton Thomas. Vetus Testamentum Supplement 3. Leiden: Brill, 1955.

Donner, Herbert. Der "Freund des Königs." *Zeitschrift für die Alttestamentliche Wissenschaft* 73 (1961) 269–77.

Malamat, Abraham. Organs of Statecraft in the Israelite Monarchy. *Biblical Archaeologist* 28 (1965) 34–65. Reprinted as vol. 3: pp. 163–98 in *The Biblical Archaeologist Reader.* Edited by Edward F. Campbell Jr. and David N. Freedman. Garden City, New York: Doubleday, 1970.

Mettinger, Tryggve N. D. *Solomonic State Officials: A Study of the Civil Government Officials of the Israelite Monarchy.* Coniectanea Biblica: Old Testament Series 5. Gleerup: Lund, 1971.

Rütersworden, Udo. *Die Beamten der israelitischen Königszeit: Eine Studie zu śr und vergleichbaren Begriffen.* Beiträge zur Wissenschaft vom Alten und Neuen Testament 6/17 (= 117). Stuttgart: Kohlhammer, 1985.

van Selms, Adrianus. The Origin of the Title "the King's Friend." *Journal of Near Eastern Studies* 16 (1957) 118–23.

de Vaux, Roland. Titres et Fonctionnaires Égyptiens à la Cour de David et de Salomon. *Revue Biblique* 48 (1939) 394–405. Reprinted as pp. 189–201 in *Bible et Orient.* Paris: Cerf, 1967.

Virolleaud, Charles. *Le Palais Royal d'Ugarit.* Volume 2: *Textes en Cunéiformes Alphabétiques des Archives Est, Ouest et Centrales.* Mission de Ras Shamra 7. Paris: Imprimerie Nationale/Klincksieck, 1957.

Weisberg, David B. *Guild Structure and Political Allegiance in Early Achaemenid Mesopotamia.* Yale Near Eastern Researches 1. New Haven: Yale University Press, 1967.


## 8. THE ROLES OF INTELLECTUALS IN ANTIQUITY

Kerferd, George B. The Wise Man in Greece before Plato. Pp. 17–28 in *Images of Man in Ancient and Medieval Thought: Studia Gerardo Verbeke . . . dictata.* Edited by F. Bossier. Louvain: Leuven University Press, 1976.

Oppenheim, A. Leo. The Position of the Intellectual in Mesopotamian Society. *Daedalus* 104/2 (Spring 1975) 34–46.

Vatai, Frank L.   *Intellectuals in Politics in the Greek World from Early Times to the Hellenistic Age.* London: Croom Helm, 1984.

Whybray, Roger N.   *The Intellectual Tradition in the Old Testament.* Beiheft zur Zeitschrift für die Alttestamentliche Wissenschaft 135. Berlin/New York: de Gruyter, 1974.

Wider, K.   Women Philosophers in the Ancient Greek World: Donning the Mantle. *Hypatia: A Journal of Feminist Philosophy* 1 (Spring 1985) 21–62

Williams, Ronald J.   The Sages in Ancient Egypt in the Light of Recent Scholarship. *Journal of the American Oriental Society* 101 (1981) 1–19.

## 9. CLASS, SOCIAL BACKGROUND, AND SOCIOLOGY

Albertz, Rainier.   Der sozialgeschichtliche Hintergrund des Hiobbuches und der "Babylonischen Theodizee." Pp. 349–72 in *Die Botschaft und die Boten: Festschrift für Hans Walter Wolff zum 70. Geburtstag.* Edited by Jörg Jeremias and Lothar Perlitt. Neukirchen-Vluyn: Neukirchener Verlag, 1981.

Edzard, Dietz O. (editor).   *Gesellschaftsklassen im Alten Zweistromland und in den angrenzenden Gebieten: XVIII Rencontre Assyriologique Internationale, München, 29. Juni bis 3. Juli 1970.* Munich: Bayerischen Akademie der Wissenschaften/Beck, 1972.

Gaspar, Joseph W.   *Social Ideas in the Wisdom Literature of the Old Testament.* Studies in Sacred Theology 2/8. Washington, DC: Catholic University of America Press, 1947.

Gordis, Robert.   The Social Background of Wisdom Literature. *Hebrew Union College Annual* 18 (1944) 77–118.

Kippenberg, Hans G.   *Religion und Klassenbildung im antiken Judäa: Eine religionssoziologische Studie zum Verhältnis von Tradition und gesellschaftlicher Entwicklung.* Studien zur Umwelt des Neuen Testaments 14. Göttingen: Vandenhoeck & Ruprecht, 1978.

Kovacs, Brian W.   Is There a Class-Ethic in Proverbs? Pp. 171–89 in *Essays in Old Testament Ethics: J. Philip Hyatt, In Memoriam.* Edited by James L. Crenshaw and John T. Willis. New York: Ktav, 1974.

Levine, Lee I.   *The Rabbinic Class in Palestine during the Talmudic Period.* Jerusalem: Zvi Institute, 1985 [Hebrew].

Neusner, Jacob.   *School, Court, Public Administration: Judaism and Its Institutions in Talmudic Babylonia.* Brown Judaic Studies 83. Atlanta: Scholars Press, 1987.

Perdue, Leo G.   Liminality as a Social Setting for Wisdom Instructions. *Zeitschrift für die Alttestamentliche Wissenschaft* 93 (1981) 114–26.

Schottroff, Willy.   Arbeit und sozialer Konflikt im nachexilischen Juda. Pp. 104–8 in *Mitarbeiter der Schöpfung.* Edited by Luise Schottroff and Willy Schottroff. Munich: Kaiser, 1983.

Urbach, Ephraim E.   Class-Status and Leadership in the World of the Palestinian Sages. *Proceedings of the Israel Academy of Sciences and Humanities* 2 (1968) 38–74.

## 10. WOMEN IN WISDOM

Asher-Greve, Julia M. *Frauen in altsumerischer Zeit.* Bibliotheca Mesopotamica 18. Malibu, California: Undena, 1985.

Batto, Bernard F. *Studies on Women at Mari.* Baltimore: Johns Hopkins University Press, 1974.

de Boer, Pieter A. H. *Fatherhood and Motherhood in Israelite and Judean Piety.* Leiden: Brill, 1974.

Boström, Gustav. *Proverbiastudien: Die Weisheit und das fremde Weib in Sprüche 1–9.* Lunds Universitets Årsskrift 30/3. Lund: Gleerup, 1935.

Brenner, Athalya. *The Israelite Woman: Social Role and Literary Type in Biblical Narrative.* The Biblical Seminar 2. Sheffield: JSOT Press, 1985.

Brooten, Bernadette J. *Women Leaders in the Ancient Synagogue: Inscriptional Evidences and Background Issues.* Brown Judaic Studies 36. Chico, California: Scholars Press, 1982.

Brueggemann, Walter A. The Wise Women of 2 Samuel: A Role Model for Women in Early Israel? *Catholic Biblical Quarterly* 43 (1981) 14–29.

Camp, Claudia. *Wisdom and the Feminine in the Book of Proverbs.* Bible and Literature Series 11. Sheffield: Almond, 1985.

———. Wise and Strange: An Interpretation of the Female Imagery in Proverbs in Light of Trickster Mythology. *Semeia* 42 (1988) 14–36. [Special issue: *Reasoning with the Foxes: Female Wit in a World of Male Power.* Edited by J. Cheryl Exum and Johanna W. H. Bos.]

Fuchs, Esther. The Literary Characterization of Mothers and Sexual Politics in the Hebrew Bible. Pp. 117–36 in *Feminist Perspectives on Biblical Scholarship.* Edited by Adela Y. Collins. Chico, California: Scholars Press, 1985.

Harris, Rivkah. The *nadītu* Woman. Pp. 106–35 in *Studies Presented to A. Leo Oppenheim.* Chicago: The Oriental Institute of the University of Chicago, 1964.

Lesko, Barbara S. *The Remarkable Women of Ancient Egypt.* Providence: B. C. Scribe, 1987.

Pomeroy, Sarah B. *Goddesses, Whores, Wives, and Slaves: Women in Classical Antiquity.* New York: Schocken, 1975.

Trenchard, Warren. *Ben Sira's View of Women: A Literary Analysis.* Brown Judaic Studies 38. Chico, California: Scholars Press, 1982.

Ward, William A. *Essays on Feminine Titles of the Middle Kingdom and Related Subjects.* Beirut: American University of Beirut Press, 1986.

## 11. WISDOM AND APOCALYPTIC

Collins, John J. *The Apocalyptic Imagination: An Introduction to the Jewish Matrix of Christianity.* New York: Crossroad, 1984.

———. Cosmos and Salvation: Jewish Wisdom and Apocalyptic in the Hellenistic Age. *History of Religions* 17 (1977) 121–42.

Gammie, John G. Spatial and Ethical Dualism in Jewish Wisdom and Apocalyptic Literature. *Journal of Biblical Literature* 93 (1974) 356–85.

Müller, Hans-Peter. Mantische Weisheit und Apokalyptik. Pp. 268-293 in *Congress Volume: Uppsala 1971*. Vetus Testamentum Supplement 22. Leiden: Brill, 1972.

Niditch, Susan. The Visionary. Pp. 153-79 in *Ideal Figures in Ancient Judaism*. Edited by John J. Collins and George W. E. Nickelsburg. Society of Biblical Literature Septuagint and Cognate Studies 12. Chico, California: Scholars Press, 1980.

von Rad, Gerhard. The Divine Determination of Times. Pp. 262-83 in *Wisdom in Israel*. Translated by James D. Martin. Nashville: Abingdon/London: SCM, 1972.

Smith, Jonathan Z. Wisdom and Apocalyptic. Pp. 131-56 in *Religious Syncretism in Antiquity: Essays in Conversation with Geo Widengren*. Edited by Birger A. Pearson. Missoula, Montana: Scholars Press for the American Academy of Religion and the Institute of Religious Studies at the University of California, Santa Barbara, 1975. Reprinted as pp. 100-120 in *Visionaries and Their Apocalypses*. Edited by Paul D. Hanson. Issues in Religion and Theology 2. Philadelphia: Fortress/London: SCM, 1983.

Stone, Michael E. *Scriptures, Sects, and Visions: A Profile of Judaism from Ezra to the Jewish Revolts*. Philadelphia: Fortress/London: Collins, 1980.

VanderKam, James C. *Enoch and the Growth of an Apocalyptic Tradition*. Catholic Biblical Quarterly Monograph Series 16. Washington, DC: Catholic Biblical Association, 1984.

## 12. WISDOM IN RELATION TO LAW, ETHICS, AND ORDER

Blenkinsopp, Joseph. *Wisdom and Law in the Old Testament: The Ordering of Life in Israel and Early Judaism*. Oxford: Oxford University Press, 1983.

Fensham, F. Charles. Widow, Orphan, and the Poor in Ancient Near Eastern Legal and Wisdom Literature. *Journal of Near Eastern Studies* 21 (1962) 129-39. Reprinted as pp. 161-71 in *Studies in Ancient Israelite Wisdom*. Edited by James L. Crenshaw. New York: Ktav, 1976.

Fohrer, Georg. The Righteous Man in Job 31. Pp. 1-22 in *Essays in Old Testament Ethics: J. Philip Hyatt, In Memoriam*. Edited by James L. Crenshaw and John T. Willis. New York: Ktav, 1974.

Gerstenberger, Erhard. *Wesen und Herkunft des sogenannten "apodiktischen Rechts" im Alten Testament*. Wissenschaftliche Monographien zum Alten und Neuen Testament 20. Neukirchen-Vluyn: Neukirchener Verlag, 1965.

Richter, Wolfgang. *Recht und Ethos: Versuch einer Ortung des weisheitlichen Mahnspruches*. Studien zum Alten und Neuen Testament 15. Munich: Kösel, 1966.

Schmid, Hans H. *Gerechtigkeit als Weltordnung*. Beiträge zur Historischen Theologie 40. Tübingen: Mohr (Siebeck), 1968.

## 13. WISDOM: PERSONIFICATION, OBJECTIFICATION, HYPOSTATIZATION

Habel, Norman C. The Symbolism of Wisdom in Proverbs 1-9. *Interpretation* 26 (1972) 131-57.

Ringgren, Helmèr. *Word and Wisdom: Studies in the Hypostatization of Divine Qualities and Functions in the Ancient Near East.* Lund: Ohlssons, 1947.

Terrien, Samuel. The Play of Wisdom. Pp. 350–89 in *The Elusive Presence: Toward a New Biblical Theology.* Religious Perspectives 26. San Francisco: Harper & Row, 1978.

## 14. THE BOOK OF PROVERBS

Bauer-Kayatz, Christa. *Studien zu Proverbien 1–9.* Wissenschaftliche Monographien zum Alten und Neuen Testament 22. Neukirchen-Vluyn: Neukirchener Verlag, 1966.

Hermisson, Hans-Jürgen. *Studien zur israelitischen Spruchweisheit.* Wissenschaftliche Monographien zum Alten und Neuen Testament 28. Neukirchen-Vluyn: Neukirchener Verlag, 1968.

Humphreys, W. Lee. The Motif of the Wise Courtier in the Book of Proverbs. Pp. 177–90 in *Israelite Wisdom: Theological and Literary Essays in Honor of Samuel Terrien.* Edited by John G. Gammie, Walter A. Brueggemann, W. Lee Humphreys, and James M. Ward. Missoula, Montana: Scholars Press for Union Theological Seminary, 1978.

Lang, Bernhard. *Wisdom and the Book of Proverbs: A Hebrew Goddess Redefined.* New York: Pilgrim, 1986.

Shupak, Nili. The "Sitz im Leben" of the Book of Proverbs in the Light of a Comparison of Biblical and Egyptian Wisdom Literature. *Revue Biblique* 94 (1987) 98–119.

Skladny, Udo. *Die ältesten Spruchsammlungen in Israel.* Göttingen: Vandenhoeck & Ruprecht, 1962.

Whybray, Roger N. *Wisdom in Proverbs: The Concept of Wisdom in Proverbs 1–9.* Studies in Biblical Theology 45. London: SCM/Naperville, Illinois: Allenson, 1965.

## 15. THE BOOK OF JOB

Ceresko, Anthony R. *Job 29–31 in the Light of Northwest Semitic: A Translation and Philological Commentary.* Biblica et Orientalia 36. Rome: Pontifical Biblical Institute, 1980.

Gordis, Robert. *The Book of God and Man: A Study of Job.* Chicago: University of Chicago Press, 1963.

Keel, Othmar. *Jahwes Entgegnungen an Ijob.* Forschungen zur Religion und Literatur des Alten und Neuen Testaments 121. Göttingen: Vandenhoeck & Ruprecht, 1978.

Kubina, Veronika. *Die Gottesreden im Buche Hiob: Ein Beitrag zur Discussion um die Einheit von Hiob 38,1–42,6.* Freiburger Theologische Studien 115. Freiburg im Breisgau: Herder, 1979.

Lévêque, Jean. *Job et son Dieu: Essai d'Exégèse et de Théologie Biblique.* Études Bibliques. Paris: Gabalda, 1970.

Müller, Hans-Peter. *Das Hiobproblem: Seine Stellung und Entstehung im Alten Orient und im Alten Testament.* Erträge der Forschung 84. Darmstadt: Wissenschaftliche Buchgesellschaft, 1980.

Terrien, Samuel. *Job: Poet of Existence.* Indianapolis/New York: Bobbs-Merrill, 1957.

Westermann, Claus. *The Structure of the Book of Job: A Form-Critical Analysis.* Translated by Charles A. Muenchow. Philadelphia: Fortress, 1981.

## 16. THE BOOK OF ECCLESIASTES

Braun, Rainer. *Kohelet und die frühhellenistische Popularphilosophie.* Beiheft zur Zeitschrift für die Alttestamentliche Wissenschaft 130. Berlin/New York: de Gruyter, 1973.

Crenshaw, James L. Qoheleth in Current Research. *Hebrew Annual Review* 7 (1983) 41–56.

Crüsemann, Frank. The Unchangeable World: The "Crisis of Wisdom" in Koheleth. Pp. 57–77 in *God of the Lowly: Socio-historical Interpretations of the Bible.* Edited by Willy Schottroff and Wolfgang Stegemann. Translated by Matthew J. O'Connell. Maryknoll, New York: Orbis, 1984.

Gordis, Robert. *Koheleth—The Man and His World.* 3d edition. New York: Schocken, 1968.

Loader, James A. *Polar Structures in the Book of Qohelet.* Beiheft zur Zeitschrift für die Alttestamentliche Wissenschaft 152. Berlin/New York: de Gruyter, 1979.

Loretz, Oswald. *Qohelet und der Alte Orient: Untersuchungen zu Stil und theologischer Thematik des Buches Qohelet.* Freiburg im Breisgau: Herder, 1964.

## 17. WISDOM OUTSIDE THE WISDOM BOOKS IN THE HEBREW BIBLE

Alonso-Schökel, Luis. Sapiential and Covenant Themes in Genesis 2–3. *Theology Digest* 13 (1965) 3–10. Reprinted as pp. 468–80 in *Studies in Ancient Israelite Wisdom.* Edited by James L. Crenshaw. New York: Ktav, 1976.

Brueggemann, Walter A. *In Man We Trust: The Neglected Side of Biblical Faith.* Atlanta: John Knox, 1972.

Crenshaw, James L. Method in Determining Wisdom Influence Upon "Historical" Literature. *Journal of Biblical Literature* 88 (1969) 129–42. Reprinted as pp. 481–94 in *Studies in Ancient Israelite Wisdom.* Edited by James L. Crenshaw. New York: Ktav, 1976.

Exum, J. Cheryl. A Literary and Structural Analysis of the Song of Songs. *Zeitschrift für die Alttestamentliche Wissenschaft* 85 (1973) 47–79.

Fishbane, Michael. *Biblical Interpretation in Ancient Israel.* Oxford: Clarendon, 1985.

Fontaine, Carole R. *Traditional Sayings in the Old Testament: A Contextual Study.* Bible and Literature Series 5. Sheffield: Almond, 1982.

Jensen, Joseph. *The Use of tôrâ by Isaiah: His Debate with the Wisdom Tradition.* Catholic Biblical Quarterly Monograph Series 3. Washington, DC: Catholic Biblical Association, 1973.

Kuntz, J. Kenneth. The Canonical Wisdom Psalms of Ancient Israel: Their Rhetorical, Thematic, and Formal Dimensions. Pp. 186-222 in *Rhetorical Criticism: Essays in Honor of James Muilenburg*. Edited by Jared J. Jackson and Martin Kessler. Pittsburgh Theological Monograph Series 1. Pittsburgh: Pickwick, 1974.

Lindblom, Johannes. Wisdom in the Old Testament Prophets. Pp. 192-204 in *Wisdom in Israel and in the Ancient Near East: Presented to Professor Harold Henry Rowley*. Edited by Martin Noth and D. Winton Thomas. Vetus Testamentum Supplement 3. Leiden: Brill, 1955.

McKane, William. *Prophets and Wise Men*. Studies in Biblical Theology 44. London: SCM/Naperville, Illinois: Allenson, 1965.

Meyers, Carol L. Gender Imagery in the Song of Songs. *Hebrew Annual Review* 10 (1986) 209-23.

Morgan, Donn F. *Wisdom in the Old Testament Traditions*. Atlanta: John Knox/Oxford: Blackwell, 1981.

Mowinckel, Sigmund. Psalms and Wisdom. Pp. 205-24 in *Wisdom in Israel and in the Ancient Near East: Presented to Professor Harold Henry Rowley*. Edited by Martin Noth and D. Winton Thomas. Vetus Testamentum Supplement 3. Leiden: Brill, 1955.

Murphy, Roland E. A Consideration of the Classification "Wisdom Psalms." Pp. 156-67 in *Congress Volume: Bonn 1962*. Vetus Testamentum Supplement 9. Leiden: Brill, 1963. Reprinted as pp. 456-67 in *Studies in Ancient Israelite Wisdom*. Edited by James L. Crenshaw. New York: Ktav, 1976.

_____. Form-Critical Studies in the Song of Songs. *Interpretation* 27 (1973) 413-22.

_____. Towards a Commentary on the Song of Songs. *Catholic Biblical Quarterly* 39 (1977) 482-96.

von Rad, Gerhard. The Joseph Narrative and Ancient Wisdom. Pp. 292-300 in *The Problem of the Hexateuch and Other Essays*. Translated by E. W. T. Dickens. Edinburgh: Oliver & Boyd, 1966. Reprinted as pp. 439-47 in *Studies in Ancient Israelite Wisdom*. Edited by James L. Crenshaw. Clarendon, 1972.

Whedbee, J. William. *Isaiah and Wisdom*. Nashville: Abingdon, 1971.

White, John B. *A Study of the Language of Love in the Song of Songs and Ancient Egyptian Poetry*. Society of Biblical Literature Dissertation Series 38. Missoula, Montana: Scholars Press, 1978.

Whybray, Roger N. *The Succession Narrative: A Study of II Samuel 8-20; I Kings 1 and 2*. Studies in Biblical Theology 2/9. London: SCM/Naperville, Illinois: Allenson, 1968.

## 18. THE BOOK OF SIRACH

Haspecker, Josef. *Gottesfurcht bei Jesus Sirach: Ihre religiöse Struktur und ihre literarische und doktrinäre Bedeutung*. Analecta Biblica 30. Rome: Pontifical Biblical Institute, 1967.

Mack, Burton L. *Wisdom and the Hebrew Epic: Ben Sira's Hymn in Praise of the Fathers*. Chicago: University of Chicago Press, 1985.

Marböck, Johann. *Weisheit im Wandel: Untersuchungen zur Weisheitstheologie bei Ben Sira*. Bonner Biblische Beiträge 37. Bonn: Peter Hanstein, 1971.

Middendorp, Theophil. *Die Stellung Jesu Ben Sira zwischen Judentum und Hellenismus*. Leiden: Brill, 1973.

Stadelmann, Helge. *Ben Sira als Schriftgelehrter: Eine Untersuchung zum Berufsbild des vor-makkabäischen Sōfēr under Berücksichtigung seines Verhältnisses zu Priester-, Propheten- und Weisheitslehrertum*. Wissenschaftliche Untersuchungen zum Neuen Testament 2/6. Tübingen: Mohr (Siebeck), 1980.

## 19. THE WISDOM OF SOLOMON

Larcher, Chrysostome. *Études sur le Livre de la Sagesse*. Études Bibliques. Paris: Gabalda, 1969.

_____. *Le Livre de la Sagesse; ou, La Sagesse de Salomon*. 2 vols. Études Bibliques, n.s. 1, 3. Paris: Gabalda, 1983-1984.

Reese, James M. *Hellenistic Influences on the Book of Wisdom and Its Consequences*. Analecta Biblica 41. Rome: Pontifical Biblical Institute, 1970.

## 20. WISDOM IN THE NEW TESTAMENT

Beardslee, William A. Uses of the Proverb in the Synoptic Gospels. *Interpretation* 24 (1970) 61-73.

_____. The Wisdom Tradition and the Synoptic Gospels. *Journal of the American Academy of Religion* 35 (1967) 231-40.

Crossan, John D. *In Fragments: The Aphorisms of Jesus*. San Francisco: Harper & Row, 1983.

Fiore, Benjamin. *The Function of Personal Example in the Socratic and Pastoral Epistles*. Analecta Biblica 105. Rome: Pontifical Biblical Institute, 1986.

Fiorenza, Elisabeth Schüssler. *In Memory of Her: A Feminist Theological Reconstruction of Christian Origins*. New York: Crossroad, 1983.

Jeremias, Joachim. *The Parables of Jesus*. Translated by Samuel H. Hooke. New York: Scribner/London: SCM, 1972.

Kloppenborg, John S. *The Formation of Q: Trajectories in Ancient Wisdom Collections*. Philadelphia: Fortress, 1987.

Mullins, Terence Y. Jewish Wisdom Literature in the New Testament. *Journal of Biblical Literature* 68 (1949) 335-39.

Perdue, Leo G. Paraenesis and the Epistle of James. *Zeitschrift für die Neutestamentliche Wissenschaft* 72 (1981) 241-56.

Scott, Bernard B. *Hear Then the Parable: A Commentary on the Parables of Jesus*. Minneapolis: Fortress, 1989.

_____. *Jesus, Symbol Maker for the Kingdom*. Philadelphia: Fortress, 1981.

Williams, James G. Parable and Chreia: From Q to Narrative Gospel. *Semeia* 43 (1988) 85-114. [Special issue: *Genre, Narrativity, and Theology*. Edited by Mary Gerhart and James G. Williams.]

_____. *Those Who Ponder Proverbs: Aphoristic Thinking and Biblical Literature*. Bible and Literature Series 2. Sheffield: Almond, 1981.

Zeller, Dieter. *Die weisheitlichen Mahnsprüche bei den Synoptikern.* Forschung zur Bibel 17. Würzburg: Echter, 1977.


## 21. WISDOM AND THE RABBIS

Daube, David. Rabbinic Methods of Interpretation and Hellenistic Rhetoric. *Hebrew Union College Annual* 22 (1949) 239–64.

Fischel, Henry A. *Rabbinic Literature and Greco-Roman Philosophy: A Study of Epicurea and Rhetorica in Early Midrashic Writings.* Studia Post-Biblica 21. Leiden: Brill, 1973.

Neusner, Jacob. Death-Scenes and Farewell Stories: An Aspect of the Master-Disciple Relationship in Mark and in Some Talmudic Tales. Pp. 187–97 in *Christians among Jews and Gentiles: Essays in Honor of Krister Stendahl on His Sixty-fifth Birthday.* Edited by George W. E. Nickelsburg and George W. MacRae. Philadelphia: Fortress, 1986.

Saldarini, Anthony J. Last Words and Deathbed Scenes in Rabbinic Literature. *Jewish Quarterly Review* 68 (1977) 28–45.

Urbach, Ephraim E. *The Sages: Their Concepts and Beliefs.* 2 vols. Translated by Israel Abrahams. Jerusalem: Magnes, 1979.


## 22. WISDOM AT QUMRAN

Denis, Albert M. *Les Thèmes de Connaissance dans le Document de Damas.* Studia Hellenistica 15. Louvain: University of Leuven Press, 1967.

Hengel, Martin. The Theology of Early Essenism. Vol. 1: pp. 218–24 in *Judaism and Hellenism: Studies in Their Encounter in Palestine during the Early Hellenistic Period.* Translated by John Bowden. Philadelphia: Fortress/London: SCM, 1974.

Tanzer, S. J. *The Sages at Qumran: Wisdom in the Hodayot.* Ph.D. diss., Harvard University, 1987.

Worrell, John E. *Concepts of Wisdom in the Dead Sea Scrolls.* Ph.D. diss., Claremont Graduate School, 1968.

# INDEX OF MODERN AUTHORS

# INDEX OF CLASSICAL AUTHORS

# INDEX OF ANCIENT
# NEAR EASTERN WRITINGS

## EGYPTIAN WRITINGS

## IRANIAN WRITINGS

## SUMERO-AKKADIAN LITERARY COMPOSITIONS

## SUMERO-AKKADIAN TEXTS
### (by publication or museum number)

## UGARITIC LITERARY COMPOSITIONS

## UGARITIC TEXTS
### (by publication or find number)

# INDEX OF SCRIPTURE AND RELATED LITERATURE

## OLD TESTAMENT

*Proverbs (cont'd.)*

14:34 . . . . . . . . 458, 491
14:35 . . . . . . . . . . . 359
15–16 . . . . . . 214 n. 35
15:3 . . . . . . . . . 486, 491
15:9 . . . . . . . . . . . . 459
15:11 . . . . . . . 236, 359,
486, 491
15:20 . . . . . . . . 161, 192
15:22 . . . . . . . 135, 157,
473 n. 36
15:23 . . . . . . . . . . . 430
15:27 . . . . . . . . . . . 174
15:28–22:16 . . 301 n. 29
15:29 . . . . . . . . 359, 459
15:31 . . . . . . . . . . . 174
15:33 . . . . . . . . 178, 359
16:2 . . . . . . . . . 486, 491
16:3 . . . . . . . . . . . . 241
16:6 . . . . . . . . . . . . 359
16:7 . . . . . . . . . . . . 241
16:9 . . . . . . . . . . . . 463
16:10 . . . . . . . . 214, 302
16:10–15 . . . . . . . . 173,
473 n. 36
16:11 . . . . . . . . . . . 491
16:12 . . . . 302, 473, 491
16:12–13 . . . . . . . . 214
16:13 . . . . . . . . 302, 458
16:14 . . . . . . . . . . . 487
16:14–15 . . . . . . . . 214
16:15 . . . . . . . . . . . 487
16:16 . . . . . . . . . . . 174,
257 n. 42, 302
16:20–24 . . . . . . . . 462
16:23 . . . . 157, 311 n. 13
16:31 . . . . . . . . . . . 304
17:3 . . . . . . . . . . . . 241
17:7 . . . . . . . . 473 n. 36
19:4 . . . . . . . . 254 n. 34
19:10 . . . . . . . 473 n. 36
19:12 . . . . . . . 473 n. 36
19:14 . . . . . . . . 194, 463
19:15 . . . . . . . . . . . 157
19:20 . . . . . . . . 157, 174
19:21 . . . . . . . . 302, 463
20:1 . . . . . . . . 302, 359
20:2 . . . . . . . . 473 n. 36
20:4 . . . . . . . . . . . . 173
20:5 . . . . . . . . . . . . 157
20:8 . . . . . . . . 473 n. 36
20:11 . . . . . . . . . . . 173

*Proverbs (cont'd.)*

20:18 . . . . 157, 214, 302,
473 n. 36, 491
20:20 . . . . . . . 161, 192
20:25–26 . . . . . . . . 359
20:26 . . . . . . . . . . . 302
20:26–27 . . . . . . . . 486
20:28 . . . . . . . . . . 302,
473 n. 36, 491
20:29 . . . . . . . . 304, 474
21:1 . . . . . 473 n. 36, 486
21:2 . . . . . . . . . . . . 241
21:3 . . . . . 458, 459, 491
21:5 . . . . . . . . . . . . 157
21:11 . . . . . . . 311 n. 13
21:12 . . . . . . . . . . . 484
21:15 . . . . . . . . . . . 491
21:21 . . . . . . . . . . . 459
21:22 . . . 157, 257 n. 42,
473 n. 36
21:30 . . . . . . . . 302, 491
21:30–31 . . . . . 302, 463
22:1 . . . . . . . . . . . . 485
22:3 . . . . . . . . 246 n. 12
22:4 . . . . . . . . . . . . 359
22:6 . . . . . . . . . . . . 173
22:8 . . . . . . . . . . . . 491
22:9 . . . . . . . . . . . . 173
22:11 . . . . . . . 473 n. 36
22:15 . . . . . . . . . . . 173
22:17 . . . . . . . 138, 174,
206 n. 3, 211
22:17–21 . . . . . . . . 206
22:17–23:12 . . . 172, 173
22:17–23:14 . . . . . . 23
22:17–24:22 . . . 138, 139,
206, 216
22:19 . . . . . . . 253 n. 29
22:29 . . . . 211, 473 n. 36
23:1 . . . . . . . . 473 n. 36
23:13 . . . . . . . . 173, 175
23:17–19 . . . . 253 n. 29
23:19–21 . . . . . . . . 192
23:22 . . . . . . . . . . . 161
23:22–28 . . . . . . . . 192
23:25 . . . . . . . . . . . 161
23:26–28 . . . . . . . . 359
24:3 . . . . . . . . . . . . 133
24:5 . . . . . . . . 257 n. 42
24:5–6 . . . . . . 473 n. 36
24:6 . . . . 135, 157, 302
24:21–22 . . . . 473 n. 36

*Proverbs (cont'd.)*

24:23 . . . . . . . 138, 211
24:23–26 . . . . . . . . 157
24:23–34 . . . . . . . . 211
24:24 . . . . . . . . . . . 491
24:30–34 . . . . . 157, 211
25 . . . . . . . . . 129 n. 35
25–29 . . . . . . 211, 212,
212 n. 30
25:1 . . . . . . . . 118, 138,
297, 302
25:1–7 . . . . . . 473 n. 36
25:2 . . . . . . . . . 463, 487
25:2–15 . . . . . . . . . 173
25:3 . . . . . . . . . . . . 486
25:5 . . . . . 302, 458, 474
25:6–7 . . . . . . . . . . 135
25:9–10 . . . . . . . . . 359
25:15 . . . . 135, 157, 359,
473 n. 36
25:21–22 . . . . . . . . 241
26:4–5 . . . . . . . . . . 267
26:5 . . . . . . . . . 299, 302
26:11 . . . . . . . . . . . 461
26:12 . . . . . . . . 299, 302
26:16 . . . . . . . . 299, 302
26:20 . . . . . . . . . . . 461
27:13 . . . . . . . 246 n. 12
27:23–27 . . . . 157, 173,
466, 473 n. 36
28–29 . . . . . . . . . . 214
28:2 . . . . . . . . 473 n. 36
28:4 . . . . . . . . . . . . 174
28:7 . . . . . . . . . . . . 174
28:9 . . . . . . . . . . . . 174
28:11 . . . . . . . . 299, 302
28:12 . . . . . . . . . . . 458
28:15–16 . . . . 473 n. 36
28:19 . . . . . . . . . . . 173
28:24 . . . . . . . . . . . 161
29:2 . . . . . 458, 473 n. 36
29:4 . . . . 302, 473 n. 36,
487
29:7 . . . . . . . . . . . . 302
29:12 . . . . . . . 473 n. 36
29:14 . . . . . . . . . . 302,
473 n. 36, 487
29:15 . . . . . . . . . . . 175
29:17 . . . . . . . . . . . 175
29:18 . . . . . . . . . . . 174
29:26 . . . . . . . 241, 302,
473 n. 36

## DEUTEROCANONICAL BOOKS

## NEW TESTAMENT

## PSEUDEPIGRAPHA

## DEAD SEA SCROLLS

## MISHNAIC AND OTHER RABBINIC WRITINGS

## NAG HAMMADI

## JOSEPHUS